Praise for

Myra MacPherson's *"All Governments Lie"*

"[A] lovely biography. Ideally timed for the moment when reporters in Washington are once again rightly (and too late) flailing themselves. . . . I am utterly sure that the recent allegation from the crackpot, Ann Coulterish right of [Stone's] having been on the KGB payrol' ' 'se. MacPherson rips the 'evidence' of these people to shreds."

istopher Hitchens, *Vanity Fair*

"Highly recommended . . . a biogra ' rich context."

"Engaging. [Stone] seemed born to the newspaper trade in ay ﬁichitz was born to the fiddle."

—*The Wall Street Journal*

"Lively and well-researched . . . more than a biography, it's a study of the press and government."

—*USA Today*

"'All governments lie,' Stone's maxim, ought to be plastered across every journalist's desk."

—*The New York Times Book Review*

"Thorough and honest."

—*The New Yorker*

"Lovingly recounts Stone's journalistic and political journey."

—*Chicago Tribune*

"In her fine and useful biography, veteran reporter Myra MacPherson traces . . . the triumphant arc of the man."

—*The Nation*

"[A] sweeping biography . . . skillfully covers not just the details of Stone's life but also how his career fit into the evolution of alternative journalism."

—*Mother Jones*

"Timely . . . valuable . . . not only a biography of Stone but a detailed history."

—*Columbia Journalism Review*

"Captures Stone's zest for the business and his bravery in persevering."

—*Rocky Mountain News*

"What fabulous stories—newspaper stories, political stories, world history, and the greatest tabloid there ever was, all crammed into one life. . . . Now is the time for all good journalists to read this book and remember what it is all about."

—Molly Ivins, author of *Who Let the Dogs In?*

"The right book at the right time. It is not only the fascinating story of an American original, it is also a sophisticated history of what went wrong between American journalism and American government."

—Richard Reeves, author of *President Reagan: The Triumph of Imagination*

"Myra MacPherson is a brilliant writer who has written a great book about a journalistic idol—Izzy Stone. Would that he were alive today to lead our country to its greatest ideals again."

—Helen Thomas, author of *Watchdogs of Democracy?*

"This book is an important contribution to the current debate about the future and the nature of journalism and why the public as well as journalists should be involved in that debate."

—Bill Kovach, founding chairman, Committee of Concerned Journalists

"Despite its size, this book is not a doorstop. It's a brain stop. Read it!"

—Gore Vidal

ALSO BY MYRA MACPHERSON

She Came to Live Out Loud:
An Inspiring Family Journey Through Illness, Loss, and Grief

Long Time Passing:
Vietnam and the Haunted Generation

The Power Lovers:
An Intimate Look at Politicians and Their Marriages

"ALL GOVERNMENTS LIE"

THE LIFE AND TIMES OF REBEL JOURNALIST I. F. STONE

Myra MacPherson

A LISA DREW BOOK
SCRIBNER
New York   London   Toronto   Sydney

A LISA DREW BOOK/SCRIBNER
A Division of Simon & Schuster, Inc.
1230 Avenue of the Americas
New York, NY 10020

First Lisa Drew/Scribner trade paperback edition April 2008

SCRIBNER and design are trademarks of
Macmillan Library Reference USA, Inc., used under license
by Simon & Schuster, the publisher of this work.

A LISA DREW BOOK is a trademark of
Simon & Schuster, Inc.

For information about special discounts for bulk purchases,
please contact Simon & Schuster Special Sales at
1-800-456-6798 or business@simonandschuster.com.

DESIGNED BY LAUREN SIMONETTI
Text set in Minion

Manufactured in the United States of America

1   3   5   7   9   10   8   6   4   2

Library of Congress Control Number: 2006042389

ISBN-13: 978-0-684-80713-3
ISBN-10: 0-684-80713-0
ISBN-13: 978-1-4165-5679-4 (pbk)
ISBN-10: 1-4165-5679-6 (pbk)

In memory of JACK D. GORDON,
the love of my life, who fought courageously
to make this a better world.

And in memory of Molly Ivins,
who did the same as a great journalist.

CONTENTS

All governments lie, but disaster lies in wait for countries whose officials smoke the same hashish they give out.

—I. F. Stone

FOREWORD:
THE IMPORTANCE OF BEING IZZY AND THE DEATH OF DISSENT IN JOURNALISM

You've really got to wear a chastity belt in Washington to preserve your journalistic virginity. Once the secretary of state invites you to lunch and asks your opinion, you're sunk.
> —I. F. Stone on government manipulation of the media

In writing this book it has not been easy keeping up with the fast-breaking news about a man who has been dead for eighteen years. Lest you think I jest, reflect on this.

In 2004, Philip Roth gave I. F. Stone a walk-on part in his masterful work of fact and fiction *The Plot Against America*. In Roth's mesmerizing "it can happen here" tale of fascism triumphant, Charles A. Lindbergh, in real life the international aviation ace and Hitler admirer, has defeated FDR. On page 316 of the novel, I. F. Stone is carted off with FDR New Dealers Bernard Baruch, Supreme Court justice Felix Frankfurter, and other real famous men by President Lindbergh's gestapo-style FBI as pogroms begin in America. Roth's novel vividly relates the fear among American Jews in 1942 when fascism was a real threat. Back then, journalist I. F. Stone was among the alarmed who excoriated isolationist Lindbergh's coziness with the Third Reich.

Uncanny echoes of Stone are heard in concert halls, on radio, or on CDs of the Kronos Quartet as his distinctive voice dips in and out of the music. With a continued war in Iraq, the Kronos Quartet and composer Scott Johnson found new poignancy and symbolism in Stone's antiwar lectures for peace taped decades ago.

What appears to be a fleeting apparition of owl-eyed Izzy rushes by in the background of real footage of a McCarthy hearing in George Clooney's award-winning 2005 movie on Edward R. Murrow, *Good Night, and Good Luck*.

The twentieth century's premier independent journalist, known to everyone from the corner grocer to Einstein as Izzy, is honored on campuses that award I. F. Stone chairs, fellowships, and scholarships. Institutions rank his tiny one-man *Weekly* in the Greatest Hits of twentieth-century journalism. In one major study, Stone's *Weekly* placed number 16 in the top 100, behind coverage of Hiroshima, Watergate, the Pentagon Papers, My Lai, and the work of early-century muckrakers. As an individual voice, he placed ahead of Harrison Salisbury, Dorothy Thompson, Neil Sheehan, William Shirer, James Baldwin, Joan Didion, Murray Kempton, and other worthies. Some who once ruled Georgetown and political society, such as columnist Joe Alsop and the acerbic H. L. Mencken, did not make the cut. Walter Lippmann placed 64. Such are the vicissitudes of life for journalists who once stood so high. "This kind of list is needed in journalism," said Mitchell Stephens, of NYU. "Nobody thinks of journalism in terms of decades or centuries." It is important to examine why some endure.

And Stone endures. He is quoted in the *New Yorker* and the *New York Times,* remembered as an inspiration by Bill Moyers and Seymour Hersh —arguably the best investigative reporter today—and anyone else who despairs of modern journalism, especially the unquestioning acceptance of governmental spin. He is a lone "courageous" voice remembered by Michael Cross-Barnet in a 2005 recollection of his own father's ruined career during the Red Scare: *"The New York Times* Shafted My Father." Defending the *Times* editor Melvin Barnet, Stone had asked back then, "How can the *Times* editorially support the Fifth Amendment and discharge those who invoke it?" Bloggers bill themselves as the next Izzy.

Stone went from a young iconoclast in the 1930s to an icon during the Vietnam War. In the fifties, he spoke to mere handfuls who dared surface to protest Cold War loyalty oaths and witch hunts. A decade later, he spoke to half a million who massed for anti–Vietnam War rallies. He became world famous.

Today, Izzy's remarkable immediacy leaps off the pages. Not only is he a sheer joy to read, his views take on vital importance, as if he had written them just this morning, illuminating the tumultuous first years of the twenty-first century.

"There was increased reliance at home and abroad on suppression by force and an increasingly arrogant determination to 'go it alone' in the world." This was not written when George W. Bush ignored the United Nations, colleagues, international treaties, and advice of allies and started a war but by Stone during Cold War escalation.

"All governments are run by liars . . ." This was not about the weapons of mass destruction or subsequent other Iraq War lies but those told during the Vietnam War.

"It is not a private quarrel between the Israelis and Arabs. It's a world concern—and of great concern to America, as a great power, to have stability and peace. And there is no way to have peace without some modicum of justice. The Arabs can not be held in second-class citizenship and bondage. If something isn't done pretty soon the lines may harden, each side will destroy its own moderates—and then they will move on to destroy each other." That was not about today's discord or the wall built by the Israelis to keep out the Palestinians in 2004, but Stone's sorrowful warning years ago.

"Almost every generation in American history has had to face what appeared to be a menace of so frightening an order as to justify the limitation of basic liberties—the Francophiles in the days of the Alien and Sedition laws, the Abolitionists, the Anarchists, the Socialists in the days of Debs; Fascists, anti-Semites and Communists in our own time." Some saw "compelling arguments for suppression." Stone argued against this, claiming that a country founded on basic freedoms had "managed to get through before." This was not about the excesses of the Patriot Act but about investigative assaults and secret surveillance of citizens in 1949. Then as now, fear galvanized citizens into silent support. The terrorists of 9/11 and continuing worldwide terrorism made it easy to sell the Patriot Act— and to resell it to a cowardly Congress as 2005 drew to a close. Even that performance was topped by a Democratic-controlled congress caving to "soft on terror" slurs in 2007. Congress gave the president unprecedented authority to escalate warrantless spying. (By then, some mainstream editorialists had had enough. The action prompted such slogans as "That's o.k., I wasn't using my civil liberties anyway," and "America, One Nation, Under Surveillance.")

Today's tone echoes words deployed in the Cold War Red Scare, when congressional inquisitors decided who was "un-American" and President Truman instituted the "Loyalty Oath." Stone would have led the pack in uncovering—once again—illegal domestic spying in this century and ripped into the Patriot Act for its trampling on the Bill of Rights, which included forcing clerks and librarians to turn over lists of what citizens read, and detaining a thousand "suspects" with no evidence. Jailed without charge, forbidden to see lawyers or family, the vast majority were innocent of federal crimes of terrorism. Bush's team had grossly inflated the number of terrorist actions. Justice Department stonewalling thwarted media access, yet available reports were overlooked. Such documents would have had hound dog Stone salivating at the joy of the hunt.

* * *

This book combines biography, a historical treatise on the press, and Stone's running commentary on twentieth-century America. All are necessary to draw some present-day lessons from the life and times of I. F. Stone. At pivotal points in their careers I have twinned outsider I. F. Stone with insider Walter Lippmann because they are dynamic examples of opposing approaches to journalism. Presidents and kings were so much a part of Lippmann's life that when he visited Paris, his forwarding address was in care of Charles de Gaulle. He wrote speeches for presidents and never saw the dichotomy, lecturing younger colleagues like James (Scotty) Reston to remain detached. "Walter was more engaged with more presidents from Wilson to Lyndon Johnson than *anybody* in the press! He was always in the White House," Reston once exclaimed to me. Meanwhile, Stone was blackballed by the National Press Club after his premature gesture of civility in a Jim Crow era, inviting a black to lunch there.

A vital companion theme is the repression of dissent that Stone and others faced in the twentieth century and which continues to this day. Stone never confused dissent with disloyalty, as mainstream media and the government so often do. Stone fervently loved this country, viewing dissenting voices as crucial for keeping it true to its ideals.

Since Stone wrote and thought everything out loud in the public arena, there are no private papers or memos and only sparse correspondence—the stuff of conventional biographies. Because of this, one extraordinary lie has been promulgated by the far right bent on besmirching Stone's legacy. They repeat the falsehood that Stone's family burned his papers, hinting at some dark conspiracy. They deduced this from *Nation* writer D. D. Guttenplan's innocent observations that Stone had left no papers. After more than a decade of examining Stone, I can sadly attest to Guttenplan's accuracy and applaud his continual debunking of Izzy-the-spy lies that the neocons spread. However, I hope to provide new insights from numerous unpublished reminiscences of family and friends, unpublished interviews with Stone, his massive and unpublished FBI file, recently declassified Russian, Chinese, and North Korean documents, and his own riveting words that flowed by the millions during nearly seventy years of writing and speaking. Stone's style combined a comic's gift for one-liners, an eye for the "significant trifle," and trenchant analysis of world affairs.

Major reasons underscore the importance of revisiting Izzy. His life was fascinating, his observations of a half century ago ring with amazing significance today, his work and methods should be taught in all journalism classes. As this book will show, he is a sheer delight to read, evocative, provocative, and witty. He needs to be known by journalism students and a young audience. Finally, he needs to be defended from posthumous lies perpetuated by today's right-wing media.

His work helps evaluate the best and the worst in today's journalism. Although Stone inspired many, he was too much of an original to be fully emulated. His vibrancy and zest for life, his enthusiasms for everything from disco dancing to Demosthenes, his curiosity and hound-dog tenacity, would have made I. F. Stone unique in any arena. But he was especially so in Washington. Most of the time, he simply didn't give a damn if he was an outcast. He slaved to make history and current events "fun"—a favorite word. He struggled always to write his "soufflés," articles and books as airy as confections despite the substance larded into each sentence.

Best of all, commented journalist and novelist Nicholas Von Hoffman, "There are so few troublemakers and he was a wonderful troublemaker. He had such wonderful guts. He defied the social fears which make cowards of most of us. He was his own person in the ice age of big, controlling institutions and organizations. He could stand alone and stand apart and therefore stand for what he believed in." Stone was nothing like today's prepackaged bloviators pickled in self-importance who offend and lampoon easy targets that feed their flocks' prejudices. An equal-opportunity deflator, when Stone perceived injustice, inequity, or lies billed as truth, he sometimes turned intimate fans into intimate foes. Izzy collected countless critics left, right, and center, alienating just about everyone at one time or another. He loathed pontificating, thumb-sucking pundits and carefully crafted a breezy, provocative style. Never far from his autodidactic grounding in the classics and philosophy, Stone possessed a memory of confounding accuracy; a scholar's grasp of the past that he applied to current events with dazzling relevance; a trial lawyer's proclivity for the tough question. Coupled with these attributes, Stone's skepticism regarding the professed nobility of government intentions served him well.

In the same year that Stone died, 1989, *Nightline*'s anchor, Ted Koppel, said of the establishment media, "We are a discouragingly timid lot . . . people whose job it is to manipulate the media know that . . . many of us are truly only comfortable when we travel in a herd." Stone was comfortable traveling alone.

Government leaks tossed out at private dinner parties were as suspicious as hand grenades to him. And a reporter had to "bone up" in advance and ask good questions to get both news and respect from officials. "You can't just sit on their lap and ask them to feed you secrets—then they'll just give you a lot of crap." The First Amendment was Stone's bible and Jefferson his God. Stone never stopped preaching against secrecy in government. "Inevitably such organizations [the FBI, CIA, NSA] become means of inhibiting the exercise of freedom of liberties and intimidate people." Few but Stone had the nerve to ridicule FBI director J. Edgar Hoover at the height of his power, calling him a "glorified Dick Tracy" and "the sacred cow," knowing full well that Hoover would retaliate. From the thirties to his death in 1972, Hoover endlessly hounded Stone, amassing thousands of pages, staking out such subversive activities as buying cigars, picking out groceries, writing letters to his hearing-aid company. The FBI bugged his phone and pawed through his garbage. Comrades in the hunt were the CIA, State Department, Army, Internal Revenue Service, U.S. Post Office, and U.S. Passport Office.

For most of the nightmare years of Bush's reign, marked by defiant secrecy, a compliant White House press corps, known to some in the trade as "access whores"; a conglomerate Murdochian right-wing drift; "liars for hire" paid by the administration to tout its programs; deferential acceptance of administration fibs—all were disgraceful capitulations to power. It is frustrating to observe such follies where mainstream media shy from accurately informing the public, burying major stories in an avalanche of celebrity trash. During the Iraq invasion, jingoism replaced journalism.

Instead of reporting scandals, establishment newspapers created them. Fiction appeared in articles in the *New York Times,* the self-proclaimed newspaper of record. Both the *Times* and the *Washington Post* were forced to issue postmortem mea culpas for their unquestioning hype of Bush's WMD false raison d'être for war. Their admission that they'd buried stories expressing doubts—written by a fine *Post* reporter, Walter Pincus, who was inspired by Stone—demonstrated the folly when administrative sources are sacrosanct. Which illustrates Stone's dry comment "Establishment reporters undoubtedly know a lot of things I don't. But a lot of what they know isn't true."

A miracle would be the day that the media did not show up for hollow photo ops such as the "Mission Accomplished" and "Plan for Victory" obscenities. As 2005 came to an end, indictments fell like snowflakes, and journalists began reporting on a host of Republican scandals, leading with the resignation of Cheney's top aide, Scooter Libby, after his indictment on five counts—obstruction of justice, perjury, and false statements—in the probe of White House leaks to journalists regarding the outing of CIA agent Valerie Plame. (In 2007, Bush swiftly commuted Libby's thirty-month prison term.) The *Washington Post*'s Dana Priest broke the story of CIA torture prisons in Europe; the *Los Angeles Times* broke the story of a Defense Department contractor that paid Iraqi journalists to run fake upbeat war stories in Baghdad media; *Time*'s embedded reporter Michael Ware exposed phony administration claims that an assault was primarily led by Iraqi forces. Still, it took the *New York Times* a full year to disclose that it had learned of warrantless wiretapping of U.S. citizens.

No discussion of a free press is without a heated look at "objectivity"—a deceptively simple concept. At its very worst, what is collected in an "objective" fashion can be a major trap (witness every single story garnered from a spin-minded administration source; the prime example is the *New York Times*'s Judith Miller's—as well as reporters on other publications—credulous reporting on WMDs, which obviously seemed "objectively accurate" to their editors at the time). Because it was the vaunted *Times*, television followed with inaccuracies based on its coverage.* After the *Times* finally chastised Miller for her blind acceptance of false WMD information and her dealings with Libby, her career there was over. It is time to resurrect Stone's warning: "You cannot get intimate with officials and maintain your independence. No matter whether they are good guys or bad guys don't get intimate with them or you'll lose your independence and they'll use you."

The fifteen-second sound bite is carefully crafted by spin doctors to mask or deflect news and is religiously regurgitated on TV.

This was no more evident than the straight-faced TV and front page repeats of Karl Rove's excuse for leaving the White House in 2007. The mastermind of campaign dirty tricks and leaker of smears, trailed by a Senate subpoena, was departing to "spend more time with the family"—

---

*See "Buying the War," *Bill Moyers Journal* with McClatchy reporters Jonathan Landay and Warren Strobel, first broadcast on PBS, 4/25/07. The WMD–*New York Times* debacle exposed a sad truth about media clout. Superior reporting by the Knight-Ridder bureau (now McClatchy) revealing the lack of WMDs was ignored by other media and deemed unimportant because the chain had no outlets within the Beltway or in Manhattan. Some papers in the chain dumped their accurate reporting to run the *New York Times* articles.

the first refuge of those embraced by trouble. The *New York Times* was tough but many mainstream editorials heaped farewell praise on Rove— ignoring the flat-out lies of his victory-at-all-costs tactics, his demonizing of "unpatriotic" anti-war politicians, and his helping to set in motion domestic and foreign disasters that will take years to repair.

Stone would have applauded CBS News's Bill Plante, forced to shout a question because the president wasn't taking any, as Rove and Bush exited the Rose Garden: "If he's so smart, why did you lose Congress?" Plante was lambasted for his "unprofessional" act. "Reporters are not here as guests," Plante said. "We're here to ask questions. If we were ever to agree to 'behave' we'd be walking away from our First Amendment role—and then we really would be the shills we're so often accused of being." And now a 2003 view from the enraptured *Washington Post*'s David Broder: "Let me disclose my own bias. I like Karl Rove." Broder had enjoyed eating quail with Rove and "long and rewarding talks," in which it can be assured that crafty Karl said nothing he didn't want used.

Stone rejected the idea of the reporter as a robot with no political passion or insight. "Without forgoing accuracy and documentation," Stone argued, reporters did not need to be "neutral." "There's no use interviewing anybody," he said, "if you're only going to ask them baby questions." Said Izzy, "A newspaperman ought to use his power on behalf of those who were getting the dirty end of the deal. . . . And when he has something to say, he ought not to be afraid to raise his voice above a decorous mumble, and to use forty-eight-point bold." "Izzy's point was that reporters were not stenographers," said investigative reporter and author Scott Armstrong, who organized the campaign that convinced President Clinton to veto the Official Secrets Act—a provision that would have for the first time in U.S. history criminalized the unauthorized disclosure of government information by federal employees and whistle blowers. "Izzy was eternally disappointed that so many were not willing to find the public records and say, 'These two points have been said and it's wrong. Here's what the record *shows*.'"

Or, as Stone put it, what often bothered him more than the *presence* of opinion was the *lack* of news in articles. As British publisher Lord Northcliff uttered, "News is something someone wants to suppress. Everything else is advertising."

Finding Real News means searching beyond the carefully crafted word of official dissemblers. Faux objectivity is when one gets lies, in the guise of formal statements, from the Robert McNamaras and the Scooter Libbys and Tom DeLays and Kenneth Lays and presidents and prime ministers. Real objectivity is when reporters dig into documents, find a credible whistle-blower source, or learn things on their own and verify them.

As a columnist, when he was not doing straight reporting, Stone committed no crime when he voiced his opinions or marshaled facts to fit his ideology and principles. Nonetheless, his enemies on the right, who consistently do the same, castigate him for the sin of having opinions. Stone advised young writers to keep in the back of their minds, no matter how impassioned their feelings, that "you may be full of BS" and, unlike many pundits, was not overly concerned about being viewed as right or wrong. He knew that such analysis depended on the prevailing political, social, and cultural framework of the moment. "Either you're going to sit on your ass and write your preconceptions or you're going to be a good reporter and that means being inconsistent. You change your mind or admit an error because things are very complicated and people do change and it's fascinating to watch them." Stone also learned to "go into the bowels of government where the really good sources are. They are good public servants, very often breaking their hearts with frustration. They're the best kind of source."

As Bill Kovach, chairman of the Committee of Concerned Journalists, notes, "Izzy's lasting strength rests on his fierce independence *and* on documentation. His independence is what inspired us and in many cases shamed most of us much of the time. But it was the material Izzy produced from his close reading of the official record and careful listening of official words that was valuable to the public and to history. When Izzy allowed his deep beliefs to override his journalism or verification he got himself into trouble. But his objective method—his objectivity as a journalist—is what brought him back to earth."

Scotty Reston recalled his tribute when Lippmann turned seventy-five: "I said that the great achievement of Lippmann was that he was a great definer of issues and that he used the news as a peg for his philosophy of government. He defined the *issues* better than anybody else. Well, he didn't like that. He wanted to be judged on the basis of whether what he had written and what he had proposed was right or wrong. And that record was *not* very good."

Stone was far from a mere dissenting polemicist. "Izzy realized some things that most journalists forget—when the decision on the controversy is taken, it is only then that you really begin to have available to you the facts that brought the crisis about," reflected Reston. "Most reporters, I among them, usually when the decision is taken, go on to something else, but not Izzy. . . . He would go back and read and interview and then bring together a story about what had really happened—which was usually so much better and accurate than the day-to-day coverage."

At Stone's death in 1989, a laudatory *Washington Post* editorial nonetheless chided Stone for "misappraising" some societies and rulers. Scoffed Von Hoffman, "They should look to themselves and the establishment press who urged going slow on the 'Negro question' when Izzy was taking black judges to lunch, couldn't see—and even defended—Vietnam while Izzy was seeing something else, or when they played into Cold War fanaticism and helped the China lobby to exist for years." A longtime anti-Stalinist, Von Hoffman said, "On Russia, certainly Izzy can be criticized, but in so many other arenas his vision stands up far better than most establishment journalism." Stone was far ahead of the pack regarding pivotal trends in twentieth-century history: the American labor movement, Hitler and the rise of Fascism, disastrous Cold War foreign policies, domestic purges, covert actions of the FBI and the CIA, the greatness of the civil rights movement, the horror of Vietnam, the strengths and weaknesses of the anti-war movement, the disgrace of Iran-contra, and the class greed of Reaganomics.

Initial research on this book began in 1990 when Google and bloggers were unknown terms. The Library of Congress was home while studying Stone's roots and political leanings, early socialist and labor movements, the New Deal, the cold war and the "Red Menace" decade, Stone's controversial book on Korea, and civil rights.

Many of the 1960s civil rights activists and anti–Vietnam War protestors who made *I. F. Stone's Weekly* a success never knew his rich past. Child publisher at fourteen, in 1933 the twenty-five-year-old Stone was the youngest editorial writer on a major daily, slashing away at Hitler, whose ascendancy was largely ignored by Walter Lippmann. As a thirties radical, Stone mingled with the famous: Charlie Chaplin and Orson Welles, Clifford Odets and John Dos Passos, James Thurber and Heywood Broun, Lillian Hellman and Dashiell Hammett. Future talents who were teenagers in the forties—Joseph Heller and Jules Feiffer and Philip Roth and E. L. Doctorow—read Stone in *PM* and *The Nation*.

Stone wrote millions upon millions of words on everything from Woodrow Wilson's peace initiatives to Ronald Reagan's Star Wars. He had a roiling history with fellow Jews; beloved when he became the first reporter in the world to travel illegally with holocaust survivors to Palestine, he was soon denounced by some as a Jew hater for championing the rights of displaced Palestinians.

Stone achieved the remarkable: he reached the age of eighty-one without growing old. Buoyed by a childlike ebullience, he often used a line that Moyers now loves to repeat when he praises Stone: "I am having so much fun I ought to be arrested."

During the Vietnam War, Stone's truth became so popular that his *Weekly* made money. A toiler outside the system, Stone was never one to take a vow of poverty and reveled in buying his wife a mink coat, joking that he had become a war profiteer. His irredeemable optimism made it all sound simple, but he worked long and furiously, relying on his own digging so that by the time he approached an official he was ready to confront him with facts. Stone's digging brought no cozy enshrinement in Washington's power circles during the dark days of McCarthyism. A stunning change occurred in the last years of his life. When Stone died, mainstream journalists who had once ignored him were stumbling all over themselves to laud "Izzy."

Then came posthumous vilification. After Stone was safely dead, right-wingers displayed their estimable courage by slandering Stone as a Soviet spy. By misrepresenting information found in decrypted Russian memos unearthed a half century after the fact, they continue their calumny into the present. Worse, mainstream media have repeated these lies, often unquestioningly.

One would like to simply dismiss, for example, the rants of Ann Coulter, the Queen of Sleaze, whose aversion to the truth is matched by an utter lack of decency. Before the Internet, talk radio, and cable TV, such extremists were relegated to fringe publications. Today, the far right, no matter how baseless their arguments, have found prominence and financial heaven. Sadly, every uncorrected falsehood, such as her lies about Stone, remains in the blogosphere, often repeated by a mainstream media scrambling for an audience.

Therefore when it applies to Stone or his work, material that surfaced well after his death has been addressed in the body of the book. Unfortunately, Stone cannot defend himself as he did so aptly in life.

He once described to me how he felt about politicians and journalists who had shunned him during the fifties: "I used to walk across the lawn at the Capitol and I would think, 'Screw you, you sons of bitches. I may be just a goddamn Jew Red to you, but I'm keeping Jefferson alive!'"

Stone was lauded for his ability to find exposés in documents that other journalists were too lazy to read or overlooked when they did read them. Again, it is not so easy to take a fresh look, to disabuse oneself of the perceived wisdom that is the stock-in-trade of government documents and press conferences. Friend and fellow journalist Christopher Lydon said, "Izzy was the only journalist, surely, who comes close to the notion of genius."

Stone would not have disputed that opinion. Fresh from his best-selling triumph *The Trial of Socrates*, eighty-year-old Stone told an audience that he had written a speech for Socrates. In fact, he said, it was a damn good speech. In fact, "I think that if Socrates had delivered *it* to the jury, he would have gotten acquitted." Stone enjoyed the ensuing laughter but in no way felt his assessment was a joke.

One criticism of Stone is that he gave Communist dictators more slack than right-wing demagogues during the thirties and forties. Even friendly critics argued that he was late to voice full-fledged criticism of Stalin's horrors. When he did, in the mid-fifties, his passionate admission lost him subscribers who still clung to the Bolshevik dream. However, his critics are incorrect when they paint him as uncritical of the USSR or American Communists; as far back as the thirties, Stone was assailing the system's repression. He belittled the "little Stalins" in the American Communist Party (CPUSA). During McCarthyism, Stone repeatedly advised America to not "go the way of Russia." Stone's inconsistencies as well as his thinking on this subject are addressed.

Stone was attacked for thinking that the road to peace with Communist regimes was through diplomacy rather than tough threats of war. Irony did not escape him in 1988, at the age of eighty. "Who would have thought it?" he remarked. "First, President Richard Nixon—that old Red-baiter—met with Mao. Now Reagan, the great opponent of the 'evil empire'! Who would have dreamt that he would head for a summit with Gorbachev and drop back from the nuclear abyss?" (Stone chuckled at how Reagan's actions had alienated all of the "kooks" in his corner.) Stone couldn't have been more pleased that these two heroes of the right had approached the Communists in the manner that Stone had been vilified for advocating all along.

The terrorizing predictions of a unified international Communism never happened. Long ago, Stone was alone in American journalism when he argued that the domino theory was wrong, that Communist leaders played one against the other and their ideological internationalists were subdued by pragmatists. Vietnam is a prosperous free-enterprise partner with the United States now, after all that bloodshed.

Stone did not live to see the collapse of the Soviet Union, but he had traveled a long road since his adolescent enthusiasm for the 1917 Russian Revolution. In later life he ardently befriended Communist dissidents. "There are great risks in a free society, but the risks of dictatorship are even greater. . . . The only thing that made it look good was the absence of a free press and a solid wall around it."

After a long detour, I returned to Stone in 2002, having received the last of some five thousand pages of FBI files. I realized rudimentary explanations were in order for a new generation, most of whom no doubt think that a person speaking of HUAC is referring to some man named Hugh Ack, as did a transcriber of my audiotape interview with the eminent John Kenneth Galbraith. That inquisitional body which terrorized leftists for decades, the House Un-American Activities Committee, was no longer recognized by its famous abbreviation.

By then, my office was a canyon of FBI boxes. Many Stone files are redacted and missing, despite fruitless years of appeals; Stone was dead, informants—FBI "moochers" Stone termed them—were dead, the USSR had collapsed, no conceivable threats to national security existed. Still, the remaining files form a fascinating paper trail of invasions and assaults on private citizens. Hoover spent a great deal of taxpayers' money, sometimes illegally and always secretively and unethically, on what any sane person would think was a fairly needless exercise. On pain of death Stone could not have contained himself from writing and saying everything he thought.

Stone took the long view. American history had always "been marked by recurrent periods of paranoia, bigotry and fear of new ideas," he noted, but he remained optimistic and loyal. In the slaughterhouse that is human history, despite its flaws, America's democracy was one of the few "bright spots," he always said. This did not mean that Stone ever stopped trying to goad it toward a more perfect union.

People often mistook Stone's passionate arguments for personal animus. Stone never hated anyone, with the exception of Cold Warrior John Foster Dulles, whom he dismissed as the "Cracked Cato of Capitalism." If Stone had been a sour, curdled gadfly, his legacy would have been spent long ago, like those of Walter Winchell and Westbrook Pegler. Like all interesting people, Stone was as complex as he was controversial. He could be prickly and kind, generous and unconcerned, self-absorbed but consumed with society's underdogs. He could be peevishly impatient on deadline, then all smiles at dinner. He suffered fools not at all, but spent hours encouraging young writers.

"I used to get extremely discouraged, but he *never* did," said his longtime friend and editor of the *Progressive* magazine, the late Erwin Knoll. He said Stone's mistakes came from his idealism, "incurable optimism," and the desire to think the best of mankind.

The great caricaturist David Levine portrayed Stone with a demonic gleam in his eye, digging out the dirt in Congress. Stone said, however, "I don't think the primary job of a free journalist in a free society is digging out the dirt. That's part of it, I suppose. The real problem is to provide greater understanding of the complexities in which your country and your people and your time find themselves enmeshed. That's our job, to translate these issues, to study them. The primary job is not to disgrace anybody or defame them, but to provide understanding."

As Stone often pointed out, the press, as it used to be called, was never as good as the myth. Historically, the control of news by the powerful was rampant. In Stone's day, family newspaper dynasties, wealthy businessmen, and government allies predominantly shaped the news and were typically antilabor, anti–New Deal, anti-civil-rights. Yet one could still find diversity and dissent printed by courageous publishers more interested in telling the truth than in large profits.

Today's vast media monopoly is no longer a fresh story but remains a disastrous new low, blocking diversity, severely hampering the public's right to know and substituting pap for truth. The far right are richly endowed by those with a vested interest in staying wealthy; their radio and television stations, newspapers, magazines, books, and Web sites disgorge to a global audience misleading information on everything from Bush tax cuts to the war on terrorism. The success of the right's media takeover was capped by Rupert Murdoch's 2007 purchase of *The Wall Street Journal*, a publication praised by Stone, who noted its curious schizophrenia. Tough front-page exposés of corporate scandals were often attacked in the *Journal*'s own reactionary editorials. If Murdoch's Fox News, *New York Post,* and other journalistic atrocities are indications, look for a *Journal* front page that will match its editorials. Such ravenous gobbling of media outlets was made possible when Congress passed and President Clinton signed into law the 1996 Telecommunications Act, characterized by journalist Bill Moyers as a "monstrous assault on democracy" and "a welfare giveaway to the largest, richest and most powerful media conglomerates in the world."

Ideology is matched by ignorance, dispensed to an often uncaring or gullible audience. On CNN in 2004, a morning-show host, Jack Cafferty, quipped that the start-up liberal-based network, Air America, was a "Communist radio network." When his cohost suggested liberalism wasn't the same as communism, Cafferty answered, "Aren't they synonymous?" That old canard, the myth of the liberal media, still sells; neocons know that they only have to use the word in a title and mainstream media will anxiously interview them or review their books to prove that the word does not apply to them. Cowardice should not be confused with credibility, but it is.

Telecommunication has transformed news gathering like no other revolution since the printing press. Those who started in journalism pounding typewriters and prowling libraries find Web sites an unfathomable miracle. In five minutes on the Internet, for instance, I was able to pull up the translated telegrams of Stalin to Mao during the Korean War. Yet this lightning ability to disseminate information has produced a troublesome database of lies as well as fact, trash and flash as well as insight. Rummaging through the blogosphere attic necessitates inexhaustible, exhausting attempts to separate truth from fiction.

Stone has been called, in effect, a Stone Age blogger. The best of blogs—such as Josh Marshall's scandal-busting "Talking Points Memo"—resemble him in shoe leather reporting. However, Stone's muckraking was mostly about improving the common good, with none of the rants found in many blogs. And it was arduous work to produce his dining table *Weekly*. Failing eyes were his search engine. He trudged to a printer, who typeset his prose, then he loaded his product into the trunk of his car, and his wife mailed it out.

There is one similarity to today's "nowhere to hide" technology. Stone's *Weekly* boxes, bordered in black, pioneered what YouTube, Jon Stewart's *Daily Show,* and blogs do with lightning relevancy as well as irreverence. Just as today's politicians and leaders are skewered by their own conflicting lies via video, Stone delighted in juxtaposing what Kissinger, for example, said on one day with a prevarication he said the next.

Now blogs are in danger of becoming as respectable as Stone was in his final days, with presidential candidates flocking to YouTube debates and mainstream media covering blog conventions.

Countless media watchdog groups, authors, and columnists such as the *Nation*'s Eric Alterman and the *New York Times*'s Frank Rich, have brilliantly addressed the good, the bad, and the ugly in today's megamonopoly media. Luckily, a host of the best journalists, many of whom were influenced by Stone, are still found in such publications as the *New York Review of Books,* the *New Yorker,* the *Nation,* and in smaller magazines like the *Washington Monthly.* In sad capitulation to the right, *Los Angeles Times* columnist Bob Scheer was fired in 2005 and replaced with neocon columnists. Luckily, voices of truth survive in media watchdog organizations such as FAIR, on the Web, and in independents like Jim Hightower and Bill Moyers. Many continue to see Stone as a beacon. The late great Molly Ivins, the leader in an unpopular posse pursuing and exposing George W. Bush, said, "I get courage just knowing Izzy is out there." Note that she did not use the past tense. Let us hope there will be a regenerative process with future generations, although the comments of one journalism professor at a major university are despairing; he told me that only 14 percent of his pupils were interested in print journalism. Stone would have regarded that as terrific odds. "All you can do, if you're lucky," he used to say to young journalists, "is change the odds a little. . . . You mustn't feel like a martyr. You've got to enjoy it."

Stone once protested, "I don't have a pessimistic view—I have a *long* view. If you want to change the human race overnight in a couple of meager centuries, of course it looks pessimistic. I have a basic democratic faith that there is a modicum of reason in all of us. And that's all we have to build on. And that's very precious." At the age of eighty, Stone sounded a warning much needed today: "Without that faith there is no reason for being a journalist. It's all we have to work with. That's supposed to be what motivates us."

He paused. "That is the heritage we have from Jefferson."

AUGUST 2007

PART ONE

The Making of a Maverick

1

COMING TO AMERICA

It was 1951, a harsh year during one of the darkest decades in American history for public, or even private, dissent. Friends were "naming names," telling the government of Communist, or merely fellow-traveler, friendships. Often the connection was tenuous, to a life buried in a distant past, but lives were being ruined. The FBI was spending millions in man-hours and money to stalk "Reds," that four-letter invective for anyone who might have embraced the Russian Revolution in the twenties or joined the Communist Party in the thirties or simply defended similar goals, such as organizing workers or fighting for civil liberties. Friends fled to Mexico, committed suicide, turned on one another. Even one's books could wreak havoc if a friend informed on a well-kept leftist library to the House Un-American Activities Committee, known as HUAC.

Isador Feinstein Stone was sickened by what he viewed as America's dangerous tilt toward fascism. He had traveled to Europe on a writing assignment, then urgently commanded his wife, Esther, and his two teenage sons, Jeremy and Christopher, to join him. Now they were living outside Paris.

It was Passover, a religious holiday that Stone had been known to pass over. Throughout his life, I. F. Stone loved to present a nonpious persona, joking that he was a "pious Jewish atheist." Still, he kept his bar mitzvah gift of Graetz's *History of the Jews* until his death and always felt "deeply Jewish." Now, in 1951, Stone decided to have a seder and asked his youngest son, Christopher, to invite a French Jew from school. As Stone read about the ancient exodus of Jews from Egypt and phrases of oppression and slavery, his voice choked and he stumbled over the words. Christopher thought his father was faltering on the Hebrew, but, looking over, saw tears in Stone's eyes. Christopher squirmed with teenage embarrassment that a friend might see his father crying.

A man more often of robust optimism, Stone never discussed the tears. From what wellspring did that emotion stem? Was he thinking of the centuries of Jewish persecution? Of the 6 million recently slaughtered in Hitler's ovens? Of the holocaust survivors with whom he had formed a strong bond five years before? His memories of 1946 were fresh. That year Stone, as the first journalist in the world to travel with European Jews on their illegal journey to Israel, endured the stench of their dank hold as they ran the British blockade. Crowded with him were Jews whose nightmares were as indelible as the numbers tattooed on their arms. Stone wept and hugged them when he said good-bye. Now, six years later in Paris as he read from the Haggadah, was Stone crying for his troubled America, so under the spell of hatred for "Reds" as to have lost all regard for those special American freedoms guaranteed in the Constitution? Stone was seriously considering self-imposed exile, in Israel.

His tears could have been for all of these reasons. There were, in that ugly time, so many reasons for which to weep.

Being a Jew whose family had fled czarist Russia was an important factor in shaping Isador Feinstein Stone, his mind and his theories, his decisions and his life, and drew him until the end of his days into controversy and ostracism. Isador's very being was in itself barely removed from the shtetl. His father, Bernard Feinstein, fled to America from Russia in 1905, only two years before Stone's birth—a time when Lenin, Trotsky, and Stalin belonged to the future.

Bernard was but five in 1881 when cataclysmic events shaped a harsh future for all Russian Jews. On a sunny day in March, a woman waited determinedly by a St. Petersburg canal for the passing of a sledge escorted by Cossacks. As it came in sight, she waved a handkerchief. Her signal was followed by an explosion, and "on the snow, huddled against the canal wall, lay a man with greying side-whiskers, whose legs and belly had been blown to shreds." The murder of Czar Alexander II was blamed on the Jews. In retaliation, new decrees destroyed the economic core of Jewish life, lasting until the 1917 revolution. They could not move from village to village, and rural commerce and community were all but eradicated. Doctors and lawyers could not practice, merchants could sell nothing but what they made by hand. Synagogues were silenced. Driven into poverty, 40 percent of Russian Jews were completely dependent on charity by the end of the nineteenth century.

Czar Nicholas II had succeeded Alexander III in 1894. His rule made the life of Jews during Bernard Feinstein's last ten years in Russia particularly intolerable. It was easy to dismiss a czar who was, at the age of twenty-six, still playing hide-and-seek with friends, but the weak and infantile Nicholas was dangerously pliable and abetted by his legacy, Alexander's reactionary court. The leading anti-Semite was its religious leader, Constantin Pobedonostsev. Some forty years before Hitler's final solution, Pobedonostsev plotted his own form of extermination. A group of Jews who petitioned him in 1898 were told that "one-third [of you] will die out, one-third will leave the country, and one-third will be completely dissolved in the surrounding population." When revolutionaries fought back, Czar Nicholas and his followers systematically pitted restive peasants against the Jews, who comprised a disproportionately large part of the revolutionary underground.

Jew baiting had worked successfully for eons throughout Europe, often providing a distracting antidote to revolutionary fervor. In 1903, orchestration was nevertheless needed to arouse the typical Russian peasant into murdering en masse. For that, newspapers were employed. In the province of Bessarabia the sole newspaper, the *Bessarabetz*, was a "sensation-mongering anti-Semitic journal." Its editor was subsidized by the czar's minister of the interior from a special slush fund. When the mutilated body of a Russian boy was discovered near Kishinev, the editor repaid the czar's largesse. The boy's uncle openly confessed to the murder, but headlines blared that it was a Jewish ritual murder. Handbills printed on the newspaper press called for the people of Kishinev to avenge the murder with "bloody punishment." The illiterate were whipped into a frenzy by those who could read.

On an April day in 1903, the massacre of Kishinev Jews began. For two days the police studiously remained in their barracks. Russian eyewitnesses described people torn in two, babies' brains splattered, bellies split open, tongues cut out, women's breasts cut off, men castrated, blinded, hanged, hacked to death.

This time, it was a pogrom to live in infamy; not only the Russian intelligentsia but Europeans and Americans, Jews and Christians, organized mass protests in major capitals. Pogroms continued nonetheless. The indifference of most Russian gentiles to the Kishinev slaughter was a warning to Jews throughout that snow-swept world. Bernard Feinstein, twenty-seven at the time, had been born into this unrelenting nightmare in a Ukrainian village called Gronov, not far from the Bessarabian province.

Feinstein never spoke to his children about those years. Like many Jews so subjugated, his education was nonexistent. He was the youngest of seven, with four brothers and two sisters. His mother, Rachel Tonkonogy, owned and operated an inn and raised seven children alone after her husband, Judah, died when Bernard was an infant. Rachel was daring enough to chase the Cossacks away with a whip when they came to the inn, a family legend that enthralled young Izzy.

Rachel was strikingly independent. One of her daughters, Eta, came to Rachel one day with a problem. She didn't think she really loved the man who was smitten with her. "What should I do?" she asked. "Marry him," Rachel advised. "If it doesn't work out, you can always get a get" (a religious divorce). Aunt Eta came to America and eventually married three times. Although all seven of Rachel's children escaped czarist Russia, Rachel never left Gronov.

How this Russian family acquired the Germanic name Feinstein remains a mystery. Bernard's grandfather was Mordecai Baer Tsvilichovsky. Like many Jews, some in the Tonkonogy-Tsvilichovsky clan compounded the confusion by giving each son a different last name in order to hide them from Russian Army conscription rolls. Desperate Jews even maimed their sons to save them from conscription. Of the six hundred anti-Jewish decrees enacted from 1825 to 1855, one sealed the fate of Jewish sons. The age of conscription for Jews was lowered to twelve. At that age, Bernard ran away from home, no doubt to escape conscription, but nonetheless became one of those poor Jewish children pressed into service. By 1905, when he was twenty-nine, Bernard had spent several years in the Army, no small testament to his ability to survive; conscription for Jews meant death or virtual life imprisonment. In his memoirs, Alexander Herzen mourned for conscripted Jewish boys: "these sick children, without care or kindness . . . were going to their graves." Conscription was a means of forced conversion to Christianity. Barracks masters beat, starved, and whipped Jewish boys to make them attend church services. Meanwhile, grieving parents said the kaddish, the mourner's prayer for the dead, for sons who had never even been bar mitzvahed.

After years of such hardship, Izzy's father planned his escape in 1905.

By virtue of inclination or circumstances, Bernard, unlike his firstborn son to be, was not a man who challenged existing conditions. He was not among the young Jewish Russian revolutionaries, socialists and anarchists who read Karl Marx and dreamed of overthrowing czars and organizing workers. When the Russian Army marched off en masse to Manchuria to fight the Japanese in 1904, revolutionaries seized the moment. As the year 1905 dawned, it looked as if a united workers' front might triumph. On Sunday, January 22, throngs of unarmed workers marched toward the czar's palace in nonviolent protest, armed with nothing more than icons, religious pictures, and banners. Songs and chants turned into screams and shrieks, only to be silenced by the steady blast of rifle fire from the palace guard. Children and women were deliberately trampled to death by Cossacks on horseback. At day's end, more than fifteen hundred men, women, and children lay dead or wounded in the crimson snow.

This massacre, forever known as Bloody Sunday, galvanized workers and students throughout Russia, and by that autumn they had organized a paralyzing general strike. After months of uprisings, assassinations, strikes, and mutinies, Czar Nicholas II was forced to meet the people's demands. A parliament, or Duma, to be elected by the people was established. Jews would be addressed for the first time by that title of freedom, *citizens*. They could live and work where they wanted, attend universities. No longer the pogroms. "No longer," however, was short-lived. By December, the czar had repelled the revolution and quickly revoked the constitution. The workers' soviet (council) was dissolved, its members imprisoned. And Jews were massacred in pogroms fueled by the czar. Inflamed by a revolution gone wrong, peasants savagely responded to the government's anti-Semitic demagoguery.

Kiev's pogrom haunted Sholem Aleichem forever. Known primarily in America as the dispenser of gaiety and humor in his *Fiddler on the Roof* versions of shtetl life, Aleichem re-created in his novel *In the Storm* the harsher reality he had personally witnessed. Seeking refuge in a Kiev hotel, Aleichem and his family awakened to shrill cries. It was the beginning of a three-night blood feast. In the street below Aleichem's hotel room, hoodlums beat a young Jew to death with heavy sticks as a policeman casually looked on. Aleichem's fiction retains the immediacy of truth. Russians were "breaking down doors, shattering windows, throwing, flinging, whipping, and hurling." With the cry of "Death to the Jews!" echoing, Aleichem's novel moves to a train station on a wet, cold morning after the pogroms. Jews crowded so close it was almost impossible to breathe, waiting for trains to take them to a new world; old women in babushkas, silent children in shock, mothers gripping bundles of cloth that held all that was left of family possessions. "The word *America* was heard more often than any other. . . . They imagined America to be a kind of heaven."

Bernard Feinstein was among that historic Jewish emigration to America. Nearly half a million streamed to America from 1904 to 1907, predominantly from eastern Europe. In the decade from 1900 to 1910 the total was 1,037,000. When word had passed through Bernard's outfit that they might soon be sent to fight in the Russo-Japanese War, he crept away from camp and headed toward Poland. A deserter and a Jew who could have been shot on sight, Bernard trudged torturous miles until he reached Hamburg, Germany. There, he boarded the next ship bound for Liverpool.

In his new, uncertain world and speaking only Yiddish, Bernard gratefully embraced his scholarly older brother Ithamar (called Shumer), who had settled in Cardiff, Wales, when fleeing Russia a few years before. After a short stay with Shumer, Bernard made the final leg of his journey.

Bernard was medium built and short, with blue eyes and curly black hair. Toughened by years of hardship, he was energetic and ready to savor the American dream along with countless other greenhorns. For days Bernard endured the reeking filth of steerage with its open troughs for toilets. He joined a long line of weak and groggy immigrants prodded along by immigration officials grown callous to this daily flood. The sickly or suspect, marked with colored chalk—*H* for "heart," *K* for "hernia," *Sc* for "scalp," *X* for "mental defects"—would be sent back. Petrified children watched as consumptive or frail relatives were pulled out of line and disappeared.*

By the time Bernard arrived, he was a familiar, unwelcome species. The previous wave of Jews, arriving in the mid to late 1800s, had settled in the Lower East Side of New York. Many had moved on and some had prospered handsomely. Now there was growing concern; what repressions could be in store for all Jews if Americans tired of this flood of penniless foreigners? Already there had been attacks from everyone— wealthy WASPs fearful that a glut of foreigners would wreck their carefully constructed caste system, and American workers fearing competition in

---

*In the spring of 1907, more than fifteen thousand immigrants arrived at Ellis Island in one day, although the maximum number had been set at five thousand. Haste resulted in criminally unsanitary practices; in 1922, British ambassador A. C. Geddes witnessed one doctor examining a line of males for venereal diseases or hernias. As he inspected their private parts, the doctor wore rubber gloves. "I saw him 'do' nine or ten men," reported Geddes. "His gloves were not cleansed between cases." Howe, *World of Our Fathers.*

the labor market. This new crop, with their stuttering attempts at English, faced hostility, scorn, and ridicule, not just from Americans, but from German Jews who had been off the boat for fifty years.

By 1907, the ninety thousand Jews arriving in New York City annually were mostly from Russia and Poland. Jews numbered roughly one-quarter of the city's total. They were the pushcart peddlers, garment cutters, and tailors who huddled in the Jewish quarter, where rats swarmed through open garbage and scurried across beds at night. Infants and elderly died from diseases caused by open sewers. There was no hiding from violence and crime, always twin companions in such hovels.

Just as German Jews had earlier endured the scorn of haughty and well-established Sephardim from Spain, it was now the Russian Jews' turn. Embarrassed that these "wild Asiatics" could be considered kin, prosperous German Jews saw themselves more as Americans of German descent than Jewish. Anti-Semitism poured from pages of the German Jewish press. The *Hebrew Standard* sneered that the "thoroughly acclimated Jew . . . is closer to the Christian sentiment around him than to the Judaism of these miserable darkened Hebrews." The German Jew created the slur of anti-Semites, *kike,* to describe the Russian Jew, because so many of their names ended in *ki.*

The Germanic Feinstein might have shielded Bernard, but his Yiddish was a giveaway. Yiddish was "piggish jargon"; German Jews tried to insist that it was understood only by Poles and Russians, when in reality Yiddish is a Judeo-German combination easily familiar to German Jews.

For all poor immigrants, America's paradise in reality became tenements and tireless work. Jewish newcomers were consigned to the lowliest jobs in the overwhelmingly Jewish garment trades. Young women developed curvature of the spine from hand-operating twenty-five-pound pressing irons. Old men in yarmulkes who stood for fifteen hours a day, cleaning and pressing cloth, walked forever stooped.

A 1903 report on the New York slums recounted the dangers of these firetraps with their vile privies, rickety stairs, broken plumbing pipes emitting sewer gas throughout the dark and fetid houses, pigs, goats, and horses in the cellars. Here, immigrants provided millions of dollars annually in rent, and slumlords were quick to denounce any who protested their living and working conditions. Labels, to be hurled against workers with fury and resilient effectiveness throughout the twentieth century, were used to diminish the protests of slum Jews. They were "radicals," "traitors," and "anarchists." Meanwhile, slumlords came in all denominations. Collecting millions in revenues from disease-ridden tenements, resisting the barest of health codes, was New York City's oldest, richest, and most fashionable religious parish, Trinity Church.

Reformers and socialists forced some tenement reforms, and a few conscientious newspapers alerted readers to the plight of immigrants. Jane Addams compared the "happy condition of Philadelphia" to other urban slums, but she had not inspected Philadelphia and only voiced popular hearsay. When Bernard arrived in Philadelphia, the majority of homes had no indoor water. Foul seepage from broken and open sewers and outdoor toilets or "vaults" (the labor department report felt the need to qualify) "may" have been responsible for Philadelphia's high typhoid fever rate.

Feinstein headed for Philadelphia because relatives were there. Prohibited in Europe from owning land and excluded from most professions, Jews had by default turned to merchandising. In their adopted country Jews continued to abound in commerce—from the wealthiest manufacturer to the poorest back peddler. Russian arrivals heard of immense wealth accumulated by German Jews and legendary figures such as Joseph Seligman. He started as a peddler and became a multimillionaire merchant and financier, a member of the exalted "Our Crowd," which aped the WASP 400 in opulence and conspicuous consumption.

By 1905, fortunes via this route were far from certain, but it remained one of the few avenues for poorly educated newcomers. And so Feinstein became a peddler. It was as if he had taken a page from Joseph Seligman's blueprint: "Sell anything that can be bought cheaply, sold quickly at a little profit, small enough to place inside a pack and light enough to carry." Bernard sold watches, slim and light and glistening in his case as he walked the streets of Philadelphia.

One of Bernard's friends was David Novack. David had one brother, Raphael, and three sisters, Celia, Bella, and Katy. These five were all that survived of thirteen children born in Odessa. Like many immigrants, the Novacks set sail in shifts, sending for other relatives when they could get the money. Katy had left with her father, who later sent for her mother. Katy was a favorite of brother David's. When she smiled, dimples creased her cheeks. David was happy to introduce the lively Katy to his friend.

She was ten years younger than Bernard. In March of 1907, Bernard married the twenty-one-year-old Katy. Soon she was pregnant. On a

night that gentiles everywhere were celebrating, Bernard and Katy Feinstein's first son was born. It was Christmas eve, December 24, 1907.

They called him Isador—which was quickly and irrevocably shortened to Izzy.

2

BEGINNINGS

When I. F. Stone became famous, his features seemed made for political cartoonists such as David Levine and Jules Feiffer. They captured a cheerful curmudgeon: round cheeks deeply dented by dimples, jolly wattles, cherubic smile, the gleam in those slightly bulging eyes peering out from behind incredibly thick glasses. Writers strained for descriptions. He was "a dumpling of a man, who appears to have the head of an owl on the body of a penguin." Aware that literary allusions might escape a TV-drenched generation, some writers compared him to cinema characters Yoda or E.T. It took Stone to provide a distinctive description, as he watched himself in a taped television interview looking short and squat, his full lids rhythmically blinking behind those glasses. "Good God," he said, "I look like a Jewish bullfrog!"

In earlier years, Stone found little humor in his looks, which later settled into character and caricature. It was something to make fun of when one felt as secure and, in his own iconoclastic fashion, as institutionalized as Stone and so well-known that *New Yorker* and other national cartoon captions referred to him simply as Izzy.

Izzy once revealed paradoxical feelings: "When you grow up a short, little Jew, funny-looking, with those funny-looking glasses, and you adore these six-foot WASP beauties who won't look at you . . ." A screen came down on that insecure recollection. "Personally I felt I was Galahad, but I was Isador. Who calls anybody Isador?" For his first thirty years, Stone was Isador Feinstein. In 1937, he created the name I. F. Stone.

Infant Izzy was as cherubic as he was in old age. Dark ringlets curled in profusion, his chubby cheeks were pierced by dimples, and his eyes held a steady gaze. For the first three years of his life, Stone was surrounded by an enraptured mother, one set of grandparents, several aunts and uncles. Whatever strife the often-absent, hardworking Bernard experi-enced as he grasped English and the peddler's trade were unknown to his toddler son. In one early photograph, the family is the picture of middle-class respectability. Bernard stands beside Katy, his hand resting on the back of her high-backed chair, wearing a dark suit, starched shirt, and bow tie, slightly askew. He has kindly eyes, the barest impression of a smile. Katy is buxom and wears a high-necked dark dress, adorned with embroidery at the wrists and neck and a gold watch pinned to her left lapel. Her curly brunette hair is constrained in a rolled pompadour. Izzy and his mother share a quizzical gaze. Her left hand firmly holds Izzy's right as he leans against her knee. Izzy's hair is slicked down; he wears a starched white dress and a look of perplexed dissatisfaction, left arm reaching out as if to bolt from this confining exercise.

Katy was Izzy's blanket of security. For five years, Izzy had his mother to himself. In those five years, Izzy and his mother forged a deep bond, not to be superseded or broken by the arrival of three other children. Izzy benefited from such special treatment, enjoying a lasting self-confidence, sometimes with displays of autocratic petulance. As Freud noted, "A man who has been the indisputable favorite of his mother keeps for life the feeling of a conqueror, that confidence of suc-cess that often induces real success." Such an idolized firstborn looks upon himself as "his majesty, the baby." In later life, Izzy often assumed that people would indulge him.

But that pampered childhood had dark shadows. During his infancy, Izzy's vivacious mother fell ill with one of the first episodes of a manic-depressive, or bipolar, psychosis that pursued Katy Feinstein all of her life. Izzy was abandoned, in a sense, during his mother's breakdown, and he was cared for by his mother's parents, who spoke only Yiddish, which became Izzy's first language.

When Izzy was about three, there was a major uprooting. Life was not all bliss in the melding of Feinsteins and Novacks. To put distance be-tween Katy and her family, the trio left Philadelphia at Bernard's urging. Katy's illness may have been exacerbated by her relationship with her mother. Perhaps Bernard's avowed agnosticism did not set well with his in-laws, who refused to visit unless Katy and the unobservant Bernard followed Orthodox dietary laws. At any rate, the trio settled in Rich-mond, Indiana, far west in those 1910 horse-and-buggy days. Izzy star-tled the neighbors in this "very small gentile town." As he toddled down the street, he greeted surprised strangers in Yiddish.

Peddlers had to sell to gentiles to make a living. Perhaps Izzy was ashamed of his father's peddling; he never mentioned it in numerous interviews and once said that his father bought a store in Richmond. Other family members vividly recall that Feinstein set out every day with horse and wagon to sell and sometimes took the train to more distant towns. Katy and her toddler son were left alone, and waiting to be fed in the barn was the horse. Katy feared the beast. Years later she would delight Izzy, dramatizing how she would open the top half of the double door, fling in an armload of hay, than flee to the kitchen.

Izzy was almost five when his first brother was born, on September 6, 1912. For seventeen years of his life, he was known as Max. Only when Max dug out his birth certificate to obtain a driver's license did the Feinsteins see *Marcus*. ("It must have been the creative effort of some country clerk," recalls brother Lou, who was born in 1917.) After that, Stone's brother was always called Marc.

When Max/Marcus came along, Izzy had a new diversion. Three months shy of five, he started kindergarten. In a class picture, Izzy is the only child smiling, albeit slightly. He wears a navy blue sailor suit and high button shoes. His expression conveys a slightly bored haughtiness. In love almost from birth with the written word, he was never equally enamored of school and often felt above the level of his particular class.

Lonesome for family, Katy persuaded Bernard to return to Philadelphia with Izzy and infant Max. The last straw was a terrifying night of thunderstorms. As a nearby river flooded, they scrambled to the top of a hill and the railroad station. They took the first train east, never to return.

In Camden, New Jersey, Bernard unsuccessfully tried to run a butcher shop. The family then moved six miles east, to the village of Haddonfield, where Bernard and Katy opened Feinstein's Dry Goods Emporium, later called Ladies and Gents Furnishings, in what had been the 1859 town meeting hall. It stood on the corner of the main street, Kings Highway, and looked like the setting for a Western movie with its watering trough and hitching post and one step leading to a long, low porch. The family lived above the store and in two spacious rooms at the rear.

In this quiet Protestant community, Izzy was aware that the Feinsteins were different, along with a handful of other Jews in the trades. Many residents were middle-class Republicans who worked as junior executives in Camden and Philadelphia for RCA, Campbell's Soup, insurance companies, banks, and public utilities. Izzy's parents were only casual Democrats, but Stone recalled that the only other Democrat in his class was an Irish Catholic. There were no Catholic churches or synagogues in Haddonfield.

During World War I, this town of five thousand mirrored the rest of small-town America—observing rationing and exuding patriotism and xenophobia. Postwar normalcy brought prosperity, "rugged individualism," and hostility to things foreign or challenging to a myopic status quo. It was a time of Babbittry and God-fearing bigotry, when "Bolsheviks" and blacks could be run out on a rail with no thought to one's churchgoing conscience by "homo boobiens," as H. L. Mencken termed them.

Izzy vividly recalled his first brush with racial bigotry, when he witnessed a brave act of protest in small-town America. Eight-year-old Izzy was awakened by the sound of chanting and looked out the bay window in his second-floor bedroom. A group of blacks had left their segregated part of town to picket the showing of D. W. Griffith's *Birth of a Nation* at the movie house down the street. As he watched this gathering in the shadowy light, young Izzy felt that something was terribly wrong for grown men and women to resort to such measures. Griffith's 1915 landmark epic exalted a post–Civil War South where white sheets didn't stay on the clothesline. No matter his revolutionary film technique, Griffith's racist thrust, with the Ku Klux Klan riding to the rescue, caused rioting in some cities. A few years later, a flourishing Klan, half a million strong across the nation, paraded in sheets and hoods past the White House and in small towns, spewing hatred of blacks, Jews, Catholics, and immigrants, lynching and beating and branding.

Even in small-town Haddonfield, the Klan staged a hooded march down Kings Highway. Haddonfield's handful of Jews apprehensively closed their doors. As the Klan surveyed onlookers from behind their hoods, Bernard determined to make a small sign of protest. He stood in front of his store, staring them down. Standing next to his father, Lou recognized from his shoes and height a Klan customer who often joked with him. The next day, the man walked past. "Hi, I saw you in the parade yesterday," piped up Louie. Bernard grabbed his son by the arm and steered him inside the store with a smart swat on the behind. Only years later did Louie realize that one did not publicly recognize a Klansman—particularly when he was the town's police chief.

Roughly divided in half by tracks of the Reading Railroad Seashore Line, Haddonfield's West Side boasted spacious homes and a private eighteen-hole golf course. The Feinsteins lived comfortably enough over the store but did not associate with this wealthy world except through customers. There were rare ripples of excitement when the horse-and-buggy fire brigade dashed out of the firehouse across the street. On Saturdays, farmers came to town, hitching their horses at the Feinstein's Dry Goods Emporium's watering trough, stomping into the store in heavy work boots, perfuming the store, which Katy would air out afterward, with manure and sweat.

Outside the store, trolley cars clanged to a stop on their six-mile journey to Camden. Next door was the candy store, run by two old maids and their deaf brother. Down the street was the pool hall, cigar store, hardware store, and the meeting hall of the Independent Order of Odd Fellows. Kings Highway was originally built by British troops during the revolution; some of the buildings were pockmarked by bullet holes, reminders of battles between American and Hessian troops. In 1931, eighteen-year-old Marc published a directory of Haddonfield, and his twenty-three-year-old brother attempted to liven up his contribution. Izzy reported a 1752 occurrence: "the hussy," an Irish servant girl, ran off with a manservant. "Even in those days," added Izzy, "the servant problem was acute." Izzy archly overreached by paraphrasing *Hamlet* as he described an eighteenth-century suitor: "Estaugh, if not sicklied over, was at least greatly slowed up in his lovemaking, by the pale cast of thought."

The Feinsteins prospered enough to afford a live-in maid, a situation so foreign to one cousin that he remembered it a half century later. The maid was a necessity for Katy. She had become an excellent businesswoman, despite cooking and caring for what must have seemed a continuous round of "only" children: Marc was five years younger than Izzy, Louie was born another five years later, and Judy, the youngest, was born seventeen years after Izzy. Katy raced from her kitchen to the front store to wait on customers and, unusual for a woman in those days, went on buying trips to Philadelphia, striking hard bargains for merchandise. Soon Feinstein's was the rival of Fowlers Department Store, their main competition.

Filling the store were bolts of cloth, ready-made dresses, men's caps and hats, overalls, work pants, stiffly starched shirts, silk stockings, corsets, and brassieres. The Feinstein brothers began clerking young and by the time they were teenagers were so expert at sizing up women that they could suggest a size 36 or 38 bra with assurance. Old patterns were never discarded; they became the specialty of the Feinstein bathroom. Izzy and his brothers never saw toilet paper until they left home.

Between waiting on customers, Katy concocted superb meals. Her fruit strudel and hamantaschen, served at Purim, were unsurpassed. The Jewish Sabbath was not observed because Saturday was the busiest day in the store, but Friday-night candles were lit and prayers said before the traditional dinner of chopped liver, chicken soup, and boiled chicken. The kitchen opened onto a back porch where a barrel filled with marinating garlic pickles stood. White brine on her sons' hands instantly informed Katy when they had raided the barrel. Over the store was a roomy upstairs with a library-playroom, rear enclosed porch used as a sleeping room in summer, large living room, and three bedrooms. Bay windows faced Kings Highway, and young Izzy would watch trolley-car lights dancing across the ceiling at night.

In those upstairs rooms, lying on a couch, gorging on pretzels and books, Izzy found a world that took him far from the dreariness of waiting on customers, far from other boys and girls whose thoughts were on such foreign amusements as sledding, baseball, and congregating at the ice cream parlor.

"Izzy was a child of the Enlightenment," reasoned one friend, Marcus Raskin. "His optimism came from his belief in reason and knowledge. His idea was that the more you knew and the more that you could put things into a historical context, the more science there was, the more enlightenment there was, the more progress there would be. And so the idea of doubt about the kinds of positivist rationality which had developed over the course of his lifetime was never strong. It really almost didn't exist."

Even as a small child, Izzy had begun his lifelong inclination to question, to search for facts. He was very much afraid of ghosts. One night, Izzy forced himself to stand, wide-eyed in one corner of the room in the dark, waiting for ghosts to come and do whatever ghosts do to little boys. After quaking and blinking into the darkness, Izzy deduced that ghosts did not exist and went to bed. He slept ghost-free nights from then on and said with finality and certitude that ghosts did not exist. A child less certain of the empirical evidence of one night could have hypothesized a more angst-filled scenario; that it was, say, merely the ghosts' night off. But not Izzy.

With his hunger for books and ideas, Izzy was a misfit. Such a loner's childhood, not uncommon for writers and thinkers, often provides a necessary solitude for intellectual reflection. For the alien, the critical eye is nurtured. In later life, Izzy's selective memory painted an idyllic childhood in a "wonderful town," but sometimes a different picture surfaced, and Stone would admit that it was lonesome being a radical bookworm in a very small *Main Street* kind of town. "I was kind of a freak," he said. As he walked down the streets, taunts of "four eyes" and "bookworm" and "kike" trailed Izzy, epithets that made Marc cringe and vow never to be like his brother. Izzy made up his own world, filled with characters and ideas from another time and place.

Before he could read, Izzy would sit in a trolley car with a book in front of him and pretend, moving his lips. Then came one of the "biggest thrills of my life," Izzy recalled, still with enthusiasm, when he was in his sixties. Young Izzy was poring through his first-grade reader "with the lovely pastel illustrations showing a bird on a windowsill, and the words underneath it saying . . . 'The bird sat on the windowsill,' and being able to figure it out was just tremendous! And I've been reading ever since."

Stone cherished books as a wealthy dowager prizes emeralds, an art collector his Rubens, an addict his drugs. Never an unimpassioned intellectual, he devoured ideas and philosophies, then distilled them into his own thinking, his intellectualism vibrating with zest, passion, outrage, romanticism. Throughout his life Stone turned long-dead heroes into intimate friends. "I've been on a Horace binge lately," he said late in life, fondling his collection of poems by the ancient Roman satirist like a lovesick teenager holding a collection of love letters. "Memorized five or six poems in the last two weeks. Horace was such a great artist. *I'm just in love with him.* I wake up at night and do some Horace in my head. It's like fingering a string of pearls."

This is but a fragment of one of those bursting-with-energy monologues, when Izzy was in his sixties: "I remember coming home after school in the fourth or fifth grade with three or four books and gobbling them up all in one afternoon. Later I remember the thrill of reading Marlowe's *Tamburlaine* with that wonderful line 'Is it not passing brave to be a king and march in triumph through Persepolis?' And I can remember the thrill of discovering Milton, and being out in the woods . . . reading Keats and Shelley and Wordsworth. While I was in high school, I discovered the Fragments of Heraclitus. He was the founder of the dialectic, and in his work you get it in its pure form—his first mystical insight into the identity of opposites. Then I read Plato and a bit of Aristotle, though I didn't care much for him, and through a forgotten book of Giovanni Papini's called *Thirteen Men* I first heard of the Chinese philosopher Kwang-tzu, who was a kind of Chinese Heraclitus, a follower of Taoism, but many ways much greater than Lao-tzu. . . . Oh, wait, I just remembered—one of the books I loved most as a child was *Don Quixote.* I can remember . . . bursting into tears at the moment of tragic lucidity when Don Quixote wavers and sees that he has been living in a world of illusion."

After reading about Herbert Spencer, Izzy set about finding his works. "There were very few places in town that had books," he recalled to writer Andrew Patner, then related this anecdote. Izzy heard that a woman named Groves had Herbert Spencer's *First Principles.* One day when Izzy came home from school, his mother said, "Mrs. Groves came around today, and we had a very odd conversation. She wanted to know if you were an invalid," Mrs. Feinstein said in her thick Jewish accent. "So, I said, 'No, Isador's not an invalid. He's not *sports*—but he's not an invalid.' And then she asked if she could loan you some book you had asked her for." Izzy realized that Mrs. Groves had asked his mother if Izzy was an *infidel.* "This was a very church town, and she wanted to clear things with my mother before she gave me such a heretical book."

There was much about the Feinstein family to like. Katy was often bright and gay and loved to dance, whirling with abandon to folk dances. Next to walking, it was the one expression of physical exercise that appealed to her son Izzy all of his life. Katy saw humor in her everyday world, making up nicknames for customers that reflected weaknesses. When one woman, who bought only sale items, entered the store, Katy would whisper in Yiddish to her sons, "Here comes the Remnants Lady."

Instead of belaboring his hardships in czarist Russia, Bernard concentrated on life in America. "He was full of tricks," recalls Lou Stone. One time Katy was preparing a feast for nearby relatives. She made a Jewish dish, similar to dumplings, with a mixture of potatoes and onions drawn up into a pouch of dough. Bernard spied the dumplings and remade one, inserting cotton balls instead of the potato-and-onion mixture. Bernard boiled it in water, then served it to one of his relatives. His sons, in on the gag, tried not to laugh as they watched the man trying to chew the dumpling.

Izzy's parents talked to each other almost exclusively in Yiddish. With little formal education, they were bright and read both the English and Yiddish newspapers. "You could always tell the politics of a Jewish household in those days by which Jewish paper they subscribed to," Izzy recalled. "If they were Communists, they got the *Freiheit;* if they were so-cialists, they got the *Forvits,* the *Forward;* if they were religious, they got the *Morning Journal;* if they were liberal, they got the *Tug,* the *Day.* We took the *Tug.*" Not radical enough for young Izzy, the *Tug* was "from a literary point of view, the best, the most literate of the papers."

Interesting characters filled Izzy's extended family, such as the thrice-wed Aunt Eta, who sold dresses in a teeming outdoor market in Philadel-phia. Other children in the family were intrigued with the bustle, the bargaining in exotic tongues, but Izzy distanced himself from many such outings. There were also regular Sunday visits to Katy's parents. Izzy's love of humor—"he prized wit above all," said his daughter, Celia—was like a congenital trait. Esther used to joke that his side of the family would "kill their Grandmother for a good joke." Actually, Izzy adored Katy's mother, who was much like her grandson—a nonstop talker who "held everyone spellbound with her stories." (When she first met the apolitical Esther, Izzy's fervent Zionist grandmother surprised her by asking her for donations for Palestine.)

Yet "he was going his own way, very young," recalls Lou. "He was not family-oriented." Izzy was, in fact, regarded as a snob by cousins because he cared so little for the family or their interests. The one family member who really intrigued Izzy was Uncle Shumer, who had befriended Izzy's father in Cardiff on his journey to America. Shumer now lived in nearby Philadelphia. Poverty had forced the scholarly uncle to work as a cap maker. He was an ardent Zionist who wrote eloquently, and his religios-ity and pride in being Jewish were the cornerstones of his life. In his will he admonished his children, "Do not permit your children to assimilate; above all, do not permit your children to marry those of another faith. Be proud of your Jewish ancestry, which is the pride and bulwark of all civilization." Remaining a "Pintele Yid" (a Jew to the minutest detail) meant "more to me than my very life."

Izzy eschewed his uncle's religious fervor, although he loved reading the Bible: "It's full of barbarism, horror, brutality, and primitivism, but it's also full of some of the most extraordinarily vivid writing, and some of the great teaching of mankind." All of his life, Stone laced his one-liners with biblical references. Wrestling in old age with new technology, Stone sighed and said, "The only thing God didn't give Job was a computer." And, after mastering ancient Greek: "Perhaps I should learn Hebrew, too, so that I can complain to God in his own tongue."

Izzy's love for Shumer was boundless. In 1934, when Izzy was twenty-six, he wrote this eulogy: "I shall always remember what fun it was as a small boy" to visit his tanta Elka and uncle Shumer. ". . . There were always books aplenty at Uncle Shumer's, to read in bed in the mornings." His aunt was "lovable," and Uncle Shumer was "framed always in a certain majesty; calm, dignified, patient—a veritable Jove of an uncle to an admiring small boy, full of the grandest stories, answering the very hardest questions. So it seemed to a small boy. And to a small boy grown up, seems still a figure, spiritually beautiful—scholar, philosopher, gentleman, learned yet kind and simple, without bitterness or rancor or envy. Human."

By then, Izzy was not so much of an atheist that he couldn't add, "When God walked with the sons of men, He must have walked with such as my Uncle Shumer."

Izzy gravitated to Uncle Shumer in part because he was not close to his own father. Shumer seems to have been the ideal father substitute, the scholar Izzy wished to emulate. Izzy and his father argued frequently, and the tension between them was palpable enough for even young Louie to notice. Some of the problem stemmed from the typical demands a father places on a firstborn son, and subsequent rebellion. This cultural pattern was intensified in early-twentieth-century Jewish-immigrant households where sons were encouraged to excel academically, only to regard their uneducated Yiddish-speaking fathers contemptuously. In *The Jews in America,* Arthur Hertzberg persuasively argues that "the children of the immigrants had no role models." Sons angry at their "powerless fathers . . . had no choice but to invent themselves, as Jews and Americans." Many observers inaccurately characterized Eastern European immigrants as dominated by socially conscious firebrands when, in fact, Stone's father was typical of the majority of Jewish immigrants, who were merely struggling to survive, not to change the world.

"The only political act by my father I remember was that when the armistice was declared to the First World War . . . my father wanted to ring the bell [of the local fire department]." It would be a false alarm and "he'd be fined five dollars," Stone said, laughing as he recalled the incident to Patner. "So he paid the five dollars and rang the bell!"

His parents were not entirely devoid of political interests. When Stone was twelve, his mother took him to visit friends who ran a south Jersey summer resort. "Their daughter was a good friend of Felix Frankfurter. And on their library table I found, for the first time, *Nation* and *New Republic*," he told Patner. After that, his mother bought him the magazines. By the time he was in his twenties, Stone would be writing for both.

Like other children from his background, adolescent Izzy drifted toward intellectual socialists for inspiration. Sholem Asch presented this picture in his novel *America 1918*: "In their children there awoke a yearning for unshackled liberty." They admired Jewish intellectuals who argued that Jews should stand up against bosses for the rights of labor, not cower before anti-Semites, and "confront their tormentors." The theme of socialist novels and essays was one of fighting back. That feisty pattern seemed bred in the bone of Izzy.

Coupled with the denigration of the father was the "Invention of the Jewish Mother" as Hertzberg termed it. "Contrary to popular mythology, the Jewish-American immigrant mother was not a transplant from Europe; she never existed in the traditional Jewish culture" (although in the Old World wives did run shops while their husbands read the Talmud or prayed). In America, however, "her labor helped eke out the family budget and made survival and schooling possible. Her own anger with the schlemiel, the father, helped to feed the rebellion of the children. She raised her sons to achieve for her what her husband had failed to do." This general description mirrors much in Stone's early years—his scorn for his father and the dry goods business, the flashing example of an energetic mother emancipated from subservience by virtue of being an equal breadwinner. High-spirited Katy was no silent Victorian wife. She fought often with Bernard about the store and how it should be run.

And the couple quarreled over the battles between Izzy and Marc. During their intense clashes of sibling rivalry, Katy so clearly favored Izzy that Marc would howl in indignation. The best pieces of chicken were always for Izzy, Marc sobbed. Such seemingly insignificant childhood incidents are often burned into one's memory, emblematic of a condition that created long-lasting insecurity, anger, or conflict. Years later, Marc recalled this still gnawing act of unfairness. He "strived in many ways to compete for Mom's love," scrubbing her kitchen floors, cleaning her stove, and once racing home from the drugstore to present her with a gift of perfume. This was not enough to receive the affection lavished on Izzy, who took it for granted.

Katy slipped money from the cash register to Izzy, so that he could buy ties in Philadelphia at Wanamaker's. Bernard stormed at her for aiding his son in such perfidy. His own ties were not good enough for this adolescent, who had taken to wearing his prized Wanamaker's ties in a bohemian manner, flipping one end over the other, without a knot. Stone was his own master of the universe, determined to go his own way. His father's hopes of having the firstborn as a partner were dashed early; unlike his brothers, Izzy balked at even helping in the store. In no way did he envision a future as a petit bourgeois shopkeeper.

Bernard's chances for the scholarly pursuits Izzy so admired had been thwarted by his impoverished childhood and the demands of earning a living. Stone recalled a few shared moments with his father, such as trips to the Philadelphia Yiddish theater, but Marc and Louie profited from the tension between Izzy and his father and eagerly accepted the roller and ice skates, bicycles, and jackets he bought them. According to Marc, Bernard was not demonstrative or affectionate, but Lou disagrees. Tears welled up when he recalled of his father, "He was not stern. I remember as a little boy standing behind the counter, how he would put his hand on my head, stroke it, because he loved me. I belonged to the Boy Scouts, and he would take me to camp, help me participate in overnight hiking, bought me a bike."

Determined not to follow in his father's footsteps, Izzy was nonetheless deeply influenced by both parents—struck by their honesty, hard work, and ebullient storytelling. His father's agnosticism and skepticism made a lasting impact. Izzy's father held all politicians in scorn. His customary comment—that they came around only during elections and were never seen or heard from again—mirrored Izzy's sardonic opinion of power players. Izzy developed some of his father's traits, from the sublime—his gift at storytelling—to the ridiculous—his inability to drive a car. The curse was apparently congenital; Izzy behind the wheel was a notoriously lethal weapon.

Marc had no desire to emulate Izzy, this "shadowy figure." He craved to be the opposite, "to play school sports, bowl, hang out at the drugstore and ice cream parlor with the 'in' crowd." He shot pool and played craps. Still, "the cruel childish taunts of Kike and Christ Killer continued into the teens. Though I might hang out with the drugstore crowd, I was not invited to their parties." Like Izzy, Marc was a "Jew with eyes only for shiksas." The pain of being snubbed was "deep and lasting. It was many years before I learned to handle the many faces of anti-Semitism, including my own."

Although Izzy often contended that being Jewish was no curse, he could recall only one high school friend, a gentile with the improbable name of Gerhardt van Arckle. He later became general counsel to the National Labor Relations Board and remained "quite friendly to me during the witch hunt, when he was 'respectable' and I was not," Stone told Patner.

In his teens, Izzy was well on his way to becoming a quintessential outsider. Recalled classmate Margaret Hartel Farrington, "He was not popular. Would I call him a nerd? Well . . . oh, that's a word that came to life long after my time. As far as I was concerned, Izzy was so intellectual he was far above my comprehension. He sure was different. He had too many brains upstairs for me to know him well." Mystification remains in her voice nearly seventy years later when she says, "He *loved* Latin." Stone portrayed his love of Latin differently: "I had four years of high school Latin and absolutely hated it. They were cramming it down my throat— here I was, a bookworm and a lover of poetry, hating Latin!—and then Gissing, with his love of the classics, and Montaigne and Gibbon (which had the dirty parts in Latin and the real dirty parts in Greek) made me realize what I was missing. After I graduated from high school I bought one of my great treasures, an edition of Catullus, Tibullus, and Propertius. And I began to read Latin with such joy and pleasure."

Izzy and Margaret were in extemporaneous-speaking contests. Izzy's high-pitched voice was overshadowed by the eloquence of his words. "He was shy socially but he could get up and express himself beautifully," recalls Farrington. Hardly the class clown, Izzy was once suspended after he closed the windows and opened some overripe Limburger cheese he had brought to class, hoping that the teacher would be assaulted by the smell when she opened the door.

The *Shield,* the yearbook for Haddonfield's graduates of 1924, graphically demonstrates an atypical sixteen-year-old Izzy. Most descriptions were typical of high school student yearbooks: amiable, lively, happy, cheery, stylish, debonair, cute, winsome, dreamy. Hobbies included talking, making friends, getting rich, a Victrola, football, golf, giggling, dates, and dances. The "Noted For" column included flapper haircuts, good looks, "that car," "tickling the ivories." What was needed most: "a chaperon," "some snap," "a haircut," "a new laugh." All this was absent in Izzy's entry, where his name was misspelled "Issy." His hobby was reading. He was noted for "his theories." What he needed most was "common sense." Favorite expressions mirrored the twenties vernacular: "Oh gee!" "Step on it!" "Holy smoke!" "Hey, goofus!" "Golly!" Izzy's was dour denunciation: "There is no truth." Judging from his friend van Arckle's entries, he was Izzy's stylish opposite. He was "cosmopolitan," his hobby was "everything," what he needed most was "a new line."

Izzy's intelligence either awed or bored most Haddonfield classmates, who, said Farrington, were "content to remain right here" after graduation. The painful effort at wit in the class prophecy said, "I wandered down Main Street and stopped expectantly at Feinsteins [*sic*] store. Izzy was there, but he was busy convincing his mathematics teacher that the square of the hypotenuse could not possibly equal the sum of the squares of the other two sides because to a certain extent the hypotenuse is longer than either of the other two sides. I made a bee line for the door."

In the yearbook, Izzy's picture is opposite Farrington's. She was wearing a flapper headband and beads. Izzy was dressed in a tie, hair slicked back, face slightly to the side. His glasses were removed; Izzy looked almost matinee-idol handsome. "That's the best picture you'll ever see of him," remarked Farrington. Izzy's extracurricular activities were slim: president of the chess club his sophomore year, small parts in the junior sketch and senior play, extemporaneous-speaking contests his freshman and senior years. "Knowledge is power" was the phrase used to sum up Izzy. The paean to his intelligence continued, "And he is our philosopher! It doesn't seem believable that one head could hold so many theories, ideas, etc. The sad part about his 'wisdom' is, that we Seniors find it too profound for our mental capacity to grasp."

Such praise gives no hint of Izzy's third-place finish—third from the end, that is. "School interfered with my reading," he once quipped. "I wasn't dumb, I just didn't do any homework." That pattern continued, and Izzy dropped out of the University of Pennsylvania a few years later. The thrills he lovingly recalled were not in the classroom but in the woods near his home—reading Keats and Shelley and Wordsworth and Plato and Aristotle. "I felt very romantic after I left school," Stone recalled of his dropout days. "I'd go to the library and read two books on Lucretius in Latin and French, a poem of Sappho, and have a wonderful time."

Stone was enormously inspired by writers who battled the entrenched ills of capitalism and political corruption. "I wanted to fight for the disadvantaged. So I became a young radical." Stone was no help to those who tried to analyze what made him so inclined. He displayed a lifelong aversion to self-analysis and a rather astounding myopia when it came to examining emotions or behavior. Stone seldom engaged in introspection or spoke of his private feelings. Definitely not a man for the couch, Stone never embraced Freud or the 1920s parlor fad of discussing ids and egos that greeted the famed psychoanalyst's controversial findings. Although he was fond of quoting Freud's observation "we overlook what we do not wish to see," Stone referred to this in the context of why reporters missed pertinent information, not in the sense of self-analysis. When he was eighty years old, Stone spent a morning tracking down an out-of-town reporter to praise the writer for using the word "psychobabble" to criticize journalists attempting to psychoanalyze Jesse Jackson's mind and motives.

Stone could weep at poetry or a divinely written passage, speak and write passionately against or for an issue, rip into mendacious politicians, but, paradoxically, never applied the same microscope to himself. People who profess lifelong "friendship" with Stone have been known to stop in midsentence and, stunned, recognize how little they knew of his private thoughts and feelings or, even, the facts about his life. No doubt Stone would have made a poor novelist; absent was that grist of familial and childhood remembrances that so well serve the best fiction.

Instead of being exposed, the personal was tucked into darkness. This was not an uncommon characteristic in Stone's era, and one could even call it a merciful contrast to today's dreary celebrity confessionals. His wife, Esther, put the most positive face on this trait: "Izzy never looks back. He's never talked about his childhood or the past. He has a zest for life, for every new day, that I've never seen in anyone else."

His son Christopher feels that Stone's reticence did not stem from lack of sensitivity but from lack of interest in what he viewed as trivial. However, even Christopher acknowledges that his father took this trait to puzzling lengths. "He was a very private person and he didn't share, except with Mom."

Childhood was seldom recalled. Nor was Katy's devastating mental illness or the shattering effect that the depression had on Stone's parents. Good times were seldom mentioned, the worst were simply taboo. "I've got to tell you, these folks are strange," says Christopher, referring to his parents' "undiscussable" attitude.

In later years, when Stone was lionized by young interviewers, he resisted attempts to examine him, replying with such superficial comments as "I was a cocky son-of-a-bitch kid." He steered away from questions of what motivated him, replying with such stock answers as "I was born a liberal and for the underdog." While simplistic and guarded, that answer nonetheless contains significance. Who else but another underdog could empathize to the degree that Stone did? But his "underdog" status did not stem from poverty, as did that of the slum people he inexplicably dreamed of as a fourteen-year-old and vowed from then on to help. Stone's penchant for the underdog, some critics feel, turned into more of a shtick in his later prosperous life, but an early empathy stemmed from a combination of both insecurities and intellectual gifts.

"What made Izzy tick?" mused his friend Marc Raskin. "I think there are two things. One, he started from *enormous* insecurity in life: height, looks, didn't finish college, on the left, Jewish. All of those things that, in fact, *hardened* him to criticism and made it necessary, in his own mind, to be better than others. When I say insecurity, it was long since gone by the time Izzy was an adult, but I think it was an instrument to propel him forward, in the sense that he didn't have certain things that others had. The second factor is that *voracious* appetite for knowledge, that encyclopedic sense, that extraordinary memory, made it possible for him to see any specific particular in a much grander conception than most people."

Stone's son Christopher feels that his father's outsider role as a Jew in Haddonfield created a heightened awareness and suspicion to "not accept the status quo. He didn't have this [suspicion] to a level of piercing annoyance. He benefited from being the stranger. It wasn't corrosive. It didn't make him less, it made him *more*."

Stone once admitted, "It's a help to be born a Jew because you have an extra perspective as an outsider." However, he quickly protested, "But I had a wonderful time growing up in a WASP town. I didn't feel persecuted or discriminated against."

Chris felt his father's "acute instinct for lies and a suspicious character" were crucial to his work. "He was able to harness these elements—that could have been deployed in destructive ways—to real advantage as a journalist; distrust and flashes of biblical anger and righteousness and all of these things. Journalism is a good career for that. He had an instinct that somebody was trying to put something over on him."

Stone's brother Lou, regarded as the "sweet one" in the family, dispenses with the intellectual exercise and says simply that "egotism" played a strong part in Stone's drive. "Izzy was an egotist from the very beginning. He used to get bawled out by my mother and father for being so self-centered. He felt that he was right and other people were wrong. He believed in himself. He was self-centered in the sense that he was always motivated to concentrate on what his interests were," says Lou, but softens the comment, "At the same time he could be very generous and thoughtful."

Judy, the sister born seventeen years after Stone, is his staunchest defender. Despite the distance in ages, Judy and Stone became close friends later in life. She saw Stone's self-absorption in a different light. "People would say that Izzy was self-centered—when Lou or Marc would say it, it used to really get me angry. I felt it was *not* self-centered—because what he was centered *on* was the state of the world, and not himself. With Izzy, it wasn't *me, me* and *I, I*. He wasn't talking about himself, but rather the substance of the conversation." Other friends have referred to Stone as an "incorrigible monument to opinionation" and argue that his ego took the form of having to dominate the conversation, no matter how world-directed.

All three of Izzy's siblings chose writing careers and similar leftist politics even though that meant remaining in their older brother's shadow. They considered him possessed of a genius unlike that of any other family member, however bright they all were.

When Izzy was thirteen, a chance meeting occurred that seemed as unpromising as it seemed mundane. It became so pivotal that it shaped the course of his entire life. A stylish young matron, Jill Lit Stern, heiress of Lit's, Philadelphia's largest department store, was living in Haddonfield. At four feet eleven inches, with fair skin and delicate features, her Dresden-shepherdess appearance hid an iron will. Spoiled and bossy, Mrs. Stern had her peculiarities, among them, decorating herself and her house almost entirely in shades of blue, to enhance her eyes. Eventually her family could not abide the color.

One afternoon Mrs. Stern walked into Feinstein's Dry Goods Emporium to buy some blue ribbons. Inside the darkened store was a lone child, wearing huge round glasses, hunched over a book. Izzy had been dragooned into watching the store. He did not look up when she entered, nor did he make any attempt to disengage himself. Mrs. Stern cleared her throat. Still, he did nothing. She said rather sternly, "Young man, I see you're reading a book." Izzy stopped long enough to reply, "Yes." Taken aback by his indifference to waiting on her, Mrs. Stern then commanded, "*What* are you reading?"

Izzy startled her speechless. Looking up, this gnome, with his owlish gaze, gave a withering, one-word reply: "Spinoza."

3
BOY PUBLISHER

J ill Lit Stern was stunned and intrigued by this strange creature behind the dry goods counter, reading Baruch Spinoza, that seventeenth-century renegade Jewish philosopher and scourge of rabbis. Twenty-one years older than Izzy, she had recently settled in Haddonfield, a choice preferable to stultifying upper-class Philadelphia. A Bryn Mawr graduate, Jill Stern "fashioned herself an intellectual," said her daughter, Jill Capron, and pursued Yeats, Swinburne, Barrie, Coleridge. The imperious Mrs. Stern was stopped in her tracks by her new acquaintance, who took her, a Jew, to task for being a "Quaker assimilationist." Surviving such impertinence, Izzy became her protégé and lifelong friend.

The Stern mansion, built in 1816, contained luxurious paneling, sweeping staircases, exquisite fireplaces. Its book-crammed library became Izzy's second home. According to legend, the house contained the ghost of Walt Whitman, America's great poet, who had lived his last years in a tiny house on Camden's Mickle Street, six miles away. Jill Stern took charge of restoring Whitman's Camden house and, during the renovation, invited the custodian to spend the night in her Haddonfield mansion, where he abruptly had a stroke and just as abruptly died. Soon the Stern cook was telling the world that Whitman's ghost had obviously resented the intrusion, followed the custodian to the Stern home, contributed to his untimely demise, and set up shop.

Superstition aside, Whitman was among the many giants who figuratively lurked alongside Izzy in his new heaven on earth. Izzy wallowed in everything from the great romantic writers—Emily Dickinson and Flaubert and Trollope and "the Russians"—to the evolutionary tomes of Herbert Spencer. (Spencer would have been a kindred spirit: the two shared a repugnance for the ordinariness of the classroom.)

Whitman, another voracious autodidact, was a favorite—"a great influence in my life," Izzy said. "From him I got a feeling of naturalness and purity about sex." Whitman's poems, combining exquisite tenderness and a sexuality shocking for that era, hypnotized many an ardent youth.

Izzy was also deeply drawn to Whitman's fiercely independent journalism. As the feisty twenty-two-year-old editor of New York's *Aurora,* Whitman composed a coda for Izzy's young mind to emulate: His newspaper "is bound to no party." It is "fearless, open and frank in its tone." He attacked crooked politicians, police harassment, and cheap wages that sent poverty-stricken women into prostitution, and called for regulation and inspection in brothels. Whitman fought legislation that would divert public money to parochial schools. His church-and-state-separation stance took no quarter. After a mob attacked St. Patrick's Cathedral and stoned the bishop's residence, Whitman wrote, "Had it been the reverend hypocrite's head, instead of his windows, we could hardly find it in our soul to be sorrowful."

Whitman grew accustomed to the inevitable quarrels with publishers and to being fired. Whitman's clarion call to youthful Izzy was to resist much and to wage "heavy" war against pernicious influences.

At fourteen, Izzy started his newspaper, *The Progress.* While many a teenager tinkers with creating a broadsheet, *The Progress* was not concerned with high school fare. In the first edition Izzy quoted from *Antigone:* "Nothing in use by man for power of ill can equal money." Izzy crusaded for Gandhi's fight to free India and supported President Woodrow Wilson's peace plan. Izzy lovingly kept a few issues wrapped in plastic until he died.

Izzy was at his prophetic best with this comment on political parties: "To stay in power has become the fundamental purpose of the Democratic and Republican parties. . . . Parties are no longer the organ of a part of the people, they have simply become hereditary things like blue eyes and cancer." At that time the country was in the throes of President Warren G. Harding's mediocrity.

Four years before his death, Izzy told a friend, "I was a strong Wilsonian at elementary school. I still think Wilson was a great president in many ways, although he was a terrible imperialist in Latin America, I realize." Stone did not assess Wilson's role in crushing dissent when the president encouraged the passage of the Espionage Act of 1917 and the Sedition Act of 1918, which began decades of abusing constitutional freedoms. Izzy's editorials were on page one. One radical notion no doubt made him blush in later years: "Why not give the President the powers of a premier? Give him the power to dissolve Congress and ask for another election." With Harding at the helm, it is hard to believe that Izzy could have found this a viable solution.

In 1925 the Scopes "monkey" trial captured the nation's attention with former presidential candidate William Jennings Bryan battling famed lawyer Clarence Darrow. Tennessee schoolteacher John T. Scopes was charged with violating Tennessee law that prohibited teaching the theory of evolution. The nation's press crowded into that small Southern courtroom, and H. L. Mencken captured the aura of God Almighty ignorance with his poison pen. Giggling flappers in short dresses and rouged knees watched shaggy-haired Darrow, stripped of his coat in the steaming heat, thumb linked in a purple suspender, destroy Bryan.

Three years before the trial, Izzy triumphantly headlined an April 1922 *Progress* editorial "Bigotry Defeated Again!" Izzy wrote that Bryan's "new role as a modern Torquemada failed when the Kentucky Legislature turned down a bill to prohibit the teaching of Darwinism, agnosticism, atheism and evolution in the public schools by a vote of 42–41. [Torquemada, the head of the Spanish Inquisition, became a style tic, invoked by Stone all of his life to illustrate nefarious actions.] However there still seem to be many worthy gentlemen in Kentucky who wish to anchor the world in a sea of narrow minds (including their own) and hold it there, lest it move forward. . . . Bryon [*sic*—Izzy often said that "typos are worse than fascism," but one of his hated typos had escaped scrutiny] and the 41 gentlemen from Kentucky are a thousand years behind the times." The spark of Izzy's later vibrancy surfaced: "They belong to the Middle Ages when free thinkers, philosophers and Jews were considered the best fuel for bonfires (there was never lack of fuel). They are utterly out of place in this age of rationalism." Bigotry's defeat was short-lived. The Kentucky legislature passed the bill in a subsequent session, and the famous ensuing trial wound up with Scopes being convicted, then acquitted on a technicality.

Izzy's paper also contained silliness: a "Nut-E Poem" . . . "When the whales of Wales wails . . ." And fiction, redeemed in Izzy's eyes no doubt because the woman eschews a rich man's gold for a poor man's "silver of romance."

The four-page sheet was printed in the shop of a local weekly. After setting radical fare such as Izzy's call for the cancellation of war debts and a twenty-five-year international arms-suspension agreement, the linotypist predicted, "between meditative squirts of tobacco juice, that I would come to a bad end." Izzy coaxed brother Marc to sell the three-cent paper to commuters on the train. A quarter bought a subscription for the whole year, which was, alas, an optimist's dream.

The third issue of *The Progress* attempted to capture a popular following. It plugged the upcoming installment of a novel, the adventures of Clay Lindsay, a cowboy who "cleaned up New York gangsters." But Lindsay rode off in a cloud of dust; there were no more issues. Bernard halted his son's enterprise after three issues, concerned that Izzy might well flunk high school. Izzy proudly listed his embryonic endeavor in his *Who's Who* listing: "editor and publisher of the Haddonfield *Progress.*"

The premature death of *The Progress* did little to halt Izzy's addiction to newsprint. A defiant Izzy got a job on the *Haddonfield Public Press,* and as a fifteen-year-old high school junior he was stringing for the *Camden Courier.* He was fond of joking, "I started as a publisher and worked my way down."

During his freshmen year at the University of Pennsylvania, the philosophy major was at a crossroads—whether to become an academician or pursue the scruffier profession of journalism. Stuffy lost out to scruffy. "The smell of a newspaper shop was more enticing than the spinsterish atmosphere of a college faculty."

As a young journalist Izzy began to perfect his blend of scholar and reporter. He pounded out stories on deadline, cigarette dangling, peppering his sentences with the *goddammit*s and easy slang of newspaperdom. ("I was a natural bird dog," he once boasted. "Some fellas are bird dogs. They like to sniff things out. I was like that.") Over the years Izzy became an eclectic craftsman—indefatigable straight reporter, editorial writer, polemicist, essayist, columnist, book, theater, and political critic.

The teenage reporter haunted libraries and secondhand book stores the way other newspapermen savored saloons. He read the Persian poets and mystics and haltingly tried to learn Chinese. He gobbled up Gide, then Balzac and most of Flaubert. His German was "mostly Yiddish, but it's good enough to read Heine." As a cub reporter he discovered Charles Beard, the progressive historian. "His historical materialism is somewhat oversimplified, I think now, but what an eye-opener then!" One of the first books Izzy bought was *The Decline and Fall of the Roman Empire*; $2 at a secondhand store paid for Gibbon's six-volume edition. Izzy kept the set all of his life. He had an early love for Santayana but hated Hegel. "I think the dialectic is very important, but I feel that he was a real belly-crawling servant of the Prussian state."

Still, by 1925, one year after high school and not yet eighteen, Izzy had learned something about the less aesthetic Jazz Age, even discounting the braggadocio in his letter to Michael (Si) Blankfort, a friend from University of Pennsylvania days who later became a prominent Hollywood screenwriter and novelist. Writing to Blankfort, who was in Marienbad, Izzy crackles with enthusiasm as he leaps from topic to topic on hastily typed sheets filled with typos, grammatical mistakes, and atrocious misspellings: "Were [sic] just going [sic] the news here of the anti-American feeling in France. I'd have loved to have been in one of those fist-fights between students American and French holigans [sic]."

But it was Izzy's roaring social life that would have struck dumb his old Haddonfield classmates. "Four-eyes" Izzy, who had never had a date in high school, "went to Atlantic City for a week-end with [two male friends] and a sweet little brunette who works on the paper, has a deuced lot of sound sense, lives utterly out of my world—beauty, dizziness, etc.—has a lovely body, is hot as hell, and I'm going to drop her soon for fear the thing's getting too serious." Schoolboy swagger and sexism marches across the page: "I'd love to have her as a mistress but she's not the kind who was made for it (not enough intellect, independence) born to be a wife and mother. . . . By the way, I just finished Shaw's preface to *Getting Married.*" Izzy counseled Blankfort to read the misogynist's views "before you marry. Wow of a lot of sense. (my prose is neither decorous nor grammatical but its late afternoon here in the office and hot as hell and I'm too damned tired to worry about. Prose)." Izzy then shifted back to sex: "Went to a grand booze party Sunday night with Jack, Sid and brunette and met a nymphomaniac restaraunteure [sic] (female of course in case you don't know what an N. is), a police chief, a docter [sic] from Iowa and his bride and had hell of a good time."

The rest of the letter revealed Izzy's more public passions—politics, books, theater: "Great things doing over here. Coolidge is slipping fast as hell, insurgency growing strong in Congress, four or five Coolidge candidates severely beaten, a colossal scandal in Pennsylvania. Been having a hell of a lot of fun on the paper. At present general assignment, rewrites and city hall . . . Also helping on theaters." Bragged Izzy, a director phoned to say "mine was only intelligent review he got." Izzy panned Pirandello's *Six Characters in Search of an Author,* which he "razzed" as "melodrama thinly disguised with pretentious platitudes." Izzy thought he might become dramatic editor of the *Camden Morning Post* next season. "If so you shall have shot at dramatic criticism."

Izzy was still struggling with college. "I get up at six every morning to go to work and get home about six thirty and believe me I'm too damned tired to do much studying. Or reading. Read Gilbert Canaan's 'Round the Corner,' a fine and beautiful work, Thomas Hardy's poems (gnarled as oak trees, one grapples them with the mind), a lot of Shaw who is becoming old-fashioned in many of his plays but who has a remarkably sane common sense mind."

A cryptic sentence regarding the health of his ever-bad eyes follows: "Going to see eye doctor this week." And then: "If you made some real observations on Fascism in Italy, *things seen more than things thought* [emphasis added], write it up and send it to me. If its good we'd love to print it. Hope my letter hasn't been too long and all that. In revenge you can inflict one as long on me. . . . Iz." "Cum veritate" followed. Izzy could not resist a touch of the intellectual show-off—"ablative, by the way."

Independent thinkers always deeply influenced the teenager. In his library/shrine in the Stern mansion he gravitated not only to the radical words of Whitman, but to the revolutionary socialism of Jack London, the utopian anarchism of Kropotkin, and the militant muckraking of Lincoln Steffens, Upton Sinclair, and Ida Tarbell. They were rebels all, battling the system despite all odds. "For me, a newspaperman was a cross between Randolph Hearst and Galahad. Galahad, because you're always going and rescuing maidens in distress." Stone's choice of Hearst, the titan of yellow journalism, may seem curious to those unfamiliar with Hearst in his incarnation as a socialist reformer, as publisher of the pre–World War I *Cosmopolitan*, then one of America's great muckraking journals. "He was pretty progressive before the First World War. In those days he was a marvelous all-round newspaperman."

While Stone was bent toward radical thought, it cannot be stressed enough that he was also a man of his times—at least the times as defined by the intellectuals of his era. To understand Stone's intellectual and political base, one has to look at the development of ideas by American intellectuals and activists that preceded him. He was among those 1930s activists who "revealed, however unconsciously, a far greater sense of their relation to and dependence on the past," notes historian Richard H.

Pells. The New Deal was, in effect, born in turn-of-the-century activism, which molded the outlook and expectations of those who later shaped FDR's policies.

The czarist subjugation of Jews like his father solidified Stone's detestation of authority and his awareness of persecution. Pivotal in forming his radicalism was the popularity of socialist reformers and the phenomenal success of turn-of-the-century muckrakers who exposed the worst of capitalism. These progressives had an abiding faith in rational persuasion and social change through education—an ideal lure for writers "who eagerly enlisted in the army of reformers," noted Pells.

In later years, the word *iconoclast* was affixed to Stone's name, as if linked by a computer key. But in truth, young Izzy was a conformist of sorts, in step with an influential group of questioning and dissenting young rebels of the twenties and thirties—a more potent force than their numbers suggest. "My introduction to radicalism and to socialism was through books," he said, and enthusiastically recalled how those who inspired him were not outsiders in their day. "Socialism was definitely part of the American mainstream. [There were] a lot of good WASP socialists and a lot of wonderful working-class intellectuals from Europe, and we had a lot of WASP idealists," he related to Todd Gitlin. "The Emerson crowd. Wonderful combination of very socially minded people and strong individualists. Pro labor union."

Again, Stone, although precocious, was reading rather popular fare for his crowd. "There was a big market in popular editions of radical writers. . . . The one I remember most was Kropotkin." One has to travel eighty-six years into the past to understand the world Stone knew in 1920 when he was reading Kropotkin, just three years after the Russian Revolution had upended the world. The collapse of the czars and the rise of Bolshevik Russia was a monumental shift as historically phenomenal as its death in 1989 with the collapse of the Berlin Wall. For the first time, a communal vision imagined by socialists was being tried on a grand scale. Amidst the chaos of 1917, radical intellectuals saw hope; standing behind the Communist manifesto were 160 million people inhabiting one-sixth of the globe. Bolshevik leader Nikolai Bukharin was predicting that "social classes will transform themselves completely and new classes will rise from their ruins."

At first, the revolution did liberate a nation from a dark and bloody past. While many idealists, including Stone, clung to the theory behind the revolution, if not the application, Stones's friend Bertrand Russell, among others, repudiated his pro-Communist stance as early as 1920. Visiting Russia, Russell witnessed none of the "kindliness and tolerance" he revered, but a Communism in which immense power was concentrated in the hands of the few. He warned American socialists against "slavish imitation," even while he was persecuted in America, jailed for protesting World War I.

When the red flag first flew in Moscow, who would have predicted that the Communists would one day be called "conservatives," a hard-line old guard toppled by today's free-market "revolutionaries"? That Bukharin's "social classes" would indeed transform themselves—from apparatchiks to *biznesmeni* and *konsooltants*? And that Mafia-style corruption would prevail in the new capitalistic society?

In that long ago, revolutionaries such as Kropotkin risked death to free men from despotic czars. Not the stereotypical anarchist bomb thrower, Kropotkin abhorred violence. He detoured from pacifism to support Russia against Germany in World War I. Prince Peter (spelled *Pyetr* in some accounts) Alekseyevich Kropotkin came from the highest ranks of Russian aristocracy; he romanticized the "great-heartedness" of the serfs and naively rested all his belief in the common man.

Kropotkin's saintliness captivated young Stone. Arrested in 1887 and imprisoned in France in 1882 for his support of "revolutionary propaganda," Kropotkin escaped to London and spent many years in England and Europe. Continuously imprisoned and hounded for his beliefs, Kropotkin managed to attain a popular following.

In *Conquest of Bread*, written more than one hundred years ago, the idealism that lured Stone is obvious, but even then Kropotkin feared that Russia's collectivism would lead to reactionary takeover. His hopes destroyed, Kropotkin excoriated Lenin in 1920 for the "repulsive" act of taking political prisoners. "Vladimir Ilyich, your concrete actions are completely unworthy of the ideas you pretend to hold . . . you have no right to soil the ideas you defend by shameful methods." He presciently added, "What future lies in store for Communism when one of its most important defenders tramples in this way on every honest feeling?"

Despite listening to the messages of Kropotkin and Bertrand Russell, Stone was also hearing the opinion of another hero and muckraker, Lincoln Steffens, who after visiting Russia pronounced his famous "I have seen the future—and it works."

* * *

One reason for resisting criticisms of Russia back then was because the often inaccurate and antirevolutionary American conservative press bred a sense of mistrust regarding accounts from the closed society. When U.S. soldiers invaded Russia in 1919 and 1920 as allies of the White Russian army, mainstream papers applauded America's attempt to kill the revolution and lied to the American public about the United States' role in this civil war. Then, in the late twenties and early thirties, during a respite from blazing anticommunism, correspondents for leading newspapers such as the *Christian Science Monitor* and the *New York Times* printed glowing accounts of the new Russia. Unfortunately, these accounts were as untruthful as previous right-wing attacks.

For descendants of Russian Jews such as Stone, it seemed that anything had to be better than the anti-Semitic czars. In those heady early revolutionary days, when one of their own, Leon Trotsky (né Lev Davidovich Bronstein), was included among its leaders, the plight of Russian serf and Jew alike did look better.

Karl Marx has been both sympathetically interpreted and criticized through the years; what Marx really meant is still being argued, especially since Russia's Communism has resoundingly failed. Before his death in 1883, even Marx was heard to grumble that, given all the interpretations of his work, "I am not a Marxist."

The Communist Manifesto, Marx and Engels's fiery call to arms written for the International Communist League, explodes with bitter protest: "Wherever the bourgeoisie has risen to power . . . it has left no other bond between man and man but crude self-interest and callous 'cash-payment.'"

Marx saw "Communism" as "the positive abolition of private property," necessary to end terrible inequities: "Bourgeois claptrap about the family and education . . . becomes all the more disgusting . . . by the action of modern industry, all family ties among the proletarians are torn asunder, and their children transformed into simple articles of commerce and instruments of labor." At that time, the concept of a just and democratic capitalism was unknown. In England, as Stone pointed out, the working class had not yet won the vote. Europe was ruled by monarchs and despots. America was being raped by robber barons making their fortunes through child and immigrant labor. In one Manchester factory in 1862, a person's average workweek—during one six-week period—was eighty-four hours.

Marx saw as inevitable the internal collapse of capitalism and an afterlife where the means of production, distribution, and exchange would be socially owned; its guiding principle would become, in his famous words, "from each according to his capacity, to each according to his need." Marx wrote little about what this new society would be like. (The architect of actual socialism was Lenin, the interpreter of Marx for Russia.)

Marx's brilliant analysis of capitalism, *Das Kapital,* took the poverty-stricken Marx eighteen years to write. There were flaws in Marx's theories, but as Heilbroner writes, "The astonishing fact is that so many of these predictions have come true . . . how profits fell, how capitalists sought new machinery, how each boom ended in a crash, how small businesses were absorbed in each debacle by the larger firms."

The problems Marx diagnosed within the capitalist system remain hauntingly troublesome, especially today's disparity between rich and poor, which exceeds even that of the robber-baron era. However, Marx misread the proletariat mind. History shows that workers wished to emulate the bourgeoisie, to be allowed "inside," to possess the same rewards of private property and money rather than to sack the system.

For years, Stone's glib analysis of what he felt an ideal government should be was a "fusion of Jefferson and Marx." He was seldom asked to define how this would actually work. The radical youth who thought that the "abolition of private property was the answer" subsequently "lost that faith when I saw what has happened to the Soviet Bloc." Where Marx went wrong, Stone believed, was in thinking that the proletariat would become an overwhelming majority. "In none of the advanced industrial countries is the industrial working class the majority. There's a new middle class." Stone had long called for a melding of ideas that included the middle class, a position consistently rejected by dogmatic leftists in his day. But Stone was no economist and did not really apply his mind to understanding economic theories. In truth, "socialist" Stone was too independent to embrace socialism or any ism. He once said, "I call myself a socialist—but I *hate* collective action!" In later years, he recognized that he "was sort of a socialist by conviction in a general sense but an individualist by temperament." Stone would have been a collectivist state's nightmare, clapped in jail inside of a week had he lived and written in Russia, Cuba, or China.

During the 1948 witch hunts he quipped, "I know that if the Communists came to power I'd soon find myself eating cold kasha in a concentration camp in Kansas *gubernya.*"

* * *

Jeffersonian democracy was another matter. Stone retained a schoolboy's fervor for Jefferson and America's foundation of free thought and speech unknown in Marxist countries. Like many journalists, Stone cherished Jefferson's stirring and oft-quoted imprimatur: "Were it left to me to decide whether we should have a government without newspapers or newspapers without a government, I should not hesitate a moment to prefer the latter." Stone overlooked Jefferson's own vices in that department. Vilified by opposition papers, Jefferson suggested that editors categorize the contents of their papers under four chapters: Truths ("the first chapter would be very short"), Probabilities, Possibilities, and Lies. As president, Jefferson lured a friendly publisher to set up shop in the nation's capital with printing-contract patronage. Such blatant news management assured that political journalism was dominated by Jefferson's party press.

Unlike modern historians who offer a discriminating view of Jefferson, the slave-owning father of slaves who sided with fellow Southern agrarians at the expense of federalism, Stone uncritically extolled the Founding Father. Stone spoke of Jefferson as if he were a flesh-and-blood friend, a colleague with whom to slip out for a brandy—tossing in asides such as "that's what Jefferson thought" during conversations. "Jefferson brought the Enlightenment to this country. He gave newspapermen a status they'd never have otherwise. It doesn't exist in England or anywhere in Europe. There they just follow the upper class around like street sweepers."

Stone's intense belief in the foundations of this country was why he could write and speak so critically of administrations and politicians that he felt were violating those precepts. "America is the first nation in modern times where the common man could stand erect. In ancient Greek society every damned aristocrat believed his great-grandmother was fucked by a god," he exclaimed to writer Bill Thomas. "So he had Olympian blood; he was different from the rabble." At another time, Stone said, "In no other society . . . do nonconformists have stronger built-in constitutional safeguards they can appeal to. And nowhere else is freedom of the press so fundamental, so much a part of a secular national ideology."

Another intimate was the seventeenth century's John Milton. Stone once seemed shocked that a young reporter had never heard of Milton's *Areopagitica*. (Others would be surprised that this generation had heard of *Milton*.) Stone constantly touted *Areopagitica*, "the most eloquent defense of a free press ever written—a malediction on journalism schools which do not make their students read it!" In 1643, Parliament passed an act requiring that all books be licensed by an official censor before publication, a major attempt to silence political and religious opposition. Threatened by this prepublication censorship were Milton's works, which included tracts arguing for the right to divorce in the case of incompatibility, a contention no doubt induced by his own unhappy marriage.

Areopagitica, written in 1644, was his answer to the censors. A rhetorical showpiece, it has survived as a great tract because it went beyond the confines of a parochial debate on prepublication censorship. Milton argued that suppressing a good book suppresses what is highest and best in man. Censors would doubtlessly be ignorant men who could not possibly judge what had been written. He further argued that if there was vice in the offing, so be it, contending that it is essential to learn about vice in order to know virtue. Stone's favorite passage is "Who kills a Man kills a reasonable creature, God's Image; but he who destroyes a good Booke, kills reason itselfe."

4

RAKING THE MUCK
AND RED, WHITE,
AND BLUE PATRIOTISM

[The arrested were] kept in jail for five months; beaten, starved, suffocated, tortured and threatened with death in futile attempts to extract admissions.

—Official report detailing abuses of
1920s Justice Department raids

Since the beginning of the republic, politicians and newspaper publishers have routinely paid homage to the First Amendment, but history is replete with dismal acts by them and the courts to curb freedom of speech and thought. As Jefferson said, "Freedom of the press . . . is . . . the first shut up by those who fear the investigation of their actions." Generally a rich, conservative, and cautious species, publishers are often content to squelch the truth if it offends those who feed them—advertisers, corporate interests, or friends in high places; a publisher was often, said Stone, "a man who made a million bucks selling toilet paper and bought a newspaper as a tax loss."

Stone admired the exceptions, such as abolitionist agitators who were beaten by angry mobs and sometimes murdered for their antislavery publications. The greatest influence on Stone was a band of courageous journalists and publishers who took on big business and machine politics at the beginning of the twentieth century. Their exposés reached eager millions. The era of "muckraking" had an impact beyond its years, transforming laws and igniting the next generation of reporters like Stone.

Such influences are regenerative; the best journalists can point to those from the past who inspired them, and they, in turn, make an impact on the next generation. For Stone, men like socialist Eugene Debs and his fearless band were lasting inspirations.

By 1900, a nation of struggling immigrants had endured the worst of the industrial revolution. During the post–Civil War years, the continent had been "looted on a scale unrivaled in the history of human greed . . . made possible by use of brute force, by the devious throat-cutting of business rivals, by an almost universal system of bribery and corruption," wrote historian Fred J. Cook. Wildly popular were journals that "gave voice to deep-seated and long-lasting anxieties, grievances and suspicions."

George Seldes, whose hard-hitting *In Fact* was Stone's "model for my weekly," wrote, "All muckraking, crusading, debunking, reforming, and investigative reporting aimed at exposing corruption and enlightening the public has been the work of the liberals. There has never been exposure of corruption, crookedness, falsification of history, robbery of the public, or propaganda to manipulate the public mind originating or engaged in by the right."

The American Socialist Party was a vibrant six-year-old when Izzy was born in 1907. Its charismatic leader and an editor of an astoundingly popular socialist paper, Debs struck a chord with toilers across the country—New York immigrant garment workers, Kentucky coal miners, Oregon loggers, Washington timbermen, Kansas farmers. Immigrants who could read English joined conscious-stricken members of the middle class in following Debs and the passionate *Appeal to Reason*. Under the headline "All Hail the King!" a 1908 article noted that Standard Oil's net profit for $25^{1}/_{2}$ years was $929 million—more than was "paid to all the kings of Europe and presidents of North and South American nations." Foes falsely painted Debs, whose appeal truly was to reason, as a murderous revolutionary: "I believe in change—but by perfectly peaceable and orderly means." With his bald dome, thin lips, and high-buttoned suits, Debs looked like the capitalists he opposed, but looks deceived thoroughly; Debs began working on the railroads at fourteen, and from that day on "my heart has been with the working class." His rhapsodic thoughts mesmerized audiences: "Gold is god and rules the affairs of men."

"I met him once," said Stone. "*Marvelous* guy. Debs had a sense of humor" and wrote "in real indigenous lingo. *Appeal to Reason* had a half million readers at one point!" Stone was off by a quarter of a million; in 1913, paid circulation reached 760,000, a phenomenal figure for any paper, no matter its politics. During political crises and campaigns when Debs was the Socialist candidate for president of the United States, the

Appeal cranked out single-issue mailings that reached 4 million. Read and reread, passed on to friends, for more than two decades the *Appeal* was like an impassioned chain letter, the most influential radical publication ever published in the United States.

An early champion of equality for women and blacks, the *Appeal* pushed reforms that came to pass decades later. Carl Sandburg's antiwar poems and Helen Keller's "dear comrade" letters to Debs graced its pages. One of Keller's letters, opposing the "unrighteous conviction" of an *Appeal* editor, included the poignant phrase "in light of the constitution, which I have under my fingers."

Debs was given an astonishing ten years in prison in 1919 for delivering an antiwar speech. As he was being sentenced, Debs told the judge, "Five percent control two-thirds of our wealth. . . . John D. Rockefeller has today an income of sixty million dollars a year, five million dollars a month." That was a grotesque "two hundred thousand dollars a day" at a time when average wages were only pennies an hour. Debs continued, Rockefeller "does not produce a penny of it. . . . I have no quarrel with Mr. Rockefeller personally, nor with any other capitalist. I am simply opposing a social order in which it is possible for one man who does absolutely nothing that is useful to amass a fortune of hundreds of millions of dollars, while millions of men and women who work all the days of their lives secure barely enough for an existence."

The *New York Times* reported Debs's conviction, but ignored his plea for child workers and their parents. For that, one had to read the *Appeal.* Izzy was twelve and enthralled with the message of Debs and his newspaper. The *Appeal* was the most exciting, but more than three hundred socialist papers and periodicals, including five English-language and eight foreign-language dailies, flourished during Izzy's early childhood.

Such radical spirit encouraged Izzy, who became a party activist for the first and last time in his life during his late teens. In 1925 Izzy supported Norman Thomas, who spearheaded the party after Eugene Debs. In later years, Stone was fond of saying, "I came in just as everyone else was leaving."

With no regard for the Constitution, the U.S. government killed free speech and socialist dissent. The establishment press was an eager handmaiden in that destruction, and all too often this unique chapter in political movements has been slighted in selective and watered-down history. Men such as Debs and Norman Thomas occasionally receive "fugitive mention," but in the main these leading thinkers and their movements "have been relegated to oblivion" by political scientists and historians.

Such historical blindness obscures the fact that virtually every humanitarian advancement, from child labor laws and workmen's compensation to welfare, came as the result of left-wing agitation. What was once a radical concept, that workers would run the operation, pushed by the Socialist Party eighty years ago, is today considered good management in enlightened companies and school systems.

To be sure, the left had a hand in its own demise. Conflicting visions of how to institute change made it difficult to sustain cohesive and lasting strength. Left-wing radicalism was pulled apart by three "diametrically opposed tendencies: socialism, syndicalism, and anarchism." Anarchists believed that a new society could happen only after the destruction of the state. Syndicalists felt that unionized workers would revise society through strikes, not the ballot box or barricades. Within the Socialist Party, warring factions disagreed as to whether the ballot and reform within the present system would work, or whether a revolution—nonviolent, they stressed—could bring about their goal of collective ownership and democratic management of land and capital. Until 1917, most Socialists were wedded to the idea of democracy. After the Bolshevik revolution, the party splintered with disastrous results.

However, during the first twelve years of this century, Socialist dreams seemed possible. Atheist Debs managed to unify the Populist, Christian, Marxist, and militant trade-union traditions that gathered under the Socialist Party umbrella in 1901.

Socialists were an enthusiastic audience for that investigative group of reporters called muckrakers, coined as a pejorative by Teddy Roosevelt. Adversarial and investigative reporters have inflamed presidents from George Washington to George W. Bush, and all presidents have used and abused journalists with varying success. By 1906, Roosevelt had successfully manipulated the quiescent White House press corps for four years. However, Roosevelt and the country were also reading firebrands who didn't collect White House press releases.

When turn-of-the-century muckraking began, the doctrine of "individualism" was potently peddled. This image remained so entrenched in the public's mind that Herbert Hoover was popularly applauded when he added a modifier and exalted "rugged" individualism. Decades later,

Ronald Reagan successfully employed the term. Pushing the concept in the late nineteenth century were conservative scholars and publishers, among them the lapsed socialist Charles A. Dana of the *New York Sun*. The cult of individualism was the ultimate in cynicism, selling "get ahead at all costs" greed as ideal and accessible to anyone. "Individualism" sanctified America's financiers and businessmen as generous men who made fortunes free from government interference by dint of brains and hard work. This artfully crafted myth ignored corruption, bribery, government deals, and slave wages, which were the norm along the robber barons' path to riches.

The epitome was John D. Rockefeller, who became one of the richest men in the world by bribing politicians and destroying competitors' refineries. Muckraking exposed the truth behind Rockefeller's Standard Oil, and much more: Policemen in most cities were so corrupt that they planned burglaries with the mob. Meatpacking factories packaged into breakfast sausage such delicacies as rats and even the remains of workers unfortunate enough to get too close to open vats.

At first, Teddy Roosevelt showed little concern that wealthy Republicans were being gored and even allowed Lincoln Steffens, the premier investigator of municipal graft, a daily audience during his barber hour. But by 1906, Steffens and company had gone too far. The U.S. Senate—which was not elected at that time but handpicked by machine bosses—was exposed by David Graham Phillips in Hearst's *Cosmopolitan* magazine as a band of hired whores with no intent to democratically serve the public. (His series sparked a nationwide movement and the passage of the Seventeenth Amendment, which called for the popular election of senators. This gesture to democracy often only marginally improved quality; financiers simply bankrolled the campaigns of hired politicians, a practice still much in evidence today.)

Then, on April 14, 1906, Roosevelt spoke to political allies skewered by socialist reporters. Right arm flailing, Roosevelt began a rambling reference to Bunyan's *Pilgrim's Progress:* "You may recall the description of the man with the muckrake" . . . a man who "fixes his eyes with solemn intentness only on that which is vile and debasing." It didn't matter that Roosevelt had his analogy wrong. Bunyan's muckraker wastes his life raking in the muck for *money*—the very target of crusading journalists. Enemies of investigative journalism, including the conservative press, seized Roosevelt's *muckraker* epithet as a cudgel, and this presidential slur paved the way for unprecedented political attacks and financial pressure, which doomed this unique journalistic movement. Stone disliked the *muckraker* pejorative but praised the writers it excoriated. He demurred when compared to them.

Content to expose, muckrakers seldom saw their job as formulating solutions. Still, for such a brief incarnation, muckrakers were a major influence, helping to create a wave of progressive reform in the first sixteen years of the last century and influencing many intellectual leftists who followed. Few journalists—especially those who sit at the table with presidents and business tycoons—can boast such a legacy.

S. S. McClure was as astute as he was brave and recognized gold in Lincoln Steffens's exposés of municipal graft and began publishing him in *McClure's* in 1902. The magazine, a blend of hard reporting and easy reading (fiction, travel articles, essays on such shocking topics as careers versus marriage), reached 350,000 homes in 1900. Brashness was not unknown to *McClure's* star, Steffens. When one timber millionaire dismissed Steffens's interview request with "I don't care for write-ups," Steffens shot back, "I don't propose to write you up. I propose to write you down."

McClure also employed an unknown reporter whose manner was cool and detached. McClure gave this reporter immense freedom—five years of research before a line was printed. Stone idolized this journalist, one of the most remarkable in history, a woman in a man's profession. Ida Tarbell's assignment was to investigate Rockefeller and his Standard Oil Company, a task for which she had a burning interest. Her father, Frank Tarbell, was one of many independent oil producers who went into debt as a result of Standard Oil's nefarious monopoly tactics, which included blowing up competitors' refineries. Ruined by Standard, Tarbell's partner shot himself, leaving Tarbell in desperate straits. He warned his daughter that Standard Oil would ruin her and the magazine. But she was not to be deterred. At the age of fourteen she had prayed to God to save her from marriage: "I must be free and to be free I must be a spinster." As a reporter, Tarbell dressed the spinster in severe high-collared shirtwaists. With single-minded obsession, Tarbell ransacked files of ancient lawsuits and congressional records concerning a mysteriously suppressed investigation. She found sources who talked despite Rockefeller's clout.

Alarmed Standard Oil executives chose a powerful intermediary, Mark Twain, who protested to the publisher, a time-honored route of businessmen who wish to intimidate reporters. McClure did not oblige. When Twain asked him what the report would contain, McClure tersely replied, "You'll have to ask Ida."

Her series, begun in 1902, detailed Rockefeller's crooked rise to power, disclosing secret deals in which Standard Oil was granted a shipping rate far below that given competitors. She wrote in terms any reader could understand: the rates were the "equivalent to renting a railroad for their own private use." Friendly judges proffered wrist-slapping fines for its sabotage of enemy refineries. Standard Oil's purchase of the Ohio legislature was so flagrant that it went down in history as the Coal Oil Legislature.

Publishers were as corrupt as politicians. In exchange for advertising, at least 110 Ohio newspapers had signed contracts with Standard to print editorials and "news" furnished by its public relations team. Hired guns vilified Tarbell in standard sexist fashion: "Hysterical Woman Versus Historical Facts." When a Harvard economist attacked her, Standard bought and distributed five thousand copies of his book.

Tarbell's flawless research withstood all assaults; her book's fame brought twenty-one antitrust suits against Standard Oil in state courts within three years. President Roosevelt was forced to order antitrust action to break up Standard's monopoly. Although the case dragged on for years, the U.S. Supreme Court issued a decree ordering the breakup of Standard Oil in 1911. It dissolved into the famous Seven Sisters oil cartel. Following the dissolution order, Rockefeller lost millions. For a man of such vast fortune this might seem slight punishment, but it pained Rockefeller. Although he was also a philanthropist, generations of Rockefellers have not been able to erase Tarbell's devastating portrait of founding father John D.

While Tarbell was all cool steel, another famous muckraker, Upton Sinclair, was molten lava. By the time Izzy was twelve, he was pressing copies of Sinclair's most famous work, *The Jungle,* on a visiting cousin and urging anyone he knew to read it. In 1904, *Appeal to Reason* commissioned Sinclair to write about immigrant workers in Chicago's meatpacking houses, giving him a $500 advance. The serialization became an instant best seller in book form, an international hit published in seventeen languages. Such success, however, belies the war waged against Sinclair by the Beef Trust to foil the publication of *The Jungle.*

Sinclair's carefully documented findings were so explosive that he resorted to weaving the facts as a novel. Filled with passages of sorrow and pain, this masterpiece rivaled the best of Zola and Dickens. Sinclair described an underfed child's workday of at least ten hours, the kind of toil experienced by 1.75 million of America's children at the time.

> *Hour after hour, day after day, year after year, it was fated that he should stand upon a certain square foot of floor . . . making never a motion and thinking never a thought, save for the setting of lard cans. In summer the stench of the warm lard would be nauseating, and in winter the cans would all but freeze to his naked little fingers in the unheated cellar. . . . He would never know what the sun looked like on weekdays. And for this, at the end of the week, he would carry home three dollars to his family . . . five cents per hour.*

For $6 a week, men and women endured torturous conditions:

> *There was no heat . . . The men would tie up their feet in newspapers and old sacks, and these would be soaked in blood and frozen, and then soaked again, and so on, until by night-time a man would be walking on great lumps the size of the feet of an elephant. . . . All of those who used knives were unable to wear gloves, and their arms would be white with frost and their hands would grow numb, and then of course, there would be accidents.*

There was no leaving the stench of blood and excrement and death for lunch. In the summer, the killing beds became a stagnant, dripping furnace; the smell never left a worker's nostrils. Carcasses were moved along an assembly line at such a fierce pace that no workman was unscarred; the loss of a thumb or finger was common.

The suddenly rich and famous Sinclair was everlastingly bitter that, for all its success, *The Jungle* did little to convert readers to agitate for socialism or labor reforms. He famously commented, "I aimed at the public's heart, and by accident I hit it in the stomach." As countless readers suddenly became temporary vegetarians, Sinclair said, "I realized with bitterness that I had been made into a 'celebrity,' not because the public cared anything about the sufferings of these workers, but simply because the public did not want to eat tubercular beef."

Six months after publication, the explosive fact that Americans were being fed tubercular and rotten meat forced even a bought Congress to pass the Pure Food and Drug Act and the Beef Inspection Act. While it abolished the worst abuses, Sinclair noted, "The lobbyists of the packers had their way in Washington; the meat inspection bill was deprived of all its sharpest teeth."

Sinclair persisted in vain to persuade Roosevelt to agitate for workers. A decade after *The Jungle,* Sinclair sadly reported that his classic had done nothing for the "wage slaves in those huge brick packing houses," as a new investigation proved. Magazines friendly to the Beef Trust, such as the *Saturday Evening Post,* gave meatpacking boss J. Ogden Armour full rein to rebut the book. (A former Armour executive, George Horace Lorimer, just happened to be the editor of the *Post.*) The conservative *New York Times* ripped into Sinclair, while an editorial by the flamboyant Arthur Brisbane in Hearst's *New York Evening Journal* praised Sinclair. Recognizing its sensational worth, Hearst serialized the novel. In England, a young reviewer named Winston Churchill lauded the book, which "pierces the thickest skull and most leathery heart."

Even with his fame, Sinclair could nonetheless find no publisher for *The Brass Check,* his exposé of the prostitution of newspapers in alliance with corporations. He was forced to publish it himself. *The Brass Check* was Stone's bible on the subject of journalistic corruption. Stone referred to it all his life. During the 1950s organized Cold War campaign to "drive out of the 'opinion industries' any opposition to the preconceptions of the big money and the screwball fringe," Stone referred to Sinclair's exposés of the "scared and sterile" media of his time. "To see this whole affair in perspective one must go back to *The Brass Check* and its story of how Big Business finally wiped out the 'muckrake' magazines whose exposés were so valuable." Although the book is filled with self-pitying passages, the facts in *The Brass Check* remain eye-openers regarding newspaper corruption. Reading it at an early age served a skeptical Stone well.

In 2004, another great chronicler of twentieth-century America, Studs Terkel, a friend of Stone's, explained the title as he talked about the impact of *The Brass Check:* "I'll tell ya what the brass check was. It was when a guy went to a brothel, he paid two dollars, this was before inflation, and the madam gave him the brass check and he would give the brass check to the girl. At the end of the day the girl cashes in her brass checks and she gets paid a half a buck apiece. Sinclair said *The Brass Check* represents the journalists of that day. . . . Today it's more so. . . . They talk about the sins of the 'liberal media.' What an insult to our intelligence! There is no liberal media today. These were the real guys. They were exposing everybody. This was before TV and radio. Now it's worse, of course."

Sinclair's close friend Jack London wrote a "rousing manifesto," as Sinclair termed it, for *The Jungle*. At the height of their fame in 1906, it seemed inconceivable that Sinclair would later be shunned by cautious publishers, or that London would quit the Socialist Party because of its "lack of fire and fight," then commit suicide.

More than any other boyhood hero, Jack London activated Izzy; "London made me a socialist," he told Patner. *Martin Eden* was written two years after Stone was born, and by the time Stone read it at the age of twelve, London had been dead four years of a morphine overdose. While many young readers embraced London's adventures such as *The Call of the Wild* and *The Sea Wolf*, Izzy absorbed London's deeper, socialist message.

London described *Eden*, his study of class relationships, as "an attack upon the bourgeoisie. . . . It will not make me any friends." Nonetheless, many readers saw *Eden* as a paean to the very individualism that London insisted he was attacking. They can hardly be blamed. London sets Eden up as a sympathetic hero who toils in a laundry-room sweatshop for pennies and falls in love with a middle-class woman who teaches him to read. Then London's Eden espouses Nietzschean philosophy to a group of socialists who are not as strongly etched; a reader's natural sympathy lies with this young man who rises from poverty through hard work. The vacillation and ambivalence in the development of his main character give credence to Sinclair's cutting observation that London could never decide whether to be a revolutionary or a landed gentleman. Young Stone did not mistake London's message. He soaked up the anticapitalism passages and thrilled to Eden's euphoric struggle for knowledge.

The personal costs were great for muckrakers, and the more popular they became, the more they were hunted. In 1907, Benjamin B. Hampton bought a magazine near death with 12,000 circulation. Three years later, his revamped *Hampton's* was circulating to 480,000. Its chief muckraker, Charles Edward Russell, was dogged by a "slinking and malignant scrutiny"—private detectives hoping to trap him in some scandal to discredit his writing. Russell wrote on, exposing historic swindles, until he attacked the New Haven Railroad. New York banks that had lent Hampton money for years suddenly refused to honor his collateral of gilt-edged securities. The railroad had gotten to them. Thus *Hampton's* was killed by the financial interests it had exposed. Wrote Russell, "Muckraking in America came to its death by strangulation at the hands of persons and interests perfectly well known. Doubtless Respectable Business was glad. Whether the country had reason to rejoice is another question.

"Where there is no criticism there is no health."

By the time Izzy was old enough to work for the Socialist Party, little of its fire remained. One reason for its "failure" as a party was, ironically, socialism's very success. In part, the party seemed peripheral and unnecessary because some of its reforms were co-opted by the mainstream. Although its incendiary words threatened the rich and sometimes alarmed those it sought to recruit, Socialist Party *ideas* were popular enough to be incorporated by the ruling class, first the progressive wing of the Republican Party and then by the Democrats. In 1916, Woodrow Wilson, needing the progressive vote, embraced such legislation as farm credits, some child labor laws, and an eight-hour day for railroad workers. The foundation of Franklin Delano Roosevelt's New Deal stemmed from Socialist Party reforms.

In earlier days, Debsian socialism looked potently political. Sparked by *Appeal to Reason,* Debs drew almost a million votes in his 1912 presidential campaign, 6 percent of the total. That year, the Socialist Party elected almost twelve hundred public officials throughout the United States, including mayors and congressmen. Four years later, the party was in decline, sharply splintered over Debs's antiwar stance and thwarted by years of government repression. In 1920, nearly a million people again voted for Debs, even though he had to conduct his presidential campaign from a jail cell, more often the domicile of politicians *after* they have been elected.*

Socialist labor victories were won at the cost of violence and death. One of the worst class battles was the 1912 Ludlow Massacre, in which whole families were suffocated or burned to death. As flames engulfed the tents of miners striking against Rockefeller's Colorado Coal Company, screams of trapped miners, their wives, and their children echoed across the camp. Christian Socialist papers and other publications blamed Rock-

*A deceptive surge of Socialist Party voting in 1920 occurred because New York's Lower East Side Russian Jewish immigrants had lived in the United States long enough to become naturalized citizens and voted for the imprisoned Debs. Many would remain, in varying degrees, committed to a dying party.

efeller, who financed the strike-breaking militia. In most reports, a rabidly antilabor press slanted stories, blaming "agitators" for the violence.

Nonviolent strikes went virtually uncovered. In a time when the public received 90 percent of its news through newspapers, fog descended as major newspapers boycotted such facts. In many strike centers from Massachusetts to California, newspapers were owned by, or were friends of, the industrial magnates whom workers were striking against. In Montana, for example, Rockefeller's mining company owned or controlled practically every newspaper in the state. Some papers and wire services easily lied. The Associated Press gave details about how the good citizens of York, Pennsylvania, mobbed a socialist speaker, Gaylord Wilshire. There was only one problem. Delayed by a heavy schedule, Wilshire had never reached York.

Radicals were such fair game that raiding offices, burning files, and curbing free speech were applauded by newspapers and politicians. In San Diego, jailed radicals who tried to break a free-speech ban were dragged out of cells and forced to dogtrot for twenty-two miles while being beaten by local vigilantes, who were given a green light by the police. Two men were murdered. Anarchist Emma Goldman was forced by a lynch mob to flee her hotel while her manager was tarred, feathered, and left for dead.

Socialists donated large sums to IWW strikers (known as Wobblies) but relationships became increasingly strained. When IWW leader Big Bill Haywood publicly sanctioned sabotage in 1913, he was dropped from the Socialist Party's executive committee and quit. Debs deplored the union he had so enthusiastically sponsored eight years before, calling the IWW "an Anarchist organization in all except name."

Haywood relished his dark and dangerous persona, especially among rich Greenwich Villagers who found him exotic. Mabel Dodge, a wealthy dilettante and sometime girlfriend of radical writer John Reed, ran a Manhattan salon where she delighted in mixing everyone from radicals just out of jail to Harvard intellectuals slumming in black tie with their satin-clad dates. Reed's *The Masses* was a flamboyant antidote to humorless reform novels and periodicals, home to both the serious and playacting "parlor pinks" who congregated in the Village. When Haywood and Emma Goldman came to Dodge's elegant Fifth Avenue digs, no one seemed to find it ironic that, as they earnestly explained the lives of the downtrodden to her rich friends, they were being served by underpaid maids and butlers. Dodge insisted that she would host "none but more or less radical sympathizers . . . People who believed that others had the right to kill on principle, if they thought it Right: The Live and Let Live Kind of people." Such inanities filled her memoirs.

Dodge's egalitarianism did not extend to the press. When reporters entered, one bejeweled guest murmured, "Oh, horrid!" Never fear, a "heavy set young man" firmly ejected them. The bouncer was twenty-three-year-old Walter Lippmann, one of Mabel's young, if portly, finds. Lippmann was already an elitist with little sympathy for riffraff reporters, even as he was experiencing his thirty-second-or-so fling with socialism. Reporters had a devastating glimpse of the 1914 Haywood soiree, and radical papers taunted the IWW leaders who dined while their idled union members starved and slept on park benches.

Continuing relentless pressure during the Taft administration proved just how dangerous life was for muckrakers. Indictments against *Appeal to Reason* grew out of a series on the federal penitentiary at Leavenworth, Kansas, a sinkhole of corruption and graft where police brutality included sodomizing inmates. Although the story was officially corroborated, the government ignored such crimes and instead indicted the newspaper for mentioning the "unnatural acts" of the deputy warden. The *Appeal* editors, including its founder, Julius Wayland, were indicted in 1911 for sending "indecent, filthy, obscene, lewd and lascivious printed matter" through the mails. The *Appeal* won its Leavenworth case in May 1913, yet smear campaigns took their toll. In 1912 the *Los Angeles Times* falsely wrote that Wayland was guilty of seducing a fourteen-year-old orphan who had died during an abortion. On November 10, 1912, Wayland put a pistol in his mouth and blew his brains out. Before he shot himself, he tucked a despairing note inside a book at his bedside: "The struggle under the competitive system is not worth the effort, let it pass."

It was as if Wayland knew that the worst was yet to come, and it soon did. As often happens in wartime when blind patriotism reigns, World War I crushed all dissent and supplied lasting labels of *unpatriotic* and *un-American* to anyone who questioned foreign policies. During and immediately following World War I, suppression of speech and thought became orchestrated madness.

Elected on a peace platform, President Wilson had to seduce a reluctant country into supporting what was later seen as a senseless and dirty war. Millions were spent on a nationwide propaganda mill to induce a national spirit through ads, leaflets, and publicity stunts; the Committee on Public Information was headed by former reporter George Creel. Speakers—seventy-five thousand of them—blitzed five thousand American cities and towns, giving 750,000 four-minute Hun-bashing speeches. According to propaganda, Huns were so busy raping nuns it was hard to see how they found time to rape Belgium. Atrocity-of-the-minute stories were cranked out by French-allied propagandists; babies' hands and feet had been hacked off, nuns' breasts hacked away. Germans had tied a village priest to his bell and used him as a live clapper. Reporters who sought truth were unable to verify any of these atrocities.

Congress swiftly enacted legislation making it a crime to speak against the war. Hundreds were prosecuted for discouraging recruitment or saying or writing anything that could be construed as critical of the government or, even, military uniforms. Government spies roamed the nation, and raids without warrants proliferated. As war hysteria grew, anything German was suspect: Teaching the language was banned. Sauerkraut's patriotic new name was *victory cabbage*. A German-born socialist was wrapped in the American flag and hanged by a mob for a speech on socialism.

More than ever, it was open season on Wobblies, socialists, and labor activists. Many opposed the war as pacifists, while others objected to this specific war as an imperialist horror. Socialists naively felt they could speak out; Debs called war a gross act of barbarism. Indictments of *Appeal to Reason* and *Masses* editors followed, as well as harassment of the *Nation* and even Lippmann's *New Republic,* although it was largely viewed as the president's house organ. Legally banned from the mail, the *Masses* and the *Appeal* were crippled. Under the wartime Espionage and Trading with the Enemy Act, it was illegal for antiwar factions to publish and mail their views. The Espionage Act even made it a crime to suggest that a referendum should have preceded a declaration of war or to oppose the draft. It was upheld by the Supreme Court; Justice Holmes, so often cited as a voice of reason, wrote the majority opinion. Quipped the *Masses*'s Max Eastman to an audience in July 1917, "They give you ninety days for quoting the Declaration of Independence, six months for quoting the Bible, and pretty soon somebody is going to get a life sentence for quoting Woodrow Wilson in the wrong connection." Socialist dissent soon crumbled.

Friendly New York newspapers aligned with Post Office officials who leaked files on "traitors." Government officials and an antilabor press, long bent on crushing radical discourse, now had a red, white, and blue excuse. Peace rallies were attacked, Wobblies were given long prison terms, officials secretly helped vigilantes round up copper miners and haul them into the desert, a thousand Socialist Party branches and meeting halls were raided and destroyed, all files seized. The sentences were staggering: A man was given ten years for writing a letter to the *Kansas City Star* charging that the government favored profiteers. A Socialist organizer and mother of four got five years for denouncing the war. A Socialist congressional candidate was sentenced to one year for opposing conscription. When a man in Indiana shot and killed an immigrant who yelled, "To hell with the United States," a jury acquitted the murderer after deliberating two minutes.

The ugliness of war hysteria was embodied in the persecution of Debs. His party torn apart from within as well as without, his followers assaulted by cops and hooligans, Debs challenged the Espionage Act in Canton, Ohio, in June 1918. Looking out at his audience, its ranks swelled by a contingent of Secret Service agents, and then across the street to the jail where radicals were imprisoned, Debs said, "The master class has always declared the wars; the subject class has always fought the battles. . . . The subject class has had nothing to gain and all to lose, especially their lives."

At his trial, Debs quoted the First Amendment: "Congress shall make no law abridging the freedom of speech or of the press; or the right of the people peaceably to assemble, and to petition the government for a redress of grievances." If the Espionage Act does not negate the First Amendment, said Debs, "then certainly I am unable to read or understand the English language." Debs was found guilty and given ten years. In modern times, the equivalent would have been jailing George McGovern or Eugene McCarthy for speaking against the Vietnam War, or those few members of Congress who opposed President Bush's resolution for force in Iraq in 2003, or Seymour Hersh for exposing the Abu Ghraib prison atrocities.

As soon as an armistice was signed, there was an astounding about-face. Wilson admitted that the real reason the war took place was because "Germany was afraid her commercial rivals were going to get the better of her." (Secret documents later revealed that Germany was not alone in its greed; the European allies had long planned to divide up the spoils.) Now presidential candidate Warren G. Harding successfully attacked the war on his march to the White House, voicing sentiments that had led to prison for Debs and others just a few years before. Said Harding, "From the very beginning it was a lie to say that this was a war to make the world safe for democracy."

The last soldier had barely fallen in Flanders fields when the wounded began detailing bitter truths in the formerly jingoistic *New York Times.* "The war did no good to anybody. Those of its generation whom it did not kill, it crippled, wasted or used up," wrote T. S. Mathews in his review of Remarque's *All Quiet on the Western Front.*

Now Debs and other antiwar prisoners were an embarrassment. Harding commuted their sentences as a "Christmas gift." Debs was released on Christmas Day. He posed for moving-picture cameras and photographers for ten minutes. Behind barred windows, twenty-three hundred convicts roared a farewell that echoed for blocks. Debs turned to the prisoners and, tears rolling down his thin face, waved his hat to them.

With war's end, violence at home escalated. With lightning speed, leftists were transformed from being "pro-German" to "pro-Red" as the Russian Revolution entered the public's consciousness. By calling all leftists "Reds," one of the most successful, long-running propaganda campaigns of the twentieth century began, one that would repeatedly drive Stone back to his obsession with free speech and civil liberties. Although he was but a child at the time, he never forgot the infamous 1919 Palmer Raids. The Cold War was born long before the end of World War II; the concept, policy, and propaganda of a "cold war" began at the end of World War I. By 1946, this anti-Red reaction was deeply embedded in the American psyche and easily resurrected for the witch hunts.

No other country had ever legitimized the right to free speech and dissent; now federal officials were attacking every vestige of those freedoms. Well-funded superpatriot groups spurred citizens to boycott any group or publication amorphously deemed unpatriotic. Labor strikes were stamped Bolshevik agitation. After the *New York Times* and other papers wrote that the 1919 race riots in Washington, D.C., and Chicago had been "inspired by Bolsheviks and overseen by Lenin personally, virtually anything seemed credible to an America driven to political hysteria." Several thousand citizen spies were recruited to find Reds.

Simultaneously, the Socialist Party imploded; leftist factions broke and formed the Communist and Communist Labor parties. Louis Boudin, a scholar and lawyer who had dined with Trotsky before he left the United

States on the eve of the revolution, was idolized by Izzy and became a relative through marriage. He was among thousands, disgusted by incessant feuds, who left all three parties. Boudin had gone from the Socialist Party to the Communist Labor Party but, soon disillusioned, claimed that he had not "left a party of crooks to join a party of lunatics."

With the American press assisting, Red Hysteria was born. Widespread prosperity and rivalry with Russia "gave the kibosh to the left" both after World War I and World War II, Stone said in later life. The attacks on leftists after both wars remain grotesque chapters in American history and often seem unfathomable to those generations who did not experience them, and even to many who did. In 1919, Attorney General A. Mitchell Palmer envisioned Reds as a lethal infestation "eating its way into the homes of the American workman." A man uninterested in the measured phrase, Palmer saw the "sharp tongues of revolutionary heat . . . licking at the altars of the churches, leaping into the belfry of the school bell, crawling into the sacred corners of American homes, seeking to replace marriage vows with libertine laws, burning up the foundations of society." The Daughters of the American Revolution denounced immigrants as "these foreign leeches" to be "cast out."

In 1919, when two anarchists blew up Palmer's home in fashionable Dupont Circle—annihilating themselves and spraying fragments of their bodies onto the doorstep of Assistant Secretary of the Navy Franklin D. Roosevelt's home across the street—an unharmed Palmer moved into rapid action. A young zealot assisted Mitchell Palmer, assembling 260,000 files on people deemed suspicious. Thus began an eager obsession in the long and destructive life of future FBI director J. Edgar Hoover. Palmer and Hoover used the 1917 Espionage Act and the 1918 Sedition Act to launch their 1919 campaign against radicals and left-wing organizations, known as the Palmer Raids, which violently thwarted the American Constitution and continued over several months. More than ten thousand suspected Communists and anarchists were arrested. No evidence was found of a proposed revolution. Arrested without warrants, the majority were guilty of nothing more than not being born in America. Agents forged incriminating documents to deport innocent people caught in illegal raids. Government funds were illegally used to distribute free "boilerplate" releases to newspapers that favored the Justice Department's campaign of repression. Alleged anarchists and members of the Union of Russian Workers were deported without trial by the boatload. Elected Socialists were denied seats in Congress. The New York Times specialized in lopsided coverage, and both the *Times* and the *Washington Post* supported Palmer in "get the Reds" editorials.

As a forerunner to McCarthyism, teachers were suspended and librarian "Reds" were hounded. Communist Party membership—although not illegal—was declared reason enough for deportation. When the most cursory examination showed a trampling of constitutional rights, the American Civil Liberties Union (ACLU) was spawned. Finally protests against the Palmer Raids received support.

Indignation crackled in a report on the raids by impeccably credentialed lawyers, led by future Supreme Court justice Felix Frankfurter, detailing the "utterly illegal" activities of the government. Nearly a hundred men had been arrested in Bridgeport, Connecticut, "kept in jail for five months; beaten, starved, suffocated, tortured and threatened with death in futile attempts to extract admissions." Some were detained for up to sixty hours in suffocating heat over the pump room of a boiler. The report noted, "Of the men still held, at least a majority had no political views of any special nature." Workmen from Russia who spoke little or no English were "practically buried alive for five months." Innocent Russians were rounded up at concerts or at night study classes. In jail, the terrorization continued; forbidden to see family or counsel, they were forced to sleep on damp concrete floors. In Detroit, eight hundred men were imprisoned without charges for three to six days in a narrow, windowless corridor with only one toilet to share. Their crime: attending a dance class or having eaten at a Communist Party headquarters. In Boston, hundreds were shackled together and paraded before jeering mobs. The report's conclusion minced no words: "We feel justified in branding attorney general A. Mitchell Palmer as the biggest violator of the law in the United States."

No journalist was more furious than Walter Lippmann, who blamed President Wilson, for whom he had helped devise a peace plan; not since Adams and the Alien and Sedition Acts had officeholders made "so determined" and "so dangerous an attack" on constitutional liberties, he fumed. In 1922, Palmer still defended his actions, but his presidential hopes were dashed and publishers were finally denouncing proposed new legislative assaults on civil liberties. Still, Palmer's reign of terror spawned lasting repression and damage by hobbling the workers' movement and leftist activism. People feared subscribing to left-wing journals, antilabor forces sold "right to work" as "American," schoolteachers applied caution in classrooms, and voices speaking against injustice were stilled. Once the clarion publication for three-quarters of a million readers, the Socialists' *Appeal to Reason* was a broken dream. It folded in 1922. On that note, the Roaring Twenties arrived and the popular press was busily whipping up new lingo such as *ballyhoo* and *making whoopee*, roughly translated as a headlong quest for money and good times.

It was hardly the moment to come of age for a young, earnest, radical socialist named Isador Feinstein, who was born fifteen years too late to do anything but embrace in spirit the golden days of socialism. With unflagging optimism, however, Izzy struck out on his journalistic career. He was one of those ebullient souls for whom radical progressivism "remained as a memory from the past and a model for the future."

5

NEWSPAPERMAN
IN KNEE PANTS

He was the editor of a tabloid newspaper but he loved his children. So he told them he was a burglar.

—*College Humor*, circa 1927

It was 1923 and the retired publisher of the *Progress* was now a junior in high school and reluctant clerk for his father after school. One day, the publisher of the *Camden Courier Post* stopped by the store.

"I heard about you," J. David Stern told Izzy. "Would you like to be my Haddonfield correspondent?"

"Yes—sure!" shot back the excited fifteen-year-old.

When the managing editor, Harry T. Saylor, met Izzy, he looked witheringly at, as Izzy described himself years later to Patner, "a little Jewish boy in thick glasses and knee pants! And he thought, 'Jesus Christ!' He had wanted a man in there."

Izzy was certain that Saylor would fire him after a week. But Izzy had come highly recommended from the publisher's wife, Jill Lit Stern, the lady in blue who had discovered the Spinoza-reading store clerk three years earlier and was now a devoted mentor. "He had an unusually developed mind for a child of twelve," her husband remembered.

For the next fifteen years—throughout the twenties, the New Deal, the Popular Front, the Spanish Civil War, and the beginning rumblings of World War II—the dynamic Stern was Izzy's patron. He helped shape Izzy's writing and gave him a powerful platform. Izzy became America's youngest chief editorial writer on a major newspaper, first with Stern's *Philadelphia Record* and then with his *New York Evening Post*.

The team of Stern and Feinstein, as Izzy was known through most of his tenure with the publisher, was as stormy as it was serendipitous. In that era of Coolidge conservatism, it was a miracle that Izzy found the one major publisher compatible with his beliefs, a man dedicated to liberal, fair reporting. But that did not stop Izzy. Their parting was so bitter that Stern excised Izzy from his autobiography, *Memoirs of a Maverick Publisher.* "Izzy was always getting into trouble with the city editor, and I was always hiring him back at the insistence of my wife," recalled Stern.

Stern had purchased the *Courier* four years before hiring Izzy, inheriting an entire staff on the take. They were owned by Senator David Baird, whose one-man machine had ruled Camden for twenty-five years. Stern fired them all. The publisher saw gold in Camden when America's two largest advertisers, Victor Talking Machine Company and Campbell's Soup, expanded their plants. Stern emphasized local news rather than compete with Philadelphia papers with warmed-over national news.

By the time Izzy was hired, Stern had smashed the Baird machine and the paper had expanded its plant six times in seven years. Stern rapidly changed a pattern of boycotting news of strikes or trade unions. He even gave a decent account of a Camden factory strike. "Word got around that I was a dangerous radical," he noted. Advertising cancellations became so serious that Stern tried his charm on the burghers of Camden. He convinced them that if he did not print the news, unions would print their own inflammatory pamphlets. The boycott ended.

The fast-rising *Courier* benefited from lightning changes in the twenties. The Delaware Bridge, opened in 1926, granted easy access to Philadelphia and spawned Camden's real estate boom. Arthur Brisbane, Hearst's widely syndicated columnist who earned a staggering $5,000 a week, rolled into town, swilled a quart of champagne for breakfast, and pounded out a column in the *Courier* office, extolling Camden's charms.

In just a few years, Izzy would be writing about Norman Thomas and FDR, business corruption and New Deal programs, Fascist Italy and Hitler's ominous rise, but in 1923 he found himself scrambling to write anything as boy stringer from Haddonfield.

His second day on the job, an eager Izzy went in search of a story and ran into the head of Haddonfield's historical society, who had the Dickensian name of Pennypacker. He suggested that Izzy find a story in the cemetery, home of Elizabeth Haddon, the founder of Haddonfield, celebrated in Longfellow's *Tales of a Wayside Inn.* The historical society needed funds to refurbish the tarnished plaque; would Izzy write a story publicizing this? asked Pennypacker.

Sure, said Izzy, but even this neophyte realized the story hardly sang with a compelling news angle. So Izzy "diddled it up a bit," writing that an elderly gentleman raising money to refurbish the plaque was "horrified one night when he thought he saw the ghost of Elizabeth Haddon trying to polish it up." When Izzy bought a copy of the paper the next day, there it was atop page one with a two-column head and a byline.

Years later, Izzy echoed that thrill of a first byline; few newspaper writers forgot that first "name in lights" reward that kept talented writers churning out copy despite miserly paychecks. Young Izzy felt he had found Fort Knox, remarking to Patner, "I got a bonus and ten cents an inch so it came out to forty-five cents an inch for that story!"

In the 1920s, television was decades away, radio was but an infant rival, and monopoly ownership had not yet throttled individual newspaper competition. Every major city had a half dozen thriving dailies; in 1923, New York City had seventeen English-language daily newspapers in general circulation, and Philadelphia had six. City rooms abounded with rebels escaping corporate conformity, arrogant with the knowledge that if they got fired, they could find a job across the street. "I always wanted to be a newspaperman," Izzy said, a sentiment echoed by most newspapermen who entered the profession before television's lure began to eclipse that of newspapers in the late fifties.

The 1920s was a time for some very bad reporting, but the decade also spawned legendary writers. On the exemplary *World*, Herbert Bayard Swope invented the op-ed page, to be copied by newspapers worldwide. Biting wit and political prognostication abounded, and talents such as F.P.A. (Franklin P. Adams), Heywood Broun, James M. Cain (who would write the thriller *The Postman Always Rings Twice*), and Walter Lippmann became high-priced celebrities.

The Front Page, Ben Hecht and Charles MacArthur's 1928 Broadway hit and acerbic paean to the business, set the tone for newspaper movies and what reporters—nobody ever called them journalists—thought they ought to be. Clichés of gin bottles rattling in desk drawers and pictures of victims stolen from piano tops held more than a little truth. The reporter who possessed a college degree did his best to hide such a flaw. Writing was fueled by alcohol, and the best (Ring Lardner, Heywood Broun) and the worst (camp followers from Peoria to Dubuque) fell victim to enlarged livers. Many a story was composed by two, three, or more colleagues when the original owner of the byline fell stone drunk over the typewriter. Paychecks went to liar's poker, de rigueur at every press saloon. Those who entered into marriage and a family saw far more of a city room than the living room or nursery.

Chutzpah helped many a reporter, including Izzy, who related with brio to Patner his one brush with the mystifying world of sports. Shortly after Izzy's father made him fold the *Progress,* Izzy, the stringer for the *Camden Post-Telegram,* was sent to cover a major basketball game. "I was a nonsports kid," he said, a description that did little justice to his ignorance about such giants of his day as Babe Ruth, Jack Dempsey, Bobby Jones, and Bill Tilden. Izzy frantically asked anyone who would answer such rudimentary questions as "What's the object of the game? What are the goals? Was there anything dramatic?" Izzy said, "I wrote a very good story—very colorful, full of crap, and so I had a job as a sportswriter. The only time I worked as a sportswriter."

Truth was often shaded, and some newsmen were owned by political machines or mobsters. Yesteryear's reporters would have been branded certifiable dipsomaniacs if forced to take the battery of psychological tests now customary in some newspaper personnel departments. Stone's ghost would think he was inside IBM if it wandered into today's carpeted newsrooms, with their attaché-case carrying "news aides" instead of copyboys, reporters with legal degrees and a vast knowledge of the Internet, the cricket click of computers instead of the bassoon thump of old uprights.

Reporters are no longer society's outcasts and are often comfortable with the status quo of corporate America. Outsider unrest and the fun of battling the establishment was doomed as soon as reporters could afford house payments. In 1991, Scotty Reston compared the generations of reporters: "We were the children of the Depression. We lived among the poor. Your generation knows more about poverty, but we felt it more. Something has been lost," he told *Washington Post* media critic Howard Kurtz. Many today view their jobs as stepping-stones to TV. Of course, favoring the establishment is nothing new. "In the early 1930s the *New York Times* was *awful . . . ,*" recalled Stone to Patner. "Richard V. Oulihan was the chief Washington correspondent. He used to play medicine ball with Herbert Hoover every morning at the White House. That's enough to kill off a good reporter. . . . You *cannot get intimate* with officials and maintain your independence," Stone stressed. Whether they were "good guys" or "bad guys" was incidental to him. "They'll use you."

Gilt by association accrued to camp followers—personal perks, fortunes, and such establishment trinkets as the Pulitzer Prize. Even the most august were pimping in the twenties. Pulitzer Prize winner Bayard Swope excelled at promoting influential friends, including Wall Street financier Bernard Baruch. Swope worked as Baruch's public relations adviser even as he promoted him as a "financial wizard" in his *New York World* columns. In return Swope profited from insider stock market tips; Lippmann disapprovingly observed, "An ordinary newspaperman with an ordinary salary . . . ended up with about twelve million dollars." Columnist Arthur Krock enjoyed similar Baruch benefits and even moonlighted with the banking firm of Dillon, Read, delicately referring to himself as private counsel on public relations. Krock was banished from the *World*'s editorial page by Lippmann after he overheard Krock telling a Dillon, Read agent about an upcoming editorial that would likely affect the price of certain stocks.

A successful new form of journalism dawned in 1919, venerating sleaze with its own format: the tabloid. Sensational divorces, ax murders, a picture of husband-killer Ruth Snyder at the moment of her electrocution, were all forerunners of today's icons of geekiness, the specialty of TV infotainment, and other atrocities of modern journalism. The trend was epitomized by the famous New York tabloid headline "Headless Body in Topless Bar."

The timing was ripe for sensationalism. Even small-town America was casting off vestiges of Victorian prudery. The generational gap was captured in a 1927 cartoon by Art Young: a flapper, in thigh-high skirt, legs draped over a stuffed chair, says to a fat matron wearing a calf-length dress, sensible shoes, hair in a bun, and a look of apoplexy, "Mother, when you were a girl didn't you find it a *bore* to be a virgin?"

America's first tabloid, the *New York Illustrated Daily News*, was the genius of Captain Joseph Medill Patterson, who accurately prophesied that his picture paper, "aimed at the twelve-year-old mentality," was "sure to be a great success." Patterson based his argument on Army IQ tests revealing that nearly half—47.75 percent—of the population had the mentality of a twelve-year-old. When he built the *Daily News* skyscraper, Patterson cynically inscribed on its stone façade, "God must have loved the common people, he made so many of them." In his Yale days, Patterson was an idle-rich dilettante who talked of socialism as he collected his dividends. By 1919, George Seldes claimed, "there was not a socialist, radical, or even liberal trace left in the man."

Already there were fewer newspapers, and the increasing use of wires and syndicated features were standardizing them like so many Model Ts off the assembly line. This was the beginning of a consolidation that led to one-newspaper towns and giant corporate chains. In 1925, Frank Munsey, "a mass murderer of newspapers, had just . . . buried four New

York papers," wrote press critic A. J. Liebling, reducing the number of New York dailies from sixteen to twelve.

Radio now loomed as a threat to newspaper advertising. From 1922 to 1929 annual radio ad sales jumped from $60 million to nearly $843 million—an increase of 1,305 percent. Radio was to the 1920s what television was to the 1950s—the dream of hucksters and an indispensable voice to the outside world. Radio revolutionized politics; for the first time Americans had "front-row seats" listening to the fulminations and clacking of gavels as embattled Democrats met at Madison Square Garden in 1924 to pick their presidential candidate. The deadlock between William McAdoo and Al Smith lasted days; for respite, listeners turned the knobs to hear hit tunes like "Barney Google." (After the ninety-fifth ballot, delegates chose a weak compromise, John W. Davis.)

Izzy graduated from high school that year and at age sixteen became both a newspaperman and active in the campaign of third-party candidate Bob La Follette, supported by the *Nation*, one of Izzy's favorite magazines. Two years before, the remains of the non-Communist left had formed the Conference for Progressive Political Action (composed of socialists, farmer-labor groups, railway unions, and progressive Republicans). Although criticized as a last hurrah from the prairie-populist past, La Follette's message appealed to Izzy. The candidate urged government ownership of railroads and water power and called for an end to the electoral college and for congressional powers to override a conservative Supreme Court. Progressives such as Fiorello La Guardia, Ernest Gruening, Jane Addams, the *Nation*'s Oswald Garrison Villard, and future New Dealers such as Harold Ickes were on board. Felix Frankfurter was deeply critical of his friend Lippmann, who shaved the truth in *World* editorials by characterizing Davis as a liberal. The forces behind La Follette, Frankfurter argued, were "at least struggling and groping for a dream."

Davis got 8 million votes and La Follette nearly 5 million, or 16 percent, outpolling Davis in seventeen western states. Riding prosperity's bandwagon, Calvin Coolidge swamped them both. Thus 1924 ended all hope for the Socialist Party as a major national movement. Two years later, Debs's death symbolized the fate of the party.

The twenties, Izzy recalled, were a good training ground for enduring life "in the wilderness." "As a radical you couldn't have been more of a minority. Hell, the twenties were a *dull* period." As their candidate, Democrats had picked Davis, who was, said Izzy with disgust, "*J. P. Morgan's lawyer. . . .* You can't go beyond that. Still, you had a couple of great

liberal papers like the *New York World* and the [St. Louis] *Post-Dispatch*
and a smaller one in Camden where I worked."

Capitalism was king and the nation was on a spending spree, seduced by
ads pushing a new means of purchase, installment buying. "Pay as you
ride," enticed automakers. "Enjoy while you pay," cajoled ads for refriger-
ators, pianos, sewing and washing machines. Even secretaries and shoe-
shine boys invested in the stock market, and Izzy's father speculated
heavily in real estate with hard-earned profits from the store.

The Roaring Twenties would have an astounding parallel in the high-
flying 1980s and '90s, built on the quicksand of junk bonds, profligate
corporations, and high-tech speculation. In both instances no one
wanted to listen. In the 1920s, Cassandras asked, just how much credit
buying could the country stand? But the public relied on the assurances
of pop economists, such as one in *Collier's* who wrote that having large
debts was an asset because it showed that a man has a "fine line of
credit."

Movie theaters as ornate as sultan's palaces were filled with massive
organs to provide sound for the silents. Stone became a lifelong movie
fan. Charlie Chaplin, who would one day attend I. F. Stone's parties, was
the world's favorite clown. Trends and trivia spread from coast to coast:
flagpole sitting, marathon dancing until one dropped. Hemlines rose
and the most staid citizen flouted Prohibition.

Beneath the ballyhoo, so carefully whipped up by the press, lurked
appalling concerns. Farmers, miners, and textile workers were not making whoopee. Nor were unions, battling to keep socialist gains of yesteryear. The Marxist doctrine was dead; instead of capitalism withering and
dying off, American industrialists were thriving. Henry Ford set the pace,
offering high wages and mass-producing Model Ts at low prices. Except
for those experiencing it, few cared about agriculture's decade-long depression. Nor the rise in unemployment as magical machines replaced
men and women in factories. Also ignored in this postwar binge was
the increasing difficulty the average family had in paying for all those
mass-produced goods.

The culture of greed was mocked by "highbrows" (a new twentieth-
century term). Instead of focusing on political corruption and economic
inequities, targets of the previous decade, criticism centered on aimless
vulgarity. In a forerunner to attitudes in the sixties, "children of the middle class eagerly repudiated bourgeois habits, assumptions, and preju-

dices. Widely dispersed, with widely divergent views among themselves, the embattled highbrows were found in all urban centers besides its epicenter, New York."

Izzy was among them, a young Bohemian who "didn't cut my hair or tie my ties." Dilettantes and an "ill-assorted mob of faddists" clung to the coattails of a small number of talented writers who dominated American literature. Sinclair Lewis's searing satires *Main Street* and *Babbitt* revealed the cultural poverty and ugliness of mass prejudices. Fiction reflected fact. In 1925, forty thousand Ku Klux Klan members paraded down Pennsylvania Avenue and past the Capitol, secure enough to leave their hoods off. Sick-of-America expatriates settled in Europe, although both their numbers and talent were more myth than reality. Mingling with the gifted were many pseudo lost souls. An enduring misconception surrounds the term *lost generation*. Romantic as it sounds, Gertrude Stein's remark was an actual quote from a garage owner. When she complained about the bad job done on her car, he referred to the lack of skilled auto mechanics—a generation of lost workingmen who returned from the war rootless and disillusioned—not to men of arts and letters.

Izzy was among the young activists who viewed expatriates as escapists from social responsibility. The *American Mercury* magazine was launched near the end of 1923, and incipient iconoclasts were soon carrying Mencken's bible on college campuses. In 1927, Lippmann praised Mencken as the premier influence of his generation's intellectuals. Mencken despised much; socialists and anarchists were as much fools as Tennessee farmers, called "gaping primates" and "anthropoid rabble." His *American Language* remains a serious, prodigiously researched landmark history of America speaking. Yet Mencken was known most for his sardonic critiques, such as "No one ever went broke underestimating the intelligence of the American public." Today much of Mencken's vitriol sounds strident, but, like others of his generation, Stone admired Mencken for bluntly opposing all that interfered with personal liberties.

Many educated liberals who a few years before had fought for minimum-wage laws, women's suffrage, and "would have risked disinheritance to march in a Socialist parade in 1915, yawned at Socialism in 1925." Izzy was not among the yawners, nor was his boss, J. David Stern. "He was a good antifascist and he did a lot of exposé journalism," Izzy told Patner. "He was a real muckraker, and he believed in investigative journalism, and he made circulation with it." Stern's paper was the only one in the Philadelphia area to write favorably about La Follette in 1924.

It is hard to imagine what turn Izzy's life would have taken had Stone not met Jill Stern or if her husband had not hired him. Or if Izzy's wistful wish to attend Harvard had been honored, a ludicrous first choice given his mediocre grades. For reasons mystifying to those who never recognized this contradictory strain in Izzy, Harvard's rejection haunted renegade Izzy. While he missed an intellectual sojourn in America's elite school, he also avoided pretentious intellectual bickering as well as certain anti-Semitic discrimination in a mindless time when rich, young WASPs coasted along on gentlemen C's. Jews at Harvard numbered 7 percent in 1900 but had risen to 21.5 percent in 1922, just two years before Stone graduated from high school. Alarmed Ivy League gentile supremacists such as Harvard's President A. Lawrence Lowell imposed de facto quotas. Yale's Dean Frederick Jones complained that Jews were winning the top scholarships; their flaw was not in their intellect but in their "personal characteristics." Since schools could not effectively discriminate on the basis of low marks, a ban was placed on the basis of "character." At Columbia, Jews comprised 40 percent of the students in 1920, a number that was slashed in half within two years.

The University of Pennsylvania, with its open enrollment policy, had to take Izzy. He was disappointed by a lack of intellectual stimulation, but Stone found kindred souls foreign to his Haddonfield experience, a "whole gang of young, Jewish, New York intellectuals" for whom radical reform had not paled. One of them was Sidney Cohen, the future husband of the daughter of Marxist scholar Louis Boudin, who was a major influence on Stone's thinking. (To compound the close ties, Louis Boudin's nephew, Leonard, and Izzy would marry sisters.) Izzy's friendship with Cohen was deep enough that Izzy sold his two-volume edition of Dyce, "a famous mid-Victorian Elizabethan scholar," to help raise train fare for a strapped Cohen to get back to New York. Years later Izzy said with a chuckle, "It still breaks my heart to think of it."

Another university companion who became a lifelong friend was Mike Blankfort, the novelist and screenwriter. Blankfort felt terrible when Stone was blackballed by a society of radicals after he spoke endlessly at a trial meeting about a poet most had never heard of. Stone was the "most alive" person Blankfort had ever met, expounding on everything from Gibbon to birds twirping during a walk.

As a working newspaperman grounded in the real world, Izzy had no time for the ennui of disenchanted youth. As any journalist who has covered a small town knows, "it's hard as hell to find a story—you've got to think up things for the mayor to say, or a good sermon for the minister," Izzy recalled. He chuckled as he recounted his "church editor" stint; he was paid $5 for every sermon he covered. This "young Jewish atheist" helped ministers with their sermons. "The ministers were a nice bunch of guys, they liked me, and I liked them," he told Patner. "I would suggest a topic and get a good story." From sermons, Izzy ricocheted to theater reviews, a short-lived career that ended with his being banished from Philadelphia's major theaters after blasting a number of plays.

By then, Izzy had become an elected political-party official for the only time in his life. Before he could vote, he was an officer of the New Jersey Socialist Party. He soon resigned after squabbling factions drifted into sectarian suicide. As a journalist, Izzy felt uncomfortable "belonging" to anything; he wanted to have unfettered independence.

This hardly meant that Izzy was a cool observer. As a Jew, Izzy was more aware and alarmed than many colleagues by the 1920s spread of Fascism in Mussolini's Italy and Hitler's early moves to rule Germany. To many, Hitler was a buffoon whose anti-Semitic ravings, clearly spelled out in *Mein Kampf*, published in 1925, were dismissed. With that special antenna of his, Izzy, however, was deeply concerned about Hitler.

Many newspaper publishers in those days saw fascism as impressively compatible with capitalism. The Camden area contained a large numbers of Italians who were not displeased when a University of Pennsylvania professor praised the wonders of Fascist Italy at a 1926 Camden Rotary Club meeting. Izzy was already reading leftist foreign papers and had correctly sized up Mussolini. Izzy had been sent to cover the speech and was becoming more apoplectic by the moment. Unable to contain himself, the squeaky-voiced teenager jumped up from the press table and peppered the speaker with questions: "Why don't you tell the other side of the story? Why don't you tell what the Fascists are doing to the labor movement?" Getting more worked up, Izzy bellowed, *"What about the murder of Matteotti?!"*

The stunned crowd stared at this small youth, pondering just who the hell was Matteotti? The murder of socialist legislator Giacomo Matteotti, so suppressed by major news sources that most Americans were in the dark, demonstrated how much of the news from Europe was deliberately distorted at the time. Many worldwide correspondents, including American, received a monthly bribe from Mussolini in the form of five thousand words free via telegraph or cable. Moreover, international business interests—including major hotel owners, tourism and industrial groups—gave Mussolini millions to subsidize Fascism. The *Manchester Guardian* was brave enough to write this, and the *New York World* and the *St. Louis Post-Dispatch* reprinted the British accounts. But the influential Associated Press, Hearst's International News Service, and most newspapers printed only glowing stories of trains running on time, not accounts of corporations bribing Mussolini. Matteotti was killed just after announcing that he would expose a deal between Sinclair Oil Company and prominent Fascist leaders.*

In the 1920s, the *New York Daily News* was one of the first American newspapers to praise Mussolini. The trend continued into the thirties. After the 1929 crash, the Paris *Herald Tribune,* fearful of economic collapse, cozied up to the strongmen of Italy, Germany, Poland, Portugal, and Romania, hailing their regimes in "Fascism for America" editorials. Anxious to keep tourism booming (and thus Paris-edition revenues), the Paris *Tribune* ran stories extolling Mussolini's Fascisti and Hitler's emerging Nazism. As author Richard Kluger recounted, in exchange, the paper was kept afloat with continued advertising by German and Italian shipping lines and other government-controlled businesses.

After long hours at the paper, Izzy rode home on the trolley with his boss. Busily trying to perfect his papers and scheming how to buy more, an exhausted Stern often fell asleep. Recalled Izzy, "My job was to shake him awake at the end of the car line."

The Matteotti flap had just died down when Izzy was embroiled in another matter of principle. Seven years before, on May 5, 1920, a shoemaker and a fish peddler, Nicola Sacco and Bartolomeo Vanzetti, were

---

*George Seldes, who was sent to cover Italy for McCormick's *Chicago Tribune,* wondered why it was not even rumored in American papers that Mussolini had assassinated Matteotti, although confessions were widely circulated in Italy. The story that would "rock the world" had not been dispatched. A father-son team of Italian correspondents for the Associated Press and the *New York Times* were also Mussolini publicists. They suppressed the story. Seldes (the "granddaddy of us investigative journalists," who had inspired Izzy "since my boyhood") wrote the assassination story, warning the *Chicago Tribune* not to print it in their Paris edition if they ever wanted to hear from their star reporter again. The next day the Paris edition—sold throughout Europe—featured the story, with Seldes's name on it. Seldes fled on the Orient Express. At one stop, Seldes heard shouting and the words *"Dove Seldes?"* (Where is Seldes?) Spying the Blackshirts, Seldes frantically joined four British naval officers, explaining that he was a correspondent about to be killed by the Fascisti. When the gunmen peered into the compartment and shouted, *"Dove Seldes?"* the British admiral shouted, "Out, you *porco fascisti!"* Groveling before an admiral, they fled.

arrested in Brockton, Massachusetts. Charged with robbing and murdering a shoe-factory paymaster and his guard, the acknowledged anarchists were quickly tried and sentenced to death. No evidence placed them at the scene of the crime, nor did the commonwealth of Massachusetts ever connect the stolen money with these immigrants who spoke broken English. Even those unsympathetic to their politics, including some jurists, felt they were being railroaded as radical scapegoats. Neither their guilt nor innocence was settled in an unfair trial presided over by a prejudiced judge.

A decade previously, two men framed on a murder charge in the midst of a fierce textile strike were acquitted after ten months of international and national labor and left-wing protest. But in the antiradical twenties, support was not immediate for Sacco and Vanzetti. As late as 1924, Mencken was the only American writer of reputation mentioned by their Defense Committee. Then came John Dos Passos and Upton Sinclair. Massive support from American artists and intellectuals followed only after an appeal by the Defense Committee on August 8, 1927, two days before the original execution date. During a twenty-one-day reprieve, frantic appeals were made. Workers and intellectuals worldwide joined emotional demonstrations urging that Sacco and Vanzetti be spared.

Izzy was beside himself, helpless over the great injustice he felt was about to take place. With a newspaperman's passion to be part of the action, he begged to cover the story. (His paper was the only one in the Camden-Philadelphia area that supported the anarchists.) When the editor said no, Izzy quit, stormed home, grabbed an extra pair of socks, and took off for the execution. Years later, Izzy recounted with fervor, "I kept thinking, what would my grandchildren think if I didn't protest that trial?" His father sped after Izzy in his car, trying to head him off, but was unsuccessful. The hitchhiking nineteen-year-old had almost made it to Boston when he found out there was a stay in the executions. Without any contacts or money to remain in Boston and too embarrassed to return to his job, Izzy continued hitchhiking up to Bellows Falls, Vermont, to visit a friend.

Had Izzy stayed in Boston as the Sacco-Vanzetti Defense Committee lurched from passionate appeal to despair, he would have been in the company of the famous—Dos Passos, Katherine Anne Porter, Edna St. Vincent Millay, and Dorothy Parker—who were arrested along with a mixed bag of liberals, radicals, and foreigners during a famous Death March. H. G. Wells, John Galsworthy, Marie Curie, and Captain Alfred

Dreyfus, whose espionage case had ignited world opinion at the turn of the century, all wrote to ask that they be spared. As the clock struck midnight protesters counted the seconds out loud. Then on a nearby board appeared the words, "Sacco, Vanzetti Dead."

Young Izzy, without a job, far away from his urban world, wept when he heard the news. But he learned a lasting lesson: his fervently nurtured ideas and causes would often face massive indifference. During that long-ago summer, the establishment press remained aloof. Lippmann's editorials tepidly called for commutation of the death sentences. Rather than join popular leftist opinion that the anarchists were railroaded, Lippmann praised the governor. Far afield from Stone, Lippmann did not want to be "dismissed as partisan" or to "cut himself off from respectable, and respected, opinion." Outraged by Lippmann's detachment, Heywood Broun blasted the three-man commission who allowed the judge's death sentence to stand. Its leader was the president of Harvard, Lawrence Lowell. Broun, a Harvard graduate, sneered, "It is not every person who has a President of Harvard University throw the switch for him." Broun was chastised by the *New York Times* as a "cowardly bomb thrower" attacking a Harvard president.

Another thunderbolt came from Broun's typewriter, then he was silenced—proof that even the most famous and well-paid columnists were not immune to in-house censorship. The paper refused to publish any more columns on Sacco-Vanzetti. Too many Harvard sympathizers in their midst had not recovered from Broun's barbs. Broun suspected that Lippmann, the Harvard-educated editor, authored a self-righteous editorial explaining why Broun's columns were dropped. Broun's contract stated that Broun could not work for another newspaper for three years if he quit. Broun quit. He turned to the *Nation* but was rehired by the *World,* only to be fired again. Angered by a weak editorial involving a censorial Catholic Church, Broun attacked. "There is not a single New York editor who does not live in mortal terror of the power of this group."

In a few years, Izzy Stone would join forces with Broun to fight for the nation's first newspaper union.

That summer of 1927, Izzy tried in vain for work on a Vermont farm, an improbable quest given his lack of familiarity with even garden tools. Too stiff-necked to return to Stern, Izzy searched for a job on the *Philadelphia Inquirer.* With customary cockiness, he "waltzed up to this Napoleonic pip-squeak of a boss" and asked, "How would you like a good man?" The editor growled, "I could use a half dozen of them." Izzy retorted, "Well, you're looking at one." He hired Stone.

Izzy was soon to quit college. Philosophy paled in comparison to working on a newspaper. While still in school, Izzy worked ten hours in the afternoon and at night, on rewrite and on the copy desk. He was making $40 a week, big pay in those days. That fall, while charging through deadlines and attending classes, Izzy had a major distraction. He was no longer the writer of show-off letters to friends about wild boozing parties or meeting "hot as hell" girls who might become mistresses. Izzy was in love.

Izzy met Esther Roisman on a blind date in 1927. "It was just a damn lucky break. . . . I just fell in love. We were a couple of kids." One Saturday night, Izzy was waiting in line for a cheap upper-balcony seat for the Philadelphia Orchestra. A friend came up and said, "Izzy, do you want to go out on a blind date?" Although a "terrible wallflower," Izzy impetuously said yes. The next week, nineteen-year-old Izzy met eighteen-year-old Esther. Their lives couldn't have been more dissimilar. Esther was slim, petite, and pretty, "a flapper who did the Charleston," lived with her Republican family in West Philadelphia, and did not have a political thought in her head. But Esther was just as taken with Izzy as he was with her.

"I was fifteen when he came into my life, and at that time I just thought he was *horrible*," recalled Esther's younger sister, Jean Boudin. "He was certainly not what I was looking for, for my sister." Esther had finished high school and was working as a typist, "earning fifteen dollars a week, which was very good. She was allowed to keep her salary to buy clothes." Jean, a budding beauty, who became a model for a time, was the grateful recipient of Esther's clothes-lending generosity.

"Esther was pretty and she always had a date, and big black cars would drive up to the house with a chauffeur usually because the kid was too young to drive. And off she would go. Then *suddenly* one night, this guy turns up with a big stack of books under his arm. And these very thick glasses, looking quite scruffy. And my sister would flutter down the steps—to *Izzy*! Well, I couldn't believe this. And then this kept repeating, and the big black, shiny cars got fewer and fewer. And then he turns up with a tin lizzie, where you crank it. And it would make a tremendous noise. The neighbors would all be watching."

Jean taunted her sister endlessly, singing a popular song: "Whose Izzy is he, is he yours or is he mine? I'm getting dizzy watching Izzy all the time." Esther "simply ignored me totally. This was *it*. At one point they had a disagreement. It ended with him giving her a string of crystals. From then on, there was nobody else. The dimples! Esther would talk about his dimples. It meant nothing to me compared to those black Cadillacs, or whatever they were. I was in such disgrace. My friends would say, 'Who's that with the thick glasses?'"

Their father, Morris Roisman, owned the Home Preserving and Pickling Co. "He was a hardworking, loving person. A very dear man." Astonishingly, given their background, Esther and Jean Roisman both married iconoclasts, one a radical journalist, the other a civil libertarian lawyer; Leonard Boudin and Stone became lifelong friends and competitors, and both became famous. But back then "Esther was utterly indifferent to political enlightenment and my parents never discussed politics either. Socialism? We heard nothing about it at home. Never. You did for the family and that was it."

Unlike Bernard Feinstein, Morris Roisman kept kosher. "We had two sets of towels, two sets of dishes. We were very strict about that because grandmother was a bit suspicious about our stepmother, concerned that she might not carry this out right, that sort of thing. Being Jewish always felt like a burden," recalled Jean. "Certainly in my neighborhood we were a minority, and at school we were a minority. It felt like it was much better not to be Jewish. When I was seventeen, I ran into the rabbi who had confirmed me when I was sixteen. I was with my friends at a restaurant. I went over and said, 'How could you have put me through this ritual of God when you know perfectly well there is no God!' I was very indignant and very brazen."

Such an act would not have occurred to her more compliant sister. Esther's thoughtfulness made her an endearing, welcome friend and confidante. Until the end of Izzy and Esther's long life together, Esther was the one who put others at ease, the one who uttered a kind or complimentary word. Esther's innate empathy and ability to sense the problems of others stemmed in part from her own deep childhood wound, a loss from which she never fully recovered. As a child, Esther was sick a great deal. "She had diphtheria, all the things that were terrible," recalled Jean Boudin. "It seemed like my mother had the doctor there all the time and my mother just worrying so about Esther."

When that protective force died, Esther felt a morbid sense of abandonment. "Esther was about twelve or thirteen when mother died. Esther was *very, very* devoted. When mother died, it was very bad for her." In her grief, Esther actually physically changed. A child of ten or eleven, she became round-shouldered, her body turning inward in a depressed, stooped posture. "She just bent in," recalled her sister.

As the great 1917 influenza epidemic decimated families, Esther's father quickly married a rich widow to help raise his three children, including an incorrigible free-spirit son named Charles. Clinging to memories of her mother, Esther resented her stepmother all of her life. Even in middle age she would cry out for her real mother if she was in a car and thought an accident was about to happen.

When she met Izzy, Esther was eager to build a home of her own, to try to re-create the closeness she'd once known. In obvious ways, Esther was the opposite of Izzy's feisty mother, who quarreled with his father, vibrantly filled a room with her presence, and ran the store. Esther was physically frail and, friends and family believe, painfully shy and lacking in self-confidence. Yet Esther emulated Izzy's mother in one enormously essential aspect, the adoration she gave Izzy. Esther was the perfect mate for a garrulous man who needed an audience. Theirs was a symbiotic relationship of deep mutual devotion, truly a great love match. Decades after they were married, in 1947, Esther wrote Izzy when he was in war-torn Israel, "This morning I went to the shul . . . and prayed to God to continue to give you strength for your good work. To me you wear the mantle of greatness. . . . Deep love, Esther."

Esther listened raptly as Izzy confided all his dreams, ideas, and knowledge. The "miserable wallflower" took up dancing to join his Charleston-loving girlfriend, but their moonlit talks were about such romantic musings as business corruption. "When I met her, I was writing anti-big-business exposés and I would go on and on. Any normal girl would have screamed." Over the years "she's listened to the goddamnedest collection of recondite subjects. She's had 'courses' in the most dumb, far-out subjects. And even though she didn't understand a lot of what I was doing or even really sympathize with it, she was remarkably sensitive. She never interfered at all."

Shortly after Izzy and Esther began courting, Izzy plunged into the 1928 presidential campaign of socialist Norman Thomas, the pacifist who ignited audiences. Stone became a volunteer publicist. Without "a lot of gibberish" Thomas "had a wonderful way of putting socialism in American terms as a pragmatic answer to specific American problems." The Thomas campaign was Izzy's last direct involvement with political candidates. He and Stern had made up and Izzy was back on the paper, where he was placed on rewrite. In those days, a good rewrite man was the backbone of a paper, able to take a reporter's dictated raw notes and quickly mold them into readable, sometimes sparkling, copy. Izzy "worked like hell," also eagerly pinch-hitting for the vacationing editorial writer and writing an occasional column. By the time he was twenty, Isador Feinstein had accomplished the work of men years his senior; he had done everything on a newspaper "except run a Linotype machine."

In the summer of 1929, Izzy and Esther married. Izzy asked for a $5 raise in honor of the occasion and got it, boosting his income to $45 a week. Stone felt his frail wife needed to stay home. "The first thing I made her do was quit her job. I got a one-room apartment in Atlantic City and put her up there for the summer." He commuted daily to Camden. "She never worked again until the *Weekly*."

Soon there would be the stock market crash and the Depression, the terrible loss of his father's business and his mother's downward spiral into mental illness, the rise of fascism and Hitler. Two physical handicaps a reporter does not need are poor eyesight and poor hearing, and Izzy also faced the agonizing knowledge that his feeble eyesight would soon be eclipsed by deafness.

But on that July day in 1929, nothing could go wrong. Esther was radiant in a soft dress with a long lace train, holding a huge bouquet of lilies. A half century later, her poet daughter reflected in a "Portrait of My Mother on Her Wedding Day,"

> *A young woman*
> *lilies gathered to her breast—*
> *the moment of the wave*
> *before it crests—*
> *bride,*
> *incandescent,*
> *even in this sepia image*
> *dazzling me, like a wedding guest.*
> *Fifty years later I uncover*
> *in the movement of her swept-back veil*
> *the life that was to come. . . .*
> *And once again I feel*
> *how evil seems to fall away*
> *before the power of that candid gaze*

while everything in us that answers to good
crowds round her lap
hearing itself spoken for.

The bridegroom was so spruced up that even Jean approved. By then, she thought Izzy was "simply wonderful" anyway. In the formal wedding portrait, Izzy sat ramrod straight in his tuxedo, his black four-in-hand perfectly tied under a stiff collar, dark cuff links glistening on the white cuffs of his stiffly starched shirt, hair slicked back, a soft smile on his lips.

The world was theirs.

PART TWO

The Decisive Decade

This section is devoted to the 1930s because it was the most pivotal decade for shaping I. F. Stone's views and philosophy on journalism and politics in particular and life in general. This young editorial writer had a front seat for an amazing number of world-shaking events: FDR and the Depression, the expanding labor movement, the heyday of American Communism, the popular front, the Spanish Civil War, the ascendancy of two monstrous dictators, Hitler and Stalin, and the beginnings of a world war that would kill upward of 50 million people before it was over.

Although the journalist would not change his name from Feinstein to Stone until 1937 (and legally in 1938), Stone and/or Izzy will be used throughout to avoid confusion, unless Feinstein is a direct quote or a reference to his parents, who retained the name.

6

CRASHING INTO THE THIRTIES

In the last days of the Roaring Twenties, Mr. and Mrs. Isador Feinstein were "just two young kids," as Izzy recalled, entering into marriage almost like children playing house. Theirs was a "darling little apartment" in Philadelphia. Esther's earnings and gifts from her father were spent on a plush blue carpet and a splurge for goblets that cost $15 apiece, sumptuous consumption for a radical journalist in 1929. But Esther was feeling flush. Her father had given her a handsome gift, $1,000.

There would be ardent feminists in Izzy's life—colleagues and one boss—but Esther was expected to stay home, wait on him, organize his life, and raise the three children who came in quick succession. At $45 a week, a comfortable salary in a time when many reporters were making $25, Stone was buoyantly self-assured. Scarcely old enough to vote, he brashly fought his way to the top in Stern's newspaper empire. Confrontation was his style and he argued constantly with Stern and the city editor over assignments while on the *Camden Courier,* incessantly pushing to write editorials.

The year before, Stern had bought the *Philadelphia Record,* a paper with a record. Audited for falsifying net-paid figures, it was a failing conservative, pro-business paper with less than one hundred thousand circulation. Stern paid $1.25 million, half the original asking price. He immediately tangled with the president of the Pennsylvania Railroad, exposing a plot to refinance the transit system that would mean millions in railroad profits while gouging taxpayers for unneeded millions. Stern won that battle, then took on antiquated laws that banned Philadelphians from doing much of anything on Sundays. Movies, theaters, sporting events, or any form of entertainment for which admission was charged were closed on the Sabbath. The city's hotel and tourist trade lost $10 million a year thanks to these blue laws. Stern's crusade earned him subscribers and business support, so state legislators braved the wrath of Sabbatarians and granted local option on Sunday laws.

In September of 1929 the *Record* moved into a ten-story building. As the only liberal publisher, Stern enjoyed battling the alliance of business-men, Republican politicians, and conservative publishers. Stone was on board, transferred from Camden in part because of his obvious talent, in part because Stern had wearied of Izzy's relentless turf battles with edi-tors at the *Courier*.

The turmoil didn't end at the *Record*. Stone's brashness was un-bounded in his churning to get ahead. He wanted to be an editorialist in-stantly. Stern belonged to a dying breed of hands-on publishers; he dictated editorial policy and wrote many editorials himself. He was furious at his protégé's heavy-handed tactics. Stern was "very nasty," Stone re-called, and his resolve stiffened. "You son of a bitch," he thought, "I'm going to keep pestering you until you make me editorial writer." After months of pleading, he wrote an editorial and left it on Stern's desk. An as-tounded Stone reported for work the next day to find that Stern had more than relented. The *Record* customarily enlarged one editorial each day and placed it in the window. As Stone arrived, he saw his editorial on display. Years later Stone recalled the thrill of seeing it, magnified for all to view.

It was early 1931 and newspapers were in financial trouble. Stern's De-pression woes deepened. He fired his chief editorialist and other staffers to cut costs. Thus Stone, at twenty-three, became the youngest lead editorial writer on a major daily. At a time when journalists were losing jobs and taking pay cuts, Stone's salary jumped by nearly half. All around him, how-ever, he witnessed the fear and poverty of a shattered nation.

On "Black Tuesday," October 29, 1929, the stock market collapsed with breathless swiftness, like a razed skyscraper crashing floor by floor. Mil-lionaires became paupers in one day's panic, brought on by unsound stock-market practices, get-rich-quick schemes, and wild speculation. Dethroned financiers were joined by countless small investors, house-wives included, who thought the gravy train unending.

It was as if some retribution for the hedonism of the twenties was spinning the financial world back into the dark ages. Stocks of stalwarts like U.S. Steel and RCA plunged into the basement. Wall Street was clogged with some ten thousand frenzied men and women, trying to unload worthless stock. Some financiers were driven to an unfamiliar act, falling to their knees in prayer on the floor of the exchange. In this America, the richest nation in the world, there was "no precedent for such a disaster," wrote authors Gordon Thomas and Max Morgan-Witts. At least a million Americans, with some estimates as high as 3 million, were instantly and directly affected by the crash, many of them wiped out. A burlesque joke, a hotel clerk asking a customer, "Do you want a room for sleeping or jumping?" was based on reality; some former millionaires solved their problems by leaping to their deaths from skyscrapers.

The worst financial disaster in history set off the paralyzing Great Depression, rocked Europe's economies, and helped cause Germany's economic ruin, which spurred the rise of Adolf Hitler. Herbert Hoover, who had been sleepwalking through much of his term, watched his popularity disintegrate as an army of evicted jobless men and women sought shelter in box crates and tin shanties known as Hoovervilles. By the end of 1932, 15 million men and women were out of work, one-third of the workforce. Those who worked saw their incomes slashed. Sobbing depositors banged on doors of banks, trying to rescue their money, but the banks were closed.

President Harding had epitomized the whipped-cream emptiness of the twenties. The poor went hungry and the rich prospered as never before as Harding presided over a poker table with cronies who paid him back with the Teapot Dome scandal. Next, Herbert Hoover bragged that he would deliver "a chicken in every pot and two cars in every garage." After the crash, Hoover never left the White House to view the hollow-eyed at soup kitchens. Scrawny intellectuals dug ditches. The former middle class sold apples on street corners. Starving farmers, silent and unnoticed victims during the twenties boom, held off at gunpoint agents who came to foreclose. Farm children and their parents, barefoot, in torn clothes, gazed with the stare of concentration camp survivors.

For Stone's family, the Depression was no abstraction. In the 1920s, Stone's father rode the crest of the boom. He spent less time in the store and more time buying properties and building stores and small apartment houses in Haddonfield and nearby Clementon. The Russian-immigrant peddler had become a prosperous entrepreneur, but his real-estate forays caused great tension between Bernard and his wife as the responsibility for the store fell on Katy. Returning from Philadelphia, laden with heavy packages of materials for the store, Katy would collapse into a chair exhausted, crying that her feet were sore and her bunions throbbing.

Some of her anger was mollified by the beautiful large brick home Bernard had built for his family in a new section of town. Then came the crash. The Feinsteins never moved into the fancy new home. As the Depression deepened, fewer and fewer customers had money to buy even such necessities as shoes and pants and dresses. In 1933, Bernard and Katy took one last look at their empty Dry Goods Emporium. All that the young man from Ukraine and his wife from Odessa had owned in South Jersey was lost, wrote Lou Stone: "The home they never moved into, the store they had run since 1912, four stores and apartments . . . four cottages . . . two houses . . . ten stores and a theater in Clementon, plus considerable undeveloped acreage on the White Horse Pike."

Bernard refused to go into bankruptcy. He worked tirelessly to pay all his debts, although this left him virtually penniless. Bernard and Katy and their two youngest, teenage Lou and young Judy, moved to Philadelphia into crowded quarters with family. Although Judy does not remember this as a particularly hard time, her father once again peddled goods. Marc, at the University of North Carolina, survived on funds he had made putting out a Haddonfield directory.

In recalling this "calamitous time," Lou Stone speaks with pride of his father's indomitable will. "For months he carried a suitcase full of women's stockings, which he sold to relatives and friends or door-to-door. He even had to swallow his pride and take occasional sales jobs from his brother-in-law, Jacob Bell." An auctioneer, Bell frequently bought the stock from failing store owners and held "selling out" sales. "Over some business transaction of ancient vintage," Bernard and Jacob regarded each other with festering ill will. Such feuds, inexplicable to offspring, can foster lasting and emotional enmity the likes of which only blood ties can produce. Lou recalls that a "shadow" remained between the two families. It took a great deal for proud Bernard to seek Bell's help.

For many, the Depression left permanent scars, fear, anxiety, and never-mended broken dreams. Bernard seems to have been one of those victims. By the time Stone's sons were old enough to know their grandfather, the youngest, Chris, saw nothing of his humorous-practical-joker earlier days. He was "sullen and withdrawn into whatever secret collapsed ambitions and hopes he had. I think of him as part of the furniture, while Grandma's presence filled the room. Although she was very ill and in and out of mental institutions, I remember her as very bright, witty, and crackling with energy."

For Lou, those Depression days were a grim burden, magnified by "this tragedy about Mother." When the Feinsteins were struggling to hold on to the store, Katy took an overdose of pills. Judy, then about six or seven, recalls, "My first memory of all this, I think, was the night she tried to commit suicide. I had to mix and give her this soapy mixture to induce her to throw up. And I remember Izzy and Esther coming to the house." Not fathoming what was happening, only that her mother was sick, the six-year-old asked them to bring her the funny papers.

For Judy and Lou, the disintegration of family life remains indelibly painful. Recalls Judy, "It was all very hard." Seven years older than Judy, Lou shouldered much of the burden and remembers that night with his sobbing, hysterical mother. "I was the one who had to take her to the hospital. It was very rough." Lou recalls having to transport his mother by trolley to the ferry and across the river to the hospital. "My father had to take care of the store."

In those days before medicines such as lithium, manic-depressives, often the most gifted and vibrant people, were tragically without help or subjected to painful and frightening treatment. Katy was strapped down, electrodes attached to her head, a stick inserted to keep her from swallowing her tongue, and given shock treatments. "Doctors said that mother needed to be taken care of in a hospital for mental diseases, and in those days the court had to send you there, to what was then the Pennsylvania Hospital for Nervous Diseases," said Lou. "She always had to be paroled when she was well. There were periods of two or three years when she would be home and everything would be fine, and then she would . . ." Lou could not finish the sentence.

Katy's compulsion took the form of frantic sewing. "She would start making aprons like crazy and selling them through the neighborhood. Normally she was a very good seamstress. But when she was in a manic stage, she wouldn't fit things properly. The band around the waist wouldn't match the rest of the apron, but she didn't care. She would make them and try to sell them all over the place." In darker days, "she'd cry and cry. It was very unhappy and very disturbing."

In 2005, studies were made in an attempt to analyze a curious phenomenon, why some people displayed a never-ending ebullience—"restless, eager people consumed with confident curiosity"—even though they were "first-degree relatives of those with bipolar [also called manic-depressive] illness who are likely to inherit some genetic basis" for this disorder. Without being able to provide much enlightenment, Dr. Ronald C. Kessler, a professor of health-care policy at Harvard Medical

School, said, "When you look across the entire bipolar spectrum, you find that maybe ten to fifteen percent of these people never get depressed: they're just up. They were lucky enough to escape crashing mood swings." Their steadily productive lives were characterized by "currents of mental energy and concentration." This description fits every aspect of Stone's life: his never-ending ebullience and energy and an ability to scarcely ever get depressed.

During the Depression, Stone sent money to his parents from his weekly paycheck, and he persuaded David Stern to use his political clout to secure a job for his father, first with the Home Owners Loan Corporation (HOLC) and then with the U.S. Mint. The HOLC refinanced foreclosed houses with government funds. Bernard retired from the Mint in the forties. He died on August 10, 1947, when Stone was thirty-nine.

Marriage to Esther had helped soften the friction between Stone and his father, but there was no enduring, written outpouring of affection to mirror Stone's eulogy to Uncle Shumer. Lou has few details about how Stone handled the trauma of his mother and father, so crushed by the vicissitudes of life. "He was married, busy working, and had a wife and daughter. The immediate day-to-day problems pretty much fell on me."

Later, Katy was hospitalized on and off for the remainder of her life. After Bernard died in 1947, Katy survived for eleven more years, spending months in her Philadelphia home, with intermittent long stays in Norristown State Hospital. She died there on June 6, 1958. How, or if, Stone emotionally dealt with the mental illness of a mother who had so adored him is unknown. Like so much of his private feelings, her illness was never discussed, even within the family. Stone may well have been one of those who defensively recoiled; for some, such pain cannot withstand the gentlest of probes.

For all the agony of the Depression, it was an exhilarating time for writers on the left. Intellectuals whose warnings and ideas had been ignored in a time blind to social conscience now watched big business crumbling along with all that was culturally insensitive in the previous decade. For Stone and others, a restructuring of society seemed possible, if not inevitable. Many in America were desperate for change. It was a rich time for writer/witnesses. America's best talents were capturing the grit of destitution, sharing the world of blacks, farmers, migrant workers, and striking laborers.

Stone read the works of fellow writers who recorded misery: blackened clouds rising from arid dust bowls and the unceasing howling winds that drove farm wives mad. Children on pallets in tenements, too weak to walk. Desperate enough to die for a living wage, laborers were clubbed or shot in midprotest on picket lines. Stone's outrage took the form of exhortation; years of Republican rule must end, he wrote. In 1932, those further to the left of Stone—anarchists and Communists who found fertile soil in the nation's misery—viewed Franklin Delano Roosevelt as just another exploiting, bourgeois politician. Stone at times harbored deep doubts about Roosevelt's ability to bring substantive change, but ultimately felt that he could fight for a better world within the system. He threw himself into the 1932 election, devoting time, thoughts, and editorials to pointing out the ills of the Depression and Hoover's inaction and, despite tough criticism, backing FDR's candidacy.

Stone's boss was captivated by Roosevelt from the second he met this consummate flatterer who "had a knack for turning the conversation to the other fellow's interest." Stern later found out that FDR, like any other politician preparing for a meeting, had been well briefed on the publisher, but this did not diminish the charm of a "truly handsome man, so vital and robust above the waist you forgot his infirmity." Stroking Stern, Roosevelt said he'd always wanted to be a newspaper publisher. (When FDR became president, Stern used to joke with the former *Harvard Crimson* editor that he could have made something of himself if he had remained in newspapers.)

In an age of numerous newspapers, the *Record* was the first, and to Stern's recollection, only metropolitan paper to endorse before the Democratic convention the man who was termed by other papers "that Bolshevik governor from New York." In a pack of nine Republican Philadelphia papers, the lone liberal editorial page hit the reader over the head with capitalized phrases and catchy headlines. Many were churned out by Isador Feinstein. Rin Tin Tin's death occasioned a lighthearted editorial praising his loyalty but humorously branded the great German-shepherd film star a victimized working-class canine, exploited by the capitalist system.*

---

*Then as now, newspaper editorials were unsigned. However, as chief editorial writer, Stone either wrote, approved, or was in sympathy with the editorials that appear in this chapter and were written by either Stern, Stone, or another writer, Sam Grafton. In my interviews with Stone in 1979 and Grafton in 1991, neither could remember who wrote what; I have quoted from some that sound as if Stone wrote them, but have not attributed them to him unless I had positive verification from a collection of *New York Post* editorials.

For the remainder of his presidency the *Record* kept up a barrage against Hoover, charging that he had done little to assist the then 7 million unemployed and their families. What was needed was "DIRECT FEDERAL AID in sufficient amounts." "If the cause of depression could be described by one word, it would be 'selfishness,'" stated one editorial. It attacked industries for paying a "smaller percentage of gross income" in wages as plants became more efficient. It praised "Ford and other enlightened manufacturers" who saw that a high wage was the "only means of keeping consumption abreast of production." But the "inherent selfishness of big business was too strong. It went on building bigger and better factories, which would employ fewer and fewer hands, to produce more and more clothing, shoes, automobiles, radios, which less and less families could afford."

The *Record*'s drumbeat for "massive government relief" included taking over the nation's two thousand banks and restoring one-half of the $2 billion in deposits to the "innocent victims, millions of depositors." The paper also argued that "enlightened self interest" would mean restoring self-confidence to the worker by lending $1 billion to the unemployed. "The well being of each depends on the well being of all." The sentiment is consistent with Stone's beliefs, even including the final sentence, since Stone always referred to Jesus as one of the world's first socialists: "When will we realize that the philosophy of Jesus is the best philosophy for business?"

In hopes of curing America's ills, Stone and Stern became cheerleaders for the aristocrat from New York. Although the fiscally conservative Roosevelt had not differed greatly from Hoover regarding earlier recovery policies (both opposed direct federal-government relief), by the spring of 1932 he had moved sufficiently toward the Stern/Stone corner that they could praise FDR; he seemed more willing than any other candidate, including Al Smith, to provide direct relief to the unemployed.

Absent was tough criticism of Roosevelt's political finagling, including appeasing his foe William Randolph Hearst with his mighty readership at the expense of reformers, as well as Lippmann, who blasted Roosevelt as a noncrusading lightweight.

FDR's "new deal" for Americans stamped for all time his twelve years in office. The *Record* increasingly wrote valentines to the shrewd, charismatic governor—he was the "only . . . candidate with any chance of victory" who "stood for relief for all classes"—and loved FDR's pledge to aid the "forgotten man at the bottom of the economic pyramid."

The *Record* charged that reactionary and conservative papers "went out of their way to DISTORT FACTS AND DISGUISE NEWS" about Roosevelt in the primaries. Despite this general truth, some of the potshots seem unwarranted overkill; Roosevelt's campaign *was* stalling. In badly bungled Massachusetts, FDR lost three to one to Al Smith, who appealed to the state's many Irish Catholics. Yet the *Record* felt that the nomination was sewn up; soon a "timid bookkeeper" would be replaced with a "pioneer."

As breadlines stretched for blocks and soup kitchens dished up thin gruel, the Democrats' optimism about the 1932 election soared, and a mixed bag flocked to Roosevelt's camp. They were a "remarkably varied lot . . . old Harvard friends, city bosses, millionaires, Western radicals, Southern Bourbons, opportunistic Midwesterners . . . Ku Kluxers, old Wilsonites, old Bryanites, professors, high-tariff men, low-tariff men."

Prohibition created no end of hypocrisy as politicians "voted dry and drank wet," imbibing bathtub gin on the sly. When Democratic convention delegates voted four to one to repeal Prohibition, the *Record* cheered mightily. It was thrilled that the Democratic platform was the first to ever call for unemployment insurance. At that tumultuous 1932 Chicago convention, Roosevelt forces tried to repeal the two-thirds rule, a risky venture that would enable them to nominate FDR by a straight majority. Opposition forced a retreat. Although he dwarfed Smith in the first ballot, cliff-hanging moments ensued until FDR's Jim Farley won John Nance Garner's consent to release his Texas delegates, beginning the Roosevelt avalanche. Breaking with precedent, employing the theatrics he loved, Roosevelt became the first nominee in history to accept his party's candidacy at the convention, rather than waiting weeks to acknowledge, a holdover from colonial days when both news and horses traveled slowly. Far from public view, his lifeless legs lifted by aides, Roosevelt was hoisted into a flimsy trimotor, where he pored over his acceptance speech. Then the press began the gentle canard that would last for his twelve-year presidency: pictures taken after he was in position, wheelchair hidden. Editorial cartoons uniformly portrayed him as a vigorously striding leader.

When they learned of FDR's convention victory, Stone and other staffers celebrated in Stern's back office, well stocked with bootleg liquor. They were joined by wealthy citizens who shocked Stern by telling him they had been in secret accord. Stern praised his wealthy Republican board of directors, which had not tried to stop his deification of Roosevelt. "Meet Our Next President: Franklin D. Roosevelt, tall, cultured, kindly, HUMAN," gushed a postconvention editorial.

Hoover's final blow was his disastrous handling of the Bonus Army, the band of twenty thousand former soldiers camped in Anacostia in the sweltering heat of a Washington summer. The Senate rejected their demand of an immediate bonus payment. Hoover decided to rout the stragglers with help from three military men who would soon become famous, Douglas MacArthur, Dwight D. Eisenhower, and George Patton. Tanks, eight hundred troops, fixed bayonets, and tear gas were used to evacuate veterans and their families. As newspapers photographed men, women, and children grazed by frightened and whinnying horses, choking on tear gas, running from blazing shacks, Hoover declared that the challenge to authority "had been met, swiftly and firmly." Roosevelt seized the moment, calling Hoover a man filled with jelly who should have had the sense to send coffee and sandwiches to the mob. Stone never forgot that moment and referred to it decades later during the 1968 Poor People's March, when shanties were set up in Washington, and then again in 1971 when Vietnam Veterans Against the War camped near the White House.

During the 1932 general election, the *Record* offered only mild rebukes when FDR—stung by Hoover's charges of "radicalism" and "collectivism"—watered down his stand on issues such as unemployment and even promised to balance the budget, a Hoover position previously slammed by the *Record.* In November, the first paper in the country to endorse FDR in the spring crowed that it was a "Victory for All of Us."

The *Record* called Roosevelt's victory a "peaceful revolution," a correct prophecy as the next twelve years would set in place revolutionary social change. Nineteen thirty-two marked the close of a "magnificently blundering chapter" in history. "Magnificently" because "in the twelve postwar years, industrial leaders raised us to new heights of economic power and prosperity." "Blundering" because it "failed to spread that prosperity over a large enough section of the population."

FDR was criticized for his scattershot approach to economic ills as well as a pattern of trying to please everyone. Still, Stone identified with FDR and his cadre of New Dealers who rushed to Washington, bent on sweeping social and economic change that meant "nothing less than the redistribution of wealth." In 1933, they had a long way to go, but Stone praised FDR's men for a "sense of concern and devotion." He saw an idealism for humane goals unparalleled with any other in his young lifetime. Stone enthused years later, "There was an excitement and hope and it was wonderful."

Stone's opinion changed little, despite such serious flaws as FDR's inaction for European Jews seeking asylum from Hitler, his acceptance of internment camps for Japanese-Americans, his refusal to break with Southern racist politicians to sign an antilynching bill. "He was a different man in 1936 than he was in 1932," Stone recalled; "he had the greatness to grow." And again, "He was a *great* man! He was a finagler, a manipulator, all of that, but he was great. And you knew it! You knew he was a big man." Stone displayed his awe of an upper-class man who saw the same world he did: "FDR was an *aristocrat,* the fruit of the Dutch aristocrat landowners of the Hudson Valley." The devotion of leftists like Stone was all the more reason for America's rich to sniff en masse that FDR was "a traitor to his class."

In 2002, years after Stone's death, economists were agreeing with him, as columnist Paul Krugman noted in the *New York Times:* "Some—by no means all—economists trying to understand growing inequality have begun to take seriously a hypothesis that would have been considered irredeemably fuzzy-minded not long ago. This view stresses the role of social norms in setting limits to inequality. According to this view, the New Deal had a more profound impact on American society than even its most ardent admirers have suggested: it imposed norms of relative equality in pay that persisted for more than thirty years, creating the broadly middle-class society we came to take for granted. But those norms began to unravel in the 1970s and have done so at an accelerating pace."

Stone witnessed FDR's first nine months from his editorial office in Philadelphia and was immersed in the historic whirlwind; in the president's first hundred days, fifteen major laws to stimulate recovery were steamrolled through Congress.

In his first week FDR faced the banking crisis. Most of the banks were closed anyway, but FDR daringly called a four-day bank holiday and spoke in soothing tones to 60 million people via radio "about banking." He reassured them that it was better to put their money in banks than under the mattress. The Treasury issued Federal Reserve notes providing enough currency to prevent runs. Only the most solvent banks were allowed to reopen; Americans who still had money deposited it, instead of heavily withdrawing. The banking business was partially resuscitated as panic eased.

This was no panacea, and Stone's editorials gave mixed reviews to FDR's efforts for substantive change. The controversial Agricultural Adjustment Act, which paid farmers to restrict acreage at a time when people were starving, earned Stone's displeasure because it primarily aided large farm holders while furthering the dispossession of small farmers.

The controversial and eventually doomed National Recovery Act smacked of Mussolini's fascism to many leftists, who felt that it retarded recovery by limiting production. Stone correctly recognized the act's significant and lasting contributions: bringing about the abolition of child labor, federal regulation of wages and hours, the right of labor to organize and bargain collectively. Stone applauded the birth of the Civilian Conservation Corps (CCC), which put masses of unemployed youths to work on flood-control projects in national parks and forests. He championed all public works programs that put people back to work and the TVA (Tennessee Valley Authority), considered a most radical measure because it was a government corporation, which provided cheap power to destitute rural regions. However, Stone criticized the New Deal's first days for failing to do anything for the poorest of the poor, tenant farmers and sharecroppers. Stone slammed Roosevelt as a "fiscal reactionary" for his initial opposition to the Glass-Steagall Act, which created the Federal Deposit Insurance Corporation (FDIC) to insure savings deposits against possible future bank failures. Under pressure, Roosevelt reluctantly converted. Stone was prescient on this matter. It is historically regarded as one of the most significant New Deal innovations. Stone's boss and frequent White House visitor forcibly argued with Roosevelt on this issue: "FDIC turned out to be one of the most constructive laws of his administration," Stern remarked. ". . . Conservative bankers would not want it rescinded."

Despite FDR's massive efforts and government-created jobs, his administration engendered hope rather than swift change; by the summer of 1933, more than 10 million still were out of work. By January 1934, 20 million men and women were dependent on federal relief of some sort for the essentials of life.

At the age of twenty-five, Stone broke into the big time with an article in H. L. Mencken's *American Mercury*. He ripped apart Pennsylvania's multimillionaire governor Gifford Pinchot, whose life of ease included a "baronial 'Grey Towers' with its twenty-three fireplaces and enormous rooms." Stone mocked the governor and his wife for a well-publicized paupers' feast. They claimed to have fed fifty people at a dinner honoring Eleanor Roosevelt for less than five and a half cents apiece. Stone displayed his ability to burrow behind political utterance to reveal the sham. "What the nation did not hear was that the number of guests was closer to thirty-five than fifty, that the ice cream had been snuck in under 'a supplementary budget,' that a beverage, butter, sugar, salt, pepper, and salad dressing did not figure in the estimate." A French chef had "glorified" plain old hamburger in a manner "not often available to jobless families."

Stone accused Gifford of ducking the subject of unemployment insurance "in a sweetly reasonable manner typical of a Great Liberal in a Tight Corner." Stone contrasted Pinchot's suggestion of $20 million for relief for families while pushing for $104 million for highways. For his biography in Mencken's magazine, the young reporter overdid the flippancy: growing up in Haddonfield, "I read myself nearsighted, wrote bales of bad poetry and was graduated . . . 49th in a class of 52. . . . My talent for manufacturing news won me a place on the [*Camden Courier*] payroll." Stone added, "I flunked trigonometry four times at college, and was fired three times as dramatic critic of the *Camden Courier*—once after being barred from the Erlanger Theater in Philadelphia by special encyclical of the late Flo Ziegfeld. " As editorial writer on the *Record* he was now "busy saving the nation from war with Japan, inflation, the maldistribution of wealth, and the seven years' itch."

Although Mencken's remarkable influence of the twenties had begun to fade, the *Mercury* was still sassy, with a shiny, vibrant green cover. Filled with few ads, it contained short stories by serious authors and articles decrying the death rate in the Depression. In sharp contrast to Mencken's *Mercury,* one magazine geared to America's richest painted a non-Depression fantasy. It was *Fortune,* edited by Ralph Ingersoll, the eccentric genius in Henry Luce's stable who would become Stone's future friend and boss at *PM*—one of the most controversial and unusual left-leaning American newspapers of all time.

In the spring of 1932, however, Ingersoll was content to appeal to the idle rich. Despite masses of hungry unemployed, one *Fortune* ad dithered on about how one ought to be the first on the block to own a Pitcairn Autogiro (a two-seat fixed-wing plane with helicopter blades), joining the ranks of an already lucky twenty-six owners in America. *Fortune*'s ads portrayed an untroubled world for those who could afford to cruise to Europe or to buy Cadillacs, Packards, and Lincolns for $4,300, a staggering cost in Depression days. In 1930, *Fortune*'s "how-to" articles were presented as perfectly reasonable: how to live in Chicago on $25,000 (and $50,000 in Manhattan).

Fortune attempted to appeal to the more enlightened financier, rather than those who choked on the initials FDR. But most of the articles were puff pieces and even included a 1936 uncritical article on Detroit's hate-mongering Father Coughlin. It also described how capitalists saw gold in dealing with Communist Russia as it pushed toward industrialization. Making money was obviously enough of a lure to overlook Bolshevik ideology and tyranny. Corporate capitalists proved just as interested in Russia as any young radical.

7

New Deal, New Life, *New York Post*

As a newlywed, Stone set the pace that endured all of his life. His long hours on the *Philadelphia Record* were filled with awesome concentration. Then he joined Esther for dinner, doted on baby Celia, and plunged into social life with the same enthusiasm he showed when tackling editorials. The Stones were at the center of a circle filled with creative leftists. They attended the Philadelphia Orchestra and the theater, danced with overstated exuberance, and gave parties.

"Izzy was always excited about his work and bubbled all the time, and you felt it from the moment you were with him, or when he walked into a room," recounts Mildred Traube, the wife of playwright and director Shepherd Traube. "He would either say something terribly cute or funny or something fascinating about the world. Izzy was always *on*, really, but in a way that was always a great pleasure." Some people thought Stone unattractive, but to friends he was electric, transformed beyond physicality. "I adored his smile and I adored listening to him," says Traube. "You would hear the truth you weren't likely to hear other places. Izzy had a worldview."

Their rich cultural world was filled with soon-to-be-famous artists, writers, and actors earnestly escaping the dreary stuffiness of Philadelphia's German-Jewish society, which had done its best to deny the existence of literate Russian and Polish Jews. Their adored leader was Dr. Morris Vladimir Leof, known to everyone as Poppa Leof, one of the best diagnosticians in Philadelphia, a sophisticated, intellectual Russian Jew who never lost his Yiddish accent. Overseeing their salon in a four-story brownstone at 322 South Sixteenth Street (known to all simply as 322) was Leof's common-law wife, Jennie Chalfin. Defying bourgeois conformity, they lived together unmarried and raised three children. Decade after decade, Chalfin marched for civil rights—first as a suffragette and then joining the first protest of Jews against Hitler. During the witch hunt, Chalfin calmly wiped off red paint dashed on their house to signify "Communists" within.

Leof and Stone met through Socialist Party politics. Like Stone, Leof was not an obedient party member and was threatened with the loss of his burial plot for nonconformity. Leof was a moralist, given to rationalizing, for example, that he did not "believe in alcoholics or homosexuals" even as both marched through his parlor. Stocky Leof, whose crinkles spread behind eyeglasses, held forth with warmth and laughter. In the group were writer Sholem Asch, director Lee Strasberg, the Jewish tragedian Jacob Adler, Marc Blitzstein, and Michael Blankfort, Stone's longtime novelist friend.

"Whatever happened in the world was immediately reflected in that house," Leof's daughter Madi remarked. Her stepson was Blitzstein, the gifted composer who wrote the score for the impassioned socially conscious musical drama *The Cradle Will Rock*. Izzy Feinstein, as he was still known, was a favorite conversationalist, discoursing about FDR and politics, the rise of Hitler and fascism, America's labor movement, what play was being performed by the recently formed avant-garde Group Theatre. Intrigued by Stone was a budding playwright who felt he was no match for such global conversations. He sat in awe while Stone spoke. But he soon became the most famous of them all. Matinee-idol handsome, with electrifying eyes, Clifford Odets tried out his unknown works on the Leof crowd, wrote biographer Margaret Brenman-Gibson. "We stayed up all night listening to Clifford Odets recite his new plays, and we became so tired. We would think, 'Good God, will this play never be over?' " recalled Esther's younger sister, Jean, who joined the Leof crowd while in college. Odets's plays became overnight sensations—in 1935, the labor melodrama *Waiting for Lefty*, in 1937, *Golden Boy*.

During the first hundred days of Roosevelt's reign, Stone verged as far left as he ever got, supporting a Communist approach in V. F. Calverton's *Modern Monthly*. He secretly wrote slashing commentary about the New Deal under the high-flown nom de plume Abelard Stone, briefly siding with revolutionaries who called for an overthrow of capitalism, an idea not so foreign during the cataclysmic Depression. One of his four articles was titled "Roosevelt Moves Toward Fascism," a piece the *Record* would never have published. Stone was furious that Roosevelt seemed to be adopting a deflationary policy in line with the thinking of the "goddamnest bunch of Wall Streeters." Later, Stone admitted to author Robert Cottrell, "It was agony to live through that period." He recognized the failings of Communism but felt that it might be a progressive path to support, if not emulate, in his own country.

Life changed dramatically for Stone as 1933 ended. "When Stern bought the *Post,* Izzy immediately dashed up and got himself a job," said Sam Grafton, Stone's longtime sparring partner in Philadelphia and then in New York. (Brother Lou says, "Izzy sort of ensconced himself.") "I came when Stern asked me," said Grafton. "There we were at the top, aged twenty-six, and how do I account for it? First, most of the editorial writers were stuffy and Republican. And we were good writers and Stern backed people like that."

Soon Izzy and Grafton were credited with producing the liveliest editorial page in town. Feisty dissent and "often raucous and abrasive" editorials were encouraged by Stern. "The atmosphere was very jolly," recalled Grafton. "Stern would take chances. And he let us write our own editorials. Izzy and I thought that there was a new world. And Roosevelt, we adored him and admired him, but he could be quite reactionary and had to be bullied into accepting bank-deposit insurance and all sorts of things." Helping to do the bullying were Stone and Grafton.

At such a young age, these two men enjoyed real power writing editorials for a major liberal paper that was "far stronger than any around now," Grafton remarked in the latter part of the twentieth century. "One Saturday morning—we worked Saturdays—I got a phone call about nine in the morning from the governor. And he said that a hospital the state was building had about ninety rooms. 'I need one hundred and ten rooms,' he said, 'I've got to have them.' Just like that. And so we wrote about it and we got the rooms for him.

"Stern was always on the phone, trying to sell advertising." And schmoozing. No matter how famous the person Stern was trying to reach, the publisher would pull a Groucho Marx routine when his secretary put through the call: "Hello, hello. Am I calling you or are you calling me?" Grafton recalled. "He was a funny guy, a very nice guy. And Izzy just loved the guy." Stone said Stern was a "joy to work for. You could talk back to him." Comfortable with presidents of countries and corporations, Stern was also capable of rolling up his sleeves and attacking malfunctioning presses until they worked. Said Stone, "He was very informal and very likable."

Stern was not about to hide his entrance into New York publishing. The front page of Stern's first edition of the *Post* on December 11, 1933, was one of the most self-congratulatory to come off a printing press. Large headlines over best wishes sent by politicians read, "Roosevelt Heads Notables Congratulating Evening Post." Under the masthead was a blown-up letter on White House stationery to "My Dear Dave." Wrote the president, "I want to wish you all the good luck in the world in this new venture. . . . There are times when a hair shirt is a good thing for an administration. I always welcome honest and constructive criticism, as you know, and you are one of the people upon whom I can count to get honest convictions."

In December 1933, Izzy and Esther and baby Celia moved into a lovely and large New York apartment at 1 West Sixty-eighth Street with high ceilings and several rooms, for which they paid about $70 a month. There, on Christmas Eve, they celebrated Izzy's twenty-sixth birthday and toasted their new life. Stone kept a grueling pace, for six months single-handedly churning out copy, staying long hours to make up the page after he had perused countless national and foreign papers and sources to write his pro-Roosevelt editorials.

In the summer of 1934, Grafton arrived. Their friendship went back to college and was genuine, but so was their rivalry. "He used to slam my editorials and I would attack his," Grafton recalls. Perhaps Stern consciously baited his young team, knowing that as they tried to outdo one another, he would be the benefactor in the form of excellent copy. Creative tension, latter-day editors would call it.

Stern was determined to turn the old, conservative *Post* into a prominent New Deal liberal paper and succeeded; by 1937 he had quadrupled its circulation to a quarter of a million subscribers. Of the 7 million New York inhabitants, many of those who chose the *Post* were left-wing and liberal Jews who had settled in the Bronx and Brooklyn. As Stern pointed out, the president seriously needed cheerleaders like Stern, Stone, and Grafton. By 1935, FDR faced increasingly hostile publishers, columnists, and White House correspondents who had once hung on his every word. As Stern said, "We were a forceful liberal newspaper in New York such as it had not had since the *World* was absorbed by the *Telegram.*"

As Grafton and Stone became the toast of Manhattan's liberal and New Deal intellectual circles, Stone also enjoyed a lowbrow pastime, burlesque. "He would beg us all to come along," recalls Traube. "He just loved those corny jokes." Stone loved the slapstick: Ed Wynn's corn-on-the-cob typewriter carriage that rang a bell when the eater reached the end of the line, eyeglasses with windshield wipers he donned while eating grapefruit. Luckily, Izzy arrived in New York in time to write a light-hearted editorial during burlesque's heyday. Titled "Monsieur Minsky's Déshabilleuses," the editorial praised the adoration by France's Jean Cocteau of Minsky's robust strippers. Cocteau's struggle to translate *strip artist* into French came out *déshabilleuses tentatrices.* Concluded Stone, "Monsieur Minsky must be gratified" to be praised by one so famous. "It is so rarely that one great artist appreciates another."

Burlesque was one American institution to thrive during the Depression. Few could afford the $5.50 for legitimate theater or Flo Ziegfeld's Follies. A legion of jobless men scraped up pennies for burlesque's cheap seats. Wives often joined them. And what entertainment they saw. Burlesque was the farm club of legit theater for Abbott and Costello, Phil Silvers, Bert Lahr, Red Buttons, Jackie Gleason, Danny Thomas, Ed Wynn, Red Skelton, Joe E. Brown, Eddie Cantor, Fanny Brice, Robert Alda. Many incorporated burlesque routines into their glory years in legitimate theater, movies, radio, and television.

Mae West would strip down to three strategically placed signs reading, "Stop," "Go," and "Detour." Star strippers Ann Corio and Gypsy Rose Lee made an astounding $2,000 a week. As burlesque became more competitive, more clothes fell to the floor. Warring factions chose up sides on whether to kill burlesque: the Legion of Decency and the National Council on Freedom from Censorship. Guess which side Isador Feinstein was on. Burlesque's mortal blow came from New York's mayor Fiorello La Guardia, beloved by many, including Stone, for most of his positions but not for his puritanical streak. In 1935, New York police closed Minsky's. A stripper had exposed her whole body "except her private parts, which were covered by a string of beads." The Freedom from Censorship council took the case. The court ruled in favor of Minsky's, but the reprieve was short-lived. In 1937, burlesque was closed down for good, only to metamorphose years later into topless bars.

While Grafton and Stone were on the *Record,* they and their wives were so intimate that they ate dinner together and stayed overnight on weekends. In New York, differing interests strained the friendship. By 1937, Izzy and Esther had three children: Celia, born September 9, 1932; Jeremy Judah, born November 23, 1935; and Christopher, born October 3, 1937. "Izzy was puffed up about having children and we didn't have them until later. He once said, 'You know, we'd never hold it against you that you haven't had children.' He was *not* being funny. 'Never hold it against us'!?" Grafton repeated, with the same indignation he'd felt a half century before. "Izzy could be very self-righteous."

Despite the Depression, those days in New York were filled with unparalleled excitement, an awakening of literary interest in social causes, and a sense of palatable national politics for leftists. Grafton remarked, "It was very joyous to live in New York in the thirties if you had a job. If you didn't have a job, it was hell. I made $125 a week and I think so did Izzy. [Many reporters were barely getting by on $15 per week.] For that $125 salary you could get, as I had, an eight-room apartment on Central Park West, which cost $75 a month. I had a Japanese cook/butler who cost $50 a month. And steak was twenty-nine cents a pound, coffee twenty-five cents a pound. House servants cost $8 a week."

Although Grafton-style liberals were fighting to change the economic structure, there seemed little conflict about hiring at the depressed rate. There was no such thing as a minimum wage or maximum hours. The Graftons' cook/butler "worked every day until midnight, four days off a month. We lived very high on $125 a week. I didn't live as well later on when I made over $1,000 a week in Hollywood [as a screenwriter].

"There was an interest in affairs which is really missing today," Grafton reflected. "How exciting it was. We thought that the New Deal was a real turnaround in American life . . . actually, it was a window that opened for a very few years, and then slammed down again. Soon plain, ordinary people—twenty to thirty years ago making $8,000 and $10,000 a year—became conservative."

In old age Stone related to Gitlin the influences within the New Deal brigade: "The real perspective is this: When Roosevelt came along, the atmosphere in Washington changed. We were very disappointed with his weak campaign in '32, but [after the election] he was going in the right direction and he attracted idealists of all kinds—socialists, free enterprise idealists, by which I mean anti-trust busters, big-business baiters. He had a very mixed bag in Washington. There were some Communists—the numbers have been *very much* exaggerated—quite a few socialists, quite a few liberals . . . and populist trustbusters, and it was a great era of excitement because something was being done. There was a lot of compromise. *Nobody* was satisfied, but people were being fed, jobs were being created, the Depression was being combated, inflation was being ended. So people of very diverse points of view worked together and suspended a lot of their ill feelings [toward other factions] and felt they were being constructive. There was an atmosphere of hope."

Flirting with Communism was more prevalent in Manhattan than in the staid nation's capital, partly because it was chic. "The middle class was very strong for the Soviet Union," recalls Grafton. "Young people used to walk down Thirteenth Street and buy copies of the *Daily Worker* and pick up Communist literature at their bookshop."

However, conservative newspapers were quick with epithets: Hearst chains were instructed to use *Reds* in all labor coverage. Republican papers such as the *New York Herald Tribune* denounced FDR, while the conservative *New York Times* steered a centrist-right course. As a radical, one couldn't be in more of a minority, Stone often remarked. That comment, however, does not factor in the exclusive and often self-satisfied comradery enjoyed by New York's intellectual left. In this circle, to be of the left was a badge of honor. The less serious embraced the sense of Communist chic.

By the time he reached New York, Stone's abhorrence for destructive feuding among leftist factions, as childish as sandbox warfare, had reached a climax. "I knew people of all varieties in government. People who were CPs [Communist Party members] or Socialists and there wasn't the animosity. [In Philadelphia] they weren't as sectarian because they were dealing with fundamental issues and they knew damn well they couldn't apply little pissant sectarian theories." Years later, Stone's voice was emotional as he recalled the New Deal to Gitlin. "You were part of a movement. A *real American* movement." Stone saw himself as an independent voice of reason, aloof from New York's "Lilliputian universe of sectarians."

"When you grew up in a small town like I did, and [worked] in a small city like Camden, all of us radicals—communists, socialists, anarchists, Trotskyites—we all felt very friendly." New York's left, by contrast, was "filled with hatreds and rivalries, animosities and jealousies and conflicts for power of the 'ultimate' ideology," recalled Stone. "I never liked organizations or parties." One of Stone's rote answers for quitting the Socialist Party was "I felt very strongly that a newspaperman ought not get too close to a party or he'd lose his independence."

In later life, Stone said he had been a fellow traveler but never joined the Communist Party, despising its doctrinaire coercion. This suited his boss fine. A fighting liberal, Stern "hated Communists" and would not have welcomed one in his editorial office. This does not mean that Stone embraced detachment. "I felt a newspaperman ought to serve the great currents of his time if he felt called upon to do so, if he was a radical, but not to tie up."*

Stone came to New York armed with what he termed an indispensable "bible," Norman Thomas's *What's the Matter with New York*. It detailed Tammany Hall's systemic scandals, graft, and corruption and how it worked, from Mayor Jimmy Walker down to the lowest borough bagmen. It showed how corruption kept the nation's worst slums afloat. Mayor Walker had to resign on September 1, 1932. "It was *wonderful;* educated me as an editorial writer," recalled Stone.

The human fact-finding machine taught himself constitutional law "because all of the New Deal reforms were being thwarted in the court." He read every decision when the Supreme Court began to invalidate New Deal legislation in 1935. When Stern and Izzy were invited to dinner with "three great scholars, very famous in that time," Stone eagerly went along, fearful "that these guys were going to talk the boss out of our very critical treatment of Supreme Court decisions. . . . I boned up for that dinner as if I was boning up for an examination. I went back to the conciliar controversy in the Middle Ages within the Catholic Church, where the concept of a higher law started—from which constitutionalism derives—and of course Aristotle has that same conception, when he discusses the *Antigone;* and it's in Sophocles. . . . And then I just worked my way down."

The lawyers "treated us rather pompously." Years later, Stone still gleefully recalled how he had trumped the legal lions on a point of law. "My boss looked at me as if to say, 'Izzy, for God's sake, shut up! You're with the experts!'" One of the lawyers turned to another in astonishment and said of Stone, "He's in our field. He's in our *field*!" Izzy laughed recounting this to Patner. "My moment of triumph! So that consolidated me with Stern— I was the guy that handled constitutional issues on the paper." Izzy's legal writing led to his first book, *The Court Disposes,* which he dedicated to Esther.

To counter virulent antiunionists and anti–New Dealers, the president went to the people with radio fireside chats, rolling up massive victories as he took potshots at the rich. Toward the end of FDR's first term, a

---

*Although Izzy was not spared decades of hounding by the FBI, HUAC, and other government organizations, this lack of participation may well have saved him from being called before HUAC and McCarthy committee hearings during the Cold War.

growing number of newspapermen broke with the president, fearing a "dictatorship" aborning in FDR's powerful central government. FDR's favorite whipping boy was the "Tory" press, and his famous line that 85 percent of the press was against him has reverberated through the decades. Some observers of the press and presidents have contended this was one of FDR's exaggerations.* Yet it is undeniable that most of the nation's widely read columnists consistently attacked the president. Westbrook Pegler reached for an oxymoron in naming his syndicated column "Fair Enough," which reached over 5 million readers. Friends called his boat *Rancors Aweigh.* Dorothy Thompson's influential syndicated column reached 7.5 million readers. A New Deal critic, Thompson swung her support to Roosevelt during the buildup to war in 1940 and wrote material for his speeches.

At first FDR waged a two-pronged attack on the media. He flattered and cajoled White House correspondents. Some felt insulted when FDR smoothly implied that they were tools of editors: "I can appreciate what you're told to write." Yet they were mostly charmed. In contrast, FDR fiercely attacked publishers like Hearst and McCormick who dropped what tenuous hold they had on the truth. During the 1936 campaign FDR was suppressed right off the front page of the *Chicago Tribune,* which distorted news from the "dictator" and attacked "Commie" Eleanor Roosevelt. And they invented. While Stone was writing editorials urging more assistance for WPA jobs, Hearst termed them all Communists: "Taxpayers Feed 20,000 Reds on N.Y. Relief Rolls."

Now the thin-skinned FDR—who had portrayed himself to Stern as a man who "always" welcomed "honest and constructive criticism"— lashed out at "liars" in the White House press corps, even when criticisms were sound. The most personal attack came in 1943: FDR presented a reporter, John O'Donnell, with an Iron Cross on the eve of a lawsuit trial that the reporter had brought against Stern and the *Philadelphia Record* after an editorial described O'Donnell as a Naziphile and anti-Semite. Many on the left applauded FDR's act.

Mass-circulation columnist Walter Winchell remained in FDR's corner,

---

*See *FDR and the Press,* Graham J. White. FDR received favorable backing in his early years. However, most newspapers wrote unfavorable editorials regarding such matters as FDR's press conference that attacked the Supreme Court for invalidating the NRA in 1935. The DNC during the 1936 election tabulated that 123 newspapers were anti-Roosevelt and 50 pro with 31 independent. The anti-Roosevelt factions dwarfed the others in circulation by nearly 15.5 million to 6.5 million.

and Joe Alsop, a Roosevelt family member, felt some tribal loyalty. This did not counter the major defection of Lippmann. In the first two years, Lippmann had been the jewel in Roosevelt's crown. By 1935, Lippmann fought him over legislation to control holding companies; the Wealth Tax became known as "soak the rich." Lippmann feared FDR was moving away from Depression recovery measures to reform of the social structure.

Lippmann was no reformer. The usually detached columnist became hysterical. He worried that FDR was substituting "some kind of planned collectivism" for a free economy. Even though he knew it was a doomed cause, Lippmann voted for Alf Landon in 1936 and urged his readers to do the same. "Nothing could be worse," he wrote, than a "Democratic landslide." After the landslide, Stone gloated, "With 80 percent of the editors of the nation shouting 'Villain!' at the top of their lungs," FDR was returned to office. "Those newspapers" who represented the view of "special privilege and NOT the opinions of the millions of American citizens . . . were defeated in November."

A stark contrast was Lippmann's and Stone's reaction to FDR's famous court-packing plan in 1937. Lippmann led the attack against FDR, who had asked Congress to allow him to expand the Supreme Court by adding up to a maximum of six new judges for every current judge over the age of seventy. FDR angered even many Democrats who saw a despotic attempt to override checks and balances. FDR was "drunk with power," Lippmann exclaimed. Over half his columns for five months were denunciations of the court plan. Biographer Ron Steel said that Lippmann's reaction was "totally out of proportion to anything FDR had proposed or contemplated."

The *New York Post* stood alone among the major newspapers in supporting the plan. Stone, its constitutional specialist, tried to convince readers and Congress that the court-packing plan did not thwart democracy; that FDR was righting a wrong by adhering to the constitutional heritage of a government run for and by the people. The reactionary court had stifled the voice of the people who had reelected the president by a landslide, Stone argued. FDR was "unpacking" a court that "has been 'packed' for years" with reactionaries who "twisted the Constitution" and stood in the path of "almost every major piece of social legislation enacted by the elected representatives of the American people." Jefferson and Lincoln had denounced what FDR "has witnessed—four years of wholesale, systematic and unparalleled destruction" of reform programs. In capital letters, Stone asserted that such a mandate meant a vote "FOR

CONTINUATION OF THE LIBERAL POLICIES WHICH THE PRESI-
DENT INAUGURATED AND THE SUPREME COURT SABOTAGED."
Stone addressed the "heart-breaking cries" of a reactionary press who
contended that "Mr. R. has 'set a precedent for packing the Court'" that
less able or sincere presidents "might eagerly follow."

"What then?" the editorialist asked.

"The worst that could happen is that the Supreme Court would be
reduced to what the Constitution intended it to be—our highest court of
appeal. It would no longer be what the Constitution never intended it to
be—an autocratic super legislature overriding the other branches of the
Government and the will of the people." Stone optimistically argued that
"a Supreme Court once 'unpacked'" by a liberal president in response to
a popular mandate "would never again dare arrogate to itself the unconstitutional powers usurped by the present Court." He wrote, "The Fathers intended this to be a government of checks and balances—not
government by judges. It gave Congress and the President powers to
keep a tyrannical Court in line." The plan was resoundingly defeated in a
Congress with a Democratic majority.

The issue begs an examination of Stone's biases. How would he have
argued if a conservative president proposed the same measure? It is
doubtful that he would call it furthering American freedoms. His editorials showed that Stone would have made a good trial lawyer, able to
argue the facts to the benefit of his client. Certainly Stone would not be
clamoring for "court packing" under Republican rule.

For all his absorption with the law, Stone wrote often about the unbearable hardship of Depression victims. Flu and tuberculosis were giant
killers. Infant mortality soared. In 1934, life expectancy for white and
African-American males was 50.3 and 50.2 respectively. Black women
were expected to die ten years earlier than white women, 53.7 compared
to 63.7 years. The average annual income for a full-time employee was
$1,091. When most newspapers applauded cuts in the WPA (Works
Progress Administration) and the CWA (Civil Works Administration),
Stone battled to keep programs for struggling Americans. The New
Deal's chaotic progress did touch an extraordinary scope of Americans:
millions of farmers and industrial workers; hundreds of thousands of
mortgage-ridden homeowners saved by the Home Owners Loan Corporation; and, for the first time, thousands of artists, writers, actors, playwrights, and teachers supported by the WPA.

Stone was dismayed when FDR took an ax to the CWA in April 1934. Headlined "Why They Riot," his editorial told of mobs battling police and smashing city hall windows as police routed them with tear gas and the threat of guns. This was not a repeat of current French riots, he wrote, but an uprising by "the citizens of Minneapolis, one of the most stable and law-abiding of American cities. . . . Men who feel they are being cheated out of life behave about the same anywhere." Riots were deplorable "but not as deplorable as the short-sighted, pinch-penny policy that creates them."

Shortly before his 1937 inauguration, Roosevelt bowed to conservative and right-wing pressure and gutted the WPA. Again Stone assailed such capitulation. It was enough to make one think that Alf Landon had been elected, he cried. Sufficient funds were available and such "wholesale layoffs" were unnecessary, he argued. A pro-business, anti-WPA contingent wanted to force workers into private industry to create a pool of unemployment, "a surplus labor market which will keep wages down. . . . If private industry wants W.P.A. workers—let private industry compete for their services BY PAYING WAGES SUBSTANTIALLY HIGHER THAN W.P.A. WAGES.* . . . This sabotage of the recovery program was NOT what the people voted for on November 3." Despite rough waters the W.P.A. lasted through the thirties.

Stone's day began with an exuberant leap for New York's morning dailies, then breakfast prepared by Esther, often consumed in silence as her husband bent over the papers, his weak eyes skimming the pages for possible editorial topics. This was only a warm-up for the armful of New York, European, and out-of-town American newspapers and magazines Stone would devour in his editorial cubicle.

Stone would chat with the tobacconist on the ground floor of the newspaper building as he stopped by for the cigars he had acquired a taste for as a man of the world. Stone once instructed his teenage brother Lou on the specifics of smoking cigars. Lou lit the cigar and was soon

---

*The same argument was raised fifty years later, in the 1990s, amid conservative clamor for workfare as a means of getting people off welfare. The argument overlooked that the minimum wage did not reach the poverty level for a family of four and that low-paying jobs seldom provided health benefits, thus offering no incentive to work. Nor were there any day-care facilities for working mothers. Due to unprecedented prosperity in the nineties, some successes were reported, but in a downturn many former welfare recipients were struggling terribly in the new century.

puffing away down the street beside Stone, who was industriously exhaling billows of smoke. "You know, Lou," said Stone, striding and puffing, "when you walk along and you smoke a cigar, you really feel like you've got the world by the tail. You really feel great."

Informal, jousting editorial conferences with J. David Stern or his managing editor, Harry T. Saylor, were held in the morning. Everyone at the table had a hand in deciding whether proposed editorials would work, sometimes with heated discussions, followed by arguments over who would write which editorial. Then they would repair for lunch, Stone frequently borrowing a dollar from Grafton, who kept a ledger of Stone's account, a rather demanding bookkeeping chore despite the small amounts. Stone would borrow $3 one day and pay back $2 the next, then borrow $8 and pay back $6. This went on for years, with Grafton usually on the short end by a dollar or two.

Grafton and Stone hitched rides on open streetcars, then walked partway to a Lower East Side delicatessen to devour huge fifteen-cent corned-beef sandwiches. They could now drink beer in real restaurants, the first for ten cents, the third one free. After one festive lunch at a German restaurant, Stone grew so silent that Grafton glanced at him. Stone had just discovered he had polished off a rabbit. "There was Izzy, moved to tears at the thought that he'd eaten a poor little Easter bunny."

After lunch, it was back to the office for fast-paced writing, pounding out editorials for the four-thirty deadline. "We were too young to feel pressure," said Grafton. "I did a lot of domestic stuff and farm policy and humorous editorials." Stone's writing showed few flashes of his later style. None of Broun's biting wit or Lippmann's Olympian prose or Joseph Alsop's erudition. For *Post* readers, Stone produced meat-and-potatoes fare, with few ambiguities or obfuscations, but often with a sense of outrage not found in other editorialists. Professionally, "Izzy was very much the way he was later in life," reflects Grafton. "His strengths were digging and reading."

Categorizing their differences, Grafton says, "I felt that I was a trend spotter and other people were 'plot' spotters. Izzy was more of a plot spotter. It was a period of big plots and big plotters and dictators and secret organizations, and if he had a weakness, it may have been a tendency to think in terms of plots, rather than trends. He would think *somebody* was doing something terrible to the public treasury. Well, I thought so too, but I didn't mind that much." Less a crusader, Grafton shrugged it off. "Izzy believed in socialism and I did not. That was our difference."

Looking back at the thirties brand of economics, Grafton added, "But I didn't believe in capitalism either.

"He was an aginner and I was too."

Stone was unique to his trade. He comfortably called himself an intellectual, a term that would stick in the throats of most reporters then, even those who had pretensions of being one. Yet he was a very good newspaperman. "He was very happy when he got a scoop," recalls Grafton, "and he got his scoops in the library." Still using the name Feinstein, Stone was earning respect from a different audience through bylined articles in such magazines as the *New Republic* and the *Nation,* then run by legendary libertarian Oswald Garrison Villard. The college dropout was at home writing for the *Nation,* where at editorial conferences, Dorothy Parker once remarked, one couldn't "hear a thing for the clanking of Phi Beta Kappa keys."

However, Stone could not be categorized with ivory-tower pundits, who did little or no reporting. (Lippmann credited himself with inventing a new approach, informed commentating, yet this was often based on such less-than-neutral sources as secretaries of state, ambassadors, and presidents.)

While Stone considered himself primarily a newspaperman, he remained aloof from colleagues who congregated at such watering holes as Jack Bleeck's Artist and Writers' Restaurant, a former speakeasy and unofficial annex of the *Herald Tribune.* At Bleeck's (pronounced Blake's), celebrity journalists such as Heywood Broun and Ring Lardner bellied up with the lowliest cub reporters panting for an invitation to play the match game, a diversion so simple that the drunkest could play, guessing how many matches one held in a closed fist. Lucius Beebe, American journalism's answer to Oscar Wilde, swished in, in a red-velvet-lined opera cape, and played with gold matches tipped with diamonds. Outlawed at Bleeck's until the 1933 repeal of Prohibition, women were not much welcomed afterward. An exception was Tallulah Bankhead, who one night allegedly stood on her head on a table while singing "God Bless America."

Stone's absence at Bleeck's was, in part, testimony to a stable marriage, a condition in short supply in the hard-drinking newspaper world. (Some reporters even had their mail addressed to Bleeck's.) Going home to Esther, their children, and more intellectual friends meant more to him than drunken bonhomie. Though capable of collecting friends of long standing, Stone's pattern of ignoring colleagues angered many who felt he was a snob. Even that monument to snobbery, Joseph Alsop, then a top feature writer on the *Herald Tribune,* occasionally entered Bleeck's. "I don't think Izzy was a newspaperman in the truest sense," Grafton recalls. "I was more in the hurly-burly." Stone embraced newspapering, not as a shared profession, but as a lone crusader.

What Stone missed was less frivolous than it seems on the surface. Joints like Bleeck's were decompression chambers for adrenaline-charged days, sacrosanct hideouts where one could gripe about editors who gutted copy and publishers who paid miserably, and lie about the great novel that few if any would write. Rebels against conformity, most newspapermen nonetheless needed comradery.

In Bleeck's, a historic mutiny was born—the forming of the newspaper guild. In 1933, publishers, conservatives in good standing among the corporate elite, occasionally lapsed into tearstained editorials on the nobility and hardships of the working class. This in no way interfered with dispensing serflike working hours and wages to reporters. To even think of unionizing meant swift dismissal.

Then came Heywood Broun, lumbering into Bleeck's and every other watering hole that adjoined a newspaper, accomplishing two missions at once—arm-twisting colleagues to join a guild and consuming his daily quota of gin. A regular at the Algonquin Round Table, Broun reigned among America's most acerbic wits. After his painful separation from the *World* in 1927, Broun went to the *Telegram,* which then merged with the *World* in 1931. The *World* "died of a final lack of courage," said the bitter Broun. As the *World-Telegram*'s hot columnist-celebrity and one of America's highest-paid columnists, Broun hardly suffered from the merger. He lived in penthouse luxury and made $500 a week while some colleagues in the Scripps Howard chain made as little as $15 a week. Yet, during Guild strikes, the columnist was a presence on many a picket line. Once, an arresting officer identified Broun as a "rich New York Communist." "Un-uh," Broun corrected the cop, "rich New York *columnist.*" Broun's persona of the shaggy, hard-drinking raconteur hid many complexities. He shunned intimacy, could be both pugnacious and sentimental, and his outsized ego commingled with a do-gooder's outrage.

A major obstacle to unionizing was the individualist nature of reporters. Despite Depression-era large-scale layoffs and pay cuts, "gentlemen of the press" often felt it demeaning to band together like lowly Linotype operators. In New York in 1933, the average weekly salary dropped to $27 for reporters, a pay cut of $12. For most, not so cushioned as Broun, joining the union could mean losing the last job they would ever have on newspapers. When Broun's penthouse doubled as headquarters for newspapermen nervously organizing the Guild, one *New York Times* reporter brought his wife so that he could claim it was a social evening if his bosses heard he was there.

Stone was a fighting charter member of the Guild. "When Heywood Broun came down from New York to Philadelphia to organize the Guild, I joined up." Elephantine Broun and squat Izzy looked like two comic-book characters as they stood together, toasting the American Newspaper Guild's beginning and talking of a unionized future. Stone worked with others to write a strong ANG code that called for a five-day, forty-hour week, the right to bargain, and a minimum weekly salary of $14.50.

Apoplectic publishers banned together across the country, threatening with immediate dismissal any reporter who signed organization lists. FDR's National Recovery Act (NRA), designed to regulate every industry, called for shorter working hours and a decent wage. With disgraceful irony, publishers gave lip service to the NRA, but produced a watered-down code for themselves—open shops, an exemption of newsboys from child-labor provisions, and "professionals" who would not be covered by maximum-hour regulations or the forty-hour week. Publishers defined "professionals" as anyone making more than $35 a week. The next summer, publishers still ignored Guild demands as newsmen across the country seethed.

Throughout the thirties, titans like Hearst and Si Newhouse ignored the Guild, threatened activist reporters with firing, or consigned them to a newspaperman's version of purgatory, obituaries. One of the few heroes was Stone's publisher. On April 8, 1934, Stern signed a contract between the *Philadelphia Record* and the Philadelphia Guild, the first written agreement obtained by any Guild. It granted newsmen a closed shop, severance pay, a $20-per-week basic minimum wage, compensation for overtime, and paid vacations. Stern's contract gave newsmen benefits for which many stronger unions in other industries had to battle to the death.

Stern shared a curious alliance with the publisher of the *New York Daily News,* Joseph M. Patterson, a hard-boiled conservative who also agreed that reporters needed protection. The rest of the New York publishers, recalled the Guild's lawyer, Morris Ernst, "resisted . . . sniffed . . . jeered" and fought a guild of their "favorite and most important workers."

In the summer of 1934, a tough *New York Post* editorial noted that the newspaper industry was one of the few still not under the NRA code—albeit "the one which has made the most noise in asking others to 'cooperate with the President' while doing as little as possible itself." In words unmistakably Stone's, the editorial attacked publishers who had produced an alternative that "ranks among the worst codes" submitted under the National Industrial Recovery Act. "All this chiseling has been effected under the thin guise of 'Protecting' the 'Freedom of the Press.' Newspapers that had, in the past, hesitated to take a stand on anything closer to home than Child Marriage in China or Immorality in Timbuctoo suddenly began to worry about freedom of the press." This was ridiculous; "regulations as to wages and hours have no more to do with freedom of the press than regulations as to fire protection, elevator inspection or sanitation. . . . Were the Nervous Nellies sincere, they would have drawn up a real code." Stern was also heard. The *Post* disavowed "this hypocritical and evasive code. And expresses regret that a glorious phrase, 'Freedom of the Press,' has been obscured by a large, dark dollar sign."

Sad to say, the large, dark dollar sign got to Stern as well. He maintained the five-day, forty-hour week but felt the struggling *Post* could not survive with a minimum-wage proviso as well as sick leave and vacation benefits. Stern even lagged behind prevailing practices on sick leave. He was being bled dry by mob boss Moe Annenberg, the new owner of the *Philadelphia Inquirer.* Annenberg had nothing but money, until he went to jail for income tax evasion, and bragged that he could lose "five dollars to make Dave Stern lose one."

Embittered by Guild tactics in a heated Philadelphia strike, Stern never recovered his enthusiasm for newspapers. "The Guild was asking things of Stern, who was friendly, that they weren't asking the *Philadelphia Inquirer,* which was unfriendly and antiunion," said Stone to Patner. "It was hard for him to be treated like a capitalist boss. I think the Guild was rather unfair in their treatment of him."

The fight against Annenberg so drained Stern emotionally and financially that he told the *Post* staff he would have to sell the paper unless they accepted a pay cut. He raced down to the White House to warn President Roosevelt that the only New Deal paper in New York would go under unless he got help. Roosevelt talked to CIO president John L. Lewis, who called Broun. He spoke to a "Communist functionary in the New York local who rammed the pay cut down the throats of the reluctant Guild members at the *Post.*"

Dolly Schiff was able to buy the paper in 1939. Stone said Stern "just couldn't get the department store lineage." He loved Stern's bravery in the trenches. "Macy's—owned by Jews, the Straus family—was selling Nazi goods." Stern and Stone ardently supported boycotting these products. "Department-store advertising was not just revenue, it was also circulation, because women bought the . . . paper to see the ads," explained Stone. ". . . If you got Macy's, you could get the others." Macy's would not buy ads because of Stern's boycott stance. Putting principle before profits cost Stern sorely needed advertising. "There was a peace meeting arranged between my boss and Percy Straus and everything looked peaceful and he was going to get the ads, and then Percy brought up the boycott—out of the blue—and he said, 'David, how about those editorials?'" Stone suddenly grew silent as he relayed this story to Patner. Tears formed in Izzy's eyes. ". . . As I talk about it, I relive it—these were very hot issues. . . ." Gaining composure, Stone continued, "And Stern jumped up and grabbed Percy Straus, by the throat. That was the end of the peace meeting."

Stone never lost sight of human misery: children in factories and mines, unprotected by laws; farmers evicted from their land; blacks abused and arrested without warrants. Disgustedly, Stone wrote in 1938 that New Dealers "preached collective bargaining but took to bed with chills when it looked as though labor were getting somewhere; when the Chicago police shot strikers in the back the answer of the press was to assail labor for violence."

Only after reporters were beaten during a civil workers' protest did some New York papers question such typical antilabor headlines as "Reds Incite Riot." Stone meticulously examined the coverage, then blasted the press and the police in a 1934 *New Republic* article. A mostly white-collar protest began when two-thirds of thirty thousand workers were devastated by cuts in relief and payrolls. Their peaceful demands were met by police billy clubs. Those arrested for "inciting a riot" were arraigned in a court whose judicial proceedings seemed borrowed from the Dark Ages. "At a signal from the magistrate the room was cleared," Stone wrote. Police "hidden" in adjoining rooms "staged an attack so brutal that two reporters intervened." Stone indulged his lifelong penchant for attacking the *New York Times* and its paper-of-record image. While the *Times* informed its readers that no injuries were reported, two *Daily News* reporters suddenly found truth in reporting, "inspired no

doubt by their own bruises." Under a unique headline for the *News*—
"Berserk Cops Beat Couple at Red Trial"—a reporter who had been hit
by police told of a couple repeatedly knocked down, kicked, and beaten
"almost to insensibility." Ignoring its reporter's eyewitness description,
the *News* editorial blamed demonstrators for "hurling themselves on the
police" and stated that "all public order rests ultimately on force—police
and military." Stone archly asked, "Was the *News* trying to teach the
Communist Doctrine that the state and its armed forces were instruments of the ruling class?"

Stone noted that the protesting group was "partially Communist in
its leadership" before dissecting negative accounts of the demonstration
in paper after paper. The *Mirror* proclaimed "no quarter for Red Agitators" and called the Communists "skulking rats . . . six thousand police
are available for a war to exterminate them." The *Mirror*'s scare tactics
included the "fact" that "there are 200,000 known Reds in New York
City." Stone dryly wrote, "This must have been news to the Communists." The *Herald Tribune* assailed the unemployed demonstrators as
"Yellow Rats." Most important, wrote Stone, "None of the 'capitalist'
press bothered to tell their readers what the riot was all about."

Then Stone sounded a warning, one that consumed him then and
again in the fifties. "A swing to the Right is perceptible all along the
line. . . . The Red Menace is being used to stifle free expression and criticism in the schools. Anti-Nazi activists are meeting with ever greater police hostility." Stone described a "respectable . . . Harvard man, club man,
financial man, who wrote a letter to the police commissioner protesting
police brutality against anti-Nazi demonstrators. Within hours, employees told him that plainclothesmen questioned them about his political
beliefs and affiliations." The man's charges of brutality were not investigated. Stone ended his article with a right-wing compilation of an "Alien
and Criminal Squads" handbook. Its "Who's Who in Radicalism" included "Bishop McConnell, Rabbi Wise, Mrs. Franklin D. Roosevelt,"
and New York's Mayor La Guardia, who had, in fact, been "hushing up
the news in good reactionary fashion."

Despite his fealty to unions, Stone exposed racketeering scandals, although he concentrated on the anticommunist AFL (American Federation of Labor) more than the CIO. "Powerful and militant unions" were
vital during "the growing menace of fascism," he noted, but the "dry rot
of dictatorship and racketeering" were dangerously weakening the AFL.
Stone combed an exhaustive report for the Department of Public Mar-

kets to uncover riveting facts about how unions kept poultry producers and sellers in line. Gas bombs blew up chickens. Poisoned feed was thrown into crates, trucks wrecked, and chickens set afire. "Crooked politicians protected the rackets for a share in the spoils."

Building-industry racketeers used union funds to defend crooks and gangsters "against charges of helping themselves to these same funds." Studying mounds of affidavits, Stone gleaned how union election "victories" were assured. A painters' union candidate had just been beaten up and was in an exhausted condition. For every man who voted, two gangsters observed him in the booth. Repeat voters were welcomed.

Stone was most effective when he contrasted hypocrisy with reality. In a long *Nation* article he applied his scalpel to the *New York Times*, comparing its lack of daily coverage of social issues to its sob-story annual Christmas Campaign, New York's One Hundred Neediest Cases. The headline took a swipe at the *Times*'s lofty "All the News That's Fit to Print"; Stone's article was titled "Not Fit to Print."

"Each of these cases unfolds a world of suffering. 'Please Make My Daddy Well,' 'Old and Alone,' 'At Nineteen—Breadwinner for Ten.' " Stone noted, "These captions make the more sophisticated shrink. But the misery behind them is real." Then he attacked: "The *Times* every year gives its readers a glimpse of news it did not think fit to print before. . . . I do not recall that the *Times* ever commented editorially on the inadequacy of relief in New York City or anywhere else.

" 'Crippled Hands' tells an illuminating story." After years of making hats, a worker's hands were misshapen and he was chronically ill from breathing damp air in his factory. "Has anyone ever heard the *Times* appeal for workmen's compensation in occupational ailments?" an outraged Stone asked. The *Times* was moved "just before Christmas. But you will find comparatively little in the *Times*, or most other newspapers, about the *100,000,000* Neediest, about social insurance, about the necessity for better relief, about the helplessness of the small investor, about the misery of the great masses of workers." Christmas tearjerkers could not make up for the *Times*'s lack of support for vital legislative and social changes and most papers "were content to blast the unemployed" as demanding grumps and "mostly foreigners." By 1936, Stone flailed, "Millions of Americans are living on a third-, fourth- and fifth-class diet" because FDR "for all his Tory trouncing—insists on cutting relief."

* * *

No thinker caught in the swirling madness of the thirties could concentrate solely on domestic issues. This was but one facet of Stone's prodigious outpouring. More than many, Stone envisioned an ominous future for the world—agonizing over the Spanish Civil War, Hitler's march through Europe, German Bundist fascists in America, the Stalin-Hitler Pact.

By 1937, Isador Feinstein was also struggling with a very personal decision. He took Lou for a walk and "told me that the fight against fascism was so important, and that there was a tendency, when you had a writer by the name of Feinstein, to discount whatever he wrote because he was Jewish. The 'What can you expect from a Jewish writer?' viewpoint. Consequently, we all decided to change the name together."

Stone legally changed his name as 1938 dawned—mercifully rejecting the hopelessly romantic "Geoffrey Duprion." His parents remained Feinstein, although his children's changes never bothered Bernard, who had not come from a long line of Feinsteins. Like many Russian Jews, his family name had been changed at least once by an ancestor.

In the thirties there was alarming support for Hitler, with American-style brownshirts proliferating, and rampant anti-Semitism. Jews often viewed changing one's name as necessary. Sam Grafton, for example, had changed his last name in 1932 from Lifshutz, to please Stern, who did not want his writers' names to sound "too Jewish." Stone's new name was hardly a camouflage. *Stone* is *stein* in German; the *F* stands for no name and is a nod to the original Feinstein. For Stone's enemies, his name change hardly made a difference. Thanks to his FBI file, begun by then, *Feinstein* would be used against him in public anti-Semitic slurs by some of the nation's most powerful.

"It was just about the time of our third baby and I thought in part if he had a neutral-sounding name maybe it would save him some trouble," Stone explained, although he revealed some guilt about the name change later. For all of Stone's zest, recalls his son, "He could summon up deep gloom. His fear of fascism was very strong. He named me, a Jewish boy, Christopher, after Christopher Marlowe, but it would also protect me if fascism spread. He had a keen eye for specters of tragedy, and there was a self-protective element. But there also wasn't much investment in the [German] name Feinstein."

Stone was facing another tragedy; he was going deaf. "Neither of my parents ever discussed illness," recalled Christopher. "It was like something immoral." And so Stone uncomplainingly used hearing aids. The liability became an asset, as it forced him to burrow further into documents. His hearing apparatus was connected by a cord to a black box hung around his neck and looked a bit like an early Walkman. When bored with the conversation, Stone turned down the volume.

One of the first I. F. Stone bylines graced a *New Republic* book review on December 29, 1937, of *Our Reigning Families* by Ferdinand Lundberg, author of *Imperial Hearst.* Stone praised this "comprehensive study of the power exercised by our wealthiest families" and polished off his best phrases. "The gigantic thieveries of Wall Street are perfumed and pomaded for public inspection." Lundberg had bared the plutocrats' "alley-cat moral code"; "the concentration of economic power in a few hands has weathered each successive spasm of protest and is today . . . greater than ever." After 150 years of "Barn-Burners, Abolitionists, Populists, Progressives and New Dealers; muckrakers, denouncers, investigators and crusaders, Mr. Lundberg can write, 'The United States is owned and dominated today by a hierarchy of sixty of the richest families. . . .'

"No one who reads [Lundberg] will ever feel the same again about Theodore Roosevelt's progressivism or Woodrow Wilson's New Freedom. J. P. Morgan and Company made its greatest progress under the 'trust buster' *with his cooperation*" [Stone's emphasis]. As "the scion of the Dodge copper fortune," Wilson was abetted in his presidential quest. Yet Stone wished Lundberg were "more judicious. . . . The fact that rich families often endow special hospital or medical facilities for diseases from which they or their families have suffered can hardly be condemned as mere self-interest."

Stone was recognizing that the New Deal meant reform only within the system, perhaps the best that could be hoped for. He was at odds with and more prescient than America's most exalted columnist. Lippmann "seriously misread the New Deal, viewing it as revolutionary rather than reformist," wrote his biographer Steel. He saw "diabolical method in the New Deal where there was only haphazard experiment." By that time, leftists were denouncing Lippmann as a Wall Street reactionary.

At times Stone harshly criticized the New Deal from the left. The NRA ultimately helped corporations more than labor; social reforms were never totally solidified; it did not end the Depression. Yet, in gauging the long-term effects, Stone was more sanguine and accurate than the soured Lippmann. There was the minimum-wage act of 1938, pushed by Claude Pepper; the princely sum of twenty-five cents an hour was a vital beginning in a still unending struggle for decent wages. Social Security was one of the New Deal's greatest achievements: "at last the national government had acted to underpin the future security of Americans."

Stone recounted the snail's pace of reform in his *New Republic* essay, contrasting his opinions with those of William Allen White, who called himself a "neolithic liberal" of the progressive era. "We of the New Deal generation are but Bronze Age. . . . They went forth to grapple with big business by regulatory commission. No sooner had they gripped the demon in one form than he was loose in another. . . . We had a simpler solution; the lion of profit and the lamb of need would lie down together if only we increased mass purchasing power. But each time we pushed purchasing power up a little by means of higher wages and relief expenditures, it fell back twice as far under the weight of higher prices and profits. We stemmed vaguely from Mr. Keynes; he taught us to believe that public works are a form of perpetual motion, that the parallel lines of production for use and production for profit can be made to meet in a Central Bank, and that faith will move the mountains of deficit; a new generation from the hills sneers that this is neo-Euclidean economics. We may be on our way to the doghouse, too. . . ." Still, "the New Deal will leave behind it: a strengthened trade-union movement, the basis of a real bulwark against fascism and a real check on the power of concentrated capital."

Noting that a dark unknown awaits, Stone wrote, "We barricade ourselves and Mr. White against despair with the thought that history is less logical than man; cuts its own patterns; picks its own instruments; eludes our formulas; is perverse, eccentric, whimsical. . . . This hope is but a crumb on which to feed self-esteem; but we bring it with us to the doghouse and invite Mr. White to dine."

8

AMERICAN DICTATORS
AND (NOT ALWAYS)
POPULAR FRONTS

"The Fascist experience in Italy [in the twenties] was very vivid to me," recalled Izzy. Coupled with Hitler's rise to power, this made Izzy a "strong popular fronter *before* there was a popular front." In later years, I. F. Stone was criticized even by admirers for a double standard. Like many on the left, the alarmed and prescient crusader against Hitler voiced only tepid criticism of Stalin's brutalities in the thirties.

Stone defended noncommunists like himself who embraced the popular front so wholeheartedly that unity meant suspending, or ignoring, hard truths. In later life, Stone contended that he was more aware and critical of Stalin's brutal reign than critics claimed. "Nevertheless the background was that *there had to be unity*" to stop Hitler. "I'm just trying to explain my attitude toward Communists," Stone told a friend, Todd Gitlin, in the mid-eighties. "I wasn't wedded to them—even by hatred or repulsion," said Stone, accurately depicting the hold that Communism had on various enemies—rabid right-wing adversaries, socialists who had long sparred with them, and CP defectors who during the Cold War denounced former comrades.

Stone viewed himself as an independent steering through the ideological shoals in that wild rapids of 1930s leftist rhetoric and dissension. Stone believed that a united left throughout Europe and America during the thirties could have thwarted fascism. Therefore, "I was friendly with socialists—left and right—and Communists and Communist dissidents and Trotskyites. In their eyes I was just a goddamn liberal, so to speak." He wanted to avoid the disasters in Germany where "the internecine struggle of the Communists and Socialists was a scandal." As he re-flected, at the age of seventy-seven, Stone spoke with the same passion about the issues of a half century past as he did about the most current perils in the world. "It was divisions on the left that gave us fascism—you've got to admit, even in Germany, Hitler never got a majority." It was "political suicide" for leftists not to coalesce in a prewar popular front. "The main issue was to fight fascism, fight Hitlerism, that a *war* was coming."

Only an optimist like Stone could have hoped for a united left in the thirties. Communist Party members were venomous to socialists, old-guard socialists were battling new-guard socialists, mutant strains of Marxists were battling one another. Working-class ideologues were joined by middle- and upper-class Ivy League graduates who played at being radically chic Marxists.

Stone's allegiance to leftist unity, however, did not mean abject silence in the face of violence. He condemned Communists who threw chairs from the balconies of Madison Square Garden down on trade-union so-cialists at a 1934 rally. "Only Nazi hoodlums" could rival the Commu-nists' performance.

For the far left, FDR's New Deal was but a pinprick in the inflated balloon of capitalism, halting real socialist progress. Meanwhile, right-wing demagogues appealed to bitter unemployed Americans. An alarmed Stone warned New Dealers that, while Communist rallies could not start a revolution, poverty and hunger could.

Stone's editorials slammed as fascistic the dictatorial powers of two inflammatory orators who reached dizzying heights of popularity in the thirties—Father Coughlin and Huey Long. Stone condemned them, but embraced their right to free speech. To do otherwise, he argued, would mean a disintegration into Hitlerism. Lippmann opposed such blanket freedom. Never a free speech absolutist, the columnist argued against ac-quiescing to the "overthrow of a democracy" if a dictator such as Long received a majority of votes. Calling for restraints, Lippmann wrote, "The right of free speech belongs to those who are willing to preserve it."

Throughout the twentieth century, an ironic political phenomenon endured. Artful dictators on the right rose to power by espousing the very socialism they successfully railed against as Communism. Hitler and Mussolini began under socialist banners. Both Long and Coughlin preached that they were instruments of the common man.

* * *

The thirties was an era of stirring orators. Handlers did not create their words or devise ads honed to say nothing. From miles around, farmers and townsfolk rode and walked to packed courthouse and town squares to listen to stump speeches, which had not disintegrated into backdrops for sound bites and ads. Radio was television's equivalent for reaching nationwide audiences, but radio gave politicians the time to speak in phrases, not three-word sentences.

Radio was a boon for the spellbinding theatricality of FDR, Long, Coughlin, Norman Thomas. Roosevelt's patrician tones stirred farmers in Tuscaloosa as they did liberal intellectuals in Manhattan. Huey Long, with his distinctive cleft chin and curly hair, decked out in expensive double-breasted suits and fedoras, exhorted mobs at rallies and those tuned in to radio as he spoke in rhythms to ignite. The worst politicians, unrestrained in an age of raw racist, anti-Semitic, and xenophobic sentiments, let fly verbal attacks on "niggers" and "Jews" and "Red furriners." Political foes were "pusillanimous polecats."

Enemies called Long the Messiah of the Rednecks and Whoey the 14th. Long reached into the barnyard, calling opponents trough feeders and buzzard brains. Crowds roared as he vowed to skin, flay, stomp, and "brain fry" his adversaries. Long's larger-than-life spirit captivated reporters and followers, no matter his dictatorial reign based on graft, corruption, cruelty, and patronage. Long never came silently into the night; his long and loud cavalcade was led by Long's brass band, bodyguards and henchmen, gun-toting troopers in tan uniforms with jackboots and Smokey the Bear hats. Long was among the first to use sound trucks, which amplified his fiery delivery to the farthest edges of immense crowds. When Long spoke, it was a "dynamic experience. . . . Even though you hated every word he said, you had to admire his delivery, the way he manipulated the crowd," commented Betty Carter, the widow of Hodding Carter, the Pulitzer Prize–winning civil-rights publisher of the Greenville, Mississippi, *Delta Democrat Times*. Carter got his journalistic start in Louisiana, where he learned to loathe Long close up.

Long posed as the savior of the dispossessed. With studied indignation he would reveal that J. P. Morgan owned a hundred suits, "each one stolen from the back of a workingman." Both Long and his audience ignored his own extravagant wardrobe. His country-boy pose masked the fact that Long had bludgeoned his way into more personal state political power and fortune than any other man in America.

New Dealers discovered almost too late that it was a mistake to discount Long as a country buffoon and his 1936 bid for the presidency as a joke. A secret poll taken by FDR in 1935 revealed that a Long third-party run could drain off 4 million Democratic votes and throw the 1936 election into the House. At the Democratic convention three years earlier, Long's iron hold on Southern delegates had halted a bolt from FDR's ranks. Now FDR was a "liar and a faker" as Long challenged him with his "Share Our Wealth Program," which would make "Every Man a King."

As chief editorial writer, Stone presided over *New York Post* editorials that strongly attacked Long as Hitlerian, but Stone shared an ambivalence with many. Years later, Stone said, "He certainly was an extremely able politician. He was very much like Caesar in ancient Rome. He leveled the liberties of the republic, but did give some aid to the poor." For Stone and other Northern integrationists, Long was a rare and welcome commodity, a 1930s Southern politician who did not resort to race-baiting. Long did more and in the quickest amount of time than any other governor in Louisiana's memory, Stone noted. He abolished the poll tax, cut telephone, gas, and electricity rates, constructed university buildings, a medical school. All schoolchildren got free textbooks and free school buses in rural districts; night schools were opened for the illiterate. He improved hospitals for the poor. He paved Louisiana "from pigsty to bayou" with concrete, asphalt, and gravel. More than a hundred bridges went up. In the Depression gloom of 1931, 10 percent of all the men working on building bridges and roads in the United States were employed by Louisiana.

Yet Long extracted a huge price. Beloved by the poor, the Kingfish turned Louisiana into his fascistic fiefdom. His own brother told a Senate investigating committee that in 1932, the day after an election, Long and a crony juggled the votes in one parish so that a winning opponent lost by a landslide. Free speech against the Kingfish was unheard of. He had nothing but contempt for the politicians he bribed; turning away from one, he sneered, "I paid for you, I don't have to shake your hand."

By 1935 Stone was an alarmed New Dealer who saw Long ram through legislation that dismantled democracy, giving him control of municipalities, the highway commission, the levee board, and the board of education. He controlled patronage on everything from hospitals and schools to prisons. His "dee-duct box" was filled with money from the 10 percent subtracted monthly from each state worker's salary, a practice utilized by many state patronage systems. With that deduct box, Long financed his political campaigns, traveled in style, bribed politicians. None of this fazed his followers; he was a Teflon leader before Teflon was invented. When he won a seat in the U.S. Senate, Long made certain that the state legislature approved a new towering private castle, known as the State Capitol. When an anti-Long legislator balked, Long ordered a hole drilled in the ceiling of the old Capitol. As water from the leaking roof streamed onto his head, the legislator reconsidered his vote. Long's new Capitol went up. Now from the nation's capital, he continued his stranglehold on Louisiana with no legal authority.

This was too much for Stone and the *New York Post.* On July 9, 1935, an editorial included an italicized preamble: *"One of Hitler's first acts on taking power in Germany was the virtual extinction of local self-government.*

"For all practical purposes local self-government was abolished in Louisiana this week. Dictator Long gave the signal and the Legislature he owns, body and soul, put the ripper legislation through for him."

Long said his seizure of power was to help the common people; however, Long's legislature "defeated a bill to give Louisiana the benefits of the new Federal old-age pensions because the Long administration would have had to match Federal contributions, dollar for dollar," the *Post* continued. "This is the same Long who has the effrontery to call the President a 'liar' and a 'faker.' " The editorial asked, "What will happen to any local official, property owner or plain citizen in Louisiana who disagrees with or opposes the ruling politicians?"The editorial answered with another question: "What happens in Germany?"

Two weeks after Long announced his 1935 presidential candidacy, the *Post* weighed in again: "Disgust is a mild word for the reactions of the American people to the stupid and selfish filibuster" of Senator Long, which had stalled progress; the administration was left "without funds to launch its social security program. The aged, the blind and the crippled will be the ones to suffer from the handiwork of the Senator." The editorial rang with indignation: "The great self-appointed spokesman of the downtrodden shows no hesitancy in putting his obsession for political vengeance ahead of any human consideration. . . . It is unthinkable that he can ever exert any national influence. Whatever public respect he may have had he has forfeited."

For antifascists like Stone, Long's twin terror was the Reverend Charles E. Coughlin. Broadcasting from the Church of the Little Flower in Royal

Oak, Michigan, Father Coughlin was a monumental lightning rod in politics. During the height of his power in 1933, Coughlin filled a New York auditorium by the thousands while thousands more shivered outside, listening to their hero through loudspeakers. On Sunday afternoons, community football games were halted so that players, coaches, and families could tune in to Coughlin. In the summer, Coughlin's radio voice floated into the air from open door after open door. One could walk for blocks without missing a word. His broadcasts reached as many as 40 million people, and a pamphlet containing his radio speeches swiftly sold nearly a million copies, a kind of following of which the left could only dream.

Long and Coughlin forces aligned in an attempt to capture the White House in 1935. At first Coughlin's hate was reserved for Communists on one hand and exploiting financiers and "money changers" on the other. He praised FDR's progressivism; his "New Deal was Christ's Deal!" Later, wearing his clerical-collar talisman of Christian goodness, Coughlin referred to the New Deal as the "Jew Deal."

Coughlin's indictments of wealthy exploiters resonated with millions mired in the Depression; even Stone's father supported the Catholic priest for a short time. For sensitive Jewish writers like Stone, however, code words were warning enough before the priest's descent into open anti-Semitism. When Coughlin attacked financiers of all backgrounds, he called them "shylocks" and "usurers." In the early thirties, however, both Coughlin and Long appealed less to anti-Semitism, racism, or fascism. Their magnetism centered on simple populism, attacking the rich with such crowd pleasers as Long's "pigs swilling in the trough of luxury." Coughlin's tirades did not prevent him from dealing with stockbrokers and financiers after he profited from attacking them.

Stone's hero Norman Thomas exposed the delusional qualities of Long's "share the wealth" plan in a 1934 public debate in New York. Yet Socialist Party members left his ranks for Long's uncomplicated appeal. When Thomas tried to organize poor farmers in an interracial coalition—a wild dream in 1935—he had to contend not only with men cowed by lynch mobs but disaffected former farmers reduced to poor tenant workers, now Long admirers.

The simplistic and often fuzzy message of Long and Coughlin appealed to a basic premise: radicalism was abhorrent to most Americans throughout history. The irony is that as these dictators denounced the abuses of the wealthy, they sang a collectivist song. As they attacked socialism, they stole the words of Eugene Debs. In addition, Coughlin's rhetoric, especially, contained not-so-veiled Babbittry; blacks, Jews, left-ists, and foreign-born people were absent in his idealized communities. They were convenient scapegoats for disenfranchised whites. Such se-ductive ammunition was used by successive politicians; Ronald Reagan tapped a nostalgia for past good times that most had never experienced and fed their anger by chastising mythical "welfare queens" living off food stamps.

As Coughlin's scurrilous voice emerged, Stone's *New York Post* attacked Coughlin as a cohort in fascism with publisher William Randolph Hearst. Coughlin should be considered "in the light of another great orator, Adolf Hitler," who "preached an unscientific socialism far more 'radical' than that of the Marxists whom he attacked. And he denounced everything he opposed as Communism. . . . And when the payoff came, Herr Hitler, of course, turned out to be a dummy" for the "great industrial interest in Germany. Now Coughlin, the 'friend of the common man,' turns out to be working with millionaire William Randolph Hearst. . . . America knows now in which direction the Fascist danger lies."

What might have resulted from the political union of Coughlin and the potent force of Long died in the corridor of the Lousiana State Capi-tol on Sunday, September 8, 1935. As Long strutted through the marble monument to himself, Dr. Carl Weiss, the thirty-year-old relative of one of Long's political victims, eased close enough to shoot Long in the stomach. Weiss was instantly killed by a fusillade of sixty bullets from Long's bodyguards. Tens of thousands came to view Long's coffin. Even famed lawyer Clarence Darrow called him a "great force of character, and a valuable liberal."

The *Post*'s editorial picked its way through the delicate task of writing an obituary about a man Stone and Stern had excoriated. "Senator Huey Pierce Long is beaten, not by ballots as he should have been beaten, but by the bullet of an assassin." Noting that "millions are grievously shocked . . . ," the *Post* said, "yet it must be admitted that millions more, though opposed to bloodshed in politics, draw a deep breath of relief that a potential dictator is no more. Senator Long was the only impor-tant American political leader since the Civil War to set up a powerful organization against the Government of the United States. . . . The mur-der . . . is a blot upon an American democracy. . . . It is also a warning that the path of a dictator on this continent is overhung by peril."

A few years before his own death, I. F. Stone said, "It's a terrible thing to say—I was very glad when they shot him. I don't believe in terrorism or assassination, but he could have become an American dictator."

The insurgency died with Long. Coughlin could not sing his song alone, although he continued to be a voice of hate despite his diminished influence. A *Post* editorial in November 1936 voiced Stone's sentiments: FDR's landslide victory proved that Coughlin was through as a power. "For his own sake, for the sake of his Church and of American unity and intelligent political discussion, we suggest that Father Coughlin sign off—permanently." Coughlin never followed the suggestion. In 1939, emboldened by Hitler's successes, he and other reactionaries whipped up Christian Front hysteria to alarming proportions. "There was genuine fear that a fascist movement had finally taken root in New York," wrote author James Wechsler. Steeped in Coughlin's vitriol, hooligans instigated street brawls and anti-Semitic raids that aped the Nazi Youth movement. By 1939, prominent men, among them aviator hero Charles Lindbergh, preached pro-Hitler isolationism and were attacked by Stone, as their supporters unleashed even fiercer anti-Semitism in America.

On the left, the Communist Party was appealing to another group of disenfranchised and disillusioned working men and women, along with intellectual idealists. A small band of zealots all but eclipsed in the twenties, the CP now saw fertile turf in the barren land of the Depression. Their numbers were small (at its height during the popular front the CP counted seventy thousand members), but they were strengthened by cadres of fellow travelers and sympathizers. Among that category were the nation's leading intellects, academicians, playwrights, novelists, most of whom became disillusioned with Communism. John Dos Passos, Sinclair Lewis, Upton Sinclair, Arthur Koestler, Ernest Hemingway, Lillian Hellman, James Thurber, Dashiell Hammett, Clifford Odets, Irwin Shaw, Marc Blitzstein, and Sidney Howard were among the famous who embraced leftist social justice but were too individualistic to accept CP dictates for long.

Those who knew Stone then universally commented that he was far too opinionated and independent to join anything. Wechsler, a fallen-away Young Communist League member, critically characterized Stone in 1953, at the height of the Cold War and McCarthyism, as a romantic follower but noncommunist. Of the late-thirties staff at the *Nation,* Wechsler wrote, "The communist unknown seemed to have a mysterious attraction for those who had never entered it. This was particularly true of I. F. Stone, who to this day [1953] persists in regarding the communists as just a colorful if eccentric group of political dare devils cast in more heroic mold than any other sect, and therefore to be forgiven their admittedly strange conduct. . . . I always had the feeling Stone could remain a fairly regular apologist for the communists, with intermittent sorties to the left and right, only by staying out of the organized movement; like other instinctive mavericks, he would not have lasted very long inside."

To Stone's credit, he wrote more charitably of Wechsler. Free from the enmity that existed between socialists and Communists, Stone saw good in both camps and in later years said, "You can't blame all the evils of Stalinism on the old left or hide the fact that the old left did a lot of useful things in the thirties, as part of a wider reform movement. As did the Socialists. In the organization of sharecroppers and tenant farmers, in the south especially, the parties did very good work."

Stone's dream of leftist unity faded, but he clung to the hope that a larger purpose would prevail. "For the majority of writers who were associated in some way or another with the movement, it was the times, not the party, that made them radicals," explained writer Daniel Aaron. He described the attraction of the CP for intellectuals: "It alone seemed to have a correct diagnosis of America's social sickness and a remedy for it. The overwhelming majority never joined the party . . . but the issues that preoccupied the party during the first half of the thirties—the plight of the hungry and the evicted, the exploitation of the Negro, the miseries of the unemployed, the persecution in Germany, the struggles of labor—became their preoccupation . . . in no other decade did writers take their social roles more devotionally."

The Communist Party certainly made it difficult for sympathizers. Members slashed away at anarchists and Trotskyists, damned Stone's friends La Follette and Thomas as "social fascists," slammed the New Deal. CP leaders took orders from Moscow, as their critics claimed and their cadres disbelieved. Leaders who went against Stalin, as Earl Browder did in 1945, were broken and expelled. For the smallest deviation members were as shunned as any Amish who disobeys the edicts of his sect.

As doubts emerged, party members often held their silence, for fear of losing friends and a purpose in life. As one former CP member, Bill Bailey, said, "Once you kicked somebody out, you put him on a 'non-association clause,' which meant that you couldn't even talk to him on the phone. I used to sneak around to see them at night. It was a great relief when I did get out of the party and I felt free to see these people."

During the Depression, the romance of Communism, however, remained strong among both idealistic intellectuals and laborers. In New York, the "heartland of American Communism," Jews predominated. During the great garment workers' strike of 1933, the Communists in the locals even cooperated with their sworn rivals, the Socialists who dominated the ILGWU and called out the entire dress trade. "For a Jew to scab was as unthinkable as to become a Christian convert," wrote historian Irving Howe. ". . . Even in the 'outside' neighborhoods where the gentiles lived, radical sentiments were starting to gain a foothold. In 1934, why not?"

Two voices from that era describe the attraction. One was Bailey, an American-Irish seaman, and the other was a woman from a poor Jewish immigrant family who worked for unionism during the halcyon days of the popular front when the party was remodeling itself as a friend to all on the left. A brilliant teacher, she hid her fleeting and unimportant rank-and-file CP past, certain that she would have lost her career during the McCarthy era. In this new century she still does not want her name used. As for many on the left, I. F. Stone's *Weekly* became her bible during the fifties and sixties. Recalling the thirties, she said, "We were so filled with hope. You'd go to a friend's house and they would all share. Years later I ran into a man whom I had known as Ninel. His parents had named him that—*Lenin* spelled backwards. I called out, 'Ninel!' and he glowered and whispered, 'Please, it's *Leonard.*' Everybody wanted to forget."

Bailey met Jewish friends for the first time through the Communist Party. "We used to believe that there was a great republic [in Russia] run by Jews, for Jews. Now we understand it was a goddamn mess. I'd talk to Jews and say, 'It must be paradise.' I had nothing to tell me otherwise." The Jewish teacher agrees; the image of Russia as a haven following czarist oppression made many Stalinist believers out of American Jews. "It was in the constitution! I used to hate selling the *Daily Worker*," she recalls. "People would spit at you or call you a 'dirty Red,' yet I did it." For an intellectual, probing such obedience remains difficult and mystifying. Like many, she now finds it incomprehensible that she didn't question. "People would say it was 'Moscow gold' that was fueling the party. We would shake our heads in firm conviction and say, 'Ohhhh, no.' "

Bailey tried to explain. "Inside, you know something is wrong, but you don't want to admit it because to admit it means that 'I was wrong all the time.' " The 1956 Hungarian revolution was the final end for Bailey. "People have a beef over in Hungary and what do they get? Army tanks and guns and clubs, and that's when I said, 'Screw you, something's wrong.' And that's when I got out."

The common cliché, comparing Communism with religion, contains its truth for Bailey. "To a Communist, 'Stalin said it' was the same as 'God said it' to a Catholic." The son of Irish immigrants, Bailey was born into searing poverty, became a seaman and Communist, fought in the Spanish Civil War, was blacklisted in the fifties. Later exonerated, he was honored by his former union and became the perfect leftist Everyman for moviemakers eager to dramatize that era. Warm and colorful, Bailey was resurrected in such acclaimed documentaries as *The Good Fight* and *Seeing Red.* He played Bruce Dern's pro-union father in an obscure film, *On the Edge,* and had a bit part in Robert De Niro's 1991 movie *Guilty by Suspicion.*

De Niro played a Hollywood director caught up in the HUAC investigation of the movie industry. When Bailey first met De Niro and the film crew, the director asked Bailey to say a few words. "I said, 'The greatest pleasure I get out of this picture is that all the people that done harm to us, McCarthy and all that scum, the pleasure is that the damn bastards are long gone. And we're living and we're in a better position to piss on their graves. And that's a great feeling.' Well, they all thought it was great. And it's the same with Stone, you know. He felt that way."

In the sad days when Bailey was unable to find work, he wrote a letter to I. F. Stone, telling him that his *Weekly* had given Bailey strength. "I just told him what a rare good human being he was. Basically it [the letter] was just appreciative of the fact that he really put out, for all of us, and tried to make the world a better place."

Although they did not know each other, Stone and Bailey shared historic moments, including the day Bailey famously instigated an anti-Nazi incident, tearing down the swastika from a German ship, the *Bremen,* docked in New York. When Bailey was being beaten and jailed for organizing the Marine Workers Industrial Union, Stone was supporting their strikes. His 1936 editorial referred to "shocking testimony" on working conditions—"seamen fainting in temperatures of 150 degrees, served rotten food." Stone cited a damaging government report that had been withheld from the public, detailing abuses that had systematically been ignored by others in the press and by politicians.

Bailey's son became a seaman. "I tell him about the old conditions: rats, eggs on Sunday if you're lucky, an apple maybe once a week. And he says, 'Why did it take you so long?' I said, 'Well, what the hell do you think the thirties strike was all about? Why is it now that you're in a room all by yourself with a television set and intercom and this and that? Because jackasses like me got roughed up trying to get these for you.' " Bailey's story, and how persuasive the Communist Party could be, are potent reminders of how terrible life was for American workers before collective bargaining, which Stone championed so strongly. Sailors lived in vile quarters "too large for a coffin and too small for a grave." Bribery ruled in hiring and firing. As Bailey recalls, "Every day it was something, you had to kick in ten cents or fifteen cents or two bits to some of the rackets they had going. It was a dirty, rotten business."

Bailey's involvement with the Communist Party is similar to that of thousands of Depression victims. Bailey's Irish parents "came over here to pick gold up out of the streets. And it was one hell of a mess. Every time he took his pants off they had a baby. They ended up with thirteen kids and seven of 'em died, fortunately for her and fortunately for the six that lived, and most of the dying was by malnutrition or diseases." After leaving his drunken father, the family scattered. "At fourteen I started hustling the waterfront." His mother hounded an Irishman who lived in the tenement, "a walking boy for some big wheel on the waterfront" who hired Bailey. "I took home $23.52 for six full days, working all the time. We called it 'your head down and your ass up.' That's what the boss wanted to see."

Lying that he was twenty-one, Bailey shipped out on a freighter, only to experience firsthand the conditions Stone wrote about. When the ship anchored in Houston, Bailey recalled, "The first thing I saw was a drinking fountain that said for 'colored only.' And ten feet away there was one for 'whites only.' I thought, 'What the hell's going on?' Then that night I got on a bus and the driver wouldn't let me go in the back where I felt comfortable. I couldn't understand, until somebody put it to me, about what the hell was going on in the South."

Bailey recognized his creeping bitterness when, one day bored at sea, he looked at a copy of the *Industrial Worker*. "A Wobbly starts telling me, 'The working class is *you,* you dumb son of a bitch. The guy who owns this ship is the *capitalist* class.' That left a big impression." Bailey joined the CP and long remembered the closeness of the "rank and file—the greatest part of the left in those days. You're running away from an environment which is 'Screw you, I'm for myself, I don't care if you drop dead,' to an environment were somebody's saying, 'Have you eaten lately? Are you sleeping well? You're a comrade.' At night you'd end up with three or four people, a bowl of stew, and someone to say, 'I'm concerned about you.' " Words that the Bill Baileys of the world had never heard before.

* * *

To counter the emergence of powerful unions, politicians, financiers, and big business exploited the Red Scare. Stone battled them in print and speeches, pointing out that there was nothing illegal about being a member of the Communist Party. If a Communist-led CIO or ILGWU meant a better life, Stone was for it. Meanwhile, union control was the priority of the CP. Only the most fanatical could tolerate their tactics, waiting out nonmembers at meetings until the bored and yawning would leave, then ramming through their slates.

The emergence of the CIO heralded the rise of politically conscious workers committed to overhauling, but not, as the Communists wanted, dismantling the profit system. John L. Lewis would eventually throw the Communists out, but at that time the Communist-fueled CIO made international press with a successful barrage of sit-down strikes against General Motors and U.S. Steel. The CP's goals, however, conflicted with the goals of rank-and-file workers—who desired union protection to get higher wages, shorter hours, and better work conditions far more than proletarian solidarity. Risking their jobs and sometimes their lives on picket lines was "not so much for the sake of revolution as for a fair share of capitalism's rewards." Still, members in the American Communist Party pushed, as Stone said, "a lot of good things." Even the CP's harsh Socialist critics, themselves collapsing through internal squabbles, had to admit that CP members trod a dauntless path in urban streets and a perilous and lonely one in the South, where they attempted biracial organizing.

The CP blundered by calling for a separate black republic; most blacks desired dignity and equality within the system. Also threatening the movement was a general black distrust of any white man's recruitment, plus the sheer terror of lynch mobs at a time when FDR chose expediency over principle. In 1935, the NAACP reported one lynching every six days during a six-week period. Yet an antilynching bill was stalled, with no help from the president, who feared alienating Southern Democrats in Congress.

The CP nonetheless drew respect from many blacks by becoming the only group in America to systematically woo them, particularly by appropriating the legal case of the Scottsboro Boys. For Stone, the Scottsboro case became as much a cause célèbre as Sacco and Vanzetti. (It figured so little in Lippmann's work that it is unmentioned in his biography.) Nine bewildered young blacks were charged with raping two white women on a freight train in 1931. One of the women, Ruby Bates, not only recanted her testimony but spoke at Scottsboro defense rallies. NAACP lawyers ducked defending the youths in their first trial, which was doomed by prejudice; eight were sentenced to die. As appeals dragged on, the CP seized the day, denouncing the NAACP for its failure to conduct a militant campaign.

The CP's International Labor Defense mounted a vigorous defense. The party had a larger agenda than the lives of nine young blacks railroaded to impending death, exploiting them to launch international propaganda against America. U.S. legations, embassies, and consulates were picketed and stoned, mass protests were held in Europe and Latin America. Exposing a hypocritical justice system did not gain all of the boys' freedom. A later compromise resulted in the release of four, but five were imprisoned.

In 1935, middle-of-the-road liberals and politicians of all stripes watched with astonishment, then acceptance, the stunning public about-face of the Communist Party. Socialists were no longer "fascists" and "vermin." FDR was now a man of brilliance. Party members quoted Stone's beloved Jefferson. The Communist Party now seemed content with "unionized" not "radical" workers." This sea change was prompted not by a reversal in Stalin's thinking, but by Hitler's fascist threat to Russia and his vow to eradicate Communism. Still, it allowed the American Communist Party to shed its pariah image. "During the Popular Front, resistance to working with the Party crumbled nearly everywhere on the American Left." Even cautious politicians saw the Communists as useful, "welcome ideologues." Stone was the lone publisher to print an article by former CP leader Browder during the fifties witch hunt that exposed prominent Republican anticommunist politicians who had been strange bedfellows during the thirties popular-front era. No establishment publications would tackle such anticommunist sacred cows in the McCarthy era.

After World War II, Browder openly opposed Stalin's "stupid," sudden, and dangerous shift in policies, which resulted in "one of the first steps toward the Cold War"—a "catastrophe for every nation involved." Expelled from the party in 1945, Browder became a marked man, vilified by Communists and anticommunists alike. Stone commented that it "took a great deal of courage" for Browder to write the article that Stone printed in 1954.

Browder recalled that an ambitious Republican solicited Communist support for his first election campaign in 1937 for New York County district attorney. The Communists obliged through a trade union committee headed by a well-known Communist, Louis Weinstock. At a victory celebration the smiling new district attorney was photographed arm-in-arm with Weinstock. The Republican exposed by Browder in *Stone's Weekly* was none other than an embarrassed Governor Thomas E. Dewey. In his Cold War, 1948 presidential quest, Dewey had attacked opponent Harold Stassen as soft on Communism, pushed to outlaw the Communist party, and slammed Truman as coddling Communists in the administration. In 1954, Stone wrote that Dewey, as a Republican administration strategist, was as "unscrupulous as McCarthy." Browder had no illusions that the earlier 1937 Dewey deal was anything but a "political marriage with no love on either side. . . . Dewey got his office and the Communists got some racketeer enemies cleaned out of the New York Painters and Food Workers unions."

Robert A. Taft, known as the "doggedly uncompromising champion of Republican orthodoxy," was also exposed by Browder in Stone's paper. In 1938, Taft asked to speak at a national meeting of the American Youth Congress (AYC). He was told yes, as long as he didn't mind sharing the platform with Communist Browder. No problem. Browder and Taft were "photographed grinning at each other in a brotherly fashion." What a "far cry" this was from 1950, Browder reflected in the *Weekly*, when Millard Tydings was "defeated for the Senate by a faked photograph ostensibly showing him in my company, a photo manufactured by, so I am told, Mr. Don Surino of Senator McCarthy's staff." By the fifties, the AYC was declared "subversive," and any youthful member back in the thirties, Browder wrote, would have a "long and rough path to a security clearance." The list of HUAC, McCarthy, and FBI Cold War "subversive groups," many of them so named long after they had disbanded, seemed ludicrous; "not even the Communist Party itself" was considered subversive "in the broad circles of public opinion" in the thirties. As late as 1945, Browder was asked, along with senators and professors, to speak on an American Bar Association radio panel.

For many who did not live through that period, it seems unfathomable that McCarthyism could make such past legal memberships so perilous.

During the popular front, less radical leftists now felt safe to join the bandwagon. The American Writers Congress (AWC) was formed and dominated by Communists. One member was Stone's friend Michael

Blankfort, who later became president of the Screenwriters Guild. Party members and fellow travelers controlled the first meeting: Granville Hicks, Richard Wright, Malcolm Cowley, Lincoln Steffens, Browder. The *New Masses,* a successor to the *Masses,* attracted celebrity writers, many of them noncommunists. Circulation jumped from six thousand as a monthly to twenty-four thousand per week, outselling the *New Republic* and within nine thousand of the *Nation's* circulation. Eclipsed by mass-circulation magazines, leftist publications were nonetheless disproportionately influential, defining, shaping, and voicing opinions.

The League of American Writers read like a famous who's who: Thomas Mann, Steinbeck, Hemingway, Dreiser, Farrell, Archibald MacLeish, Lewis Mumford, Lillian Hellman, William Carlos Williams, Nelson Algren, Saroyan, Nathanael West, Clifton Fadiman, even pop psychologist Dale Carnegie. Most did no more than sign an occasional petition. Most were party members or fellow travelers for but a brief time.

Stone was never a League member, but Sam Grafton was briefly. Neither a Communist nor a socialist, Grafton "was sucked into it by a friend. They didn't tell us, until we were safely in, that it was the Moscow branch of an international union of writers. They took anybody," Grafton joked. "If you'd written a *menu* for a restaurant they took you!"

Exciting changes were occurring in American theater. Some of the most awful dramas were agitprop plays. But the radical Group Theatre—termed Grope Theatre at first by unimpressed critics—electrified New York with CP member Clifford Odets's fiercely proletariat play *Waiting for Lefty.* Stone thrilled to the phenomenal success of his old Philadelphia friend, the words transformed from the Leof's living room to the stage, spoken by Luther Adler and Odets himself. Two years later another of Stone's acquaintances, John Garfield, became the luminous boxer in Odets's *Golden Boy* and then a Hollywood star who was hauled before the HUAC in the fifties.

Lefty's audience erupted on opening night. When actors, positioned in the audience, shouted the militant question "Well, what's the answer?" the audience with a spontaneous roar answered, "Strike! Strike!" *Lefty's* message "was the birth cry of the thirties . . . a call to join the good fight." Twenty-eight curtain calls lasted nearly as long as the one-hour play. The audience hurled hats and coats into the air and rushed onto the stage. Within twenty-four hours, unions, antiwar and antifascist student groups, political parties, professional and amateur theater companies, and fraternal orders begged the Group Theatre for permission to produce *Lefty*. Overcome by dollar signs, Broadway even staged the radical play. "More than any play in theater history, *Waiting for Lefty* would be more frequently produced and more frequently banned all over the world—from Union Square to Moscow, from Tokyo to Johannesburg," wrote Odets's biographer Margaret Brenman-Gibson.

When Odets headed a League of American Writers team to investigate labor and social conditions in Cuba under the Mendieta-Batista dictatorship, Stone championed the visit. The *Post* bannered the trip on page one: "Odets Tells Own Story of Cuban Arrest and Deportation!" The playwright and fourteen others, including five women, were seized by Cuban officials. "The whole place bristles with guns. One of the delegation tries to insist on our rights . . . but nobody listens," recounted Odets of those pre-Castro days. "Our baggage is ripped open. All our papers, notes and books are confiscated. . . . The police try to prove that the mechanism of Nathan Shaffer's false leg is a concealed weapon. . . . They insist I must be Russian because of my long hair." In the prison camp, "a captain . . . swings on one of our Negro members." While Odets sat in prison in Cuba, police at home were raiding Newark's Ukrainian Hall. The audience's guilt? Watching a performance of *Waiting for Lefty*. It was the sixth such assault on the play in as many weeks.

In this vibrant time, politics at home still consumed Stone, but his preoccupation with the growing menace of fascism abroad vied for center stage in his thoughts and his writing.

9

HITLER, LIPPMANN, IZZY, AND THE JEWS

Stone was among the first American writers to view Hitler's rise with dismay. "At a very early time, Stone was way ahead of his American contemporaries, knowing exactly what was going on in Germany. He took Hitler seriously, which a lot more people should have done," remarked a German historian, Bernd Greiner, sixty years later. "Had they, maybe history would have ended differently."

As early as 1929, when Stone was merely twenty-one, he recognized a road map for annihilation and world conquest in what others dismissed as the lunatic ravings of *Mein Kampf*. Stone predicted in 1932, "Today or tomorrow the shifty-eyed little Austrian paperhanger, Hitler, may step into the mighty shoes of Bismarck as Chancellor of the Reich." At twenty-four, Stone shaped prophetic editorials for the *Record*, lucidly denouncing the dictator in the spring of 1933: "The danger to Europe and the world is that he may seek a way out in war." Stone's words throughout the 1930s stand in stark contrast to the silence of Lippmann, regarded as America's most influential voice. Lippman's lack of concern, relegating Hitler to "Europe's problem," was thus all the more damaging. Not only his mass of readers, but other journalists and, Lippmann felt, world leaders took their cue from him. His influence was so strong that *Time* magazine cited him as their excuse for a do-nothing policy. Lippmann must have been aghast when the magazine deemed him America's "most statesmanly Jewish pundit."

William Shirer, a wire-service correspondent in Germany at that time, later noted how atypical Stone was. "Our ignorance was inexcusable," he recalled, even after witnessing months of Nazi persecution of Jews. "All of us in the west, our political leaders and our newspapers above all, had underestimated Adolf Hitler and his domination of this

land and its people." Almost two years after Stone's warnings, Shirer concluded that most Germans had easily followed Hitler: "They couldn't
have cared less" about their loss of freedom and other democratic rights.

Stone's editorials railed against Hitler's intensified war on Jews, and the
Record's front pages were filled with news of Hitler's swift repression,
begun as soon as he took office in 1933. Early on, the paper reported terror tactics and raw humiliation: Jewish shop owners were thrust into jeering mobs by storm troopers, their pants gapingly unbuttoned after the
Nazis had checked for telltale signs of circumcision. Nazi pickets pasted
stamps on the foreheads of shoppers leaving Jewish stores: "We traitors
bought from JEWS." Jewish shops were required to display "Juden" signs.
In 1933, huge bonfires seemed to touch the heavens as Nazi storm troopers and hooligans, grinning and stumbling with their arms full, cheered on
by mobs, threw thousands upon thousands of books onto funeral pyres
for education. The books burned were written by Jews and liberals. Einstein's theory of relativity was mocked as a bid for "Jewish world rule." The
"wandering Jew," as the brilliant scientist was called, renounced his German citizenship and would later become a friend of Stone's.

From the first days of the Third Reich, Jewish judges, lawyers, and
clerks were evicted from the courts. Professors were thrown out of universities as Hitler instituted "science and race" classes. While many German Jews were still rationalizing that such a madman could not last,
public acts of anti-Semitism were everywhere. On July 20, 1933, three
hundred Jewish shopkeepers in Nuremberg were paraded through the
city to the jeers of laughing crowds as storm troopers kicked the slow-
moving elderly or yanked their beards. That same day, mobs in Stuttgart
cursed and spit on four hundred men, women, and children who were
forced to lick the dirty pavement and to pull up grass with their hands.

Germans who after the war professed to know "nothing about such
Nazi activities" were exposed decades later as holocaust scholars cited
frantic memos sent to the State Department and the White House from
envoys in Germany in the 1930s. Arthur D. Morse in his towering chronicle of apathy, *While Six Million Died*, cited instance after instance to
prove that "from the advent of the Hitler onslaught, the actions taken
against the Jews were carried out with the full knowledge of the German
public." Entire communities competed with one another to post signs at
town limits boasting that they were *Judenfrei*.

In July 1934, a *New York Post* editorial reflected the historical depth,
passion, and prescience that Stone displayed so young. "Peace Hangs

Upon a Thread" claimed the bold-faced editorial. "Unless Germany is faced, at once, with an array of hostile Powers so overwhelming as to make opposition hopeless, Austria and world peace are lost. To hesitate, to split hairs, as Great Britain did during the Austrian crisis ... is not to safeguard peace, but to insure war by encouraging Nazi aggression."

When correspondents during the early thirties did report the daily acceleration of Hitler's attacks on Communists and Socialists, the Catholic Church and Jews, newspapers often buried their stories in snippets back with the advertisements. In sheer volume, the *New York Times* had the most complete coverage, but readers had to search to find the articles, including one in April 1932 mentioning the building of a concentration camp at Dachau. Witnesses noted that four thousand new inmates were being sent to join the five hundred working inside the prison with its high voltage wire fences and rifle-bearing guards. Unlike many urban publications, small Midwestern newspapers, appealing to conscious-stricken socialist readers, protested that Germany was no longer a part of the civilized world.

Had Lippmann done the same, he might have swayed public opinion and possibly stirred FDR into action, although the latter is debatable. Well-informed through internal State Department memos both before and during the worst of the holocaust, Roosevelt himself remained scandalously silent. Nevertheless, Lippmann's public abandonment of the Jews lasted for five amazing years. In 1938, he broke his half-decade silence only to recommend that Europe's "overpopulation" problem (he did not mention Jews) could be solved by shipping the Jews to Africa. Lippmann "showed a surprising insensitivity to the human dimension of the Nazi threat, especially as it concerned the Jews," wrote his biographer Ronald Steel. Like many journalists, Lippmann touted an early cynical speech of "peace" by Hitler, but Lippmann went further, praising Hitler as "statesmanlike" and the "authentic voice of a genuinely civilized people."

Like Stone, Shirer shared none of Lippmann's sentiments but felt handcuffed by the "neutrality" of wire-service reporting. Hitler's "peace" proposals were, confided Shirer to his diary, "pure fraud." He added, "And if I had any guts, or American journalism had any, I would have said so in my dispatch tonight. But I am not supposed to be 'editorial.'" The reporter's stock refuge and subterfuge—quoting an official who said what the reporter felt—was impossible in Nazi Germany, therefore such views went unvoiced.

Lippmann dug a deeper hole by including a Jewish slur as he wrote that one could not judge an entire body of people by the actions of some: "Would it be fair to judge the French by The Terror, Protestantism by the Ku Klux Klan, the Catholic Church by the Inquisition," or "the Jews by their parvenus?" Not only did this sound like an excuse for Hitler's anti-Semitism, it smeared Jews with a condemnatory cliché: their rich were vulgarians—as if there were no such analogous WASPs. (Lippmann, obviously embarrassed, did not include the column in a collection of his pieces published two years later.) His columns caused Felix Frankfurter, the New Dealer who became a Supreme Court judge, to dissolve their friendship.

No wonder Stone as chief editor of the *Philadelphia Record* sanctioned this caveat above Lippmann's column: "EDITOR'S NOTE:—Walter Lippmann's articles are published by The Record because Mr. Lippmann is one of America's foremost *publicists* [italics mine; a trivializing description that must have stung Lippmann]. The opinions he expresses are strictly his own. They often disagree with the editorial policies of this newspaper."

The day an insensitive Lippmann column ran in 1933, the *Record* was filled with stories of Hitler's inhumanity to Jews. A month before Lippmann's praise of Hitler's false cry for peace, actions should have left little doubt of Hitler's intentions. Berlin mobs and police arrested Jews as they left synagogues. On April 1, a large photo on the front page of the *Record*'s second section showed four storm troopers boycotting a branch of an American chain store. Resplendent in swastika armbands, brown shirts, and puttees, legs apart, mouths agape as they sang Nazi songs, the quartet still looked like thugs; Hitler had elevated Germany's scum by giving them uniforms and weapons. The last of a six-part series was headlined "Germany's Future Dark as Dictator Strives to Crush All Opposition." Most American newspapers wrote about this boycott, but the *Record* bannered it on page one, reporting that Jews had no place to run as all passports were being withdrawn. Yet one correspondent blithely wrote, "Freed of the one-day anti-Jewish boycott, business appeared to be going on in Berlin as usual."

The State Department had already caved. The American Jewish Congress had staged a large protest meeting in Madison Square Garden but was pushed into silence the day after the boycott. "In deference to the wishes of the State Department," read a cursory statement, the American Jewish Congress "announced today that it refrains at this time from making comment upon the tragic situation of the Jews in Germany." No explanation was given, reported Stone's paper.

While many had underestimated the plight of European Jews, Lippmann's dismissal remained reprehensible. As late as 1939, he wrote nothing about Jews who were refused asylum on a refugee ship. In 1942, when the death camps were known and some newspapers printed graphic descriptions, Lippmann wrote nothing. When others criticized the State Department for repressing knowledge of Hitler's extermination plans, Lippmann wrote nothing. By contrast, Stone was frantically and vainly urging—along with ordinary citizens, a handful of other concerned writers, and religious groups from synagogues to Quaker meeting halls—that Congress and President Roosevelt relax U.S. immigration policies to admit more European Jewish refugees. Lippmann argued against changing the quota, a prevailing sentiment in Depression-weary America, where the unemployed feared foreign competition.

While Lippmann's columns do not stand the test of time, Izzy's work was singled out for praise by holocaust historians more than half a century later. "The dispassion, if not indifference, of most of the press becomes all the more noteworthy when it is compared to the behavior of publications such as the *New York Post, The Nation, The New Republic, Commonweal* and *PM,*" wrote Deborah Lipstadt. "I. F. Stone, Dorothy Thompson, William Shirer, Arthur Koestler, Max Lerner, Freda Kirchwey and a few others . . . had no more information than the rest of their colleagues. In fact, some of them depended on reports in other major dailies for their information. . . . The real difference between these publications and the vast majority of the rest of the press is not between belief and disbelief, but between action and inaction, passion and equanimity." They were convinced that the Allies could do something if they would stop behaving as if "the Jews were expendable."

Stone himself ran into sentiments from American Jews not dissimilar to Lippmann's. "I remember one German-Jewish reader coming to me, about '31 or '32," Izzy recalled to Patner. "He said, 'Why are you writing these editorials against Hitler? He's only against *Ostjuden*'" (Eastern Jews). (As a class, German Jews sneered at Eastern Jews and, at that time, felt spared from Hitler's persecution.)

The comparison between Lippmann and Stone reveals a fascinating schism among Jews in the thirties, when overt anti-Semitism ruled the world of politics and business, journalism and judgeships, universities and executive boards. Even Stone's revered FDR, while appointing Jews to prominent positions, was not above private anti-Semitism. He once infuriated *New York Times* publisher Sulzberger by labeling some business deal a "dirty Jewish trick."

Lippmann and Stone were Jews from opposite sides of the ghetto. Lippmann's childhood was lined with gold, his parents were second generation, of German stock. He brought expensive suits to Harvard by the trunkful. Assimilation was a goal for upper-class Jews such as Lippmann, who were generally taught from birth to disparage the masses of Yiddish-speaking Russian and Polish Jews, the world from which Izzy sprang.

Everything about them was a study in contrast: Lippmann cultivated a disinterested, elevated, and cool style. Stone was red-hot, passionate, and spoke for the masses. If Stone erred on the side of ideological fervor, Lippmann was flawed by an absence of it. Lippmann was a celebrity journalist early in life; Stone's glory came late in life. Friends never shortened *Walter,* and no stranger had a nickname for Lippmann. Hordes of strangers called Stone *Izzy.* Stone felt that being an outsider was the only way to cover politics, that governments needed constant watching. Lippmann reveled in being an insider, dealing with kings and presidents, financiers and titans. His columns at times scorned the idea that democracy should be left to the vote of the inferior average citizen, and at one stage, Lippmann put his faith in Wall Street to handle government.

As early as 1916 Lippmann had perfected his views that the Jews brought much of their troubles on themselves. Noted Steel, "He criticized the Jews for being 'different' rather than the Gentiles for emphasizing and punishing those differences." Such thoughts were anathema to Stone. Despite his name change, he proudly identified himself as a Jew to clarify his position on a subject. Stone empathized with European Jews and wrote passionately about their homeland in Palestine (only later to be excoriated by fellow Jews for criticizing Israeli treatment of the Palestinians.) Lippmann ignored them.

To the very end, Lippmann sought to hide his Jewishness. When a childhood friend, Carl Binger, was asked to write a biography of Lippmann for a book of essays honoring his seventieth birthday, Binger faced a quandary. He "could not say that Walter was Jewish. Otherwise Walter would never forgive him, and would never speak to him again," author David Halberstam reported. Binger snuck in the suggestion of Lippmann's heritage by mentioning that Lippmann had attended Dr. Sachs's School for Boys, where wealthy Jewish families sent their sons.

Lippmann was far from alone among the journalistic elite in his effort to hide Jewish roots. The head of CBS, Bill Paley, edgy about his Russian-Jewish heritage, associated with ultra-WASPs and feared being tagged as a Jew, which he was by Washington's F Street Club, the WASP gentlemen's club that blackballed him. He turned down a chance to back *Fiddler on the Roof* with the comment, "It's good, but don't you think it's too Jewish?" The Jewish owners of the *New York Times* held to an unspoken code denying Jews high-level positions. (In later years, the *Times* was said to be owned by Jews, edited by Catholics, and read by Protestants.) Arthur Hays Sulzberger married Adolph Ochs's daughter Iphigene, and in the midthirties became editor of the *Times*. His influential wife and her family were "determined that the paper not seem too Jewish," wrote Halberstam. In 1937, Sulzberger flatly asserted, "In all the years I've been here we have never put a Jew in the showcase." Washington Bureau chief Arthur Krock hid his own Jewishness and refused to have Jewish reporters in his bureau. In 1939, Sulzberger was among Jewish leaders who urged Franklin Roosevelt not to appoint Frankfurter to the Supreme Court for fear that it might increase anti-Semitism. As late as 1952, Cy Sulzberger, nephew of Arthur Sulzberger, told Daniel Shorr, then a stringer in Europe, he wouldn't staff him because "we have too many Jews in Europe," wrote Harrison Salisbury. It was worse on the *New York Herald Tribune,* the guardian of mainstream Republicanism. The presence or advancement of Jews was "not encouraged," wrote author Richard Kluger. They were stereotypically viewed as too crude, radical, or pushy. Lippmann was the sort of Jew with whom WASP publishers felt comfortable: a Harvard man who favored Jewish quotas for admissions to his alma mater.*

Given this atmosphere, few major papers were sensitized to the problems of Jews either at home or abroad. The *Herald Tribune*'s edict on European coverage was the most reprehensible. Paris correspondents were told to write lavishly about Europe's glamour in order to induce American tourism, which would boost the European edition's circulation. The *Tribune* slashed news coverage at a vital time; it had no correspondent

---

*Far into the second half of the last century, discrimination was still so openly practiced in the media against African-Americans and women that such unspoken but unequal hiring policies would not be challenged or changed until the late 1960s, and a glass-ceiling concept remains into the twenty-first century in many corporate media offices. The push for women's and African-Americans' equality came some time after males with Jewish names had gained relative access, especially on metropolitan publications.

on the scene when Nazi Germany seized Austria, for example. The paper appeased fascist regimes, wrote historian Richard Kluger, "all because its owners were unwilling to deprive themselves of personal luxury or seek adequate outside financing." The *Tribune's* excuse was "We cannot take the definite risk of antagonizing other nations or in frightening tourists by presuming to tell the former the faults of their regime or the latter by explaining to them, through our columns, the dangers of an immediate armed conflict over here."

The proud Jew I. F. Stone would not have been hired by or survived on such newspapers. His blessing was to connect with J. David Stern, one of the few prominent Jewish publishers who never hid his Jewishness or his concern for social causes, even though he urged his writers to alter their Jewish names.

Like Lippmann, Stone did join the conventional chorus of those who blamed Hitler's rise on the combination of Germany's Depression woes and the post–World War I Versailles Treaty, which demanded, Stone wrote, "insane amounts as reparations."

Wrote Stone in the early thirties, "Germany was . . . deprived of one-tenth of her area and her population, cut in twain by the Polish Corridor and crippled industrially by the loss of 30 percent of her coal and 75 percent of her iron." Undermining the German republic "brought into being a noisy windbag irresponsibly waving a sword." Other dictators, including Turkey's Kemal, Italy's Mussolini, and Russia's Stalin, "have been men of character and purpose," wrote Stone, blindly ignoring their brutal methods on the way to what they described as socialism.

Stone accurately predicted that Hitler would promise anything to become chancellor—"but Hitler's promises are not worth much. . . . The presence of Hitler at the head of the Government" would lead to "bloody civil war and class struggle." Like everyone else, Stone was wrong in underestimating the ease with which Hitler inspired a nation into roars of *"Sieg Heil!"* and Heil Hitler salutes. Years later, he commented, "There was never any revolt of the German proletariat, as there had been in 1918."

In January of 1933, a *Record* lead editorial headline bemoaned "the twilight of Capitalism and Democracy in Germany." Hitler, the "shifty-eyed loud mouthed demagogue with a Chaplin mustache," leader of a "Central European Ku Klux Klan," was named chancellor by President von Hindenburg. A month later, the famed burning of the Reichstag, the German parliament building, turned Hitler into an overnight hero.

He claimed that the assault was masterminded by Communists, although historians generally accept that the Nazis had planned the arson to garner sympathy. Hitler instituted a war on terror, abrogating such constitutional protections as free speech, a free press, the right of assembly, and protection against unlawful searches and seizures. He also put in place the Storm Troops (SA) and Special Security (SS) federal police agencies. With such ruthless suppression the Nazis routed opposition in the upcoming election. On March 5, 1933, the Nazis received a 44 percent plurality in the Reichstag.

Neither the United States or other free countries had the foresight to back Hitler's opposition. Moreover, Britain's Prime Minister Neville Chamberlain vowed that allowing Hitler's preemptive strikes would assure "peace in our time." When he invaded Austria, Hitler said that the Germans came "not as tyrants . . . but liberators," as Austrians cheered mightily. All internal dissent was suppressed in the name of national security. Hitler flailed his arms and hysterically shouted in speech after speech that the *Juden* must go. Hundreds of thousands of men, women, and children roared back their approval. Archival footage at the Holocaust Memorial and a half century of collected evidence give the lie to common postwar statements that Germans did not know Hitler's intent at the beginning.

Diverting their attention by persecuting the Jews was the way to "keep his followers together" while "baiting the Jew," said Stone. He wrote about this tactic with passionate outrage, not Lippmann's callousness. Wrote Lippmann, "the persecution of the Jews" acted as a " kind of lightning rod *which protects Europe*" (emphasis added).

While Stone dissented from America's majority stance of isolationism, denial, disinterest, and, for some, support for Hitler, Lippmann "would not go against the powerful tide of American isolationism." He wrote in 1933, "As long as Europe prepares for war, America must prepare for neutrality." A stable Europe was vital, but Lippmann refused to support any commitments to sustain it, wrote Steel. "Despite his low esteem for the public's wisdom, he was no less confused than the average man."

At that early stage, hope vied with pessimism as Stone optimistically argued that reality would set in when Germans understood that boycotting Jewish business would result in vast losses to German banking and would disrupt profitable trading between gentiles and Jews. But Stone was applying rationality to an irrational regime.

* * *

One 1935 act of defiance by American seamen became an international incident that was wrongly interpreted by the nation's press. This New York act was simply a fortuitous excuse for Hitler's planned and lethal crackdown on Jews with his 1935 Nuremberg laws, which officially deprived German Jews of their citizenship, and, within months, their lives. But the nation's press depicted the New York incident as touching off Hitler's actions. Angered at seeing the Nazi swastika waving from a German ship docked in New York's harbor, six American seamen boarded the *Bremen* and ripped it down. In an America conditioned to hate Bolsheviks more than Hitler, "Reds" attacking the swastika was a provocative headline. The *New York Times* gave the nod to Hitler: "BERLIN IS ANGERED BY SHIP RIOT HERE." The first line began, "The Communist raid on the liner Bremen early yesterday quickly became an international incident."

Louis Brodsky, the New York magistrate, released the men with an enlightened comment (there was no evidence that they had done it). A "pirate" flag such as the swastika was seen by many "of our citizenry as a gratuitously brazen flaunting of an emblem which symbolizes all that is antithetical to American ideals." Stone's *Post* initially joined the chorus in calling the act "deplorable"—which must have been penned by Stone's anticommunist boss. Stone protested that German outrages overshadowed the trashing of the swastika. A far more "deplorable" act by the Nazis precipitated the *Bremen* folly, he wrote: "Nazi secret police took an American seaman, Lawrence Simpson, from the *Manhattan* in the harbor of Hamburg and jailed him without trial and without bail on charges of 'conspiracy.'" Bold type followed: **Simpson is still in jail and his seizure led American seamen to protest by pulling down the swastika from the Bremen.**

That the swastika fracas could overshadow the sweeping terrorism of the Nuremberg laws shows appalling news judgment. The laws were a fait accompli three months before the July *Bremen* affair. On April 28, 1935, the Nazis had publicly announced that all German Jews would be deprived of their citizenship. Stone and the *New York Post* had it right. Hitler's anger regarding the *Bremen* was "more feigned than real," they noted, adding, "The Nazis undoubtedly will attempt to make capital out of the incident to justify further persecutions at home."

The Nuremberg laws sealed the Jews' fate and made terrorism legal. Jews could no longer work in the government or "Aryan" businesses, serve in the army, vote, or—no great loss—fly the German swastika. They could not marry or engage in sexual relationships with "Aryans." There would be no escape; borders were closed to such noncitizens. Either fearing or supporting the Nazis, Germans averted their gaze and shut out the screams of neighbors carted off. For the Jews it was slow strangulation. Children watched as parents sold off family heirlooms for food. No longer allowed in schools, they huddled with parents, trembling that the storm troopers might arrive. The United States' meek and apologetic response to the *Bremen* incident merely gave Hitler a green light.

Stone's drumbeat continued. He quoted from Gibbon on the Roman emperor Commodus as he assailed Hitler's "mad charges that the Catholic Church is linked with 'Communists' in a plot against the regime." He attacked Mussollini's crushing of Ethiopia "by use of poison gas," which was in "violation of international agreements." He indicted the weak League of Nations and warned that Ethiopia's fate could be repeated "tomorrow" in Europe. "Fascists have made the discovery that poison gas, bullets and torture chambers are more than human flesh can bear." He cited his favorite villain. "The Torquemadas who used it before learned what their modern imitators will also learn," Stone wrote with hope, "what human flesh cannot bear the human spirit can survive." Then his fears returned: "Every week brings evidence . . . that a dangerously large section of the population of the United States is fertile seed for Fascism."

Deborah Lipstadt's *Beyond Belief,* published in 1986, is harsher on the press than Morse's *While Six Million Died,* written eighteen years before. Morse claims that readers in the United States could have been more enlightened had they read more carefully. Both authors make excellent cases. Major events such as the Nuremberg laws, the 1936 Berlin Olympics, the Anschluss, and the *Kristallnacht* pogrom were often well reported, but consistent coverage of Hitler's daily anti-Jewish blitz was sparse. In addition, analysis in periodicals often contained tortured reasoning to explain Hitler's barbaric treatment of Jews, everything from the view that Hitler was helpless to control "ad hoc" ruffians to the theory that the Jews had brought much of this upon themselves. Few questioned the inherent anti-Semitism of Hitler's mad design, which he had announced as early as 1920.

Right-wing revisionists and twenty-first-century authors and media are still trying to psychoanalyze Hitler, humanizing a demon by hypothesizing and searching for childhood explanations for acts that remain in-

explicable. This infuriates holocaust researchers such as Frenchman
Claude Lanzmann, who compiled the searing documentary on Nazism
Shoah. Any psychobabble attempt to explain Hitler, said Lanzmann, "is
an obscenity." One such contribution is a documentary shown in the
United States in 2003 and 2004, antiseptically titled *Blind Spot: Hitler's
Secretary.* Although Traudl Junge began working for Hitler in 1942 and
was in his bunker until the end, the film allowed her to peddle the ancient, repellent defense that she knew nothing about the concentration
camps.

Lipstadt observed the disingenuousness surrounding the claims of
reporters and editors that they had also been unknowing until the camps
were open: "Why their protestations of ignorance? . . . Why did most of
the press react so dispassionately?"

One exception among conservative publishers was William Randolph
Hearst. Some observers felt that Hearst's strong stand on rescuing Jews
and his outspoken support of a Jewish homeland in Palestine were motivated by his loathing for the British. Whatever the reason, Hearst's response was in sharp contrast to that of other mass publications. "Many
government officials, members of the press, and leaders of other religions
behaved as if Jewish lives were a cheap commodity," stated Lipstadt.

Although recent books further document the U.S. government's early
internal knowledge of Hitler's final solution, *While Six Million Died,*
published twenty years after the war, remains the premier shattering indictment of the State Department and the White House. Through classified documents it details years of stalling by the government, despite
urgent and precise memos sped to Washington from European consulates from the beginning of Hitler's reign. It presents the government's
complicity in withholding information and relates the decision not to
bomb railroads leading into concentration camps, which might have
saved countless victims. "Democracy in Germany has received a blow
from which it may never recover," informed the U.S. ambassador to Germany, Frederick Sackett, on March 9, 1933. American diplomats
throughout Germany dashed off dire observations as they watched the
swift obliteration of German Jews. By July 8, 1933, just months after
Hitler gained power, "consistently and relentlessly the Jews are being
eliminated from practically all walks of life."

Stone and the *Post* reported what official Washington ignored: In
1935, a strong leftist contingent, among them Socialists and trade union-
ists, packed Madison Square Garden with more than thirty thousand de-

manding that the United States protest Nazi persecutions. Groups representing millions of Americans favored boycotting the 1936 Olympics. Lifting the immigration quotas for Jews, while not popular in polls, was championed by the critically influential. Yet Roosevelt and the State Department remained silent. Reports of persecution were exaggerated, stated Secretary Hull. The official line was silence. Interference, went the excuse, would only exacerbate the problem.

Thus, Morse wrote in *While Six Million Died,* "the greatest mass murder in history" was set in motion while the United States acquiesced. This sentence was written in 1967—long after Stalin's murderous regime was known and in the midst of America's benighted war in Vietnam—but it was before full exposure of Mao's Cultural Revolution. Yet to come were Cambodia's rotting killing fields, massacres in Bosnia and Rwanda, terrorist assaults on America, the Iraq war, Darfur. Despite the millions upon millions slaughtered since then, Hitler's mass killings remain so dreadful in part because of the sheer technological precision masterminded for wholesale genocide: the massive crematorium readied for Auschwitz by the end of 1942 that refined the process, the amethyst blue crystals of hydrogen cyanide pellets tossed into the "shower room" while naked men, women, and children fought for breath before the convulsions of suffocation. The efficiency of Germany's engineers still chills; Auschwitz greatly raised the murder rate from the ninety who could be packed in at one time for asphyxiation in the first mobile gas vans used in Poland in 1939. Gone were such lapses as diesel-fuel failures, when it took more than an hour to kill.

Meanwhile, overseas journalists fought specific problems. Authors of articles injurious to the Reich met with a swift ouster from Germany. Yet the best reporters, such as Frederick T. Birchall, warned in the *New York Times* that the Aryan principles "most warmly defended by the Germans" would lead "even to extermination—the word is the Nazis' own—of the non-Aryans, if it can be established without too much world disturbance." Despite the *New York Herald*'s edict to report the light and fluffy, Hitler's horrors were revealed by some courageous reporters who reported in the New York edition that Hitler was "seeking to rid the world of Jews." While condemnatory at times, the *New York Times* editorials, unlike those written by Stone, settled for the ad-hoc-ruffian theory, despite evidence of overwhelming governmental orchestration. When American Jews protested that "it is inconceivable that the American government should stand passively by at these violations of human rights," the State Department responded with polite murmurs of sympathy.

Following the Nuremberg laws, nothing jarred so deeply a divided citizenry than the upcoming 1936 Nazi Olympics. There were fierce anti-Olympic boycotts and protests in America, but American and International Olympic Committee head Avery Brundage and his aide, Brigadier General Charles H. Sherrill, refused all pleas. One poll of sportswriters found them almost evenly divided about whether the team should go. A strong opponent was Shirley Povich of the *Washington Post.* Years later, the uncompromising prize-winning columnist fumed at the age of eighty-eight with clarity and moral fervor, collectively referring to Brundage and Sherrill as "those sons of bitches" who ignored the protests to boycott.

Stone's editorials noted that the American Federation of Labor's stand against taking part in the Olympics was "only one more sign of a sentiment which has been visibly growing in this country." He pushed leaders to arouse opposition in other countries; it was vital "to send a signal to Germany and Hitler that they can't get away with it." The U.S. participation in the 1936 Nazi Olympics, with its worldwide coverage, was a huge coup for Hitler and bolstered his belief that he could further pursue his policies.

There was some retribution when the great black sprinter Jesse Owens won four gold medals. Hitler screamed at being photographed with Owens and refused to see him. Said one *New York Post* editorial, "We like to think of that moment: Hitler, his racial dogma made ridiculous by the performances on the track before him, scurrying under the stands to get away from the truth, while Jesse Owens, a great Negro, walked in the sun before a cheering German crowd." Caught in the euphoria, the editorial visualized a hopeful but incorrect ending for Europe: "Every tape broken by Owens is an answer to Hitler that the burning of a thousand books cannot wipe out."

The Olympics brought to Germany prominent American businessmen—among them newspaper publishers who left even less enlightened than when they'd arrived. They saw a Potemkin village of Hitler's making: anti-Jewish signs removed from highways and cities, spit-and-polish cleanliness on the streets and heel-clicking obeisance at lavish parties. Shirer wrote caustically, "All Jew baiting is officially off in Germany during the Olympics." He arranged a luncheon for America's junketeers to meet the U.S. commercial attaché, one of the best-informed men on

Germany. A frustrated Shirer watched as "the genial tycoons told *him* what the situation in Nazi Germany was"—a land of no strikes, no troubling unions, no agitators, no Communists.

Aviation hero Charles Lindbergh was the prime ward of Hermann Göring, the rotund chief of the German air force. At one lavish Olympic party, Lindbergh, who had been avoiding the media, walked near the press table. Shirer hoped to enlighten him, but Lindbergh expressed his admiration for the Nazis. On October 18, 1938, Lindbergh accepted Hitler's Service Cross of the German Eagle with Star, the highest German decoration that could be conferred on a foreigner. Lindbergh's insensitivity and ignorance seemed boundless. Less than a month after Lindbergh's crowning, on November 9, 1938, the worst German pogrom that the Jews had experienced up to that time, *Kristallnacht,* the Night of the Broken Glass, signaled Hitler's triumph. Lindbergh remained a German ally. Even as front-page stories reported the mass roundup of fifty thousand Jews, Lindbergh and his family were house hunting for a winter's stay in Berlin, made easier, a wire-service report observed, by "the recent abandonment of many Jewish homes."

In July 1939, world leaders frolicked at Évian-les-Bains as they discussed the "Jewish problem." Australians said, "As we have no real racial problems, we are not desirous of importing one." The French were noncommittal. The United States, battered by the deepening Depression since 1937, was hostile to changes in asylum quotas. And Lippmann favored the suggestion of sending Jews to Africa. Many editorials railed against aiding the refugees. Meanwhile Stone was frantically speaking at benefits for refugees, writing editorials and magazine articles, fighting to change America's immigration policy. In 1937, he had described the anti-Semitism "virus" that "sets Frenchman against Frenchman, Englishman against Englishman, American against American.... There is, second, the bogey of communism. Fascism frightens dominant classes in the democracies with the hobgoblin, then offers them protection—at a price."

The Anschluss, annexing of Austria, meant death for Austria's two hundred thousand Jews. It was the end of a career for many European correspondents and the exposing of others. Shirer recalled how his former assistant in Vienna, Emil Maass, "swaggered" into a café filled with reporters. " 'Well, *meine Damen und Herren,*' he smirked, 'it was about time.' He turned over his coat lapel, unpinned his hidden swastika party button and ostentatiously pinned it on the outside over the buttonhole." An even chillier defection was that of Bob Best of the United Press wire service, whose articles had filled many American newspapers, including Stern's. He then joined Hitler's forces to broadcast over the Nazi airwaves. Shirer's personal indignation rose when an editor, thinking only of dollar signs, asked him to get Hermann Göring to write a column.

For concerned writers like Stone, the continuing train wreck of Nazism was agony. He wrote stinging columns about Roosevelt's inaction and pointed out that a cowardly State Department had done nothing when other countries were taking in refugees. The international press was finally startled by *Kristallnacht,* and close to one thousand condemnatory editorials were written in the next few weeks. Still, isolationism and anti-Semitism skewed the reporting. "Numerous papers dismissed the idea that the Nazis were motivated by racial hatred." Not Stone. "Germany's Moral Leprosy" was the editorial headline following *Kristallnacht.* "The annals of the Third Reich contain nothing quite so wanton, brutal and cowardly as the mass onslaught on her Jewish and partly Jewish citizens. . . . Its purpose is criminal on a huge scale." The editorial warned that Jews "are to be shut up in ghettos, with no release but death." FDR was attacked for his inaction. "Not to speak is to acquiesce; to acquiesce is to accept as natural the horrible inhumanity of the Nazi regime." Even then, in 1938, the British Foreign Office confirmed daily deaths at Buchenwald. Families had to pay three marks to get the ashes of relatives who had been killed. FDR finally spoke of his "shock," ordering the ambassador to Germany back for "consultation," but shunned permitting more refugees into the United States. And, as I. F. Stone wrote, U.S. companies continued their relations with the Third Reich.

Studies in the twenty-first century that demonstrated that "the rise of National Socialism was underwritten and materially supported—both before and during World War II—by U.S.-based multinationals, as well as Morgan, Chase, Rockefeller, and Warburg banking interests," were greeted as news. Stone was exposing this at the time.

As the thirties moved toward a horrible end, one incident captured all that was terrible about worldwide vacillation. On May 13, 1939, the *St. Louis* set sail from Hamburg to Cuba. On it were 930 Jews, among the last hoping to escape Hitler's gas chambers. Their journey was legal; they had paid and had quota numbers that would permit them to enter the United States. Suddenly, the Cuban president invalidated their landing certificates. During a week of frantic negotiations, they drifted off the shore of Cuba, then were forced to set sail back to Germany. Panicky passengers viewed the fading faces of families who had waited for days at the dock. After a former concentration camp inmate slashed his wrists, passengers formed suicide patrols. Children played a game with deck chairs as barriers. As each one came to the "guard," seeking entrance, they were asked, "Are you a Jew?" When they replied yes, the guard shouted, *"Jews not admitted!"* The response was "Oh, please, let me in. I'm only a very little Jew."

Hardened newspapermen in nearby launches wept openly as these doomed souls lined the rails pleading for mercy. While the *St. Louis* hovered off Miami's coast, desperate American Jewish leaders offered money to Cuba's President Bru to relent. Night after drifting night, lights onshore beckoned to those imprisoned on the saddest ship at sea. President Roosevelt, the State Department, and Congress did nothing. Passengers wrote to Roosevelt pleading that four hundred of them were women and children. There was no reply.

Many factors played into this policy, which "cries to high heaven of man's inhumanity to man," a 1939 *New York Times* editorial stated. Entrenched anti-Semites in the State Department and Congress were receptive to Americans who wanted no softening of immigration barriers. America firsters, pro-Nazis, and a majority of Americans clamored for neutrality. Rather than antagonize them or, more shamefully, Hitler, Roosevelt chose to expend the Jews.

Countless newspapers denounced the *St. Louis* episode, but many blamed Germany and Cuba, not the United States. It would be hard to find a more callous editorial than that of the *Christian Science Monitor,* which charged that ingrate Jewish refugees "apparently have no taste for the pioneering necessary" to embrace suggestions to unload them in "uncivilized" and "unexplored" places somewhere in Africa. Finally, Britain, Belgium, Holland, and France took the refugees. Except for those who went to Britain, freedom was short-lived. Emboldened by such lack of intervention, Hitler soon invaded Belgium, Holland, and France. Many from the *St. Louis* died in gas chambers.

Stone anxiously watched the unfolding nightmare. He was also consumed with yet another high-stakes battle that was a dangerous dress rehearsal for a second world war.

10

"My Heart Is with the Spanish Loyalists"

A watershed tragedy for Stone was the Spanish Civil War. Years later, Stone's earnest reminiscences captured his obsession with halting global carnage. "A *war* was coming—and Spain was the preview of it. Without the popular front, Spain would have gone under much earlier," he told Gitlin.

While many Americans remained impervious to the agony played out daily on Spanish soil, it fostered ardent partisan battles, the kind that would not be replayed again until the incendiary days of the Vietnam War. For American leftists Spain's Civil War finally meant unified allegiance. This was a black-and-white duel; fascism had to be halted by supporting the officially elected Republic, also known as Loyalists. Stone eagerly joined those who felt this was a frantic last stand to stop Hitler. The Catholic Church and other Americans on the right, including most newspaper publishers, felt that Communism, not fascism, was the scourge that had to be stopped by supporting Franco's Nationalists.

In this war of lies and deceit, Loyalists were doomed on an unfair field. Franco's powerful allies, Hitler and Mussolini, scorned a noninterventionist pact and provided him with planes, guns, and troops. Britain, France, and the United States refused to condemn Germany and Italy or to intercede on the side of the legally elected Loyalists. For sheer drama and impassioned allegiances, this war had it all. Journalists took up sides, either censoring or manufacturing "news" to suit their publishers or themselves. A battalion of famous and talented writers covered the war, which heightened international interest. Among them were André Malraux, Stephen Spender, Arthur Koestler, Antoine de Saint-Exupéry, George Orwell, and Ernest Hemingway. They saw no conflict in reporting the war and participating in it, mostly on the side of the Loyalists (Hemingway, the Republic's ambulance driver; Malraux, who trained pilots and flew for its air force). British and Irish intellectuals like W. H. Auden, Rebecca West, Aldous Huxley, and Sean O'Casey paraded their support.

Hemingway's ostensibly factual reporting was fiction at its worst. Relying on a Soviet correspondent, Hemingway boasted that the Russian-backed Republicans had a good chance of winning. Six months later, the Republic was soundly defeated. Crucial among Hemingway's shortcomings as a war correspondent, wrote Phillip Knightley, in *The First Casualty*, was his "total failure to report the Communist persecution, imprisonment, and summary execution of 'untrustworthy elements' on the Loyalist side, when he knew this was happening and when disclosing it might well have prevented further horrors."

Stone was among the many leftists guilty of ignoring truths written by a disillusioned George Orwell, who detailed such Communist perfidy. "We didn't want to listen to the message that Orwell brought back," Stone recalled many years later. "It was just too terrible, what was going on, particularly the last days of the Spanish Republic. So there was a terrible conflict."

The fierce divisions on the left included a kaleidoscope of political parties. Prominent was the POUM (Party of Marxist Unification). The Communists stood for centralized power and, at least for the moment, propping up the Republic, while the POUM sought universal revolt by workers. Orwell noted the irony: "The [conservative and anticommunist] *Daily Mail* with its tales of red revolution financed by Moscow was even more wildly wrong than usual." Among these leftist factions supporting the liberal government, "the Communist party stood on the extreme right."

Many leftist journalists felt that the POUM was a dangerous hindrance to the main goal of defeating fascism. Knightley writes that the "failure of correspondents to report the imperfect face of the Republican side does not seem to have been due, except in the case of confessed propagandists [among them, Arthur Koestler], to any policy of duplicity, but to their preoccupation with the effect that the war was having upon them personally." This was the case with Stone, and as an editorial commentator he was freer than a straight reporter to argue the cause and speak at fund-raising rallies. "We didn't have much patience for the POUM, the anarchists, and the red-hot anticommunists," Stone later explained, revealing the extent to which he refused to deal with reality, *"even though we knew that a lot of what they were saying was true"* (emphasis added).

Orwell was a singular leftist voice speaking the truth about the atrocities. An idealist, Orwell would have fought with any group on the left, but by happenstance wound up with the POUM. This group was easy enough to dislike, noted Orwell, but the Communists were not into mild rebukes. Anyone connected with the POUM that the Communist secret police could find was imprisoned, and many were executed as fascist spies, including "wounded men . . . nurses, wives . . . and in some cases, even children. . . . Not a scrap of evidence was ever produced except the unsupported statements in the Communist Press.

"Nearly all the newspaper accounts . . . were manufactured by journalists at a distance . . . intentionally misleading," wrote Orwell, regarding one battle between the Communists and the POUM characterized as an insurrection solely instigated by the POUM. Known facts were ignored. Many members of the Communist Party "openly expressed" their intent to liquidate the POUM once the war with Franco was won.

Orwell's indictment, *Homage to Catalonia,* published in 1938 during the war, did not change Orwell's views on the need to fight fascism. Soured on the Communists, he nonetheless felt that "whatever faults the post-war government might have, Franco's regime would certainly be worse."

In the beginning, during the summer heat of 1936, it was indeed a civil war. A broad coalition toppled the dictatorship, and the Republic Loyalists were duly elected. This set the stage for murderous revenge by the Nationalists, who tortured, murdered, and starved opponents. Although leftist factions tangled fiercely among themselves, they were united in their hatred; twin enemies were the Nationalists and the Catholic Church, which had become their handmaiden. Soon, civil war became a misnomer for what happened to the men, women, and children slaughtered as international forces engaged in a dress rehearsal for global war. Stone predicted early that Spain would be a "grim prelude" to all-out war if the fascists won: "a war between Russia on one side, Germany and probably Italy on the other." His boss must have helped compose this editorial, which noted, "We of America have no truck with either Fascism or Communism. Both are alien here. . . . Yet Americans cannot ignore the perilous possibility of European conflict."

The busiest appeaser of them all was Britain. It forced Léon Blum, France's Socialist leader, to halt his initial support for the Loyalists; if France went to war with Germany over Spain, Britain warned, it would not be bound to aid France. Some secret assistance continued, but France swiftly joined the nonintervention agreement. Six months into the war, Stone mocked the sham Neutrality Act and denounced the United States for inaction. He called Britain's foreign minister, Anthony Eden, a liar when he vowed that Britain would not permit any foreign power to dominate Spain: "Even as Eden spoke, his government was and is now permitting Hitler and Mussolini to pour soldiers into Spain, and helping them dominate the peninsula by calling off all aid and volunteers from Britain to the lawful Spanish government." While masses of the British and Americans protested their governments' positions, American companies such as Texaco willingly broke the Neutrality Act and sent oil to Franco, as Stone's exposés showed. FDR and American publishers cowered before the powerful pro-Franco Catholic Church.

Walter Lippmann applauded the United States's refusal to lift the arms embargo and then complained when the Loyalists, abandoned by the West, accepted arms from Russia. Neutrality meant consigning Spain's government to a brutal and unequal siege. Said Steel, "The logic of everything he had written about the European crisis dictated that the United States should abandon neutrality and forge a defense alliance with Britain and France. This alone might have prevented" Hitler's aggression and "brought Russia into the balance against Hitler." Lippmann knew this, but was unwilling to "race too far ahead of the pack." Even after Mussolini flouted all rules by sending planes and troops to the fascist-led rebels, Lippmann coolly insisted that somehow the sides were even. The Spaniards "must work out their own salvation until a favorable moment presents itself for conciliation."

While Stone, like many on the left, was guilty of ignoring ugly facts about the Communists during the war, he was more correct than Lippmann in assessing the double standard applied by those who decried Russia's participation in Spain. Stalin had sent planes, cannons, munitions, tanks, arms, and men. And no condemnation of Russia's aid would be "too severe," wrote Stone, if Germany and Italy had honored "their obligations under the nonintervention agreement to cease supplying [Franco's] soldiers. . . . It would seem that the democratic powers are now resigned to a 'nonintervention' agreement that cuts off aid only to the established government while Hitler and Mussolini pour in men and funds" to aid the rebels. "There is bitter irony in the drift of European events," continued Stone. "Fascism, which pretends to be a bulwark against revolution, has fomented revolution in one country after another—Rumania, Greece, Spain. Hitler cries poverty but spends $180,000,000 in subsidizing rebellion in Spain."

Stone, however, ended with a misguided defense: "The Soviets, openly revolutionary in philosophy, rapidly become the one source to which the smaller democratic nations of Europe can look for help in preserving the status quo." In reality, Stalin was as indifferent to Spain's future as were other global powers. His decision to support the Loyalists was ruthlessly examined. His objective was to get Britain and France in his corner, aligned against Hitler. Stalin feared that a fascist victory in Spain would allow Hitler to freely attack Russia if he overpowered France. So Stalin aided the Republic, but abandoned it when it was not prudent. His help shored up the Republic for a time, but only prolonged defeat.

Meanwhile, Lippmann was equally off base, floating the idea that London and Paris could arrange a "simple and disinterested" truce acceptable to Franco, although there was no evidence to support that belief.

The difference between the response to Lippmann and Stone was that when Lippmann was wrong, he was, in the eyes of the establishment, *acceptably* wrong; in fact, he was not even viewed as wrong. His international clout did not suffer (except with the left) when Lippmann careened off the deep end. One reason is that his errors in judgment were often mirror reflections of the status quo—his denigration of the New Deal, his myopia regarding Hitler's rise, his neutrality regarding Spain, his isolationism when it was clearly ruinous. On the other hand, when Stone was wrong, he erred on the side of the unacceptable left— which earned him a barrage of attacks, lifelong surveillance by the FBI, and scorn from establishment journalists and publishers.

Both Lippmann and Stone were powerful opinion shapers in the thirties, and thus their blind spots were all the more harmful. Lippmann spoke to entrenched establishment thinking. Stone was a spokesman for, and shaped opinion among, a significant New Deal group of leftists. Unlike Stone, Lippmann was motivated neither by war's human slaughter nor the concept that Spain's battle was a moral contest between good and evil. "I never took a passionate, partisan interest in the Spanish Civil War," Lippmann later revealed in a private conversation. "I feared it as a thing which was going to start a European war. . . . My hope was that it could be quieted, pacified, rather than exacerbated. I thought the nonintervention program was critical and futile, but *I didn't concern myself with it* [emphasis added]. My mind works like a spotlight on things, and it wasn't one of the things that I was interested in at that time." He displayed little comprehension of this war's global repercussions and disregarded the human cost of Hitler's daily blitzkrieg, "strafing city after city, dropping ten thousand bombs a day to obliterate once peaceful towns like Valencia." Although there had been limited use of airplanes in World War I, advanced technology now produced bombs and aircraft that spared few villagers. It was a new form of killing, a prelude to the mass terror bombings of World War II.

On April 26, 1937, the bombing of a small Basque town would live as a ghastly reminder of what this new era of warfare could inflict. Guernica was crowded on market day. Church bells announced the approach of enemy planes minutes before waves of bombers passed over every twenty minutes for three hours. More than sixteen hundred villagers were killed, another thousand wounded, the center of the town destroyed. Those who tried to flee were machine-gunned to death on the road. At a time when such bombings of towns and cities had not taken on the banality of routine warfare, Guernica turned the tide for many publications; influential *Time, Life,* and *Newsweek* became supporters of the left Republic. Pablo Picasso's masterpiece *Guernica* showed the horror—bodies disjointed, limbs everywhere, a mouth open in a silent scream in a face gone mad with terror, a fallen horse's distorted face. Outraged democratic governments protested, but still remained neutral as such destruction continued for two more years.*

Pressured by citizens horrified by the mass bombing of Guernica, Britain and France finally provided ships to carry several thousand Basque refugee children to safety. But in America, "neutrality was so strictly enforced" that a plan for the reception of Basque children was dropped "in the name of nonintervention."

The press lost little time living up to the axiom that truth is the first casualty in war as writers and publishers openly produced fiction—lying to the public, matching false atrocities with false atrocities. The British papers that Stone read daily were representative of the polarization. The *Manchester Guardian* was the only paper that left Orwell with an "increas-

*Responding to international condemnation, the fascists outrageously blamed the Basques for setting their own fires. Then they stated that Guernica, a mecca for Basque Catholics, who were among the few Catholics supporting the Republic, was a "military" target. Guernica was a prelude to the twentieth-century warfare of mass terrorizing and obliterating of innocents, from World War II's London and Dresden to Vietnam's thatched hamlets.

ing respect for honesty." Dispassionate correspondents were nearly impossible to find. To its credit, the conservative *Chicago Tribune* printed a highly damaging report of mass slaughter by Franco's Nationalists. Its reporter, Jay Allen, had discovered thousands of men, and some women, who were lined up and executed in a twelve-hour span in a bullring. Wrote Allen, "There is more blood than you would think in 1,800 bodies."

The Catholic press was nothing more than a propaganda arm of Franco's; they inflamed with often fake atrocity accounts about Republican assaults on nuns and priests. A colleague in crime was an Associated Press reporter who filed undocumented tales about the sexual mutilation of priests. (These gonads-in-the-mouth atrocities seem to be a staple of war tales, repeated during the Vietnam War.) The left was hardly better. Louis Fischer of the *Nation* was a Russian shill, briefing Russian ambassadors, citing victory based on wishful thinking. Like Hemingway and Malraux, he saw no conflict between being on active duty for the Republic and his reporter's role. (He even purchased arms for the Republic, which curtailed his time for writing.)

Hemingway saved the truth for his novel *For Whom the Bell Tolls,* admitting to editor Maxwell Perkins in 1938 what he had not told readers as a correspondent: the Spanish war was a "carnival of treachery and rottenness on both sides."

The *New York Times* correspondent Herbert Matthews described the attitude of leftist reporters. The Republic government "was, on balance, the cause of justice, legality, morality, decency. . . . We were right. . . . We knew, we just *knew.*" The majority of those who held that view, including Stone, remained adamant years later. Matthews, accused of bias in his coverage of the Spanish Civil War and later coverage of Castro's revolution, defended his view: "I would always opt for honest, open bias. A newspaperman should work with his heart as well as his mind." His argument goes to the heart of a major conflict in journalism. "I always felt the falseness and hypocrisy of those who claimed to be unbiased and the foolish, if not rank, stupidity of editors and readers who demand objectivity or impartiality of correspondents writing about the war. . . . A reader has a right to ask for all the facts; he has no right to ask that a journalist or historian agree with him." However, upon reflection, Matthews felt that he, too, had incorrectly ignored the battle between Spanish leftist factions.

Some publications that purported to be objective, then as now, slipped bias into their accounts by such illusive methods as burying a story or conversely playing it on page one. "I did my best, night after night, to keep out of the paper anything that might hurt [the Germans'] sensibilities," the London *Times* editor Geoffrey Dawson admitted in a letter to a friend. No reader, expecting objectivity, would have a clue about this sort of censoring, but by changing copy, burying or featuring a story, editors are making subjective and often biased judgments.

Matthews let his biases show, but he did give the facts, which was rare in this war. When Matthews was viciously attacked by the Catholic press, the *New York Times* felt it wise to give voice to both sides and hired William P. Carney, a Catholic and Franco sympathizer who was with the rebel forces in Spain. The paper twinned the stories. Carney's reports were not burdened by facts, thus readers ended up with inaccurate information that was given the same weight as Matthews's. Carney's inventions were quickly refuted by Matthews, whose reporting was so strong that the *Times* was forced to print his rebuttal to Carney, as Knightley reported.

At that time, the *Times*'s senior editors were predominantly Catholic and often played up anticommunist stories. They controlled what appeared in the "paper of record." The most flagrant violation of Matthews's copy occurred when he scooped everyone with an eyewitness account of Italian troops in Spain, a presence that Franco forces were denying. This significant political story was butchered by editors. That the troops were "Italian and nothing but Italian" was ridiculously changed to "they were Insurgent and nothing but Insurgent" (a term for Franco's forces), recalled author Phillip Knightley.

In the earlier glory days of the war, youths from all over the world came to fight with the Loyalists. They thrilled to La Pasionaria, the voice of Loyalist Spain, demanding arms for workers in her Radio Madrid broadcasts, urging women to fight with knives and burning oil, crying, "It is better to die on your feet than to live on your knees! ¡*No pasarán!*" This became the Republic's call to arms. The Communists formed an International Brigade of volunteers forty thousand strong from America, Britain, France, Hungaria, Yugoslavia, Czechoslovakia, Poland, and Albania, and leftists from Italy and Germany.

With Hemingway, the king of bravura journalism, leading the way, no battalion was more eulogized than the Abraham Lincoln brigade, led by Robert Merriman, a twenty-eight-year-old college professor. These battalions were young and idealistic and brave. Former pacifists, poets, and artists joined or came to drive ambulances in a noble crusade. Stalin's cold-blooded cynicism dictated his misuse of this heroism. Survivors of the brave International Brigade knew years later that they and their dead comrades were pawns in a horrific international chess game.

Six months before Franco's forces crushed the Loyalists, Stalin considered an alliance with Hitler, abandoning hope of an anti-Hitler alliance with France and Britain. With this shift in thinking, Stalin deserted the Loyalists. In a last-ditch effort to rally help from fellow democracies, the Republic, to show neutrality, ordered the International Brigade home. On November 15, 1938, Bill Bailey, the seaman who had ripped down the swastika from the *Bremen* in 1935, was among the departing members of the worldwide brigade, veterans of the war's bloodiest battles. "They *made* us leave, the big parade and all that. Many of us had made a commitment to ourselves that if we had won, there would be such a need for engineers and plumbers and electricians that we would stay to help. You made so many friends with so many people there."

They marched through the streets of Barcelona as a huge turnout cheered, cried and sang farewell. La Pasionaria ignited the crowd: "Mothers! Women! . . . When the wounds of war are stanched . . . speak to your children. Tell them how, coming over seas and mountains, crossing frontiers bristling with bayonets . . . these men reached our country as crusaders for freedom. They gave up everything . . . and they came and told us: 'We are here, your cause, Spain's cause, is ours.' . . . We shall not forget you!"

Meanwhile, on the home front, squads of writers, poets, intellectuals, actors and artists massed together in New York and Hollywood as they did in London and Paris, holding fund-raisers, urging support for a popular front, cheering the volunteer brigades, singing the stirring "Internationale." Irving Howe, the anticommunist socialist, bitingly recalled the radical-chic element at play: "Spain made possible a vicarious participation, a thrill over cocktails." Easy to spoof, these people at least tried to help. Howe ripped into an article about a "highly successful benefit for Spanish refugee children" sponsored by Eleanor Roosevelt (even as her husband stayed neutral) unfortunately called "The Spanish Fiesta." It sounded more like a thirties movie in which Carmen Miranda was about to rumba across the stage into the arms of Cesar Romero. The land of glitz then aped this successful event with the "Hollywood Fiesta Committee" to raise funds for the children.

Like other pacifists, I. F. Stone supported war for the first time in his life. In a 1937 *Nation* article headlined "Neutrality—a Dangerous Myth"

Stone passionately wrote under the name of Geoffrey Stone, "I hate fascism. My heart is with the Spanish Loyalists. Yet if it were possible to insulate the United States from the world, to retire into our shell, to plow our fields and write our books and raise our children untouched by quarrels across the sea . . . I would be for isolationist neutrality legislation. . . . But I do not believe insulation and isolation possible. . . . Neutrality legislation is nothing more than a breeder of illusions. Must we play nursemaid to the world? I am afraid so."

Stone warned, "Another world war is coming, that we shall ultimately be drawn in; that it would be better for us . . . to throw our weight on the side of peace and against aggression. I see no other possible way of averting war. I see no way to keep out of another world war, once it starts." Stone tried to appeal to isolationists through global economics, not emotional pleas, a repeated theme as he watched Hitler crush country after country while the United States remained isolationist. "The devastating effects of isolation on whole areas of our economy and our country rise to view." Some 2 million Americans "are directly dependent on foreign trade for their bread and butter." Texas cotton growers and California fruit pickers, Midwestern wheat and corn farmers, workers at "our great ports. These would be struck, as though by a plague, by isolation. What are we to do about the bread lines, the unemployment, the falling prices, the panicky markets, the bankruptcies, the dispossessed croppers, that would follow in the wake of the neutrality embargos required to keep us out of a world war?"

Hitler had already made America "no longer free . . . because forces beyond our control are forcing us to choose. In the context of our time, isolation is an unreal, a classroom solution." He urged "international cooperation. . . . The weight of our power might turn the trick, halt the aggressor nations, prevent war," he wrote. "Nothing else can."

Despite the pain and horror of war, a postscript was even more crushing for surviving International Brigade members. Those who had enlisted from Eastern Europe were victims of Stalin's crazed paranoia, presumably for having fought side by side with anarchists, socialists, and other noncommunists. Some were shot in purges, others were outcasts until Stalin's death. In America, as 1950s paranoia gripped the country, the Abraham Lincoln and Washington battalions were tarred for their Communist affiliation.

His heart heavy, Stone wept at war's end. In the sweltering summer of

1939 an estimated 1 million lay dead, over two hundred thousand were in prison. Untold billions of dollars' worth of homes, buildings, livestock were destroyed. More than 180 towns were obliterated. Land stood empty, devoid of farmers, who were among the half million refugees who had fled to foreign soil. The parties of the left were wrecked.

The future of war in Europe was now ominously certain, and Stone turned all his efforts toward making his readers understand the urgency of this peril.

On the home front, further rifts on the left would immerse Stone in battles that, in many cases, only ended with the deaths in old age of some of the participants and, in some cases, not even then.

11

WHEN TYRANTS RULED

The simultaneous rise to power of two mad tyrants, Josef Stalin and Adolf Hitler, produced a twentieth-century bloodbath of still unfathomable proportions. Stalin, in his paranoia and ruthless march to collectivize and modernize Russia, murdered no less than 20 million of his countrymen. Hitler murdered 6 million Jews and 6 million other "undesirables"—Catholics, Gypsies, homosexuals, Protestants, political enemies—in his gas chambers alone. This does not begin to count the millions of nonincarcerated civilians who perished in World War II or the millions of dead soldiers strewn across European and Asian battlefields.

In hindsight, as is so often the case, it seems easy to condemn them equally. In the years leading up to the war, however, passions of the moment, the unwillingness to see, the murky dissemination of news, all helped to cloud vision on all sides. Apolitical pacifists opposed entry into war no matter how morally justified it might seem to others. And partisan leftists overlooked Stalin's brutalities just as pro-fascists did Hitler's. "The great anomaly of the time was that one group saw one set of mass murderers and another could see another set of mass murderers. An insignificant number could see both," commented author Nicholas Von Hoffman, a longtime friend of Stone's, a liberal who has always been strongly anticommunist.

Like many leftists, Stone had blind spots that marred his typically clear-eyed skepticism. Stone insisted later that he knew Stalin's infamous purge trials of the thirties were a fraud. "As the news began to filter out, a *great* disillusionment began to grow," Stone recalled. "Popular fronters realized it was true. I can remember arguing with Freda [Kirchwey, editor of the *Nation*] about the Moscow trials being just a frame-up."

Nonetheless, as Stone said many times, a united alliance against fascism meant cooperation with all on the left. His writing reflected an agonizing vacillation as he toned down his rhetoric after the Communist Party shifted gears in 1935 with its United Front sloganeering to appease other leftists. Previously, in 1934, Stone was outraged at the executions following the murder of a Party official, which were a prelude to Stalin's show trials. "Whether one agrees with its tenets or not, the Russian revolution was at least the work of men with ideals. Their government cannot resort to the methods of Fascist thugs and racketeers." He attacked Stalin for shutting off free speech and due process. However, by January of 1937, Stone's criticism softened due to the "prominence of the Soviet Union within the antifascist camp," wrote historian Robert C. Cottrell.

What puzzled some observers was that no accused Soviet leader denied the charges, even though they knew that confession was no reprieve from death. A *Post* editorial reflected this confusion with a showstopping headline: a series of question marks. While he harbored doubts about the sincerity of the confessions, Stone's faith in socialism and the antifascist front were so great that he waffled. One can imagine what he would have done with Stalin's bizarre inconsistencies and "facts" in order to execute valiant revolutionaries had these come from Hitler, Mussolini, or Franco.

Lippmann was much more prophetic. As Steel commented, his poor judgment regarding Hitler was countered with a "far better sense than his left wing critics of the realities of Soviet-style Communism." He wrote in 1937 that Stalin's purges could help free Western liberals "from the dominion that Russian communism has exercised over their minds in the past twenty years. To have realized that the present Russian government repudiates the principles of truth and justice must, I think, eventually lead to the realization that this is not a corruption of, but the inevitable consequences of, the ideals of communism."

Stone believed for decades that socialism was an inevitable worldwide course and never totally abandoned it as his ideal, although he strongly denounced Russia's Communism. Stone was guided by "pessimism of the intellect, optimism of the will," remarked Erwin Knoll, publisher of the *Progressive*. "Izzy understood the fallibility of human beings and of human institutions, but never saw that as a reason to abandon hope. The only mistakes Izzy made were the mistakes of the heart, of optimism."

The Russian Revolution replaced a "decayed, semi-feudal, absolutist monarchy . . . corrupt to its core," which "exuded the characteristic odor of all dying Western civilizations—anti-Semitism," argued Stone in 1937. While not perfect, "its ruling party is seeking to transform" this "most backward of the great European nations."

Stone's beliefs were formed in the crucible of his time: America's biased coverage of the Bolshevik Revolution, the repression of the Palmer Raids, workers' strikes reported with an anti-"Red" slant, distortions about the New Deal, the tenacious influence of unchecked capitalism on presidents and publishers alike—all this made it impossible for many leftists to believe the negative news filtering out of Russia. The U.S. media was often discounted, not without reason, for perpetuating anti-Stalinist lies to bolster right-wing viewpoints. For many who were organizing workers, America's police and judicial system and biased reporting made it easy to discount negatives about Russia. In 1930s film clips, sixteen-year-old Dorothy Healy stands behind prison bars in California after being beaten and jailed for organizing farmworkers. No paper was more viciously antilabor than the *Los Angeles Times*, which used Red Scares to crush labor and social welfare legislation. Its distortions and fabrications were well-known. So leftists like Healy, who later formed a friendship with Stone, discounted anything printed in the *Times*.

Still, it remains easy for Stone's critics to attack him for a double standard of reporting. No matter the cost, even to his own tenets as a journalist, the united front against fascism had to be preserved.

Meanwhile, a more cynical collection of Americans dealt with Russia, the very group who excoriated American leftists as "radical Reds." Concerned not with human rights but with making money in Stalin's Russia, American financiers willingly overlooked Stalin's murderous path to industrialization. Companies had begun trading with Stalin even as they gave lip service to President Hoover's avowal never to recognize the U.S.S.R. This alliance would continue unabated throughout the thirties, despite purges and pacts.

Fortune, the bible for free-enterprise moguls, devoted its March 1932 issue to Russia's Communism. The article noted the lethal powers of Russia's secret police, yet added that such tactics didn't start with the Communists: "peasants and proletariats who remember how the Czar's Cossacks liquidated objectors before the Revolution" accepted Stalin's brutality with an equanimity that "visitors would find scandalous."

Stalin was naively depicted as a warm family man, even though he had already slaughtered and starved millions into collectivism. But, according to *Fortune,* the Five Year Plan was progressing positively. *Fortune* seemed agog over Russia's massive industrial transformation: tractor factories, munitions plants, and the Dnieper Dam, built by American and Russian engineers with a major amount of General Electric equipment.

Ads urged businessmen to visit Russia for grand investment opportunities. More than fifty illustrious American corporations were heavily trading, beginning with Allis-Chalmers farm equipment and ending with Westinghouse electrical equipment. In between were such giants as Bethlehem Steel, U.S. Steel, Standard Oil, Marshall Field, R. H. Macy, Chase National Bank, Caterpillar Tractor, Deere & Co., and RCA.

Such capitalist presence legitimized Stalin in the eyes of many Americans.

Stalin's great purge trials of the thirties strained ever-quarreling leftist factions and fostered an irrevocable rift between Stone and his boss. In a barrage of anti-Stalin editorials, Stern saw the trials for the sham that they were, mocked popular fronters like his chief editorialist for trying to mix democracy with dictatorships, and compared Stalin's strong-arm tactics to Hitler's. " 'Liquidation' under the Russian constitution would seem to be guaranteed even more certainly than freedom of the press."

A test of faith was certainly provided by Stalin's long-running purges. The elite of the 1917 revolution were accused of forming a terrorist bloc to assassinate Soviet leaders, collusion with the Nazis, and plotting the return of capitalism. Virtually the entire general staff of the Red Army had been executed. Many alleged conspirators conveniently died under mysterious circumstances; others "disappeared." Mocking the charges against Trotsky, historian Harvey Klein wrote, "He had somehow united left-wing Zinovievites, right-wing Bukharinites, and disgruntled Stalinists . . . and then plotted with both Nazi Germany and Imperial Japan to overthrow the Soviet regime and install capitalism."

While Stone fell further away from his "fellow traveling," he was also "terribly unhappy" at the Post in 1938, arguing more and more with his mentor who had, he thought, drifted perilously to the right. Stern proudly took credit for the editorials in which he "came out four square against the united front." The CPUSA about-face was a fraud and "many New Dealers had been taken in by this hypocrisy."

In those ominous times, fear of fascism escalated, which solidified many leftists. Democracy's claim that "it can't happen here" was heard less often as Nazi Bundists drew huge crowds in America. They were disturbing imitations of Hitler's throngs, complete with uniformed storm troopers and swastikas. Grateful New Dealers observed that the Communists were the one group attempting to heckle or break up Nazi rallies. Wrote Stern, "Extremists and muddleheads, in both liberal and conservative camps, had public thinking in a fine state of confusion."

No confusion could be found in *Post* editorials, increasingly written by Stern. In an unusual front-page editorial, Stern's 1938 attack spanned two columns. Those who favored the popular front to fight fascism should now see that "the one ism is as evil as the other." His attack was a direct hit on Stone's position. Any group that elected or appointed a Communist to office was bringing in a revolutionary "sworn to destroy our system," blasted Stern. To Stone, who knew many rank-and-file Communists dedicated only to America's workers and civil rights, this was tarring with a wide brush.

Should any 1938 reader miss Stern's message, the accompanying editorial cartoon—they were never long on subtlety in the *Post*—showed Stalin holding a dagger dripping blood behind his back while grinning at an Uncle Sam figure entitled "Labor." That evening, Stern took his young daughter to a party at the home of George Seldes, who had been expelled from Russia in the twenties for smuggling information past censors. As they walked into the party, Stern told his daughter that she would meet friends "who really appreciate your father." Stern was greeted by "a dozen avant-garde liberals" who berated him for his "abominable editorial." Fists were shaken in his face, and his daughter collapsed in laughter. "Dad," she said, "they certainly appreciate you."

Finding out what was really happening in Russia was difficult. Foreign reporting, always a nightmare in heavily censored Russia, tended to support Stalin. Some correspondents were taken in, others were unable to sneak harsher reports past the censors or faced indifference and butchering by editors back in the States.

It is important to examine the coverage in Russia to understand why popular fronters like Stone could justify their support of Stalin. Readers of the *New York Times,* for example, were exceedingly ill served by their man in Moscow, Walter Duranty. In 1939, Stone referred to Duranty as the "unofficial spokesman for the Kremlin"—a rather benign description of this bon vivant who had lost one leg in a train accident and came to Russia fresh from opium dens and sex orgies among the fashionably decadent in European capitals. Proud of his cynical indifference, Duranty cared not that he greatly underestimated the deaths in the Ukrainian famine, so brilliantly reported by the *Chicago Tribune*'s Frank Gibbons, who horrified the world with descriptions of massed corpses and living skeletons. Duranty did not even visit the area. This was a prelude to reportage that earned Duranty such condemnations as "fashionable liar" and "journalistic shill." He ensconced himself in Moscow with a mistress, maids, caviar, and vodka, and was the official greeter for touring celebrities, taken in by his *Times* position and a Pulitzer Prize he had astonishingly won. His famous retort to complaints of Stalin's brutal collectivism (at times attributed to the dictator) eased those who hoped this was but a temporary stage: "You can't make an omelet without breaking a few eggs."

Duranty's slanted history-in-the-making was deplorable given his influential role of international authority bestowed on the *Times* correspondents. Duranty's glowing reports of Russia's metamorphosis from backward peasantry to industrial force were instrumental in President Roosevelt's recognition of the revolutionary regime in 1933. All the while Duranty hid the huge cost of Russia's rise. Colleagues felt he had made a deal in exchange for privileged treatment.

New York Times readers were thus left in the dark regarding the famines. Duranty sang a different song at dinner parties. Companions feasting on his caviar heard a much higher number of famine deaths than what he reported. Duranty concluded with a shrug and the tagline of an old joke: "But they're only Russians."

Historians would later ponder how Stalin was able to cover up his mad master plan. The best coverage had to wait until a reporter left the country to expose what had been heavily censored. There were no press conferences or access to commissars, phones were tapped, sources imprisoned. This pattern continued for decades. In the 1940s, one of America's best reporters, Harrison Salisbury, chafed at the gutting of his *New York Times* dispatches and feared readers would infer a pro-Soviet slant. Salisbury urged the *Times* to print what seems like a perfect solution to the problem—a warning at the top of each article: "Passed by censorship." Unfortunately, the *New York Times* rejected his idea, which bothered Salisbury for decades.

In 1930 there were only a half dozen correspondents in Moscow. While the kulaks were being terrorized, driven from land, exiled to Siberia, and liquidated by the millions, the Soviets enforced strict censorship and banned visits to famine areas. In 1933, William Stoneman of the *Chicago Daily News* and Ralph Barnes, Duranty's rival at the *New York Herald Tribune,* snuck into famine-stricken regions, were arrested and sent back to Moscow. By smuggling out dispatches, they alerted American readers to the slaughter; swollen bellies and matchstick-thin legs, flesh so shrunk that faces looked like death masks, mirror images of what would be found in Hitler's concentration camps. Duranty persisted that "the famine is mostly bunk" while the *Tribune* bannered Barnes's report with "Millions Feared Dead in South Russia." Three weeks later, Duranty swept through the heart of the famine district for the first time and wrote that "any talk of famine" was a "sheer absurdity," although he acknowledged seeing starving children. In a devastating response, "The Famine the *Times* Couldn't Find," scholar Marco Carynnyk wrote that while people died at the rate of six thousand per day in World War I, Russian peasants during the famine were dying at the rate of twenty-five thousand a day.

By all accounts, Duranty should have been fired, but the *Times* refrained. Editors and publishers have always been suckers for exclusive interviews, even if it means toadying to the prominent who reveal nothing more than a self-aggrandizing "scoop." Duranty got his exclusives with Stalin, but, unfortunately, his fraudulent dispatches affected world opinion. As biographer S. J. Taylor noted, "Had Duranty, a Pulitzer Prize winner . . . spoken out loud and clear in . . . the *New York Times*, the world could not have ignored him . . . and events might, just conceivably, have taken a different turn."

Duranty and the *Nation*'s Louis Fischer, who wrote nothing of the famine, were not alone in witting or unwitting compliance to hide the facts about Russia. Consumed with depression at home, Western newspapers gave no priority to far-flung disasters. Nor did Western diplomats wish to intercede in a country viewed as a possible ally. Censorship at home also took a heavy toll. For Moscow reporter Joe Barnes (no relation to his predecessor Ralph Barnes), the *Herald Tribune* of 1937 was endlessly frustrating. Its skimping on finances to the detriment of coverage infuriated Barnes, who saw history unfolding and was told to hold down his copy while his censored purge-trial reports were further mangled by a pro-Soviet editor in New York.

Duranty saw nothing "sufficiently remarkable . . . to justify comment" about the purge trials. Disarray among journalists and diplomats inside Russia was crucial to shaping opinion. U.S. ambassador Joseph E. Davies told reporters he believed that the trials showed "the threads of a conspiracy to overthrow the Soviet regime."

An American leftist, David Prensky, whose disillusion came later, recalled, "Duranty did what we considered to be real honest reporting. And more important to our thinking was Joseph Davies. You can't imagine the effect of this very wealthy trial lawyer who had tremendous experience with courtroom procedures and was present at the trials."

The culmination of skewed and censored reporting certainly contributed to the American left's benign attitude toward Russia. However, even hard facts were ignored. Eugene Lyons went to Russia in the late twenties to cover his "Utopia." He turned from believer to sour observer to rabid enemy. His *Assignment in Utopia,* written without censorship after he left Russia, was the first major book to expose the dark reality of Stalin's regime. It was denounced by American Communists and Soviet sympathizers. Thus, there was firsthand news by 1937, the time of the second trials, but Stone was among those who regarded Lyons as an unreliably bitter source.

Lyons asked the mystery questions: Where were the families of these convicted men? What kind of hostages did Stalin hold in return for such acquiescence to improbable charges? Nikolai Ivanovich Bukharin's widow answered that in her autobiography in 1988 as she spoke of one man's torture: "His denial of guilt would not endure. He was . . . forced to 'confess'—that is, to lie—." She herself was taken from her infant son, tortured, and imprisoned for being married to an "enemy of the people," a founding father of the Revolution. As she lay starving and freezing in a damp prison hole, she learned of her husband's execution, this "horrifying travesty."

A battle among New York's intellectuals who supported Trotsky and those who supported Stalin erupted during the trials. Many later became fierce anticommunists. Arthur Koestler's indictment of the purges, *Darkness at Noon,* was published in 1941. His searing novel told of innocent men cast into jail, listening to the screams of torture that produced "confessions" from heroes of another time. Koestler's hero is forced to confess and knowingly meets his fate; dragged down a corridor, out of sight, shot to death by a police officer placing the gun close to his temple. Many on the left chose to ignore Koestler. The *Nation,* however, reviewed his book favorably.

Meanwhile, the conflicted alliance of Stone and Stern finally shattered. Stone's explanation in later years was that he felt Stern, beset by financial and advertising difficulties, had moved "too far to the right." But the story of Stone's final break in 1939 with his mentor is a Rashomon tale, varying with each narrator.

Family and friends remember vague stories about a fight for principle. Said Stone's brother Lou: "I think it was over editorials on the Spanish Civil War, which Izzy was writing. Stern had a lot of pressure brought upon him by Cardinal Dougherty, and Izzy was told, 'Lay off support for the Loyalists,' and Izzy said he wouldn't." Sam Grafton: "Ideological differences had absolutely nothing to do with it." Grafton recalled that one day, instead of his writing an editorial, the managing editor had asked to write it. The next morning at conference, Izzy, unaware that it had been written by the managing editor, "lit into the editorial, criticizing it kind of shabbily. I wanted to signal Izzy [to lay off], but as he continued hammering on the editorial that Izzy thought was mine, I thought to myself, 'Why should I?' Well, that was the end of it, he was good and fired off the editorial page." Stern's daughter said of Grafton's version, "Well, Izzy and Sam were sort of rivals, and in later years Sam became reactionary, comparatively speaking, and Izzy stayed extremely to the left. I think Sam was jealous because Izzy became a national hero."

J. David Stern's version, told in the early fifties, creates further confusion; he places the time as "during the first years of my ownership of the *Post*," when, in fact, Izzy was demoted in 1938. (The publisher sold the paper to Dorothy Schiff in the summer of 1939.) According to Stern, the *Post* had taken a position opposing a refinancing plan for the New York transit system. "Izzy made an intensive study and wrote a great many editorials on the subject. They sounded very erudite . . . but they were always in opposition." Meeting Stone in the corridor one day, Stern recalled, "Izzy, it's been on my mind to ask you why you don't offer a constructive program to replace the present [refinancing plan]. What is your solution?"

"Let the city foreclose."

"You mean the city should wipe out all the investors?"

"Why not?"

Stern argued, "The city shouldn't take advantage of this situation and it isn't moral or decent for it to act in such a way."

"I don't see why not," retorted Izzy. "Businessmen would act that way towards the city if they were in the saddle."

Stern walked off, but kept worrying about Stone's "juvenile attitude towards this problem. I sent a note to Izzy and the managing editor that hereafter he would work with the news department as a special writer at the same pay. Izzy never spoke to me about it, but he induced the Newspaper Guild to bring charges against management for unfair practices. According to his contention, the publisher did not have the right to choose his editorial writers. The matter went to arbitration. The arbiter was Francis Biddle, then judge of the United States Court of Appeals for the third district, and later attorney general. Biddle rendered a very forthright opinion that it was entirely within the province of management to decide what work writers should do. Thereupon Izzy resigned."

Izzy's version was colorfully described to Patner: "In 1939 Stern wanted me to write an editorial" saying that secondary picketing of a department store was unconstitutional. Stone: "Look, the Supreme Court recently upheld secondary picketing. I can't write that." Stern: "Goddammit, I need that editorial to get the department-store advertising." Stone: "Goddammit, why didn't you tell me that in the first place? I've been in a whorehouse long enough to know what one's supposed to do!" Stone reflected that he probably never wrote the editorial, but this fight compounded the aggravation. "I guess he didn't want to fire me; he'd have to pay me an awful lot of severance pay, so he demoted me to reporter. . . . Much to his surprise—much to everybody's surprise—I just had one hell of a good time in the newsroom, and the first day, I got a page-one story. It was fun to be back on the street. . . . Everybody looked at me askance; I was the fair-haired boy and here I was demoted. Then they caught on that I was having too much fun, so they stopped giving me general assignments. Charles Evans Hughes was about to die so they set me up to prepare an obituary. So I went to the library . . . I read everything Charles Evans Hughes did on the Supreme Court. . . . But Hughes didn't die, and they would just keep me sitting there. So I did pieces for the *Nation*. And then I brought a Guild case for my severance pay, arguing that my demotion was constructive discharge, and . . . Biddle ruled for my boss. So, when I lost, I left."

It was hardly an opportune time for Stone, now the father of three children, to quit. Although he was writing regularly for the *Nation,* the magazine paid little. Stone lost an important niche as an editorial writer on an influential daily. He also lost the friendship of a man who had employed the writer for half of his life, from his days as a fifteen-year-old reporter, and who was in many ways a surrogate father. "He was very bitter and angry at Izzy," recalled Stern's daughter. He even left Stone out of his memoirs. Stone, however, spoke glowingly about Stern for the rest of his life.

For the American left, the worst was yet to come, a bombshell that annihilated the popular front. In the spring of 1939, a manifesto against totalitarian regimes was published by the Committee for Cultural Freedom in America. No matter how prescient they sound today, at the time many were Trotskyists whose hatred of Stalin made their views suspect to other leftists. Freda Kirchwey published the manifesto in her May 27, 1939, issue of the *Nation* and then wrote a scolding editorial. "I have no doubt that they really want to defend intellectual freedom, but I think they also intended to drop a bomb on the ranks of the liberal and left groups in the United States." Kirchwey and others were upset by the insistence of this group, led by writer Sidney Hook, on lumping Stalin with Hitler and Mussolini.

Kirchwey wrote that the Communist Party's tactics were "invariably provocative and often destructive," and they "have been guilty of unscrupulous and callous attacks against their enemies," but then added, "with all their faults, the Communists perform necessary functions in the confused struggle of our time." Whether organizations "known as 'fronts' by their opponents" were "sincere or strategical," they were now working for democracy and should be accepted. She called for "factional disarmament."

Stone took a harsher stance and along with four hundred cosigners slammed Hook and the committee in a letter that appeared on August 10 in the *Nation*. Among those who signed were writers and playwrights Dashiell Hammett, Granville Hicks, George S. Kaufman, Max Lerner, Clifford Odets, S. J. Perelman, Vincent Sheean, Maxwell S. Stewart, Louis Untermeyer, James Thurber, William Carlos Williams. Kirchwey distanced herself from Stone and Max Lerner, the only other *Nation* writer to sign. Titled "To All Active Supporters of Democracy and Peace," the letter castigated Hook's group for "their chief . . . objective," maligning the Soviet people and "their government." The Soviet Union, the letter said, "continues as always to be a bulwark against war and aggression, and works unceasingly for a peaceful international order." Stalin's Russia "has eliminated racial and national prejudices . . . fed the minority peoples enslaved under the czars, stimulated the culture and economic welfare of these peoples, and made the expression of anti-Semitism or any racial animosity a criminal offence."

The letter exalted Russia for its "nationwide socialist planning, emancipating women and developed an advanced system of child care." It depicted the Soviet Union as "one of the most far reaching cultural and educational advances in all history. . . . Writers and thinkers whose books have been burned by the Nazis are published in the Soviet Union." The requisite caveat followed: "The Soviet Union considers political dictatorships a transitional form. . . . There exists a sound and permanent basis in mutual idealistic cooperation between the USA and USSR in behalf of world peace."

This might have been just another internecine spat, one in which Stone's side looked gullible, were it not for the timing. On August 23, Stalin and Hitler signed a nonaggression pact, forging an alliance that stunned the world. World War II, which Stone had written and worried about for more than a decade, was a certainty. And now Hitler was aided by Russia, the country Stone had just enthusiastically endorsed. A week after signing the pact, Germany invaded Poland. Britain and France declared war.

America's press corps had no end of fun mocking the leftists, and this episode guaranteed Stone a footnote in later history books. Journalist Richard Rovere, who later became one of Stone's more virulent critics, remarked that at the time of the Stalin-Hitler Pact "no one" was "more outraged by that outrageous document" than Stone. Still, signing such a fulsome pro-Soviet letter aimed at whitewashing the purge trials and Stalin—especially since Stone had already decided that the trials were "phony"—damaged his reputation and diluted his influence. It was "unquestionably the most foolish and dishonest action of his entire career," wrote biographer Cottrell. Stone's admission years later that he had been "something of an apologist" was an anemic admission from the journalist who privately questioned Stalin at the time. In letters to his friend Blankfort, Stone displayed deep anger. The pact and propaganda excuses "turned my stomach . . . the party and its organs have stunk pretty badly." He despised their "robotic . . . flip-flop" on cue from Moscow and was through with "fellow traveling."

Immediately after the Stalin-Hitler Pact, Stone wrote an angry two-thousand-word *Nation* article: "All of us who felt that the Soviet Union was the core of the world front against fascism" shared an "indignation and contemptuous disbelief" that Stalin would sign with Hitler. Stalin was the "Moscow Machiavelli." Stone assailed the CPUSA and other "apologists-after-the-fact" for their "red faced excuses" that the treaty was a way to "stiffen the democracies" and "prevent a Munich."

The headline was more one-sided than the article, calling it (British prime minister Neville) "Chamberlain's Stalin-Hitler Pact." Stone chastised journalists who, for ideological reasons, had dismissed two stories in conservative newspapers that had speculated on a possible rapprochement between the USSR and Nazi Germany and a third by Duranty, who had finally become more observant. Months before the pact he warned that the only obstacle to an agreement was "Hitler's fanatic fury against what he calls 'Judeo-Bolshevism.'" But in no way could Stone accept Duranty's "cynical and shocking" claim that "Stalin has shot more Jews in two years of purges than were ever killed in Germany." Duranty must have been "off on some queer tangent of his own."

Stone then switched to Chamberlain's disastrous appeasement policy, which Stone argued had left Russia adrift. Chamberlain, the "little man with the umbrella," was sucked into every "peaceful" claim of Hitler's and ignored every subsequent crushing of country after country. After Nazi troops occupied Prague in March of 1938, wrote Stone, even the pro-fascist "London *Times,* the Cliveden set, and the formerly pro-Nazi *Observer*" had joined "the demand in Britain for a Russian alliance. . . . If Chamberlain had shared the popular revulsion in Britain against Munichism, these scattered hints alone would have been sufficient to make him hasten negotiation of a pact with the Soviets."

As the prime minister toyed with him, Stalin fumed and carried on secret negotiations with Berlin while still trying to deal with Britain and France. Winston Churchill had harshly criticized Chamberlain for his failure to respond to a Soviet offer of a French-Soviet-British alliance against Germany. "I beg his Majesty's Government to get some brutal truths into their heads . . . without Russia there can be no effective Eastern front.'"

In later years, Shirer, among many, agreed with Stone's 1939 criticisms of Chamberlain. Speculated the war correspondent, if Chamberlain had enthusiastically greeted Russia's overtures, " 'Let us three band together and break Hitler's neck,' Parliament would have approved . . . history might have taken a different course. At least it could not have taken a worse." Still, wrote Shirer, who was then in Berlin, "I remained woefully ignorant of the secret rapprochement of Nazi Germany and Communist Russia."

Two months into the war, Stone blamed both Stalin and Chamberlain for Hitler's invasion of Poland. Chamberlain had tried to save face in a blue book the British issued on the origins of the war, saying that these documents would prove that "the responsibility for this terrible catastrophe lies on the shoulders of one man," Hitler. Stone called this accounting "history with its face lifted. . . . Hitler caused the war, but who 'caused' Hitler? Britain's Tories share the final honors." He added Russia to the mix: "The hammer-and-sickle, as well as the umbrella, is linked with the swastika in responsibility for the attack on Poland. . . . Agonized cries for help from Warsaw echo unanswered in the Blue Book."

Years later, Max Lerner, who was responsible for Stone's being hired by the *Nation,* reflected on that period. "Did I feel duped? I think we were ignorant. This was true of the political culture of our time and particularly true of those liberals who had come to identify with the Russian Revolution. Sidney [Hook] was ahead of the culture, and all honor to him. Alas, most of us had not learned how things were in Russia." During the purge trials, Lerner was political editor of the *Nation.* "I was beginning to have doubts. Doubts which were further strengthened by the fact that Louis Fischer had come back from Russia and told us that things were pretty bad. He wanted us to concentrate on the Spanish war and not try to defend the trials. Freda was the farthest out in supporting them. Writing the editorials was an agony because I was feeling so split."

As for denouncing Hook's manifesto, "the only answer I can give you is that we had conveniently decided that Sidney had taken a particular view of his own. We took our stereotype of Sidney [as of the violently anti-Stalin socialist left] and used it to dispel what we had learned from the trials. I did not apply what I had learned about the trials."

After the pact, Stone joined Lerner at his home to start a noncommunist New Beginnings Group to replace the collapsed popular front. They felt an urgency to "form some new credo for an independent left," recalled Lerner. "Some had already left the fellow travelers' train—and I think most were ready to." A new left group fizzled because "None of us were organizers. We saw at the end of the road a splinter party." By then, Lerner felt that "Marxism was not a satisfying creed. My emphasis was not on rejecting or accepting capitalism but an emphasis on democracy. Stay within capitalism, but one that is more collectivist, a democratic collectivism." Stone had called for a blend of Marxism and Jefferson. "That's *his* version," said Lerner. "No, I was not going to blend it."

Lerner addressed the question of why intelligent people would not break with or probe Stalin as they would another faction in the face of evidence. "Once they made a commitment, their whole sense of selfhood was tied to it." To think otherwise would be a "betrayal of what was most valuable about themselves. This was the kind of hold Communism had on liberals and intellectuals. That dream world." Lerner said, "It took me some doing" to break with the dream, "but I look back with content on my intellectual journey. Izzy held on much longer."

As this decisive decade came to an end, Stone celebrated his thirty-second birthday. His soaring career on New York's leading liberal paper had crashed. His popular front was in crumbles. His view of Russia had curdled. Nazis marched through Europe. It was only a matter of time before the United States would be drawn into war. In this cataclysmic moment in time, he watched right-wing America firsters and America's Stalinists become the strangest of bedfellows in their heated isolationist stance.

Stone's personal future was as uncertain as that of the world.

PART THREE

Washington Wars, Hot and Cold

12

NATION ON THE BRINK

Does he mix with Negroes? Does he . . . have too many Jewish
friends? Does his face light up when the Red Army is mentioned?
—Stone 1943 exposé of FBI questions of government employees

For a brief time, when Stone combined the *New York Post* and his
part-time *Nation* job, the writer was faring well financially. Freda
Kirchwey had assured him that as soon as she could afford it, she
would hire him full-time. Such a position on the influential but always
financially strapped magazine would hardly guarantee riches. As hu-
morist Calvin Trillin famously quipped, "The *Nation* pays in the high
two figures."

But with his combined salaries, Stone was able to buy a 1932 Dodge.
He drove it with reckless but cheerful disregard as to which was the
clutch and which was the brake. And this urbanite tried something
new—a home in the country, in Northport, Long Island. The rent was
paid by subletting the Manhattan apartment. Stone loved the train commute, using the time to absorb the news about Europe's emerging war.
At home, he seldom stopped working, reading late into the night. Still,
his letters to Blankfort were filled with chitchat; Stone had begun roller
skating and had endearing nicknames for Jeremy, "Jay Jay," and Christopher, "Criffy." Esther and the children were thriving. Stone joked in one
letter that Jay was recovering from a major disappointment. A school-
mate had a policeman for a father—"Jay seemed resigned when he asked
Esther about my not being one."

Stone's tumultuous departure from the *New York Post* left him
searching for additional income. For a while he was semi-adrift, writing
part-time for the *Nation* and taking the odd freelance job. Kirchwey had
suggested in 1938 that Stone take a press officer's job at the Department
of the Interior and work for her on the side. Stone did not see how he
could be "a press agent *and* an independent journalist" and said no. The
Stones moved to a smaller house and let the maid go, saving $100 a

month. In the summer of 1939, Stone worked for an institute that ana-
lyzed propaganda from an antiunion farmers' association. Writing a
book sounded like fun, but a $500 advance from Modern Age Books to
write a history of agribusiness ignited no productivity. Stone briefly
joined George Seldes to write for a muckraking investors' paper, and he
and brother Lou began researching another book that never materialized. In September 1939, Stone was hired as publicist and speechwriter
for famed opera singer Lawrence Tibbett, head of the American Guild of
Musical Artists, who was fighting a union takeover by mobster James C.
Petrillo. His $250 weekly paycheck staggered Stone. It was the most
lucrative job he had ever had. And the shortest.

Three weeks later, Kirchwey offered him a full-time job at the *Nation*
as an associate editor. Stone jumped at the chance to write under his
name again for $75 a week plus $10 for expenses, a medium-sized income for reporters in those days. In 1940 he was made the national
Washington correspondent, and he and Esther packed up the children
and were off to the capital, renting a small house off upper Connecticut
Avenue on Nebraska Avenue in northwest D.C. It would become home
for nearly three decades.

It was a modest house by any standards—"a little squish of a house,"
one friend said—but friends loved its book-lined coziness. There was no
foyer and one walked directly into the small living room from the front
door. The dining room, which Stone often usurped as an office, was directly behind the living room. Upstairs were three bedrooms. The second-floor landing was bulging with floor-to-ceiling books. The Stones
were lucky in their timing. The capital was still a sleepy Southern town,
abundant with magnolias and mosquitoes, where it seemed as if the hu-
midity could be wrung from the summer's air like a damp cloth. Then,
when Washington went to war, it doubled in size and was quickly filled
with such disparate newcomers as dollar-a-year industrialists, sailors,
secretaries, reporters, Nazi and Russian spies, pimps and prostitutes who
serviced young soldiers passing through.

A monstrous military building was being erected across the Potomac
that would house an entire city of military and government workers,
some forty thousand. It was said that one could get lost in the Pentagon
and wander its corridors for months. An oft-told joke was of the pregnant
woman who gasped to a guard that she was in labor and needed help to
get to the hospital. He said, "Madam, you should not have come in here in
that condition." "When I came in here," she answered, "I wasn't."

The housing shortage was so acute that strangers knocked on doors, begging to rent rooms. One joke claimed that a man saw another drowning in the Potomac, shouted for his address, and raced to the man's abode, where he was told that the room was already taken. "But I just left him drowning in the river," the man protested. "That's right," replied the landlord, "but the man who pushed him in got here first."

Stone's indefatigable energy, curiosity, and obsession with the big issues of the day were ideal for his new job. He was ecstatic about being in the New Deal's epicenter on the brink of cataclysmic change. Soon his exposés of FBI racist and anti-Semitic tactics would make him a famous enemy, and his exposés of business scandals and antiwar production would earn praise from a future president of the United States.

Although no feminist, Stone respected his first, and only, female boss, even though his bullying interviewing technique and tiffs with staff members drove Kirchwey to firing off reprimanding memos. A product of the twentieth century's first wave of feminism, Freda Kirchwey was an inordinately powerful force in any era of journalism. Only a handful of twentieth-century women—Cissy Patterson, Katharine Graham, Dorothy Schiff—would take such powerful personal roles in shaping major publications. Kirchwey's controversial signed editorials would alienate editors, writers, and readers. Some felt her intense antifascism badly skewed her judgment on Russia. On the other hand, pacifists decried her push for the United States to aid Loyalists in Spain, and, later, to fight Hitler.

Founded in 1865, by abolitionist E. L. Godkin, the *Nation* grew into a broader-based crusading opinion magazine under Oswald Garrison Villard, tackling international as well as national affairs. A reformer dedicated to ending racism and providing freedom for all, Villard kept Godkin's spirit alive. As Stone wrote, the *Nation* kept its "moralistic approach to politics and politicians." As a pacifist, Villard and his *Nation* opposed U.S. entrance into World War I, a position that assured questions of "patriotism." J. Edgar Hoover's FBI would continue to spy on the *Nation* and its writers for decades.

The daughter of progressive parents—her father was dean of the Columbia Law School—Kirchwey was born agitating. She was voted both "the most beautiful" and "the most likely to succeed" by her 1915 Barnard classmates. She gave a feminist valedictorian address and rode in a suffragette parade wearing a filmy white cheesecloth robe over jodhpurs. Kirchwey kept her own name when she married Evans Clark that year, and scandalized some in her husband's family by writing for the *New York Morning Telegraph,* noted mostly for its racing tips.

In 1918, Kirchwey interviewed for a job at the *Nation,* stressing her interest in women's suffrage and the peace movement, both of which pleased Villard. Only twenty-five years old, Kirchwey had already experienced a searing tragedy. She had quit the *Telegraph* to raise her firstborn son, Brewster, recording every minutia of babyhood. When the baby died at eight months, the grief-stricken Kirchwey was unable to write professionally for eight more months. The *Nation* then became a refuge, a crowded office filled with avant-garde colleagues. Pregnant women were mostly confined to homes and dismissed from jobs, but during Kirchwey's next attempt at motherhood, no one "made any protest against the extremely pregnant Miss Kirchwey strolling about the office, interviewing foreign authors." Still, her embarrassed mentor, Villard, when introducing her as "Miss Freda Kirchwey," would go on to explain, "but she is really Mrs. Evans Clark."

When her second son was born, Kirchwey determined to work as hard at her career as at child rearing. She wrote with dash, pushing for the radical idea of birth control, detailing the plight of coal miners' wives, or decrying anti-Soviet positions of U.S. policies. For nine months she walked across the Brooklyn Bridge daily to breast-feed her son. She recalled that combining motherhood and a career "was very hard."

By the time I. F. Stone began freelance writing for the *Nation,* Kirchwey had experienced two more tragedies, the shattering death of her mother and then, after years of caring for her third son, Jeffrey, his death from TB and spinal meningitis. Kirchwey retreated from her career and essentially from life, seeking help through psychoanalysis, then returned to the *Nation* after a three-year absence. She spoke eloquently about the strains and ambivalence of combining motherhood and a career, but was now ready to throw herself into the *Nation* with the passion and energy of a woman running from a private life of such sorrows. By the mid-forties she was known as a witty, fun-loving editor and publisher of a magazine that was, in contrast to her personal style, loaded with gravitas. By 1946, Kirchwey was in her early fifties. She impressed and charmed many with her intelligence and youthful looks, which she took pains to heighten. One female reporter during the war remembers an editorial discussion "in a beauty parlor, having to shout because Freda was under the damn hair dryer."

Despite wrangling leftist forces, Kirchwey amassed a collection of famous writers and friends for the *Nation*. Her constant worries about finances escalated when thousands of pacifists canceled subscriptions in protest of Kirchwey's position that the United States might have to enter the war to stop Hitler.

Facing the grim probability of his country at war, Stone hesitated. He aligned neither with isolationists nor with all-out interventionists, feeling that the United States should support the Allies with aid, but, like the vast majority of Americans, wavered about sending troops. His *Nation* columns sometimes reflected turmoil; morally certain that Hitler was evil, Stone nonetheless abhorred war. And with Russia now aligned with Germany, he no longer saw it as a black-and-white battle between fascism and socialism.

It is ludicrous, as some critics have charged, however, that Stone remained neutral because it was the pro-Communist position during the Stalin-Hitler Pact. He supported lend-lease to Britain, and his brilliant exposés of corporations in cahoots with Nazi cartels totally refute such lies. Well before other journalists began to look at "business as usual," Stone became a superb investigative critic of politicians and corporations that not only opposed war production but continued to do business with Germany, Japan, and Italy. Stone produced scoop after scoop about American financiers, who included John Foster Dulles, and their dealings with Axis powers. Half a century later, historians would dredge up such relationships of American super-WASPs with German cartels, but Stone was reporting about them at the time.

Stone observed that their dealings with Nazis stemmed from pure moneymaking interests. Following the war, when John Foster Dulles pled for leniency for the Germans, Stone choked on his "ostentatious" piety. Dulles gave speeches in Europe preaching that man is created in the image of God. Stone said, "I want to hear him say it in Atlanta, where one of those images, done in charcoal, has been strung up to a tree. I do not want to hear him deplore materialism as long as he devotes his life . . . to defending the rights of a few to monopolize its blessing. The man who keeps Mammon for a client shouldn't talk so much about God. If Jesus had been as this man . . . he would have opened a law office in Jerusalem, catering to the wealthiest of the Pharisees." Stone despised Dulles for his phony "conversion" to God in light of his business actions before and during the war. His firm, Sullivan & Cromwell, "numbered among their clients leading German cartels Hitler used in his attempt at world conquest." At no time back then did Dulles denounce totalitarianism, Stone lashed out. "He did not attack Nazi paganism nor reject retainers in protest against concentration camps." Now, in 1948, Dulles, "who had never risen to plead for the victims, asked mercy in defeat for the oppressors."

In 1940, Stone bitingly attacked Secretary of State Hull, infuriating him not for the last time. The stiffly Victorian, white-haired statesmen was much given to subterfuge when dealing with the press. As Germany, Italy, and Japan united in a critical alliance, Stone dissected the State Department's maladroit response. "Nowhere in Washington was the news of the Berlin-Rome-Tokyo pact greeted with so elaborate a lack of surprise as in the State Department," wrote Stone. " 'We knew it all the time' was the refrain the Secretary of State gave the press. . . . He went on to declare that it 'merely makes clear a situation which has long existed in effect and to which this government has repeatedly called attention.' " Commented Stone, "It is impossible to take these words at their face value without passing a harsh verdict on our diplomats. For if the announcement of the [Axis] pact does not alter a situation which has existed for several years and if that situation was 'fully taken into account' . . . why did the State Department so long refuse to embargo war materials which armed one of the principal participants in the most dangerous alliance that has ever confronted this country?" Stone enumerated years of foot-dragging by the United States on embargoing materials to make weapons in Japan, thus "protecting the profits accruing to American business from the aggressions we were so nobly denouncing. It was not until July of 1939, after almost eight years of Sino-Japanese warfare, that the State Department finally gave notice of intention to abrogate our commercial treaty with Japan, a necessary step if an embargo was to be imposed with full legal decorum."

Regulations put in place the previous summer (1939) were meaningless, charged Stone. "It is now revealed that few if any licenses were denied under these regulations. Now, when an embargo is finally to be placed on all the seventy-five varieties of iron and steel scrap instead of on just one, the Japanese are given almost three weeks' notice, and will therefore be able to add another 100,000 to 200,000 tons of scrap to the 9,000,000 tons we have so generously supplied to them."

Two weeks later, in October 1940, Stone attacked Republicans who gutted funds to investigate Axis alliances: "American companies have

$2,000,000,000 invested in Germany. To what extent has this been made a basis for blackmail?" His exposés led to congressional hearings.

Enemies of Stone who falsely insist that he was an apologist for Russia during the time of the Stalin-Hitler Pact would do well to read him. Stone wrote contemptuously of both. "The Nazis were ready to give up their hatred for bolshevism when a pact with the USSR suited their purposes. The USSR was ready to revise the 'line' of the Comintern for a pact with Berlin." Nor were "the Allies" much better; they had been "cultivating the friendship of those well-known democrats, Franco and Mussolini," and could possibly join the Nazis. Indeed, Britain's wealthy Cliveden set, the pro-Nazi faction who frequented Lady Astor's Cliveden estate, were so enthralled by Hitler that the specter of England becoming a puppet state if he won was not a casual fear. In a pox-on-all-your-houses mood, Stone wrote, "I see no issue here that warrants American intervention. I see no solution to this conflict that could possibly compensate us for the expenditure of lives and money, and for the bigotry, madness, and folly inevitably unchained by war. This struggle among England, France, Germany, and Russia," with shifting alliances "as strategy dictates, has been going on ever since the appearance of the European state."

Again Stone attacked Stalin in 1940: "In an attempt to make Russia safe for cartels and capitalism I am not prepared to champion the present Russian regime." But "whatever the true nature of the regime in Moscow," he wrote, a "holy war against it" would lead to the "fiercest kind of repression at home of all who believe in social reform, though it be of the modest variety." As the war escalated, both Stone and Kirchwey resorted to harsher rhetoric against the USSR, resulting in angry letters from pro-Stalinist readers. At every step, Stone consistently opposed both left- and right-wing isolationists during the months of the Stalin-Hitler Pact when groups dominated by the CPUSA fiercely opposed the Lend-Lease Act to aid Britain. Stone championed the bill throughout its arduous slog through congress and cheered its passage in the Senate in March of 1941.

It took far more courage to vote for aid to Britain than any future generation steeped in World War II Greatest Generation hype could imagine. Polls showed that a vast majority favored no action. "Only 12 percent were willing to aid the Allies while staying out of the war." Shortly before Paris fell in 1940, Senator Claude Pepper introduced the first lend-lease bill. Giving aid to Britain so that it could resist Hitler's blitz was the only way for America to avoid combat, he argued. Fierce opposition resulted in a watered-down bill that was finally passed the following spring. Meanwhile, dozens of women calling themselves the Congress of American Mothers marched on the capital and hanged Pepper in effigy. Pepper kept the scraggly stuffed effigy all of his long life.

Stone understood that, for some, neutrality was a genuine and understandable position. The horrible loss of lives in World War I was but twenty years past, and some veterans were still wasting away in VA hospitals. But the mixed bag of isolationists was more complex than that. It included everyone from beer-drinking fascists to the Communists who did their 180-degree turn overnight, anti–New Dealers, anti-Semites, and tycoons. Landlocked Midwesterners saw no reason to rescue those on a far-off continent. Stone did not question the patriotism of most isolationist senators, "but there was also a minority of appeasers. . . . Their strategy is to inherit power in a debacle. A little anti-Semitism fits in with their plans. Their chief campaigning grounds will be in the isolationist farm belt," warned Stone. He combined reportorial digging, examination of articles and radio shows, interviews with New Deal sources, and personal criticism to systematically excoriate right-wingers in congress who had opposed the lend-lease bill—"a measure no more extraordinary than the times in which we live." The legislation gave President Roosevelt the power to sell, transfer, exchange, or lend equipment to any country (with the bulk of the aid going to Britain) to help defend itself against the Axis powers. Stone noted that the first ships to Britain sent food to prevent starvation, which was "as dire as the need for steel for guns. 'Starve' does not exaggerate."

Stone explained, "The hope is to obtain war-time powers at home, as abroad, without actual participation in war. . . . An opposition crystalized and united by the fight against the lease-lend bill will do its best to represent the defense effort in a sinister light, although this opposition is itself infected with the totalitarian virus." He assailed isolationist Senator Burton Wheeler of Montana for "his excursion into Coughlinite demagogy," noting that Wheeler had named only Jews in his condemnation of the rich who supported intervention—"the Sassoons of the Orient . . . the Rothschilds and Warburgs of Europe"—who, said Wheeler, wanted to save their overseas investments.

"Even more disturbing to one who wishes to believe that the Senator's recent tone is due to a temporary hysteria and not a considered position was the conversation I had with Mrs. Wheeler, who is said to exert a strong influence over her husband. The Senator, she said, was in her opinion much too tolerant of the Jews, often defending them unjustifiably in conversations in the Wheeler home."

All the while Stone was exposing foot-dragging congressmen and flaws in the U.S. defense program, championing preparation for war, and supporting the universally unpopular cause of helping countries who were fighting Germany, Stalin adhered to his nonaggression pact with Hitler. Stone's entire views were antithetical to Communist sloganeering. Then on June 22, 1941, Germany attacked Russia. In the first days of Operation Barbarossa, the German Luftwaffe massacred the Red Air Force. Russia suffered huge casualties—20,500 tanks, thousands of aircraft, and more than 3 million prisoners of war by December 1941, most of whom would die. Many on the left rested easier now that the United States and Russia were allies.

Because of his near deafness, Stone continually examined documents, thus his depth of knowledge trumped most in the trade. Contrary, however, to the myth that Stone seldom covered events or interviewed high-level sources, he attended press conferences and larded essays and articles with facts and opinions gleaned from prominent New Dealers. He tangled with some and was admired by others.

John Kenneth Galbraith, who would become a force in politics, a giant in economics, and a master of the felicitous phrase, endeared himself to generations of readers with such irreverent comments as "the experience of being disastrously wrong is salutary; no economist should be denied it, and not many are."

He was a young man in FDR's administration at a time when the country faced a devastating shortage of wartime materials exacerbated by reluctant executives loath to gamble on profits. "Before and even after Pearl Harbor it was very difficult to get many of the large corporations to take the war seriously. They weren't willing to give up the production of civilian goods. The automobile industry was the prime case," Galbraith recalled. "It was a bitter fight and a number of journalists were involved, but Izzy was by far and away the leading and best one." Galbraith wanted "immediate shutdown" of civilian production in the auto industry and "all effort put into conversion, but [Leon] Henderson [the administrator of the Office of Price Administration and Civilian Supply] made a [secret] concession that they could manufacture automobiles for another couple of months and use up their inventories. No one wanted the press to know what had transpired. There was an enormous press conference and Izzy was in the front row."

Stone was about to do battle with Henderson. A half century later, Galbraith recalled with a smile, "I can still see Izzy, in the front row. He had a perpetually tough expression on his face. Although he was liberal in his orientation, he was ruthless in his demand for the facts, whatever the politics of the person involved.

"That day, Henderson gave a brilliant defense for letting the automobile companies go on for another two or three months" of civilian production of cars. "Henderson pulled out all the stops, saying that automobiles produced in that time would be used for [military] staff cars, giving it a war-production angle. He'd practiced it all day!" In the silence of other reporters scribbling, one voice piped up. Henderson's argument was "totally exploded by Izzy, who asked, 'Mr. Henderson, can we assume that this is a deal?'" Henderson fumed in red-faced agitation as the other reporters took their cue from Stone to see the facts behind his spiel. As Stone had so aptly remarked a few years before, "The cash register never did march to the front trenches, and fascism cultivated for all it is worth the innate imperviousness of money to sentiment."

Stone was "then, as for generations, the most intractably independent of reporters," said Galbraith. During a liberal administration, "Izzy was not vilified for his views. He was vilified for his methods. He was relentless in exposing evasion and made no concessions to the person who was improving on the truth. If you didn't resort to phony explanations, you had no problem with Izzy, and I very early on learned that."

Even after Pearl Harbor, Charles E. Wilson, president of General Motors, came to Washington on behalf of automobile-industry leaders who continued to resist all-out mobilization. The press was locked out of Wilson's meeting with William S. Knudsen of the Office of Productions Management. Among the reporters was Stone, wearing his hearing-aid receiver clipped to his coat pocket with separate wires running up to earpieces. "Stone pressed his receiver flat against the conference room door, turned up the volume, and as the door vibrated from the sounds inside, he heard everything said in the meeting and repeated it to the others," recalled David Brinkley. Thus the Washington press corps heard in great detail Wilson's plea to go on building cars and the final curt refusal from Knudsen: "No, Charley." As Brinkley wrote, "With those two words, the Roosevelt administration shut down the largest industry in the world and forced it into other work." That Stone had helped make this nationally known by use of his hearing aid always drew a chuckle from Brinkley.

In addition to his *Nation* work, Stone managed to write a critically acclaimed book, *Business as Usual,* published in 1941. This was no cut-and-paste of published columns but a thorough clarifying exposé on mobilization. The book was praised by the chairman of the Senate Committee Investigating Defense as "absolutely essential in the public interest. This is the first book to show the way in which monopoly practices and big business control hamper mobilization of America's resources for defense," wrote the senator. This was no faint praise from a senator who used Stone's work to expose the scandals of Axis cartels and was credited with prodding business into wartime production. Within a few years he would become the president of the United States, Harry S. Truman.

At times there were evocative human details in Stone's reporting, such as his you-are-there piece on Washington's reaction to the Japanese attack on Pearl Harbor on December 7, 1941. Stone got the bead on reporters because he was at work on a Sunday at the National Press Building where wire tickers flashed the news. He raced to the White House as a crowd gathered, then talked to the Chinese ambassador on the phone, who said "he felt 'really sad' and sounded as though he meant it." Around town, Stone witnessed the first awakening of war: "Soldiers in helmets, carrying guns with fixed bayonets, guarded the entrance to the War Department . . . looked awkward and uncomfortable. . . . In the Navy Department reference room women employees, hastily summoned from their homes, sent out for sandwiches and joked about Japanese bombers." Everywhere he "encountered a sense of excitement, of adventure, and of relief that a long-expected storm had finally broken. . . . We are going into this war lightly, but I have a feeling that it will weigh heavily upon us all before we are through."

However, most of Stone's work during this period featured investigative pieces. If readers were justifiably outraged, felt Stone, it would come from what he uncovered more than from personal polemic. Stone was proudly carrying on the tradition of his boyhood heroes Upton Sinclair, Lincoln Steffens, and Ida Tarbell.

Stone and his boss agreed that exploiting the fear of a Communist revolution remained Hitler's one ace in the hole as the war progressed. Anticommunist fear in the United States also gave J. Edgar Hoover untrammeled authority to snoop on U.S. government workers. Stone told

Kirchwey that he could expose FBI assaults on civil liberties through an anonymous source. Although she was deeply troubled by FBI tactics, Kirchwey was repelled by the use of anonymous material. "There was a time when I would have objected to printing any anonymous article in the *Nation* which made serious charges against individuals or government agencies," she wrote to Stone, and warned him in tough terms, "When [Attorney General] Francis Biddle calls me up the day after the first article appears, I want to be able to say that I know who the writer is, that I consider him a responsible and reliable person, and that I can vouch for the authenticity of the facts."

Stone's source would not reveal his identity to anyone else. So Kirchwey took the train from New York to Washington to see for herself if the FBI's "character investigation" violated the civil liberties of government workers. Wrote Kirchwey's biographer, Sara Alpern, "Talks with a Cabinet member, the head of a federal agency, and two other prominent government officials convinced her that the 'inquisition was aimed at ridding the government service of as many New Dealer and other progressives as possible.' Based on these facts, trust in Stone's integrity, and the importance of the charges, she risked the consequences and published."

Thus Stone's anonymous informant became the forerunner to such secret whistle-blowers as Watergate's Deep Throat, thirty years later, who remained unknown until the summer of 2005. He too turned out to be an angry top FBI agent, W. Mark Felt. Stone's blockbuster series was titled "Washington Gestapo," with the provocative byline of "by X X X." Kirchwey wrote an explanatory paragraph: The "author has deemed it necessary to guard his anonymity. His identity has been revealed only to our Washington editor, I. F. Stone, who as a friend of long standing, is able to vouch for his absolute reliability. . . ." Her government sources "fully bear out his charges."

The anonymous official explained the " 'character investigation' to which all workers in war agencies are subjected to by the FBI, sometimes over and over again." The disclosures of invasion of privacy remain chilling. In addition to the typical quiz of what books someone read, the FBI questions put to government workers about colleagues included "Does he mix with Negroes? Does he seem to have too many Jewish friends? Does his face light up when the Red Army is mentioned? Does he turn first to Russian news in the paper? Is he always criticizing Vichy France? Is he faithful to his wife? Does he think the colored races are as good as the white? Why do you suppose he has hired so many Jews? Is it true that he reads the *Nation* and the *New Republic*? Does he buy out-of-town newspapers? How often does he read *PM*? Does he talk a lot against the poll tax? Do you think he is excessive in opposing fascism or Nazism? Does he support the Newspaper Guild? Did you ever hear him whistle or sing the communistic 'Internationale' or other subversive songs?"

Stone noted, "Questions like these are being used as a sieve to strain anti-fascists and liberals out of the government. They serve no other purpose. You don't look for enemy agents or sympathizers among people who read *PM*, the *Nation*, the *New Republic*; among people who believe in the dignity and equality of all men; among people who condemn the poll tax, Vichy France, [House Representative Martin] Dies, Jim Crow; among people who admire unions, cooperatives, and the heroic exploits of the Red Army."

Warned Stone, "Ordinary, decent people" were being singled out. A woman was dismissed from her job because she was accused of having "mixed parties" (the first definition of *mixed* was Negroes and whites, and then it was "cautiously modified" to "boys and girls"). A scientist was deemed "unsuitable" for a government job because he was among those who helped organize the concert by Marian Anderson "after she had been jimcrowed by the D.A.R." (After the DAR refused to let her perform in their hall, the famous black opera singer, backed by Eleanor Roosevelt, stirred hundreds of thousands of listeners when her voice rang out from the Lincoln Memorial.)

The article tore into J. Edgar Hoover's racist sentiments and expounded on guilt-by-association harassment and "stupid prejudices and absurd evidence" of the investigators. "The penalty for an investigatory finding of guilt is peremptory dismissal from the government. This means being blacklisted for life. . . . No government employee is safe from such an obscene attack on the elemental decencies."

Stone wrote light-heartedly but pointedly, "President Roosevelt himself could not qualify for work in a war agency. Did he not entertain the Soviet Premier, Molotov, in the White House?" This did not please Kirchwey, who dashed off a memo to Stone: "In the middle of a war, when one is forced to denounce the President it is probably better strategy to do it in an extremely serious, dignified way—however bitterly."

The series revealed Stone's appreciation of the absurd as he described a visit from an FBI investigator to his anonymous source: "A curiously fanatical look came into his eyes. 'Could I tell him why Bill Smith had grown a beard? What did he have to conceal?' " Added Stone, "He was trying to hide a receding chin about which he is inordinately self-conscious." Stone commented, "The quality of the work done by the FBI . . . is about what one might expect from detectives diverted from their normal pursuit of bank robbers and white-slavers into the misty world of opinion and intellect."

Stone's enmity for Hoover was returned. "Stone is known to the bureau because of his hostile editorial comments made against the FBI as early as 1936," noted Stone's FBI file. "He has repeatedly attacked and vilified the Director and the FBI." As Stone continually damned Hoover and the agency in well-documented essays and scoops, Hoover fumed and resorted to customary vengefulness. At the time of the 1943 FBI "Gestapo" series, Stone had been watched by the FBI since 1936 and had been singled out personally by the director for at least two years. A July 29, 1941, memo noted that an informant, the name blacked out, "dropped in this morning and stated that I. F. Stone, writer for the Daily Worker [incorrect] and other radical publications, has been in Washington and BLANK listened to him place two telephone calls, one to BLANK in Solicitor General Biddle's office and one to BLANK, a recent addition to the Solicitor General's office." That a legitimate reporter would be calling legitimate news sources did not seem to penetrate the mind of Hoover's G-men. In FBI-speak, the memo hinted at dark doings: "Stone has a rather close and possible intimate contact with these gentlemen as he had no difficulty in reaching and talked with them rather familiarly."

Then followed an underlined anti-Semitic notation: "The Director *will recall that Stone is not his correct name* [again, incorrect]. *He is of Jewish descent and BLANK advises that he is very arrogant, very loud spoken, wears thick, heavy glasses and is most obnoxious personally.*" Once again, a blacked-out informant "*thought we would be interested of knowing this contact.*"

Hoover scrawled back, with his signature use of "H," two questions: "What is his name?" And more ominously and tersely: "What have we got on him?"

Until Hoover's death in 1972 the search was on to "get" something on Stone. Following the *Nation* series, the FBI stepped up what had already been a prodigious surveillance of a man who never stopped openly saying or writing what he thought. Stone kept the FBI busy throughout the forties; he was now speaking to every imaginable left-wing audience and writing for not one but two "subversive" publications.

Stone was participating in one of the great experiments of journalism in the twentieth century, an effort both praised and maligned. The New York paper would not last a decade, but managed to live on in almost mystical memory for the rest of the century.

It was, quite simply, called *PM*.

13

GREAT EXPECTATIONS

In 1940, Ralph Ingersoll produced the most daring newspaper experiment of the twentieth century. *PM* was a tabloid that refused to pander: there were no racing sheets, no stock market reports, no pictures of stripteasers being hauled off to jail. But his major revolution stunned the publishing world: Ingersoll was going to try to make money or at least break even with no advertising. Instead, leftist political columnists and hard-hitting exposés were juxtaposed with full-page photos, often of leggy young women, in the "only daily picture magazine in the world."

Ingersoll was a wealthy, neurotic, flamboyant genius who breathed confidence, although the derisive comment around *PM* was that he couldn't make a move without consulting his psychoanalyst; in those days, only the rich and famous thought there was some benefit in lying on a couch talking exclusively about themselves for an hour.

Unlike publishers who were primarily ignorant about the products they sold, Ingersoll was a gifted writer; Stone always praised his World War II book as akin to *The Red Badge of Courage*. He also wrote a classic roman à clef, *The Great Ones,* which skewered that international couple Clare Boothe and Henry Luce.

Stone was among the best in Ingersoll's stable of investigative reporters. In November of 1941, Stone's exposé of profiteering U.S. oil companies still shipping oil to Hitler's Germany by way of Franco's Spain forced the companies to stop the oil flow. He called the State Department flabby-minded censors: "The remedy, in the opinion of the State Department, is not to shut off the oil but to shut off the information." Stone referred to a censorship bill moving through Congress: "under the terms of this bill a reporter revealing information declared confidential by any government department would be liable to a $5,000 fine or two years in jail or both." The bill was being pushed by J. Edgar Hoover.

Once again, Stone had found an editor who gave him freedom. Stone recalled to Patner that Ingersoll was just "wonderful. I just loved the guy, the way I loved Stern." And Ingersoll repaid the compliment. "Ralph absolutely *adored* Izzy," recalled his last wife, Toby Ingersoll. "And what Izzy loved about Ralph was his independence—he's the only man I heard of who turned down a luncheon invitation from Nixon at the White House. He gave Izzy a free rein. Ralph was *violently* alive himself." The friendship lasted for years, until Ingersoll's death in 1985. In terms of appearance, they were an odd match. At six feet four inches, Ingersoll was a towering hulk next to Stone. Ingersoll's shuffling gait and occasional lisp hid his lightning-quick intellectual energy. What was left of his hair was black, circling a prominently balding dome.

Ingersoll was thirty-nine and Izzy was almost thirty-two when Ingersoll began his quest in 1939 to publish *PM* following an already famous career in journalism. He had been the managing editor of the *New Yorker*, the brains behind *Life* and *Fortune* magazines, and Henry Luce's top editor at *Time*. Before he saw the light, Ingersoll was just another happy capitalist in the world of Luce. As Wolcott Gibbs wrote in a *New Yorker* profile, "Few men of our time have risen to fame as crusaders in the face of such an aggressively respectable background."

Liberal to the core and vigorously antifascist in an era when most prominent and affluent Americans were not, Ingersoll nonetheless loved a rich high life unimaginable to his writers. There were four wives, three divorces, and several affairs. He fished with Hemingway. Dined with presidents. Before his stockholders grounded him, Ingersoll flew his own blue Fairchild monoplane, "roaring down out of the sky at a hundred and twenty-five miles an hour with his briefcase under his arm." In his briefcase were the names of what he called VRM (Very Rich Men) whom he would put the bite on to invest in his unorthodox paper.

PM often scored in crusades that mainstream, corporate-friendly newspapers largely ignored. It exposed the practice of the American Red Cross to segregate blood, deeming that the blood from black donors could not be used for white soldiers. Remarkable for its time, *PM* attacked segregation and lynchings like no other newspaper catering to white audiences.

In the first year and a half, *PM* exposed the Standard Oil Company, the Aluminum Trust, life insurance scams. It dogged Charles A. Lindbergh's romance with Nazi Germany and isolationist William Randolph Hearst. It took on Father Coughlin and the powerful Catholic Church.

Freed from advertisers, it passionately supported unions and workers' rights, including the controversial right to strike during wartime. Stone crusaded for an increase in the minimum wage. Companies that were profiting handsomely throughout the war could well afford to pay for an elevated standard of living for their wartime workers, he argued. Stone's exposés about seamy cartel dealings with the Axis were given prominent display. Housing codes that barred Jews were detailed long before one of Ingersoll's girlfriends, Laura Hobson, wrote *Gentleman's Agreement*, a novel depicting anti-Semitism in suburban America. "We pressured for the establishment of the first biracial hospital in New York," recalled Rae Weimer, one of the two top editors. "We weren't at all on the popular side." In other words, it was a perfect place for I. F. Stone.

Ingersoll was no stranger to personal journalism; his stories could have been briefer if the *I* key on his typewriter had broken. He reported at length his private audiences with Chiang Kai-shek, Stalin, Churchill. A "Dear Ralph" letter from FDR was framed. Eleanor Roosevelt praised *PM* in her column. Five months before Pearl Harbor, Ingersoll obtained a worldwide scoop when Lieutenant General Walter C. Short told him that "war with Japan was imminent." Ingersoll went to war, but unlike thousands of soldiers, his patriotic gesture was covered on page one of *PM*. (Stone was no grand specimen for the army. He flunked the physical.)

While many staff members were garden-variety liberals, political infighting was vicious between pro- and anticommunist factions. Some staff members remember *PM* as it was depicted by the Hearst empire, a "Commie" rag, but others proudly remember it as a heroic attempt. "The paper was often sloppy, screwy, and exasperating," said Stone, who single-handedly boosted circulation to 250,000 with his 1946 series detailing his adventures traveling underground to Palestine with Jewish refugees. "But it wasn't dull. Between endless griping we were proud to be PM-ers." Well, not everyone. Former staffer Shirley Katzander hated the intolerance of its leftists. "If you had dinner with one, you were a Stalinist; if you had dinner with Jimmy Wechsler, you were a Trotskyite." She laughed. "All you could do was eat alone. . . . If you were in the middle [she rolled her eyes], it was dreadful." Years later she remained loyal to fervent anticommunist Wechsler, a former CP member who sowed dissension and informed on at least one staffer to the FBI; Penn Kimball discovered that Wechsler was spreading lies about him to the FBI when he obtained his FOIA files.

Ingersoll captured idealistic journalists, intellectuals, and potential readers who fell in love with the prospect of journalism unfettered by greedy advertisers and reactionary publishers. *PM* was "against people who push other people around . . . whether they flourish in this country or abroad. We are against fraud and deceit and greed and cruelty and we will seek to expose their practitioners." Ingersoll roped in as his principal backer Marshall Field III, heir to Chicago's department store and once named "the richest boy in the world."

The rush to *PM* was like nothing ever seen in the newspaper business. More than ten *thousand* reporters applied for the two hundred available jobs. Ingersoll's first wave of recruits included friends who were famous or on their way to fame. And all too many of the staff had never been inside a newsroom. Dashiell Hammett, the author of *The Thin Man* and other popular detective novels, read copy for a brief, disastrous spell. James Thurber, Dorothy Parker, Ben Hecht, and Lillian Hellman wrote for *PM*. Gossip columnist Walter Winchell moonlighted, writing under the improbable sobriquet Paul Revere. The world's most famous photographer, Margaret Bourke-White, snapped pictures for *PM*. A doctor who gave baby advice in an anonymous column would later be known around the world as Dr. Spock. An illustrator who had spent seventeen years writing bug-spray advertising copy did scathing cartoons about Hitler, Mussolini, Japanese leaders, and America firsters like Lindbergh. He would become famous to generation after generation of book reading children as Dr. Seuss. An unknown James Baldwin was a copyboy.

PM's first edition arrived on June 18, 1940, four days after the fall of France. Ingersoll had so hyped his new venture that people stormed the delivery trucks and yanked copies off news racks. On the left-hand side at the top was its large, distinctive logo, *PM* in white italics on a sharp red background. Red borders outlined the front page. *PM* pioneered color, first-rate investigative journalism, innovative design, and consumer news. It also had the wildly successful cartoon *Barnaby. PM* cost five cents—two more than the *New York Times*—but scalpers were able to sell the first edition for half a dollar. This issue, with its enormous boldfaced headline "Hitler Arrives in Munich to Meet Mussolini," sold out its 450,000 copies before the day was over.

A. J. Liebling, the wise and witty *New Yorker* critic, was forever lamenting corporate takeovers and media mergers. One-paper towns stifled dissenting voices and wrought flabby complacency. Making money

through competition was "immaterial" to the takeover publishers because there was much more to be made "by selling out and pocketing a
capital gain, or buying the other fellow and then sweating the serfs." *PM*
"marked the first increase in the roster [of New York City papers] in
nearly twenty years," noted Liebling. "We greeted it with the delight that
bird-watchers manifest when the Department of the Interior reports the
birth of a new whooping Crane."

"One of the good things about *PM* was that it was different from any
other New York paper, and the differences were irreconcilable." There
was no way it could have been folded into any other existing paper. "Also,
it was pure in heart." Liebling's customary humor did not spare the
pure-in-heart paper: "The injustices it whacked away at were genuine
enough, but an awful lot of whacks seemed to fall on the same injustices.
A girl to whom I gave a subscription to *PM* in 1946 asked me after a
time, 'Doesn't *anybody* have any trouble except the Jews and the colored
people?' [From such thinking came the play on words to describe *PM*:
"Man Bites Underdog."] Still, while other papers were inventing anecdotes to discredit price control or lamenting the hard lot of large corporations, *PM* kept the facts of the case available to anybody who would
bother to read them."

The erratic ebb and flow of churning out a daily, staff dissension, ha-
rangues by reactionary competitors and congressmen, a natural disappointment after so high an expectation—all of this contributed to the
eventual death of the paper, but it lasted until Marshall Field III sold *PM*
to lawyer Bartley Crum on May 1, 1948. After the first few issues, the
rush to read it quickly subsided. *PM* slid down to 31,000 readers. One
disenchanted reader purportedly wrote to cancel his subscription, but
enclosed a wistful plea to just keep sending the high-minded prospectus
because it sounded so good.

The paper regained a steady audience of 125,000. This was not
enough to break even, but with Field's vital injections it survived for several more years. "I really liked Marshall Field an awful lot," recalled Stone
to Patner. "He was very good to me. It was very hard for a man of high
social position . . . to support a bunch of nondescript radicals and
pinkos. . . . I could just imagine him going to his clubs. . . . It would be
hard to take."

A hapless neophyte when it came to daily deadlines, Ingersoll
nonetheless brought his magazine skills to the daily. "He got us to write a

news story as a *story,* and not to put in the guy's name and address and his grandmother's name in the first paragraph," Stone emphasized. News was traditionally assembled with clunky, top-heavy paragraphs and lesser information trailing in order of importance. (This reverse-pyramid style evolved so that if an editor chopped off the bottom, not an unknown practice, at least the major facts survived.) Ingersoll encouraged more creative storytelling.

Not given to humor about his *PM* baby, Ingersoll did once joke, "We need both screwballs and competent technicians. So far I've been concentrating pretty heavily on the screwballs." His first labor editor (before *PM* there was no such beat) made a big display of rolling paper into his typewriter and raising his fingers as would a master pianist over the keys. Then he stopped. He didn't know how to type. Ingersoll spent more money to hire a secretary to do his typing. And somehow one hundred thousand pre-subscribers never got their paper. When *PM* finally discovered this enormous error, no one could find the valuable list. "Ingersoll wasn't a very practical man. He hired a *schoolteacher* for education editor," said Rae Weimer with the contempt of an old-line newspaperman, one of the few at *PM* who could run a paper. "He wasn't going to have a copy desk 'ruining copy.' The reporter was going to write his own headlines and send it down! Hell, there isn't anybody so good that a good copyreader can't improve. He paid Margaret Bourke-White $122,500! An awful high salary."

Above all, "we were trying to be a complete paper, and we didn't have the resources," recalled Stone. "It was nonsense." He argued with Ingersoll that he had to face that "we were a secondary paper. We should focus on exclusives and not do little feeble rewrites of stuff in the *Times.* Focus on two or three good stories. Scream it and sell." A decade later Stone would employ that formula in his own *Weekly.*

PM's hope of attracting working-class readers was a bust. They never caught the idea that an ad-free paper might give them straighter news. In fact, they missed the ads. However, *PM* had an absolutely devoted following. The famed author Joseph Heller, having grown up in Coney Island, elucidated how different the reading experience of New Yorkers was, compared to most of the country. "I never was aware that there was any suppression of liberal thought. I always had access to liberal newspapers, including one or two that Izzy wrote for. There was the *New Republic,* there was the *Nation,* there was *New Masses, PM,* and the *Star,* there was the *New York Post.* The *Times* I always regarded as being conservative or right-wing." One could tell a lot about the demographics and ethnic-ity of a neighborhood by what was being read on the subway, said Heller. "There was a subway station where people switching to another train would get off, the Fifty-ninth Street station, and everyone on the subway car who was reading the *Journal* or the Scripps Howard newspaper would get off at that stop. Everyone reading the *New York Post* would continue to Brighton Beach or Coney Island. That would be from 1937 to 1942. And then it was *PM*."

Looking at *PM* a half century after its demise, it is puzzling that it was so criticized. True, the complete newshound had to read other papers to find stories that *PM* missed, but *PM* covered what other papers had missed as well. It was biased, but openly so in the mode of European publications, not like papers that pretend otherwise. The pictures and layout were eye-catching, and stories were diverse and provocative: "Ar-gentina: Where the Nazis Have a Foothold" (October 5, 1941), "After the War—What U.S.A. Is Doing to Head Off the Crash" (May 10, 1942), "Jean Muir Demands Fair Deal for Negro Themes in Movies."

At times "we hit like a sledgehammer when we should have been smooth," admitted Weimer. Lindbergh's famous incendiary speech was handled in kind. Cascading down the page, one word per line, a huge headline on October 5, 1941, blared, "Lindbergh Lays Foundation for Fascist Revolt in U.S.A." Two articles stretched across four full pages, at-tacking Lindbergh and his America-first fulminations in Des Moines, Iowa. Lindbergh warned Jews of retribution for being "war agitators" along with an "undemocratic" Roosevelt and Britain. This was bad enough, but he added, "Their [the Jews'] greatest danger to this country lies in their large ownership and influence in our motion pictures, our press, our radio and our Government." His wife later wrote a mea culpa of sorts; her husband's speech was "at best unconsciously a bid for anti-Semitism. It is a match lit near a pile of excelsior."

PM's irreverent nose-thumbing enraged hard-line reactionaries and racists, much to the delight of its staff, especially the paper's treatment of the avowed leading racist and anti-Semite on Capitol Hill, Congressman John Rankin. "We always spelled his name in lowercase. It just infuriated him," said Weimer.

Stone feared that a pro-fascist force would disastrously shape postwar policies. He urged that Secretary Hull be fired for his "incorrigible deter-mination to play pat-a-cake" with France's pro-Nazi Vichy government (set up as a puppet government when the Germans occupied France) while ignoring de Gaulle's Free French forces. In 1940, when the secretary of state appeared before a congressional hearing, Stone had complimented Hull on his "ability to say little at great length." And two years later, Stone wrote that Hull had incensed America's allies when he had belittled the Free French. "Hull and the undemocratic little clique of decayed pseudo-aristocrats and backsliding liberals who dominate the State Department do not speak for the American people."

After relaxed censorship in North Africa in 1943, establishment publications, such as *Time* magazine, reported what Stone had already written a year before; such shoring up of fascist enemies imperiled the United States' relationship with its allies. At one press conference Stone asked Hull a tough question about his support of Vichy France, which provoked a sorry display of temper and anti-Semitism from the Southern politician. Recalled Madeline Amgott, who was covering the State Department, "Izzy would never get angry but asked these tough questions in a nice way that quickly got to the heart of the matter, and Hull would absolutely turn purple." There were usually about thirty reporters, all standing around a conference table. Hull faced them from the far side, only occasionally deigning to look up at the reporter asking a question. His Southern accent was accompanied by a "slight speech defect, almost a lisp," wrote Stone. "Unlike some old men, there is no youth in his eyes."

At one press conference Hull's attack on Stone warranted coverage. He had already accused Lippmann, but not by name, of "vicious, venomous vituperation." Stone had asked Hull if the State Department had or had not opposed the appointment of a former collaborator, Marcel Payrouton, as governor-general of Algeria. Hull didn't answer. Instead he demanded, "What's your name?"

"Stone," replied the reporter.

Hull pointedly responded, "You have some other name too, have you not?"

The reporter's name had not been anything but Stone for six years, and Hull had obviously been briefed about Stone's original name by the FBI. Reporters at the conference were shocked into silence, understanding the anti-Semitic implications of Hull's response. "Hull's whole demeanor and the contemptuous look in his eyes were so obvious; it was as if he was saying, 'This little Jew guy from the streets of Philadelphia,'" recalled Amgott. Hull's public temper tantrum was all Congressman Rankin needed. He stood up in the House and asked if Congressman

Martin Dies, another Red-baiter, "had noticed lately that these crackpots led by a man by the name of I. F. Stone, of *PM*, *I think his name is Feinstein*, are now attacking and attempting to besmirch Cordell Hull, secretary of state." The next day Rankin continued to attack "this Bernstein or Feinstein—one of the pen pushers on this communistic publication known as *PM*."

A *Washington Post* editorial decried Hull's shameful actions, and the *New York Herald Tribune* hammered Hull for scolding "those who have dared to question the perfect wisdom responsible for the present mess in North Africa." In the *Nation*, Hull was assailed for his "petty attack." Instead of answering a reporter's vital question, Hull was "dabbling in dirty waters," which gave an opening for "Congressional Jew-baiters" like Rankin. None of this quieted Stone, who continued to rile officials by sweetly asking the toughest questions in town, which prompted this crack after one tony correspondent asked a hard question: "Who does he think he is? The rich man's Izzy Stone?"

During the months of the Stalin-Hitler Pact, Ingersoll, like Stone, was hit by both Stalinists and isolationists for urging that the United States enter the war. "Our stance was that we were for anybody who was killing Nazis," said Weimer. "You had to understand the times, the tremendous power of all the big antiliberal papers." The fact that *PM* did not carry ads was one reason to attack it. "If we could succeed, it would be a definite threat to the way they did business." Many of *PM*'s strengths were adopted by newspapers long after its death. Later newspapers would follow Ingersoll's thrust for more vivid writing. In the 1960s the *New York Herald Tribune* became known as a "writer's paper." The *Washington Post*'s editor, Ben Bradlee, scrapped the women's page in 1969 and created the Style section, which profiled politicians, and covered politics, arts, and theater. This successful venture was copied across the country. Before *PM*, no paper had provided consumer and health news, which are now common.

"You can count on my honesty and sincerity. But I am sometimes gauche, tactless, overeager. If I should sometimes offend or rub you the wrong way, I will appreciate it and take it in good part if you tell me so frankly." This rather remarkable admission was written by Stone to Max Lerner after the well-known columnist helped Stone get his *PM* job. Yet, while admitting his faults, Stone did not change his volatility, which led to conflict with colleagues and bosses as well as those he exposed in print.

To Shirley Katzander, Stone was a humorless sexist who bore no resemblance to the colorful character of later years. But she respected his professionalism. "Izzy was *not* a Communist. No way," she said decisively. "Izzy made sense, a *lot* of sense, and wouldn't have been taken in by them. Izzy was very Jewish in the sense of being a 'good boy,' and he was a 'good boy' as a journalist." He was not one to play around or drink, she said. Did she think he developed a personality later in life? "I gather," she answered dryly. "He didn't have it when I knew him."

Katzander deplored the paper's left slant, and her admiration for Ingersoll could have filled a shot glass. "Ingersoll was such an ass. When I say I worked at *PM,* some people get down on their knees to genuflect. But I was *appalled* at it. I was told when I went out to cover a story, 'This is what we want.' I would never do it. And no one could tell Izzy what to do. He just wouldn't do it." She paused. "And that was quite splendid, really. If anyone tried to change his copy, he'd have a stroke. He was prickly and independent."

Katzander worked on a few stories with Stone, who was "very demanding." She felt that he barely trusted her to get correct information. "My God, he was a sexist." (Stone's attitude was not reserved for women alone, however; male assistants in later years got the same treatment.) Katzander felt that Stone's research was so superior that "although there was always a slant, he could back it up; he was dredging up a lot of government stuff that was hidden and needed to be exposed. He was one helluva reporter."

Stone's mercurial nature engendered an opposite response from *PM* editor Weimer. "Izzy was one of the most gentle, kindly people, besides being an extremely good reporter. His writing was low-key. You didn't know he was digging into something until you found you didn't have any pants on. He was always so inconspicuous and quiet-spoken." Again, this is in contrast to Stone's *Nation* editor. Although Kirchwey liked and respected him, her upbraiding memos to Stone scolded him after a colleague had been subjected "to the second abusive display of yours within a few months." She sharply urged Stone to tone down his combative questions and caustic comments, especially about "back sliding" liberals in the New Deal. "We cannot afford to throw overboard too lightly the few progressives we have in high office." Fearing libel, she rewrote a column and told him that without being able to back it up on legal grounds, "it was hardly advisable to call corporate heads 'traitors.' " She rebuked him for the "violence of your language."

Weimer remembered no such temper tantrums or writer's pique at *PM*. "Izzy was very accommodating. If I asked him to do something, he never argued with you. He might tell you it couldn't be done, but he said it quietly. A very popular guy, everybody loved him. In the early days Ingersoll would have all of us editors up to his apartment on Friday night. We would drink his beer and eat his food and Ralph and Lillian Hellman would take off for the theater. Stone sometimes joined in when he was in New York, but when he came up, it was pretty much all business."

A famous line that has lasted through the ages is attributed to the *New Yorker*'s Harold Ross. The seriously earnest men putting out *PM* "were a bunch of young fogies." And Liebling twitted them as well: "*PM*'s editors were not humorous men, but they realized that the paper lacked gaiety, and every now and then they brought in professional funny men to run columns. It never did any good. The humorists took to reading Max Lerner and became ashamed of themselves."

However, no newspaper worth its salt was ever free of pranksters, and *PM* had its share of frivolity. They worked "like hell" to put out the paper and pulled pranks to relieve the tension. As Ingersoll took off for Russia, the two top men he had just put in charge dropped firecrackers on him from the second floor. *PM*'s office in a crumbling, ancient converted factory loft had a skylight, kept open in hopes of catching a faint summer's breeze in a sweltering non-air-conditioned era. "Special nights after working late on a story, like the Roosevelt campaign, some of us would go up on the roof and dump a bucket of water down on the copydesk and everyone reading below," said Weimer. The copy was a mess, but the editors pretended nothing had happened and worked on. Because it was so hot, some had stripped down to their underwear anyway.

Stone used his near deafness as a ploy. "If he didn't want to hear you, he pretended you weren't around," said Weimer. Once while editing his copy, Weimer asked Stone a question and Stone didn't answer. "So I dropped a one-dollar bill and said, 'Izzy, you dropped some money on the floor.' And he went right for it."

Penn Kimball formed an active dislike of Stone, who he felt was a young fogy after he gave Stone a hotfoot (a match stuck in a shoe sole). The shoe didn't explode, but Stone did. "He had no sense of humor that I could discern. He was a very self-centered fellow," continued Kimball.

"And I admire him greatly as a reporter. He was a terrier at it, but he also had some crazy ideas. For someone who viewed himself as a fact finder, there are instances to prove that he certainly bent them when it became an ideological concern."

Stone's work was more complex than that. Since his articles were often critical of government transgressions, it was easy to brand him as biased, but there were no protests about his meticulous research. His viewpoint pieces were slugged in large type "OPINION." His investigative pieces summarized documents and press conferences and were supplemented with interviews, and he balanced his material. In his capacity as a columnist for the *Nation, PM,* and the subsequent *Star* and *Compass,* Stone was free to express viewpoints as all columnists do. But just as quickly, Stone could switch from commentary to investigative reporting.

Stone had the satisfaction of substantive results. His three-part exposé of Standard Oil led to Truman's firing an official who had withheld vital information. After a Stone series revealed that a handful of big business firms monopolized defense orders under OPM (Office of Price Management), the administration set up a branch to help small businesses get contracts. He experienced the power of the pen when the Economic Defense Board halted U.S. oil shipments to Franco and revoked licenses for export of oil to fascist Spain. The Treasury Department was forced to admit that Stone's figures on oil sent to the dictator were authentic. A month later, Stone reported that business as usual was sinking the arms program; he exposed OPM bungling in Detroit and revealed that plants ran at a fraction of capacity. FDR then scrapped OPM and set up a new War Production Board to expedite wartime production and procurement. When a Stone series revealed that the administration had slashed Russian requests for aid, the administration revised the aid allotment. In 1943, Stone revealed that Hull had forced the United States to put frozen funds in pro-Vichy hands.

In 1944, a small explosion against the rich occurred after Stone revealed that Palm Beach real estate interests were pushing the army to vacate the posh Breakers Hotel, which had been turned into a hospital for wounded servicemen. The publicity following Stone's scoop forced the army to delay closing the hotel hospital for four months.

The Red Scare was already in full swing, and another Stone series revealed that Civil Service Commission investigators were victimizing government employees suspected of liberal beliefs. At first the commission protested. Stone replied to the commission with tough editorials. A few weeks later, the Civil Service Commission issued a new code of regulations giving more protection to people investigated.

Then it was back to the war: SKF, a Swedish ball-bearing trust—with a Philadelphia subsidiary—was supplying the Nazis with vital ball bearings. Stone traced SKF's origins to a German combine. A few days after the series, United Press reported that SKF would cut sales to the Nazis. And so it went, on and on, one *PM* exposé after another, one *Nation* column after another. Well before most, Stone had in 1942 prophetically written in the *Nation* about the unfolding holocaust, "a murder of a people so appalling . . . that men would shudder at its horrors for years to come."

When Ingersoll returned to the paper after serving in the war, his battle with Wechsler, who Stone said was "smearing Ralph as a party-liner," escalated into the biggest public fight in *PM*'s stormy history. Besieged by advisers and investors who said that *PM* had to take advertising to survive, Ingersoll stubbornly refused, engendering the quip "Failure has gone to his head." As a cost-cutting necessity, Ingersoll told Wechsler to fire three people in the eight-man Washington bureau. Wechsler shoutingly told Ingersoll to fire Stone and one other reporter instead. There was no way Ingersoll would fire Stone. Ingersoll demoted Wechsler. He offered Wechsler's three reporters jobs in New York; they refused, and he fired them. The Newspaper Guild sued but a judge upheld Ingersoll's position. Wechsler quit, taking all but one reporter in the bureau with him. He carried on a vendetta for years against Ingersoll and Stone and decried their left-wing sentiments during Cold War investigations. A defender of Ingersoll's and an award-winning reporter, Tom O'Connor, said, "This whole affair reminds me of Gulliver in Lilliput—only Swift's little men never thought of trying to kill the great big guy with sour grapes." Ingersoll put Stone in charge of the bureau, and he "really hated" the job. "The only time I've ever been an executive. I hated having to fire people," he told Patner. "Just awful."

A disorganized Stone was guilt-ridden about unanswered letters from readers. Virginia Reid, a young mother whose paper had gone on strike, sought a temporary job with Stone. His secretary was away and Stone needed a good typist. "He would just pay ten dollars a day out of petty cash" for her temporary three-week job. The first day, she opened a drawer and found "about three hundred little scraps of paper . . . envelope scraps, with return addresses torn off and scraps with names to write letters to." When Reid asked Stone what to do with them, he sighed, muttering that he had always intended to answer them. He told her to write some responses. "Well, Virginia, tell him he's a wonderful person and a nice human being, but I can't do anything for him—but say it nicely."

Yet another woman literally sacrificed her future by giving Stone a sensational scoop about the United States' cushy dealings with German cartels. Her story illustrates one of Stone's edicts for reporters to search for help from those lower down in the government: "They are the ones who do the work and know things."

The war was winding down when Barbara Bick worked on an Antioch College co-op job in the Alien Property Custodian department in D.C. in 1944. The agency's job was to seize enemy properties. Bick discovered that many of the top managers of German corporations had become naturalized American citizens, either with "canny foresight or as part of long-term planning." One of the companies was I. G. Farben, the chemical cartel that made the gas pellets for Hitler's exterminating chambers. Her boss had discovered that the agency was about to turn over Farben's assets to its former German managers, now naturalized American citizens.

One morning her boss "rushed in and pulled me into the hall." She was leaving immediately to be with her husband for the last few days before his army unit left. She shocked Bick, whispering that she had been leaking the story to Stone. The woman thrust a document-filled folder at Bick, begging her to meet Stone that evening for her. Bick smuggled out the heavy folders. She felt the same as her colleague; what the Alien Property Custodian was doing was wrong. "Isn't that the reasoning of all whistle-blowers?"

The exposé exploded on the front page of *PM*. The United States had allowed the seized I. G. Farben firm to slip back into the hands of German murderers; Stone blamed Alien Property Custodian director Leo Crowley. Through Bick's leak, Stone proved that Crowley's Standard Gas cohorts were really dictating what went on in the Alien Property division. The next day, FDR at a press conference announced that Crowley would resign.

"There was a huge uproar at the office. Who had leaked the documents?" recalled Bick. The petrified college student was among those to be questioned by the FBI. Her mother, "perhaps from her youth in czarist Russia, knew instinctively what had to be done. 'You know *nothing* about this,' she drilled me, her dark eyes hard upon mine. 'Nothing!'"

Bick got through two interrogations. Months later, she was in San Francisco on her next co-op job when she was called to Antioch for a meeting. The administrators asked her about the incident. She gave them a full account, trusting in their doctrine of activism. A stunned Bick was suspended from college. "Izzy was outraged. He always felt a bit guilty, but it was not his fault. He wanted to make a cause célèbre of it. But my parents wanted no publicity."

During the Cold War years Bick never went to another college; "my husband was afraid that I might still be held accountable for leaking classified government documents." Only after Daniel Ellsberg's leak of the Pentagon Papers did Bick realize that she would probably not have been prosecuted. Without a college degree, Bick lost out on many opportunities. Still, her experience with Stone "has been a keynote of my life. 'Trust no government.' A free press, courageous journalists, and an alert citizenry are the only guarantees for a democratic society."

And "Izzy became a lifelong friend."

14

LIVING WITH IZZY

Stone's life was ruled by the tyranny of deadlines, as son Christopher so eloquently said. Stone's standard line to friends was "I'm working like hell" coupled with "I am having so much fun I ought to be arrested." His absorption, concentration, and constant deadline pressure did not always make life a lot of fun for the family. "Dad's life pulsed and we pulsed with it—or steered out of the way," recalled Christopher.

His children were lulled to sleep by the rhythms of a thumping typewriter. They awoke to the knife-sharp harshness of morning papers being ripped down the spine; Stone opened the papers like a book, gripping the sides with each hand, tore them down the center, then assembled the pages flat. Through the years he traveled many miles in his desk chair, circling as he went from one pile of documents or books to another until the wheels wore a grooved circle in the carpet.

The cycles of daily living were impressed upon Stone's daughter at an early age. "My father worked, my mother mothered. Father and his work were one, and to that one we were all of secondary importance," wrote Celia Gilbert. "When father napped, we tiptoed; when he was hungry, we ate. If he wanted to sleep at nine o'clock, mother was corralled upstairs." Dinner guests were expected to listen if he sat down at the piano. "If the teacup wasn't filled to the brim, he raged as though he had uncovered a plot to destroy him." Then, with her father's same glancing humor, she reflected, "I felt at home reading memoirs about Louis XIV."

The luckiest day in Stone's life was when he married Esther. Throughout their long marriage, friends and family watched her cater to Stone's whims and often wondered how she endured his sometimes peevish demands. At the couple's fiftieth wedding anniversary in 1979, Stone's kid sister, Judy, who had been a flower girl at their 1929 wedding, quipped that Esther deserved "some kind of a Purple Heart" for her longevity. Although she adored her older brother, Judy explained,

"Sometimes Izzy could be impossible in arguments, and Esther would sometimes timidly insert a word." His sister imitated Stone's impatience, with a brush of her hand in the air to stop the comment, " 'Wait a minute, Esther. Be quiet!' " His sister repeated what everyone else who knew them well said: "But he really loved her with a passion. He really knew how important she was to his life and told her all the time."

One of Stone's assistants during the seventeen years of his *Weekly* enterprise, Chuck Nathanson, said, "I thought Izzy was an enormously decent man in his political role. I also didn't think—aside from the way he treated Esther—that there was anything mean about him, and even *that* meanness seemed to have to do with whether he was ever going to be able to meet his deadline or not. Esther was always making sure that Izzy was not upset. 'He wasn't to be disturbed. He should *not* be.' It was clear that he loved and was devoted to her, but he just couldn't control himself." Nathanson marveled at how "it just seemed to roll off Esther." The irascibility faded as soon as the *Weekly* was put to bed, and Stone would be off in search of his favorite dim sum delicacies in Chinatown. By then, he "was always all relaxed and full of laughs."

Esther instinctively knew that Stone's obsession and anxiety—searching through documents, rereading notes and books to get a point exactly right, quizzing some source on the phone, pounding furiously to finish the article by deadline, constantly hawking prospective subscribers to make a living—was for Stone a tremendous pressure cooker. She did not take his outbursts personally.

Esther was a mother hen to all of Stone's assistants. "She is the most perfect human being I can think of," said Andy Moursand. "Without her I don't think Izzy would have had a chance. She had a wonderful sense of humor. If Izzy would sometimes blow up at me, she would just say, 'Oh, don't worry, he's always like that.' "

Said Peter Osnos, who later became a writer and editor at the *Washington Post* and then an editor at Random House before becoming the founder and publisher of PublicAffairs books, "Izzy's negatives were the flip side of his virtues. He was so focused and expected the world to revolve around him. I don't think of this as a great crime. All those sort of conventional list of flaws—sloth, greed, adultery, boozing—are absurd when considering Izzy. He sure as hell was not a hypocrite, he sure as hell was not a sycophant, he sure as hell was not greedy—except for information. He was very strong-willed, courageous, tough-minded, impatient, with enormously high standards for everybody and hugely high standards for himself. He could be abrasive but he was not angry or bitter. It's very hard to be a very good reporter for your whole life unless you truly believe in something. If there was a rage in Izzy, it was a rage for justice. In the end the only thing that could be criticized was the price other people paid for him—basically his wife and children, but Esther never thought that way, and if the children ever thought that way, they sure as hell have come to terms with it as adults."

The stories about Izzy and Esther seemed at times to portray an intellectual Archie and Edith Bunker of the leftist set. "At a party in the sixties, Izzy was holding forth brilliantly," recalls a friend. "It was a stormy night and the fire was in need of another log. Esther puts on a scarf and coat and steps into the night and comes staggering in with a load of logs, and Izzy points his hand to where she should drop the load and without missing a beat continued with his conversation." Esther's sister, Jean, remembers visiting the couple in later years. *"Esther!"* shouted Stone from upstairs one early morning. "Where the hell are my papers!? I can't find my papers!" Esther came from the kitchen to the bottom of the stairs and called up to him. Jean imitated Esther's delicate voice: "Izzy, they're right on your desk. Underneath the books. Remember? I put them there this morning and you said, 'Put the books on top because I need them'?" Admonished her sister, "Esther, how *can* you let him talk to you like that?" Esther responded, "Oh. Oh," in a perfectly reasonable voice, "he just can't find them." "Celia was always saying, 'He doesn't *talk* to her right.' I would just laugh at her. I knew my sister had her way whenever she wanted it."

When Stone finished his last book, *The Trial of Socrates,* he crowed to a friend and writer, Judith Viorst, "This is the best thing I've ever written." He had passed his eightieth birthday, but Stone jumped up and down like a child and said, "It is a *soufflé* of a book!" He quickly added, "I couldn't have done this or anything without Esther." Viorst was "very moved. I didn't really know that he had ever told her that. And I asked Esther how often he praised her that way and she smiled and said, 'Every day.' "

After thirty-four years of marriage, Stone was still saying of Esther, "She's an angel and I love her tenderly," adding that his wife "still loves me insanely." She "must have fallen on her head as a baby to like a funny-looking guy like me." In the feminist days of the late sixties and seventies, women friends and family were upset enough to speak to Esther about Stone's treatment of her. At age seventy, Esther said, "You know, my daughter, Celia, feels very strongly that I gave up something of my own talent. I simply don't care. I am completely fulfilled in Izzy's life. His energies and enthusiasms and excitements are just so great. When you live with a man who slides down the banister to get the news and can't wait for his first corny joke of the day, you have an experience. His life so fascinated me. It was as though I was hypnotized. Some people need complete attention, and Izzy is one. Complete attention, complete devotion, a complete feeling of being the creative person." Her job was to serve that end. Years later, Stone was asked if he agreed with Esther. "That's what Esther said. It's the way she feels." Women certainly had the same rights as men to do what they wanted to, said Stone, then added a bit defensively, "But women who like to be a wife and mother like my wife should be allowed."

Esther was attracted to Stone's impulsive bursts of romanticism, which lasted all of his life. In 1987, while attending a conference in Europe, he turned to a male companion who was walking with him and said, like a love-struck boy, "You know, today is the sixtieth anniversary of my first walk with Esther." Stone dedicated one of his books to Esther, "the best of me." In his first book, *The Court Disposes,* Stone inscribed his love to her in Latin: "You are to me a respite from care. You are to me light even in the black night and, in solitary places, you are for me world enough."

And he was world enough for Esther.

Esther was filled with contagious warmth. She always seemed ready to embrace a new venture or a new friend as long as it didn't interfere with her time with Stone. In their sixties they were the oldest couple on the dance floor, rocking to the beat at a San Francisco joint called Dance Your Ass Off. Stone loved the "freedom" of the dances of a younger generation; one didn't have to hold someone and lead, you could just do what you wanted to. Because of his near deafness until an operation in the mid-sixties, Stone loved to dance to a loud band, feeling the rhythm through his feet. When rock came along, he loved the thundering rhythm. No one ever called him a great dancer, but Stone carried on with gusto throughout the night.

Esther was wise to the ways of life beyond a sheltered existence; a woman acquaintance once hinted to Esther about her unhappy marriage and was astounded when Esther nodded her head sympathetically and murmured, "Sex is *madly* important in a good marriage." One of her granddaughters, Jessica, thought Esther was "so wise and so accepting and nothing you tell her can shock her."

"Esther is so much more understanding than I am," Stone once proudly admitted. "Within five minutes, people are stretched out on an imaginary couch telling her all kinds of intimate things. She's never malicious. She has a green thumb with people; she knows how to say a healing word. I tell her she's just a goddamn Florence Nightingale going around binding people's wounds. She's read a tremendous amount of Freud, but she instinctively knew everything Freud taught."

To Celia, her mother "was the mirror image of Father: he could only be happy satisfying himself; she others. She had her own order of priorities: personal loyalties, love of family, friends, her daily relationships." That combination and the complex array of gifts both parents gave their children created three individualistic adults, who, like their parents, have had lifelong single marriages and intellectual interests. Celia became a published poet, writing with powerful elegance. Mathematician Jeremy served as president of the Federation of American Scientists for thirty years. Christopher teaches environmental law, ethics, and globalization at the University of Southern California, where he holds the J. Thomas McCarthy Trustee Chair in Law.

It was a lively household where Stone took phone calls from the famous and erudite all over the world who were not hostages to America's Cold War scare. Many times during the repressive Cold War era home was an island cut off from a hostile world, awash in books and papers and stacks of Stone's files and documents. There were tempestuous political conversations in the living room. Poetry was forever spouted in snatches by Stone, who would jump up from the dining room table to find his beloved Horace, Whitman, *Agonistes,* or Blake.

Although some women acquaintances felt Stone was a sexist, this certainly was not true in his attitude toward daughter Celia. "There was an enormous bond between my father and me," she recalled. "When he was dying in the hospital he called me 'my alter ego.' We thought alike on most things in a spiritual way" and they reacted symbiotically to the same people, art, poetry.

Stone delighted in his daughter. He took her to parties, on interviews, trips and his endless round of bookstores. At Fire Island parties, "he liked to announce, 'My wife is the prettiest, my daughter the wittiest in the room.'" Although plagued by the rush of deadlines, Stone did not seem like an absent father to his daughter. When he was on trips, his loving letters to Esther always contained special messages for the three children. "He was proud of all of us." His whirlwind energy filled the house. "When he was away the house was very quiet and when he burst in through the door we all gathered around him excitedly, waiting our turn to be hugged after mother and to get his attention."

There were many family outings to the beach and the Smithsonian, and weekend picnics in Rock Creek Park, but what Celia and Izzy shared the most was their love of the written word. Early on, Celia became a sounding board for his work. "He was always showing me what he wrote as he pounded away on his typewriter at home." As he tore out sheets of paper and marked up his copy with thick black pencil, Stone would ask his daughter her opinion, "not about the politics but about the writing of it."

A cherished memory is the day when she was about ten and her father handed Celia a copy of *Roan Stallion and Other Poems* by Robinson Jeffers and said, "To be a poet is the greatest thing in the world." After she became an evocative poet, Stone's admiration was boundless. He proudly visited her at Smith. "He loved it that I was studying Greek, inspired by him, and gave me his own Liddell and Scott lexicon to take with me."

Stone had a passion for walking and talking that permeated his relationships with friends and family all his life. The conversation on those walks always "blossomed into lectures or diatribes or sermons, depending on Pop's mood," remarked Christopher. These talks were not just along some sylvan path. Trudging up and down the hill from his home to Connecticut Avenue, chasing seaside waves, crossing an urban street impervious to approaching cars, shopping in a supermarket, Stone could retain a steady, erudite stream. Patner's *Portrait* vividly captures Stone breaking into Greek and Latin poetry at the store's fish counter or dashing through *The Rise and Fall of the Third Reich* or the conditions in Nicaragua while examining the tomatoes.

In later life he had so often been interviewed that Stone's thoughts were distilled into shtick, but what shtick it was; whole, literate paragraphs would emerge, as if he were at a lectern, with hardly a pause as he paid a checkout clerk or stopped to give a beggar some money, as Patner observed. "I hate to pass a beggar," commented Stone. "I think they need to make a minimum wage. Even if they're professional beggars."

Adults meeting Stone for the first time were often amazed at the breadth of conversation; with an artist he would discuss arcane aspects

of a little-known sculptor, with poets he could talk about and quote son-
nets from several centuries; historians got a run for their money from
Stone's appraisals—he could easily summon the twists and turns of
worldwide ancient and present-day regimes. For him, arcane Greek
came alive and he would quote passages the same way he spoke French,
in a terrible accent, oblivious to the grimaces of his audiences. One of his
granddaughters joked that no one in the family could quite figure out
how to dissuade him from mangling poems in their original language.

His children absorbed his knowledge, spongelike, but it was Esther to
whom they "turned for love and unmatched wisdom," Christopher said.
And, said Celia, Esther "saw into the heart as clearly and profoundly as
Father did into the body politic." Christopher said he meant no implica-
tion that his father was uncaring about his family, but he always needed
friends and readers, "from whom he drew his zest."

Christopher acknowledged that all three of Stone's children had had
their problems with this "rather difficult" man, yet they were also "united
in common admiration" for him. Stone himself admitted, "I was a rather
absent father, I must say." Oblivious to his children's feelings, Stone startled them at dinner just before he left on a dangerous assignment to
cover the Israeli war in 1948. "I don't mind if I get shot by the Arabs,"
said Stone between mouthfuls, "but I'd hate like hell to be shot by the
Jews."

By all accounts of family and friends, Jeremy, the eldest son, had a
prickly relationship with his father, repeating Stone's pattern with his
own father. Jeremy adored his mother and resented the way Stone
treated her; he once bought a machine that aided her in the arduous task
of tabulating checks from subscribers to the *Weekly,* something that had
apparently not occurred to his father. Before that, Stone stuffed checks in
drawers to molder away. Helen Dudman, a lifelong friend and a former
Washington Post editor, felt that Jeremy had "a lot to work out about Izzy.
After his memorial service I sought Jeremy out. I said, 'The family all
spoke but you didn't speak. Why not?' Jeremy's answer to me was 'Helen,
you're too much of a reporter.' And that was all."

Jeremy was the acknowledged scientific genius in the house; in later life
he became the expert his father turned to for information on nuclear defense. At an early age Jeremy was playing three-dimensional chess. One
day Esther decided to give a party for her son's chess club. She was expecting a group of twelve-year-olds. Who showed up? "All these old men," said
Esther.

When they were grown-ups, any of Celia's or Christopher's childhood problems had faded into insignificance. Christopher recalled their father's "rare and wonderful life." Stone's quirks had long been turned into cherished anecdotes. One that summed up his myopic view of life around him was about the time the family went for an outing. Celia and Chris sat in the backseat, jerking back and forth to the pulsing, lurching rhythm of Stone's foot on the gas pedal, gunning it and then receding, then gunning it again in gut-wrenching sequence. All the while, Stone yelled cheerily to the carsick children, "Isn't this *fun*, kids?"

"I *need to practice*," Stone admitted to his reporter friend Madeline Amgott, in order to get a driver's license. Attempting to teach Stone how to drive was painful. Finally, he went with her to take the driving test. Stone put the car in reverse, gave it the gas, and promptly knocked down one of the blocks indicating where he should park. "He got the license," she said, "but that is no reason anyone should have ever driven with him."

She recalled that "Izzy was very comfortable in his own person." She arrived at the house one night to see Esther and Stone giggling like children. They were lugging a Christmas tree up the stairs, to hide it from a group of young American Jews. "He'd been training young people for the Haganah, to fight and create the state of Israel. Can you imagine him doing that? They were actually out in the yard, marching with sticks! But that was Izzy. He wanted to have a Christmas tree *and* the state of Israel." "Thank God Izzy had a sense of humor," remarks his sister, Judy. "Because with a brain like that, if he couldn't laugh at things, he would have been unbearable."

Stone was a complex character, mercurially cranky and good natured. He hated gossip and never participated in it. Many acquaintances have remarked that they learned nothing about his family from Stone. "He never talked about them on any of the occasions I was with him, or said that we ought to meet them," said *Washington Post* reporter Walter Pincus, who knew him socially for years. "I literally don't know anything about his past. He was always talking about the here and now."

Talking about the here and now could get him into trouble. Said Judy, "He was always very gregarious," but was incapable of masking his true feelings, a unique quality in the varnished world of Washington media and politics. As Esther said, "He loved to go to parties, but he'd insult people and then he'd wonder why he wasn't invited back." Esther used to blanch at times when he "caused a spectacle." Even among friends he didn't want to hurt, Stone could not dissemble. During the tough times of the movie-industry blacklisting, Stone made a speech at a Hollywood party, then made a few cracks about the Hollywood "proletariats" living the rich life. "No one would speak to him after that," recalls Judy, except actress Shelley Winters, who "got him a glass of cognac. They were pretty angry because they were under siege and here was Izzy, after giving this fine talk, having to ruin it all by criticizing this rich and famous lifestyle." When Christopher was eleven, his father took him to the movies. The newsreel came on and the face of China's leader, Chiang Kai-shek, filled the screen. Suddenly there was one sound in the audience, Izzy Stone, hissing and booing. Then someone said, "There's a Commie in the house!" Christopher shrank in his seat. "I'm very proud now of Dad for doing that, but at the time I just wanted to disappear."

There were other moments more wonderful. Many Washington classmates were the sons and daughters of whoever was the seasonal royalty, anointed by the politics of a particular moment. But rare was the father who knew someone as world famous as Albert Einstein and who thought to take his sons to meet him. "He was like he was advertised to be," said Chris. "The sweatshirt, sneakers, the towering corona of white hair. The most impressive thing to me was how slowly Einstein thought and spoke. He was much more reflective than Dad in this way, but clearly he was evaluating Dad's view on things. They talked about politics in America and the conditions in Germany. Dad was rapid-fire, and Einstein had this distinct voice with German culture and universities with unpronounceable names lurking in the background."

When they were ready to leave, Einstein said, "Do the boys haff any questions?" recalled Christopher in a fair imitation of his accent. Einstein said, "I will answer them if I can." Christopher, who felt "it was like being in the presence of God," couldn't speak. "I literally could not open my mouth. I was dumbstruck." There were other brushes with the famous, including one that did not impress Esther. When the family lived outside Paris in 1950, Jean-Paul Sartre came for a visit. Esther watched Sartre peel oranges and indifferently toss the peelings into her immaculate garden. As far as Esther was concerned, that was it for existentialism.

For many years, the Stone family had a little cottage on Fire Island in an enclave of leftist writers, thinkers, lawyers, and actors, such as the witty and amusing comedians Jack Guilford and Carl Reiner, and the ever-dramatic Lee J. Cobb. Stone was idolized by many who had read him in the *Nation,* the *New York Post,* and *PM* before his later fame with the *Weekly.* After Stone had pounded out a piece on his typewriter on the porch, he and Esther would take long walks on the beach; his brother-in-law, Leonard Boudin—who would later experience national Red Hunt turmoil and family scandal—organized the ball games with the children; there were cookouts on the beach and always political conversations and sometimes famous guests, such as Charles Chaplin, who drank cocktails on the Stones' porch.

Like many neighbors, Ruth Smallberg waited expectantly on first meeting for Izzy to say something brilliant. "He just sat there, quietly, with this wonderful dimpled smile, listening to us," said Smallberg. "It wasn't until later that his daughter came over and said that he wasn't listening to half of what we were saying because he had his hearing aid turned off."

"I had a wonderful relationship with the Stone children," said Smallberg. "They were my babysitters. They were all wonderful children, but Chris was the most open. And fun! There were no cars on the island, so children with their wagons would line up to meet the boats to get the luggage. Chris at about the age of ten got all these wagoners together." Christopher unionized them. "He got them all to agree not to bid against each other when the boats came in and to agree on a uniform rate. That rate was determined by how many blocks you had to walk from the boat.

"Chris also organized the babysitting service at a very young age. He got the movie house to run an ad about it, with his name on it. And a grown woman, a nanny from London, wanted to use his service. She came to the door and asked for 'Mr. Christopher Stone.' Esther said, 'He's taking a nap.'

"There was such a warm feeling in that house," recalled Smallberg. "I think Esther was the main one keeping it all together."

Neither parent disciplined the children, and consequently, Christopher never had any incidences of rebellion. A neighbor, a career navy officer, gave Christopher his first and last spanking. "His son Timmy and I were messing around with some dye and it got on the floor. Timmy couldn't believe that I had never been spanked. That shocking discovery was enough to almost numb his pain."

The atmosphere in the home gave the children a sense of freedom to think and do what they wanted. Stone wasn't a father with whom to have heart-to-heart talks, or to watch Christopher play sports; even when Christopher was on the Harvard lacrosse team, his father barely made one game. On occasions this hurt, but never translated into a feeling that

his father was uncaring. Stone seldom brooked differing viewpoints in his conversations with his children but, at the same time, was neither critical nor interfered with their careers or other choices. While Christopher appreciated the role his parents played, he is shaped by a newer generation's concept of fatherhood for himself. "In raising my own children, I am much more participatory."

Christopher had other males in the family who entranced him, especially his uncle Charlie, his mother's black-sheep brother who outraged Esther's middle-class sensibilities. "A real character and just terrific," said Christopher. "He represented the Black Muslims and Eartha Kitt and patented Dizzy Gillespie's horn. I used to upset my mother enormously by saying, 'You know, Mom, of all the people in the family, I really think I'm most like Charlie.' She would say, 'Oh, no! You don't know what you're saying.' " Christopher's wife, Ann, said Esther was the complete opposite of the meddling mother-in-law. She never interfered and was unflappable—"except when you said that Chris is like Charlie—that always rattled her."

Christopher has a self-deprecating ease about himself. "I was the slow-witted one in the family; my brother and sister were prodigies, and I think Mom was really pleased when I came along: 'Thank God, I've got a normal one.' I just obliged everyone by running around in the woods and playing sports and being interested in the girls. Jay [Jeremy] was intensely reading books and trying to teach me. Celia was embarrassed that I didn't know a foreign language, and she tried to teach me at a very young age." She set up a small desk and chair on the upstairs landing and would try to drill Chris in French. "She gave up." He was in awe of his sister, five years older, who was "very sophisticated and mature and had crossed bridges into literature which gave her insights that I couldn't aspire to." As the two women in the house, Celia and her mother shared a special closeness. They "would huddle in a sort of conspiratorial way drawing harsh judgments about men—particularly Father." It was a feminine entitlement that excluded Christopher. "I always sided more with my father. Of *course* he was impossible. He was running at his own pace, but that didn't seem to be so bad. He was following his own will."

As close as Celia was to her mother, she resented the expectation that was passed on from mother to daughter that Celia should submerge her own talents.

"As long as I was exclusively a wife and mother, I knew I had my

mother's full approval; to deviate from that path would threaten me with the loss of her love."

Yet Celia received conflicting signals because her father encouraged her to "speak up and be as direct as I please." She could be independent in a way that her mother would never be. This left Celia "confused and superficially rebellious." Her mother insisted that she give way to her father and brothers. When Celia protested her father's treatment of Esther, her mother insisted, as she did to everyone, that he was entitled to his "outbursts of anger as necessary outlets for the tension of his work."

Stone himself was rather underwhelmed by the new wave of 1960s feminism, unprepared for the tearing down of structured gender roles. He ardently supported such cataclysmic changes as the antiwar and civil rights movements, but did not take up the cause of women. Later, he encouraged younger women in journalism, and as one friend said, so quaintly, "He had an eye for the pretty young women." Celia absorbed different feelings as a child. The women who talked politics with him were either "homely, which depressed him, or opinionated, which unsexed him," she recalled. "But I, I was different." Celia would become the writer but in her father's image: "He could see that I was 'just like him.' "

No woman in her family had yet combined a career and marriage. Celia bonded with her mother's poetry-writing sister, Jean, and with Stone's sister, Judy, who was "independent and energetic, well satisfied with her bachelor girl life," a newspaper writer and movie critic who traveled the world to interview international directors. Her mother's comment was 'Poor thing, she's all *alone.*"

As Celia got ready to leave for a date when in high school, Stone would crack, "Now for God's sake, act dumb." Recalls Celia, it was "a joke of course," but privately she thought, wasn't that dumb-Dora act an aspect of her parents' marriage? "Wasn't Mother *serious* when she would whisper triumphantly, 'He's going to do exactly what I suggested last night, but of course he thinks it's his idea.' "

From the time she was very little, Celia heard conversations in the home about writing and books that friends were writing. "Poetry was woven into the fabric of his life and work." Still, Celia could not shake off the image of what a wife and mother should be, gleaned from Esther. And so Celia put away her poetry and ran away to get married at a young age.

Not wanting a lot of fuss, Celia and her fiancé borrowed Izzy's car and drove across the District line and were married by a justice of the peace. On the way home they stopped to buy some glasses and wine to

celebrate and then phoned Esther. "My announcement was so unexpected that it took Mother and Dad by surprise but Izzy knew one thing." "Look," said the absorbed publisher, in a response that became a long-standing family anecdote, "this [phone announcement] may be a joke or serious, but get the car down here. I need to deliver the papers!"

That she had married well and into a family of longtime friends pleased both her parents. Her husband, Walter Gilbert, a scientific genius, became a Nobel Prize winner in chemistry for his work on DNA and then made a fortune when he helped start one of America's first big biotech companies. For a decade Celia adopted her mother's role, molding her own marriage to match it—having three children in five years, as had Esther, accommodating her husband's career, giving academic dinner parties, leaving poems unwritten, desires unvoiced.

In the early 1970s "consciousness-raising" era, Celia, then in her late thirties, self-consciously took writing classes at Harvard, feeling not only older than the rest but unprepared. "It took a long time" to give herself permission to emerge as an individual, and in 1977, at forty-five, Celia wrote brilliantly of that struggle in an aptly named "gentle manifesto." When she did give voice to her creativity, Celia's poetry was published in the New Yorker and by Viking. When she first tried to talk to Esther about poems she was writing, Celia was plunged into the past. Esther would say, "That's good," then quickly, "But how are the children?" "I felt betrayed again as I had when a child, as though her love was bestowed only when I took care of others," wrote Celia. "I couldn't understand then her terrible lack of self-confidence, projected onto me."

Esther's reaction was similar when Ralph Ingersoll's widow, Toby, told her that she was designing and selling needlepoint. "She didn't want to listen. She only was interested in what I did for Ralph. I felt as if she was a little bitter. One of the last trips we went on with them on the QE2 before the cataract operations, when Izzy couldn't see; she didn't have a minute to herself. But she thought he was worth it. Esther once told me, 'In sixty-five years of marriage, that man has never bored me.'"

Although Celia felt that her parents' marriage was "out of the nineteenth century," in truth her mother's role was not dissimilar to that of other women of her era raised in middle-class households—and aspiring daughters of Celia's age often felt thwarted and uncomfortable by the housewife role model such mothers presented. After World War II, society still espoused marriages in which the wife was the helpmate. The relatively few wives who had independent careers were applauded for a private "at home" existence perpetuated by *Ladies' Home Journal.*

"If he didn't like this or that, I changed this and that. It might be qualities which I personally valued. It did not matter. I changed them. . . . We ate what he liked. We did what he liked. We lived a life which he liked. This gave me great pleasure. The thought that this was pleasing to him." And who said that? Katharine Hepburn, about her long-standing liaison with Spencer Tracy. In real life she was acting out the last reel of her movies where she routinely returned home as a "proper" wife or girlfriend.

Several women friends felt that Esther lacked self-confidence in the domestic life she had chosen. "Esther was no cook. I taught her how to fry eggs," said Toby Ingersoll. "Esther felt inadequate as a wife and a mother, I believe," said Helen Dudman. "If we would have them over for roast turkey, she thought it was the most amazing thing that somebody could roast a turkey." Toby Ingersoll sensed that "Esther was longing for women friendships," which naturally took second billing to Stone. "If Izzy wasn't present, she would chatter like a magpie. I have a good sense of fashion, but Esther didn't. The only time it mattered about her clothes was when Izzy thought something was too sexy and didn't like her wearing it. I bought her a see-through blouse—they were all the rage at one time—and she said, 'Izzy isn't going to like it.' Izzy was a real sort of Old Testament Jew in that way. There were a lot of sexist qualities."

Esther was often fearful for Stone when he was on assignment in Europe, even though she outwardly showed nothing but approval for his ventures when he was discussing impending trips. "Izzy would take off for Israel, and Ralph looked after Esther and the children. Esther went wild, trying to find where Izzy was. She was frantic on the phone to Ralph, 'Where is Izzy!?'" recalled Ingersoll's widow. One time, Esther had reason for her fear. While he was overseas, Esther heard that a man named Stone had been shot. After hours of intense, frantic waiting, Esther learned that it was not Izzy.

Esther's small insecurities and fear of losing someone close are understandable if one looks at her childhood. "If I could venture one psychological insight, which I don't usually like to do, but it is so obvious in this case," said Christopher. The loss of her mother "remains *beyond question* the major event in her life. Mom was shattered by her death. I think she felt she had to serve her father. And then he remarried. Mom felt basically that her identity was in testing her mettle, in going through ordeals. She saw herself, her existence, her identity, as meeting these Herculean tests. I think there was perhaps a tendency to magnify these domestic difficulties of life with Dad, as a test." He thinks that Celia, in tune with feminist values, was influenced "by a more contemporary politically correct view of things—that some talent of Mom's was nipped in the bud or sacrificed to Dad. Mom, as far as I could see, was just fully satisfied." Judy Stone agrees: "I think Celia wanted to liberate her, but I don't think she really understood. Esther was really totally devoted to Izzy."

As for her father, Celia reflected, he had become her kinsman who supported her work. "The secret of the power of his writing was and is that it reposes in and takes energy from a past that was always present to him. At all times he was surrounded by, as Emily Dickinson wrote, 'his kinsmen of the shelf.' "

No matter, Stone faced a common angst that possesses even the best of writers. Ruminating about the 3 million words he had written during twelve years at the *Nation* and New York papers by 1952, he felt that "only other newspapermen will fully realize the agony of turning out so much copy; the perpetual gap between what one would have liked to get down on paper and what finally did get itself written and printed, *the constant feeling of inadequacy.*" And he echoed the tireless theme of deadline writers: "If only one had a few hours more, how much better the copy might have been!"

In the six years that he had two full-time jobs, writing for the *Nation* and *PM,* Stone consistently wrote a punishing six columns a week. He described one high-pressure day to Patner. After missing a Friday deadline for the *Nation,* Stone took an early Friday flight to New York, raced to the magazine, and wrote not only his weekly letter but an editorial and another small piece, ate a steak at an all-night restaurant, took a Turkish bath, dashed over to *PM* to write a major page-one story, and caught a train home.

Writers can identify with Stone's sensation of bolting up in the middle of the night long after a deadline had passed and there was no hope of repairing or amending copy. "I rarely had doubts about those I defended. I often had doubts about those I attacked. Had I been fair? Was I being a self-righteous prig, without charity or compassion?" Then followed self-flagellation: "How little I understood about human beings, the conflicts within them, the compulsions under which they operated, the compartmentalized lives they led. . . . How easy, and how shameful, to be a newspaper pundit, a petty moral magistrate sitting in judgement of others!" Those were, however, the musings of a sleepless night, swept away with the dawn. He awoke in the morning "unregenerate and cheerful."

Despite the wealth of knowledge resting in his brain ready for retrieval, Stone worked hard at his craft. "He used to revise a thousand times. He had a way with a phrase, but he always worked it over," said Andy Moursand, one of his *Weekly* assistants. "He had a spontaneous wit, but the point was, he had all this substance behind it."

Stone longed to be a great writer and succeeded in composing remarkably impassioned, zestful, and wise prose over the years, but while trying to perfect a style, he coped with a feeling of inadequacy that seized many writers. Yet, to the reader, his sentences were often a lilting joy to read.

His pithy comments have been passed on through the years: After listening to Governor Thomas Dewey, he summed up the canned qualities of his cadences and "measured emphasis" as "too perfect to be pleasant." He sounded a Menckenian note at the July 8, 1944, Republican convention: It "required a strong stomach and a robust taste for humanity, not in the raw, where idealists may savor it, but in the pretentious and ribald package, human hamburger served up as Salisbury steak with a sprig of parsley. For this was country-club America. . . . The Chicago convention was the convention of a do-nothing party run by say-nothing politicians hankering for the past but afraid to speak up for it." Some lines seemed to be tossed off by a borscht-belt comedian: "It was hard to listen to [Senator] Goldwater and realize that a man could be half Jewish and yet sometimes appear to be twice as dense as the normal gentile." Standing alone, the one-liners could be harshly funny, but Stone balanced them with keen and thoughtful analysis.

Writing was one subject that engendered empathy from Stone. "I used to feel consoled when I was struggling over some dumb review," said his sister, "and Izzy would be so sympathetic. 'You know, Judy, it's *hard*. It's *hard* to write.' We'd be having this discussion over three thousand miles, on the phone, while I was in San Francisco." If the article had already appeared in the paper, he would rave about it. However, the need to be teacher, judge, and jury overcame Stone when he saw her raw copy. "When I sent him something *beforehand, that* copy he would criticize." She laughed. "I would have done better with a coldhearted editor."

British journalist Peter Pringle and his wife, Eleanor Randolph, now an editorial writer for the *New York Times,* became friends with the

Stones in the 1970s. Early-morning phone calls from Stone began by his mentioning something he had read either by Pringle or Randolph. "He would surprise you completely by calling you up," said Pringle. "He was nearly blind at that time and you would be flattered, thinking how long it took him to read anything. And then he would say, 'Just one small thing . . . In the third and fourth paragraph, and y'know . . . just something's not quite right.' And you'd think, 'Goddammit, why can't he just say nice things? What is this?' Of course, he'd be right!"

Stone's enthusiasm for life astounded Pringle. "He was always calling up saying, 'There's this marvelous Japanese film, just come to town. Now we *must* go on Friday.' How did he know there was a good Japanese film? *I* didn't have time to find these things out. He was just irrepressible. God, if I had half that energy right now!"

A lasting memory of Pringle's is an afternoon when Stone dropped by. Their daughter was an infant, lying on a blanket on the floor. Pringle went to the kitchen to bring out a drink and food. As he returned, he saw Stone, then in his seventies, lying on the floor next to the baby. His curiosity had overcome him once more. Stone was peering at the baby not only through his very thick glasses. In his hand, through which he was examining every detail of her features, was a magnifying glass.

15

Blood and Billions and Going Underground

Terrible things have been done to human bodies and to human minds.
—I. F. Stone, August 12, 1945

On a pleasant April day in 1945, Stone stood in Lafayette Square opposite the White House, watching a gathering crowd waiting for a glimpse of FDR's flag-draped coffin. In recent months Stone had seen up close the dark circles under FDR's eyes and the trembling hands of a wasted man. Still, the president's sudden death from a brain hemorrhage was shattering. The leader Stone revered was gone, and now he and other New Dealers faced trepidation as well as sadness. War still raged and the direction for peacetime planning was precarious; Stone worried that disastrous policies might ensue.

He wrote about the extraordinary events that quickly followed the passing of FDR: the birth of the United Nations. The Potsdam conference of Stalin, Churchill, and Truman. The victory in Europe. The incineration of Hiroshima and Nagasaki by the greatest mass-destruction weapon created. The atomic bomb would forever alter world diplomacy and spawn generations of critics, General Eisenhower and Stone among them, who questioned the necessity and the morality of using such devastating force.

For that April day, however, Stone was capturing his pain and that of millions who were saying good-bye to a hero. The strength of Stone's writing was not in an individual phrase but in the accumulation of detail: "The gray tip of the Washington Monument showed above the White House. . . . We could hear the harsh tones of command as the guard of honor lined up on the White House lawn. Florists' trucks pulled up at the door, and huge wreaths were taken inside. . . . Camera men were perched on high ladders on the sidewalks. Birds sang but the crowd was silent. . . . Motorcycle police herald the procession's approach." Planes roared in stilted formation overhead. "The marching men, the solemn bands, the armored cars, the regiment of Negro soldiers, the uniformed women's detachments, the trucks filled with soldiers, and the black limousine carrying officials and the President's family went by slowly." Stone watched with tears in his eyes. It seemed part of an unreal pageant "by comparison with the one glimpse of what we had come to see—the coffin covered with a flag. . . . In that one quick look thousands of us said our goodbye to a great and good man, and to an era."

Although FDR had ruled from a wheelchair, his presence often seemed monumental. By comparison, Truman, with his flat, nasal Midwestern tone and the most ordinary of countenances, seemed small for the job. The contrast between the patrician and the plebeian was startling. Truman looked like what he had been, a haberdasher, outfitted in snappy suits as if he were a short, stuffed mannequin.

Stone sounded hopeful that Truman would carry on FDR's vision. The year before, Stone had wrongly predicted that Roosevelt would again choose Henry Wallace as his running mate. Truman thought he had no chance either. Roosevelt had played his cards so adroitly that none of the likely candidates knew whom he would choose.

"I hate to confess it, but I think Mr. Roosevelt was astute and farsighted" in picking Truman, wrote Stone after FDR's death. "At this particular moment . . . Mr. Truman can do a better job. Mr. Wallace's accession might have split the country wide open, not because of Mr. Wallace but because of the feeling against him on the right."

Stone quickly lost faith. "So long as Mr. Roosevelt was alive, the 'hard peace' idea had the ascendancy, but since his death a change is already perceptible. . . . The State Department opposition to drastic action against Germany has stiffened." The drift toward going soft on Nazi war criminals and businessmen was "also fed by cartel and commercial considerations, here as in Britain." On the eve of the signing of the United Nations charter Stone pessimistically predicted that these strong forces in Britain and America "impel us to the reconstitution of pretty much the same kind of Germany and Japan we are spending blood and billions to crush." He followed with a misguided view of Russia: "The example of racial equality in the Soviet Union will be a constant reproach and irritant to colonialism, as Soviet full employment will be to capitalism."

In May, Stone joined worldwide celebrities and press to cover the signing of the United Nations charter in San Francisco. For one of the few times in his life, Stone recalled, "I was a mainline journalist because of the New Deal and Roosevelt. So I was 'in.' " He rode the special train taking press and dignitaries to San Francisco. On board, the radical lunched with some of the country's richest Democrats and chatted with administration officials. He lightly observed the scene in the packed and gigantic Palace Hotel. Izzy, as "goggle-eyed as any movie fan," met suave Charles Boyer and Edward G. Robinson, Hollywood's best-known faux gangster. Correspondents, he dryly observed, "obtain much of their mysteriously authoritative inside information by interviewing each other at the crowded bars."

Stone filled his letters home to Esther with descriptions of the celebrities, his being admired, and the jokes he was telling at the endless round of parties, where drinks were plentiful. He also wrote with deep longing for Esther, "Dear Dolly: I love you. I'm getting awfully tired of this place and I wish I were back home with you and the kids going to corner movie, to bed at 9:30, playing the piano and have a drink once every two weeks. You're the most wonderful woman in the world for me and I wouldn't swap you for a brace of Hollywood glamor girls. Please write more. Your letters are awfully good." Stone added, "But I'm glad I came and I'd like to stick it out if possible. There are really terrible possibilities here and I'm glad I came out and saw for myself what is hardly believable. The anti-Soviet obsession here, the danger of a new war, I want to see it and watch it and warn against it."

On opening night in the Opera House, where "flashlight bulbs kept going off like summer lightning," Stone stared at four brown pillars, symbols of the four freedoms, "connected at the tip by what appeared to be large segments of a boa constrictor."

Truman's speech was filled with "windy moralisms, turgid periods, and the kind of untruths which are regarded as inspirational." It was "hooey," Stone announced. He had enjoyed Truman as a senator and wrote that "in private Mr. Truman would say, 'It's a tough job. I'm not sure we can do it. But we're going to try our best.' Why doesn't he say it in public?" Most of the speeches "depressed" Stone. "The occasion was so momentous; the danger so grave; the need so great; the utterance so mediocre."

Stone summed up the international cast of characters who were cobbling together the "first tentative framework of a world order" and emphasized that it was a lost cause unless the "big powers stick together." He complimented Lippmann's observation that there was a tendency to assume "that because Germany is prostrate, the German problem is no longer the paramount problem of the world." The preoccupation of many at the UN meeting, wrote Lippmann, "has not been Germany, but the Soviet Union." Stone quoted Lippmann's warning: "Our relations with the USSR would become hopeless 'if we yield at all to those who, to say it flatly, are thinking of the international organization as a means of policing the Soviet Union.'" In one short week since Lippmann's views had appeared, the "anti-Soviet atmosphere has grown," wrote Stone. "To be quite frank about it, the conference, for all its glamour, is a meeting of pretty much those same old codgers to whose fumbling we owe World War II."

Stone, however, deeply embraced the precepts of the United Nations, as he had the League of Nations when he was fourteen years old. Within days of the UN gathering, the Axis collapsed. Mussolini was killed by partisans and hung upside down in a provincial town square as crowds cheered. Hitler committed suicide inside his bunker. On May 7, what was left of the Nazi high command surrendered. The horrible, costly six-year war in Europe ended in mass celebrations, but then the hard work of securing peace began.

International alliances are primarily a matter of perceived necessity rather than genuine accord. For Stone, the litmus test for doing business with Communist postwar leaders was to compare them with past regimes. "With the exception of Czechoslovakia" none of the Eastern-bloc countries had known liberty or democracy before the war, when "rightist repression and feudal exploitation were the rule." These conditions made "'revolutionary methods,' *with all their dreadful abuses* [italics added] almost inevitable." Stone conceded "these were not lands of liberty in the Western sense," but argued "they are not one-party states, either, in the Russian manner."

The cloak of a people's revolution served left-wing dictators well in the twentieth century. They often applied the same tyrannical rule, mass murder, death squads, liquidation of enemies, and subjugation that are common to rightist regimes historically backed by the United States. At the time, however, there was reason to believe that leftist dictatorships offered preferable alternatives, although Stone admitted that individual freedom was sorely absent, illustrating this with a denunciation of Bulgaria's recent execution of a dissenting politician.

No blind follower, Stone had been attacked by American Stalinists and the *Daily Worker* for supporting Trotskyists tried under the Smith Act in 1941. The *Daily Worker* and the CPUSA harshly condemned Stone for championing Yugoslavia's leader Marshal Josip Tito after Stalin expelled him from the Communist bloc in 1948. In the aftermath of World War II, Stone was critical of Stalin, especially for his rejection of the Marshall Plan. Yet Stone continued to see Stalin as a nationalist, not an aggressor. Stone argued that the Communist leader needed to surround himself with friendly countries in his Eastern-bloc sphere of influence, just as the United States was fortifying itself in Germany, France, Greece, Turkey, and Latin America.

An economic and geopolitical alliance of the two big powers was essential, he declared. Throughout the world, a deep-seated apprehension was born with the A-bomb. The ability to produce annihilation now made cautious diplomacy mandatory, a fact that hard-line warriors discounted. Now a concerned Stone watched as the uneasy alliance forged in war swiftly disintegrated. Cold War actions were set in place before peace came. Both superpowers were frozen in mutual paranoia, fear, and hostility in what would be the long "war of nerves," as Truman called it.

The mystery, or perhaps the secret, of world-champion mass murderers is that they can electrify the masses and also disarm sophisticated adversaries with a mask of deception. Stalin's soft voice and quiet demeanor were easily misjudged as affability. Churchill, FDR, Truman, and Eisenhower all reacted favorably to Stalin in person, and such personal impressions were no trivial concern when great powers met to carve up the world. Even the prime minister, a strong critic of the "Iron Curtain" that descended on Eastern Europe, lavishly praised him. Stalin "invited personal friendship and comradeship," Churchill commented. "He seems a man of exceptional character." Roosevelt was unstinting in his praise after their meeting at Yalta in February 1945. Stalin "combines a tremendous, relentless determination with a stalwart good humor. I believe he is truly representative of the heart and soul of Russia." Stalin "was capable of being kind to me, but he was utterly ruthless," recalled eighty-five-year-old Averell Harriman, who had been the ambassador to Russia and was with FDR at Yalta. Asked how Stalin, the jovial toastmaster, could also be the century's greatest mass murderer, Harriman shook his head. "It is still totally ununderstandable."

The major surprise upon meeting Stalin was his size. Forceful portraits, with his full head of hair and bristling mustache, cultivated the impression of a large, imposing leader. He was at most five feet four inches, and some accounts indicate he was barely over five feet. Truman was seated at a desk in the cavernous palace at Potsdam when he first met Stalin. He looked up to see this "little bit of a squirt" standing in front of him. Stalin was so charming at a caviar and vodka dinner that Truman praised him in letters home to his wife and in conversations with Henry Wallace. In fact, Truman was more irritated with the brandy-swilling Churchill, who was given to tiresome monologues.

At Potsdam, the suburb of Berlin occupied by Russian soldiers, Truman scored one victory: Stalin stood by his Yalta agreement to enter the war against Japan. Although Stalin was obdurate in not giving up Russian-controlled regions in Europe, their meetings were not bellicose. After all the toasts, the cordial smiles, the wishes for safe trips home, Truman felt that Stalin also liked him and that future relationships would go well. Stalin's private assessment, however, was that Truman was "worthless." It took Truman "dozens of years" to admit that he had been naive, and he bitterly recalled, "I liked the little Son of a Bitch." Roosevelt may have dealt more forcefully with Stalin, but his neophyte successor, to be fair, had little bargaining power when Stalin refused to budge; the sticking point was dividing up Germany and Poland. The war could not have been won without tenacious Red Army victories; the tremendous loss of Russian soldiers and citizens, estimated at 30 million, could not lightly be dismissed.

Thus, an exhilarated Stone cheered the outcome of the Potsdam conference, which accepted, "with some modification, the idea embodied in the so-called Morgenthau Plan which was also Franklin D. Roosevelt's plan. . . . The safest and wisest course was to reduce the industrial and therefore the war making potential of the Reich." This was "perhaps the greatest achievement of this historic conference." However, Potsdam solidarity soon collapsed as Stalin reneged on agreements.

All the while at Potsdam, Truman was reading secret alerts on preparations to drop the atomic bomb. He and Churchill consulted frequently, but Truman spoke only vaguely to Stalin about a new powerful weapon. (Only later was it revealed that Stalin had known for years about atomic secrets through Klaus Fuchs, a British naturalized citizen, Los Alamos physicist, and Russian spy.) Even though Truman triumphantly predicted in his diary that Russia's imminent entry meant the end of Japan, he always said that dropping the bomb was necessary to halt U.S. invasion casualties. Eisenhower had argued, as did intelligence reports, that the Japanese were crumbling and it was not necessary to hit them with such terrible force. For decades, Americans accepted Truman's explanation. Exultant cheers erupted from American soldiers and civilians alike when they heard that the bomb had been dropped. In a pre-TV era there were no immediate pictures. No understanding of the mass devastation. No questions about the necessity to drop a second bomb on Nagasaki even as a million Russian troops streamed into Manchuria to aid in the war. A Strangelovian aspect of the second bombing was that Truman gave no additional orders, nothing beyond the original military directive that stated "additional bombs would be delivered" on targets as soon as they were ready.

Dissension still fuels historians' viewpoints. Some argue that the massive land attack that would have caused great American casualties was not scheduled for months and conventional warfare would have brought victory before then. Historian Gar Alperovitz states that it is now generally accepted that dropping the bomb was unnecessary. However, resistance to that theory remains.

The official U.S. argument was that they had softened their edict of unconditional surrender by Emperor Hirohito to only unconditional surrender of Japan's armed forces. In the end the United States accepted what had been proposed before the A-bomb attacks; the emperor was allowed to remain. Pearl Harbor had hardened many Americans, including Stone. The fierce defender of civil liberties did not write one line of protest when Japanese-Americans were herded into concentration camps, losing their homes, jobs, and freedom in this wartime security measure. (Later, in 1949, Stone referred to the "terrible racistic implications" of this internment program.)

Within days of Hiroshima, however, he wrote that the use of the A-bomb was "terrifying" and "abhorrent." The bomb dropped on August 6, 1945, instantly killed eighty thousand, mostly civilians. Some were burned to cinders. Others tried to run as skin melted to the bone. Another sixty thousand would die within months. Thousands more would continue to die over the years from radiation poisoning and thermal burns, while others lived with hideously scarred bodies and faces. An estimated seventy thousand more died at Nagasaki; more would have been killed but the bomb was dropped two miles off target.

Despite initial euphoria, trepidation characterized many of America's editorials. The *St. Louis Post-Dispatch* felt that science might have "signed the mammalian world's death warrant." Hanson Baldwin wrote in the *New York Times* that "we clinched the victory . . . but we sowed the whirlwind." Stone wrote, "More terrifying than the atomic bomb is the casual way we all seem to be taking the end of the war."

Fighting fascism had been necessary, but Stone disturbingly saw little realization of war's awful destruction. Perhaps people were "punch drunk on horror and sensation," he reflected. "Terrible things have been done to human bodies and to human minds." The United States had not had a "vivid conception of what hell has reigned in parts of Europe and Asia." The use of "democracy and freedom" by those who had never known its cost was so repetitive that "the words have grown shabby and nauseating. . . . How many of us are thankful that our own country was spared, that our children did not jump from their beds as the warning air-raid sirens screamed in the nights, that we did not huddle with our families in the subways, that our daughters were not shipped into slavery and our mothers sealed into death cars . . . that our cities are not gutted by bombs, our children's faces pinched by hunger."

In this new century, after years of hostility with Russia and peace and prosperity with Germany, albeit while sustaining a U.S. military presence there for sixty years, it may be difficult to understand the anxiety that overtures to Germany created in the immediate aftermath of World War II. Former first lady Eleanor Roosevelt, Stone's friend, wrote in her popular "My Day" column that the United States should insist "there shall be no rebuilding of heavy industry of the kind which would permit Germany again to become a great industrial nation and rebuild a war machine." Nothing should be done, she wrote, to "allow Germany again to become a potential war breeder."

It was an edgy, emotional time. As the enormity of Hitler's holocaust was revealed, deep revulsion, anger, and the sickening knowledge that ordinary citizens had participated in such systematic savagery astounded millions. Doctors had participated in barbaric torture under the guise of scientific experiments. Burghers in town after town had loaded the trains with humans herded to slaughter. By the spring of 1945, the skeletal wreckage of Dachau, Treblinka, Auschwitz, and Bergen-Belsen had been liberated. Pictures haunt viewers still: hollow eyes in cadaverous faces, matchstick legs of the barely alive, mounds of hair and eyeglasses taken from prisoners, gaping ovens. The need to disarm a country forever that had started two world wars was a passionate concern to Stone and many others. It was especially so among American Jews.

Henry Morgenthau, FDR's secretary of the treasury, was one of those proud, rich Jews who labeled himself an "American" and felt above the concerns of his kinsmen until he saw what the Nazis had done and be-

came "very pro-Zionist." He was furious at fellow Jews like Felix Frankfurter who did nothing to "push Roosevelt in the direction of assisting
the Jewish victims of Hitler." Morgenthau became a man obsessed, fighting vehemently for his plan to demilitarize and deindustrialize Germany,
making it dependent on light industry and agriculture. FDR's death
meant the end of Morgenthau's plan, and Truman soon fired him. Stone
defended Morgenthau's efforts: "The plan did not, as its critics alleged,
seek to 'turn the Reich into a goat pasture.' It sought permanently to end
the danger of German military revival by placing the Ruhr under international control."

Stone tracked America's capitulation to Germany, digging up a December 1946 congressional report, widely ignored by the media, that
leaned toward Germany's retaining "its twin key war industries, synthetic oil and synthetic rubber." Revitalizing Germany and crippling
Russia was the order of the day "less than two years after the war." Stone
saw his country preparing for World War III, "this time against Russia."
The report sought stringent curbs on reconstruction aid to war-ravished
Russia and urged the State Department to put "maximum pressure" on
Britain and European countries to do likewise. Stone acidly observed,
"Merely to refuse a loan to Russia is not enough." Six months before, he
wrote, "To make German revival the prime consideration . . . is not the
same as fitting Germany into an overall plan for recovery. . . . Britain as
well as France is getting stepchild treatment in our new emphasis."

Stone never let up on the cozy cartels. He wrote in cold fury of the
whitewashing of Farben, which had begun even before the war ended,
and the eagerness to resume business with the company that had mass-
produced the gas to kill millions of Jews.

Years later a young German historian, Bernd Greiner, noted that, to liberals worldwide, "the spelling of the Marshall Plan was M-A-R-T-I-A-L
Plan—rehabilitating the German economy and leaving the major German
war-making industries intact. They did crack out I. G. Farben, but we all
know that was just a farce."

Greiner was among a young generation of German scholars probing a
painful past in which their fathers had participated. In 1991, he marveled
at Stone's work fifty years before. "His pieces still hold comparison with
anything later historians have written. His work at *PM* was extraordinary!
As we now know, American business did not restrain from dealing with
Germany as a 'silent partner' during the buildup to war." Greiner cited two
American companies that sold airplane navigational patents to a Berlin

company, "which allowed them to speed up Göring's strategic project." For an address he was giving in Washington, Greiner had a copy of a 1943 *PM* Stone column that assuredly piqued Secretary of State Hull at the time: "State Dept. Blocks Plan to Rescue European Jews."

Stone's outrage in 1946 still rings with immediacy. "The rebirth of I. G. Farben," he wrote, "is just around the corner." Meanwhile, another birth was filling Stone with hope, the creation of a sanctuary for Jews in Palestine.

For the first time in his life, Stone visited Europe, just after World War II ended. The stench of rotting bodies underneath the gray dust and rubble of what had been thriving cities sickened him. Hunger was everywhere; he watched homeless urchins raid the garbage of the occupation forces. An initial sense of liberation faded as the Jews were forced to remain in the same concentration camps, many seriously ill from malnutrition, existing on bread and coffee, clothed in the tattered remains of their prison garb or "ignominiously in S.S. uniforms left behind by their oppressors." Stone railed at the Allies for doing little for these hundred thousand souls and exclaimed that "the liberated are treated far worse than the defeated."

Still Stone sounded like a scriptwriter for a travelogue when he returned from his six weeks' trip, "drunk on the beauties of the world": "St. Paul's, mighty and melancholy amid the bomb ruins in a London dusk; Paris as one had dreamed of . . . ; a savage sunset over the wild Balkan headlands flying into Greece; . . . dawn over the Negev . . . Jerusalem, clean, white, and lovely on its ancient hills." Tears coursed down his cheeks when Stone entered the immensely grand and hushed Notre Dame Cathedral, and when he wound through the narrow passages of Jerusalem's Old City and came upon the gleaming whiteness of the Wailing Wall.

Then Stone addressed politics. He "hated" Egypt. "I had never seen so much poverty." He was heartened to see that in Palestine, where Jews had been settling for decades, their presence "has not degraded the Arab but lifted his living standards." He was thrilled that this was "one place in the world where Jews seem completely unafraid. . . . In Palestine a Jew can be a Jew." An ardent proselytizer for a Jewish homeland, Stone nonetheless immediately voiced concerns that only grew stronger with time, alienated him from many Jews, and created arguments and enmity even with friends and relatives. Visiting a Jewish settlement, Stone felt "painfully impelled to disagree with the majority opinion" of the group. "I am not in favor of a Jewish state in Palestine." A binational state, "created on a parity principle, is ethically right." He understood the passions of Jewish settlers and praised the "passionate" and "mystical national faith" that had enabled them to "colonize areas the goats despised." But he warned that the Arabs, "who are also human beings and who also have historic rights here, are prepared to fight against any subjection to a Jewish state. . . . No one likes to be ruled by an alien people."

With canny precision Stone in 1945 predicted a dire future because of the "blind alley into which Palestinian Jewry is being led by the failure to achieve any political understanding with the Arabs. . . . Political agreement will be impossible so long as a single Jewish state in Palestine is demanded." Stone would return to this land and this argument many times, as violence, not peace, continued its heartbreaking passage well into the twenty-first century. Some Israeli soldiers would refuse to fight what they termed an immoral war among Palestinian civilians. Palestinian terrorists would blow themselves and any Israelis nearby to kingdom come. More than a half century later, Stone's arguments were voiced by mainstream forces.

Fearful of a warring Middle East future, Stone was equally obsessed with finding a home for Hitler's victims. Stone followed unfolding events with alarm. Some six hundred thousand Jews were already in Palestine; the British were obdurately resisting immigration of displaced Jews and aligning with hard-line Arab leaders. Oil, then as now, motivated political and business decisions. Terrorism escalated on all sides. Stone argued the old premise that one man's terrorist is another man's freedom fighter. As 1946 dawned, Stone praised the Haganah as a "Democratic militia" more restrained than the Stern Gang and the "quasi-fascist Irgun," who ruthlessly attacked Arabs. The *Nation* column was pointedly titled "Gangsters or Patriots?" Haganah members, he argued, were "no more gangsters" than Thomas Jefferson or George Washington.

Stone's praise for the Haganah paid off in a memorable international exclusive. The group allowed him to travel on one of their illegal ships running the British blockade into the Holy Land, a journey no reporter had experienced. It would be treacherous, with many snags, Stone was told. He would be passed from one anonymous source to another. It was absolutely imperative to tell no one; unmasked Haganah members would be in jeopardy. Stone told only Ingersoll, *PM*'s managing editor, John Lewis, and Esther, "the most discreet woman I know." He fabricated a story for the *Nation;* he was taking a leave of absence to cover the Paris Peace Conference for *PM.*

Then he started a fascinating, winding, legal and illegal journey to Palestine.

A quarter of a million New York readers rushed to buy each *PM* installment splashed across the pages and hyped in advance with large headlines. Stone later expanded those stories into a book, the most lyrical of his works, filled with pathos but also hilarious personal adventures. He was not there simply as a reporter, he told his New York audience, many of whom could identify with his personal story. "I am an American and I am also and inescapably—the world being what it is—a Jew.... My parents were born in Russia," wrote Stone. "Had they not emigrated . . . I might have gone to the gas chambers. I might have been a DP, ragged and homeless. . . . I did not go to join them as a tourist in search of the picturesque, nor even as a newspaperman merely in search of a good story, but as a kinsman, fulfilling a moral obligation."

As Stone set out, he remained haunted by what he had seen at war's end: in "battered railroad yards . . . half-wrecked freight cars and ancient third-class coaches jam-packed with refugees from the extermination camps of Nazi Germany," they were "among the lucky few" who had survived, a roaming mass of more than one hundred thousand Eastern and Central European Jews "with no homes to return to."

Now, a year and a half later, many still lived in appalling conditions in the worst DP (displaced persons) camps. Stone gagged at the overpowering smell of the overflowing latrines. At refugee reception centers, bomb-damaged walls were blanketed in the graffiti of the lost. Names and hometowns were scrawled in hopes that relatives or friends might see them. Yet Stone found hope. The suffering of the Jews was an "old story, grown weary." The "real news" was a spirit of optimism as they traveled "on a journey many of them would take months, or forever, to complete. . . . Everywhere else in Europe I felt a defeatist spirit."

Stone's cloak-and-dagger meetings with contacts read like a Graham Greene novel: Stone at a far table in a dim café or grungy bar, waiting for someone he did not know to lead him to his next destination. Waiting in Munich, Stone observed the capriciousness of bombardment: while only a "few crazy brick skeletons" remained, "an undamaged bathtub protruded dizzily from a precarious bit of wall." He spent one morning in Nuremberg at the war criminals trial and leafed through the mountain of documents. "I was struck by one vivid passage. It was in the testimony of Rudolph Hess, the former Auschwitz commandant.* Of the gas chambers, he said, 'We knew when the people were dead because they stopped screaming. . . . Very frequently women would hide their children under their clothes, but of course when we found them we would send the children in to be exterminated.'" At Hitler's Berchtesgaden hideaway, GIs had written on the walls and American Jewish soldiers had drawn the Magen David star. As Stone looked out from a shattered glass wall, he thought that the magnificent view of the Alps "made megalomania almost inescapable for anyone who lived there." Stone had a moment of satisfaction: "Solemnly I committed a primitive act of contempt."

Stone got lost and went to a German city called Amberg instead of his destination, Bamberg. He knew not a soul and no one was expecting him. Stone was wearing a military correspondent's uniform, which earned him a stay in a small officers' club. The next morning he strolled through this "Hans Christian Andersen" kind of town, now knowing "what horrors can come out of these quaint little places with their ancient churches, arched bridges and the stork's nests on the chimneys." Stone learned that the town harbored militant Nazis and that 40 percent could not vote because they had been in the Nazi Party. A citizen told Stone that they would rush to embrace the Reich again.

In a small Czech town, Stone ran to catch an ancient train with a locomotive that "looked as if it would burst its boilers." The packed refugees clung to him, asking if he knew a cousin in *Jigago* or an aunt in *Nefyork*. In Yiddish and halting German, Stone extracted memories as indelible as the concentration camp numbers tattooed on their arms. A pro-Russian feeling solidified as Stone observed those streaming out of war-torn Russia: "Out of the Soviet Union alone came the miracle of whole Jewish families." Stone saw continuing virulent anti-Semitism among Germans and Poles. "Most of the Poles I encountered hated the Jews more than ever," said one woman. Another who came across the border from Russia said that the first shouts they heard from Poles were " 'Jew Communists!' . . . We were only more Jews to kill." Some wore head bandages after being beaten by Polish guards at one crossing.

---

*The use of "Rudolph Hess" was either an error or a typing mistake in the original *Underground to Palestine.* The lesser-known former Auschwitz commandant was Rudolf *Höss.* In 1941 that other Nazi, Rudolf Hess, flew a Messerschmitt to Scotland, bailed out, and remained in British captivity until war's end, when he was returned to Germany for trial.

* * *

Stone's conversations continued far into the night in lurching, smelly third-class cars. One teenage passenger, Abram, adored by the elders, was nine when the war started. Abram's mother, father, and two older brothers had already died in the Lodz ghetto. When the Nazis obliterated the ghetto, Abram managed to slip away as they loaded up the death wagons. Alone, his only hope for survival was to sneak into another concentration camp. A German Communist hid him from the guards. He was alive when the Americans liberated Buchenwald. Abram's tale ended happier than most. Haunted by the dream that his sister might still be alive, he hooked a ride on a repatriation train to Lodz. "I found her," he told Stone. "There she is." He pointed to the smiling nineteen-year-old listening to him. Stone was stunned to see the two siblings together. This was "little less than a miracle." Abram's sister, Sarah, recounted a story of kind bravery by a German. In Bergen-Belsen she was put to work in a munitions camp. "I would stand at the machine and cry so much that I couldn't see through my tears." A German forewoman asked her why she was crying. "These bullets are killing the people I love," said Sarah, crying harder. The German boss secretly showed her how to wreck the bullets so that they would not work. Both would have been killed had they been discovered.

Stone heard one other humanitarian story. A Jewish resistance fighter was captured by Hitler's SS men at the Hungarian border. He had false Aryan papers, but the guards were suspicious. A passing German doctor surveyed the scene and assured the Nazis that he would examine him to make sure he was an Aryan. The doctor took him to a nearby hut and the Jew trembled. The doctor said nothing as he saw that the man was circumcised. He called the guards. The Jew held his breath. "This man is an Aryan," said the doctor, saving his life. He was sent to an Aryan labor camp instead of the death camps for Jews.

Stone was immensely invigorated by the people he met. There were hugs and tears as he passed from one group to the next on his way to a ship bound for Palestine. As one ancient train chugged through the night, Stone leaned into the vestibule's welcoming breeze, then climbed up to the roof. He found it "cool and comfortable provided one kept an eye out for the low bridges." Later, he recounted to Shirley Katzander, then living in Paris, how he had ridden out of Eastern Europe on top of the train. "I just loved it!" he exclaimed. Hearing the story, writer Nat Hentoff said, "I wish there were photographs of Izzy, with his thick glasses and quizzical look, riding high through the perilous Czechoslovakian countryside—an emblem of the free press."

Stone finally reached Italy and moved toward the harbor. His story took on all the aspects of an Italian comic opera, with Stone in the lead, making swift costume changes, mangling accents, and browbeating attendant spear-carriers—the local police who had captured him. As he approached a ship bound for Palestine, Stone donned a Basque beret in order to play a joke on a young man on board whom he had met in New York. He strutted up the gangplank and was halted by a guard. Stone demanded, in his bad accent, *"Où est le capitaine?"* Asked his name, Stone suddenly became Jacques Pirandel—from the French FBI. Worrying that no one recognized him, Stone laughed heartily and pulled out his *PM* reporter's identity card. The crew member laughed too; he was a faithful *PM* reader.

It was too dangerous for Stone to board the ship in the harbor because there were no arriving passengers on the manifest. So Stone and two companions drove to a rendezvous point farther down the coast. In midnight darkness they sat on the beach to wait. An hour later, "far out to sea, we saw a tiny triangle of light moving toward us. . . . It looked as if a ghost ship were moving slowly toward the beach." Headlights lit the winding coastal road as a convoy of twelve trucks carrying refugees pulled up, stopping just long enough for the refugees to jump quickly off, then sped away, leaving the people "huddled together like a herd of seals on the shore." Signals were flashed. The ship did not immediately move in; fear gripped the refugees.

Around 3 a.m. the ship landed and let down a rickety gangplank. At that very moment, six Italian police sprang out of the dark beach, shouting, as Stone translated it, "Hey, fellas, here are a bunch of Jews!" In the chaos that followed, the refugees began to scramble up the gangplank and Stone found himself sparring with the carabinieri. Guessing that the police would respect authority, Stone whipped out his "most impressive reporter's card, a red State Department card with a gold Eagle on it," officiously demanding the policeman's name and rank. Through a translator, Stone began to browbeat the police captain, threatening to write an exposé of "what you and your men do on this beach tonight." All the while Stone was passing out Camel cigarettes, which "visibly softened" the carabinieri as Stone demanded they let the people go. Gripped by indecision as this little man from America kept up a torrent of unfamiliar words, the police watched helplessly as the refugees streamed on board.

Stone was taken to the police station, where an Italian companion shouted that Stone was a famous journalist and a "good friend of [President] Truman." Rapid-fire Italian references to "Tru-MON" ensued. A policeman rushed into the room shouting the boat had gotten away. "I pretended to be furious," recalled Stone, and he bellowed "This will ruin me professionally!" He demanded to be allowed to change into his correspondent's uniform to prove that he was an American. He managed to quickly hide his notes in his fresh army socks just as the whole brigade marched in to watch him dress. "The colonel was very much impressed with my new green officer's uniform."

When the Italians finally let him go, a discouraged Stone was stranded in Italy. His mission seemed doomed. In another town he luckily found a ship due to leave the next morning. Stone's job was to tour one dive after another, rousting sailors to duty. After too many drinks, he stumbled onto the ship the next morning. It was so crowded that "our decks looked like Orchard Beach or Coney Island on a hot Sunday." Then they transferred to an even-more-jammed ship. Izzy insisted that the young and able make room for the sick to lie on deck. Although refugee males objected, Stone took his turn in the horrifically smelling hold, where the closely packed had vomited, then thrashed his way through the sweating humans clustered around the ladder, to reach air.

As they neared land, the group decided voluntarily to give themselves up. A British ship escorted them into harbor, and the crew defiantly hoisted the blue and white Israeli flag. Surprisingly, the British did not take it down. Stone again put on his uniform and authoritatively made his way to a British Navy coast-guard cutter. It was an emotional farewell. "They waved and cheered and cried *shalom*. I stood on the cutter among the rather startled Britishers . . . and shouted *shalom* and threw kisses. . . . These Jews were my own people and I had come to love them." They were the lucky ones, said Stone. "They were among the last shiploads of illegal immigrants permitted to land." Stone's heart was filled with passion. It was a "moral obligation" of Jews and Christians alike to lend "full support of the so-called illegal immigration."

"And if those ships are illegal," Stone reminded his readers as he ended his book, "so was the Boston Tea Party."

A postscript occurred more than three decades later. In 1980 Stone called a *Washington Post* reporter and said he had a great story; you *have* to meet this woman from Israel, you *have* to write her story, you *have* to get your editor to say yes. Stone had long perfected his persuasive, goading requests of mainstream journalist friends to write about whatever was firing him up at the moment.

Stone was right. The woman's fascinating story began when she was six, smuggled with her parents out of the Warsaw ghetto, concealed among forced laborers leaving for a day's work. She raced into the woods with her aunt. Her parents were caught and taken to Treblinka. For three years, the girl posed as an Aryan in a Catholic orphanage. One day, she was brought into a room to meet a Pole and a German official, who had a discussion about her in German. The Pole was certain she was a Jew. The nine-year-old chattered in seeming innocence, "The most interesting person is my *Italian* grandmother. Everyone says I resemble her." Her German was perfect with no telltale traces of Yiddish. "Soon they were all smiles—and I was passed over."

In 1946, her aunt, who had escaped the concentration camp with forged Aryan papers, came for the child. On their crowded, listing ship to Palestine, a man was taking notes. She smiled at him when he talked to her. "Our oldest passenger was seventy-eight; our youngest, ten . . . a dark haired Polish-Jewish girl," recounted Stone. "She was clever, sharp-tongued and precocious and wrote poetry in Polish. She had crossed five borders illegally to reach that ship." Thirty-four years later, she had found I. F. Stone again in Washington. As a child she had been Judith Greenberg. In 1980 she was Yoella Har-Shefi, forty-four, a leading Israeli journalist and former war correspondent. The two shared more than memories of a distant passage. They both deplored the Israeli government's Palestinian policy, which, Stone predicted, "will push Israel into an endless sea of troubles." A frontline correspondent during the Yom Kippur War, Har-Shefi was among the vocal minority peace movement. She was fired from her mainstream newspaper for expressing her beliefs. In 1980 she was a political columnist for a left-wing publication.

"The only valid way for Israelis and Palestinians to stop bleeding each other to death is by mutual reconciliation and coexistence," said Har-Shefi. "If they don't have their country, we won't have ours. We cannot be racist in our treatment of them, just because the Holocaust happened to us." The "root of evil," she said, was the growing Israeli settlements in the West Bank. "We should not—and cannot—be allowed the luxury of our excesses."

* * *

When Stone returned to the States, he was a hero to American Jews. Requests to speak poured in from synagogues and Hadassah chapters. His book *Underground to Palestine* received enthusiastic reviews, particularly for "tenderly" handling such emotional stories and avoiding the pitfalls of cloying prose. Sixty years later it is still riveting, filled with significant details to rival the best fiction as Stone fleshed out an amazing cast of people bound for freedom. The *New York Herald Tribune* praised Stone's "extraordinary tale." Stone had reached a level of "three dimensional reporting" and had produced a "notable journalistic achievement," said the *New York Times*. He received a medal from the Haganah.

It also looked as if Stone would be rich for the first time in his life. Leaders in the Zionist movement, including a partner in one of the nation's leading advertising firms, approached Stone. They would spend $25,000 on publicity—a most substantial sum in 1946. In exchange they wanted "just a sentence or two" excised from the text: they wanted Stone to remove his suggestion for a binational solution.

"No," said Stone. Ralph Ingersoll had printed it that way in *PM*, and "he would have a low opinion of me, quite rightly, if I submitted to such censorship for the sake of an advertising campaign."

Recalled Stone, "That was the end of lunch." And the book. "It was in effect boycotted."

16

GUILTY UNTIL
PROVEN INNOCENT

Stone returned from his postwar examination of a devastated Europe and a tense Middle East, determined to spread the idea of peaceful solutions to world conflicts. In 1947, he penned "The ABC's of an Effective Foreign Policy," notable for clarity. "You cannot kill an idea. You cannot substitute bullets for bread. You cannot make misery more palatable by putting it under guard. You cannot build a stable society on exploitation and corruption. When Mr. Truman understands this as fully as Mr. Roosevelt did, American foreign policy will begin to look like something more than a futile attempt to build bulwarks against Soviet expansion on the quicksand of bankrupt ruling classes."

Stone later summarized what he was fighting for: civil liberty, free speech, peace in the world, truth in government, and a humane society. The Cold War at home made a mockery of these values. "Through headlines and Congressional 'investigations' three simple ideas are being hammered into the American consciousness. One is that we will have to fight Russia. The second is that we must rebuild Germany. The third is that Roosevelt was no good." All "part of one package, neatly tied with a bright red ribbon, by the old hate-Roosevelt brigade." After witnessing famished Europeans, Stone despised the complacency and blustery jingoism at home. "To listen in on the constant tidal roar of yammer and complaint that is politics in America was a sour experience."

At this time, Truman's Loyalty Program, deliberately designed to foster panic, was born. Senator Arthur Vandenberg told Truman that he must "scare hell out of the country" if he wanted support for his costly European recovery programs. And that was exactly what Truman did.

HUAC, in business since 1938, now had a green light to escalate attacks. "In an America being mobilized emotionally for war against Russia, it was easy to drive radicals and liberals of all kinds out of positions of influence and thus make a new successful period of peaceful reform impossible," said Stone. "As long as Truman made faces at Stalin, it was more difficult to accuse the Democrats of being communistic."

The manufactured Red Scare at home became a successful gambit for decades, weakening the left, stifling independent thought, fostering militaristic muscle, and bringing to power those bent on dismantling New Deal social programs. Truman never apologized for the devastation caused by the Loyalty Program, although he admitted privately to Joseph L. Rauh Jr., the famous Americans for Democratic Action lawyer, that it was a "terrible" mistake.

Truman's executive order, signed on March 21, 1947, went against all tenets of the American Constitution, leading to the persecution of thoughts, not deeds. The Loyalty Program allowed sweeping investigations of federal employees and job applicants. Loyalty boards were established to rule on vague allegations of disloyalty or subversion. To have ever been a Communist Party member, which was not illegal, was equal to being a closet Benedict Arnold. Becoming a snitch was honorable and Hoover was king. Just one of the voluminous edicts stated, "Each department and agency of the executive branch . . . shall submit, to the Federal Bureau of Investigation . . . the names (and such other necessary identifying material" as the FBI "may require) of all of its incumbent employees." Another: "There shall also be established and maintained in the Civil Service Commission a central master index covering all persons on whom loyalty investigations have been made by any department or agency since September 1, 1939."

Human misery was matched by a huge cost to taxpayers to implement the program.: By 1951, 3 million employees had been investigated by the Civil Service Commission and another several thousand by the FBI. Some two hundred were dismissed for "questionable loyalty" but no one was indicted and no evidence of espionage was found.* Still, the mere presence of the Loyalty Program induced nervous bosses to fire everyone from schoolteachers to cafeteria workers, who, Stone consistently noted, had no access to vital secrets.

---

*Half a century after the fact and six years after Stone's death, newly released, decrypted Russian files would lend credence to some of yesteryear's high-government-level spy charges, but nothing to justify such wholesale purge practices. Decoded Russian files in no way exonerate the abuses of the Loyalty Program and McCarthyism. (For more on this, see chapter 19, "Lies and Spies.")

Years later, the major architect of the Loyalty Program conceded that it had been a blatant political move, a point that Stone made constantly at the time. Facing a tough election, Truman needed to dispel charges that he was "soft on Communism." Garry Wills, one of America's most thoughtful historians, indicts the Loyalty Oath's mastermind, the suave and slippery Clark Clifford, Mr. Fix-it for many presidents and then counsel to President Truman. "As much as anyone he created the national security state, its rationale and its organization," wrote Wills. When Truman read Clifford's combative policy memo, he ordered all copies destroyed and locked his own in a desk. A disastrous leak would "blow the roof off" of both "the White House and the Kremlin," said Truman. In his 1991 sanitized memoirs, Clifford never indicated what had startled Truman, but he had given an unexpurgated version to columnist Arthur Krock, who ran it in an appendix in his 1968 memoirs. In 1991, Wills looked up Krock's version and found that Clifford's report showed a "disquieting enthusiasm for germ warfare." To maintain leverage against the Russians, wrote Clifford, "the United States must be prepared to wage atomic and biological warfare." Clifford's amazing and chilling admission of politics at any price was given to journalist Carl Bernstein in 1978: Truman felt that the Communist scare was "a lot of baloney. . . . I felt the whole thing was being manufactured. . . . We never had a serious discussion about a loyalty problem. . . . There was no substantive problem. We had a presidential campaign . . . and here was a great issue, a very damaging issue, so he set up this whole kind of [clearance] machinery."

The Loyalty Oath became a terrorizing tool for the right wing and helped Truman sell his "get tough" foreign policy. Stone championed the Marshall Plan (officially called the European Recovery Plan). He blasted Stalin and the CPUSA for rejecting it and pulling the Eastern European countries out of the America-dominated assistance program. The Russian excuse was that the United States had never bargained seriously. (An unacceptable stipulation to them was that the USSR would have to provide funds to rebuild parts of Western and Central Europe.) One witness to Cold War maneuvers, Lord Gladwyn, adviser to the British foreign secretary Ernest Bevin, felt that "an impossible situation would have arisen if Russia *had* cooperated . . . it would have been very difficult to get the money out of Congress." Stalin's rejection was Truman's victory. A hard sell with a price tag of $17 billion, the Marshall Plan was now seen as thwarting the rise of Communist governments. Congress resoundingly approved it in April 1948.

A separate move that greatly troubled Stone was Truman's military assistance to Greek rightists who were fighting Communist rebels. For many observers this Truman Doctrine, which included aid to Turkey, seemed a belligerent and sweeping threat to Russia. Truman said it was necessary to protect "free peoples who are resisting attempted subjugation." Stone assailed Truman's support of a "coalition of crooks, incompetents, ex-Axis agents and decayed monarchists." "The Marshall Plan as originally conceived was to avert revolution by feeding the discontented. The military assistance program was to avert it by shooting them."

In 1947 the Republican Congress overwhelmingly approved the $400 million military aid package to Greece and Turkey, setting the tone for subsequent decades of foreign policy. Unlike Stone, Lippmann approved assisting Greece, but he also worried that Truman's bellicose rhetoric was an unsettling call to arms. The rest of the nation's journalists cheered the doctrine in breathtaking unison. Reporters who had chortled at such plays on words as "to err is Truman" and "I'm Just Mild about Harry" busily switched gears, painting the "new," "bold" Truman as no longer FDR's pale successor.

However, Stone's prediction that America's foreign policy was on the road to "harsh and cynical collaboration with crooked and dictatorial elements" proved remarkably accurate. By 1947, wrote Stone, "we seem to have opened a military shopping service for dictators, guns for the asking to anti-Democratic regimes from Iraq and Turkey to Brazil and Argentina, guns for use against their own peoples, guns marked U.S.A., not the best kind of advertising." Stone continued to minimize harsh regimes on the left, hoping that they would evolve and not ape Russia, which was ruled by "a system harsh, ruthless and single-minded enough to underfeed and underclothe a whole generation for the sake of the future." He wrote, "The world is not going Communist, Russian model, unless American policy is so incredibly stupid as to leave the masses abroad no middle road." Capitalists feared "social ownership and control of the means of production," but it was an idea "at least as old as Jesus and his first followers" and was "the most potent idea in modern times." For readers who did not routinely read the Bible, he appended his column, "see Acts 2:44–45." [One sentence in Acts ends, "and distribution was made unto every man according as he had need.")

Equating dissent with disloyalty has ever been the hallmark of the right, who habitually label opposing views "unpatriotic." Stone never stopped extolling the freedoms of American democracy, stressing that it was not only a right but an obligation to dissent. That opinion was obliterated in the fifties. Senator Joseph McCarthy entered the arena in 1950, three years after the Loyalty Program was launched. By then Cold War hype and hysteria was an art form. Friendly HUAC witnesses, warbling their high-decibel guilt and naming names, "all claimed to have been Communists who cursed God every morning before they brushed their teeth, and then went out and looked for secrets to betray," mocked A. J. Liebling.

Stone used humor as well. " 'I was a Communist but left the party out of sheer boredom' might well be telling the unvarnished truth. . . . If the Communist Party were one-tenth as glamorous as renegades and FBI moochers make out, it just might be possible for them to elect a candidate or pay decent wages to the minuscule staff of the *Daily Worker*." Whenever Hoover went before Congress to plead for Red-hunting appropriations (always granted), he hyped the CPUSA membership; Stone ridiculed him by saying that half its members were FBI agents. He mocked the brightly lit Senate hearings: the "sprinkling of priests, for whom obsequious attendants hastened to provide special chairs," the ex-Communist informers who were "regarded as oracles; crowds shiver in expectation. . . . The longer they are out of the party the more they remember of frightful conspiracy."

In later years, Stone chuckled at how reactionary congressmen became devoted *Daily Worker* readers. "Around the hearing table were at least two or three volumes of the *Daily Worker*. It was a kind of Talmudic exegesis as to whether something had in fact appeared on page one or three, like the Kremlinologists read *Pravda*. It was the *devil's* text, but it was almost a sacred text," he told Gitlin. Most of his memories were grimmer. "People who had been Communists were scared to death. They didn't want to rat on their friends, but they didn't want to get in trouble. Many were older people and *good* people."

Although the glamorous Hollywood Ten HUAC hearings accelerated publicity, ordinary innocent citizens—schoolteachers, union laborers, and government employees—lost their jobs and were stigmatized for life. Without a right to confront accusers, or to even know who they were or what the charge was, employees could be fired for "reasonable grounds" of disloyalty—whatever "disloyalty" meant. By 1951, only reasonable "doubt" of a person's "loyalty" as determined by a government board was needed. "Loyalty" and "disloyalty," however, were never defined.

Mini-versions of House and Senate investigating committees spread from state to state; to be even an anticommunist liberal often meant political suicide. A liberal was depicted by opponents as being a closet Communist. Few profiles of courage were found in journalism and fewer in politics. Anonymous paid informants felt no discomfort in peddling hearsay, gossip, and slander to the FBI. And why should they? Their names remain buried under the heavy black pen of FBI censors more than half a century later.

When alleged subversives were interrogated about their Communist affiliations, denial was no proof of innocence. Committee members argued that the KGB would not want to compromise their top sources with "card-carrying" records, hence anyone could be labeled a concealed Communist. Since providing cover was standard practice in every spy network from the KGB to the CIA, it was hard to prove one's innocence once targeted by congressional committees.

"It was a dreadful, dreadful time," recalled New York lawyer Victor Rabinowitz, who handled many loyalty cases. The question "Are you now or have you ever been a Communist" was frighteningly sinister, no matter that Republicans, including 1948 presidential candidate Dewey, had sought Communist Party endorsement just a decade earlier. Many of the accused were members or fellow travelers during the Depression but had long abandoned the party. To argue that one's political views were no one else's business (as guaranteed by the First Amendment) or that one could not be forced to incriminate oneself (the Fifth Amendment) was no help. "Taking the First or Fifth was an absolute sign of 'guilt' to employers," said Rabinowitz. "And just as we got no support from the press, we got very little support from the courts.

"People were completely destroyed professionally. Some were substitute teachers—you can't get any lower than that in the public school system—but nevertheless they were unceremoniously fired because the New York board of education had ruled that anyone who took the Fifth was immediately fired. When that was held to be unconstitutional, they changed it a little—they fired these same people—for *insubordination*. For every case that was won—which took years and had to go up to the top courts—I would say there were five hundred people who didn't have the ability or the money to fight it through.

"It is hard to describe how terrible it was. Roy Cohn and the committee would subpoena somebody on short notice and there was no way to get out of it. Being called was a death knell. Time after time I would go down to Washington with these poor people and they would be sobbing on the train, saying, 'I'm going to lose my job.' There are only five or six people I really hated, but Cohn was at the top of the list. Cohn was really malevolent. I thought McCarthy was just a drunken opportunist who was riding a wave."

Meanwhile, the left was doing a fine job of disintegrating on its own, splitting hopelessly and venomously. Former popular fronters like Stone were critical of the CPUSA but defended its First Amendment freedoms. The newly formed Americans for Democratic Action (ADA) were anti-communist liberals who saw the CPUSA as a threat to the left's survival. Stone derided some ADA actions but scathingly attacked the CPUSA. "The purpose of independence is to avoid the stultification and idiocies, the splits and the heresy hunts, which make the Communists so ludicrous a spectacle half the time," he wrote in 1950. The party "oscillates between calling for a broad front against fascism and a 'pure revolutionary' line, in accordance with what its leaders think is the wind blowing from Moscow," and was run by rigid and mediocre men.

"If you had Communist friends in the thirties, and just about everybody did, you saw that their whole movement was filled with little Stalins. Petty little dictators," Stone remarked to Patner in retrospect. By 1948, Stone was using harsh words to describe Russia: its system depended upon "outlawry, suppression and terror."

In 1952, Stone wrote to Dashiell Hammett, declining to sponsor a rally for the CPUSA's V. J. Jerome, one of the Smith Act defendants. "V.J. is a hell of a nice guy personally but . . . he has tried to ride herd on the intellectuals in a way most offensive to anyone who believes in intellectual and cultural freedom. . . . I'd feel like a stultified ass to speak . . . for Jerome without making clear my own sharp differences with the dogmatic, Talmudic, and dictatorial mentality he represents." Stone would continue to defend him as a Smith Act victim, but "I can't pretend he is a libertarian so I'd better stay away."

Stone had challenged the Smith Act in 1940, always mocking Stalinists who said nothing because it was aimed at their sworn enemies, Trotskyists. Named the Smith Act for its sponsor, segregationist Congressman Howard Smith of Virginia, the Alien and Registration Act of 1940 was signed into law by FDR. It made mere advocacy of ideas a federal crime. J. Edgar Hoover later suggested to Truman that the act be used against the Communist Party. As he had for the Trotskyists in 1940,

Stone argued that its use in 1949 against eleven Communists was wrong. They were not charged with any overt acts but for conspiring "willfully to advocate and teach the principles of Marxism-Leninism," which the government interpreted as "overthrowing and destroying the government of the United States by force and violence" at some unspecified future time. Ten were given five-year prison sentences. Robert G. Thompson, who won the World War II Distinguished Service Cross for bravery, was given three years. While in prison Thompson was murdered by inmates.

The convictions dealt a blow to all on the left. "From the first to last the government has not alleged or sought to prove that the defendants committed any act which was unlawful," wrote Stone. "They were not accused of trying to put a bomb under the Capitol or of inciting others to do so or of drilling a private armed force with which to march on Washington. They were accused of disseminating revolutionary ideas. . . . There are revolutionary ideas in the Declaration of Independence and in Lincoln's First Inaugural, the right to utter revolutionary ideas is protected by freedom of speech."

At no time did the government try to use the "clear and present danger" defense, of which Stone approved when warranted (the government has the right to step in when advocacy of an idea threatens a "clear and present danger"). "For there was no evidence to show that after thirty years of legal existence the tiny Communist Party did in fact in any way represent a 'clear and present' danger of overthrowing the government." Stone called the Smith Act trials the "Dirty Derby." "There has not been so hollow a case as this since the similar anti-Red hysteria which followed World War I. . . . This scandalous prosecution was initiated by the Truman administration as a pre-election campaign against the Wallace movement." Each of the defense attorneys was cited for contempt and served a prison sentence. "Not many lawyers still have the courage to defend an accused radical of any kind. . . . The effect is to weaken so basic a right as that of representation by counsel." Three days later, Stone blasted an "appalling anthology of fatuity"; the *New York Times,* the *New York Herald Tribune,* the *Washington Post,* and the *Baltimore Sun,* "which championed fundamental American principles in years past, seem to have collapsed into doddering senility. Only cowardice" could explain approval of the convictions.

The next year, 1950, a despairing Stone wrote "Washington was becoming more and more like Moscow in rigidity, suspicion, and imposed conformity." Stone's nonconformist leftism was noted as far back as 1940 by an informant who advised the FBI that Stone was "not a member of the Communist Party." In fact, the informant confided, Stone frequently took positions that deviated from the "progressive" and "even the liberal" line. The informant defined the terms for the FBI: a progressive adhered to the Communist Party line; a liberal did not follow the party line and held mostly socialistic positions. Another former CP member, who had never met Stone, assured the FBI that Stone was frequently belittled as "half baked" by CPUSA members. When Stone joined Western leaders in applauding Yugoslavia's Marshal Tito's break with Stalin, no one was angrier than John Gates, the editor of the *Daily Worker,* who vowed, "A struggle must be conducted against such miserable instances as that of I. F. Stone."

"No group likes nonconformists," Stone told Patner. "I was *of* the left but a nonconformist." Many who renounced the left "hated me because I was still on the left, and those on the left were contemptuous of me because I fell off 'the locomotive of history.'" Many on the left and the right could never get straight what Stone was all about: defending the right of any person or group, no matter how odious, to speak freely. In 1949, for example, he defended a "Jew-baiting suspended priest, Terminiello, against a $100 fine for breach of peace. . . . I am, I suppose, exactly what Terminiello in his harangues meant by an 'atheistic, communistic, Zionistic Jew,' [but] I would not demean myself or my people by denying him the right to say it." Stone did not hold the "liberties I enjoy as an American in so little esteem that I am prepared to run from them like a rabbit" when one utters "gutter paranoia."

Privately Stone could be testy with more radical friends. "He was angry at me once in a while," said Victor Rabinowitz, who was Leonard Boudin's law partner. "He considered me to be too much of an apologist for the party line." Stone argued with Rabinowitz that CPUSA "support of Stalin and Russian policies was making the situation in the United States worse; it was counterproductive, it was helping McCarthy."

Publicly Stone often took the "no enemies on the left" stance because unity was vital. However, he shifted course in a few years, arguing that other leftists should disassociate themselves from the party and suggesting in bitter tones that the CPUSA could do everyone on the left a favor by disbanding. Years later he had no answer for one of history's what-ifs: If there had not been the Cold War, would there have been better foreign relations? asked Patner. "I just don't know the answer. Each side was just so suspicious of each other. . . . The Russians are really very paranoid. And *we're* very paranoid."

For all their faults, Stone felt that the Russian Revolution, and then the Chinese revolution in 1949, were inevitable consequences of the abject rule of emperors, czars, and corrupt despots. The USSR offered "substantial advantages for the peasants and working class," Stone argued, emphasizing that he was not comparing Russia with "Western freedom and standards of living." Mao Tse-tung was the direct result of the rotten Kuomintang, he argued, and saw his rule as a beneficial change. Yet, rather than casting off the atrocities of past regimes, China's Chairman Mao, like Stalin, aped them, living luxuriously while starving and murdering millions. The disastrous Great Leap Forward was followed by Mao's appalling Cultural Revolution from 1966 to 1976. A generation was destroyed. Those who survived physically were victims of antieducationalism, and numbing ignorance was their lot. Through it all, the murdering despot fooled the outside world. "Foreigners who met him often insisted that he was modest, warmhearted, even Lincolnesque."

Such revelations were all in the future. In 1950 Stone urged the United States to recognize the new Chinese Communist regime, which had come to power only because "the great mass of its people were disgusted" with the "corrupt, tawdry and murderous Kuomintang government." It was an accurate assessment, accepted by many observers. The powerful right-wing China Lobby who championed Chiang Kai-shek in exile in Formosa had cowed the Democrats in Congress, wrote Stone. "China has a right to rule its own destiny." Dabbling in intervention and blockades hurt not only America but "our own satellites in the Far East, especially Japan. . . . An adult policy must recognize that trade is a necessity between nations irrespective of ideology." It would take a quarter of a century and a Republican president to open relations with China. Stone cheerfully noted that President Nixon dealt with the ruler who had been a convenient enemy for Congressman Nixon when he'd smeared Democrats for having "lost" China.

In 1950 Stone was in accord with mainstream journalists like Lippmann, who tried to weaken the China Lobby's influence on the administration, even though Stone chided the columnist. "For all the welcome good sense . . . on the China question," Lippmann still held a "negative" position, "thinking in terms of alliances against the Chinese Reds." Used to wielding influence, Lippmann, Edward R. Murrow, and other noted journalists met privately at the home of *Washington Post* columnist Marquis Childs for a discussion with Secretary of State Dean Acheson.* They were trying to persuade Acheson to reveal what they had found in Treasury files. The China Lobby was bankrolled by drug money and American aid that had been sent to China, which was then secretly returned to the United States for the Lobby's public relations and kickback schemes. Acheson never used the information.

Stone devastatingly excoriated Acheson, who "has so stooped to placate his Congressional critics that he is now half his normal size."

Repression at home had escalated as the attorney general named "Communist fronts," deeming as subversive the aging veterans of the Abraham Lincoln Brigade and little old ladies who had sent wartime relief packages to Russia. Many of these harmless or disbanded organizations were now targeted retroactively. In "The Case of the Legless Veteran," Stone revealed the heinousness of Truman's Loyalty Program.** In 1948, a $42-a-week clerk in the Veterans Administration had "lost his legs to a German shell and his livelihood to American hysteria," wrote Stone. The veteran was fired because he was a member of the Socialist Workers Party, an anti-Stalin Trotskyist group. As Stone observed, "No one could suspect a Trotskyist of trying to steal the atom bomb and ship it to the Kremlin, except perhaps with mechanism attached to make it go off when Stalin turned the spigot on the office samovar." There was nothing sensitive about the man's job, there was no explanation given, and he was clearly fired only for belonging to a group the government had blacklisted. Stone ended with a jab at Truman: "More pitiable than a man without legs is a President without firm principles."

Stone made it a point to speak to front organizations, taunting the FBI informants who invariably appeared when few members dared show up. On one wintry night, Stone spoke to a near-empty room, joking that it was too cold even for the FBI. On November 8, 1949, Stone spoke at a

---

*Lippmann and Acheson had previously tangled at a Georgetown party when Acheson accused Lippmann of "sabotaging" the Truman Doctrine with his criticisms. Both men shouted at each other as guests watched in gleeful fascination. (Ronald Steel, *Walter Lippmann and the American Century,* 439).

**This incident remarkably parallels the 2002 fate of Senator Max Cleland, who lost both legs and an arm in Vietnam but was nonetheless tarred as "unpatriotic" by his opponent because he opposed U.S. entry into the Iraq war. The charge contributed to Cleland's defeat.

meeting sponsored by the Washington Book Shop, another "front" because it sold leftist material. Stone joked that he had joined the Book Shop that night and "have my card here to show for it." An FBI informant scribbled down Stone's speech at a May 25, 1950, Progressive Party meeting. Stone tailored his speeches somewhat to fit his audience. To this radical group he was quoted as saying, "What's the matter with the Russians? They got rid of the rottenest religion in the world." He mockingly (the FBI files characterized it as "sarcastically") added that it was time to "import some more Reds as the Republicans are running out of them and will have nothing to attack."

People with "radical ideas" should be heard, one informant reported Stone as saying, because a healthy range of political thought was the only way to develop a "middle-of-the-road" policy that was "advantageous to all people. . . . Only in a country which has a Communist or revolutionary party functioning without interference do you have a real democratic country." Stone frequently said and wrote that the most un-American and subversive person in the United States was the attorney general. In 1951 Stone spoke to a group so subversive that it was called the Baltimore Committee to Defend the Bill of Rights. In a time of pervasive segregation, this was, remarkably, a racially mixed group. More than four hundred "Negro and white citizens" had gathered at the Odd Fellows Hall in Baltimore. Six months later (July 25, 1951) Stone spoke to three thousand at a National Council of the Arts, Sciences and Professions affair. The turnout "makes one feel we are not alone. We are here to thumb our noses at the law. . . . I respect the rights of others to speak."

Such respect was seldom accorded Stone by the right-wing press. Stone ridiculed the *New York Herald Tribune* "Red Underground" column, which included Eleanor Roosevelt in its list of subversives. The column "has begun to expose the fact that I have been making speeches around the country against the Smith Act," wrote Stone in 1951. "I have heard of more sensational exposés. . . . I have written thousands of words about the Act. . . . I have made twelve speeches in nine cities against the Act" in six months. His appearances at the Boston Conservatory of Music and at Chicago's Chopin Hall "were not advertised as violin recitals. I did not pretend to be a lecturer sent out by the National Geographic Society. . . . The meetings were open to the public. Except for a few jokes in Yiddish, they were carried on in . . . English." To label the meetings as "underground" smeared all who had attended. "In a febrile search for hurtful material" the "Red Underground" column quoted

"We were just a couple of kids," said Izzy, spiffy in a tuxedo, with slicked-back hair and a boutonniere, at his wedding to Esther Roisman, July 7, 1929. [Celia Gilbert, family collection]

Esther the bride, with lilies and resplendent in satin and lace, displaying, as their daughter, Celia, wrote, "the power of that candid gaze . . ." [Celia Gilbert, family collection]

Izzy in his earlier smoking days. [Jacobi; Celia Gilbert, family collection]

Esther and Izzy, all dressed up for cocktails and dinner at the Waldorf-Astoria, circa late 1940s–early 1950s. [Celia Gilbert, family collection]

As a younger journalist, Izzy enjoys a scoop on the phone as he
punches the typewriter with his right hand.
[Celia Gilbert, family collection]

The Stones arriving in New York by ship from Paris in 1951. [Courtesy of Jeremy Stone]

Cartoonist David Levine captures I. F. Stone digging out the dirt from beneath the U.S. Capitol, 1968, for the *New York Review of Books*. [Copyright © David Levine, Kathy Hayes Associates]

Esther and Izzy say goodbye to their daughter, Celia, as she sails for Paris for her junior year abroad, early 1950s. [Celia Gilbert, family collection]

Izzy peering at a copy of *I. F. Stone's Weekly* rolling off the press. [Still from a documentary by Jerry Bruck, early 1970s]

I. F. Stone hunting and pecking his way through Ancient Greek research in March 1977. [*Washington Post* staff photo by Charles Del Vecchio]

The Stones on their fiftieth wedding anniversary, flanked by their best man, Chester Roberts, and their flower girl, Izzy's younger sister, Judy Stone. [*Washington Post* staff photo by Linda Wheeler, July 7, 1979]

During the Vietnam War, I. F. Stone takes notes from French scholar and Vietnam historian Bernard Fall in his Washington, D.C., study. [Dorothy Fall collection]

By 1972 I. F. Stone had become so famous that the *New Yorker* referred to him by nickname for the punch line of this cartoon. [Copyright © The New Yorker Collection, 1972, Lee Lorenz, from cartoonbank.com. All rights reserved.]

"Bucky Fuller. Scotty Reston. Izzy Stone. I may assume, then, that you are personally acquainted with these gentlemen?"

At long last, the college dropout receives one of his many honorary graduate degrees. [*Washington Post* staff photo by Larry Morris, May 14, 1978]

Izzy on his favorite outing; a long walk to a bookstore to rummage through the outdoor rack. [Copyright © Neil Selkirk, 1978]

I. F. Stone at eighty, in his office at home. [*Washington Post* staff photo by Craig Herndon, March 10, 1988]

"Good Night, and Good Luck"; Izzy waving farewell to a friend
on the streets of New York. [Copyright © Neil Selkirk, 1978]

These proposals did not come from a lunatic fringe, noted Stone. "Its members and directors make up a veritable Social Register of American Big Business (General Mills, Standard Oil, Monsanto Chemical, General Motors, picked at random)." The chamber was a "widely organized network for influencing legislation and opinion." Stone enumerated its influential blueprints that had been adopted by the government. In 1946, the chamber recommended the loyalty purge and investigation of Communists in Hollywood, which came to pass the next year. In January of 1947, the chamber suggested that the Department of Justice publish a "certified list of . . . front organizations and labor unions." This practice was soon begun. "The 1948 report called for action to bar Communists as teachers, librarians, social workers and book reviewers." A reign of terror soon followed in these professions. The CIO and ADA were criticized for opposing the Smith Act. Stone dryly wrote that the Chamber of Commerce had seen a "Communist plot": somehow thousands of anti-Communist ADA liberals who were fighting for civil liberties had been tools of the Communist Party, not independent thinkers.

Stone faced not only a troubled world of politics but ominous times in journalism. He cited the "organized campaign to use Cold War fears to drive out of the 'opinion industries' any opposition to the preconceptions of the big money and the screwball fringe it mobilizes." The myth of a dominating liberal media has had an astonishing run in America, exploited for decades by the right, and continues into this century. In June of 1950, at a time when radio sponsors and owners were quavering and caving, Stone mocked Hoover's assertion that "Communist fellow travelers and stooges" were controlling opinion. Instead, "hardly a liberal voice is to be heard on the air" in the world of "scared and sterile radio."

In the late forties, Stone was an occasional guest commentator on *Meet the Press* on radio and then when it began airing on television in 1947. The country's swing to the right put him in the role of the token "hot radical" trotted out as a passing nod to fairness while the rest of the panel "barbecued . . . some poor Red or 'Near-Red.'" Stone complained in private and sarcastically panned the show in his *Compass* columns. When Stone pushed Major General Patrick Hurley, Chiang Kai-shek's friend, as to why the United States should continue to waste billions on the dictator, Hurley yelled over the airwaves, "Quit following the Red line with me," then shouted, "Go back to Jerusalem." On the other hand, Stone was blasted by the *Daily Worker* as a "dirty counter-revolutionary" when he didn't follow the "rubbish of the Cominform." Stone tangled with the original producer and moderator of *Meet the Press*, Lawrence E. Spivak, a prickly anti-Red. At the age of ninety-one, Spivak said that Izzy was a "legitimate reporter. I thought he was appropriate [for the show], although I didn't always agree with his point of view." He added testily, "Most considered him off-base on a good number of things and considered him a Communist, although I didn't think he was ever a member of the Communist Party."

Stone's angry departure in 1949 left him without a national audience and, as *Meet the Press* grew in prominence, the chance for relative fame. Writing outlets were dwindling also. When Stone returned from his Palestine venture, he correctly sensed that there would be no happy homecoming at the *Nation*. *PM* was also in trouble. While Stone was away, Ingersoll had had one too many battles with Field. When Field's advisers convinced him that ads would put the paper in the black, Ingersoll told Field that he had no choice except to leave. "I resigned one sentence before I would have been fired," Ingersoll cracked at the time, but felt bitterly betrayed for years. Ingersoll's 1946 departure and the arrival of advertising signaled the end of an era, wrote newsmen at other papers where advertising was always paramount.

Stone hung on, but ads did not increase circulation enough. Field sold his costly venture in 1948 to Bartley Crum, a major lawyer for the Hollywood Ten who quietly changed its name to the *Star*, with barely a mention of *PM*'s demise. He and former *New York Herald Tribune* correspondent Joseph Barnes ran it for seven months, then gave up. *PM* "was a gallant defeat," Stone commented, "which is more glorious than a victory because it was something original, courageous and different." Ingersoll pioneered techniques that had lasting impact; "newspapers as a matter of course now cover labor, radio, the press and consumer news," said Ingersoll's biographer, Roy Hoopes, in 1989.

On February 18, 1949, Liebling's "grim duty" was to write *PM/Star*'s obituary. He had a sick feeling that he was witnessing "an Irreversible Trend." The *Star* was "making progress" in changing over from *PM*, "although the process resembled changing clothes under water." New York was now left with "three fewer papers than it had twenty-four years ago, although the population has increased by at least two million, and indicates how quickly the consolidation of control over the sale of news has advanced," wrote Liebling.

"On all the papers I worked for, we were always afraid that they would close the following Monday—and they always did," Stone quipped years later, but it was no joke at the time. Liebling referred to New York's papers as "our all-out Tory press," and Stone wrote in 1952, "The small circulation of the non standardized opposition press speaks for itself. Five more years of the present trend and it will be as impossible for a dissident voice to be heard in Washington as it is in Moscow."

When the *Star* went under at the end of January 1949, Ted Thackrey, the editorial-page editor of the *New York Post*, rushed to publish Stone's column, quoting a handsome salary. Stone did not miss a day's work—but after a few weeks he noticed he wasn't getting paid. Thackrey had "improvised" the deal without asking Dolly Schiff, the publisher, who was also Thackrey's wife for a time. Luckily for Stone, Thackrey bought the *PM/Star* premises and began the last fling in New York leftist newspapers, the *Daily Compass*, undoubtedly the only American newspaper to serialize Victor Hugo's classic *Les Misérables* in its comics.

Stone penned his strenuous six columns a week until the *Compass* folded in 1952, writing for a fiercely loyal but increasingly smaller audience. "The red label cannot be avoided in these days of hysteria," he warned the left in 1950. "The rightists" had broadened their attacks to include "the ADA and Truman, and the *New York Herald Tribune* is being called the 'uptown edition of the *Daily Worker*.' The red label is something which can only be handled with a laugh and a 'Nuts to you.'"

17

A Hot War and a
Cold Murder

In June of 1950, only five years after the end of World War II, stunned families again sent young men into combat, this time in a distant Asian country, Korea.

In a New York hotel, Stone jokingly told a sweltering crowd of leftists to "prepare your tomatoes." He plunged. "I'm sorry but I must say the North Koreans attacked the South Koreans" with Stalin's blessing. Many sat in stony silence as the journalist assailed both the United States and the USSR. "There is hypocrisy on both sides. . . . Both . . . want the markets of the world. God help any country occupied by the Russians or the Americans. . . . They should leave things to the Asiatics and get the hell out of there." To angry questioners, he kept repeating, "This is only my opinion."

Truman, MacArthur, Acheson, and Dulles instantly drummed into the American conscience that North Korea's attack on the South was Stalin's "naked act of Soviet aggression" to test the United States in its drive to worldwide expansion. UN troops, led by U.S. forces, rushed to counter Stalin and his North Korean "puppet" brigade. For decades this was accepted history. One major work termed the invasion a "Soviet War Plan," and another stated that Stalin "planned, prepared and initiated" the attack.

Had Stone maintained his original stance, he would have been in the mainstream. However, he changed his mind and was slaughtered by reviews condemning his uncharacteristic whodunit theories on the war's origins in *The Hidden History of the Korean War*. Written as the war raged, Stone's history argued that South Korea's leader, Syngman Rhee, "deliberately provoked" an attack by the North, with "secret support from Chiang Kai-shek and some elements of the U.S. government." "Possible" American suspects were the hubris-laden General Douglas MacArthur and Cold Warrior Secretary of State Dulles. Stone's theory seemed not only heretical but preposterous because the North quickly subdued an unprepared South and pushed through to Seoul. Years later, Stone traveled the same road to distance himself from his sensational theory that the South had jump-started the war. He told Patner, "It's hard to believe that the *South* provoked the war. I don't know; but if they *did,* it's very odd that the North was able to get all the way down to the end of the peninsula within a few days."

Although Stone was very wrong in his theory about the South starting the war, new evidence shows that he was correct in refuting the historical presumption that Stalin masterminded the war. Captured North Korean documents and Russian and Chinese documents show that, just as Stone wrote, both superpowers did not want to risk World War III by going to the aid of either North or South Korea. "At no point in his deliberations . . . was he [Stalin] willing to allow the conflict to draw him into a direct military confrontation with the United States. On the contrary, at every juncture he took steps to prevent such an escalation," wrote historian Kathryn Weathersby. Fifty-six-year-old Russian documents show Stalin wavering for months, seeking guarantees from North Korea's Kim Il Sung that the United States would not assist South Korea in a civil war. (Scholars are still analyzing and arguing about interpretation of this material, with some continuing to give Stalin a more central role in the decision to strike.)

At the time, Stone was among the few who accurately sensed Stalin's nervous concern about fighting the United States over Korea. The dictator urged Kim to beef up his forces, but played a cagey distancing game with both North Korea and China. With emerging revelations, other aspects of Stone's book prove more correct than the criticism he received in the fifties, when Stalin was seen as bullying his way toward World War III. Paranoia and distrust prevailed on all sides. Decades of Cold War hostilities, thousands upon thousands of dead and wounded American soldiers, millions of Southeast Asian civilian casualties, ruined countries, and a costly nuclear arms race might have been avoided had direct diplomatic negotiations ensued between the two great powers. While Russia and the United States were reluctant to back a war of their Korean satellites, neither was willing to directly negotiate.

One of Stone's ancient assessments seems greatly perceptive in the light of new evidence. Truth was "not to be found in the simplistic propaganda of either side," he wrote when the war began. "I believe that in Korea the big powers were the victims, among other things, of headstrong satellites itching for a showdown which Washington, Moscow and Peking had long anticipated but were alike anxious to avoid."

The United States had issued a hands-off policy in early 1950, trumpeted in a famous National Press Club speech by Acheson and broadly disseminated by the administration; neither South Korea nor Formosa were in its sphere of influence, and the U.S. would not commit troops to defend them. Stalin was willing to believe that this was no mere propaganda because the United States had not interfered in China's recent civil war. The Russians were similarly "seeking to restrain hothead Korean leaders," writes historian Bruce Cumings after examining the declassified documents. In the spring of 1950, Congress approved a $100 million economic and military aid package for South Korea and alarmed Stalin by cozying up to Japan, but "Stalin still hoped for a limited engagement." Then he disastrously gambled, supporting an "immediate advance along the whole front line," which solidified Western alliances. An alarmed Truman "abruptly reversed the meticulously considered policy," wrote Weathersby. The Korean War became a defining Cold War watershed; the portrait of the Soviets as "naked aggressors" shaped U.S. foreign policy for decades. Truman hastily concluded his separate peace with Japan, which gave the United States an Asian ally. And he "moved quickly to implement the massive rearmament plan drawn up earlier that year to defend Chiang Kai-shek's Taiwan [Formosa] and the French position in Indochina."

Stone, Lippmann, and other alarmed commentators watched Truman's swift embrace of Axis enemies who had been considered evil forces just a few years before. His rapprochement with Japan and his push to bring Germany into NATO, as well as his defense of the ousted Chinese dictator in Formosa, all made relations with Russia extremely precarious.

Interpretations of history seldom remain static, and this is nowhere more obvious than in arguments about the Korean War. What greatly incensed Stone's critics was his insinuation that General MacArthur, Dulles, and other leaders willingly continued the war on behalf of South Korea's unpopular leader Syngman Rhee and Chiang Kai-shek, who had been driven out of China by Mao's Communists in 1949. Stone himself had been prone to discount conspiracy theories before. Aside from this questionable gambit, Stone developed an interesting theory that the North

Korean attack was not the surprise the United States had claimed. He cited a number of advance warnings, including memos that MacArthur ignored. He used accounts of press conferences in the *New York Times,* the Paris edition of the *Herald Tribune,* government sources, and public UN documents that many American journalists had overlooked. Stone referred to a UN commission document in the State Department's White Paper dated June 24, the day before the fighting began, which noted that UN field observers reported two weeks earlier that "developments" along the thirty-eighth parallel were "likely to involve military conflict." Stone showed that MacArthur and others had been privy to previous CIA warnings of "extensive build up of forces and equipment on the 38th Parallel" but did not agree on the "imminence of any danger" although war broke out six weeks later. Stone asked why "had nothing been done" in light of advance warnings?

His suppositions proved so incendiary that publishers refused to print his book. (It was eventually published by the leftist Monthly Review Press.) In 1954, Colonel W. A. Perry of the U.S. Army security division notified the FBI director that recommendations had been made to remove the book "from Army libraries throughout the Department of the Army." The army asked Hoover whether its contents were "inimicable" [below, "inimical" was scrawled in handwriting, followed by a question mark] to the best interest of the United States government." A corresponding confidential memo noted that "during interrogation on 14 August 1953, [blanked out] stated that he had read a book by I. F. STONE . . . while he [blanked out] was a PW [prisoner of war]."

Stone could not be accused of writing the official view. "When there was reason to believe North Korea might be preparing an aggression against South Korea, neither [MacArthur or Dulles] uttered a word of warning. Is it possible that the outbreak of war . . . was preceded and followed by a chain of errors, falsehoods, forgeries and negligence so extraordinary as to leave MacArthur unaware of what was going on? It would be easier to believe in the light of what happened afterward—when the Korean War reversed American policy not only on Korea but also on Formosa—that MacArthur preferred to 'play dumb,' that Korea was a pawn to be sacrificed in a bigger game." Then Stone equivocated. "This is only surmise . . ." if this was the war's "unsavory secret history no outsider yet knows."

The remainder of the text builds a strong case that MacArthur was eager to take on the Chinese Communists and relates the snafus that led to a tragic stalemate. A man unhampered by humility, MacArthur challenged Truman's authority by going directly to China Lobby congressmen who favored widening the war by bombing China and bringing Chiang Kai-shek's forces into the battle. Such arrogant insubordination led to Truman's thunderbolt firing of the war hero in 1951.

Lippmann, who by that time saw the disastrous consequences of the war, also blamed Acheson and Truman for heedlessly urging MacArthur's drive to the Yalu. He was as caustic as Stone; the Truman administration was "almost prostrate with its inferiority complex in the presence of generals, aware of its mediocrity and inexperience." Lippmann and Stone correctly saw Truman paralyzed by charges that he was soft on Communism, and both backed Eisenhower in 1952 on the grounds that a Republican might be able to negotiate peace better than a Democrat.

While even the *Nation* termed Stone's book "tendentious," a stinging vendetta by Richard Rovere accused Stone of writing "heavily documented rubbish" with a pro-Communist slant. The review was preserved by Hoover in Stone's FBI files, with passages regarding Communists heavily underlined: "*Never, I think, has the communist line been upheld with such an elaborate display of the mechanics of research.*" Rovere wrote that Stone "once gave every promise of becoming one of the most accomplished journalists in the country." Considerations of libel informed Rovere's writing—he noted that Stone was a "free agent" and never was and "is still not a Communist"—but charged that he is "a man who thinks up good arguments for poor Communist positions." Stone once remarked to Patner that his nonconformity angered everyone: "Rovere hated me because I was still on the Left; and those in the Left were contemptuous of me" when he disagreed. "Rovere . . . was an ex-Communist. And ex's have to prove their apostasy."

Korean experts, such as Rutherford (Rudd) Poats, a United Press reporter who covered the Korean War from its beginning, disagreed with Rovere. Years later he avowed that Stone's book was "no blind-ideologue Communist crap but a very sophisticated analysis by a fellow who can see all sides. Stone presented a well-developed alternative view. The South *had* been conducting forays for months, and the North would hammer them back." Poats faults Stone, nonetheless, for being "totally myopic about the Communist side. I found very little criticism of the Chinese in his work; they were 'dutifully protecting their territory.' Izzy was blind to the faults and tended to see Communism as simply another socialist movement, just a little stronger."

In the sixties, when disillusionment set in after revelations that the Gulf of Tonkin incident was a false pretext that began the Vietnam War, a new audience breathed new life into Stone's *Hidden History,* finding the "timely parallels" to be "both obvious and frightening. . . . In pinpointing how severely we were brainwashed by our own propaganda [Stone] forces us to scrutinize Vietnam with the same microscope," wrote a 1969 reviewer of the republished edition. Historians continue to cite Stone for correctly challenging the dominant view of Western scholars that China joined the Korean War as part of a well-ordered monolithic Communist plot to rule the world. (In 1994, Chinese scholar Chen Jian noted that this was the standard interpretation "except for a few books . . . such as Isador F. Stone's *The Hidden History of the Korean War.*")

Stone was wiser than most American journalists on two pivotal foreign-policy points. He challenged condescending assumptions that led to decades of disastrous foreign policy in Asia. "The comfortable notion that the Russians were a backward enslaved people, allied with even more backward colored Asiatics, and that technological proficiency in air warfare was not to be expected from either of them was one of the casualties of the Korean War," wrote Stone in early 1952. "That truth had not penetrated" a general feeling of "cocky complacency and American superiority." He cannily prophesied the folly of Vietnam. There would be no "swift and easy Buck-Rogers-style victory over helpless masses of 'gooks,' 'Chinks' and 'Russkies,'" wrote Stone more than a decade before Vietnam.

Especially, he saw through the myth of a united Communism. Indeed, months before the Korean War, wily Kim Il Sung was playing Moscow off against Beijing and Stalin was waffling. The tense struggle between Mao and Stalin seemed to abate in 1949 when Mao gave his famous "lean to one side" speech, indicating that he would align with Stalin. Yet when MacArthur advanced toward the Chinese-Korean border in September 1950, Stalin inflamed Mao by initially reneging on his promise of aid. "But in those days," recalled Poats, "we were used to a monolithic view of the Communist bloc. Stone was doing a very good job of demonstrating that it wasn't really true then, but we were inculcated with John Foster Dulles viewpoints."

Many of Stone's Korean-era evaluations were echoed by later historians. Nearly fifty years later, evidence in Chinese documents revealed that MacArthur's advance to the Chinese border and his unconditional-surrender demands to Kim were largely responsible for China's entry into the war. However, Russian documents revealed that Mao had discussed plans with Stalin to enter the war as early as July 1950, shortly after it began. Some historians now conclude that, driven by a "divine destiny" vision of dominance, Mao would have entered the war with or without MacArthur's advance.

Never one to view war with detachment, Stone wrote that the harsh terms of unconditional surrender brought additional months of "futile slaughter." "An average of 4,666 American casualties was the price paid for every month's delay in the truce negotiations—the price paid for American insistence on carrying on the fighting while talks proceeded," he wrote. Tracking the inconsistencies in official tallies of enemy casualties, he termed them "sheer statistical slapstick." The public had grown so sour on these inflated claims "that even the Hearst *New York Journal American* protested."

As peace talks stalled in late 1951, Stone explosively charged that American leaders wished to continue the war for economic, geopolitical, and ideological reasons at the expense of human lives. "One could almost feel the relief in Washington as the truce talks bogged down again in an endless wrangle over air bases and the exchange of prisoners. . . . Chiang Kai-shek and Rhee still feared that peace would be the end of them," Stone argued. "Dulles feared that peace would fatally interfere with the plan to rebuild the old Axis powers for a new anti-Soviet crusade. Truman and Acheson feared that peace would confront them anew in an election year with the need to face up to the Far Eastern problem and recognize the government of Communist China. . . . It looked as if extension of the war . . . was necessary if the cold-war front was to be held together." And again: "Leaders were gripped by dread of the consequences of peace upon the economy."

Rovere and others saw Stone's overused phrase "fear of peace" as "sheer poppycock" and the reason that Stone should no longer be taken seriously. To suggest that leaders would deliberately extend the killing of American troops for geopolitical or economic reasons was an incredibly damning charge to many. "The great watershed that made Izzy a pariah was his book on the Korean War," recalled Murray Kempton. "All of us— particularly those of us who have romantic and somewhat hyperbolic views of our roles as soldiers in the Second World War—thought at the time that Korea was a 'just' war. We all felt then that he was basically a

Soviet apologist." Stone's journalist friend Stanley Karnow, who wrote definitively of the Vietnam War, felt that "Izzy had a somewhat contorted" view; "it seems as if he was bending his right elbow around to scratch his left ear." Stone was in part blindsided by ideology, yet Communist machinations to stall the peace talks remained hidden from Western scholars and journalists for decades until well after Stone's death.

Still, Stone's tendency to blame only the United States was questionable at the time and properly excoriated. CBS correspondent Bob Pierpoint, who covered the talks at P'anmunjom off and on for two years, pointedly recalled that progress began "within weeks, if not days, after Stalin died." Indeed, Stalin's death in March of 1953 was a major factor in the peace process as his successors scrambled to end the war. Stalin, who had supplied aircraft and other military equipment, had also advised Mao and Kim to stall on peace talks. When the Chinese had repelled UN forces, Stalin had telegrammed Mao to go slow: "A drawn-out war . . . shakes up the Truman regime . . . and harms the military prestige of Anglo-American troops." As the Chinese and North Koreans sustained huge casualties, Stalin still endorsed stalling tactics: Mao should "pursue a hard line, not showing haste and not displaying interest in a rapid end to the negotiations."

Stone was the harshest critic of American policy, but as peace talks stalled, even conservative papers were critical in milder tones. In November 1951, the *Wall Street Journal* suspiciously observed that peace would hamper America's role in Europe's rearmament: "If there is peace in Korea the position of the United States as the prime mover of European defense will be more difficult—and much more costly." This was just after a promising cease-fire compromise was thwarted when Acheson publicly attacked the Chinese as worse than "barbarians," hardly a winning diplomatic course. Stone quoted Reston: "Even officials . . . [in Washington] conceded that it might look to the world as if the United States was purposely trying to avoid a cease-fire in Korea."

A specious charge against Stone, which continued after his death, was that he spread Communist germ-warfare propaganda. In 1952, Chinese Communists accused the United States of air-dropping diseased rodents and insects that would spread anthrax, cholera, and other plagues. In a 1952 *Compass* column, Stone strongly refuted the charges as false: "I do not believe them. I start from the premise that a certain amount of lying, some bare-faced, some quite sincere, is inseparable from the heat of warfare." Atrocity reports should not be believed unless proof "objective enough to be persuasive on either side" was presented. Lippmann took the insider's viewpoint: the accusations could not possibly be true because two top officials "who happen to be old friends" had told him they were false. The United States long denied such actions, but not until forty-six years had passed was proof available. In 1998 the Japanese newspaper *Sankei Shimbun* printed "explicit and detailed evidence that the charges were contrived and fraudulent," based on Soviet archives.

Stone was too charitable about the Communist lie at the time: "I am inclined to believe the germ war charges grew like Topsy from plausible suspicion to fervent conviction in the hateful atmosphere of war." Yet he telegraphed what was to come in Vietnam: "The napalm bomb, our favorite device for burning out suspected villages, is worse than the germ." Stone suggested that the United States look at how its enemies perceive its actions. "The American refusal to support a ban on germ warfare can hardly seem a mere tactical or technical matter to them." But he scoffed at the "alleged confessions" of downed American pilots broadcast by the Chinese. "Confessions obtained under conditions of duress are suspect"; these were filled with "Communist clichés and slogans that ring quite phoney."

Stone pushed for a UN hearing with the Chinese and North Koreans, which the United States opposed. (His position seems naive. Documents later revealed that they were willing to inject corpses with cholera if an international inquiry ensued.)

Stone brought unusual skepticism to war coverage and made a new generation of reporters aware of the lies presented in press conferences. He belittled official reports from Tokyo headquarters, just as the next generation of reporters would label the euphemisms, evasions, and syllogisms emerging from Vietnam's daily briefings "the Five O'Clock Follies." And yet another generation would report "news" from the 2003 Iraq war on a glitzed-up media stage. Wrote Stone, Tokyo headquarters "had a gift for making the war sound as if it were being run by men temporarily on leave from the more juicy advertising agencies."

Stone sympathetically pointed out that "correspondents are subject to reprisals, ranging from denying them some bit of news given a competitor to withdrawing their accreditation." In the *New York Times*, Hanson Baldwin complained that "embellished adjectives had replaced facts." Reporting conditions were Stone Age primitive compared to today. Film sent to New York took a minimum of three days to get on the air. Poats tried carrier pigeons but abandoned that after the first bird took eleven days to fly from Korea to Tokyo. Since Vietnam, said Poats (in an interview that preceded unquestioning reporting on WMDs, the Patriot Act, and the Iraq war), "It is accepted that journalists are highly skeptical of authority. In those days it was out-of-bounds. MacArthur had to be covered straightforwardly. There was not enough independent research and reporting. Stone certainly had another view of the role of Dulles at that time. I don't recall anybody covering it the way that he did."

Echoes of Stone's skepticism followed in Vietnam and afterward. While some argue that Korea was a just cause because the South remained free from Communism, others still question now, as Stone did then, the cost of a war in which a country ended as divided as it began despite the huge human price in casualties, a stalemate that has resulted in fifty-three years of U.S. military patrols, a long and difficult road to democracy in the South, and today's edgy clash over North Korea's nuclear arsenal.

A few weeks after the Korean War began, Stone left for India, urged by his *Compass* publisher to meet with Prime Minister Jawaharlal Nehru, whom Stone had met in the States in 1949. He hoped that Nehru could mediate the war. "Nehru was a neutralist. At that time neutralism was a bad word in both Moscow and Washington." (Nehru had passed on a memo through Scotty Reston at the *New York Times* to Acheson six months after the war began in which Peking offered a peace proposal in exchange for negotiations on Formosa. Acheson appalled Reston by dismissing it out of hand.)

In 1949, Stone could not resist a quick stiletto to open his column about Nehru's appearance before the all-male and segregated National Press Club. The club had "lifted its Jim Crow rules for a colored man. It gave a luncheon for Pandit Nehru." (Stone had quit the club in 1941 when it had refused to serve him and a black guest, and had asked a "friendly member to take me to hear Nehru.") Stone was startled to see Nehru in Western garb and was disappointed in Nehru's press debut— he "skillfully said nothing at all" in an "almost fussily nervous and precise" manner, giving the impression of a "slightly effeminate English barrister." The eyes alone "gave promise. They were set in dark caverns, and their deep brown seemed to smolder, as if with some inconvenient vision ill-repressed."

The next night, Nehru's rousing speech at Columbia University was a welcome change; it "was an attack on the cold war, a critique of the Truman foreign policy, a protest against the pressure Washington is exerting on other countries to line them up for war, and a warning from the colonial world's foremost living spokesman against the doctrines of racial, and in particular of white, supremacy. This, from a supplicant for financial aid, took nerve." Stone's meeting with Nehru in India was futile. He left certain that Nehru would not or could not do anything to intervene in Korea.

Stone did not go home. For the first time in his life, he was not, as Esther said, "sliding down the banister to see what news awaited." Washington's oppressive Cold War climate had penetrated his natural ebullience. Before he left for India, Stone groused around the house that he could not stand "this goddamn town." Stone went to Paris and felt at home in a thriving left intellectual atmosphere. Claude Bourdet, the editor of *L'Observateur* and a romantic former member of the French Resistance, published Stone's columns on the Korean War, which were more palatable to a liberal foreign audience. In his tiny hotel room under the eaves, Stone looked out on a "raw, cold and rainy day" and wryly wrote, "Were this any place but Paris I would describe the day as miserable." He was genuinely fearful of returning to a country that seemed dangerously tilting toward fascism. Urgently calling Esther, Stone told her she must come immediately. The *Queen Elizabeth* was sailing in 10 days and she and the boys should be on it. (Celia was in college.) For Esther it was an unquestioned command. For her two sons, it meant a disruption of school and friendships.

Esther had no money for this venture, but rather than sell the house she followed Stone's advice to mortgage it and take out a loan. Stone also had a large war correspondent's insurance policy. Esther managed to rent the house and pack up within ten days and set sail. Stone met them in Cherbourg. Christopher was struck by how tired and worn-out his father looked. The forty-two-year-old journalist had been up all night traveling from Belgrade, where he had interviewed Marshal Tito. He bubbled with enthusiasm about Tito and hoped that he was the face of a new socialism. Despite troubling crackdowns on dissidents, Stone felt a sense of promise in Yugoslavia that was absent in much of Europe.

Stone had rented a house on an estate outside of Paris in Jouy-en-Josas. It belonged to the widow of the former French premier Léon Blum.

Christopher adapted to his French school and France, but Jay hated it. Stone was at home among French intellectuals such as Jean-Paul Sartre and Albert Camus and thumped away at the typewriter on his Korean War manuscript. Claude Bourdet introduced Stone to Stanley Karnow, who was "just a kid" from New York, enthralled to be starting his career in Paris. Karnow recalled that Bourdet was more neutral and nuanced than the famous Sartre. "He wasn't anticommunist but he wasn't a Communist by any means, and none of the people around him were." Paris harbored leftists of all stripes in those days, so soon after Hitler's occupation. "There was a real Stalinist group [whom Stone's sister referred to as 'crazies'] but Izzy was never involved with people like that," said Karnow. Stone comfortably invaded the staid *New York Times* Paris bureau when he needed the bustle of a newspaper office, recalled Karnow.

Karnow, then in his midtwenties, was thrilled to meet Stone. "Izzy was a great hero for anyone who was from New York and had aspirations to be a journalist. He was very big in the Jewish community and was a name to anyone who read the *New York Post* or *PM*. In those days, things were pretty rough in France. Izzy's place wasn't very luxurious; kind of quaint. He was terribly nice to me. And funny and fun to be with."

For Stone's family there was a feeling that they were in exile and an "uncertainty as to where we were going to wind up," said Christopher. "There was a whole community of exiles from McCarthyism, from the blacklist, who spoke to one another in ways that amplified their mutual fears of the United States. The expatriate group in Paris did see one another a lot. They came from the same intellectual, social background. A lot of them were writers and in films. Being abroad, we only heard the worst because the self-supporting community was wholesaling the paranoia."

After several months in France, the question of whether they would return to the United States enmeshed the family. The *Daily Compass* publisher desperately wanted Stone back in the United States and told his leading columnist that the paper would go under without him. Stone's brother Marc was "very active brokering the return of Dad," said Christopher. So was his sister, who passionately implored her brother to return to fight McCarthyism. "There was this one really very dramatic scene," Judy Stone recalled with a laugh. "I remember bursting into tears—which I could do at the drop of a hat—and saying, 'Well, if *you* won't come back, there are other people who will stay in the United States and *fight*.' He finally decided to go back. I had less to do with it than just the fact that Esther and the boys were really unhappy."

Stone was contemplating Israel, which sounded perfectly dreadful to Christopher. He tiptoed into his father's bedroom with a cup of tea while the grand decision was being made. "He had fallen asleep, for crissakes, in the middle of the biggest decision of our lives!" The next morning Stone announced, "We're going back." They booked passage on the *Liberté* and the family "very quickly got out of there."

As they pulled into New York harbor that June of 1951, Chris leaned over the boat's edge, "watching the tugboats nudging us in. We suddenly got called on the loudspeaker—'Would I. F. Stone and his family please report to the purser on the main deck.' We thought, 'This is it.' Were we going to be arrested? Was Pop going to be arrested? It was really scary. There was a big barrel-chested guy who said, 'Let me see your passports.'" (Passports were being denied to radicals at the time.) The man stared and said in a Brooklyn accent, "Is youse the Stone that writes for *PM*?"

"Yes," Stone replied. The man suddenly replied, as he stamped the passport, with a big smile, *"Gei gesund"*—"Go in good health" or "Be well" in Yiddish. Behind him came the man who had requested the singling out of the Stone family. He turned out to be a photographer from the *Compass*. An article on Stone's triumphal return was quickly added to Stone's voluminous FBI file. Three months later a State Department agent walked into Stone's office and demanded his passport. Stone refused repeatedly. He was warned that any future plans to travel abroad might be denied.

Stone refused to return to D.C., that "goddamn town," and rented an apartment at 1133 Park Avenue. It was not the posh address distorted by right-wing enemies who charged after Stone's death that it might have been paid for with "Moscow gold." The Stones got a lucky break in the postwar era of rent-controlled apartments. A friend bought the apartment for a virtual song when it went co-op, and rented it cheaply to Izzy and Esther.

Despite Stone's initial trepidation, he returned to the United States with renewed vigor, more defiant than ever. He hit the ground running, both in print and in person, in a resounding defense of the Bill of Rights and especially First Amendment freedoms. He now tangled with the right and the left, many of whom were caving under the assault of McCarthyism. In disgust at the American Civil Liberties Union, which hedged on its duty to defend the rights of political outcasts, Stone helped found the Emergency Civil Liberties Committee (ECLC). The ACLU's lawyer, Morris Ernst, was now enthralled by J. Edgar Hoover, writing the director gushing letters, dining with him at the Stork Club, and eagerly joining his hunt for suspected Communists. Stone railed at the ACLU expulsion of board member Elizabeth Gurley Flynn because she was a Communist and its refusal to aid lawyers, among them his brother-in-law Boudin, who defended Communists. Little did Stone know that Ernst was feeding Hoover personal letters written by the journalist and others who broke with the ACLU.

Stone seemed more determined than ever to attack mainstream media support of Cold War fulminations. "A world in which neither side can attack the other without disaster is a world in which the alternatives are mutual destruction or co-existence," he warned. He lampooned a ludicrous *Collier's* edition that turned an entire issue over to a "preview of the war we do not want" that included this cover line: "Russia's Defeat and Occupation, 1952–1960." The issue featured garish paintings—fleets silhouetted in moonlight with bombs bursting and American paratroops outlined in flame-red skies parachuting into Russia's Ural Mountains, also with requisite bombs bursting. Famous authors and journalists weighed in—Robert E. Sherwood, Arthur Koestler, Walter Winchell, Lowell Thomas, Edward R. Murrow, World War II cartoonist Bill Mauldin—on various fictional aspects of a "winning" war. The United States would be victorious—despite the numerous atomic bombs dropped by the Russians and after Detroit, New York, Philadelphia, and the nation's capital were ravaged.

Stone was obsessed by the absurdity of the *Collier's* issue, precisely because it asked to be taken seriously, intoning that "this is a sober document" that took months of research. Stone devoted several columns, one headlined, "Easy, One Hand: *Collier's* Wipes Out Russia." "*Collier's* says, in effect, 'Well, now, an atomic war wouldn't be so terrible.' . . . This is war propaganda of the most wicked sort." The magazine did not "try to lift the curtain on the terrible hysteria and Red-phobia which would accompany such a war once bombs began to fall on our own soil." Stone added, "There is no way to wage a war of liberation with atom bombs."

In 1952, Stone saved his most blistering attack for Walter Lippmann and other distinguished journalists in an outraged five-part exposé under blazing headlines: "I. F. Stone Exposes Polk Murder Case Whitewash." "The Crime of Hush-Up." His columns remain among the most salient of that era.

Four years earlier, a body had been fished out of Salonika Bay in Greece—with the back of his head blown off. The face was unrecognizable after days in the water. In life, he had been a dashing foreign correspondent; photographs portray the fine features and slicked-back-hair elegance of matinee idols. In death he was mottled and bloated. His hands and feet were bound with rope, execution-style, and he was thrown into the bay while still alive. There had been no attempt to hide his identity; ID papers were in the pockets of his camel-hair jacket, and on his wrist was a metal bracelet etched with the name of George Polk, a thirty-five-year-old CBS radio correspondent covering the battle between the U.S.-backed Greek government and Communist rebels. His body was found on May 16, 1948.

At first the murder caused a sensation among journalists. Polk had been one of famed Edward R. Murrow's "boys," as his radio reporters were called. Correspondents had been killed in warfare, but this was cold-blooded murder, an act of reprisal and a message of horror. Fearing that the Greek government was involved or, at the very least, would wink at the murder investigation, American reporters pushed for an independent inquiry. Walter Lippmann headed the committee and picked General William J. (Wild Bill) Donovan, recently of the OSS, to run the investigation.

The choice of Donovan should have been suspect at the time, noted Stone; a man so closely linked to the State Department was "too easily reachable by government officials." Lippmann had to prod Donovan for years to get a report, which was finally made public in 1952. Stone was the only journalist at the time who pegged the belated report a "feeble bit of whitewash" that endorsed a "farcical" 1949 Greek-government trial pinning the murder on Communists. In his shabby *Compass* office in Manhattan's warehouse district, Stone waded through the report's attached appendices. (He always told reporters to read documents from back to front.) Stone concluded that "the Truman Administration had as big a stake politically in the outcome of the Polk Affair as the Greek government." Stone stingingly rebuked the Lippmann committee. A "cub reporter" could have done better; it was clear that both the Greek and American governments had prevented a real investigation of the murder and had succeeded in "making an accomplice of this bunch of journalistic stuffed shirts." What is worse, Lippmann expressed private doubts but, wrote Steel, "accepted a verdict that seemed feasible and had the inestimable virtue of not upsetting cold war politics."

"To a surprising degree," wrote Steel, Lippmann endorsed the assumptions that Cold War policies were essentially defensive. "He criticized the policy makers, but rarely what lay behind their policies." There could be no greater contrast than his and Stone's approach to the ramifications of Polk's murder. Stone blasted Donovan for his part in a high-stakes political murder cover-up: "It is extraordinary how much he managed not to see in that courtroom." Stone ridiculed a speech given by Lippmann when presenting an inscribed bowl to Donovan on behalf of the committee. Lippmann cloyingly praised Donovan—"We have learned that your sense of justice is the equal of your courage"—a sentiment uttered "on behalf of men whose profession it is to have few illusions." Retorted Stone, "For men with few illusions they certainly managed to be gulled by the Greek and American governments."

In 1947, the United States began pouring millions into the Greek regime, the first front in its global containment of Communism. "A cardinal point" of the Truman Doctrine, wrote Stone, was its support of the rightist government against leftist rebels. What had been a Greek civil war became a vital forerunner in the domino theory of foreign affairs. Independent-minded journalists at that time were the victims of a "kind of guerrilla war" campaign by the Greek rightist press and the State Department, wrote Stone in 1952. They were "smeared as Communists," and letters of complaint were sent to their home offices. For example, Homer Bigart of the *New York Herald Tribune,* which could scarcely be called a Commie rag, was called a "distorter of truth in Greece" by Administer of American Aid to Greece Dwight Griswold.

Polk was an honest reporter, "a decent and fine young man," wrote Stone, who had met Polk in Cairo. He was "no radical" but a "fearless" reporter who was "not the kind who used handouts and not the kind who fell for soft-soap." On his CBS broadcasts, Polk did not hesitate to criticize both sides, but decried America's support of the corrupt Greek government; the Greek Army was a "military monster"; the Truman Doctrine program was a "poor investment."

Although the Lippmann report noted that Polk was a "severe critic" of the regime, it nonetheless endorsed the improbable verdict of the Greek trial and lamely added that "it was not self-evident what the political motive was." Stone scoffed at "this lush double-talk." He exposed this sham endorsement of an "incredibly one-sided" trial; witnesses were suppressed and American-style cross-examination was not allowed. A leftist Greek journalist, Gregory Staktopoulos, was convicted of being an accomplice.

The accused assassins, two high-level Communist officials, were never found and were sentenced to death in absentia, while Staktopoulos received life imprisonment. Donovan declared himself satisfied that justice had prevailed, and the Lippmann committee bragged that "we can say with entire conviction" that the man who had led Polk to his death was in prison. Stone and several members of the New York Newspaper Guild formed their own group to investigate, but attempts at inquiry "were discouraged by Lippmann on the grounds that a second investigative group would complicate efforts to win the cooperation of Greek and U.S. officials," wrote Steel. "The most vocal dissenter was I. F. Stone."

Typically, Stone found nuggets buried in the fine print staring at anyone who had cared to examine it. There was the skeptical Harvard criminal-law professor, E. M. Morgan, who concluded that the many and several "confessions of Staktopoulos" were "so inherently weak as to be practically worthless." The Greek's entire testimony "cries aloud for cross-examination." The Morgan analysis, "ignored in newspaper coverage of the Lippmann report, would have severely damaged the official theory" had it been published at the time, argued Stone, who was furious that this view had been withheld "until now" (1952) when Polk's murder "has been all but forgotten."

Stone assailed the committee and the media for ignoring another major clue: they showed only mild concern that Lieutenant Colonel G. L. Kellis, Donovan's assistant, was recalled "although he was the only investigator working on clues . . . which pointed to the Rightists" as the authors of the crime.

Stone's work remains a piercingly accurate indictment, but more remarkable is that the evidence was right there in the attached appendices, including CBS radio's fair but harsh coverage of the trial. Fifty years later Stone was singled out by several newly intrigued authors for his courage in taking on the leaders in journalism, exposing woeful timidity and lackluster pursuit of the truth. They utilized documents unavailable to Stone at the time to reinforce his argument that the crime was committed by the rightists and that the truth was deliberately suppressed. At the time, however, Stone experienced the frustrating fate of writing for a fringe publication. His concise analysis was ignored amidst Korea and Cold War saber rattling.

"Only I. F. Stone can be said to have seen and said it all at the time," wrote journalist Christopher Lydon in a 1996 *New York Times* book review of the latest exploration, *Who Killed George Polk?* Fresh details made interesting reading, Lydon wrote, but "there is no improving on I. F. Stone's succinct judgment."

Stone had remarked in 1952, "Some day perhaps the truth will be known and these men will blush for their role in its unfolding." By the time the Polk murder was reexamined, it was too late for blushes. Staktopoulos, released from prison, publicly recanted his confession years later, stating that he had been tortured by government officials; Kellis, who had maintained more than two decades of silence, charged that "the entire inquiry and trial had been a cover-up," which was why he had been removed after unearthing a trail leading to right-wing assassins. But by the time widespread interest occurred, both Stone and Lippmann were dead. A committee member, James (Scotty) Reston, the *New York Times* columnist, said in 1990, "I do not have one single memory of that committee."

Reston spoke fondly of Stone. When told that Stone had accused the committee of gullibly accepting Donovan's judgment, Reston said, "If we did, we were stupid. I wouldn't trust Donovan's judgment on anything. I wouldn't have put it past Donovan for one minute to engage in cover-up of that kind, but Lippmann, Joe Harsch, Reston, and so on? That we would have covered up a murder of one of our own colleagues is unthinkable. Did I ever see the report? I don't remember that either."

"His murder was an outrage," noted Steel in 1991. "At the least, Lippmann can be criticized for showing too much faith in Donovan and allowing himself to be led into a solution that suited everyone's convenience." The committee "and particularly Lippmann, should have been more skeptical." However, Steel argued, the committee had no access to Donovan's private files, did not know of the "open collusion that took place between U.S. and Greek officials." They were all too comfortable accepting a verdict that did not disturb the Cold War status quo. The inexcusable fact was that they "should not have been so credulous. They failed in their responsibility. But this is not the same thing as a cover-up. Here Donovan is the far more likely candidate." Steel's latter-day comments were reasonable, but the fact remains that Stone came to a far different conclusion with no more evidence than the committee at the time.

In the summer of 1952, Stone once again faced an uncertain future. The Polk series was one of the last he would write for the *Compass*. He fired several more salvos at the Truman administration's foreign and domestic policies. Then on the night that Truman's presidency came to an end, so did the financially strapped *Compass*. Stone was a month shy of forty-five years old with children and a wife to support. But a radical dissenter in the Cold War era had few options. He would write millions more words in the next thirty-five years, become famous in circles from Paris to London and on nearly every campus in America, yet he would never again be put on staff by a newspaper publisher.

Stone's future seemed as chilly as that cold November night.

PART FOUR
Going It Alone

18

CHASING IZZY

"Washington DC: November 6, 1953: Surveillance was instituted in the vicinity of the subject's residence at 7:50 p.m." So began one of the thousands of pages of endless spying on Stone. That year Stone had moved back to Washington to start a risky venture, his own newspaper. This report was spiced with Chekhovian gloom: "Heavy snow fell. . . . Many of the streets were impassable to automobile traffic."

The FBI had received incorrect information that Izzy and Esther Stone were giving a party—a fine opportunity to take down license plate numbers and "attempt to identify visitors." The Stones and two other couples emerged. The report allowed a cloak-and-dagger moment: "It was noted that all lights were extinguished in the subject's residence when the group departed." The six trudged through heavy snowdrifts up to the corner of Nebraska Avenue and Thirty-first Street NW and entered a "light grey 1952 four-door Pontiac sedan." (Stone's car was detailed in files as a green 1952 Nash.)

The FBI followed the car to the National Theater. Stone and party went inside. Stone was observed in the lobby, holding the tickets. He was overheard telling "the other members of the group, 'Marty didn't come.'" Surely a hidden code.

Having no tickets for cultural edification, what were the agents to do? They slogged through the snow to the group's parked car. They illegally searched the car and glove compartment and found the automobile registration card, an envelope postmarked from New York with a return address, a map of Princeton, New Jersey, with an address circled and marked, a postcard from New Jersey, and numerous automobile maps of East Coast states.

No one in Stone's theater party ever knew that they had been identified by name and tagged for lifelong inspection through this illegal FBI search and seizure. (Their names were blacked out in files released a half century later.)

Like thousands, this report reveals nothing more than how agents spent their days and nights observing American citizens at work and play in their guilt-by-association scattershot spy hunt. For nearly forty years, the FBI trailed Stone in every conceivable fashion, including pawing through his garbage. Hoover's infringement on civil liberties seems most odious reading recounts of surveillance titled "Trash Picked Up." The purpose was to find "persons largely in the Washington Metropolitan area which appeared in the trash of the subject [Stone] on dates set out concerning whom there is no identifiable data in the files of this office." In the trash picked up were "addressors [sic] or names written on scraps" by Stone. There are indications that this initial report was made in 1952, but this notation was listed as May 20, 1954.

Stone's mountainous file bulges with his speeches and articles, which remain monuments to his crusade against spurious trials and hearings, blacklists and wiretaps, deportations and loyalty oaths. They reveal FBI inaccuracies, innuendos, and persistent anti-Semitism, as well as numerous inventive ways to spell his name, such as Irving and Finkelstein. Memos stated that Stone was "not his true name," although Hoover knew that Stone had legally changed his name decades before. Augmenting Hoover were the CIA, State Department, Army, Internal Revenue Service, and the U.S. Post Office.

At times several agents were detailed to follow Stone, writing up tedious reports in longhand: September 27, 1951, 7:00 a.m. Agents positioned in front of Stone's New York City apartment. 10:55 a.m.: "Stone came out . . . and proceeded on foot east on 91st to Lexington Avenue." Two minutes later "Stone entered Max Schwartz's cigar store." One minute later Stone exited, no doubt in possession of at least one more cigar than when he went in. Three minutes later "Stone entered a grocery store on the west side of Lexington Ave. between 89 and 90th street." Six minutes later: Stone came out of the grocery store with a bag of groceries and proceeded north on Lexington Avenue and west on Ninety-first Street. By 11:08, the subject, no slow study in the shopping department, was back home. Nothing happened for four hours, in which time an agent could presumably yawn himself to death. Down the block, into the subway, out of the subway, and a walk to the *Compass* offices ensued from 3 p.m. to 3:29 p.m. At 6:30, with Stone still holed up in the office, surveillance was discontinued.

For those whose memories of Hoover go back no further than some recent biographies depicting him as a cross-dressing homosexual who answered to the name of Mary on festive occasions, it is hard to imagine the courage it took to battle the director during his absolute reign. Hoover fed Cold War inquisitors raw files of unchecked suspicions and lies in one of the most pernicious decades in American history. HUAC spawned mini-HUACs and vigilantes across the country who infiltrated civil rights and peace movements. Files were available for corporate blacklists.

It is impossible to know what lies beneath blacked-out paragraphs, in pages not granted through FOIA or listed only as "destroyed." Certainly Hoover would have leaked to congressional and journalistic allies anything to torpedo his nemesis, but Stone's file reflects the futility of hounding a man so publicly opinionated. When asked why he was never called before HUAC or any other investigative committees, Stone remarked, "What was McCarthy going to do to me? Expose me? It would be like exposing Gypsy Rose Lee. I was exposing myself every week anyway."

Years of surveillance reveal an outrageous concentration of time and taxpayers' expense on a reporter who had no military or classified secrets to pass to a friendly ally, much less to an enemy. He had no massive audience to sway as an "agent of influence"—murky spy-talk so ambiguous that it could include any columnist who advocated peaceful action that coincided with Russia's avowed aims or revealed what had been told to him by government sources. After the FDR era, Stone had few high-level contacts to give him scoops, and those leaks he quickly published anyway.

The FBI, CIA, the Army, the State Department, and the U.S. Postal Service relentlessly tracked Stone across the United States and Europe. They grilled family and friends about his activities, and memos frequently mention that brother Marc had once been a member of the Communist Party. Agents opened packages and boxes, tapped his phone calls, recorded the names of those who entered his house, covered his speeches, clipped his articles, and kept dossiers on meetings with sources, friends, relatives, neighbors, other journalists, or alleged Communists—all of whom Stone cheerfully acknowledged knowing, including more than twenty organizations retroactively deemed by various attorneys general to be "Communist fronts," cataloging them from A (Abraham Lincoln Brigade) to W (Washington Book Store.)

It did the FBI no good to link Stone with Earl Browder, the head of the American Communist Party until 1945, or labor leader Harry Bridges, whom the U.S. government tried unsuccessfully to deport for decades. Stone never disguised knowing them. He also knew that supporting Wallace and his CP-filled Progressive Party "automatically got you on the subversive list." Stone fiercely defended the Communist Party's right to exist in a free society. He refused to answer questions about his own political affiliations "as a matter of principle" when applying for a passport. Later Stone signed a statement that he had never been a member of the Communist Party in order to get passport approval for a 1956 overseas reporting trip. As an old man he sighed, remembering that capitulation.

When Stone traveled, the FBI could have saved themselves the expense of tracking him on airplanes, bribing hotel bellboys and desk clerks to give them information on phone calls (mostly to home) and visitors (few), eavesdropping on lunches with suspicious suspects. Had they bought a copy in the next day or two of whatever paper Stone was working on, they would have found his report of his travels, whom he had met, and what had been said.

Despite such extraordinary effort, if the FBI ever collected anything incriminating, it is not in released FOIA files. And one FBI official who saw them before they were redacted noted, "Hoover thought Stone was something more than he said he was—but I never saw anything to indicate that. I never saw anything startling in his files. Hoover really had a pathological hatred of this man." The FBI official ventured a reason: "Hoover disliked him because he was a man of great imagination, where Hoover was stolid and disapproving of such freethinkers. He saw him flitting hither and yon, touching on so many different subjects, always from a leftist slant. I find him fascinating, an intellectual butterfly. Hoover tended to be rabid about people, and I think he was about Stone. Izzy was a moving target because he wrote so much." The FBI official added a tantalizing tease and would not elaborate: "The stuff withheld is much more interesting than what you'll get. Izzy's file was a bailiwick of very very sensitive informants. In general, if that was declassified, it could make the Bureau look very good." However, he repeated, nothing he read would make Stone look bad.

Stone had no more inveterate reader than Hoover. The FBI files became a mini–Library of Congress on Stone, his articles copied from the midthirties through the seventies, his endless speeches scribbled down.

Alas for the trailing FBI agents, they found no trysts with steamy Svetlanas. Dreary page after page document Esther and Izzy constantly together, the kind of fidelity that could bring tears to a gumshoe's eyes. "At 6:45 p.m. on July 24, 1951 subject left his office carrying two suitcases and a third small carton and proceeded by taxi to Union Station" is about as gamy as it gets.

Red hunters held the First Amendment in scant regard. Journalists who expressed views that were anti-FBI, antifascist, pro–New Deal, pro–civil rights, and pro-peace (regarded as suspiciously pro-Russian to the FBI) were suspect. "Connections" with "questionable" news sources were diligently dogged. In Hoover's war on free expression, journalists who criticized the thin-skinned director were as subversive as political dissenters. Files were kept on many of America's great twentieth-century writers primarily because they dared mock or lambast Hoover. They include James Agee, Nelson Algren, Sherwood Anderson, James Baldwin, Ludwig Bemelmans, Heywood Broun, Pearl S. Buck, Truman Capote, Dale Carnegie, Willa Cather, John Cheever, e. e. cummings, E. L. Doctorow, John Dos Passos, Faulkner, Fitzgerald, Hammett, Ben Hecht, Lillian Hellman, Hemingway, Ring Lardner Jr., Lippmann, Norman Mailer, H. L. Mencken, Jessica Mitford, Ogden Nash, Anaïs Nin, Clifford Odets, Grace Paley, Dorothy Parker, Damon Runyon, William Saroyan, John Steinbeck, James Thurber, Thornton Wilder, Thomas Wolfe, Herman Wouk, and so forth. Dossiers were kept on gossip hounds Hedda Hopper, Louella Parsons, and Walter Winchell (who later became a faithful Hoover lapdog).

When Stone admirer and Pulitzer Prize winner Murray Kempton read his own files, he concluded that Hoover was "stark, raving mad," consumed with Kempton's satirical digs, not his politics. Kempton amusingly recounted that the FBI had not even known that he was briefly a Communist Party member in the midthirties ("almost mandatory," he recalled, for his seaman's job). Kempton himself candidly told them in the 1950s. Instead, "my file was all about Hoover." Likewise, Hoover's paranoid trailing of Stone began with Stone's trashing of Hoover in the midthirties.

Hoover forever warned FBI agents to practice deep cover; "in view of Stone's profession and his frequent castigations of the Bureau, it is felt that extreme caution is needed." When Stone returned from Europe in

1951, FBI agents complained of difficulty spotting him in Manhattan's grungy produce district where "between 8 a.m. and 6 p.m. trucks completely obscure the entrance to the *Compass* building. . . . It is necessary to practically stand in the doorway. . . . As a result, surveillance cannot be maintained there for any long period of time."

The Stones' tiny Fire Island cottage—"the second house on the left from Bay Walk in Ozone Beach" (the FBI's misspelling of Ocean Beach)—was also a bust in the lurking department. No cars were allowed on the island, and there was no phone in the house. Stone "must use the public phones located in the Western Union Office." The informant said Stone would be unlikely to discuss "any confidential business" over these phones "inasmuch as he was hard of hearing and would have to speak in a very loud voice."

Island surveillance was "not deemed feasible," but the memo assured Hoover that "informants are covering telegraph, mail and ferryboats." They discovered such clandestine correspondence as letters from his hearing-aid company. Skulking terms predominated: They learned through a "a pretext telephone call" that Stone was in his office. "On August 24, 1951, informant [blanked out] advised that Stone had taken the 4:10 PM ferry boat . . . to Fire Island. Informant said that Stone was having a 'meeting' on the Island the next evening." This meeting of "undetermined nature" was so hush-hush that "about 100 people would attend."

It was darkly noted that Stone was "friendly" with civil liberties lawyer Leonard Boudin, which was advantageous, considering that they were brothers-in-law.

When Stone started the *Weekly* in 1953, Hoover was apoplectic, going through tortured motions to subscribe without Stone knowing. In 1955, Hoover let one of two subscriptions lapse. An FBI memo stated that "extensive investigation has failed to establish any espionage activity on the part of subject and has established no current CP activity on his part." Agents were instructed to continue reviewing the *Weekly*, "which refers with rather great frequency in a critical and derogatory manner, particularly to Director Hoover, the FBI and Attorney General." "Nasty" treatment of Hoover was noted. Hoover furiously scrawled comments on the reports. At one time, the Justice Department criminal division wanted the Bureau to interview Stone, hoping that he would reveal the name of a writer whose articles Stone had submitted to the *Nation*. "NO!" Hoover angrily scrawled on the memo. "We will not do so under any circumstances. If they want him interviewed, they will have to do so themselves."

Hoover's creepy vendetta against outspoken journalists, as well as his obsession with the sexual proclivities of political leaders, saved Hoover from Stone's wistful hope that a president one day would fire him. "Hoover's closet is well stocked with skeletons," wrote Stone. "Many in the capital fear the stray bones he may rattle." The nation's chief smut collector had his own dark secret, which may have propelled him to get the goods on others. Hoover was deeply bothered by pervasive rumors about his homosexuality. Hoover's gnarled private life even led to a secret grudge against his friend William F. Buckley Jr. In his *National Review,* a 1967 satiric piece issued a mock front page of the *New York Times,* with a notation that Hoover had resigned after being arrested on a "morals charge." Hoover never forgave Buckley.

Hoover was steeped in sexual conflict; he called homosexuals "deviants" but cavorted with closeted Roy Cohn and his gay friends and suspected ones like Cardinal Francis Spellman. (Hoover's files contained numerous allegations that his friend Spellman was "a very active homosexual.") Hoover was never outed during his lifetime; in today's sex-celebrity era, bachelor Hoover's extraordinary relationship with Clyde Tolson, his associate director and hatchet man, would be fair game. They rode to and from work together, partied and dined constantly together, took vacations together, and, as biographer Richard Gid Powers wrote, had a "spousal relationship."

Stone would never have hinted at Hoover's private life. It was his public life he despised; he had nothing but contempt for Hoover's use of raw and scurrilous sexual data. During one notorious Cold War spy case, Stone's brother-in-law Leonard Boudin successfully appealed the conviction of Justice Department worker Judith Coplon by proving that the FBI had illegally tapped her phone, planted documents as bait, and arrested Coplon without a warrant, charging her with passing secret documents to the Russians. (Nearly fifty years later, it became known that Hoover possessed incriminating KGB files that had triggered the FBI pursuit of Coplon, who was a spy.)

Coplon's affairs, introduced in trial, were slapped across tabloids. This "incredible vomit of slander, gossip and suspicion pouring out of the FBI files," Stone argued, had nothing to do with identifying her as a spy. (Stone carefully did not defend her innocence.) Stone correctly defined the troika of trash collectors who were "synchronized in thought control." The FBI was feeding HUAC and McCarthy, a fact long denied by Hoover, tidbits from his "mountainous mass of garbage." The "anonymous gossip and slander on which the congressional investigators feed so lushly" was "exactly the same mishmash the Coplon case turned up in FBI files." It was "dirty business. . . . If FBI men can gather sex stories and salt them away in those files . . . 'fornication' can be said to obtain conviction in many kinds of cases."

When Boudin revealed the director's abhorrent tactics, Truman wanted to fire Hoover, but the president was persuaded that he had to retain the Red-baiting hero during his reelection battle. Hoover merely scurried underground. He stored secret files in the basement of the FBI, under guard. (Many such files, including some on Stone, were destroyed during the sixties.) In December 1950, Hoover's congressional friends passed a helpful law following the botched Coplon case. FBI agents could make arrests without warrants if it involved (with no clear definition) "espionage."

"Secret police agents are very dangerous," Stone forever railed. At age eighty he said, "The American Constitution, the American system and the countervailing elements of a free press to check it—these are the good and only safeguards. Secret police agents are no substitute."

"TOP SECRET" was stamped on each page of Stone's file. By far the most serious FBI attempt to connect Stone with anything clandestine began with Elizabeth Bentley, who walked into an FBI office in 1945 and told a sensational story of a massive spy ring operating at the top level of government during World War II. Bentley gave the FBI details about spies in the State and Treasury departments, OSS, the Pentagon, and named such top officials as White House aide Lauchlin Currie, OSS major operative Duncan Lee, and Assistant Secretary of the Treasury Harry Dexter White. She claimed this ring was run by a New Deal economist named Nathan Gregory Silvermaster; the FBI named Bentley's file "Gregory."

Like many reporters, Stone knew several of these men as sources and was especially fond of White. Since Bentley named Stone—a man she had never met—as an acquaintance of some she accused, Stone's file was elevated from "security" matters to the "Gregory espionage" case. In 1945, Bentley was a bitter defector, furious that Moscow had sent Soviet professionals to run her job. Bentley was more important in the spy game than the mousy mole she appeared as; her unsubstantiated charges would usher in the Cold War and the biggest spy hunt in American history, dramatically described by Bentley biographer Kathryn Olmsted.

Bentley said she was ready to confess because she feared being murdered, with good reason. Soviet archives show that agents contemplated shooting her, faking a fatal car or subway accident, administering a slow-acting poison. In the end they did nothing. Bentley told the FBI that she had operated a high-level Soviet spy network. At first she named fourteen, then eighty, and then still more. The most prominent, powerful, and respected were Currie and White, a chief architect of the Bretton Woods International Monetary Plan and the World Bank. Bentley claimed that White had used his "influence to place C.P. members and fellow travelers in strategic positions in government." If true, this would have been analogous to other administrations harboring secret members of the KKK, the John Birch Society, fascist German-American Bund sympathizers, or open racists—all of which happened in the twentieth century. If White had knowingly planted someone involved in espionage, that would have been a different story, but Bentley's proof was nonexistent. The celebrated ex-Communist defector Whittaker Chambers said nothing about espionage when he first named Alger Hiss and never even mentioned White until after White was dead. But the era was devastating for anyone viewed as pro-Communist, and if people lied about Communist connections, they risked perjury convictions. By the time Bentley first went public, in 1948, it was nearly forgotten that the USSR had been America's ally during the time frame she detailed.

Hoover grilled Bentley from 1945 to 1948 in secret, beefing up surveillance of anyone she had mentioned. In 1948, Stone joined many doubters who assailed the "secondhand hearsay gossip" Bentley "unsuccessfully retailed to a grand jury."

Uncharacteristically an insider during the New Deal and World War II, Stone of course dealt with these officials. For decades, until the FOIA release of FBI documents, few except Hoover's circle of HUAC and McCarthy committee colleagues knew that Bentley had mentioned Stone. Only after Stone's death and the release of his files would Hoover's tenuous rationale for his intense scrutiny of Stone be exposed.

The FBI first honed in on whether someone had been or was a member of the not-illegal CPUSA. On her FBI visit in 1945, Bentley gave them a memorandum concerning "persons who she claimed to be active members of the Communist Party." Stone was a correspondent of the *Nation,* she said, and then termed the magazine "a CP organ that helps to place members of the CP in federal positions." FBI repeats of Bentley's account botched the sentence, omitting reference to the *Nation,* so that it appeared in numerous subsequent mimeographed copies that Stone himself was charged with placing CP members in federal positions.

A 1946 notation mentions that Stone knew people whose "activities had come under scrutiny in the Gregory investigation," but clearly adds, *"The extent of his relation to these persons was unknown"* [italics added]. If this came from Bentley, she was pointedly unfamiliar with Stone's name: "His full name was set forth as Isadore Finklestein Stone." Another 1946 memo stated that the "WFO [Washington Field Office] identified Stone as a close contact of several subjects in the Gregory Case." Either informants were so hazy that they did not know Stone's correct name or reports were especially sloppy: One who "thinks" Stone was a Communist called him "Irving." Another informant—who said Stone's middle name was "Finklestein"—also incorrectly thought Stone was related to publisher J. David Stern.

From 1945 until 1948, while the FBI spent three years trying to substantiate Bentley's charges, they stepped up their already heavy surveillance of Stone. From then until the Bentley case was closed in 1954, it was open season on Stone. A former editor at the *New York Post* who admitted his dislike for Stone after the journalist sued the paper contended that Stone feigned barely knowing CP leader Earl Browder when Stone set up an editorial meeting with him in the thirties. This implied secretiveness on Stone's part offers nothing but malicious observation. So was the view that he "may" have been either a Communist or hard-line sympathizer in the thirties "when it was fashionable."

At no time did anyone ever remotely hint that Stone was a spy.

Moreover, Stone's FBI files prove that he was often excoriated by Communists and the *Daily Worker.* In what had to be a wiretapped phone conversation, in 1945, an unnamed Communist lambasted the journalist: "Stone doesn't get that sense of defending the Soviet Union all the time. How can a real radical, or liberal, even, not have that feeling?!" The test of loyalty was "Do you trust the Soviet Union through thick and thin, regardless of what anybody says? . . . And you got to defend that with your last drop of blood, and Izzy Stone hasn't done it all the time and there's no excuse for it!"

Some sense of accuracy compelled Hoover to write that Joseph Starobin of the *Daily Worker* criticized Stone in 1944 for lumping the USSR with Germany and Japan in its loss of freedoms; "Isn't it about time people like Stone admitted that the vigilance of the GPU [Soviet Secret Police] wiped out Hitler's fifth column in the Soviet Union, a service from which the entire world is today benefitting?" said Starobin. Another entry included this damaging evidence: "It is this informant's impression that Stone thought the United States was a wonderful country in which to live, and that it provided more opportunities for the foreign born than their ancestors had ever experienced, in spite of certain laws such as the Smith and Walter-McCarran Acts."

About the same time that Bentley defected, British spy Kim Philby tipped off the Russians that Washington and London were beginning to decode KGB cables, some of which included names that Bentley had cited. Therefore, just as Hoover was beefing up his forces to catch those accused by Bentley, the KGB hastily dismantled its operations. There had been some "witches" after all, but the witch hunt actually began long after the fact, after such espionage had been halted. Had Hoover not zealously guarded the KGB files—eventually named Venona for no particular reason—perhaps much of the Cold War's vicious domestic turmoil could have been evaded. However, it seems likely that those early Cold Warriors would have deployed these ambiguous and fragmented KGB files to scapegoat any New Dealers who thought they were furthering the war against Hitler through such back-channel connections.

At the time, heavy surveillance revealed no espionage, and most of Bentley's accusations were discounted. As Olmsted recounted, both KGB and FBI files remarked on the instability of their alcoholic source, who aggrandized her drab past and painted herself as a naive waif. In truth, she was shrewd and smart and for a time both misled the KGB and successfully blackmailed Hoover. The FBI soon realized she could lie as easily as she told the truth. Her virtue was manufactured; some friends knew her as a licentious bisexual. She became a spy out of love for a major KGB kingpin, not ideology.

More important than character flaws were Bentley's flawed evidence and admissions that she had never met many she had incriminated. Bentley had no evidence except overheard conversations as to who was a Communist, a fellow traveler, or simply an idealistic New Dealer. She could not say whether some knew they were involved with Russia or believed they were just helping the CPUSA or merely cooperating in the antifascist cause to defeat the Germans during wartime. She had kept no copies of anything to substantiate her claims. Even Gregory Silvermaster, who indeed ran a spy ring, evaded conviction after taking the Fifth. Bentley at first basked in Mata Hari fame, revamped by the tabloids as the sensational Red Spy Queen. Running out of factual material, Bentley embellished, exaggerated, and told outright lies as she testified. After rousing herself for the klieg lights, Bentley would then descend into drunken self-pity, telling a friend that Roy Cohn and other inquisitors had pressured her to exaggerate when she had nothing new to expose.

In fact, Hoover feared putting her on the stand but had no choice. By 1948, Hoover and Attorney General Tom Clark worried that if they sought no action, HUAC might accuse them of bungling the case. Hoover knew that exaggerated or uncorroborated evidence would not dissuade congressional members bent on stardom; one mission of the hearings was to publicly shame or discredit someone by merely calling him or her to testify. Just as Stone often wrote, Hoover was sending his secret slush to HUAC, including Bentley's unsubstantiated files. Clark knew a grand jury had no basis on which to indict but convened one anyway to save face. If HUAC questioned its effectiveness, Clark could counter that the Justice Department had made the effort. Hoover panicked when a leak stated that the anonymous defector was a female. So did Bentley.

After bigger fish, and not knowing that Russia had closed down its operations, the FBI dared not threaten their only cooperative witness with prison. Hoover's star witness became his chief headache as Bentley demanded hush money and threatened to go public. Partly as a smoke screen, Hoover and the Justice Department pushed the grand jury to investigate a more viable case. On July 20, 1948, the grand jury indicted twelve CPUSA leaders for violating the Smith Act. The successful case was attacked by Stone as trampling on their constitutional rights of free expression.

Unbeknownst to Hoover, Bentley had already talked to a New York reporter, who tarted her up in page-one stories as an anonymous sexy blonde. Bentley was neither blond nor sexy, as became obvious when she finally surfaced in a print dress, dowdy hat, and glasses. But such publicity forced Hoover to reluctantly proceed with a weak case. Without any corroboration, Bentley became famous overnight as she testified to grand juries, HUAC, and the world. (Whittaker Chambers, locked in his battle with Alger Hiss, would second some of her claims and crowd her for front-page coverage.)

The famous spy case, which brought no indictments or convictions, was unceremoniously dropped by the FBI in 1954. Historians would rate it as Hoover's longest, most expensive, and most fruitless failure. Meanwhile one of Bentley's lesser contacts, William Remington, successfully sued, but was later convicted of perjury. In prison, Remington was bludgeoned to death by an inmate who hated "Commies."

The woman who helped start the Cold War died in 1963, derided as a lying alcoholic. Bentley never knew Hoover had hoarded evidence that could support some of her charges. It took thirty more years before the public would know.

One of the clearest points to be made is that Stone always viewed that passing atomic or military secrets was punishable treason. "Every government necessarily and properly seeks to protect itself and its secrets from such activities," he wrote in the early 1950s. In 1953, the world was mesmerized by the drama as Julius and Ethel Rosenberg awaited execution as America's most famous atomic-spy couple. The FBI recorded that Stone talked with their lawyer Emanuel Bloch at Sing Sing prison, and that Bloch had scheduled a visit to Fire Island to confer with Stone about them. Stone was both reporting on the Rosenbergs and actively fighting to commute their sentences. However, unlike many on the left, Stone never argued their innocence.

"It would be easy if one could dismiss talk of Soviet atomic espionage as a myth," wrote Stone at the time. "Unfortunately, the fact is undeniable. Allan Nunn May in Canada, Klaus Fuchs in England, David Greenglass and Harry Gold in this country, all confessed to such espionage on behalf of the Russians." Rosenberg supporters were wrong in arguing that there "has long been no secret about the atom bomb. It cannot honestly be argued that many processes and much of the know-how were not secret. The Russians were eager to get just such information. . . . There is little doubt" that spies gave them "useful information" that hastened the Soviet atomic energy program.

"I have kept silent on the case so far," Stone continued, "because I was never persuaded by the campaign on behalf of the Rosenbergs. This campaign aroused many people but in some ways did more harm than good with its sentimentality, its distorted presentation of the facts, and its wild charges of anti-Semitism." These were grim words for both Stone readers and the keepers of such reasonableness in the Collected Works of I. F. Stone as Compiled by the FBI.

Stone took an unpopular position on the left. He had "never been persuaded that the case was a frame-up," then added, "But I do believe the sentence imposed upon the Rosenbergs is barbaric, savage and way out of line with justice. It is fantastic and shameful that Rosenberg and his wife should be sent to the chair when Fuchs and May got fourteen and ten years in jail," he wrote. (May was released after only seven years.) Greenglass, who implicated the Rosenbergs, was sentenced to thirty years. Stone's was part of the worldwide appeals that included the pope's, exhorting Truman "in the name of human decency" to commute the Rosenbergs' sentence to thirty years imprisonment, "which is the alternative provided in the statute."

Stone's views against the death penalty were bolstered decades later. Three years before Stone died, the FBI admitted that seeking the death penalty was a ploy to get the Rosenbergs to reveal other spies. At the time of her execution, the FBI knew there was no case against Ethel and she should have been spared the death penalty, said the FBI's chief spy chaser, Robert J. Lamphere. He recommended death for Julius but only if the judge made it clear that the "sentence would be reduced if he cooperated with the F.B.I." In 1997, the Russian who had dealt with the Rosenbergs, Aleksandr Feklisov, also said they were unjustly executed. He claimed Julius passed military secrets, but provided no useful atom-bomb material. Ethel's sentence was particularly tragic, he said, because she was not an active spy.

As the world waited, Stone frantically tried to effect a stay of execution. "I had thought of Stone as the great reporter, and here he was Bloch's 'adviser' for the day in how to handle his effort to save the Rosenbergs," recalled Al Spivak, who was an INS wire-service reporter covering the White House. "I heard Izzy saying to Bloch, 'Why don't you take the appeal directly to the White House? Try to see the president?' Now anybody in his right mind knew you just didn't pick up the phone on the night of the Rosenberg execution and say, 'Mr. President, I want to discuss this matter with you.' " The lawyers "on the advice of Stone" saw this as good publicity and a stalling maneuver, said Spivak. They "spread the word through the media that they were going to the northwest gate of the White House to deliver a letter to the president.

Izzy became a participant, rather than an observer," said Spivak. "That repelled me."*

As the Rosenbergs were put to death, the press found dramatic symbolism in a blazing sunset reflected in the Hudson River. The execution was especially gruesome. It took three jolts of electricity to kill Julius and five to kill Ethel. Stone was among those who listened to the news and wept.

On December 16, 1954, an FBI memo stated that the Washington Field Office was "closing this case . . . inasmuch as there are no outstanding leads." With typical sloppiness, some FBI raw files continued to be classified as espionage. In 1955, the FBI recommended that Stone be removed from the security index. "WFO has no information that subject has membership in or participated in the activities of a basic revolutionary organization within the past five years." However, a year later, the FBI still sent advisories overseas regarding Stone's travels. Two copies were sent to a blacked-out source in London and another to a foreign liaison office: "It should be noted" that the *Weekly* on April 2, 1956, informed its readers that there would be "no issues for the next two weeks while I. F. Stone goes abroad. 'The next issue, April 23, will be from Israel and after that (we hope) from Moscow.'" The FBI again reactivated Stone's file during his civil rights and anti–Vietnam War activism. Not until Hoover's final years and the end of the *Weekly* did they stop hounding him.

For their illegal bugging efforts, the FBI heard many long, arduous interviews, which proved only that Stone was guilty of exhausting a subject to death. The near deaf Stone was often heard saying, *"What?!"* followed by repeated answers. These tapped phone calls strongly show that Stone never thought of himself as a Communist, always referring to CPers as "they," never "we." In seeking clarification of puzzling grand jury testimony, Stone quoted from the record that an unidentified man

*Spivak, however, revealed just how subjective one's feelings can be. He recounted another incident in which he praised a highly respected *Baltimore Sun* reporter, Phil Potter, for actively participating in defeating McCarthy. Potter persuaded a committee member to leak the army memorandum that accused McCarthy of trying to sabotage the army, which led to his downfall. So wasn't Spivak admitting that Potter was not just an observing reporter? "Yeah," said Spivak with a laugh, "it's just that I liked the way he did it." Potter included several reporters in the deal, sacrificing an exclusive. "He knew if it just appeared in the *Baltimore Sun,* what good would it do? Potter didn't want a Pulitzer. He wanted to get McCarthy." Spivak to MM, 1990.

entered a CP meeting and allegedly said, "Young men in the C.P. must get into the Army so that we can disintegrate the morale of the men. . . . In this way we could soon overthrow the capitalists and also take over the control of the Army." Stone then commented to the lawyer, "It sounds so much like a piece of tailor-made testimony to fit the preconceptions of the FBI. . . . This business that 'we could soon overthrow the capitalists by taking control of the Army'—I don't think any Commie is so *meshugah* [crazy] to think quite that way." Referring to other testimony, Stone asked the lawyer, "Are the Communists screwy enough to take in a new member, introduce him to a National Committeeman and take him into a private meeting of seven people the very same night?" "You got me, pal," answered the lawyer.

In his David-and-Goliath battle, Stone repeatedly told audiences to thumb their noses at Hoover, HUAC, and McCarthy. The "real evil," he stormed, was "the very idea that Congress has a *right* to interrogate people on their political views." Stone managed to incense Communists and Hoover at the same time when he called the FBI America's near equivalent of Russia's secret police. "Today in America," Stone often reiterated, "it is a crime even to think."

During McCarthy's reign, many journalists were goaded into silence by the McCarthy-Hoover Axis, as Stone nicknamed it—some by nervous publishers, some caught in the implacable, often silly, and complicit journalistic practice of having to quote authorities on deadline, no matter how suspect the comment. (Retractions or real facts typically appeared in small type later.) Others were wooed into friendly drinking bouts with McCarthy or favored sensational stories. Stone often attacked with humor. In 1950, McCarthy made his Red-baiting debut, waving a sheet of paper—without names, as it turned out—saying, "I have here in my hand" the names of State Department spies. Soon after, Stone opened a 1950 Carnegie Hall rally against the H-bomb with, "Greetings, FBI agents and fellow subversives." A few weeks later, Stone was greeted by laughter when he came onstage trailed by a midget with a huge red card. Stone said, "This is one of the card-carrying Communists I picked up in the State Department." Hoover's informants were there to record it all.

Congressional hearings were "unconstitutional inquisitions," wrote Stone, where suspects could not face their accusers. He likened them to England's medieval Star Chamber, so named because the roof was ornamented with stars. This royal tribunal (abolished in 1641) was notorious for its secret sessions without jury, its torture, and its harsh and arbitrary judgment. What strikes one today about early Cold War inquisitions is the chillingly banal acceptance by Americans who remained unharmed, unaware, and oblivious. In contrast, the leftist world Stone knew was awash in anger, fear, and agonizing frustration as friends were dishonored by innuendo. Stone pounded a *New York Times* editorial stating that congressional committees had the right to "question teachers and scientists or to seek out subversives wherever they can find them" before it lamely criticized the "profoundly wrong" manner in which some hearings were conducted. Stone tartly responded, "To accept ideological interrogation is to make nonconformist views of any kind hazardous. . . . To permit Congress to seek out something as vague, undefined and undefinable as 'subversion' or 'un-Americanism' is to acquiesce in a heresy hunt. . . . One man's 'subversion' is another man's progress; all change subverts the old in preparing the way for the new. 'Un-American' is an epithet, not a legal standard."

Stone constantly attacked the Walter-McCarran and Smith acts, which allowed the United States to deport aliens and members of the CPUSA for their political beliefs. Rounded up were labor militants and elderly editors of foreign-language newspapers. Immigrants were threatened with deportation if they did not end pro-labor activities or refused to turn in Communist Party relatives. Homes were invaded without warrants. "People are afraid to look. . . . This is how good folk in Germany walked hurriedly by and shut their ears discreetly to telltale screams."

The American public shut its ears. HUAC began well before McCarthy and sailed on after the senator was ruined. The initial Dickstein-McCormack Committee "set up to investigate purveyors of racist and fascist views was converted in the hands of Martin Dies into a means of attacking the New Deal and the left-of-center," wrote Stone.

Union workers and intellectuals alike were fair game. Directed by the FBI, HUAC interrogated Joseph Papirofsky, then a stage manager for CBS and a theater producer. A Missouri congressman knowingly asked him about injecting Communist propaganda into his productions. "Sir," said Papirofsky, "the plays we do are Shakespeare."

The famous Joe Papp (né Papirofsky) produced the New York Shakespeare Festival. The step-by-step technique was graphically described in

2001. "The committee members tried to bait him [Papp] into a jail term for admitting contempt for HUAC," wrote Rick Perlstein in the *New York Times*. As usual, demanding that he name former colleagues was a ploy because the congressmen already knew them. "The only honorable way to answer the question then, while avoiding legal jeopardy, was to take the Fifth Amendment. But that just completed the humiliation, because it seemed to imply you had done something illegal, something you wanted to hide. And taking the Fifth was what moved you from the committee's witness list to the blacklists."

HUAC's persecutions became infamous during the 1947 Hollywood Ten interrogations into the political beliefs of leftist writers, directors, and actors. Ronald Reagan could thank his lucky presidential stars that the Communist Party had turned him down when he wanted to join in 1938. A decade later, Reagan was an eager, "friendly" witness, telling HUAC what he knew about leftist colleagues.

Screenwriter Ring Lardner Jr.'s life is an apt lesson on the toll it took to be an unfriendly witness. Stone was infuriated as HUAC chairman Parnell Thomas grilled Lardner in 1947. Five years before, at age twenty-six, Lardner had shared Hollywood's 1942 Oscar for best screenplay for the witty *Woman of the Year,* costarring Spencer Tracy and Katharine Hepburn. Now the committee charged that he was a possible Communist who planted subversive propaganda in movies. Thomas thundered, "Are you now or have you ever been a member of the Communist Party?" Lardner puckishly replied, "I could answer it, but if I did, I would hate myself in the morning."

For this, Lardner spent nine months in prison, convicted of contempt of Congress. While in jail, Lardner ran across his famous former inquisitor. Thomas had been caught defrauding the government—a delicious irony that Stone reminded readers about frequently. This legendary conversation supposedly took place during work duty: Lardner was cutting grass with a sickle and HUAC's former chair was cleaning up a chicken yard. Thomas yelled to the writer, "I see you've got part of your old Communist emblem. Where's the hammer to go with the sickle?" Lardner replied, "I see you're up to your old tricks, Congressman—shoveling chicken shit."

By 1948, anticommunism was rampant, led by the American Legion, the Catholic Church, the Hearst and Scripps Howard newspaper chains, and ad hoc committees who would have made great use of such modern conveniences as blogs. The Legion organized anticommunist letter-writers to demand that radio and TV sponsors fire the offenders. Rush Limbaugh–style tirades began ages ago: "YOU DON'T HAVE TO PROVE ANYTHING . . . YOU SIMPLY HAVE TO SAY YOU DO NOT LIKE SO-AND-SO ON THEIR PROGRAMS."

It remains frightening that the whole nation was influenced by these tactics, which affected the entire media and involved the interrogation of those who posed no threat to security. Writers, performers, guests, and editors were fired or demoted at the behest of sponsors; leading newspapers such as the *New York Times*, radio, and the budding TV networks were as guilty as Hollywood moguls. (The unemployable Lardner had no mantel for his Oscar; he was forced to sell his home.)

Ironically the espionage act had only a three-year statute of limitations during peacetime, while the false blacklist could damage one forever. John Henry Faulk, a political satirist with a witty cracker-barrel delivery, was billed as "the new Will Rogers" by CBS—until Faulk took a detour into principle. He opposed a major broadcast blacklist organization, Aware Inc., in the midfifties. Stone cheered as Faulk headed an entertainers' union antiblacklist election slate to halt this practice. Aware Inc. then falsely branded Faulk a Communist. Displaying the moral courage so familiar to television, CBS fired Faulk. Famed lawyer Louis Nizer took Faulk's landmark case. At trial's end, jurors asked if they could award *more* than Faulk's request for damages. Their $3 million award was a pyrrhic victory. Aware Inc. was by then defunct.

Stone and Edward R. Murrow (who gave $10,000 to the unemployed Faulk during his struggle) remained the humorist's few journalistic heroes. Faulk's trial broke the blacklist, but it took seven years; by then Faulk had lost his early fame and was broke. Faulk considered Stone a friend and "coreligionist" in First Amendment fidelity. "Izzy felt the First Amendment placed on him as a journalist a very great burden to practice and maintain," said Faulk. Like Stone, Faulk had little use for the zealotry of CP members, but felt that "a Communist had as much right to work as a Seventh-Day Adventist or anyone else, just like Izzy said. Izzy always said, 'Everybody has a right to work unmolested in America.'" Like Stone, Faulk was tarred for dining with a "known Soviet agent." It was the Astor Hotel, 1946, and the "agent" was Andrey Gromyko, the Soviet ambassador to the United States. Eleanor Roosevelt and several hundred others were present. It was the first anniversary of the United Nations.

Such insanity muted any sober attempt to uncover true espionage. Faulk was among the civil libertarians who loathed what Stone termed the "crawl," abject recantations to prove one's loyalty. Faulk never publicly criticized the Communist Party. For years, Stone was loath to do so, also in part for the same reason his friend Molly Ivins attributed to Faulk: "Americans hear so much anti-communist propaganda already there's no point in adding another scintilla to it." "Pop hated sellouts," said Stone's son Christopher. "He didn't want to be in league with that and it seemed all too easy to knock Russia. There was plenty to write about without that."

Stone often stated that the small, ineffective CPUSA could hardly overthrow anything. (A viewpoint as hotly argued by today's neocons as it was by the fifties Red-baiters.) Stone's view jibes with historically accepted views; even some neocons admit that "most" CP members were not spies. By 1959 the party was reduced to five thousand members; so many were FBI informants that Hoover flirted with taking it over.

In all of Stone's file, what appears to be only one anonymous person claimed that Stone had once been a member of the Communist Party. Verification, the informant stated, came from Stone's brother Marc, who was briefly a party member, and other blacked-out sources. (Other family members, friends, and even those who disliked Stone continue to vigorously deny this.) This claim was repeatedly photocopied for inclusion in the pages of Stone FBI lore. Yet a preponderant number of informants, names blacked out, did not know, did not believe, or had no knowledge that Stone was a Communist. Perhaps the most underwhelming FBI observation was that Stone "defended Communists" and those with Communist "sympathies."

As mentioned, the biggest New Dealer the FBI hoped to catch on Bentley's list was Stone's friend Harry Dexter White. They broke into White's home and listened to his wife, Anne, discussing a column of Stone's on their constantly tapped phone. The FBI deduced that the other person did not personally know Stone but "from the conversation it appears possible that Anne knew him." Another memo noted that Stone and his wife were among several unnamed individuals invited to the Whites' for a party in November 1946. (It does not specify whether they attended.)

The FBI was concerned with Stone's efforts to aid European Jews in their illegal exodus to Palestine, as well as finding out what the Whites knew. "On August 30, 1946, Anne White was contacted by Bernice Bernstein, who stated that her husband, Bernie Bernstein [an aide and financial adviser to Dwight D. Eisenhower], was in Europe." The two women talked about Stone's articles in *PM* and remarked that, according to FBI notes, Stone urged that "the Jews of the world should organize and buy ships to haul Jews out of DP camps . . . to Palestine and should run the blockade."

Stone was both angry and grieving when White died suddenly—a dramatic incident during the HUAC/Bentley hearings that did much to tarnish the Red hunts. In 1948, White requested an appearance before HUAC to deny the charges made by Bentley and Chambers. Stone was among the crush of reporters who watched White in the cavernous congressional hearing room on August 13, 1948. Harsh flashbulbs glinted off White's eyeglasses. He squinted for a second, then spoke so defiantly about his Americanism that the room burst into spontaneous applause. Many committee members felt White was "utterly convincing." White readily admitted that he knew all the alleged subversives and said that he played Ping-Pong with the Silvermasters in the basement where a darkroom was located; Bentley had charged that Silvermaster developed documents there to send to Russia. White subsequently asked if he could be permitted periodic rests because of his heart condition. Chairman Thomas caustically commented, "For a person who had a severe heart condition, you certainly play a lot of sports." That afternoon, White boarded a train for his summer home in New Hampshire. Pain gripped his chest. Three days later he died of a heart attack.

White's family received worldwide condolences. International and national editorials cast White as a badgered victim and assailed HUAC for its "shoddy" treatment of a sick man. HUAC could not be charged with his death, wrote the *New York Times,* but it could be charged with "having denied him the true protection of laws, with having permitted witnesses to make unsubstantiated claims . . . which the accused learned only through public sources, and by so doing, ignoring the Bill of Rights."

Stone's emotions ran high. "I certainly knew Harry White better than the inquisitorial bigots who put the final unbearable strain on his ailing heart. And I do not think Harry White was a Communist," Stone wrote, ambiguously adding, "if the word is to be used correctly and without quotation marks." White was an idealist who desired to "hammer out necessary social changes on the clamorous but firm anvil of Democratic processes. . . . The United States never had more devoted servants than men of White's kind." In describing White, Stone explained the core of his own thinking: "These men hated fascism, as all decent men must. They were friendly to the Soviet Union, for they understood the dreadful circumstances out of which the Russian Revolution sprang. They hoped that in time the Soviet dictatorship, given peaceful conditions, would swing back toward Democratic methods. They wanted to build a new and better world after the war. . . . White had an internationalist outlook, as must every intelligent man in our time."

Stone referred to his association with White: "Those who had the privilege of talking with him off the record . . . knew that White was no softy, that under the surface he had an unexpected vein of American nationalism." In no way, wrote Stone, would White let the Russians or the British "take the shirt off Uncle Sam's back."

Stone, among many, countered charges against White by noting that he worked tirelessly to hammer out a postwar international capitalist system beneficial to the United States. Peaceful coexistence meant including the Russian regime; White recognized the difficulties of dealing with the Soviets, said Stone, but envisioned an otherwise disastrous "inevitable corollary," a breakdown between the West and the USSR and a fateful "rebirth of the German menace" that America had "twice been forced to fight." This view was shared by New Dealers and other Americans absorbing the full extent of the horrors of Nazi concentration camps.

White "fought for his country . . . in World War I and worked for it as faithfully and honorably in World War II," wrote Stone. "His crime was that he belonged to a group of men who helped to make democracy work at home and hoped to make international collaboration work abroad. I would not demean the memory of Harry Dexter White by saying he was not a Communist," Stone again ambiguously said. "If he was one, Communists had reason to be proud." Said an emotional Stone, "Killing White was but an incident in the war being waged to kill the free America which bred him."

After Stone died, some historians used new evidence to call White a "spy"—a charge his family has protested—others termed him an "agent of influence," and still others tried to put his clandestine World War II dealings with Russia in the same context that Stone had in 1948.

19

LIES AND SPIES

By 1944, paranoia coursed through the Kremlin as FDR refused to divulge his plans for postwar Europe until victory was reached. The USSR and the United States had been cozy enough during the war to consider an alliance of their secret spy agencies. Now Stalin knew from his spies that FDR warily tried to keep him in the dark on crucial matters while publicly encouraging cooperation with Moscow. This only increased Stalin's paranoia, and he desperately sought insider knowledge.

With that in mind, which of these two cases deciphered in secret Russian archives sounds as if the person was an "agent of influence" for the USSR during this crucial year in the battle against Hitler?

Case Number One: Two long 1944 memos detail meetings of an NKGB [as it was then called] agent named "Sergei" and an American journalist, identified with the initial *I*. The first, dated May 16, mentions that journalist *I* felt the United States was positive about success in its impending invasion of Europe and told Sergei that Churchill no longer objected to an "operation of this kind." *I* told the Russian that the United States considered "the question of the participation of the USSR in the war against Japan a stumbling block in Soviet-American relations." *I* agreed with Sergei that arguments on this matter be kept from the press, but contended that Russia should enter the war against Japan to insure postwar cooperation. (*I* elaborated on this theme in a subsequent meeting.) Also, *I* told the agent, "The Americans by the end of 1944 hope to seize the Philippines, Formosa, Singapore . . ." At this point the decoders were unable to decipher any more of the memo.

Another memo involving *I* is dated June 15, 1944. Sergei gleaned from not one but four American journalists "who have close contacts" in the government that "the question of France's future is very disturbing." *I* reported that FDR and Hull clashed over the future of France. (FDR's petty refusal to recognize Charles de Gaulle and his Free French forces continued until the fall of 1944.) *I* reported that State Department factions feared continued snubs of de Gaulle could "lead France into the sphere of influence of the USSR." Russia was vitally concerned about U.S. plans for carving up Europe. Sensitive negotiations were proceeding between the USSR and centrist Polish leader Stanislaus Mikolajczyk, who was avoiding Stalin. *I* told Sergei that the Polish leader was backing away because State Department factions were pushing to replace him with an anti-Soviet coalition. *I* advised that Stalin make a "temporary concession" in dealing with Poland. Russia sought information on the upcoming election between Republican Thomas E. Dewey (code-name KULAK) and FDR (code-name KAPITAN). *I* hoped to toughen Dewey's soft position on postwar Germany. Contrary to its previous intentions, "the U.S. is not now supporting the dismemberment of Germany although it still regards the award of East Prussia to Poland as essential."

Case Number Two: Three memos relate the frustrating attempts of the same Russian secret agent, Sergei, to meet another American journalist code-named Blin/Pancake. A September 13, 1944, memo stated that Sergei had "three times attempted to effect liaison" with a journalist. "Each time he declined on the grounds of being busy on trips." On October 10, 1944, Sergei reported that the journalist was continuing to avoid him. Two weeks later, October 23, Sergei finally "made the acquaintance" of the journalist. A thirdhand paraphrased account was sent to Moscow by New York agent Stepan Apresyan, posing as a furrier. The alleged reason for the journalist's reluctance to meet with Sergei was fear of jeopardizing his career or being observed by the FBI. When Sergei asked about further meetings, the journalist reportedly said he would be "glad to meet but rarely visited New York." On December 23, the journalist was mentioned in a joint conversation with three other American reporters, who told Sergei that America's "General Staff" was "very much alarmed at the German offensive which may delay for several months the renewal of the American general offensive which is calculated to crush Germany in concert with us." End of Case Number Two.

It would be easy to assume that the first reporter was the more eager and capable informer. The initial *I* was not for "Izzy," however. *I* stood for "Imperialist," which the FBI labeled none other than Walter Lippmann. Case Number Two involves the few references in the KGB files of trying to meet "Blin" or "Pancake," and one alleged insignificant conversation with several other American reporters. After a farcical pursuit of journalists, the FBI had decided in 1951 that Stone *"appears"* to be Blin.

Critics automatically assume that the FBI identification of Stone as Blin is accurate. But even this identification of Stone as Blin was iffy, characterized by a confusing caper as FBI agents wrangled over two journalists who might be Blin.

Both Lippmann and Stone were among many journalists courted by Sergei, aka Vladimir Pravdin, in his official capacity as the TASS news agency correspondent. He approached Blin/Pancake legally and officially "in the line of cover." During the crucial World War II alliance, journalists met routinely with TASS representatives, swapping information. Lippmann probably told Pravdin nothing that millions did not read in his columns—while Stone is never reported as having done anything but evade Pravdin, except for a casual reference of being with him and three other journalists. Yet, in numerous books about the KGB decrypts, many of them written with a right-wing slant, Lippmann's meetings with Pravdin create no stir while Stone has been branded a "spy" with no evidence but these meager mentions in KGB memos and the misinterpreted words of a former Russian spy. Despite vast evidence to the contrary, old HUAC hacks like Herbert Romerstein and extremists like Ann Coulter and Robert Novak still spread such lies. So let's answer these accusations: First, Stone never had access to classified secrets to barter. Second, journalists naturally sought information about Russia from a TASS correspondent, Pravdin's official role. And as files reveal, Lippmann told far more than Stone ever did in meetings with Pravdin.*

*Here are verbatim the pertinent Venona transcripts on Blin (aka Pancake): Sent by New York KGB resident Stepan Apresyan (code-named MAJ) to Lieutenant General P. M. Fitin (code-name VICTOR) in Moscow. *September 13, 1944:* "Sergei [Vladimir Pravdin] has three times attempted to effect liaison with PANCAKE ... *in the line of cover* [emphasis added] but each time PANCAKE declined on the grounds of being busy with trips. IDE [Samuel Krafsur, a TASS reporter and agent with extensive journalistic contacts] has carefully attempted to sound him but PANCAKE did not react. PANCAKE occupies a very prominent position in the journalistic world and has vast connections. To determine precisely his relations to us we will commission ECHO [Bernard Schuster, a well-known CP member]" (#54, p. 333 of Venona transcripts). In an *October 10, 1944,* operational report on possible recruits, PANCAKE was mentioned as "avoiding Sergei" (p. 349, Venona transcripts). The next memo, *October 23, 1944:* Sergei "has made the acquaintance of PANCAKE. Earlier Sergei had several times tried to contact him personally and also through IDE but the impression has been created that PANCAKE was avoiding a meeting. At the first conversation Sergei told him that he had very much desired to make his acquaintance since he greatly valued his work as a correspondent and had likewise heard flattering [twenty-three groups unrecoverable] PANCAKE to give us information. PANCAKE said that he had noticed our attempts to contact him, particularly the attempts of IDE and a couple of the TRUST

* * *

The flap over Stone began in 1992, three years after his death, when neo-cons misconstrued comments of a former Soviet agent, Oleg Kalugin, whose cover in the sixties was the Soviet embassy's press attaché. Stone, they cried, was a paid spy! This ludicrous accusation stemmed from a speech that Kalugin had given to students in England. He was quoted as saying, "We had an agent—a well-known American journalist," but "after the invasion of Czechoslovakia . . . he said he would never again take any money from us." After the brouhaha Andrew Brown, who wrote the article for the *Independent,* clarified the quotes in the *New York Review of Books.* An editor had asked Brown for an anecdote on deadline and he threw in this one, cutting the reference of Kalugin's that specified that he was only talking about the journalist's refusal to let him pay for lunch.

Further proof came from the *Nation*'s D. D. Guttenplan, who employed a tool unknown to those intent on smearing Stone: he did some reporting. Kalugin repeated that he only bought lunch on occasion for Stone and in his official role. Mainstream editorials defended Stone, but the lies continued. When long-buried Soviet decrypted files were released in 1995 and 1996, with slim mentions of a journalist code-named Blin, this was Red meat for the far right, now in full chorus that Izzy was a spy.

It is nothing short of astounding—but connotes the right wing's media power—that Stone's critics are insufficiently challenged by mainstream media for their continued lies that he was a "paid spy" based on

---

[Soviet embassy in Washington] but he had reacted negatively fearing the consequences. At the same time he implied that the attempts at rapprochement had been made with insufficient caution and by people who were insufficiently responsible. To Sergei's reply that naturally we did not want to subject him to unpleasant complications, PANCAKE gave him to understand that he was not refusing his aid but one should consider that he had three children and did not want to attract the attention of the HUT [FBI]. To Sergei's question how he considered it advisable to maintain liaison PANCAKE replied that he would be glad to meet but he rarely visited TYRE [New York] where he usually spent [fifty-four groups unrecoverable.] His fear is primarily explained by his unwillingness to spoil his career. Materially he is well secured[.] He earns as much as $1,500 a month but, it seems, he would not be averse to having a supplementary income. For the establishment of business contact with him we are insisting on [one group unrecovered] reciprocity. For the work is needed a qualified [two groups unrecovered] CARTHAGE [Washington, D.C.]. Telegraph your opinion" (#1506, p. 359 of Venona transcripts). The final cable was dated *December 23, 1944:* "Correspondents who have contacts with the military leaders [four code names include PANCAKE] in a conversation with Sergei maintained that the General Staff of the COUNTRY [America] is very much alarmed at the German offensive . . ." (quoted in body of text). The rest of the conversation in the memo is attributed to another unidentified journalist.

insubstantial memos and the misinterpreted Kalugin comments. (The former KGB agent, who has long disclaimed any knowledge of Stone as anything but a friendly journalist, amplified his views for this book.)

Yet as recently as the 2004 presidential campaign, Stone was smeared by columnist Robert Novak, who some colleagues inexcusably and benignly term "conservative." This reasonable adjective does not begin to describe him. Novak's disregard for truth and scruples—as in the 2004 outing of Valerie Plame, the CIA agent—are exceeded only by factual sloppiness. In 2003, when ABC's George Stephanopoulos asked then presidential candidate John Edwards to name his favorite book, he replied, "I. F. Stone's *The Trial of Socrates.*" Novak fumed on CNN, "That's incredible! Did Senator Edwards know that Izzy Stone was a *lifelong* Soviet apologist? Did he know of evidence that Stone received secret payments from the Kremlin?" Both were old and patent lies, and Novak certainly had to know this. It was common knowledge and much had been written about it. As far back as the thirties, Stone criticized Stalin's ruthless "state police" repression; for the last three decades of his life, he denounced Stalin and the entire Soviet system as "rotten to the core." He loudly championed Soviet dissidents. And, of course, there is not a shred of evidence that Stone was paid in any way by the Kremlin.

The question is why the rabid right pursues such febrile arguments with inordinate gusto. The importance given these fragmented World War II files is due to the persistence of many convinced Cold Warriors that they validate their belief in the Soviet Union's threat to the United States and Western Europe. If one follows this argument, those who supported Russia as allies or later championed peaceful solutions to East-West tensions were either stupid or Soviet apparatchiks. Only by carrying the argument this far and this late can they justify the excesses of McCarthyism. Today's neocons have a vested interest in portraying Stone as a paid Kremlin stooge because he remains an icon to those who despise all that the far right espoused.

When neocons continued to repeat the lies about Stone well after they had been refuted in books and magazines, a family spokesman took them apart with the facts. The always inaccurate Accuracy in Media in 1995 tried to cast suspicion that Moscow gold must have paid for the *Weekly* since its $5 subscription rate for a four-page newsletter was "hardly enough to pay for the postage." Here are the facts: In 1953, when Stone started the *Weekly* with five thousand subscribers, second-class postage was one-eighth of a cent, so that only six cents of the $5 subscription went for postage. Of the 99 percent remainder of his $25,000 revenues, he and his wife, as secretary, drew a total of $10,000 in salary. (This was enough money in those days that he refused to let a child apply for a scholarship at Harvard.)

Moreover, the FBI finally had to agree in 1966 that the *Weekly* was very profitable, noting that Stone's newsletter had "25,000 subscribers" and that the mom-and-pop enterprise "should clear at least $60,000." In today's dollars, Stone was saving more than a quarter million dollars a year. In his final year, Stone had seventy thousand subscribers and was grossing, in 2006 dollars, a very substantial $1.75 million. This is when he moved to a larger house, which was another reason for Romerstein, a most inaccurate crafter of the written word, to suspect skullduggery. (This is a man who twisted Guttenplan's phrase that Stone left no archives into the assertion that Stone's papers "had been destroyed.") Perhaps the unkindest cut was not only that Stone had thoroughly denounced Russia years before but that he proudly and often mentioned his success as an enterprising capitalist.

Accuracy in Media even reversed a key historical fact: Stone had often said he lost hundreds of readers after reporting on his 1956 visit to the Soviet Union. This was because of his "stubborn admiration" for the USSR. Nothing was further from the truth; he lost his leftist readers for denouncing the Soviets.

Years after Stone's death, pieces of Soviet 1940s cable traffic that the United States began decrypting fifty years ago and had then kept hidden were released with much fanfare by the CIA and NSA. The far right declared the Venona Files, as they were named for no particular reason, sacrosanct and seized them to rehabilitate McCarthy and all those who had "named names." They minimize the fact that the files cover 1942 to 1945, the war years when Russia was an ally. The files do provide a fascinating glimpse at how deeply the Russians succeeded in recruiting high-level U.S. officials. Venona's major success was in corroborating evidence regarding yesteryear's A-list of spies—the Rosenbergs, Alger Hiss, Klaus Fuchs—all of whom Stone had had doubts about and never defended at the time. They go far in corroborating Bentley's charges that Stone's friend Harry Dexter White was an agent of influence. However, analysis concerning the extent of who did what, whether American aims were subverted, what secrets were passed—except in the obvious and celebrated cases—is too often freighted with ideology. Accounts of these partial cables abound with such qualifiers as "perhaps," "maybe," "possibly"; even the neocon-friendly *Washington Times* admitted that "the Venona papers standing alone are nigh unintelligible." Yet the caveat in the Venona release—that these files should "move the debate" from the "politics and personalities" of yesteryear's spy hunt—never happened. Instead, the files prompted another era of name-calling and finger-pointing. Serious scholars make valuable historical contributions in analyzing the memos, but the most irresponsible of today's writers play connect-the-dots with scattered "clues" to smear the left once again. The files in no way absolve the excesses of McCarthyism, but nonetheless were disturbing to the left. As writer Joseph E. Persico noted, "The hardest part . . . to accept, at least for those of us who deplored the overzealous Red-hunting . . . is that the hunt rested on more substance than we cared to admit, the phony posturing of . . . McCarthy aside."

Hoarding these files did a disservice to justice and to history. Now neocon benefactors of hindsight use them to scapegoat scholars and journalists who judged these matters for a half century when no Venona Files were available. They indict anyone in the New Deal and chastise those who today challenge their sweeping interpretations as nothing less than "holocaust deniers."

One of the problems with the Venona Files at this late date is that there is no way to determine whether the Russian agents were telling the truth or trying to make themselves appear more valuable. There were compelling reasons for KGB agents to embellish their contacts—their lives, for that matter, often depended upon appearing successful in cadging important recruits. An ominous rebuke contained in the second Blin/Pancake memo indicates just how urgently Pravdin needed to heighten his authority and magnify his effectiveness. His failures were darkly examined: *"I hope that we will not have to engage in the 'theoretical' education of Sergei after all these years."* Despite such threats, nothing in the files indicate that Sergei's efforts earned him anything but an initial meeting (in which Pancake is uncharacteristically described as fearful and cautious) and a brief follow-up attended by other reporters. Nothing indicates that Pancake knew him as anything but a TASS news agency official; not only would it be normal to deal with a representative of the news agency, a reporter covering Russian affairs would of necessity have dealt with him.

Another drawback is that Venona provides but a window into the past, predominantly when Russia was a vital ally and FDR encouraged back-channel discussions. (This was also a time when Nazis abounded in Washington and had infiltrated the press.) Ironically, today's right wing takes these KGB cables as gospel while their ideological Cold War ancestors would have believed nothing coming from the Kremlin. Now the files are embellished to encompass the entire Cold War era. Coulter, for example, cannot bother with facts: The declassified Venona memos proved "the existence of a vast network of Soviet spies in America throughout the forties and fifties," she writes. There is nothing at all about the fifties in Venona. When the Kremlin learned of Bentley's defection in 1945, KGB intelligence activity was virtually frozen overnight. Pravdin was ordered to disband his operations and return home.

The KGB agents hyped Blin/Pancake as occupying "a very prominent position in the journalistic world and has vast connections." Their alleged conversations sound nothing like Stone. "P [Pancake] said that he had noticed our attempts to [contact] him . . . he had reacted negatively fearing the consequences. . . . To Sergei's reply that naturally we did not want to subject him to unpleasant complications, PANCAKE gave him to understand that he was not refusing his aid but one should consider that he had three children and did not want to attract the attention of the [FBI]. . . . His fear is partially explained by his unwillingness to spoil his career. Materially he is well secured[.] He earns as much as $1,500 a month but, it seems, he would not be averse to having a supplementary income." The stilted phrases, with several unrecovered letters, prove nothing more than that Blin/Pancake was brushing off Pravdin. As to what transpired, we have only the word of one KGB agent recounting what another agent reported that Blin/Pancake may have said, but it has been interpreted as Stone's verbatim comments. Stone's harsh attacks on Hoover had warranted FBI hounding for years by then, so avoiding Pravdin could hardly have stemmed from a fear of attracting FBI attention. No embellishment is given for the supposition "it *seems,* he would not be averse to having a supplementary income." Also out of character is "his unwillingness to spoil his career." If so, Stone would have spurned friendships with Soviet news sources and American Communists long before. Stone's leftist audience and employers would have applauded contacts with the Russians during wartime.

The Haunted Wood, arguably the most scholarly work to include Venona Files, provides damaging evidence because the authors were able to cross-reference and amplify by using Soviet documents that one of them, Alexander Vassiliev, was allowed to examine in Russia. He and coauthor Allen Weinstein do not even mention Stone. They also paint a textured picture of Americans who gave information to the Soviets during World War II as idealists often conflicted about their roles. Other scholars refer to Stone only in passing and some declare that the Venona Files exonerated him.

John Earl Haynes and Harvey Klehr unambiguously state, "There is no evidence in Venona that Stone ever was recruited by the KGB." Writes Coulter, "It has now been overwhelmingly documented that I. F. Stone was a paid Soviet agent." Whom does she source for this "proof"? None other than Klehr and Haynes, who said there was no evidence, plus Romerstein, who was discredited long before her book was published. Clearly ignoring the evidence, Coulter's comments are unconscionable, deliberate lies as she consistently refers to Stone as a "paid Soviet agent" and states that "declassified Soviet cables confirmed that he was an agent." All of this is totally false. As previously stated, nothing was "overwhelmingly documented" nor was anything "confirmed" that he was "identified as an agent."

Haynes/Klehr themselves cannot resist casting an aspersion: "Had he [Stone] thought he was simply dealing with TASS employees he would hardly have been so cautious or frightened." First they take as absolute truth these paraphrased alleged conversations reported by agents eager to explain Stone's noncooperation to their Kremlin bosses: Stone "told" Pravdin, Haynes/Klehr flat-out write, "that he had noticed our attempts to contact him." It is only an assumption in reading this passage from a KGB agent that Stone actually "said" or "told" them anything. Next they assert that Stone had to know he was dealing with the KGB because "no left-wing or even mainstream journalist in America would have been afraid to meet a TASS correspondent or think that meeting with one in 1944 would incur the wrath of the FBI." This absurd assumption implies broad-based tolerance by Hoover, the obsessive lifelong hunter of Reds. At no time did Hoover ever view Russian sources or colleagues as acceptable bedfellows with whom leftist journalists could mix without suspicion. On the contrary, the FBI constantly tried to uncover who leaked scoops to Stone.

Still others strained to finger Stone. Concocting an answer to his own question "Why were Stalin's agents so enamored of Stone?" author Philip Nobile's scurrilous solution is that "Stone was likely predisposed to treason." Nobile did not consider that the KGB pursued him because he was a major voice on the left or that agents posing as press attachés wooed countless reporters. Even if Stone, writing for leftist publications, had been given a code name by the Russians, that in itself is meaningless. Yet

Nobile termed Stone "intellectually dishonest" even after admitting that the "Venona tease is inconclusive." Such comments remain in the blogosphere.

One cannot overlook the fascinating, mind-bending pressure of those who slaved for years to crack the Soviet code; one had a nervous breakdown and another committed suicide. Their work went for naught when Hoover and others decided to keep their findings hidden. Now "too few of those dealing with American Communism today have either a real sense of perspective or an ability to make this history vivid," Jacob Weisberg aptly commented in the *New York Times*.

Far-right vendettas mirror the bluff and bluster of McCarthyism and mar attempts to provide valuable scholarship. Citing as proof the partial information that came to light a half century after the fact is tricky. Scholars who suggest a time-oriented contextual explanation for clandestine cooperation with Russia are slammed. Historian Robert Craig, for example, was backhanded in a negative *Washington Post* review by historian Ted Morgan. In his carefully researched book on Harry Dexter White, *Treasonable Doubt,* Craig agreed that the Venona Files demonstrated White was an "agent of influence" who participated in a "species of espionage" during World War II and shortly afterward. White knowingly held conversations about sensitive foreign policy matters with Russian agents, Craig concluded, and no doubt perjured himself when he told HUAC that he didn't know that his friend Silvermaster was a paid Russian spy. However, Craig echoed the judgment of those like Stone a half century ago; the idealistic White thought of himself as furthering a just cause—Russian/U.S. cooperation and shaping mutually beneficial policies.

Stalin sought classified information because he believed, correctly, that FDR avoided official channels, not wanting leaks to destroy his control of policy. White was a nervous recruit. At one point, Silvermaster complained that White "doesn't pass information or documents" any longer, believing his grander role was "to give advice on major political and economic matters." Harsher interpretations see White as "subverting" American policy and taking orders from Moscow, despite his monetary policies, which favored the United States.

What prompted these leaders to secretly aid another country, albeit an ally? This was a period when, as theologian/historian Cornel West wrote, "only the American and Soviet Empires seemed capable of combating the Nazi conquest of the world." The time lines are very important. What was seen as helping Russia then was recast as subversive in the fetid Cold War atmosphere a few years later.

Motivation seemed too dreary a subject for those occupied with a sensational blame game. A core reason to cooperate with Russia during and immediately after the war was fervent antifascism, coupled with a romanticized view of Communism. By 1944, FDR's officials were split. Some favored a "hard" approach to a defeated Germany and continuing alliance with Russia. Others favored a "soft" approach to Germany and a "tough" stance against Russia. Such polarization contained undercurrents of anti-Semitism. For American Jews in FDR's administration and writers like Stone, many of whose parents had fled Europe, compelling reasons shaped their popular-front support and a postwar alliance. They deeply feared any policy that would strengthen Germany. They either had lost real family in the holocaust or identified with the millions in the larger family of Jews. Stone felt a common bond with these men who had helped forge the New Deal.

In a caustic 1945 editorial, "The Future of the Reich," Stone lambasted advisers who "to a large extent" were "drawn from those circles in big business, finance and the corporate bar which did a great deal of business with the Reich before the war." Stone questioned whether men who had so profited from deals with the Nazis could make "wise postwar policies." He named former OSS officer Allen Dulles and David Bruce, of the Aluminum Company of America. The OSS complained to Hoover about Stone's "highly undesirable" article. The FBI tried frantically to find who'd leaked this to Stone.

One did not have to be Jewish or "pro-Stalin" to favor cooperation with Russia at that time. Lippmann pushed for a "political accord between Russia and the West that did not require an American military intervention to sustain it." He was not driven by idealistic "good will or sentimentality," but by practicalities, wrote Steel. Lippmann, Stone, and others recognized that it was "inconceivable" that the Red Army "would ever again tolerate anti-Russian regimes on the Soviet border." If the USSR was going to be the next four-hundred-pound gorilla, the United States was going to have to learn to dance with it.

Venona Files devotees charge that White was under Kremlin orders when he pushed the plan to provide German currency plates to a depleted Russia, a get-tough policy with Chiang Kai-shek and Japan prior to the war, and the Morgenthau Plan, although White actually opposed its harshest measures. In 1944, General Eisenhower emotionally told

White and Morgenthau that he favored the Treasury director's tough plan, which had caused heated international debate: "Things should be made 'good and hard' on the Germans. . . . 'Let the Germans stew in their own juice,' " Eisenhower said. He had just heard the first ghastly reports of Nazi death-camp atrocities. Such revelations affected many who strongly argued to curtail Germany's war-making and industrial powers. Optimistic about postwar cooperation with Russia, Eisenhower told Morgenthau that he would personally speak to FDR if he needed help in countering State Department proposals. Morgenthau needed such support; Hull characterized Morgenthau's proposal as "blind vengeance" against the Nazis. Postwar architect John McCloy thought him a "very dangerous advisor," too "biased because of his Semitic grievances."

Identifying spies or alleged spies and Communists or sympathizers as "Jews" was often a part of the Hoover, HUAC, and Bentley lexicon. Bentley mentioned that White was a Jew—his father was a Lithuanian peddler named Weit who had fled rampant anti-Semitism. "They all are," said Bentley, of her group led by Silvermaster, who was born in Russia. The leading anti-Semite in Congress, John Rankin, delighted in depicting American Communists or followers as "sneaky, Jewish, domineering, blood-thirsty and dumb." In earlier testimony Bentley stressed benign motives among her sources and denied that they "planned to use violence in the United States." But in front of HUAC's cameras, Bentley hyped their actions, to the pleasure of Rankin, who took the opportunity to slam two favorite targets, Jews and blacks. (Civil rights was just "communistic bunk," he always said.) When Bentley linked Silvermaster and Lauchlin Currie, Rankin roared, "How could she have taken the word of a 'man named Silvermaster' over that of a 'Scotchman'?" In hallowed halls filled with such utterances, "justice" was being rendered. Rankin was known for his headline-grabbing hunts-without-evidence. How could any journalist, especially a Jew, not cringe at this sight, consider the source, and doubt the proclamations?

Strangely, when Russia was truly a Cold War enemy in the sixties, back-channel cooperation did not incite the wrath that World War II cooperation did in the fifties Red-baiting era. In 1962, JFK authorized his attorney-general brother to hold clandestine meetings with a Russian spy who operated as press attaché, Georgi Bolshakov. Robert Kennedy was a personal friend of Georgi, as he familiarly called him. Although both Kennedys had few doubts about his KGB affiliation, the attorney general used Bolshakov as a secret emissary to Khrushchev during the Cuban missile crisis. Another friend of the agent's was the president's favorite columnist, Charles Bartlett. Of course neither Bartlett nor the Kennedys were considered "agents of influence" nor were reporters who freely trafficked with Bolshakov. Instead, they were using diplomacy.

A lingering question is why esteemed FDR officials felt the need to deal in secret. Domestic political ramifications played a major role, as Roosevelt and his administration delicately skirted the minefields of American politics dominated by a reactionary anti–New Deal Congress. As Stone's scoops so aptly exposed, many American corporations were doing business with Nazi Germany and Japan even after Pearl Harbor. Stone hammered State Department factions who encouraged recognition of France's pro-Nazi Vichy government. Stalin's 1939 pact with Hitler had created renewed alarm and became an excuse to override the Bill of Rights. FBI agents raided offices of organizations linked to the CPUSA and arrested its general secretary, Earl Browder, who was imprisoned for passport fraud.

Actions sharply reversed when Hitler invaded Russia. The hunt for Russian spies was no longer paramount; in 1944, when OSS officers bought Soviet cryptographs from the Finns, the White House instructed the OSS to relay them to the Soviets. FDR had no desire to provoke an indispensable ally, and encouraged back-channel cooperation with Russia. In 1942 Stone participated in forming a citizens committee to free Earl Browder. That year, Roosevelt commuted his sentence. (By 1945, Browder was outed from the CPUSA by more militant factions, and its influence further waned.)

Meanwhile, Hoover continued to monitor the CPUSA. The U.S. Army's Signals Security Agency (SSA)—forerunner of NSA—began collecting coded Soviet telegrams because they feared that Berlin might negotiate a separate peace with Moscow. Deciphering KGB decrypts became a grinding and steady task; by 1948, the FBI began to provide names for what had been indecipherable nicknames. Such consuming effort was for naught because of unwarranted secrecy, rivalry, and lack of cooperation among competing counterintelligence agencies. Such competitiveness and secrecy continued after the war. (Hoover tried to torpedo the CIA before it started; Bentley's charges interested him because she named alleged spies who had been his chief competitors in its previous incarnation, the OSS.) The Venona snafus have a parallel in the ineptitude, deceit, cover-ups, and infighting between rival secret agencies that led to the disaster of 9/11, WMD fabrications, and Bush's excuse for a foolhardy, disastrous war in Iraq.

The reason given for secrecy in the 1940s was that the government didn't want the Russians to know that their code was broken, but had those long-ago files been revealed, the course of Cold War history would arguably have changed. They might have halted Russian advancement on the A-bomb. Cold War domestic battles might have lessened, McCarthyism might have been stifled, the guilty tried and the innocent spared years of smears. Yet, given the incompleteness of the Venona Files, witch hunts would probably have continued. Still, had Truman not felt the need to cave in to Red-baiting in order to win in 1948, he might not have enacted loyalty tests. He might have curbed the persecution of those who had joined groups retroactively named subversive. And a forty-year campaign to prove the Rosenbergs' innocence would not have occurred.

The media's and the public's right to know, the basis of a democracy, was fatally compromised. Only when the late Senator Daniel Patrick Moynihan ordered the files released in 1995 and 1996 was Hoover's secret known. Moynihan had always argued for less secrecy, a sacred belief of Stone's. Moynihan hoped that public exposure of the Venona Files would demonstrate the folly of such secrecy and provoke salient future examination of intelligence practices, a vain hope as we have seen.

With profound understatement, the 1995 Venona release stated that "intelligence agencies . . . did not do a good job of presenting counterintelligence analyses to President [Truman] and his aides." Partisan squabbling continues about what Truman knew and when. The weary recipient of countless unproven Hoover memos, Truman demanded more proof than gossipy innuendos peddled by the Chambers/Bentley/HUAC/McCarthy brigade. Truman never saw the Venona Files. "Now then," Moynihan asked, "did the director of the FBI, who had been quite prepared the year before to rush to the president a report of an all but fictional 'enormous Soviet espionage ring in Washington,' inform the President of the possibly less than enormous but real communist spying when real evidence became available?" The answer was no.

"The secrecy system," Moynihan wrote in a 1997 commission report, "has systematically denied American historians access to the records of American history. Of late we find ourselves relying on archives of the former Soviet Union in Moscow to resolve questions of what was going on in Washington in mid-century. This is absurd."

* * *

When the Venona Files were released, suspicion arose among those long wary of Hoover's tactics. FBI raw files were loaded with misinformation and disinformation from disgruntled and unreliable paid informants as well as misspelled and illiterate memos from field officers. They even misspelled the one word that was their basic modus operandi—*surveillance* (with one *l*). Now they were being presented as providing an authentic "fit" of persons to Venona's cover names. However, other newly released files verify many of the names, while some remain mysteries.

Hoover's sleuthing attempts to identify Stone as Blin/Pancake provide instructive glimpses of bumbling activity. The spring of 1951 marked the beginning of an antlike swarm of agents in Stone's life. No Stone was unturned, if one can pardon the pun, in their search to find "Blin." Stone was still in France, and on April 6, 1951, the FBI sent a memo to unidentified authorities in England (one copy went to "legal attaché, London, England"): "We have recently instituted an investigation of Stone because of the possibility that he is identical with one BLIN. . . . We would be very interested in receiving any information you may have on I. F. Stone and Unknown Subject BLIN." The prompt response was terse: "We have no evidence that STONE is a Communist or a Communist sympathizer. He has only come to notice here as an extreme pro-Zionist in 1945 and 1946." On that same date a memo regarding Hoover's investigation was sent to the director of the CIA with attention to Major General W. G. Wyman, Office of Special Operations: "Stone is the well-known pro-Communist correspondent" is how Hoover identified him. Also on that date, an alert from Hoover was sent to the legal attaché in Paris in the confidential air pouch: "I. F. Stone (*real name* Isidor Feinstein) who is a well-known pro-Communist correspondent . . ."

FBI memos seemed as padded and hyped as any Russian agent's when Hoover used the Venona Files to try to identify Stone as Blin/Pancake. Hoover's standard line was that Stone associated with "individuals who . . . are definitely sympathetic to Russia." The Bureau added this qualifier: "It is not known at this time whether Stone was reluctant in associating with such individuals *during the pertinent period*" (italics added), referring to the Venona Files' World War II time lines.

FBI memos reveal a talent for outrageous juxtaposition and omission. "From 1940 to 1943, his [Stone's] office was reported to be in the National Press Building. It is to be noted that this building also houses the offices for Tass and the Daily Worker." The FBI did not mention that the bureaus of every respectable, legitimate, and prestigious international and American newspaper were also housed there.

In March of 1951, the search for "Blin/Pancake" was in full force. A bulletin from the director's office to the Washington Field Office cited "IRVING F. Stone" as a journalist who had long been a "security matter." Tracking Stone "should now proceed as an espionage investigation" and should be filed as "Unknown Subject BLIN."

Many FBI file references to Stone as a newspaperman with three children became clear only after the Venona Files were released well after Stone's death. The Russian memo had identified a well-known journalist code named "Blin" who "had three children." And so the FBI traced American journalists who had three children and came up with another suspect as well, Ernest K. Lindley. The Rhodes Scholar author of books on FDR was the epitome of establishment journalism. His column appeared in the *Washington Post* and the New York Tribune Syndicate, he had a radio show and was "chief of the News Week [*Newsweek*] Bureau." It is doubtful that Lindley, one of the unquestioning members of Lippmann's Polk-murder committee, would have appreciated being linked with either Blin or Stone. But an informant "indicated" that on November 9, 1945, Lindley had attended a Russian embassy reception celebrating the twenty-eighth anniversary of the "Red Revolution." As was often the case, such receptions were awash with journalists trying to find news about Russia during a vodka-filled moment. Yet, this was enough to make Lindley a marked man. Like many journalists, he was a friend of "one of the men named by Bentley as a source of information for Soviet espionage." And he too could fit the description of Blin, noted the FBI, because he was a prominent newspaperman with "a substantial income and has three children."

However, the FBI memo stated, Stone was the best suspect to pursue. "If it later developes [*sic*] that Stone is not [Blin]"* then our investigation will necessarily have to seek other suspects." Just nine days later, on April 9, a New York agent argued that "ERNEST K. LINDLEY was perhaps a better suspect and . . . I. F. Stone would *not* appear to be identical with [Blin]." A second memo (April 20, 1951) said that "Stone does not appear to warrant espionage investigation" and should be downgraded once again to a security matter. The New York FBI office offered three sensible reasons: The espionage person would have more money than Stone if he was a paid

---

*Although the code name was blanked out in most FBI mentions, it is obvious after reading the Venona cables that the redacted name was Blin. Therefore, it will be so indicated in brackets.

agent. Unlike Stone [Blin] "must have been a person whose true pro-Soviet sympathies were not known to the public and his associates." Stone was "too open in his association with Communist front groups" to conduct any espionage. The memo incorrectly said Stone "has for years been a member of the Communist party," comparing this with the Venona comment that Blin showed a "reluctance" to become involved in espionage. (Argued Hoover, this "apparent inconsistency should not eliminate Stone.") A third reason was that Stone did not have the "prominence" that [Blin] "must have acquired, according to the information furnished." Lindley, "however, would appear to be an excellent suspect." Copies of this memo were distributed nationwide to FBI offices.

Hoover indicated in a bristling memo "this office does not agree" with New York Field Office communications "which tend to eliminate Isidor F. Stone" (May 4). His income was supplemented by as "much as $200 per speech to front groups." It was "presumed" that he made supplemental income from freelance writing. He maintained a home in a "first class Washington neighborhood" (Stone's tiny house on busy Nebraska Avenue was among the more modest in "first class" northwest Washington.) His daughter was attending college. It was "extremely doubtful" that Stone could have afforded this without additional income—"the source and nature of which is not yet known to this office." The director would obtain Stone's IRS income tax returns to gauge his finances. Therefore "further investigation attention" should proceed with "Stone as a logical suspect" (May 9, 1951).

Two weeks later, on May 24, 1951, the FBI laboratory was comparing "two photostatic copies containing handwritten and typewritten specimens of suspect I. F. Stone" (which came from the originals in his State Department passport files) with the "known handwritten and typewritten specimens of Soviet espionage agents." The results? No matches were found and the test was concluded "without making an identification." Hoover was assured, however, that Stone's handwritten and typewritten "specimens" would be kept "for future comparison purposes."

The following week, June 13, 1951: "Assembled information tends to indicate that [Blin] is identical with I. F. Stone." The "assembled information" consisted of Stone's glib comments, translated as deadly serious evidence: he "openly admitted to being a Red," he was identified by one unnamed "reliable" informant as a Communist, and he was affiliated with "numerous Communist front groups." The memo noted that the *Daily Worker* quoted him, ignoring that these comments were often negative.

Stone had ricocheted from the Great Suspect to No Longer the Chief Suspect and back to the Great Suspect with lightning speed. About this time, while Stone was wrestling with returning to the States, he probably knew about such ardent FBI sleuthing from friends who were questioned. His actions offer proof of his innocence: Stone decided to return and fight Hoover and McCarthyism anyway. Stone hit the ground running, immediately speaking and writing against the Red Scare. As soon as Hoover knew Stone was back, an FBI memo noted that Stone continued "vigorous defense" in articles concerning "Communists convicted after violating the Smith Act." The Bureau authorized the New York office "to institute immediately a full time surveilance [sic] of Stone," to "establish if he is now being utilized by the Soviets in an attempt to influence the liberal thinking in the United States to advance his alleged notion that the Government is restricting freedom of thought and speech by arresting Communists." Of course the government was restricting freedom of thought and speech, but by then Stone, branded as a radical Red, was writing and speaking to increasingly smaller audiences, often further left than he, and in no position to influence "liberal" thinking. Nonetheless, instructions for heavy spying were sent to all FBI field offices: The Boston division would search for "additional pertinent background," the New York division would "check on whether the property on Fire Island is owned by Stone." New York would further interview *her* (no doubt Bentley) to find out the identify of "prominent correspondents known to her to have been friendly to Russia." Philadelphia was assigned to find out "if Stone was related to [former boss] J. David Stern and if Stone got any income from the family." Washington would "thoroughly analyze available information." Los Angeles and San Francisco would receive reports.

Several agents trailed Stone across country to San Francisco, reporting that Stone had been in "telephonic contact" with Harry Bridges's lawyer, Vincent Hallinan, and others, "all of whom have either been reported to be members of the Communist Party or to have associated with members of the Communist Party." The "nature or significance" of Stone's phone calls "was not known." Bridges had been convicted on April 4, 1950, in San Francisco's U.S. district court for perjury and conspiracy for his denial of Communist Party membership while he was naturalized as a U.S. citizen. Stone was writing about the case and the FBI was hot on his trail, noting that Stone had called the International Longshoremen's and Warehousemen's Union—and then Western Union (to file his story). A quick read of the *Compass* would instantly have told the FBI what Stone was up to.

On September 18, 1951, Lindley was "eliminated as suspect." Stone was Hoover's man, although FBI memos never flatly said he was Blin. Constant attempts were made to see if Stone lived more lavishly than the money he earned from *PM,* the *Nation,* the *Star,* and the *Compass,* the assumption being that he was paid in Moscow gold. Stone had reported his annual income in 1947—after his parting with the *Nation*—at $5,000. "Records at the Credit Bureau contained a report dated May 19, 1947, which disclosed [the FBI always used such loaded words] that Stone has resided at 5618 Nebraska NW since Sept 1, 1940." After renting for six years, the Stones bought the home on March 7, 1946, for $10,250. They held a mortgage. An informant said that Stone "appeared to be dependent on the income he received from PM and Nation." The FBI "established" that two small lots and the Fire Island cottage were in Esther's name. An informant told the FBI that Stone was "attempting to sell his home in DC and obtain an apartment at 1133 Park Avenue." (A total of fourteen copies of this memo were sent to offices nationwide.) The Stones never bought a New York apartment. The rental from the Washington home went toward their seven-room apartment, rented for $197 a month from a lawyer friend.

Today's attempts to link Stone with spying are as tawdry as they are untruthful. (Were Stone alive, he would humorously skewer these sources.) Herb Romerstein, a professional Red hunter who started by investigating Communist summer camps and charities, became the chief Republican investigator for the successor to HUAC in the 1960s, then headed Reagan's Office to Counter Soviet Disinformation, still functioning in the 1980s. In the fifties, he worked for the anti-Red blacklisting publication *Counter-Attack,* which spread lies about many, including Stone; it did a brisk business in placing names on the blacklist and then, for a fee, expunging them.

Heaven forfend that neocons should do some original reporting. Kalugin, the former KGB agent, lives not in the gulag but outside the capital. He was easily found at the end of a telephone line.

Interviewing Kalugin is like talking to the eager politician who could argue that the earth was round or flat, depending on what his audience wanted to hear. When Romerstein's claims surfaced in 1992, Guttenplan called Kalugin, quoting him saying, "I did not recruit" Stone, as proof that the journalist was no agent. After the Venona Files were released, in a conversation with this author, Kalugin at first equivocated, saying, "I did not have to recruit him. He had been recruited well before me," but quickly reversed himself, saying he had no proof Stone had ever previously been an agent and that in no way was Stone an agent when he knew him from 1966 to 1968. The journalist was just a "useful contact," not that it mattered to Romerstein, who continued his lies. Kalugin verified to this author, "We had no clandestine relationship. We had no secret arrangement. I was the press officer. I would call him and say, 'Are you interested in having lunch?' I never paid him anything. I sometimes bought lunch." In fact, in 1966 Stone suggested a luncheon with Kalugin at Harvey's, a favorite Hoover haunt, to "tweak his [Hoover's] nose."

In interviews with this author, Kalugin repeated that he had no evidence about Stone being an agent—only that he had read the public disclosures of the Venona Files. Kalugin "assumed" Stone may have been an agent because he was instructed by Moscow to resume a press attaché/journalist relationship when he arrived in the States. Many of Kalugin's answers were slippery; he was not a valued KGB agent for nothing. Washington journalists who did business with Kalugin warned that his answers were not necessarily trustworthy. All spies lie; that is the nature of a business in which morality is a sometime thing. U.S. intelligence employed Russians to spy on the Germans during World War II and, as soon as the war was over, employed former Nazi SS officers to spy on Russia. The capital was overrun with Japanese, German, Russian, and British spies before and during the war, often under cover of official business.

During the fierce battle between isolationists and interventionists at the time of the 1940 Republican Convention, British agents named Winchell, Pearson, Helen Reid, and Lippmann as having "rendered services of particular value." Meanwhile, the Republican Party's isolationist foreign-affairs plank "was taken almost verbatim" from a *New York Times* ad secretly written and paid for by Nazi agents.

Like all agents, Kalugin peddled untruths, but was fond enough of Stone to "not feed him disinformation, which I would do to other journalists." Kalugin was "very upset that Romerstein did not keep his word" in 1992. "I told him, 'Listen, I tell you in trusted confidence that he [Izzy] was an . . . well, not an agent, but a trusted man.'"

Kalugin characterized Stone as a "fellow traveler who began his cooperation with the Soviet intelligence long before me, based entirely on his view of the world. We had hundreds of people like that in the United States alone." Further questioned, Kalugin said he had absolutely no idea if Stone had ever been paid anything. It was pointed out that Blin/Pancake was mentioned only briefly in Venona transcripts and there was no corroboration of anything. Did he have actual information that Stone had ever cooperated with Soviet intelligence? "No. What I told you is what I know. Before I went to Washington I read some of the old spy stories for my enlightenment. I. F. Stone was not among those people. We were interested in more valuable assets. Stone had no access to classified documents. He did not steal anything. It was his brains" that the KGB valued. Kalugin agreed that what Stone thought during the 1940s, as well as when he knew him in the sixties, turned up in his writing for anyone to read. "That's true, he was very outspoken about his liberalism."

In a follow-up interview, Kalugin again contradicted his previous "paid agent" comment; he did not know anything, other than the public Venona Files references. Commenting on the names in the files, he said, "I always maintained that while technically they may be called spies, they were helping the Soviet Union as idealists. They did not wish for money, they did not wish to undermine the United States. In that sense, Stone belonged to the same crop, a generation of idealists. We called them 'agents of influence.' They could shape public opinion, manipulate public opinion."

Definitions of spy, espionage, subversion, and agent of influence are tossed around interchangeably in sloppy interpretations of the Venona Files. Kalugin's description of Stone is far from what could be construed as a spy. The term *agent of influence,* Kalugin admitted, could fit any journalist who disseminated anything of consequence. Even so, Stone was not that important. "I knew one guy from *Time* magazine, for instance. That was a big thing. I. F. Stone was an individual. As a true liberal and not a Communist he was not dedicated to the overthrow of the United States government," Kalugin said with a laugh. "He would not hurt or damage the United States. He was a link and was willing to perform tasks." Such as? Stone would "find out what the views of someone in the government were or some senator on such and such an issue." Kalugin agreed that Stone was doing nothing more than probe for information he would use in his work. What about Romerstein casting Stone and others as "spies"? Said Kalugin, "That's his view. I am biased in the opposite direction—these people were sympathizers of the cause in which I had profound faith."

Kalugin introduced himself to Stone on the phone in 1966 as the press attaché, saying he would like to meet him on a permanent basis. The two met for lunch infrequently, about once in every two months. Kalugin knew that Stone had denounced and refused to have anything to do with Russia after his trip to Russia and its 1956 invasion of Hungary. Their lunches ended in 1968, "when he bolted again. I wanted to get his views and that of his friends, how they assessed the Soviet intervention [in Czechoslovakia]. He was very blunt in his criticism and said, 'Listen, this is the last time I see you guys. You betrayed me once, you betrayed me now, and I don't want to see you again.'" So when I tried to pay for lunch, he said, 'No more blood money!'"—referring only to the lunch checks. (In Kalugin's book, the quote is "I will never take money from your bloody government.") They split the bill, "and that was the end of the association."

Did Stone give you anything you couldn't find in responsible newspapers? "Well, in the intelligence business you do not refer to newspaper headlines," Kalugin said, chuckling. "That's in bad taste." He commented wryly on the spy game that had so preoccupied both countries. "He may say exactly what you read in the morning's *Post*. But you needed your sources." Theirs was a press-attaché/journalist exchange, with Stone often questioning Kalugin. "He was not an 'obedient tool.'" What did he get of importance from Stone? "He was just useful, like dozens of other [media] contacts I had." For the last time Kalugin was asked, "Can you remember anything from Izzy?" "Oh, no, not anything that I can remember. I supervised a bunch of guys in Washington who had access to exceptionally valuable information." Stone was not among them. "Izzy," said Kalugin, was merely "on the fringe."

A succinct dismissal of Stone-the-spy tales came from old friend John Kenneth Galbraith. "Nobody who knew Izzy would take that seriously, and his history all denied it." He laughed. "If you were a totalitarian state . . . you didn't want Izzy."

20

A Guerrilla Warrior during the Fifties Fetish

Since the press is largely Republican and this is a Republican administration, there is little market for "exposing" the government . . . the average Washington correspondent is content to write what he is spoon-fed by the government's press officers.
—I. F. Stone, 1953

Stone felt like a ghost as he sat alone in the abandoned *Daily Compass* newspaper after it folded in the winter of 1952. In the darkened third-floor city room, startled prospective buyers stared at Stone "as if they had suddenly found the place haunted." In that crumbling brick building, "over the space of a decade there were a series of experiments in independent liberal journalism which now have come to an end," Stone wrote. "I was part of them all."

Those years had been a glorious gift; "twelve years of such freedom and opportunity for service as few American newspapermen and intellectuals in my time have enjoyed. I never had to write a word I did not believe. I was allowed to fight for whatever cause won my heart and mind. I had the greatest privilege any human being can have—I was able to earn my bread doing exactly what I liked to do."

A few weeks from forty-five, Stone was ending nearly thirty years in daily journalism. Most recently, he had been preoccupied with the Cold War's twin terrors: dangerous foreign policies and suppression of dissent at home. Stone had no ulcers and no need to consult a psychiatrist, but the Truman era had been depressing for a reporter, he admitted. It was inescapably hard on Stone's friends and acquaintances, the "wonderful collection of idealists, liberals and radicals" devoted to the New Deal. "The loyalty probe was calculated to drive such people out of the government, since there were few among them who did not have enough of a radical past to run into trouble." He called McCarthyism the "fetish of the fifties."

Stone called the Truman years "the era of the moocher," filled with "Wimpys who could be had for a hamburger." Truman's "little men" had floundered; "freedom requires courage, and peaceful coexistence requires confidence. They lacked both." With Truman, "'toughness' became a mask for weakness, and stubbornness a substitute for strength." The basic philosophy of revolutionary America, including the "separation of Church and State and respect for individual belief and conscience" became witch-hunt casualties. Stone was disgusted with false piety: "politicians and generals were constantly invoking God" but "the young were taught to distrust ideas which had been the gospel of the Founding Fathers." Stone excoriated the Catholic Church and the Chamber of Commerce for dictating the worst measures of Kremlin-style "thought control." Socialists were seen to be as potentially dangerous as Communists, and "liberals were damned for protecting the free speech of both."

Stone had no place to express such thoughts as repression of ideas spread. In this atmosphere, then congressman Nixon was a "middle-of-the-road spokesman and conservative papers like the *Washington Star* and *The New York Times*" were being classified as part of the "'left wing press.'" Necessity forced Stone to start his own four-page broadsheet of news and opinion, which he doubted would last. *I. F. Stone's Weekly* had a glorious run of nearly twenty years. His readers could thank the fifties repression; Stone would never have started this venture if he could have found a job.

Only the insanely optimistic would have begun a radical publication in January of 1953. After three years of riding the witch hunt to international notoriety, McCarthy had become chairman of the Senate committee "which he used to terrorize the left of center, the Eisenhower Administration and even his own Senate colleagues." Stone presciently kicked off his first edition: "McCarthy promises to become Eisenhower's chief headache." A man of "much daring and few scruples," McCarthy was in a position to "smear any government official who fails to do his bidding . . . ," Stone correctly wrote. "Outgoing Democrats and incoming Republicans will live equally to regret that they did not cut McCarthy down to size when they had the chance."

Stone began with jovial chutzpah, putting up a front despite private doubts: "I hope General Eisenhower feels as encouraged about his inaugural as I do mine." "In the eyes of many in cold-war Washington . . . I am regarded, I am sure, as a dangerous and subversive fellow," acknowledged Stone, joking that no one was to the left of him but the *Daily Worker*. Stone received second-class postal privileges without "political" questions being asked. He remained grateful for such press freedoms; this break was pivotal in keeping the *Weekly* afloat. He went from 5,300 charter subscribers to 20,000 by 1963 and 70,000 his final year, 1971.

Stone remained ever grateful to his charter readers garnered from mailing lists of the *Nation* and, as Victor Navasky described it, "the ghoul list" of dead leftist publications. From its inception, the *Weekly* sharply criticized the CPUSA—from Stalin's false 1953 "Doctors Plot" indictments to his brutal Eastern-bloc takeovers—knowing full well this would cost him readership. Stone's only start-up money was his $3,500 severance pay from the *Compass*, small gifts, and a friend's interest-free loan of $3,000. "It was a hard time for Esther and Izzy at the beginning," recalled Erwin Knoll, who came to work for the *Washington Post* in 1957.

Still, Stone's letters from that time are supercharged with an energy and signs that he would succeed. Celia was in Paris, on her Smith junior year abroad. Her mother wrote her on December 8, 1952, "We already have 2000 subscriptions, we are thrilled." Esther remained in New York for a month when Izzy went down to Washington to start their venture. "Father's subscriptions are over 5000 so he is considerably relieved about going ahead with the project," Esther wrote on January 12. "I am meeting him in Washington tomorrow to bring accumulated subs [subscriptions] so that the 1st edition of the [news]letter can get out to all subscribers on the 17th. From now on our little family is divided between Paris, New York and Washington."

Ten days later, Izzy weighed in with glee: "Subscriptions passed 5907 today (don't know what came in the last mail in New York)." Thus, by January 22, 1953, Stone could write, "I am in the black financially and feel very chipper. Some of the oddest and nicest people have subscribed, including a Supreme court Justice who shall be nameless till I see you again" (probably liberal chief justice William O. Douglas, who became a friend of Stone's). The *Weekly* had hit the stands when Stone wrote another letter to his daughter, February 24, 1953. "Darling. Your delightful letter just hit at press time. . . . Circulation past 6600 and newsstand distribution this week is 9300." What was vital to the newsletter's success had happened. "Got my 2nd-class permit which saves me more than $100 . . ."

He had famous early subscribers including Bertrand Russell and Eleanor Roosevelt. A framed $5 check from Albert Einstein hung in Stone's study for decades. "I asked if I could frame the check and his secretary let out a groan. Everyone framed checks from Einstein and it really screwed up the bookkeeping. So I cashed it and she sent me back the canceled check." Marilyn Monroe, who met Stone when she was married to playwright Arthur Miller, sent a subscription to every House member. "Such a lost soul," Stone sighed, recalling her suicide.

Despite such glittering readers, Stone was so shunned by colleagues, politicians, and sources that he gave up his deadly quiet office where he flipped rubber bands, waiting for the phone to ring. The *Weekly* office then consisted of the dining room table, third-floor hallway and two bedrooms, an enclosed downstairs porch where Esther kept the books and handled the mail, and the basement, where Stone later stashed his assistants. Esther did so much work that if the *Weekly* grew, joked Stone, he'd have to become a bigamist. In a home bulging with books, documents, and newspapers, no one ever sat in one armchair that had become the permanent repository of newspapers.

It is hard to imagine just how fearful people were even to be seen with a leftist. As he darted in and out of conferences or committees, Stone was regarded by big-time reporters as a scruffy nag to avoid. "There was this perception by some that he was a Communist," said David Brinkley, then a neophyte radio reporter. He began reading Stone, marveling at his digging. "He sat at home and read everything in the goddamn world. He was always quoting some report of some obscure agency you never knew about—and distilled it into something interesting."

"He had a wonderful style," remarked cartoonist-author-playwright Jules Feiffer. "Left-wing writers are usually notoriously bad stylists. Izzy was *funny.*" Stone cultivated a breezy elegance, backing up pithy comments with facts and historical reference. "You felt like you knew him from his writing. It's interesting; he was not easy to be a personal friend of, although I was. But in his writing, you became a friend." In 1973, Stone asked a new senator, Jim Abourezk of South Dakota, to lunch. Stone was intrigued with the maverick senator. "Say, how did you become such a radical?" asked Stone. "I guess by reading *I. F. Stone's Weekly* for so long," replied the senator. He explained that an older friend, a Jewish doctor, gave him his copies after reading them. "What's his name?" Stone shot back. "I don't think I had more than *one* subscriber in South Dakota."

* * *

Stone soon plunged into cataclysmic events. The Korean War ground on, Stalin died, the Rosenbergs were executed, political dissenters were imprisoned for their beliefs and their lawyers disbarred, the horribly mutilated body of a black teenager named Emmett Till kindled the embryonic civil rights movement, nuclear annihilation seemed possible, and blacklists were applauded.

After one early attempt, a men's clothing ad, Stone boasted that he was one up on Ben Franklin because he sold no advertising and was free from coercion, although finding few advertisers for a radical rag was no doubt a less lofty factor. Stone took that sole ad only to get a congressional press pass. "They told me that you had to have advertising." The owner of a Manhattan clothier advertised a bargain of $59.97 "in ready-to-wear imported Harris Tweeds, Flannels, Gabardines, Worsteds, etc." Stone didn't charge him, getting a free suit in exchange for the ad. But the keepers of the congressional passes told Stone that he needed a substantial portion of advertising revenue to qualify for a pass. Stone recalled to Patner, "It just wasn't worth it. So I never got my press pass but they gave me a 'courtesy of the gallery' pass. I could go by anytime, except when the president was there. I guess they thought I was a threat!"

Instead of huckstering for ads, Stone shamelessly and happily hustled himself and his product. He begged, pleaded, cajoled, offered cut-rate deals, all with brash cheerfulness: "Keep the ball rolling by getting a friend or two" to subscribe; "Don't forget to prod your friends into subscribing with that handy subscription blank on page 4." As a "pepper-upper" Stone was giving away a free copy of "my forthcoming book, 'The Truman Era,' with every two subscriptions." This "darn good book" was a collection "of my best pieces." Business was thriving, "though the editor and publisher (who is also the office-boy) sometimes gets a little breathless."

On continued Stone: The *Weekly* was being distributed through several hundred kiosks in New York and Brooklyn, but he urged small-town readers to tell newsstands to handle the *Weekly.* "Just a phone call to a friend," pleaded Stone, could "put the Weekly on a firm foundation. Won't you make that call today?" At the end of March, he proudly reported that the *Weekly* "now reached every state in the union, the territories of Alaska, Hawaii and Puerto Rico and six Provinces of Canada." Subscribers were in Mexico, Panama, Colombia, Brazil, Jamaica, Norway, Sweden, Belgium, England, France, Austria, the British zone of Berlin, and Israel. One subscriber was behind the Iron Curtain. No subscriber was found in Newfoundland or the Yukon, but "as soon as we can get the dog team hitched, our circulation department [aka Esther] mushes forward."

Just as it seemed that subscriptions had triumphed and dignity prevailed, Stone would pop up now and again with a plea, such as this Christmas-jingle staple. Wrote Stone: "It may not be Shakespeare but it sure went to our circulation manager's heart."

> *Keep Your Diamonds,*
> *Cashmeres, Furs,*
> *And Cadillacs Marked "His"*
> *and "Hers,"*
> *Just Give Me for My Very Own,*
> *Another Year of I. F. Stone."*

In the spirit of ecumenicalism and sales, Stone cheerfully wished everyone a merry Christmas.

Stone's informal style complemented the hard facts he was uncovering. There were no flaming headlines or exclamation points. "My idea was to make the *Weekly* radical in viewpoint but conservative in format." His famous boxes became as well read as the bloopers at the end of *New Yorker* items. Bordered in dark type, these paragraphs captured errors or contradictory positions in governmental utterances and newspapers, topped with sardonic headlines that drew smiles.

While Stone later asserted that tackling the repressive fifties was a "helluva lot of fun," the snubs of colleagues hurt him more than he cared to admit. He always shaded those early *Weekly* years with rosy memories, but his son Christopher recalls, "Dad revised his feelings. He really was angry sometimes: 'I don't want to be buried in this goddamn city.' " Christopher was sometimes startled by his father's vehemence. "He seldom swore. He accepted a lot, but he was bitter and angry, and there was sort of a stored-up rage at those who snubbed him during this period. His ebullience buoyed him over some of the sharper memories, but he was a pariah and he did not like it." Chris worked for his father during the summers. "I remember walking into the [congressional] pressroom with him and you could feel the cold stares."

A true and close friend was Richard Dudman, of the *St. Louis Post-Dispatch*. Dudman first introduced himself to Stone in 1946, shortly after Stone's famous underground trip to Palestine, seeking his advice on an impending trip there. After a while, Stone said bluntly but kindly, "Dick, I don't think you know enough about history." Stone gave Dudman a reading list, and their lives became entwined for forty years until Stone's death. The two couples formed a bond that included their children, seeing movies, and even going together on a popular diet of grapefruit and steak.

When Dudman was assigned to Washington in 1954, he and his wife, Helen, invited Esther and Izzy to dinner. Another guest who worked for the USIA called Dudman into the kitchen, ostensibly to help fix a drink. "What are you thinking of!?" he demanded. "How could you invite me to your house with I. F. Stone? I could lose my job!" Dudman was too startled to rebuke him, saying, "Izzy's a friend of mine," and hoped he would like him too. More than a decade later, the Dudmans and Stones were recounting all their happy times together and Esther said, "Do you remember that dinner party a long time ago when somebody from the government was there? Here we were at the home of a prominent Washington correspondent with people from the government, and I really thought we'd arrived." Dudman debated about telling them what had happened and thought that the now famous journalist would think it amusing. Stone was not amused. "Right away he wanted to know who that son of a bitch was."

In the fifties Dudman defended Stone from a "jerky managing editor who questioned Stone as a too radical source" for a *Post-Dispatch* editorial page article. "Everybody was scared stiff. You couldn't mention the *Nation* or people would say, 'Shut up,' afraid some informer would report you. You had to be careful what books and periodicals you had on your coffee table." Stone, Mary McGrory, Alan Barth, Drew Pearson, were "on the cutting edge, the brave ones," said Dudman. "To write something new is dangerous ground. [The press] always talk about how they want scoops, but they'd rather have something that somebody else has touched on. Access is considered the great thing. Walter Lippmann told me he voted for Nixon and I asked, 'Why would you do that?' Lippmann said, 'Because he's going to get us out of the Vietnam War.' I said, 'How do you know?' and Lippmann says, '*He's told me!*'" Dudman's eyes widened in recollection. "There's access for you."

Individualists like Dudman were later honored to be on Nixon's enemies list. "Like Izzy, I distrusted access and found better sources were lower down where they did the work. But I think that was always a disappointment to my editors; they really measure you by what access you had to the head of the CIA or the secretary of state or the president. No establishment paper is independent. But Izzy was. He was not beholden to conventional concerns." Although Stone could fracture a cozy press conference with sharp questions, Dudman noted, as did others, "Izzy had a hell of a conventional streak. When he got famous, he liked acceptance awfully well."

"The fifties were terribly lonely for him," said Bernard (Bud) Nossiter, a major *Washington Post* reporter who later went to the *New York Times*. He was introduced to Stone by the *Nation*'s editor, Carey McWilliams, in 1955. "Izzy enjoyed not being on a first-name basis. Not going to the dinners. Not being Walter Lippmann. He liked being the opposite side of the coin to Lippmann. He gloried in that, and God knows there were plenty of people that admired him for it. But at the same time he was very social. He was bloody lonely; at that time very few people would talk to Izzy." Once Chris asked his father why he had not counterattacked his enemies. Stone told him that he took the advice of William Fulbright, one of the few senators to tackle McCarthyism. He told Stone, "Don't get in a pissing match with a skunk."

During one of the congressional hearings when the USIA was being quizzed on the artistic material it sent abroad, Stone asked his son to cover. "I was sort of laughing at it all. And then I went back to get the transcript." The chief counsel of HUAC put his arm around Chris's shoulder, recognizing him from the press table.

"What paper do you work for?" the man asked. Chris answered, "*I. F. Stone's Weekly.*" The man swiftly took his arm away, "like I was the devil, and said, 'Get out.'" Chris stood his ground, saying, "I want the transcript." "I thought he was going to punch me," Chris recalled. He argued that he had a right to the public transcript. "There was a bit of a scuffle" as the man shoved him out the door. When Christopher sought out the Capitol police and told them of the incident, they refused to make a report. He went back to the pressroom. "This very conservative guy from the *Chicago Tribune* was there. Now he happened to like Pop. He always said, 'I don't agree with your dad, but he's a good reporter.' Within a couple of hours he had produced the transcript for me."

Judith Martin, the witty *Washington Post* writer who became famous as Miss Manners, was a high school classmate of Christopher's at

Wilson High, class of 1955. Back then, as an officer of the Woodrow Wilson Philosophical Society, Judy and two male classmates, Charles Miller and Edmund Games Jr., invited "Chris Stone's father" to speak to their club. Martin was among the children of New Deal liberals who populated Washington's northwest all-white, top-tier public school. "Ours was Wilson's last segregated class," she recounted. "Designs for desegregation had begun, and a bunch of us proposed a meeting with Dunbar [the distinguished school for blacks that was a mirror of Wilson in academic excellence]. The principal was furious and said, 'You can't do it as a group from the school! Don't say you're from Wilson, don't call the newspapers!'" Martin laughs. "All of which gave us perfectly good ideas we hadn't even thought of. We immediately called the *Post*, who covered us."

Recalls Charles Miller, "McCarthyism was nowhere a more insidious miasma than among public school officials in Washington, D.C. Children of congressmen and senators attended the schools, the school budget was in the hands of the House committees dominated by Southern racists, and the slightest provocation by sentient, not to say conniving, adolescents inspired nervous fear." "The principal told us we had to cancel Izzy's speech," recalled Martin. They went to Stone's house and "poured out the story to Izzy." The principal was not through with his defiant students. He told them, "If any of the three of you get into a good college, it won't be my fault." Recalls Martin, "This was quite a threat; it was no small thing when you are concerned about getting into a good college." Either he didn't carry out his threat or his influence was no match for their intelligence: Games went to Harvard, Miller to Swarthmore, and Martin to Wellesley.

Instead of speaking at the school, Stone addressed a small group at Miller's house. He had planned to speak on government but, after their experience, decided that the students needed a much more important lesson on freedom of expression. He came armed with Milton's *Areopagitica*. In that era, recalled Chris Stone, it wasn't surprising that the "principal got cold feet. The surprising thing is that somebody could even *think* that my father could speak at the high school. No one liked McCarthy and you could talk about it. Still, everyone was watching to see what was happening and was afraid."

Even as late as 1962, McCarthy's ghost was present. That year, Finlay Lewis, who became a top national journalist, was just out of basic training and was assigned to "the Army Language School preparatory to becoming an electronic snoop with the Army Security Agency . . . I carried with me vivid memories of the red-baiting witch hunts." An avid reader of Izzy's *Weekly*, Lewis was determined not to give it up, "even though it went without saying that the FBI would look into my subscriptions." During regular barracks inspections, "everything had to be openly displayed." Lewis hit upon a solution. On inspection day, when "an obnoxious West Point graduate came striding in, he immediately looked at what I was reading." He stared. Side-by-side were the radical *Weekly* and *Human Events*, "the John Birch publication." It was worth buying the reactionary rag, said Lewis. "He walked out of the room shaking his head," too dumbfounded to inspect anything else.

In hindsight, it seems ludicrous that Stone was so shunned and that a cowering mainstream media unquestioningly reported the dubious diatribes of the Hoover-McCarthy axis. But when Stone started the weekly, the grip of McCarthyism seemed endless. "My *sister* was Joe McCarthy's executive secretary during that whole horrible time," recalled David Brinkley. "We couldn't speak to each other about that whole period. I thought he was a sonovabitch, which he was, and after McCarthy died, she told me she thought he was a liar, which he was." Brinkley echoed what Stone often wrote: "Every time the appropriations were about to come out, these committees suddenly discovered a new terrible Communist conspiracy. It was strictly a racket. Stone was right about a lot of things; they were selling a scare and they used it like a club. It was manufactured by the right wing in Congress and the hard-line Republican papers would all play it big." Reflected Brinkley, "Had I been running a daily paper, I'd be very dubious about taking a hard position then, although the monumental idea of being able to destroy a paper seems strange today."

"It's a cliché," said wire service reporter Al Spivak, "but McCarthy played the press like a violin," making great use of deadline pressures. Reacting to the question of whether they were forced to quote him, even though they had major doubts about what he was saying, Spivak says, "It was a *wire* service." Spivak was referring to the traditional who-said-what-when-and-where of journalism when there were three highly competitive wire services vying to be first with their reports to national newspapers. "He made sure we had an overnight every morning, fed us tips, and on and on."

McCarthy's nasal sneer and inane giggle, his swaggering name calling and shouts of "Point of order!" made him a ridiculous figure to the sixties generation who watched reruns of the Army-McCarthy hearings in urban art theaters. In the early fifties, however, he was the hottest bully on the block. Secretary of State John Foster Dulles cleared his selections to department posts with him. He and Hoover managed to make a menace out of the rapidly disintegrating American Communist Party.

Said the great literary stylist of the twentieth century Murray Kempton, "While we were all running after McCarthy as the main man, Izzy was tracking that miserable J. Edgar Hoover stuff—you know, following the children of Jews and Communists to their school on the chance that their father might show up to speak to them, taking away the pensions of wounded veterans who had been Communists, that kind of thing. Izzy wrote a lot on Joe, but he understood how deep it went. There are people who run around like water bugs and poison the surface of the water, like Joe McCarthy. And there are people who get down in the springs and sit there and poison the springs. And that was J. Edgar Hoover. The rest of us just worked on the water; we covered the water bugs. Izzy was braver than most of us. He took on Hoover."

Before most, Stone was finding evidence that Hoover was giving his notoriously flawed files of nameless informants to McCarthy, HUAC, and other inquisitional committees, actions for which a president could justifiably fire the director, but Hoover always denied it and retained his post. He despised Stone more than ever as he saw such headlines as "McCarthy-Hoover Axis." Yet America's Blackmailer in Chief, who feared no leaders, was terrified of Stone's ridicule. Stone was never called as a witness. While the FBI was supposed to be investigating McCarthy's financial manipulations, Hoover was extolling the senator as his good friend, a red-hot conflict of interest that Stone hit hard and which few other journalists addressed.

Stone never stopped his crusade against such injustices as not being able to confront an accuser, flagrant wiretapping invasions of privacy, attacks on free speech, lifting passports, and deportation for political beliefs. In his first year of publication, 1953, when his friend Charlie Chaplin left the United States after being hounded by Hoover, Stone wrote "Charlie Chaplin's Farewell Custard." "There must be something wrong with our America if Chaplin could no longer live in it." The "voluntary exile" of the man who never became an American citizen "owes it to us and himself to put into a new film the tragicomedy overtaking of America where greasy informers are public heroes, where a Senator who is afraid to answer questions about his own financial accounts becomes the great investigator of others. . . . Turn the laugh on them, Charlie, for our country's sake. This capital needs nothing so badly as one final well-flung custard pie." Stone cheered on Einstein when he called for civil disobedience to protest the witch-hunters.

"Amazingly little attention has been paid," Stone wrote, to a portion of the Fifth Amendment: "No person shall be held to answer for a capital or otherwise infamous crime, unless on a presentment or indictment of a grand jury." As Stone pointed out, Congress constantly publicly pilloried people after grand juries had found no evidence sufficient to hold a trial. People then faced wild public accusations that could not be proved or disproved: "If a man charges that he saw Eisenhower riding a broomstick over the White House, he will never be convinced to the contrary by sworn evidence that the President was in bed reading a Western at the time." In reply to McCarthy's "silly 'Communist coddling' charges against the army," cowering Republican senators launched their own investigation, which would "merely pander to paranoia and reward demagogy" and would be greeted as a "whitewash" by McCarthy's "lunatic fringe."

Although Stone had astounded friends by supporting Eisenhower, hoping that a man who knew about the horror of war firsthand would push for peace in Korea, he rapidly found weakness in the new president's response to the witch hunts. After thirty days the president "let the State Department knuckle under . . . to McCarthy," wrote Stone. The "naked acts of submission" included killing an order "that no employee need talk to McCarthy's investigators" and that the senator's investigators could not remove files without specific permission. Scoffed Stone, "Those like Walter Lippmann who hoped wistfully that . . . Republicans under a famous General would provide sufficient . . . backbone to put the wild men under control must be bitterly disappointed."

Although Stone started earlier and never let up, he was not alone in his attacks on McCarthy. Civil libertarian Joe Alsop's right-wing foreign policy did not preclude his strong denunciations of McCarthy. Even *Time* did a 1951 cover on McCarthy that denounced his bullying tactics, if not his goals. The *Washington Post* was a struggling paper then, not wanting to take risks, but its great editorial cartoonist Herblock invented the word *McCarthyism*—lettering it on a barrel of mud, teetering on a column of several barrels of slime. The best writing came from those who were allowed interpretation. The *Washington Star*'s Mary McGrory covered the Army-McCarthy hearings like theater, Murray Marder of the *Post* wrote biting analysis, and editorial writer Alan Barth pulled no punches, although his publisher, Phil Graham, sometimes balked. The *New York Times* buckled under; reporters called before the committee were banished to obscure assignments and sometimes ousted. "You could get canned if you got your name in the paper. If you were called and used the Fifth, then the blacklist would take effect," said Kempton.

Stone's anguish was deep and wide as he spoke to audiences across the country. "When the dissemination of ideas is confused with conspiracy, it is the duty of every American to refuse to be an informer," Stone told a 1954 Los Angeles audience.

As McCarthy finally lost luster with his indiscriminate attacks, Stone said, "People are beginning to realize that anybody can be called a Communist, not just a liberal or Democrat, but . . . a General, an Army man, even the head of the Chase National Bank . . . any genuine trade unionist. The reason the term *witch hunt* is justified is because just as supernatural and magical power was attributed to these poor old women [during the Salem witch hunts], so is the supernatural and magical power attributed to the handful of Communists in our midst. It's like the days of the Inquisition, it's like the days when people believed in the power of the devil."

In speeches Stone mocked the attorney general, Herbert Brownell. When he could find no abuse of powers of Communist or alleged Communist teachers, Brownell argued that they were guilty of "spreading ideas in the classroom, ideas too subtle to be detected." When Stone caustically added, "That's how 'devilish' these teachers are," ripples of laughter came from the audience. "The idea that you can get over something too subtle to be detected in the classroom, to stick in [those] little minds, and turn them into Marxists and dialectical materialists overnight! If there are any Communist teachers, they must be immensely flattered by this kind of a description of the magical potency of their teaching powers."

Criticizing a wiretap bill, Stone said, "You get the picture from the attorney general that people are openly discussing crimes on the phone, of a guy picking up the phone saying, 'Say, Joe, how about stealing the atom bomb plans tomorrow night?' but they can't do a damn thing about it because of the lack of wiretap legislation! There are only two crimes in which the telephone is used at all—kidnaping and extortion—and both crimes were omitted from the administration wiretap bill."

Stone's polemics were nonstop: "China Lobby senators connive and conspire to get us into war, connive and conspire . . . to make people afraid to talk for peace. . . . These are the real betrayers of America."

Stone's March 19, 1954, antinuclear issue was preserved by the FBI: "The United States is the leader, organizer and paymaster of a huge coalition in a world split in two. It holds in its hands the most terrible instrument of destruction ever developed. . . . It claims the right to use these for 'instant retaliation.' . . . No one says, 'Look, the situation is so terrible we've simply got to live in peace with the Russians.' No one talks that way anymore, at least no one who can reach more than a handful of people. The country is afraid to talk of peace. It is being conditioned for war, and war will engulf all mankind."

That spring, Stone opposed American intervention in Indochina, predicting that the get-tough belligerency of Secretary of State Dulles would lead to another Korean War in that region. He assailed Dulles and his "efforts to build up support for unilateral intervention in Indo-China if necessary." He saw the country turning toward fascism as it hounded atomic scientists on the left. He abhorred the Internal Security Act, which labeled veterans of the Abraham Lincoln Brigade as members of a Communist front: "This hounded mutual aid organization representing that brave handful of men who fought Fascism in Spain will some day again be accorded the respect it deserves." Stone chided Congress for not having "the nerve to question Hoover about the leak to McCarthy of FBI material damaging to the Army."

By 1956, McCarthy was a shambling, deposed, and exiled drunken wreck, censured by the Senate in 1954 and abandoned by the press. His staff "urchins," as Stone called Roy Cohn and David Schine, had done their book-burning worst to decimate the Voice of America and State Department overseas libraries and had now scrambled off the front page. But the inquisitions continued, and Stone's nonstop ridicule of FBI and congressional Red-baiting tactics included attacks on "America's greatest paper," the *New York Times*. Stone pummeled the *Times* for firing an editor in 1955 who refused to name names: "How can the Times editorially support the 5th amendment and discharge those who invoke it?"

American journalists were quite rightly championing those who were "staking their lives on the demand for free expression in Budapest," but Stone stingingly noted "no newspapermen were demonstrating for one of their own," the mistakenly identified *New York Times* editor Robert Shelton. Found guilty of contempt for invoking his Fifth Amendment rights before the Senate Internal Security Committee, Shelton and a librarian were each given a staggering four months in jail.

"Every day we are told that freedom is the precious possession we must be ready at the drop of a bomb to defend with our lives against Them, but nobody took an hour off from work to come down to the courtroom and see whether the First Amendment was in danger." Still another *Times* employee was slated to go on trial soon. Chastised Stone, "Do we only honor Peter Zengers when long dead? When will the New York *Times* take the offensive?" It pained Stone to report that the Newspaper Guild "has done nothing to help the newspapermen caught in the committee's web." Only the then liberal *New York Post* had given the Shelton affair proper treatment, sending Kempton to cover the trial and editorializing against the verdict.

Stone punched out his disappointment in print, urging editors to look at HUAC's just published revised edition of its *Guide to Subversive Organizations and Publications*. Were journalists going to allow the "fungoid growth" of this current atmosphere to continue? That any government agency or committee "may decide which publications are subversive and which are not?"

Recalled Stone's anticommunist, liberal friend lawyer Joe Rauh, "This town was so scared. Your clients would *lie* to you," said Rauh, in hushed tones, as if still not believing it. "I would say to them, 'Tell me the worst thing you ever did for the Communist Party. Tell me anything you did.' They wouldn't even tell me they belonged to a goddamn commie bookstore. Then it comes out afterwards. And you're stuck. I finally had to have a ritual with these people and just say, 'Now, I tell you, if one thing comes out, you've lost your lawyer.' And that would get a little more cooperation."

Even Rauh's old friend Phil Graham, publisher of the *Washington Post*, drew back at times. "Outside of Izzy, the *Post* was the best, but there were real brawls between Phil and the greatest civil liberties writer of that period, Alan Barth," said Rauh. "Phil was one of my best friends. But he killed a favorable editorial of Alan's on a case of mine. He told me, 'You don't know what I'm up against with the advertisers.' Phil was a young man, trusted by the family to run a huge enterprise, worried that it would go under because it wasn't a profitable enterprise then. They still were good on McCarthy, especially compared to others, but they weren't perfect."

Reporters often felt helpless covering McCarthy's scenes staged for newspaper deadlines. If hearings were producing little news, the senator would stalk out and give a wild press conference to the herd that followed, once claiming, "I'm going to subpoena [former] President Harry Truman!" His hot-air threat never materialized, but made the headlines he sought.

An excuse by Lippmann is one often used to champion "objective" reporting. "McCarthy's charges of treason, espionage, corruption, perversion, are news which cannot be suppressed or ignored," he wrote. "They come from a United States Senator." His attacks on the State and Defense departments were "news which must be published." Richard Rovere, who wrote the quintessential biography of McCarthy, caustically responded, "It was also, of course, news that a United States Senator was lying and defrauding the people and their government."

For journalists to call an official a liar, goes the old argument that remains in effect today, some official had to call him a liar. But this is no excuse for not researching and presenting damaging documentary evidence or asking tough questions that get a point across. As Rovere noted about a McCarthy treatise with "meticulously numbered" but meaningless footnotes, "Anyone who employed them to run down sources would have seen for himself how McCarthy butchered the truth."

Stone caught McCarthy at this time and again. The *New York Times* once huffed that "just because they are usually proved false," it was "difficult, if not impossible to ignore charges by Senator McCarthy. The remedy lies in the reader." To which Rovere commented, "This was rather like saying that if a restaurant serves poisoned food, it is up to the diner to refuse it." Years later, James Reston said in his memoirs, "Putting quotation marks around McCarthy's false charges did not relieve us of complicity."

Wire-service reporter Al Spivak was afflicted by the Being Important bug of journalism. Of Stone's early reporting, Spivak argued, "If no one's reading you, who cares? I don't think he had any impact, except in a very limited area where they didn't like McCarthy anyway." Edward R. Murrow is credited with hastening McCarthy's downfall, but Murrow always admitted that he and CBS came late to their 1954 attack, repeating for TV what Stone and a handful of reporters had written for some time. At the time, Stone praised Murrow's "brilliant TV show," which exposed to a wider audience the shabby case of an Air Force officer, Milo Radulovich, who was about to be blacklisted as a "security risk" for the sole reason that he associated with a father and sister who "might" have

Communist views. Murrow's show forced the Air Force to clear Radu-lovich. McCarthy's biggest mistake was choosing to answer Murrow on television; he was a malevolent apparition, with his oily thinning hair and lifeless eyes.

Kempton argues that even early on Stone's reach was further than his 5,300 subscribers because other journalists of merit were beginning to notice what he did. Kempton had discounted Stone after his book on Korea and cracked to him, "One of my in-laws is a Commie and he's a great admirer of your newsletter." Stone snapped back, "You'd have a future if you'd be more serious." Years later, Kempton shuddered as he recalled his slur that only a Communist would read Stone. "He was very disapproving—as well he should have been because the condescension in my remark is disgusting. A deeply offensive thing to say to a man who is making his way and a very exegesis way. So I began reading the *Weekly*. And of course, it was absolutely staggering. I developed a tremendous admiration and great affection for him. He had a genius for reading documents, but he also had this great gift of historical imagination."

Eventually, McCarthyism produced change. Journalists began arguing that it was imperative to find out if officials' comments were true before printing them. However, as we have seen, rush to judgment continues to foster enormous casualties to truth. The skill or interest in challenging documentation remains inadequate in mainstream publications and nonexistent in the garbage bag of tabloids and TV cable pundits. Murrow's principled despair foreshadowed that future in his famous 1958 farewell tirade to the TV industry.

When the Senate censured McCarthy in 1954, wrote Stone, "Basically it may be said that McCarthy is being censured only for being a bully and a boor. Until McCarthy disgraced himself by running roughshod over President Eisenhower and the Army, he so well served the function of Red-baiting the Democrats for the Republican Party that they were willingly quiescent." Stone accurately wrote that McCarthy's ilk were "far from defeated." Still, his optimism surfaced at the escalating cries to censure McCarthy. "For the first time the possibility of a broad front against fascism is beginning to shape up in America." McCarthy "cared more for his publicity . . . than truth or his country." In order to look better in public, documents released a half century later revealed, McCarthy conducted private sessions behind closed doors to weed out witnesses who might be tough adversaries.

* * *

Stone was offended in later life when people thought they were praising him by calling him the first laptop publisher. "I had a *printer*," he emphasized, not referring to a machine hooked up to a computer. No one seemed to care much about Esther and Izzy or their struggling paper except the FBI agents who trailed them on their lone walks to the dingy printing plant where they disappeared for hours. Unknown to waiting FBI agents, journalistic history was being made, albeit in baby steps. Stone watched the Linotype operator set his words, shouted out requests or directions in the din of press machines, then loaded piles of the weekly into his car for distribution.

Stone's inspiration, George Seldes, was the only other man in the twentieth century who managed to make a sweeping success of hard-hitting, personal one-man publishing. (Ben Franklin continued to publish the excellent *Washington Spectator* to quieter applause until his death in 2005.) At the age of 101, his voice still strong, Seldes searched for reasons why he and Stone attempted risky ventures. "I guess we were just brought up to have a social conscience. Most newspapermen don't have a social conscience, I can assure you," said Seldes, whose *In Fact* publication regularly excoriated big business, government, and the press. "Their main thing was to get a front-page byline, no matter the consequences. That's all anybody was actually working for. Do you realize that a guy could come into an office, show the city editor the two dollars he had just paid for an ad, then take out a typewritten 'story' and order him to put it in the next edition? That was at the *Pittsburgh Leader*. I was sixteen years old, 1906."

Seldes filled the muckraking void and was "the dean and granddaddy of us investigative reporters," Stone remarked. Seldes scoops were major. In the late thirties, he was the first to warn that cigarettes could cause cancer and blasted newspaper owners who made millions from cigarette advertising while hiding this horrendous evidence. Seldes's superior reporting was often censored by the press lords of his day, who were friendly with the offended corporations he exposed. A disgusted Seldes quit mainstream reporting and began *In Fact* in 1940. He had the luck to publish for a decade when thriving unions bought in bulk. "I reached 180,000—more than all the publishers on the left put together, the *Nation, New Republic*, et cetera, not to mention the 'repeaters,' what I call the five-buck liberal who subscribes to all of them."

In Fact closed in 1950. "I'd like to just take it over from you directly," Stone proposed at that time. "No," said Seldes, explaining years later that he wanted to protect the younger Stone. "I wanted him to divorce himself as far as possible from me. I had been Red-baited out of business." Seldes refuted Stone's version of *In Fact*'s demise. Stone had said that Seldes lost his enormous circulation, bulk sales to Communist-run labor unions, when he broke with the party line on Yugoslavia. Seldes said it was Hoover, not ideological wars, that killed *In Fact*. During World War II, "the FBI established a censorship and threw out *In Fact*, the *New Republic*, and of course the Communist *Daily Worker*. They took notes on all of these soldiers who had gotten these publications." Seldes got a letter from one GI who said, "Send me *In Fact* in a plain envelope. I can't live without it but I can't let them know what I am reading." The FBI "eventually frightened the majority of our subscribers enough to cancel or not renew."

Said Stone when the ninety-one-year-old Seldes received a 1982 Polk Award, "I'm very proud to acknowledge that George was the model for my weekly. . . . He soared above the conventions of his time, a lone eagle, unafraid and indestructible. . . . He illustrates the fact that if you live long enough, the establishment will take you to its bosom."

In 1957, McCarthy flamed out spectacularly, consumed by advanced alcoholism. Stone wrote, "A black sense of failure and public rejection hastened his sodden end." He looked ahead to a fresher breeze in American politics: "While the Senate last week was burying McCarthy, the United States Supreme Court buried McCarthyism." A majority ruling in favor of two men who stood up to inquisitions "expunges two decades of carefully nurtured nightmare," exalted Stone.

However, Red-baiting would be used again and again in an attempt to taint the civil rights and anti–Vietnam War movements, but for the moment Stone was ecstatic. He turned his attention to those two great social movements of his time. But first he had to face some truth telling of his own that came in the form of an anguished confession.

21
CONFESSIONS

In the case of Russia, we have seen before how Stone's intellect collided with myopic optimism and his emotional desire for peaceful coexistence. After World War II, he was critical at times, notably when he refused to participate in the Communist-orchestrated martyrdom of the Rosenbergs. He attacked Stalin's repression and blamed the Soviets along with the United States for not deterring the nuclear arms race.

Still, Stone maintained public illusions far longer than his intellect and reputation as a fierce advocate for truth warranted. In the spring of 1953, he ricocheted from one position to another. Just after Stalin's death, Stone called him a "giant figure," a "great leader" of a "party in a new sense, like nothing the world has known since the Society of Jesus, a party ruling a one-party state." The administration's "merely 'official' " condolences were "small minded and unworthy of a great power." Without Stalin the war "would have lasted a lot longer and cost a great many more American lives."

A month later he ripped into Stalin's last murderous act before his death. The charges in the infamous Doctors' Plot were "too hideous to be credible," Stone had written during the trials. Now he asked, "What was wrong with Stalin's regime that such miscarriages of justice could occur? How many framed political prisoners were being held in camps?" Russia's long history of false show trials was produced by cynics who "assume an audience too unintelligent" to separate truth from melodrama. He wrote that Stalin's insane charges reeked of anti-Semitism, Jewish doctors plotting to poison Soviet leaders at the behest of worldwide Jewry and Zionists.

Left-wing Jewry had placed such stock in Russia's avowals of equality for Jews that many of Stone's readers could not face the lethal depths of Stalin's anti-Semitism. Stone attacked readers who protested his "astringent observations" and denounced those "trained to believe everything they are told, so long as it comes from Moscow and party higher-ups." Stone hoped that new Russian leaders would "dissipate the murk of conspiracy" by providing the right to counsel and applying "the doctrine of overt act as the test of guilt." A grasp for peace followed: such reforms would mollify Americans and "go far to dissipate those fears on which warmongers depend."

One can only wonder what Stone would have thought had he visited Russia earlier. After seeing Russia in 1956 he wrote a strongly confessional column that cost the financially strapped journalist four hundred subscribers. He would never lead with his heart on the Soviets again. With uncharacteristic timidity he began, "I am only a reporter" and "not wise enough . . . to know how much truth may be wisely given the public with our eyedroppers. . . . This is what I think. It may be wrong but it is not synthetic." For decades, Stone critics have mocked as "too mild" an oft-quoted sentence in this column, which Stone had italicized: *This is not a good society and it is not led by good men.*" However, the entire column conveys much more criticism, personal anguish, and self-reproach. Stone literally gulped for air as he faced the truth. "The way home from Moscow has been agony for me," he confided to his readers. "I . . . feel like a swimmer under water who must rise to the surface or his lungs will burst." Stone gave a reason for his less-than-candid earlier appraisals: friends had warned him to temper his criticism in the cause of a "worthy expediency"—the "fight for world peace." But he could keep silent no longer. "I hate the morass into which one wanders when one begins to withhold the truth because the consequences might be bad— *this is, indeed, the morass on which the Russian Communist state is built.* . . . I have to say what I really feel after seeing the Soviet Union. . . . No society is good in which men fear to think—much less speak— freely." The destruction of socialist ideals was everywhere. Stone had seen the fear of those with whom he'd tried to talk as shadowy figures watched; he'd heard whispered tales of murdered and imprisoned political enemies.

He indicted the entire system. "Stalinism was the natural fruit of the whole spirit of the Communist movement," Stone lashed out. "The wanton executions, the frame-ups, the unjust convictions and exiles—these would not have been possible except in a movement whose members had been taught not only to obey unquestioningly but to *hate.* . . . The liquidation of the opposition was not just a duty but a savage pleasure."

After post-Stalinist leaders executed his number one henchman, Beria, Stone scoffed, "Only persons rendered permanently idiotic by complete submergence in party-line literature will take at face value the charges that" Beria "was a British or imperialist agent." The new regime was no better; "this is how Stalin operated . . . first slander and then the firing squad. . . . And *everybody* turned out to be a foreign agent!"

Stone sharply observed, "This society is a paradise only for a rather stupid type of Communist party member . . . if you believe everything you read in the papers, lack imagination, and feel no need to think for yourself, you can be very happy." But for those who care "deeply about the basic questions of humanity and history, the USSR has been a hermetically sealed prison." The fearful press repeated only Party-line "repellent gibberish." "Whatever the shortcomings of the Western press, there is no comparison between it and the Soviet press." It horrified him to see first-hand a society in which no news entered from the outside world.

Secrecy surrounding Khrushchev's famed February speech to the 20th Party Congress angered him. Why did Communist newspapermen have to leak it to foreign newspapermen and not report about it until it had leaked back from abroad? "No one knows . . . it is amazing how little anyone knows of what really goes on in Moscow." (The text was unpublished in Russia even by the time of Khrushchev's memoir two decades later.)

Khrushchev's 1956 revelations proved that Stalin's abuses "are not figments of hostile propaganda," Stone admitted. Khrushchev's twenty-thousand-word indictment explosively detailed Stalin's reign of terror. With the intense anger of one who had once believed, Stone would not let Khrushchev's present regime off the hook. The meager changes since Stalin's death were in no way commensurate with the evils Khrushchev had exposed, and he lacked a "clean break with the Stalinist past." Khrushchev had to do more than "hang Stalin in effigy, or defame him in self-serving panic."

Stone added what would be his rallying cry for the rest of his life against the arms race and saber-rattling solutions for dealing with Russia. The United States should "strive to keep the windows open" in the "interests of peace." Yet he warned against "forgiving and forgetting" either Stalinism or what his successors were doing.

The onetime radical who had said there was nothing wrong with Communist Party members controlling Wallace's Progressive Party, who had believed in a popular front and still believed that socialism would triumph in forms other than distorted Communism, fired a final salvo at American Communists. He sounded more like ADA liberals who were accused of dividing the left. In a "fight for a better world and a better society," nothing would be gained "by joining hands with the poor deluded house-broken Communist parties of the West. They will jump back through the hoops as soon as they get new orders." Never for censorship, Stone nonetheless called upon the Communist Party to disband for the good of its members and all others on the left.

While Stone's castigations inflamed some readers, one of America's most powerful men eagerly read every line. Like a porn reader who wanted mail delivered in a plain brown wrapper, J. Edgar Hoover had his secret subscriptions to the weekly for years. Now he demanded a deep-cover search to obtain one thousand copies. In a June 15, 1956, internal memo one agent crowed that Stone, a "nasty" critic of the FBI, "has definitely been a tool of communism in one form or the other. . . . In the light of this, it is particularly significant that he has just recently apparently done a complete flip-flop." Stone "lashes out bitterly at Nikita Khrushchev and other present leaders. . . . Agents . . . are badly in need of articles of this kind. . . . Discreetly" securing "many copies" was needed in order to distribute them to agents.

Hoover delightedly cleared such efforts: "Stone has delivered a scathing denunciation of Soviet Russia. . . . Therefore, the Bureau is interested in securing a large quantity. You are requested to very discreetly and appropriately explore the possibilities of securing one thousand copies. . . . It will have to be done in such a way so that the Bureau cannot be identified." The memo requested "expeditious attention." The New York Field Office reported eleven days later that it had struck out. New York considered some technique by which to order them direct from I. F. Stone; however, no logical cover came to mind. It was suggested that Washington take on this task. Two weeks later the Washington Field Office reported that it couldn't even make contact with Stone's office. They desperately contemplated approaching Stone directly on some pretext, but Stone never answered his phone and it was too indiscreet to try his home. Officers trudged to the newsstand at Fourteenth Street and New York Avenue known to sell Stone's paper. "Without disclosing his identity" the FBI sleuth asked the newsstand owner to find out how many copies of the issue remained. He had been warned, "Under no circumstances should either the operator of the newsstand or the printer be given any indication that the Bureau is trying to locate additional copies of the captioned publication." Hoover didn't want to even think of the ridicule Stone would heap on him if he knew. After three months the trail ended. Whether they were successful in finding copies does not appear in released files. Even in the dark ages of 1956, it seems that a mimeograph machine or even a reprinting by the FBI would have served their purpose.*

In March of 1953, Stone had attempted to explain Stalin's slavish following, which was "deeply rooted in Russia's character. . . . This is a movement with a philosophy comparable to the great religions in its capacity to evoke devotion. . . . It has proved itself capable of industrializing Russia and opening new vistas to its masses." This was Communism's appeal to Asian and other poor countries and only through "peaceful competition" could the West succeed. "The surest way to wreck what remains of capitalism and intellectual freedom in the non-Communist world . . . is blindly to go on refusing to recognize" both the presence of Russia and Communism's appeal and to coexist "on the same planet." Saber-rattling Cold Warriors needed such sober warnings, but Stone was off the mark in his prior refusal to castigate USSR realities.

Russia's czarist antecedents had indeed conditioned its people by enacting horrific subjugation and slaughter. And both Stalin and Hitler borrowed the concept of modern concentration camps from imperialist regimes: Spain had set them up as instruments of torture and abuse against insurgents in colonial Cuba. British and German colonists used them during the Boer War. King Leopold II of Belgium slaughtered millions of slave workers in the Congo. Nor can Americans forget history's stains, the enslavement and gross subjugation of blacks, the slaughter and herding of Native Americans onto reservations, the internment of Japanese-Americans.

While colonialist brutalities paved the way, this does not mitigate— nor should it have prevented Stone from harshly criticizing—mid-twentieth-century Russia. Despite its closed society, some observers had by then unearthed information on the gulag, just as Stone had done so

---

*Meanwhile, right-wing pundits were congratulating Stone. In the September 22, 1956, edition of the *National Review*, William F. Buckley called Stone an "undeviating fellow traveler since 'way back when' [who] . . . has written so critically since his recent trip to Poland that the *Daily Worker* regards him as outside the fold. . . . If this is it, 'National Review' welcomes him upon his escape to freedom."

brilliantly with Nazi Germany. Yet Stone argued that "official propaganda" by the United States "has built a distorted picture of Russia. Many Americans fed constantly on the notion that the Soviet Union is a vast slave labor camp must have wondered why the masses did not rise now that the oppressor had vanished." A month later, a chastened Stone wrote about the revelations of the Doctors' Plot.

As Anne Applebaum recounts in her indictment of Stalin's gulag, there were initial differences from Hitler's camps, planned for mass extermination. At first, Stalin's objective was to fuel his industrial revolution with slave labor until the victims dropped from disease, starvation, and abuse. Then, at the very time Stalin was promoting the popular front, "the Soviet camps became the notorious mass murder camps," transformed from "indifferently managed prisons in which people died by accident."

Generations of Americans reacted less viscerally to the gulag than to Nazi death camps. For one reason, the diffuse "enemies of the people"—which included Stalin's close colleagues and relatives—were not systematically targeted as were the Jews sent to Hitler's ghastly, efficient, and unique gas chambers and massive ovens. At times, gulag prisoners were released, to fight in the war or when the camps became intolerably crowded. And while the numbers of those who perished in the Soviet Union were higher, it was over decades and less dramatically revealed. No cameras exposed the gulag as they did the German concentration camps.

Another reason for reluctance to equate them, even today, argues Applebaum, is the abiding memory of World War II as the last "good" war. "No one wants to admit that we defeated one mass murderer with the help of another," wrote Applebaum in 2003, or "how well that mass murderer got along with Western statesmen." Or, as Stone wrote, how could people forget that Stalin had saved American lives? Wartime newsreel depictions of a strong, gentle people and their Uncle Joe leader gave no hint of such barbarity.

Stone's private loathing for Stalin came well before his public anti-Stalin stance. "Around the house, he never had a good word to say about Stalin," recalled son Christopher. "He would not go public with misgivings, but way before he went to Russia, he had read Bertrand Russell. We had in the bookcases the record of the purge trials, and he had shown that to me as just a terrible atrocity of justice—'a lot of crap.' " Said Christopher, "I hate to speak for him but I think he felt there were enough critics already and there was no need to add anything. If there was one shattering experience about which everything coalesced, it seems to me it was meeting somebody in Russia who spoke Yiddish and agreed to take Dad to his house. When Dad met him at an appointed place, the guy said, 'I can't speak.' And across the street there were two KGB agents. At that point, realizing it was a complete police state, I think he was confronted with what he had read and had intellectually known."

Chris recalled, "I was at Harvard, a very conservative college then, and one of three public boys on the lacrosse team. One of the few times Dad ever came to see me play was that year. He was still in the full flush of that trip, and I was quite relieved at what he now felt—my teammates were concerned about his being a radical."

After 1956, Stone vociferously criticized Russian Communism for the rest of his life, losing some old left friends. He supported Russian dissidents, refuseniks, and famous critics like Sakharov and was a friend of such notable anticommunists as the Nobel Prize–winning poet Czeslaw Milosz, who had defected from Poland.

One of Stone's longtime friends in the battle for individual and civil rights, lawyer Joe Rauh, was firmly anticommunist and helped found the ADA in 1947. As he reminisced about important passages of twentieth-century history he shared with Stone, Rauh felt that Stone's final disillusionment with Russian Communism contributed to his success with the *Weekly.*

"I've always thought there were two reasons for Izzy's significance. One, the press was so bad on the great liberal issues that there was a great market for absolute independence. Second, he had this absolute independence precisely because he had gotten burned a little bit by *dependence.*" Rauh recounted the shock when his wife told him she had heard Stone on a TV show in 1988, the year before he died, saying that he had never been a Communist, "but I was a fellow traveler." Remembering the way people had been treated for such admissions, Rauh said to his wife, "Ollie, you must have misheard him! I don't think we should go around repeating it until I can ask Izzy."

Says Rauh, "So I was having tea with Izzy and I asked him, 'Did you say that?' and he said, 'Yes, I said that.' So part of his great independence during the *Weekly* is that he had come to terms with himself, that being a fellow traveler of anything was wrong, and that independence was the most important thing you can have in this world. I think he had brought himself to peace. It explains a great deal of the later independence. More than any other person in the press, he was emancipated."

Rauh laughed. "But I was surprised when he confirmed it. He didn't elaborate, and I sure wasn't going to elaborate." Stung by the repetitious grilling of "Are you now or have you ever been . . . ?" of McCarthyism's investigators, "with my generation, you just didn't ask people what they had done in the past," Rauh explained.

As for the criticism that Stone waited far longer than most, "Well, let me be devil's advocate for Izzy's sake," said Rauh. "With Izzy, Communism was an ally in fighting fascism. Also there could have been personal feelings of loyalty. These were his old friends." Rauh had his own disenchantment with some ADA members, "but I would never say that publicly. I wouldn't hurt these people that I worked with."

Still, Stone felt free to be a "critic of everybody, including me," said Rauh, laughing. During the witch hunts "the question of 'anonymous informers' was huge. I was arguing the right to face one's accusers, as was Izzy, and we were losing that issue left and right." In one Supreme Court case, Rauh wanted to make a "little exception" to an amicus brief for particularly difficult cases. "So we wrote in this exception and Izzy took me to task. Looking back, I am not sorry he did. There was just so much pressure from the other side; having a little pressure to hold you up straight wasn't bad. I did not think that column was unfair, but I tell you, Izzy had an ax when he got at that typewriter."

An old joke goes like this: A corrupt politician asked a candidate what he could do for him. The response was "Endorse my opponent." There was nothing better for Rauh's reputation than a knock by Stone. "Everyone else was saying I was a wild man. The greatest thing was getting criticized there, in the *Weekly!*"

The fights between the anticommunist liberal wing and other leftists dissipated energy needed in the long battle against McCarthyism, but Rauh and Stone had great respect for one another. Rauh never backed down from defending the unpopular in court, and Stone never backed down from defending them in print. Rauh's defense of Arthur Miller during HUAC hearings caused Miller to comment, "Joe thinks that the world starts and ends with the Bill of Rights." Says Rauh, "Well, Arthur's right." That is why he could both assail the Communist Party but defend the right of due process for members and accused Communists. Rauh recognized that many members adhered not to Russia but to the goals of socialism and racial equality espoused by the party. "Good God, I admire that. And McCarthy was making a vicious campaign against all on the left."

For Stone, there was no waffling or hesitation; one's political beliefs were protected by the First Amendment, period. In 1957, Stone cheered the "liberal court of Earl Warren.... June 17, 1957, will go down in the history books as the day on which the Supreme Court irreparably crippled the HUAC," which was designed as a "kind of roving grand jury acting not in traditional secrecy but in the full blaze of publicity to punish by defamation those radicals who could not be reached by criminal prosecution." The Supreme Court said that Congress "is not a law enforcement or trial agency." The decision "stresses heavily protection of academic freedom as well as political liberty from such inquisitions." It "came as close" as "probably feasible" to "declare ideological inquisition by Congress unconstitutional under the First Amendment." Hoped Stone, a few more cases and "the HUAC as we have known it for painful decades is out of business" and its state imitations would follow. Stone chortled that "who could have foreseen" that Eisenhower, the first Republican elected since 1928, "would give us a court like this one?" Members of Congress who had attacked New Deal Democrats, Stone twitted, had "investigated the wrong party." Right-wing Republicans had readied their "Impeach Earl Warren" signs.

By the end of 1956, Stone would summon up only harsh judgment of Russian Communism. On November 4, two hundred thousand Soviet troops and hundreds of tanks rolled into Budapest, mowing down thousands in a five-day battle that crushed the largest armed Eastern-bloc uprising. The radio appeal of freedom fighters was heartbreaking: "Civilized people of the world, we implore you.... Our ship is sinking. The shadows grow darker every hour over the soil of Hungary. Listen to our cry . . . and act."

"For those of us who have all our lives regarded socialism as our ideal, it is humbling to see that the leading role in the convulsions sweeping Eastern Europe is being taken by the working class," Stone admitted. "The same groups who had fought for 19th century socialism—'the workers, the idealist students, the intellectuals with a conscience'—were the very elements now fighting the ills of 20th century Marxist-Leninism in Poland and Hungary." Stone had come late to this understanding, but he bore down hard, predicting that the uprising in Hungary would play out across Europe as Eastern-bloc satellites rebelled against "the Russians and their stooges." The 1848 revolution in Paris had set off a chain reaction across Europe "against that hated combination of secret policeman and priest which was symbolized in the Holy Alliance and Metternich." Now, a hundred years later, rebellion was against a decayed "socialist bureaucracy" that "could also oppress and exploit." Those who had once led the oppressed had become modern monarchs, determining that "*they* should have the Cadillacs, the *dachas,* the more spacious apartments, the fine linens and the servants." Once again, it was Stone's actual observations that had swayed him: "Those of us who have been in Eastern Europe" have "caught that aroma of ruling class complacency which the party apparatus exudes."

Stone's optimism surfaced again: "It was a joy to see in this new revolution far off upon the Danube the rebirth of our own Jeffersonianism." The workers were demanding "the right to establish a labor press, free from control by the government." Bullets pockmarking Budapest's buildings are lasting reminders of an uprising soon crushed. The survival spirit that had kept a handful of Jews alive when Eichmann was in charge of extermination there continued on in Hungary's freedom fighters, but they received little help from Western leaders who had talked so big about battling Russia. "Faced at last with the possibility of that 'liberation' they so long preached, Mr. Dulles and his friends in Western Germany are soft-pedaling the anti-Communist revolution" which was a "signal to Moscow that it can crush the new revolution without fear of our intervention."

As the Hungarian rebellion lay in ruins, Stone noted that "in devastated Budapest, the general strike was in its second month; ninety thousand Hungarians had fled. A new war seemed to be brewing in the Middle East. . . . Europe was running out of gas, and England and France were swept by anti-American feeling. But it was quiet here in Washington." Ambassadors desperately seeking guidance found none. "The sign on the doorknob read plainly, 'do not disturb.' The leadership of 'the free world' was resting. Such silence signals to Moscow that we have adopted a complete hands-off policy toward Eastern Europe, perhaps in the hope that the Russians will thus be more ready to keep hands off the Middle East, where our material interests lie."

While Stone was never for imperialist preemptive strikes, he was among those who had "complained that the United States missed a chance to help Eastern Europe by challenging the Russians to withdraw their armies if we withdrew ours from Western Europe." Now he knew that "American policy is satisfied to have Europe divided into two zones. To revise these plans because Budapest rose against the Russians may seem sentimental nonsense to the Pentagon."

* * *

The watershed year of 1956 produced another personal confession, titled "The Mote in Mine Own Eye": "Since every man is a microcosm, in whose heart may be read all that sends armies marching, I must admit I am no better. Because so many bonds attach me to Israel, I am ready to condone preventive war; I rejoiced when my side won. Though I preach international understanding and support for the UN, I found all the excuses for Israel that warring nationalisms always find to excuse breaches of peace. . . . Israel's survival seemed worth the risk of peace. And this is how it always is and how it starts, and I offer the mote in my own eye."

"What the Russians are doing in Budapest is so dreadful that even the Indian, Icelandic and American Communist parties protest," wrote Stone. "Moscow is ready to do anything in order to keep in its 'zone of security' governments politically satisfactory to it." Stone then assailed actions that protect "what the United States considers zones of security." He despised the administration's boast "of the quick way we toppled the Arbenz government in Guatemala [through CIA action] and how we honor brave fighters for freedom—until they shoot down *our* tyrant friends in Nicaragua."

Although recognizing pitfalls in dealing with Russia, Stone argued that seeking accords on nuclear deterrents was the only way to save the world. Now that nuclear hawks had won the race to create H-bombs, "a new war may ruin the earth." Such dire threats are forgotten "when going to war seems a matter of life and death for 'one's own' . . . perhaps it will take a new menace from outside the planet to make men feel at last that all who inhabit it are their own." Stone's last line held a strong measure of self criticism: "But beware of these fine phrases. I, too, like the rest of them (and maybe even you), am a hypocrite."

Not one for dwelling on mistakes, Stone moved forward to fight witch hunt harassment, the arms race, a president who did nothing to quiet Dulles's threats against Communist China. Despite worldwide concerns, Stone next turned long years of attention to domestic violence and death in the battle for justice. Along the way, a young generation of freedom riders and marchers would discover the voice of I. F. Stone.

22

A Bloody Revolution at Home

Ours is the world's oldest and most successful experiment in
Apartheid.

—I. F. Stone, August 18, 1966

Stone was standing there on that momentous Monday in May 1954
when the ruling came down. Instead of the normal process where
opinions were handed out in the pressroom, reporters were shep-
herded into the court chamber. Stone stood in the crowded, tense, marble hall at the reading aloud of the opinion in *Brown et al. v. Board of
Education:* "Does segregation of children in public schools solely on the
basis of race, even though . . . other . . . factors may be equal, deprive the
children of the minority group of equal educational opportunities?"
Stone held his breath and leaned forward and heard the chief justice
reply, "We believe that it does."

"It was all one could do to keep from cheering," recounted Stone,
"and a few of us were moved to tears." Outside the Supreme Court,
Stone witnessed a unique moment in history. NAACP lawyers hugged
and shouted in victory. Stone choked at the sight of grown men acting
like jubilant children. Striking down segregation in schools could only
mean the eventual end of such daily indignities as "white only" bus seats;
sixty-year-old black men being called "boy" or "nigger" by white men
half their age; restaurants and pools and restrooms and libraries and
houses and front-office jobs where blacks could not trespass. Someday it
might stop more violent forms of racism—beatings, shootings, lynchings, burnings—but Stone knew that "Jim Crow will not be ended
overnight." The South proceeded with "all deliberate speed" at the rate of
a child given a choice of going to the dentist. Having observed Southern
racist Democrats in Congress for years, Stone accurately wrote that there
is "little prospect" that the Democratic Party would stay together on in-

tegration, federal aid to education, black entitlement in major industrial unions, and other struggles to come. Southern Democratic congressional racists would fight hard against "mongrelization" of the races, and Democratic Southern leaders felt free to yell out to cheering audiences that the name of the nonviolent civil rights minister was "Martin Luther Coon." The effect of the ruling depended on whether there was a prolonged outburst of bitterness in the South.

And inhumane bitterness seemed unceasing. Cross burnings, lynchings, beatings, castrations, bombings, and assassinations followed this federal step toward integration. A year later, in the summer of 1955, a fourteen-year-old boy from Chicago went to visit relatives in a Mississippi collection of shacks incongruously named Money. The centerpiece of this young boy's crime was that he either looked at, whistled at, or said something to the wife of the owner of a run-down store where he bought some candy one stifling day. Caroline Bryant was white and Emmett Till was black. Deep in the night, the store owner, Roy Bryant, and his brother-in-law, J. W. Milam, rushed into the cabin of Mose Wright, Emmett's uncle, dragged the boy out, and threw him into their car. Three days later, Till's body, tied to a cotton-gin fan, floated to the surface of a river. Before he was shot, Till had been so severely beaten that his head was caved in and one eye gouged out. When Till's mutilated body was shipped back to Chicago, his mother, Mamie Bradley, insisted that the casket remain open at his funeral, so that "all the world" could see "what they did to my son." Seventy thousand filed passed Emmett's body. The nation was horrified at the battered body pictured mostly in black magazines. In death, a fourteen-year-old boy galvanized Northern blacks and their supporters like nothing before. As his mother said, "When something happened to the Negroes in the South, I said, 'That's their business, not mine.' Now I know how wrong I was."

Northern condemnation of the "sickness in the South," as I. F. Stone named it, created resentful backlash. Even some Mississippians who had been appalled at Till's brutal murder closed ranks; five prominent lawyers stepped forward to defend Milam and Bryant. In those days it was unthinkable that a black would publicly accuse a white man of any crime in Mississippi. But Emmett's elderly uncle identified the two men. "We salute his courage," wrote Stone. Other blacks followed and were whisked out of the state for protection after testifying. Their words mattered not. Defense attorney John C. Whitten argued for fighting "outside agitators," always an effective ploy. He told the all-white jury (in a part of

Mississippi that was two-thirds black), "Your fathers will turn over in their graves if [Milam and Bryant are found guilty], and I'm sure that every last Anglo-Saxon one of you has the courage to free these men in the face of that [outside] pressure." The jury found their white brethren not guilty on September 23, 1955. It was the 166th anniversary of the signing of the Bill of Rights.

Stone assailed the jury and this "maniacal murder. Those who killed him were sick men, sick with race hatred. The murder and the trial could only have happened in a sick countryside. . . . Where else would the defense dare to put forward the idea that the murder was somehow 'framed' by the NAACP? Where else would newspapers somehow make it appear that those at fault were not the men who killed the boy but those who tried to bring the killers to justice?" Sharing a Northerner's superiority—that the sickness of race hatred belonged to the South—Stone feared "there may some day spring from its crimes an evil as immense as the crematoria of Hitlerism." But he also chastised the muffled and weak "northern white press" and "basically all of us whites, North and South, [who] acquiesce in white supremacy, and benefit from the pool of cheap labor created by it."

It was time for the blacks to mass against "this latest outrage." Stone prophetically called for a massive march on Washington. "The American Negro needs a Gandhi to lead him, and we need the American Negro to lead us." Calling for a massive peaceful protest, Stone remembered the struggles for integration in the thirties and forties; the defenders of the Scottsboro boys; the Henry Wallace Progressives. With special empathy, the predominantly Jewish activists transferred their knowledge of pogroms, purges, and discrimination to the black cause. But McCarthyism had made them cautious. White activists, "hounded out of public life and into inactivity," no longer joined blacks in Harlem, Baltimore, Chicago, and Detroit. Eight years after Stone's 1955 astounding insight, an American black Gandhi did emerge and all the world heard Martin Luther King's "I have a dream" speech. Looking down from the top of the Lincoln Memorial, the only square inch not occupied by singing, swaying people was the Reflecting Pool, and some stood knee-deep in that pond. Anyone who saw that peaceful gathering of blacks and whites was transported by buoyant optimism. Stone "suddenly [felt] no longer alone in this hot-house capital" because "out in the country people did care." Stone complained that militant blacks had curbed their speeches and King was "a little too saccharine for my taste," but he was stirred by the poor and gnarled elderly blacks singing "We Shall Not Be Moved." He thrilled to see the "unquenchables," "the old-time radicals," out in full force and "no longer lonely relics."

But after that glorious 1963 moment, the defiant crawl toward integration was marked by more bombings, maimings and murders, lynchings and castrations, burning cities and burning crosses, sit-ins and mob violence. Bombs blew up black church after black church. People around the world were shocked at newsreel photos of police dogs set upon terrified marchers; fire hoses spraying water at great strength, strong enough to knock teenagers to the ground and flatten them against walls; grinning whites pouring ketchup and sugar on the heads of blacks and whites at lunch-counter sit-ins.

Twenty-two years before King's march on Washington, Stone conducted his own little march on the National Press Club in 1941. He and his companion, the dean of the Howard Law School, who later became a judge, were served "not even a glass of water." Stone knew "few places outside the [nation's] Negro ghetto which will feed a colored man." However, except for a "few glares from some mossbacks," Stone thought the club would be above the city's stifling segregation. Stone and William H. Hastie, who was later appointed by Truman as governor of the Virgin Islands, had gotten as far as a table by the window when a waiter whispered to Stone that he was wanted on the phone. Instead, the manager, in person, was outside the door.

"Is that a colored man with you?" he asked Stone. When Stone "confessed that it was," the reporter was told that he would not be served. Stone heatedly said that as a member he insisted on service for his guest, turned around, and returned to the table. More than an hour passed with no waiter approaching. Finally the two left.

Stone tried to make a formal protest but could not get the twenty-five signatures needed to call a special meeting. "Only ten of my fellow newspapermen were willing to sign. I resigned from the club." He never let this so-called bastion of freethinkers forget it. He wrote a column in 1948 stingingly entitled "Mein Kampf with the (Lily-White) National Press Club." Seven years after his luncheon fracas, Stone was still taunting the club to desegregate: "How many Washington correspondents are willing to lift the National Press Club color bar as their contribution to the fight against Jim Crowism in the nation's capital? All the fellows here write plenty about democracy. Will they demonstrate by this simple gesture that they believe in it? I now belong to the Capital Press Club, the Negro press club. Why not signalize a change in the rules by inviting us darkies to lunch?" Stone's actions upset one member of his household, their longtime black maid, who thought he was borrowing trouble.

The siege between the National Press Club and Stone did not end for decades. A former board member, Frank Holeman, declined to attend a luncheon featuring Stone in 1988 "because I feel the event implies criticism" of earlier actions "which is not justified by the facts. . . . Mr. Stone was not expelled . . . or 'kicked out' as he has repeatedly claimed." Stone "voluntarily resigned . . . after his black guest was refused service." In a memo to the club, Holeman proudly noted that a black journalist, Louis R. Lautier, was admitted in 1955—but not before opponents threatened to sue for fear that the presence of a black member could "result in foreclosure of the multimillion dollar mortgage on the Press Building, the Club's main physical asset." Board member Holeman was magnanimous; he "personally" greeted Lautier "and showed him all the rooms."

After blacks were admitted, Stone reapplied for membership in 1956. He was blackballed. One might wonder why Stone even bothered; the club held a sizable share of the silly and stuffy, the hacks and flaks. But the club's cachet was elevated by its international luncheon speakers who were passing through the nation's capital. Women reporters had to eat brown bag lunches in the balcony into the seventies, until they were admitted to membership.

In 1972, Stone was approached by some of the young Turks (White House correspondent Helen Thomas had just become a member). Said syndicated columnist Warren Rogers, "We were anxious to have Izzy. The club was going to hell in a handbasket. We were reformers and thought it would be great symbolism. By then he was *major*—and a rock thrower, and that's what it's all about, or should be."

Rogers "danced attendance and asked Izzy if he would join the club. He bit my head off, which was not unusual. Izzy said, 'No. You're all a bunch of narrow-minded bigots.' He softened it a bit by saying, 'You're not as bad as the rest—but you're in there too.'" Rogers did not know at the time of Stone's club history, but it was no excuse for his behavior. "I still admired him for his work, but I found him very annoying, arrogant, and contemptuous of the rest of us."

Long after Stone reached icon status, his first National Press Club honor came in 1981, at age seventy-three. Forty years after he had resigned on principle, a younger generation of members gave him a standing ovation. (Earlier, Stone had refused to speak at an awards lunch given by the club that had once blackballed him.) In 1981, Stone retaliated by inviting noted leftists to his head table. He trashed mainstream editorials, saying he refused to "regurgitate the same drivel as everyone else." He indicted Reagan's policies and accurately predicted that Reagan's programs would produce huge deficits and only helped "the rich and the well-to-do" at the expense of "the little guy who can't even afford a cup of coffee." For dessert, Stone called the *New York Times*'s coverage of the Reagan administration "collaborationist."

Despite admiration for his work, Stone's lack of fraternal warmth resulted in few press corps friendships. In contrast, Rogers mentioned Pete Lisagor, a universally revered reporter who set a fine example of journalistic excellence, but was also one of the gang. "There was a difference in what they did. Pete was an *in*former. Izzy was a *re*former."

As his own publisher, Stone exercised his right to opinionated pamphleteering in the spirit of Tom Paine. His polemics were seeded with fact; reading Stone was like listening to a good debater argue his side. His fans often said that they would read the *New York Times* on an issue, then read Stone, and recognize that Stone was providing more relevant insights. His crusade for civil rights was constant and passionate, unlike the efforts of many white colleagues and mainstream newspapers who either were late to cover the movement or editorialized that civil disobedience merely stirred up trouble.

Lippmann and Arthur Krock wore as badges of honor their membership in the Cosmos Club, which had unspoken quotas regarding Jews and denied membership at that time to blacks and women. Lippmann even supported the Southern filibuster against a federal antilynching law in 1938. He hailed the *Brown* decision and applauded Eisenhower's use of federal troops to desegregate schools during the Little Rock battle of 1957, but looked to Southern liberals to "solve the race problem amicably." He did not see the urgency of the problem until blood ran in the streets.

Lippmann's personal involvement in the sixties was to second the nomination of journalist Carl Rowan for the Cosmos Club. Rowan was a tennis-playing buddy of many reporters and politicians, a "one-of-us" establishment black. There is no greater comparison between Lippmann and Stone than Stone's dismissive comment about Rowan. After Malcolm X was gunned down in 1965 by rivals in the Black Muslim movement, Stone wrote a long essay in the *New York Review of Books* on

Malcolm X's *Autobiography* (written with Alex Haley). Stone sympathetically defined Malcolm X and delved into the reasons for the fiery road he took ("If they make the Klan nonviolent," Malcolm X often said, "I'll be nonviolent"). Stone touched on Malcolm X's emerging sense of unification with whites, for which he was murdered. "In Africa and in America there was almost unanimous recognition that the Negro race had lost a gifted son," wrote Stone. "Only the then head of the U.S. Information Agency, Carl Rowan, immortalized himself with a monumental Uncle Tomism: 'All this about an ex-convict, ex-dope-peddler who became a racial fanatic,' was Rowan's obtuse and ugly comment."

Nonviolent attempts to cure centuries of mistreatment began the year following *Brown*. In 1955, a tired department-store seamstress and civil rights activist in Montgomery, Alabama, was too exhausted to go to the back of the bus, where the "colored only" seats waited. Rosa Parks sat in a kind of no-man's-land, halfway back, where blacks could sit if there were no whites needing seats. When the "whites only" section overflowed, the bus driver ordered Rosa Parks and other blacks in her row to move to the back, where they would have to stand. Some complied. But Rosa Parks stayed. Martin Luther King's SCLC (Southern Christian Leadership Conference) led the subsequent and famous Montgomery bus boycott. Those who had obediently sat for years in the colored-only section were no-shows. Buses went empty. Blacks were walking, even riding mules to work. Stone was exultant, but to segregationists, this defiance signaled all-out war.

By 1957 it was routine for nonviolence to be met by violence. Peaceful marchers were bloodied by mobs, undisturbed by local troopers, who sometimes nonchalantly tossed their own KKK robes in the backseats of patrol cars. President Eisenhower finally responded during the attempt to integrate a Little Rock, Arkansas, high school in 1957. After Governor Orval Faubus defiantly fought desegregation by calling out the National Guard, Eisenhower sent a thousand paratroopers from the 101st Airborne Division to guard nine frightened children passing through a jeering, spitting mob.

A furious Stone came out swinging at those who cautioned slower measures. "Amid the hand-wringing over Little Rock by the so-called Southern moderates, and the conferences in the White House to negotiate withdrawal of troops and to let Faubus save face, it is forgotten that for the Negro the law never looked more truly majestic than it does today in Little Rock where for once the bullies of the South have been put on notice. . . . The white South feels like an oppressed minority because the white North has interfered to prevent it from oppressing its Negro minority. The white South feels a victim of injustice, misunderstanding and brute force. That these are exactly what it visits on the helpless Negro who steps out of line merely illustrates the capacity of human beings to go on doing to others what they violently object to when done to themselves."

As soon as Chief Justice Warren read to a "tense and crowded courtroom" the order that integration proceed in Little Rock that fall, Stone headed South, caustically calling his trip "A Piece of Foreign Correspondence." Reading the *Nashville Banner,* Stone saw an editorial cartoon that was a far cry from the fiery creations of the *Washington Post*'s Herblock. "Education Be Hanged!" said the caption, with a grotesque caricature of Chief Justice Warren. In a Little Rock paper Stone read segregationist leader the Reverend Wesley Pruden: "The South will not accept this outrage, which a Communist-dominated government is trying to lay on us."

Stone found whites everywhere extolling their good relationships with blacks, some recounting how their ancestors wanted to free the slaves but the slaves "begged" them not to. "I began almost to believe that in the slaveholding south no one was a slaveholder by choice but only out of devotion to the welfare of their wards," Stone remarked. The hotel elevator operator wore the look of "simulated imbecility Negroes often wear like a protective cloak in the South." After an evening with "tortured southern liberals," one felt that Tennessee Williams had merely taken notes, Stone commented. "They feel themselves a natural elite gone to seed," appalled by the racism of others but not willing to speak out; after the bourbon flows "they begin to say 'niggers' and 'coons.' . . . One feels that the Negro doesn't just live in the South, he haunts it."

Since the media were covering the Little Rock story "almost entirely from the white side," Stone pivoted from an upscale white club to the dingy quarters of Little Rock's Harlem, where a young man refused to talk, saying "white man takes what you say and uses it against you." At a black college, no one would speak and scarcely looked at the reporter. "The silence as it piled up seemed more eloquent than anything which might have been said." Attitudes in the neighborhood of a prosperous black doctor were different. In fact, 20 percent of his patients were white. There were no definitive racial patterns, but the doctor's wife noted that she was snubbed by whites and there were no restrooms or places for her to eat in department stores.

When a young black car-rental employee followed Stone into the office to map out his journey, the manager sternly said to the black, "You're getting out of your place when you come into this office." Stone explained that it was his fault as the boy stood back with a compliant expression. The manager felt no constraint in talking to a stranger: "You're going down to nigger country . . . where they raise rice and cotton and niggers."

Nor was there much restraint at the Helena country club in Delta country. "Everybody said 'nigger' as a matter of course. 'Our better class of niggers have left,' " one woman told him. Stone caught the cadence precisely when she described her relations with a black woman who lived across the backyard. "There isn't anything I wouldn't do for her or she wouldn't do for me—but of course I wouldn't think of asking her into my parlor. It would only embarrass both of us." One man said, "Sure our niggers vote," and with no hint of irony explained that the whites paid their poll taxes and "lined 'em up to vote for the liquor interests." Often Stone heard the South's mantra: integration was coming but "we need more time." They blamed Northern agitators, the au courant theme touted by Southern leaders and J. Edgar Hoover. Speaking of poor whites, one woman said, "Why, some of them are so low that niggers won't associate with them."

It must have agonized Stone to keep quiet in order to elicit such comments. He ended caustically, "All of our new friends . . . were strong supporters of Governor Faubus."

Although Stone's contempt for the South was strong, Jim Crow aspects back home were too obvious to ignore. "Few are concerned about segregation, though it begins to burn the brand of inferiority into the Negro child from the day he enters a separate school. . . . The racially lopsided . . . system in the District of Columbia schools shows how readily de-segregation may be defeated and delayed."

At the time Stone wrote this in the fifties, a young boy squirmed as he saw daily indignities toward blacks. His parents, Al and Sylvia Bernstein, were leftist union and civil rights activists. Blacks and leftists of all stripes socialized with them in the dark days of McCarthyism, among them Esther and Izzy. One day the son, Carl Bernstein, would follow Izzy

Stone and become famous along with Bob Woodward for bringing down the president of the United States with their Watergate exposés.

At age seven, however, Carl was just a boy resentful of the demonstrations to which he was dragged by activist parents. "I hated the whole enterprise," he recalled. "I went to a segregated public school; all the city's playgrounds and swimming pools were segregated; the hotels were for whites only. . . . The municipal hospital wards were segregated. . . . Thursdays and Saturdays I'd be ripped from the neighborhood, torn from the day's game of stepball or running bases." Downtown, an organizer would "pair me with a Negro child. The black children usually wore church clothes, little girls in pink and white and lace and patent leather, boys with too-long clip-on neckties . . . jackets neatly buttoned. . . . The only place downtown where Negroes knew they could sit down to eat were the railroad station and the government cafeterias; even there, my father says, the union was constantly challenging food-service managers" who tried to enforce separate seating. Few public places allowed blacks in restrooms. "When one of the black children in the sit-down"—which they were called in those summers—"had to go to the bathroom, we would go running to the National Gallery of Art, which was about five blocks away. But more often than not it would be too late . . . and the children would cry, and sometimes their mothers and even their fathers would, too." Years later, when Bernstein covered civil rights in the South, he remembered his long-ago friends "holding their legs together and the pain on their faces." A reason for hating the demonstrations was the "knowledge that my friends were going to pee in their pants. There seemed to me to be two cruelties: the indignity of segregation, and the shame our demonstrations inflicted on my friends."

Stone's *Weekly* became a conduit for protest as he published what other newspapers were ignoring, such as verbatim testimonies at congressional hearings. The 1955 Senate testimony of NAACP executive secretary Roy Wilkins was headlined "How Mississippi Whites Terrorize Negroes Who Dare Ask De-Segregation." The Klan-infested White Citizens Council had run a full-page ad of pure intimidation that included the names and addresses of every person who signed a petition in Yazoo City to end segregation. "Of the fifty-four citizens who signed," all but six asked that their names be removed from the petition. They recanted after being either fired or so threatened. A plumbing supply company refused to give materials to a plumber who had signed, and rather than sell to him, his grocer hiked the price of a loaf of bread to $1 (a monumental charge in those days). Two registered voters in Mississippi were killed by shotgun blasts in daylight. The sheriff "cynically suggested that the shotgun pellets" in one victim's "jaw and neck could have been lead fillings in his teeth," testified Wilkins.

In 1962, the Ole Miss riot greeted James Meredith's entry into that university. Stone was enraged that "not one single student at Ole Miss has had the desire or the courage to go over and shake Meredith's hand or to sit beside him in class." He faulted the Kennedy brothers for sidestepping civil rights and using "stale Cold War rhetoric." "When is Kennedy going to mention racism?"

Stone did not ignore racism in the North: "A large section of the white South is mentally sick on the subject of race; it draws support from paranoid minorities in the North who join it in seeing the Supreme Court as the seat of Communist plotters, and integration as an artificial business stirred up by Jews from New York."

In 1963, a shotgun blast killed the NAACP's Medgar Evers as he walked from his car to his front door in Mississippi. For decades his wife searched for the murderer who had shot him in the back. William Colmer, an ardent segregationist congressman (and mentor of Trent Lott, the U.S. senator who in the twenty-first century enthusiastically recalled Strom Thurmond's segregation stance), dismissed the murder at the time as "the inevitable result of agitation by politicians, do-gooders, and those who sail under the false flag of liberalism." Thirty-one years later, Byron De La Beckwith was convicted of the murder; the FBI had known he did it all along. A Klan informant told them that Beckwith had boasted, "I killed that nigger." J. Edgar Hoover sat on this vital news to hide their informant's identity.

That same year, Birmingham violence left a permanent stain on the Southern response to integration. Early one Sunday a bomb ripped through one of Birmingham's black churches. Four little girls dressed in white for Sunday school were murdered, their remains found in the rubble. Hoover was up to his old tricks of Venona days once again: he failed to give Justice Department prosecutors information on the church bombing for fear of compromising his Klan informants.

"Looking back, I believe the South began to change inexorably that day," recalled Curtis Wilkie, a Mississippian who captured the emerging conscience of his homeland and his own odyssey toward civil rights activism in his book *Dixie*. "A long period of bitter resistance lay ahead.

But the consciences of many white people were badly shaken that Sunday. . . . The murder of . . . innocent children was unacceptable." At the time, Stone did not share such an assessment and indicted senators from all parts of the country for their "lack of contrition" and concern over the 1963 bombings in a column titled "The Wasteland in the White Man's Heart." Culling through the *Congressional Record* filled with orations on every possible topic, Stone noted that "of 100 ordinarily loquacious Senators, only four felt moved to speak. Javits of New York and Kuchel of California expressed outrage." Majority Leader Mike Mansfield was joined by only one Southern senator, William Fulbright, in condemning the actions. Senators Phil Hart from Michigan and Hubert Humphrey framed a resolution that a day be set aside for national mourning. They knew it was worthless to "even introduce it" to fellow senators and sent it to the White House, where it disappeared.

"Four centuries of white supremacy have left their indelible mark on the double standard we whites instinctively apply to race relations," wrote Stone. Noting the lingering Red Scare, he said, "If four children had been killed in the bombing of a Berlin church by Communists, the country would be on the verge of war." He laced into President Kennedy and Robert Kennedy for "rejecting a Negro appeal for Federal troops." Stone reprinted a *New York Post* report of troopers beating an aged black man who didn't move fast enough, yelling to those on porches, "Get back in the house, niggers." A *Washington Post* story repeated a common refrain: said a Birmingham housewife, the killings were "terrible" but "that's what they get for trying to force their way where they're not wanted."

The "human chill" reminded Stone of Germany after the war. "I felt the empty waste land of the German heart. I feel the same way about the hearts of my fellow white men in America, where the Negro is concerned. . . . Just as many Germans feel it was somehow the fault of the Jews that they got themselves cremated, so many whites here, North and South, feel that the bombing wouldn't have happened if the Negroes weren't so pushy."

Mocking the response to the 1954 decision to desegregate with "all deliberate speed," Stone titled a 1964 box "All Deliberate Speed—or How to Get Where You Don't Want to Go in 1,000 Years." He trod the lonely researcher's path to discover in the 1964 Civil Rights Commission report that ten years later "98.8 per cent of the South's Negro children are still in segregated schools, and even that figure is deceptively low."

The government and segregationists continued to spill Red paint on those who fought for progress. From the beginning of the civil rights movement Stone attacked Hoover, whose pathological racism and hatred of King were often ignored by the white establishment media, just as "nigger news" was considered unworthy of coverage. In 1959, Stone asked, "Why is J. Edgar Hoover so venomous and suspicious about anyone who seeks to help the Negro? . . . Year after year his testimony chimes in with Southern racist attempts to picture the Negro's struggle for justice and equality as a Red Plot." In an undated notation the FBI explained that Stone was "not interviewed" by them because "subject is an outspoken exponent of civil rights." There was no telling what a man who harbored such thoughts would do. He might, as the memo stated, "seize on the incident of contact by Bureau Agents for critizism [sic] of the Bureau."

In 1960, the FBI reopened Stone's case after his criticisms of Hoover were circulated by the Emergency Civil Liberties Committee (ECLC), and Stone's speeches to civil rights and so-called front groups were covered by informants. In his speeches Stone constantly said that the challenge of the sixties was "peace." Early on he predicted riots in the streets if blacks were not given their rights and disaster in Indochina if the United States widened its involvement in Vietnam. Stone touched on "Mr. Hoover's boundless enthusiasm as a hunter of assorted Leftists and his reluctance before the war to take on Nazis and Bundists." The FBI had become an evil that "many recognize but few talk about; it is too dangerous to fight, but it grows as a cancer within our free society."

Hoover's partners in invective were Southern senators like John Stennis and James Eastland. In 1955, Stone splashed a chutzpah-laden lawsuit against Eastland across the front page of his weekly, headlined "Why the Weekly rejected that $5 from James Eastland." Stone had received a subscription request from the Red-hunting Internal Security Subcommittee with a $5 voucher signed by Chairman Eastland. This touched off Stone's long-standing hatred of the subcommittee's hounding of journalists, its attempts to link whites and blacks in a "Communist" movement, and its guilt-by-association intimidation. Stone returned the $5, rejecting the subscription on the grounds that spending public funds would violate the First Amendment because the committee would use the newsletter "for purposes of surveillance under the 'internal security' program." Stone sued Eastland and committee members, appearing in court as his own lawyer. Of course Stone knew the case would be dismissed because such committees were not subject to judicial interference. "This was not intended merely as a man-bites-(exceptionally large)-dog story" but to show that "subcommittee hearings on press 'infiltration'—such is the vocabulary of paranoid melodrama—are sufficient indication of the subcommittee's belief that it can act as a thought police over newspapers and newspapermen." It was "hardly a secret . . . that the subcommittee has been building dossiers on the press." Eastland's *Weekly* request was part of such "morbid interest." Eastland responded to the suit with a growl: "It's bunk."

Hoover's calling sit-ins "a Communist plot" could "only encourage the racial paranoia endemic in the South," said Stone. He slammed newspapers for ignoring a report on FBI "police state" practices that included widespread use of dogs to terrorize blacks. King's associate the Reverend Fred Shuttlesworth recalled a typical headline: "Negro Pastor Heads Communist Front." Said Shuttlesworth, "I'm too American black to be a commie Red!"

Coverage of the momentous St. Augustine, Florida, protests was either buried or slanted. When the judge told three teenage girls they would be released if their parents signed petitions stating that they would desist from further picketing, they begged their parents not to sign. The girls were locked up in a reformatory for fifty-two more days, "rubbing, scrubbing, shining, and buffing the floor on our knees until our knees bled." One of the male youths, who had been beaten in jail, said decades later, "All we was asking that day of America was 'bring truth to what you're saying on paper.' " In 2004, blacks and whites sat together at a panel on Florida's civil rights movement. A white prosecutor, Dan Warren, said St. Augustine "opened my eyes at just how debased a society can become." White newspapermen apologized for their weak or nonexistence coverage of forty years before.

Stone's heroes in those long, hot summers were the "handful of young Negroes in their teens and twenties" who Norman Thomas called "secular saints." Said Stone, "They and a few white sympathizers as youthful and devoted . . . have begun a social revolution in the South with their sit-ins and their Freedom Rides. Never has a tinier minority done more for the liberation of a whole people than these few youngsters of C.O.R.E. (Congress of Racial Equality) and S.N.C.C. (Student Non-Violent Coordinating Committee)."

Three of them became martyrs of the 1964 Mississippi Freedom Summer voting rights movement. New Yorker Andrew Goodman, twenty, was paired with James Chaney, the twenty-one-year-old son of a Meridian, Mississippi, domestic. With them one night in a car was Michael Schwerner, who came from New York and was hated by Klan members for his activism as a CORE field organizer. The first white civil rights worker to be permanently based outside of the Mississippi capital, Schwerner had dodged death threats, hate mail, and police harassment for six months. The imperial wizard of the White Knights of the Ku Klux Klan, Sam Bowers, ordered Schwerner's "elimination." In his CORE application Schwerner had written that he hoped to spend the rest of his life working for an integrated society. Through informants the FBI found the bodies of the three murdered men months later.

For years Stone had written about how police brutality, especially toward blacks, was condoned. In the case of Schwerner, Chaney, and Goodman, complicity was gruesomely abundant. For no reason the three were arrested by Neshoba County deputy sheriff Cecil Price. Then Price, with official police approval, conspired with Klan buddies to release them from jail in the dark of night. The trio's station wagon was halted on a rural road by the waiting mob. The young men were beaten and shot and their bodies buried in a makeshift grave. An unhappy Klansman watched as the two white civil rights workers were killed, then complained as he shot Chaney, "Y'all didn't leave me anything but a nigger."

The state showed little interest in prosecuting the murders, but national publicity forced federal action. The strongest charge that could be brought in federal court was violating the civil rights of the murdered men. The killers grinned and laughed at the few "nigger" reporters at the trial. Some of the Klansmen were convicted, others were not.

As sickened as Stone was by these murders, he was especially tough attacking the sexual darkness that inflamed race actions. A white Detroit housewife and NAACP member, Viola Liuzzo, participated in the 1965 Selma to Montgomery March when Dr. King led twenty-five thousand people to the Alabama state capital and handed a petition to Governor George Wallace demanding voting rights for African-Americans. After the demonstration, Liuzzo volunteered to help drive marchers back to Montgomery Airport.

As four Klansmen idled their car next to hers, Liuzzo was instantly killed with two shots to the head. The South's obsession with "racial purity" fostered "that sexual sickness which made the killers feel they were carrying out a sacred duty to the white race," wrote Stone, then italicized, *"Mrs. Liuzzo was executed in her car because there was a Negro on the front seat with her;* this is the truth about the murder people shy away from." In an attempt to prejudice the case, rumors circulated that Viola was a Communist Party member and had abandoned her five children to have sexual relationships with blacks in the civil rights movement. It was later discovered that these rumors had come from the FBI.

An Alabama jury acquitted the Klansmen. By focusing on the Klan in the murder of Liuzzo, the "respectables" were laying off their guilt on redneck elements, said Stone. Along with this "regional sickness is a national sickness—that when anything goes wrong it must be due to communists." He accused President Johnson of "vulgar opportunism" when he pushed for an investigation by HUAC—"a discredited bunch of witch hunting old dodoes" that Stone nicknamed The Unamericans. He bitingly remarked, "Is study required to realize that organizations which preach hatred of Negroes, Jews and Catholics . . . are profoundly disruptive in a nation like ours?" He attacked Robert Novak, who forty years ago was "leaking 'red' smears" against CORE and SNCC.

Not all of Stone's heroes were young. In a *Weekly* box titled "I Could Hear People Screaming," Stone recounted the testimony of sharecropper Fannie Lou Hamer, who was beaten senseless in jail and became one of the famed black women of the movement. She electrified audiences with phrases such as "I'm sick and tired of being sick and tired" and "Mississippi Negroes are excluded from everything except hanging." Hamer survived polio and picking cotton from age six but suffered lifetime injuries from her jail beating. Hamer was fired from her job of eighteen years for trying to register blacks, but her stark testimony of hate was placed in the *Congressional Record.* Stone's readers relived it in his June 22, 1964, newsletter. In 1962, Hamer was fired upon sixteen times in the home where she stopped during her twenty-six-mile trek to the courthouse to try to register voters. She and other Freedom Riders were arrested after some walked into the "white only" side of a bus station. In jail, "I could hear people screaming." Hamer was placed in a cell with two black prisoners, and a policeman ordered them to beat Hamer with a "long blackjack that was loaded with something. . . . I was beat until I was exhausted. . . . I couldn't get up when they told me to. . . . My kidney was injured from the blows." She nearly lost the sight in one eye. SNCC lawyers filed suit against the police, who, to no one's surprise, were found not guilty.

At the 1964 Democratic National Convention in Atlantic City, Stone cheered Hamer and others in the Mississippi Freedom Party, who challenged the all-white Mississippi delegation. Hamer's shouts rang out: "Is this America, the land of the free and the home of the brave, where we are threatened daily because we want to live as decent human beings?" A compromise was made; two seats were given to the challengers, and the Democratic Party promised it would never again seat an all-white party. Dixiecrat segregationists bolted the convention and then the party.

Finally, that summer, Stone had reason to rejoice. When the Civil Rights Bill of 1964 was passed, Stone said, "The first comprehensive Federal civil rights legislation since the days of Reconstruction marks the arrival of the Negro as a major force in American politics." He bannered the story and praised Lyndon Johnson, the Texan who "made his debut in the Senate 15 years ago" opposing all federal civil rights legislation, even that "against lynching." Despite weakening amendments that created loopholes for both the North and the South, "The bill as passed under Johnson is better than the bill originally proposed by Kennedy. . . . Johnson's enormous gifts as a persuader and wheeler-dealer made themselves felt. . . . He was the No. 1 lobbyist for civil rights."

Two issues that obsessed Stone for decades converged in 1967 when a famous black man said he would not fight in Vietnam and a famous preacher stood up for him. Cassius Clay beat Sonny Liston and became the world's heavyweight champ in 1964. Clay announced that as a Black Muslim he was discarding his slave name; the charismatic, internationally known boxer demanded that he be called Muhammad Ali. The mostly white sports press corps reacted as if they had been slapped in the face by such an uppity act and continued to call him Clay, ignorant of Ali's powerful message for emerging militants and countercultural youth: "I don't have to be what you want me to be. I'm free."

Ali defended his title nine times, and no challenger came close to beating him, barely laying a fist on his pretty, wide-eyed face as he "floated like a butterfly and stung like a bee." In 1967, the heavyweight champion of the world refused induction into the Army, vowing that he was a Muslim minister, a conscientious objector, and that war was wrong. While privileged whites were exempted as college students or used pull to hide out in the National Guard, blacks and poor whites were bearing the burden of Vietnam. Ali either said, "I've got no quarrel with those Viet Cong," or the widely popular "No Viet Cong ever called me nigger" (also attributed to black activist Stokely Carmichael). He became a hero to the antiwar movement, all the more so when boxing officials lifted his title. The very congressmen who had no sons in Vietnam and had carefully devised loopholes that kept the privileged out of the draft vilified Ali. He was convicted of draft evasion and sentenced to five years in prison. Free on bail, pending appeals, the defrocked champion could not fight for three years.

Ali's stance influenced Dr. King, against the counsel of others, to turn his nonviolent disobedience into a denunciation of the war that had taken so many young blacks. The ills of racism, King argued, could not be cured until the war ended. By 1967, as the world waited to see if King would also be sent to jail for urging resistance to the draft, Stone warned, "It is no small national problem when the foremost Negro preacher and the foremost Negro sports idol are united in urging Negro (and white) youth not to serve." Stone quoted King's fiery call: "Every young man in this country who believes this war is abominable and unjust should file as a conscientious objector." Stone praised Ali for doing so and said of King, "He is both the foremost spokesman of America's better conscience and the Moses of 20 million Negroes, a submerged nation in an ugly mood. When and if the jail doors close on Clay [Stone still had not used his new name] and King . . . the domino effect could be far more costly than the distant fall of some Oriental despot."

In 1968, King's body lay sprawled in a puddle of blood on a motel balcony in Memphis. "He stood in the line of saints which goes back from Gandhi to Jesus," a distraught Stone wrote. The nation's ghettos erupted in riots, and the hope of nonviolent disobedience was laid to rest with King's body. Eleven years before, Stone had predicted, "A time of troubles may be beginning, the most serious conflict of our generation, poisoning our politics for years to come, capable of fomenting volcanic eruptions." How much better it would be if everyone accepted that "integration cannot be stopped." Now fiery militants ruled as the splintering civil rights movement fell into chaos. Stone angrily castigated this new direction: "A minority of his own people . . . celebrated [King's] memory with an orgy of looting while black radicals and New Leftists hailed the mindless carnival as a popular uprising. . . . Those who sneered at his non-violent teaching as obsolete now seized upon his death as a new excuse for the violence he hated."

The official response to King's murder was a "massive outpouring of hypocrisy." The president and the Washington establishment had been working "desperately" to keep King and his impending Poor People's March "out of the capital." Nothing, said Stone, "could be more deceptive than the nationwide mourning. Beneath the surface nothing has changed." King himself had once said of the mourning for assassinated civil rights workers that this was a "ten-day nation" because all would be forgotten that soon.

Stone confessed that "for whites who live like myself in almost lily-white northwest Washington," the ghetto riots "might have taken place in a distant country." Sympathetic whites were insulated not just by geography or military cordons, but by an "indiscriminate black hostility" that presaged the Black Power break with liberal whites. The hostile rejection of the young black firebrands was disturbing to a man who had spent decades fighting for civil rights, but Stone recognized the "agony of a lost race speaking." He sounded a warning, "The Fire Has Just Begun."

23

Affairs of the Heart, Plus Kennedy, Khrushchev, and Castro

The frightened journalist thought he was dying as he lay in a hospital in 1967. He "rehearsed his death," quoting Homer, while being wheeled on a stretcher into a Manhattan hospital heart unit. A few years before, a new procedure had restored Stone's hearing. The man who had for three decades lived inside his own world whenever he turned off his hearing aid was suddenly assaulted with sound. He now had to ask his children, "Can you not talk too loud? Remember, I'm not deaf."

By 1967, Stone's eyes needed correcting to avoid going blind. He had slaved over his four-page newsletter for fourteen years. His eyes had examined thousands of documents. He had cranked out millions of opinions. By April, a detached retina in his left eye was too dangerous to ignore. Without fanfare, Stone skipped a few editions in April after firing off a warning to disruptive elements in the peace movement that divisions among German leftist groups had given Hitler his victory.

Stone admired literate medical men with a leftist bent. Stone would beam and say of a doctor, "He's a reader! He's a *reader!*" Chris thought, "I wouldn't give a shit if the guy read Bill Buckley, as long as he knew what he was doing." Chris said that Stone's operation on August 7, 1967, at Manhattan's Eye, Ear and Throat Hospital was "botched." "Dad's detached retina was sewn back on badly," recalled Chris. "They kept taking his bandage off and saying, 'Do you see my finger?' and Dad would say, 'No.'" Chris and his wife, Ann, were at the hospital, "trying to mediate between these doctors who were having no success," when Stone suddenly announced, "I think I've had a heart attack."

Panicked family members called for help to transfer Stone to NYU's heart unit. Christopher was frantic as he saw his father experiencing excruciating chest pains. "It was a terrible, terrible time. He was scared, really scared. Ann and I had to create a scene to get any attention." Christopher "misrepresented myself," announcing that he was a "professor from USC—knowing they would think that I was from the University of Southern California medical school." As Stone was finally rushed into an elevator, he joked as a way of bolstering his hopes. "He was trying to bridge the seriousness with humor."

Stone had probably experienced a mild heart attack and certainly acute angina pain. As he recovered, he met up with two old pals who were also recuperating from surgeries. Stone, Ralph Ingersoll, and John Steinbeck, the famed author of *The Grapes of Wrath,* traded jokes and stories as they tooled around in their wheelchairs. Typically, Stone did not complain. "He was just incredible about that," recalls his son. "Dad had this terrible eye really sewn on in such a way that it wasn't very effective, but he never, ever made anything of it [although it contributed to his near blindness in later life]. Dad hated pain and there was no use dwelling on it when it happened." Stone started taking heart medication and walked as much as five miles a day. Walks cleared his mind, gave him stamina for the next column, and became seminars as he took friends and family along.

Days went by as a restless Stone remained for observation. Doctors ordered him to temporarily suspend the newsletter. In the fall, Stone convinced doctors that he could recuperate nicely on the SS *France.* Stimulating visits with intellectuals and fans in Paris and London put him in a fine mood. By November he was cranking out the newsletter. An FBI description of ancient vintage was handed down year in and year out: "Subject is a notoriously sloppy dresser" with unkempt hair. By then, Stone was dressing in suits, ties, and vests and was even termed dapper. Not one to adopt ludicrousness, he did not join peace-movement elders who succumbed to long hair, sandals, and jeans. But he bonded with the youth. Stone had two distinct groups of fans: grandparents who remembered him from the thirties and forties and their grandchildren who discovered him in the sixties.

Stone enjoyed being back "at the center of the storm . . . to participate in the battle even though it may seem to be again as always on the losing side." He praised those who were "moving and molding the sheep-like mass" against the war. As he hawked his wares, Stone could now add, "I'll be on the *Today* show on Thanksgiving day." There was Izzy, among the "respectables," as American as Thanksgiving Day. The alive and mostly well journalist thought it only fitting that he celebrate. His newsletter hawked tickets for his "Joint Birthday Party at New York's Town Hall (Stone's 60th, the Weekly's 15th)." On January 19, 1968, a packed crowd saw Stone toast himself. Among those paying tribute was E. Y. (Yip) Harburg. He had written the famous Depression song "Brother, Can You Spare a Dime," as well as "Over the Rainbow," and the lyrics for the musical *Finian's Rainbow.* Harburg's dazzling career was felled by the blacklist although he had never been a Communist. Stone beamed as he heard Yarburg's tribute, to the tune of "The Battle Hymn of the Republic":

> *HUAC reads him and it cites him,*
> *Alsop reads him and indicts him,*
> *Reston reads him and rewrites him,*
> *But the Stone goes rolling on!*

In fourteen years Stone had gone from a pariah tracked by the FBI to a wordsmith in demand on popular network TV shows. It took a war to make it happen. As Stone used to joke, "I became a war profiteer." "Izzy has tremendous influence," Knight columnist Ed Lahey was saying in 1968. (By then Stone had forty thousand subscribers, and the number would jump to fifty thousand the next year.) "It is catalytic. The people who read him influence others; there is a progressive geometric spiral downward to people who have never heard of Stone." Stone was gleaning from twelve papers daily, from *Le Monde* to the small York, Pennsylvania, *Gazette.*

The sixties started with only faint promise. Civil rights inched forward. McCarthyism had faded but the anticommunist Cold War nuclear arms race took on dangerous zigzags. Cuba's revolution caused jitters as did testy relations with Communist China and Berlin's divided city. Stone gave his readers a history lesson when Nixon campaigned as a peace candidate in 1968. Don't be fooled, he said. "Eisenhower and Nixon were elected as peace candidates in 1952 and . . . Eisenhower had hardly finished making peace in Korea when Nixon was ready to plunge the U.S. into war in Indochina. . . . He backed MacArthur against Truman" over Korea and "was for bombing Chinese bases, and unleashing Chiang Kaishek." In 1960 Stone had headlined a warning, "Nixon Was Wrong About Vietnam," when most Americans had no idea what was happening there.

After the 1960 Democratic convention Stone quipped, "We do not remember ever seeing before so inattentive a convention, and we regard the inattention as a sign of growing national maturity." To him, the event was mired in mediocrity. Eleanor Roosevelt, in her "hopeless" appeal for Adlai Stevenson "achieved a passionate and memorable sincerity ... and by her power overshadowed every other participant." Among the contenders were the "moronic Symington," the "sophomoric Jackson," and the able Johnson, but none of them glittered and Kennedy did. "His grace, his tact and his intelligence are unmistakable." The party's "outstanding" civil rights plank championed the sit-ins and nullified loyalty and security programs by calling for the right of the accused to confront "faceless informers."

Like the rest of the world, Stone was entranced when the youngest president ever and his wife entered the White House "as charming as any Prince and Princess out of a ... book of fairy tales." He bubbled over after witnessing the forty-three-year-old president's deft charm in his first press conference. Stone was in no danger of mellowing; soon he was decrying "the rapid deterioration in our national leadership." He warned against invading Cuba before Kennedy was elected. Just before JFK was inaugurated, Stone urged him to break with Eisenhower's policies, which included endorsing CIA assassinations. Stone cautioned that an alliance with Latin American rightwing dictatorships and duplicitous acts against Castro were dangerous. He worried about a drift toward "preventive war." With "giddy arrogance" the United States was assuring the UN Security Council that our intentions were "pure as driven snow," even as "correspondents were being given a ... not-for-attribution briefing on our plans to choke off the Castro regime with a sea and air blockade." He asked in 1961, "Why the sudden pretense ... that CIA operatives only spend their time translating *Pravda*?" (The CIA covertly and actively participated in the overthrow of Latin America leftist regimes in the 1950s.) In 1962, Stone derided Kennedy's foot-dragging on civil rights and his "foreign policies [which] keep us on the brink of war in a half-dozen far places from Vietnam to Berlin."

When the president backed the CIA-led Bay of Pigs fiasco just weeks after taking office, Stone called it "our Pearl Harbor" raid on Cuba. The invasion was bungled from beginning to end. American newspapers had written about its possibility; Castro, who read the papers, did not need spies to learn of the assault, Kennedy ruefully admitted. And, as history would repeat, there was no uprising of support for an invading "liberation" force. Stone warned of further "unilateral intervention."

The relationship between Cuban exiles in Miami and Castro's regime was as complex as it was deadly. Blood brothers in Miami fought against brothers in Cuba. Many moderate exiles had despised Batista and cheered Castro until his social reforms coexisted with the revolutionary's own oppression. Rich exiles who had lost everything vowed to fight Castro to their death. Castro rightly saw the CIA and the Kennedy brothers as enemies who plotted his assassination, were friendly with American gangsters who had controlled Havana's casinos, instigated embargoes, and planned to illegally invade his country.

There were many tragedies of the assault; the lost life of its twenty-nine-year-old commander, Jose "Pepe" San Roman, was a metaphor for the entire invasion. Tortured by the fact that he had never questioned any of the American plans, San Roman watched in horror as his troops were slaughtered while waiting in vain for promised support from the United States on April 17, 1961. San Roman's radioed pleas for help remain chilling to this day. At dawn: "Do you people realize how desperate the situation is? Do you back us or quit? All we want is low jet air cover . . . need it badly or cannot survive." An hour later, 6:13 a.m.: "Blue Beach under attack. . . . Where is promised air cover?" 7:12 a.m.: "Enemy on trucks coming from Red Beach. . . . 8:15 a.m. "Situation critical . . . need urgently air support." 9:14 a.m: "Where the hell is jet cover?" 9:55 a.m.: "Can you throw something into this vital point in battle? Anything. Just let jet pilots loose." Toward the end: "Out of ammo. Enemy closing in. . . . Send all available aircraft now." When a final call for U.S. aid was denied, San Roman replied, "And you, sir, are a son of a bitch."

San Roman did not die in the invasion. Consumed by his betrayal, San Roman—who had stood with Kennedy as throngs cheered the adroitly orchestrated propaganda parade after the debacle—killed himself when all was but a memory, the same year that Stone died, 1989.

Following the Bay of Pigs debacle, Stone and other peace activists signed an ad in the *New York Times* opposing further intervention. He bitterly opposed Kennedy's policy of "pulling down an iron curtain of our own on Cuba, of non intercourse and embargo." It had "fostered Sovietization. A more self-defeating policy would be difficult to imagine." Diplomacy with Cuba was vital: "Cuba is the one nation in the Soviet world which is still not securely either in the Russian or the Chinese camp."

No matter how disastrous the Bay of Pigs invasion was—even *Time* magazine called it "shockingly bungled"—few journalists thought it morally wrong. Conditioned to Cold War jousting, Americans rallied around Kennedy: his approval rating jumped 10 points to 83 percent in a national Gallup poll. Kennedy exclaimed that it was just like Eisenhower's performance: "The worse you do, the better they like you."

In the early 1960s Stone began speaking to a burgeoning New Left about Cuba, as CIA and FBI agents took notes. Historian and founding member of the Students for a Democratic Society (SDS) Todd Gitlin told Stone, when the journalist was in his seventies, "My recollection of your viewpoint is that Castro represented an authentic independent radicalism and that the American government was pushing him, tragically, into the arms of the Russians." "It's *still* my view," Stone shot back. "I was in Cuba three times before Castro and three times under Castro, and it changed as he got pushed more and more. He was caught in a bind between the Cuban Communist Party and American hostility and had to do some very agile political maneuvering. The Cuban Communist Party had a very checkered record in supporting Batista and was not friendly to Castro, and they felt that they could get rid of him. When the oil embargo was imposed Castro had nowhere to turn except Moscow. [Stone was talking five years before the Soviet collapse.] But I think he is the most able man in the bloc, the only one in the whole goddamn [Communist] bloc."

Stone bristled at the suggestion that he had romanticized Castro, whom he had initially called a hero worthy of America's 1776 revolutionaries. "At first the atmosphere was very different from a Soviet state, but it changed. Originally he was more like the New Left. He was not afraid of socialism, but he was not wedded to any dogma." A shrug is in Stone's voice when Gitlin brought up the view of some that Castro was "really a tinhorn dictator all along." "Well, maybe. But you see, when I was down there. . . ." Stone recalled Cuba in the summer of 1960; blacks dined in restaurants where only the rich and foreigners had been allowed, and there was a free press. He had seen Havana with all its banana-republic excesses of the subjugated poor and rampant corruption. He had great expectations for the revolution. (As did Cuban reformers, leftists, and moderates, who sided with Castro until they saw his totalitarian bent. Many who decry Castro's human rights violations continue to admire Cuba's early agrarian reform, literacy, and high medical standards.) "Now it is a Soviet state, but I blame the United States for that," continued Stone.

Long ago Stone had pushed for understanding on both sides, admonishing Castro to adopt a mixed economy and elections and urging JFK to trade with Cuba as the United States was doing with other Communist countries. "The United States could have lived with it, the revolution, but we're just the arrogant bully. We want 101 percent."

Stone's work on Cuba became something of a Rorschach test for opposing governments. When he came back from one trip following the revolution, Stone was highly critical of both the U.S. government and Castro's cult of personality. His columnist friend Edwin A. Lahey sent the *Weekly* piece to the White House. A few days later a White House report critical of Cuba included some of Stone's material. Simultaneously, the Cubans used material from the same article in a speech condemning the United States.

Castro often remarked that America's "foreign policy" toward Cuba is really a "domestic policy." Keeping hatred alive among Florida's Cuban exiles and tightening the embargo have been excellent maneuvers for decades in garnering Florida votes. Meanwhile such restrictions allowed Castro to play the *Yanqui, no* card, the David in the battle against Goliath. So far he has survived for nearly half a century.

Despite his feelings for the revolution, in 1961 Stone was sobered by the changes in Cuba since his visit the previous summer. Two months before the Bay of Pigs, one could almost hear the sigh as Stone wrote, "I might as well make a clean breast of this." Stone confronted the paradoxes in a country that was neither as horrible as the propaganda against it nor as good as the illusions of its supporters. He hoped that his country would restore diplomatic relations, cast off rigid Cold War edicts, and attempt a good-neighbor policy. That hope waned as he saw in Cuba an "infantile leftism" filled with hubris, a closed press, and a drift toward "strengthening the secret police and arbitrary legal methods." Yet Stone's ambivalence emerged: "Nothing could be harder for an observer from a rich status quo society than to understand a group of desperate idealists striving within a short time to remake a poor colonial society in the shadow of a hostile great power." He hoped that Castro would become "our Tito." Nothing was more dangerous than *Time* magazine and other publications that advocated invading Cuba again, he cried.

In the fall of 1962, Russian missiles were detected on the island. On October 22, 1962, Kennedy ordered a naval blockade of Cuba, demanding that the missiles be removed. Stone saw this as an act of war. Five days later, a fearful and agitated Stone stood with pacifists Norman Thomas and A. J. Muste, addressing two thousand protesters in front of the White House. Air Force reserve units had been called up, and Stone saw a world "on the brink of thermonuclear war."

Journalists and historians made much of the fact that Khrushchev and Kennedy went eyeball-to-eyeball and the Russian leader "blinked first." But Stone asked an important question: What if he had not blinked? Stone saw macho recklessness in Kennedy, who needed a victory after the Bay of Pigs. When insider accounts emerged, Stone ripped into them as disingenuous. Both leaders shared in the blame of duplicitous diplomacy, Stone felt, arguing that Kennedy was as concerned with the Democrats retaining a congressional majority as he was possible world destruction. "To face the November elections with these missiles intact would have been disastrous for Kennedy and the Democrats." Stone viewed with skepticism JFK aide Ted Sorenson's account of a "sentimental" Kennedy on the eve of the confrontation reflecting not on his "possible death but of all the innocent children of the world who had never had a chance or a voice." Commented dry-eyed Stone, "If Kennedy was so concerned he might have sacrificed his chances in the election to try and negotiate."

Stone acknowledged that "the look into the abyss" made both world leaders "really feel in their bones the need for co-existence," and Khrushchev's fright coupled with Kennedy's new sense of confidence were "factors in the *détente* which followed." Yet Kennedy took a grave chance. "Negotiations, however prolonged, would have been better than the risk of World War III." Stone heralded a suggestion that Lippmann had made during the crisis and blamed Kennedy for refusing this mutual face-saver that Khrushchev ultimately offered: Russia would remove the missiles from Cuba and offer a nonaggression pledge to Turkey if the United States would remove its missiles from Turkey and offer a nonaggression pledge to Cuba. Stone termed Arthur Schlesinger's account that Kennedy "regarded the idea as unacceptable, and the swap was promptly rejected" as "appallingly ethnocentric. Cuba's fate and interests are simply ignored."

Had Stone been privy to the private discussions of JFK and his advisers, he might have been less harsh on Kennedy, who had agreed with Khrushchev in private to take action on removing the missiles in Turkey. Tapes released in 1997 show that while others, such as McNamara and even Fulbright, continued to push military solutions, JFK was an agonizing, if reluctant, dove who had made a secret concession.

Soon after the missile crisis, Stone made his last trip to Cuba. Upon his return, in January 1963, Stone wrote once again that Communist countries were not monolithic. "Castro alone of all the Soviet leaders declared his neutrality between Moscow and Peking," which could be used to America's advantage. When American policy was "to some degree flexible and pragmatic, rather than rigidly ideological, this paid off. . . . We have diplomatic relations with most of the bloc. We do some business with them. We have cultural exchanges. We even extend aid to . . . Yugoslavia and Poland. But China and Cuba are outside the pale. Is it any wonder that they . . . are rigidly hostile in return?"

Stone naively extolled the Fidelistas as living "in a spring time of mankind. . . . Elsewhere youth has turned beatnik in the shadow of the mushroom cloud. In Cuba the same youth still *believes*" (italics in original). Luckily for the new revolutionaries, Stone joked, the "Yankee imperialists" had so modernized Havana that they were able to fight "the world's first air-conditioning revolution." But Stone admitted that he had not visited the prisons or studied spying units set up to police one's neighbors.

Compassion was necessary for the exiles, Stone recognized, but American policy should not be shaped only through their eyes nor should we "take to the opium pipes of our own propaganda." Then Stone admitted, "Those who try to be objective or friendly are dismissed as dupes, and sometimes—as the Stalin years demonstrate—they were." Yet he ended with a defense: "But events have also shown that in the long run the dupes prove less misleading than the doped."

On that last trip Stone was taken into custody. The day before he left Washington, Kennedy announced that he would soon impose new restrictions on other nations shipping to Cuba. Not an auspicious time for an American journalist to visit. Stone had to fly first to Mexico and from there into Cuba. At the airport, as other passengers passed through, "Every time I moved up to the immigration barrier I was waved back." Stone of course was not silent when authorities searched his bags and confiscated a large cache of medicines he was delivering to a Havana hospital. "I was tired and cross and rather relished the idea of a good fight," recalled Stone, whose shout-in with an angry young militant ended when Stone was hauled off to Havana for questioning. He refused to sleep on a cot set up for him just outside the jail cells and spent the night "alternately dozing in a chair and roaming around the police station."

His attempts to make phone calls were thwarted. Esther knew that he must have been in jail because he had not called. He was poorly guarded and, Stone hilariously remarked, "could have run away if I had known where I was." He decided a "tantrum" was in order and began kicking chairs. However, Stone felt "real alarm" when told that his was not an immigration matter but rather a "security police" case. He became much quieter after this news, remembering an Israeli reporter friend who had been arrested in Prague on a trumped-up charge and imprisoned for four years. He requested that they send word to the famous revolutionary Che Guevara, whom Stone knew. He was never sure why he had been taken into custody or why he was released a day later, but thinks he made a clinching argument when he said, "Didn't Fidel himself in a recent speech attack *bureaucracia* and isn't this an example of bureaucracy at work?"*

After a shave and hot bath at his hotel, Stone celebrated his freedom in Sloppy Joe's, a Cuban tourist hangout with the same name as the bar in Key West. He was delighted to see that the Cuban ninety-cent daiquiri "despite Marxism-Leninism . . . remains the world's best."

The bartender viewed his American customer "warily, as if I were a phantom." Making a sweeping gesture, the bartender said, "In Cuba, Americans *feenish*." It was neither a sad nor triumphant statement but delivered "objectively and with finality, as of an unalterable fact. I felt like the last Yankee imperialist, unwelcome and no longer at home."

Stone continued to criticize U.S. policies, but that trip altered his view. He no longer saw Cuba as a socialist dream and never attempted to return.

In his own country, Stone was also trailed. His constant speeches against nuclear proliferation, as he stood with Linus Pauling, Norman Thomas, Dr. Benjamin Spock, and Women Strike for Peace, were targets of the FBI. Not everyone greeted Stone with enthusiasm in 1961. When his speaking engagement at New York's Harpur College was announced that year, an

---

*When Stone speculated on his detainment years later, he said, "I think my crime was telling the Czechs to go screw themselves. We no longer had a relationship with Cuba, and I had to get a visa from the Czech embassy to go to Cuba. They called me up, wanted me to come to lunch, tried to make a big *tsimmes* out of it, and I said, 'Look, I'm very busy.' They wanted to make me beholden to them for my Cuban visa. And I didn't like the Czech party. I think it was one of the ignominious, belly-crawling Communist parties of the world. I think the Czechs put some smoke in the works."

American Legion Auxiliary anti-Cuba activist, Betty O'Hara, denounced Stone in the press, saying he wanted to abolish "our security laws" with his advocacy of free speech. His response through a reporter: The HUAC "are Communists in reverse.... They believe in hounding and smearing those with whom they disagree. I haven't met this kind of thing in years . . . as a matter of fact, I don't remember having met it since 1949."

Stone was mad enough at slurs on his patriotism to throw his speech away and "give a lecture on Americanism to the Legionnaires, the DAR, the Junior G-Men and the FBI" in the audience. He lambasted the local newspaper for printing the HUAC list of "front" organizations with which he had been involved. He was "not ashamed" of those associations but faulted the use of speeches he had "given 25 years ago. If they had bothered to call me, I would have given them some more recent ones," he said dryly. He called the local newspaper reports "droppings" that came close to "defamation of character" and said, "They make respectable people afraid to listen to you." He continued, to applause, "A free country is not one filled with rabbits who are afraid to disagree. . . . Never was a country overthrown because of too much freedom of speech." He knocked totalitarian countries, naming Russia. Despite some "idiots," said Stone, "who go up in arms every time somebody expresses an unpopular view, America is still tolerant of free speech."

During a postspeech session Stone kept turning up his hearing aid to hear the questions. When an American Legionnaire asked him how he could support the Abraham Lincoln Brigade, a HUAC-condemned "front group," Stone replied that the brigade had fought the Nazis and Italian Fascists. "What side were *you* on—the Brigade's or the Nazis'?" Stone shot back. The man tried to further grill him, but Stone shouted, "I want an answer to my question!" The Legionnaire finally said tersely, "No comment."

In November 1963, the world mourned in shocked despair when President Kennedy was shot to death in Dallas. To watch him was to be "delighted by his wit, his intelligence, his capacity and his youth," wrote Stone. "These made the terrible flash from Dallas incredible and painful." Stone then took a deep breath and plunged into an astonishingly tough column, an appraisal of Kennedy that was only replicated by writers long after the revelations of a tarnished Camelot: "Perhaps the truth is that in some ways John Fitzgerald Kennedy died just in time. He died in time to be remembered as he would like to be remembered, as ever-young, still victorious, struck down undefeated. . . ." But, Stone continued, "The Kennedy administration was approaching an impasse, certainly at home, quite possibly abroad, from which there seemed no escape. . . . The President was caught between these old men [in Congress], their faces set stubbornly towards their white supremacist past, and the advancing Negro masses, explosively demanding 'freedom now.'" In foreign affairs Kennedy was stymied by Cold Warriors when attempting any minuscule thaw with Russia.

Stone asked his readers to face deep realities and decried the tendency to either applaud or ignore covert acts of the CIA, from the killing of Patrice Lumumba in the Congo to the assassination of the Diem brothers in South Vietnam. "We all reach for the dagger, or the gun, in our thinking when it suits our political view to do so. . . . In this sense we share the guilt with Oswald and Ruby and the rightist crack-pots. Where the right to kill is so universally accepted, we should not be surprised if our young President was slain." Stone addressed the growing acceptance of "murder on the widest scale as the arbiter of controversy between nations."

Stone said it was necessary to take a "clear-sighted view" of Kennedy and his advisers, who were "in some ways a warlike Administration." It seemed ready to "send troops into Vietnam" and "in violation of our own laws and international law" embraced the inglorious Bay of Pigs invasion. As for the Cuban missile crisis, Stone asked, what if Russia had "called our bluff and war had begun and escalated?" If any historians had survived, "would they have thought us justified in blowing most of mankind to smithereens, rather than negotiate, or appeal to the UN, or even to leave in Cuba the medium-range missiles which were no different after all from those we had long aimed at the Russians from Turkey and England?" These facts should be remembered in case Johnson had a mind to imitate the slain president. "Think it over carefully before canonizing Kennedy as an apostle of peace."

Dissenting from worldwide eulogies—"funerals are always occasions for pious lying"—Stone firmly concluded, "Abroad, as at home, the problems were becoming too great for conventional leadership, and Kennedy, when the tinsel was stripped away, was a conventional leader, no more than an enlightened conservative, cautious as an old man for all his youth, with a basic distrust of the people and an astringent view of the evangelical as a tool of leadership. . . . In the clouds of incense . . . it is easy to lose one's way just when it becomes more important than ever to see where we really are."

Like Stone, Lippmann "wrote no eulogy" for Kennedy and was not into mythologizing him, remembering that the president had taken no stance against McCarthyism. Lippmann and Stone both supported the Warren Commission's "lone gunman" report on the assassination, although Lippmann privately voiced questions when others clamored for more investigation as conspiracy theories bloomed. Stone never wavered. When a conspiracy buff phoned Stone in 1966 with "important evidence," he bellowed, "I don't care about that asshole case!" and hung up. On the fortieth anniversary of Kennedy's death, conspiracy arguments incessantly abounded in articles and on TV shows. Despite new methods of examination, the Warren Report was still not disproved. In 2006, interested groups were still trying to wrestle secrets on Kennedy's murder from a balking CIA.

Stone seldom wrote an ambiguous headline, and the one addressing the country's new leader was no exception: "Johnson Far Below J.F.K. in Sophistication, Breadth and Taste." He sighed, "The hope is that men change and grow."

Johnson would earn Stone's respect for his masterful civil rights legislation. He gushed when Johnson picked Hubert Humphrey as his vice president in 1964. "No liberal in the Senate has been more effective. . . . Much of what was best in the New Frontier came from measures Humphrey launched long before it. Medicare, the Peace Corps, the National Education Act, began with Humphrey. . . . He had the nerve to make the politically dangerous issue of disarmament his own. No man in the Senate has been a firmer champion of the Negro; none worked harder to make the new Civil Rights Act the legislative triumph that it is. None has done more through Food for Peace to infuse a larger component of idealism into our foreign policy. . . . No Democrat more deserved the Vice-Presidential nomination."

Then, as Vietnam escalated into the country's longest and most divisive war, all such praise was forgotten. Stone dedicated himself to an all-out crusade for peace, saw Johnson as a duplicitous warmonger, and Humphrey as a fallen hero and faithful lapdog to LBJ.

24

THE HAUNTING WAR

When the government lies, must the press fib?
—I. F. Stone, May 3, 1961

By the midfifties, Stone was forecasting such dangers as preemptive and covert wars against countries that had not attacked the United States. Later he predicted that such actions would not be halted "by the currently fashionable proposal to take cloak-and-dagger activities out of the CIA and put them in the Pentagon." This sounds like circa 2005, but Stone was writing forty-five years ago, after the Bay of Pigs. "To embark on secret warlike activities against peoples whose governments we dislike is to set out on a course destructive of free government and of peace," he wrote in May 1961. "Is It in the National Interest to Let the Government Deceive the People?"

One November day in 1965 a busy crowd milled around outside the Pentagon, hardly noticing a young man who walked past with an infant in his arms. No one saw him until it was too late, until the flames began to engulf him. In his last gesture, the man tossed his one-year-old daughter clear of the inferno.

The incident devastated Stone, aghast at the inadvertent role his *Weekly* had played in the decision of Quaker pacifist Norman R. Morrison to immolate himself on the steps of the Pentagon. John Vanderchek, the deputy Pentagon correspondent for *Time* magazine, learned that Morrison had read Stone's *Weekly* the day before, which had printed an agonized account of death and destruction in Vietnam. When Vanderchek called Stone, "he was terribly distressed. What I had dug up was original and unknown to him. Izzy kept repeating, 'Oh, my God, oh, my goodness. This is just so awful!'"

At noon that November day, Morrison had talked of immolation with his wife, who had no idea that her husband was considering such a fiery death for himself. A picture of a Vietnamese Buddhist monk who had set himself afire to protest the war had recently shocked the world. Morrison's despair that peace demonstrations had not slowed his country's policies deepened when he read a vivid account of a Catholic priest's agony as U.S. bombs killed his people. "I have seen my faithful burned up in napalm," the sobbing priest said. "I have seen the bodies of women and children blown to bits. I have seen my village razed. By God, it's not possible!"

Morrison had read the harrowing account in the *Weekly*. Stone's inclusion of foreign accounts that did not sanitize war coverage gave his readers a tougher reality than other American publications. Stone had dedicated a full page to this *Paris Match* story when few American periodicals were addressing the toll on noncombatant civilians in a war with "free-fire zones" where one could kill anything that moved. The Vietcong had long left the priest's village, but bombs fell unceasingly through the night, pulverizing everything below. The badly hurt priest "buried as best I could the bodies. . . . I had to abandon some wounded and dying." As he lay in a Saigon clinic, Father Currien said, "Nothing remains of that region. . . . Before the bombardment, loud speakers, in the planes above . . . told them not to go into the fields and to stay in their huts. They stayed in their huts and the huts were bombarded anyway."

Father Currien had helped save the wounded for twenty years by then, beginning with the French in 1944. "We Catholics have little love" for the Vietcong, he said, but the priest reserved his most vivid indictment for the firepower that the United States rained down on them. The Americans, he said, "must settle their accounts with God."

Morrison could not forget such tragedies. Friends held a press conference after his death, saying that he "must have been motivated by a desperate search to find the way to be heard by the American people and by their leaders. We pray that all people will be able to see beyond the act to the essential message." The *Washington Post* noted that Morrison had seen the priest's story, not mentioning that he had read it in Stone's *Weekly*. In the *Post*'s excised account, the sentence "I have seen the bodies of women and children blown to bits" was omitted. Stone made no editorial comment but printed a doctor's outrage: "What Morrison Wanted McNamara to See." "Dear Mr. Stone: I have just sent this letter to Secretary McNamara and the Joint Chiefs of Staff: . . . What he was trying to say was: 'See what it is like for a man to die by fire. . . . You, who make impersonal war, devising strategies and tactics in your air-conditioned offices, look and see!' This very thing happens daily in Vietnam," continued Dr. Marian E. Manly, of Walnut Creek, California, in rage about war's "dreadful, clinging napalm fire, burning human beings to death regardless of age, sex or political belief." American peace activists who later traveled to Hanoi were startled to learn that Morrison, who had been so quickly forgotten in the United States, had become a North Vietnamese national hero.

During the midsixties the *New York Times* Washington bureau grew in strength as bureau chief Scotty Reston amassed a gifted team that included Russell Baker, Tom Wicker, Max Frankel, Felix Belair, Jack Raymond, Hedrick Smith, and Anthony Lewis. "Few newspapers were opposing the war, and certainly *Time* magazine was not—although a counterinsurgency began among writers like David Halberstam and Malcolm Browne, who saw the war from the ground and reported that it wasn't working," recalled Vanderchek. TV celebrity had not yet engulfed journalism. Sitting on Mount Olympus were print journalists Lippmann and Krock, who held no love for one another. Both were capable of pompous views and thought themselves indispensable to the workings of government. Scotty Reston, a fine reporter who could force the truth out of officials, was the clear heir apparent. Stone's friend Drew Pearson was the most powerful and highly read columnist, although loftier pundits with less influence sniffed that he was a sensationalist who used vendetta-like information from any available source. "Stone was the first independent voice and he had a niche," said Vanderchek. "All the top dogs, editors, and reporters were reading him. He was respected by a lot of us because he had no master to serve but his own conscience."

Unlike some journalists and historians who bought Defense Secretary McNamara's accounts—and later accepted as adequate expiation his bloodless concession that "mistakes" were made—Stone did not forget the lies and disregard for war's human cost displayed by the McNamaras, Rusks, Kissingers, LBJs, and Nixons. Back when others had applauded Kennedy's appointment of Dean Rusk as secretary of state, a troubled Stone, after examining Rusk's statements and past actions, predicted that he would be a hard-line Cold Warrior. Much later, Lippmann wrote that Rusk "is a very sincere man whose education stopped about 1944."

Stone began his wary watch of America's Indochina policy as early as 1946. "A history of lost opportunities" brought about the Vietnam War, he wrote in 1963. As early as 1961, Stone summarized the follies of U.S. foreign policy in an article titled "Anti-Guerrilla War—the Dazzling New

Military Toothpaste for Social Decay." "It is time we realized that the brutal surgery of military and para-military methods cannot cure complex social and economic problems. The CIA got rid of a popular reformer, Mossadegh, in Iran, but the makeshift corrupt regime with which he was replaced is now collapsing. Guatemala, where the CIA got rid of Arbenz, is ripe for new trouble. . . . If the hundreds of millions we have squandered in Laos and South Vietnam had gone into public improvements . . . both countries would be models of stability."

A translated copy of the 1957 *Revue Militaire d'Information* was "so fashionable at the Pentagon" in 1961. It was written by men "watching a dance from outside through heavy plate glass windows. They see the motions but they can't hear the music. . . . What rarely comes through to them are the injured racial feelings, the misery, the rankling slights, the hatred, the devotion, the inspiration and the desperation. So they do not really understand what leads men to abandon wife, children, home, career and friends; to take to the bush and live gun in hand like a hunted animal; to challenge overwhelming military odds rather than acquiesce any longer in humiliation, injustice or poverty." Such "military theoreticians," so "astounded by the success" that revolutionary forces can achieve "against huge and well-equipped armies," make the mistake of thinking that they can replicate counterinsurgency, combining the overthrow of governments with such actions as "economic and social reform. . . . Some of the liberals around the President seem to believe it . . . but experience is against them. We never succeeded in getting Chiang or Syngman Rhee to make reforms. . . . Can we do better with Diem in South Vietnam?" Stone said no.

When Ho Chi Minh modeled his declaration of independence after the United States', Stone felt he was "pro-American" and hoped that Truman would support his Vietminh, "who worked closely with the OSS during the second World War and took FDR's promises of colonial liberation seriously." Then Ho Chi Minh accepted a limited independence within the French Union in 1946, which permitted the French to "reoccupy Hanoi without a shot being fired." France's "promises were broken" and a colonial war began that was to cost France $5 billion—much of it financed by the United States. Small towns of France are dotted with graveyards in which lie the remains of soldiers who died before the Geneva agreement marked France's defeat in 1954.

Stone later again ruminated over "lost opportunities." Stone denounced the "heavy-handed thought control" of the Communist Party in North Vietnam in 1956, which produced "peasant uprising and widespread resentment among the intellectuals." Meanwhile Diem "was busy erecting a dictatorship of his own. In 1956 he abolished elections even for village councils. In 1957 his mobs smashed the press of the one legal opposition party." Then came "fake land reforms and concentration camps." Peasants and Buddhists were jailed, tortured, and killed by the thousands, which stirred wide rebellion "*before* [Stone's italics] North Vietnam gave support" and led "oppositionists of all kinds" to align with the Communist National Liberation Front. Vice President Johnson returned from a 1961 trip to South Vietnam and "laid it on with a shovel," extolling Diem as the "Churchill of Asia." Stone blasted Kennedy for also mythologizing Diem. When the corrupt, brutal, and unpopular Diem regime became a liability, Diem and his brother were assassinated. Kennedy wanted a coup with "plausible deniability," one of those twisted euphemisms of which administrations are so fond, planning to replace a "pseudo-democracy and ineffective police state" with "an effective military dictatorship ready to work with the United States."

No love was lost for Diem by either the right, who saw him failing, or the left. Stone mocked the lies that poured forth about upcoming "free elections." "In Saigon a street rally calling for a neutralist government was forbidden and its banners torn down. Censorship continues . . . only parties they regard as non-communist will be allowed. . . . This means that if there is to be a choice between democracy and continuance of the war, it is democracy that will go." Stone belittled American press responses. He called a *Washington Post* editorial "Orwellian with a vengeance" for arguing that "the cause of freedom need not sink with the passing of the old government!" The "'cause of freedom' is soap advertising lingo for continuation of cold and hot war." The new cabal "headed by a weak turncoat who has served any and every regime foreign and domestic will bring neither peace nor freedom to Vietnam," prophesied Stone.

Less than two weeks later Kennedy was assassinated. The following summer, Johnson received a blank check from Congress for retaliatory bombing raids on North Vietnam following a trumped-up charge that it had fired first on American ships in the Gulf of Tonkin. Thus was born America's full-scale war. Lippmann's readers found only approval of the so-called retaliatory bombings. They were "a test of American will." But this was no reflexive U.S. response. All the while Johnson had promised not to send American "boys" to do the fighting for South Vietnamese "boys," he was secretly planning to bomb North Vietnam. When an excuse came to widen the war—which Johnson carefully never called a war—he dispatched ground troops to Vietnam. Of 3 million who served in the war, some 58,000 were killed, 340,000 were wounded. Returning veterans became reviled scapegoats for the only war the United States had ever lost.

In contrast to Lippmann and other journalists who were either hawkish on the war or believed the official word, Stone was astonishing in his immediate and accurate assessment of the dubious 1964 Tonkin incident. He acknowledged that some in the press had reported for six months that the U.S. government planned to leap from commando operations to "overt attacks against the North." Stone added, however, that "very few Americans are aware" of the circumstances that "cast a very different light on the *Tonkin* affair." He was quite alone as he tore apart the "official mythology of the war." He consistently ran the remarks of the lone antiwar voices, Wayne Morse and Ernst Gruening, the only senators to vote against the Gulf of Tonkin resolution. Morse charged that U.S. warships in such proximity was "bound to be looked upon by our enemies as an act of provocation." Stone dryly observed, "The press, which dropped an Iron Curtain weeks ago on the anti-war speeches of Morse and Gruening, ignored this one, too."

Stone addressed a central problem in uncovering the facts: "The process of brain-washing the public starts with off-the-record briefings for newspapermen in which all sorts of far-fetched theories are suggested to explain why the tiny North Vietnamese navy would be mad enough to venture an attack on the Seventh Fleet, one of the world's most powerful." Everything except *"the possibility that the attack might have been provoked"* (Stone's italics). A few weeks after the Gulf of Tonkin incident, Stone exposed official fabrications that only came to light years later in the Pentagon Papers thunderbolts. Stone noted the confusion, inconsistencies, and prevarications in the Tonkin official explanations, commenting that the whole affair was "beginning to look like a barroom brawl with the lights out. . . . It is not surprising that Secretary McNamara abruptly shut off his press conference on the latest Tonkin Bay incident so he would not have to answer questions." Stone asked readers to imagine that "if Russian or Chinese destroyers prowled the Florida coast while ships they supplied Castro engaged in coastal raids, what would we do? Send hampers of Florida grapefruit to their skippers?"

In 1964, the Democrats had adroitly painted Republican presidential candidate Barry Goldwater as dangerously trigger-happy. Now Johnson and his team were considering nuclear warfare while lying to the public. In 1964, Daniel Ellsberg, who later risked prison for leaking the Pentagon Papers to the media, became a special assistant to the assistant secretary of defense for international security affairs, John T. McNaughton. He recalled the "ways of flattering and misleading journalists . . . part of the process of keeping the secrets well." One morning McNaughton told Ellsberg, "A Blue Springs drone has gone down in China. Bob is seeing the press at eight-thirty. We have ten minutes to write six alternative lies for him."

Stone did not fall for an Ellsberg attempt to further the secrets. He exposed the lies in the 1965 official White Paper that charged that Hanoi was engaged in an " 'elaborate program' to supply the Viet Cong." Stone's report was "very devastating" to the administration, recalled Ellsberg. Stone ripped into the report, using its own evidence in Appendix D. "Unfortunately few will see the appendices since even the *New York Times* did not reprint them," noted Stone, "though these are more revealing than the report."

Examining the small print, Stone found a total of 179 items captured in eighteen months that had come from Communist-bloc countries. "This," he wryly surmised, "is not a very impressive total." Stone checked Pentagon figures, which tallied an average of 7,500 weapons captured from the enemy each eighteen months in the past three years. "If only 179 communist-made weapons turned up in 18 months, that is less than 2 and ½ percent of the total." Stone concluded that the Pentagon was vastly underestimating the number of weapons the guerrillas had captured from the United States.

"Stone added it all up and said, 'Is this the best they can come up with?!' His criticism was right on," recalled Ellsberg, who had personally crafted a sentence in the report that left wiggle room for lies. "We said, right in the text, 'This is an example of the weapons we had found.' In truth, that was all we had found, but we thought we had carefully concealed it." Ellsberg laughingly added, "Stone did not quote our lies correctly."

For many journalists, Stone's White Paper refutation remains a key example of digging out the truth obscured in government lies. It also became a rallying message for the Students for a Democratic Society (SDS) peace movement, which launched its first major antiwar demonstration the following month, April 1965. Stone was a major speaker.

Issue after issue of the *Weekly* continued to mock President Johnson's reasons for war and what LBJ termed a policy of "measured response." Stone acidly commented, "Plain words are disappearing from circulation as the government floods us with counterfeit phrases of this kind." He harkened back to devious World War I phrases that the Germans had used to frighten their enemies into submission. Who else was culling from the past like that? Lippmann had the depth and breadth but was slow getting off LBJ's team.

Like other war critics with no access to the enemy side, Stone did not know how many Communist troops were traveling south. When U.S. peace groups visited Hanoi in 1965, they were "disarmed by assurances that a postwar Vietnam would be Democratic in a Western sense." Quaker pacifist Staughton Lynd was told that North Vietnamese troops were not fighting in large numbers in the South. "I had been snookered," he later said.

In war, propaganda is never clean or truthful on any side. Steeped in World War II heroics, American journalists were initially often unwilling to face this or could not convince publishers and editors to print their skepticism. Americans continued for the most part to be misled on the war, through no fault of the correspondents who were in Saigon, enduring the Five-O'clock Follies briefings that did not jibe with their own assessments. They were under strong pressure to "get on the team" by top brass, who thought nothing of leaning on their publishers, most of whom had supported the war, and top editors, who often second-guessed, countermanded, and rewrote accounts from their correspondents. A majority of editorial pages supported the war until after the Tet offensive in 1968.

Stone had read and learned enough to know that a land war was treacherous and that massive airpower was futile in guerrilla jungle warfare. He used historical references, pointing out the massive but ineffectual bombing during the Korean War. In the early days of that war in less than two months, the United States "leveled every urban and industrial target above the 38th parallel except some naval oil storage tanks too close to the Russian border to be bombed without risk, but the war went on for three more years." (Following the Korean War stalemate, a "never again" club arose in the U.S. Army, but with a caveat; "I knew that the real meaning of the 'never again a land war in Asia,'" wrote Daniel Ellsberg, was "never again a land war with China *without nuclear weapons*" (Ellsberg's italics).

After his four decades in the business Stone's keen sense of the official lie was well developed. His visits to Europe and England and his stay in France had attuned him to a different perspective, and he continued to forage constantly through foreign newspapers, periodicals, and books. While still a left-wing scourge to some in the nation's capital, Stone was friendly with major foreign intellectuals and journalists. Among his closest friends was the superb historian, journalist, and analyst on Indochina, the French-born Bernard Fall, who enhanced Stone's understanding of Vietnam's guerrilla warfare.

It remains astounding that neither McNamara nor any of the "best and brightest" architects of the Vietnam War heeded Fall's classic accounts of how and why the French failed in Vietnam. Instead, Vietnam became America's longest, most divisive, and most senselessly tragic war to date. Stone had read Fall before the two met in America in the early sixties. Fall had married a beautiful young artist, Dorothy Winer, and they lived near the Stones in northwest Washington. The couples spent much time together. Like Stone, Fall was pursued by the FBI. "In the early sixties, Bobby Kennedy thought Bernard was a French agent," recalled his widow. The great investigative reporter Seymour Hersh once told Dorothy Fall that "it was just Bernard and Izzy" who were writing correctly about Vietnam early on. Esther later told Dorothy Fall, "I'll never forget how Bernard introduced Izzy as 'my friend' when Izzy was an outcast in Washington. Nobody would have anything to do with us." Said Dorothy Fall, "This must have occurred in 1965, when Izzy was already accepted by many of the antiwar left. But in Esther's mind, it remained a prominent gesture." That year, Fall received the Polk Award for interpretive reporting and brought Stone as his guest to the ceremony. Susan Sontag was among those who rushed over to Stone, gushing her delight upon meeting him. By then, Stone had achieved something he never thought possible as a "funny-looking" teenager. "Women adored this cute little man and he was very courtly," recalled Dorothy Fall.

Unlike Esther, Dorothy never had the feeling that she and Fall were outsiders. "Bernard was controversial, but had a following." Recognized as the top expert on Vietnam among those uncommitted to the official U.S. posture, Fall was professor of international relations at Howard University and by 1965 was being listened to by doves in the administration. Fall did, however, feel "persecuted by those who did not agree with him. The powers that be did not like him and tried to shut him up in many ways," recalled Dorothy Fall. "For instance, he was denied a job with AID and found out through other channels that it was because of his views, which were contrary to officialdom."

At parties, Bernard Fall and Stone appeared as odd-couple friends, with the towering six-foot-tall Frenchman bending down to talk to Stone. At times Stone felt jealous of this younger scholar and military analyst who spoke three languages fluently and wrote in all three—English, French, and German. As a teenager Fall fought against the Nazis in the French maquis, an experience that, Stone noted, "gave him an ineradicable interest in things military, especially in guerrilla war."

Like Stone, Fall worked tirelessly—even more than he did, the older writer professed. When socializing, Fall also commanded attention at every gathering with his ironic humor and erudition. "Bernard was outspoken but not shrill or emotional as Izzy was," said Dorothy. "He always held court and was beholden to no one. He loved to share what he knew and did so with Izzy. Like Izzy, he insisted on finding and writing the truth, no matter what the consequences." And like Stone he could be "abrasive, intent on winning every argument, and controversial." Their friendship was bonded by mutual respect. "There was never any small talk, as I recall. They always talked about Vietnam. Even if joking, it was about serious stuff. They both investigated, were honest and frustrated about stupidity and deception among people who made policy."

Fall insisted on getting his material firsthand. In 1967, he made his last trip to Vietnam. On February 21, while on patrol with U.S. Marines north of Hue, Fall stepped on a land mine and was instantly killed. He was forty-one and left behind his wife and three daughters, the youngest just an infant. "I was in Hong Kong at the time," said Dorothy Fall, "and received a telegram of support and love from Izzy and Esther." The Stones were stricken at the death of Fall and remained friends with Dorothy throughout their lives.

In a *Weekly* box, with a thick black border, Stone wrote of his friend's "short but dazzling" career. "There is hardly a writer on Vietnam in Washington or elsewhere who will not miss Bernard Fall. No one in the country knew as much as he about the Vietnamese war, and none was so generous with all who consulted him. These ranged straight across the spectrum from right to left. . . . He was not a peacenik but his hatred of doubletalk often made him the ally of the peace forces. He himself prized above all the respect of the soldiers. . . . Fall understood the soldier's devotion. . . . He avoided the high brass to be with the troops, and he would much have preferred to die as he did, with the Marines, on combat patrol along that road one of his earlier books made famous as the *Street Without Joy*." Stone correctly predicted that Fall "will long be read and remembered as a soldier-scholar. . . . I will miss him as a friend."

In 1963 Stone had praised Fall's *The Two Vietnams*. Fall was able to get to Hanoi with two other foreign correspondents and interviewed North Vietnamese leaders, who told them that they were veering toward a negotiated solution and would recognize a neutral South Vietnamese state. There was no American confirmation because American journalists were not allowed into North Vietnam. Correspondents in Saigon had begun to rebel at the pressure by the American mission "to get on the team." The bureaucratic and media battles became known as the "press mess." As Phillip Knightley wrote, "President Kennedy's administration itself did everything in its power to ensure that the existence of a real war in Vietnam was kept from the American people. . . . But to the discredit of the world's press, the fact remains that in the crucial years of Diem's decline, with American involvement growing steadily, the only daily newspaper with a full-time correspondent in Saigon was the *New York Times*" (the legendary war correspondent Homer Bigart, to be followed by David Halberstam). The rest relied for daily coverage on the wire services, who were represented by such exceptional reporters as Malcolm Browne of the Associated Press; the outstanding Pulitzer Prize–winning journalist and author Neil Sheehan, then with United Press International; and *Newsweek* stringer François Sully.

After writing that the war was going badly, some were threatened with expulsion by Diem, and all were trailed by his secret police. "Their reward for reporting" the war's deterioration was a "campaign of denigration," wrote Stone, including right-wing newspaper silliness that Halberstam was "soft on communism." Kennedy famously tried to manage the media by putting pressure on the *Times* to transfer Halberstam out of Vietnam. The *Times*' publisher, Arthur Hays Sulzberger, behaved admirably, even canceling a vacation for Halberstam so as not to appear acquiescent. On the other hand, *Time* magazine behaved abominably. In1963, Charles Mohr, the magazine's tough correspondent, coauthored a piece with *Time* stringer Merton Perry. They led with an observation that Stone had used two years earlier: "The war in Vietnam is being lost."

No *Time* readers saw that sentence. It was cut and replaced by glowing words on how well the war was going and an inaccurate attack on the Saigon press corps.

Negative reports were not questioning the morality or validity of American intervention, only that it wasn't working. "We would have liked nothing better than to believe that the war was going well," Halberstam wrote later. And when Mohr quit *Time* magazine on principle over his gutted story, he was embarrassed that some saw him as an antiwar hero. He returned to cover the war for the *New York Times* and later wrote, "I didn't come to think of it as immoral until the very end." Halberstam later told Knightley, "You really should have had a third paragraph in each story which would have said 'all of this is shit and none of this means anything because we are in the same footsteps as the French and we are prisoners of their experience.' But given the rules of newspaper reporting you can't really do that. Events have to be judged by themselves, as if the past did not really exist."

Stone was at times contemptuous of such explanations. In a mostly laudatory review of books by Halberstam and Browne, who both won Pulitzer Prizes, Stone wrote that they "acquitted themselves honorably in the best tradition of American journalism, which is to be skeptical of any official statement." But "the idea that the past may help explain the present appears only rarely." Stone criticized the restrictions of daily journalism rather than the reporters: "There is no time for study and American editors do not encourage that type of journalism in depth," as did some foreign newspapers that Stone read faithfully, such as *Le Monde.* Michael Herr's *Dispatches* remains the best work at capturing the surreal nightmare of Vietnam's warfare, and he wrote in *Esquire,* "Conventional journalism could no more reveal this war than conventional power could win it."

Unlike Herr and Fall, Stone never saw combat troops in the field and subsequently did not empathize with them as they did. At the urging of Fall to see for himself, Stone made one visit to Vietnam in 1966. "He came back very excited and sat down to write the 'perceived wisdom— He Had Been to Vietnam,'" recalled Peter Osnos, who was Stone's assistant at the time. But it was not easy to write that definitive piece. "He crept around it and crept around it and got writer's block. He gave the piece to Esther and me to read. It had lots of pretty girls in flowing dresses and so forth. Esther and I looked at each other. 'Oh, dear, what are we going to do?' It was pretty thin gruel. And Izzy knew it. He walked and walked and really fretted. Then he bolted out of bed in the morning and rewrote the whole piece from beginning to end, pounding away. He sent it to Bob Silver, who thought it was terrific and included it in a book of great prose." In some of the meandering descriptions of stifling heat and teeming streets, the piece still seems like warmed-over Graham Greene and doesn't match Stone's other perceptive impressions of foreign lands. He refused visits to the field of battle, which were highly orchestrated by press officers. Stone came away with the less than remarkable acknowledgment that despite the best of intentions no outside force could heal the problems of Vietnam.

For most Americans, fed the pablum of jingoistic patriotism, any truth about Vietnam was new. A 1967 Gallup poll revealed that half of all Americans had no idea what the war was all about. Even after Tet in 1968 the unenlightened chairman of the House Appropriations Committee, whose consent was needed for appropriations, asked the U.S. Army chief of staff, "Who would you say is our enemy in this conflict?"

Stone's most acid attack on the American press came after its reaction to the historic scoop of the *New York Times*' Harrison Salisbury, who was the first U.S. journalist to visit Hanoi. In January 1967 Salisbury exposed one of the biggest military lies, that of precision bombing, and, Stone wrote, it should be recognized for "the possible saving of civilian lives in the future.... The myth that we have been bombing the North with surgical precision is dead." The U.S. military had been concerned about reactions to Hanoi's charge that civilians were killed in Johnson's December 13 and 14 "Christmas" bombing raids. A man of Salisbury's stature confirming such charges made it "impossible" for the United States to "downgrade criticism abroad as enemy propaganda or anti-American prejudice." Instead, Stone watched in anger as the U.S. press corps strafed Salisbury. Stone facetiously headlined his piece "Harrison Salisbury's Dastardly War Crime." "That America's foremost paper could send a correspondent to an enemy capital in the middle of a war and expose the misleading character of our own government's pronouncements was extraordinary. It has few parallels in history and it should make Americans proud of our free institutions [particularly the media]. But the Salisbury exploit instead of being greeted by applause has evoked as mean, petty and unworthy a reaction as I have ever seen in the press corps.... A barrage of slander has been laid down." Even the *Times* attacked Salisbury's reports as "uncritical, one-dimensional," and Reston criticized him, as did other columnists. *Newsweek* bombarded his searing reports of civilian deaths as reading "like the line" from Communist publications. "Frenzied journalism" in the *Washington Post* and the *Star* came close to calling Salisbury a traitor for reporting what was not in the "national interest." Such nonsense, Stone wrote, could be characterized as "ponji-stick journalism"—like the dung-tipped spears in Vietcong booby traps.

Lippmann was among the few establishment columnists who came to Salisbury's defense and supported his nomination for the Pulitzer Prize. However, Vietnam was still too ticklish a subject, and Pulitzer judges were overruled by an advisory board.

Years later, Salisbury chuckled over Stone's vociferous support. "Oh, I loved that. I'm sure I thanked him for it." Salisbury was hurt by a slicing column in the *Washington Post* by Chalmers Roberts. "I was very sore at him for that. . . . On the whole the *Post* was not very good. Obviously, the Pentagon went ballistic and tried hard to 'get something' on me, and there was this Communist leaflet."

Stone was apoplectic when a journalist he respected, the *Post*'s Pentagon reporter, George Wilson, revealed that Salisbury had not attributed a North Vietnamese propaganda pamphlet as a source for much of his information. "Salisbury would have been on solid ground and probably would have won the Pulitzer for doing just what he did—he got behind enemy lines and wrote that this 'surgical strike' was false," recalled Wilson. "I have no disagreement with that. But he went on at great length to say these planes did this and that, with no attribution at all. All he needed to do was say, 'according to North Vietnamese reports.'" Wilson referred to the highly competitive atmosphere that existed between the *Post* and the *Times*. "The Pentagon was suffering grievously from Salisbury's stories and so was the *Washington Post*. Here was 'the enemy' behind the enemy lines and we had nothing. The *Post* was delighted that we could knock down the *New York Times* coverage. I was the messenger who put a blight on these revelations and, indirectly, helped the Pentagon." Responded Salisbury, "Had George or any other reporter stopped to think for a moment, they would realize when you're in a Communist country, your sources *are* Communists. There aren't any other [sources] there!" What hurt was the suggestion by some that Salisbury had not seen the destruction for himself. "Of course, years later, it was revealed that the CIA had all of this information all along. I was delighted with that," said Salisbury.

Salisbury had lasting disagreements with some of Stone's views, particularly his Korean book, but he revered him. "Without people like Iz, we're dead. He was a stimulus. He kept digging and digging and had to be convinced [of information being given him], and he was *hard* to convince. He had a great nose for smelling out bad policies and politics and lies. I loved reading the *Weekly* because I never knew what he was going to get into."

Stone's blistering attack on the Washington press corps for hammering Salisbury may have been a way to vent his own anger for having so long been dismissed by them. As Stone's prominence grew during the Vietnam War, Dudman asked Stone's permission to put his name up for membership in the Overseas Writers group. Stone said "Okay—with no great enthusiasm, but he was willing." Its president, Marvin Kalb, was delighted with the idea of Stone joining. After a couple of weeks, Dudman approached Kalb, who told him, " 'There's a little snag, we'll get through it. Two old guys on the board are raising a question about does he have too much connection with the Communist Party.' Marvin thought it was all foolishness that would be smoothed out at the next monthly meeting, but I felt I had to tell Izzy that there was a delay and why. Stone was hurt and shocked and sore. 'Dick,' he said, 'I shouldn't have been in this at all. Get me out of it! I feel like I've just stepped in a great big pile of horseshit.' I tried to tell him that we'd get it through, but he told me to drop it. So we did." Kalb recalled, "I did run into opposition, and Izzy did withdraw his application in anger and disappointment. I never did understand why Izzy wanted to be a member anyway. The club was for those of us who lived off of off-the-record or deep-background sessions with 'senior officials.' Izzy lived in his own world of journalism based on on-the-record comments. He didn't care what the 'senior officials' said on 'deep background,' because I think he assumed they were lying or misleading the press in any case." In fact, Stone used to say that not being admitted to deep-background briefings was a plus because he was not bound by any of the "secrets." He could find out what went on from journalists who were present and use that information. His anger was directed more at the snub than not being a member.

As Stone grew in stature for his Vietnam reporting, a union occurred with the premier journalistic insider. It made a startling impression on those who gauge the ebb and flow of a person's station in Washington's incestuous world of media and power. Pragmatist Lippmann was nonetheless gullible when LBJ smothered him with flattery, asking his advice on the war. Lippmann believed the administration was listening to him. After a trip to France in 1965, Lippmann worried that "I've been pulling my punches" regarding Johnson's foreign policy. He tried to get the *Washington Post* to shift its pro-war stance, which did not happen until LBJ's friend Russell Wiggins, its chief editorialist, was replaced by Phil Geyelin in 1967. The final blow in Lippmann/LBJ relations came when Lippmann realized that the president "had misled me." He turned down a state dinner at the White House at the end of 1965. He remained far from Stone's peripatetic activism, however. "Although he would not identify himself publicly with the anti-war demonstrators—the constraints of civility were too strong—neither could he condemn them," wrote biographer Steel.

Now estranged from the president, Lippmann lashed out at LBJ for pursuing an imperialist, willful war that risked involving China. The president was consumed by "messianic megalomania." Harsh words filled his column by 1967: Johnson was "pathologically secretive" and was ruining America. Under LBJ, wrote Lippmann, "there was growing belief in the world" that the United States was a "bastard empire which relies on superior force to achieve its purposes, and is no longer an example of the wisdom and humanity of a free society." Helping to inform Lippmann's opinions were two people he had previously viewed as too radical, Fall and Stone. In the spring of 1966, Lippmann contacted Fall to get his opinions. Soon he was meeting with both Fall and Stone. "From these dissident journalists he learned not to believe administration reports about the conduct of the war." The great scribe, who had seldom set foot out of Georgetown, the White House, or the Cosmos Club, now dined with Izzy and Esther at the home of Bernard and Dorothy Fall. That spring, Izzy and Esther mingled on the Lippmanns' lawn at their annual mint julep party, receiving discreet glances. The absence of any important administration officials was duly noted. Except for Stone, that is. From his viewpoint, Stone could only grumble as he left the party with Esther and Dorothy that he had seen far too many administration dolts present.

Lippmann began to get a dose of what Stone had long experienced. LBJ set a team of researchers to look at old columns trying to find errors. As the war continued, shouting guests shattered Washington dinner parties, and old alliances splintered. Lippmann, snubbed by the powerful he thought were friends, was distressed. "His sense of isolation increased. The snide remarks about his age and judgment, the embarrassed encounters at his club when old acquaintances . . . averted their eyes . . . the intellectual fratricide and vendetta—all of those took a toll," wrote Steel. But Lippmann's harsh lesson forced him to see things differently about conventional explanations for the Cold War. "The war, as it had for many others, had changed his interpretation of the American past," wrote Steel.

"It was as if Walter Lippmann and I. F. Stone met at the intersection of two arcs, one declining and one ascending," wrote Andrew Patner, although he noted that Lippmann's "social 'suffering' did not continue for long." Too accustomed to being an insider, Lippmann backed Nixon over Humphrey and once again wined and dined with a president and his slippery sidekick in war, Henry Kissinger.

Until Seymour Hersh exposed the My Lai massacre in 1969—the dark and bloody tale of a "search and destroy" mission where GIs rounded up several hundred women, children, and old men and executed them—few reports of atrocities and brutality surfaced. After My Lai broke, innumerable stories of inhumane treatment were recalled by reporters who had witnessed them. GIs faced not just physical traumas, but a world of sanctioned immorality; they were given a license to kill through policies that mocked the Geneva convention, shaped by armchair officials cushioned from actual warfare. In a war of attrition, with no fixed goals, ground was taken at extreme cost to lives, then abandoned. In any war, soldiers are systematically trained to dehumanize the enemy; all Vietnamese were "mere gooks," so why have concern for "wasting" them on missions labeled search and destroy. And, in truth, the enemy could be an old lady or a twelve-year-old boy, which kept tensions high. The body count became a perverted measure for victory that included untold noncombatants. The counts were often inflated, faked, or became an incentive for killing, as officers pushed for "success." The common saying was "If it's dead, it's VC" (Vietcong). Jack McCloskey, a wounded and decorated veteran leader of a center that worked with troubled veterans, recounted, "They would set up competition. The company . . . with the biggest body count would be given in-country R and R or an extra case of beer. You're telling a nineteen-year-old kid it's okay to waste people and he will get *rewarded* for it, what do you think that does to your psyche? Years later, they're reflecting on it."

As we have seen as recently as 2005, military trials dealt with only a few "bad apple" soldiers in the Abu Ghraib tortures, just as My Lai was blamed on Lieutenant Calley. The top brass were once again successful in deflecting attention from their own guilt and the systemic realities of war strategy. Hersh, the reporter whose diligence once again exposed tortures and mayhem, continues to use a long-ago illustration that is applicable for today's audience: when the My Lai massacre was exposed, a mother of one of the soldiers who participated said, "I sent them a good boy and they made him a murderer."

In responding to My Lai, Stone recognized the kind of war American soldiers were being told to fight. His attacks were aimed at the perpetrators of the war. In an essay titled "The Atrocities Nixon Condones and Continues," he wrote, "We are dealing here not with an occasional atrocity but a deliberate policy. What a fear-crazed and hate-filled GI may do in occupying a hostile village can be put down to the brutalization of war. The real crime is higher up. . . . Our strategy . . . is to uproot or destroy the peasantry the guerrillas may have won over. . . . The safe rule . . . is to shoot first and investigate later, or just add them to the body count." Stone said as "horrible as it may sound," there was logic to this method, which "grows stronger as the spiral of hate mounts on both sides." The VC used civilians who showed "increasing willingness to fight back after their lives and homes were ruined. . . . The biggest and dirtiest booby trap of all is the filthy pit of this war itself, from which we emerge stinking in the nostrils of mankind."

Except for sympathizing with poor black draftees, Stone was guilty of writing little about the class nature of a war that asked everything of a few and nothing of most in America. The skewed draft system assured that the vast majority of the 27 million men who came of age during Vietnam could avoid military service, to say nothing of actual combat. Stone was as weak as most observers at the time. Although he saw racist aspects, the onetime socialist seldom addressed the terrible inequities of what was essentially a war fought by the poor and the working class. As a social critic, he extolled the dedicated youth in the antiwar movement (a minority of that generation) rather than examining how exempt most were through a draft riddled with loopholes: student deferments, lax medical excuses, high lottery numbers. (Only later was it popularly noted that no sons or grandsons of members of the U.S. Congress, who had devised the loopholes, had been killed in Vietnam.) Back then the reserves and the National Guard were privileged dodges for the likes of George W. Bush, and many of his current advisers had deferments. Vice President Cheney took advantage of several. However, a GOP propaganda campaign and ignorance about the Vietnam War assured Bush that he could wipe out enough traces of the past to win an election in 2004 and continue to send someone else's children to war.

Few remember at all Robert McNamara's shameful legacy, never discussed in his self-serving accounts—his brainchild, Project 100,000. By 1966, President Johnson feared that calling up the reserves or abolishing student deferments would further inflame war protesters. Even after McNamara began privately declaring the war was unwinnable, he devised Project 100,000, which systematically recruited those who had previously been rejected for failing to meet the armed services' physical and mental requirements. Recruiters swept through urban ghettos and Southern rural back roads, even taking at least one youth with an IQ of 62. In all, 354,000 men were rolled up by Project 100,000. Touted as a Great Society program that would provide remedial education and an escape from poverty, the program offered a one-way ticket to Vietnam, where "the Moron Corps," as they were piteously nicknamed, entered combat in disproportionate numbers. Johnson, the civil rights advocate, sanctioned a program that took a heavy toll on young blacks. A 1970 Defense Department study disclosed that 41 percent of Project 100,000 recruits were black, compared with 12 percent in the armed forces as a whole. And 40 percent of its recruits were trained for combat, compared with 25 percent for the services generally.

In fairness to Stone, the facts about Project 100,000 seemed to have escaped his eagle eye because they did not surface until near the end of the *Weekly*. Still, instead of examining the complexities of this class war as it escalated, Stone seemed to overlook the inequitable draft. While justifiably praising the students of SNCC and CORE who risked their lives fighting for black rights in the south in 1965—many of whom were also the early unpopular dissenters on Vietnam—Stone seemed to feel that everyone who went to Vietnam had a choice. "Unthinking enthusiasm, blind devotion, anti-communist fervor and herd-like conformity may be counted on to produce enough troops in Vietnam," he callously wrote. "It takes far more guts to fight the civil rights struggle in the south." Unfortunately for many poor blacks and whites, that was not an option.

In all other areas of the war, Stone bombarded McNamara: "Men who can so twist the truth are a menace to national security." If historic calamities such as Vietnam seem inevitable in retrospect, they did not while under way. In 1968, Stone cataloged McNamara's "Record of Dishonor." He looked up McNamara's lies of four years earlier claiming "unprovoked aggression" that stampeded Congress into giving Johnson his war resolution. Then Stone compared that testimony with McNamara's contradictory 1968 assertions before the Senate Foreign Relations Committee. McNamara was not altering the picture out of conscience; he knew that the committee now possessed incriminating Defense documents that proved that McNamara had lied four years before. He was still peddling a "deceptive picture" and "still trying hard to lie about it now."

Two factors informed Stone's unflinching prose. He had read, reread, and compared the documents and testimonies. And unlike Washington top journalists who hobnobbed with administration officials, Stone knew that he was never going to be chatting over cocktails in Georgetown drawing rooms with McNamara; it was not difficult for this outsider to finish McNamara off: "His whole performance is the shameful climax of what many had believed to be an honorable record."

In 1969, Stone blisteringly attacked the president in "The Old Nixon Surfaces Again." "No Communist regime ever rewrote history more blatantly than Richard Nixon in his November 3 speech on Vietnam." Nixon tried to blame Vietnam on the Democrats, "but the truth is that 15 years ago Nixon [as vice president] was doing his best to prevent peace from breaking out in Vietnam and he failed because Eisenhower would not support him. . . . This has been Nixon's war for a long, long time." Then Stone criticized the Democrats, who "if they had the guts would be warning the country" instead of caving in to Nixon, who Stone noted, was not averse to using tactical nuclear weapons. "Nixon still wants to contain China and to keep Vietnam as a base for that purpose." Vietnam's "self-determination" had nothing to do with it.

Since Tet many in the mainstream media were doing excellent reporting and criticism, and Stone consistently praised and credited them. The *Nation* publisher Victor Navasky aptly called Stone an "investigative reader"; as Stone and the *Weekly* aged, he did not always dig for scoops. His newsletter at times resembled a top-notch clipping service with additional commentary and edgy headlines, which explains why so many mainstream journalists found information in the *Weekly* that they couldn't find elsewhere. In one four-page edition, seven boxes were filled with critical war stories from the *Baltimore Sun,* Karnow in the *Washington Post,* ABC-TV, selections from an Agnew press conference ("A Fast Man with a Non-Sequitur"), a *Today* show transcript of Senator Muskie blasting Agnew on the SALT talks, an excerpt of a Nixon address, and a letter from a combat soldier refuting administration lies that search-

and-destroy missions had ended ("Search-and-destroy is what we do every day, though we don't call it that").

Although ill health forced Stone to close the *Weekly* before the war ended, he hammered away in the *New York Review of Books*. When Kissinger escalated harsh demands, Stone described the peace proposal as "the first time we ever heard of a con man offering the Brooklyn Bridge at half-price twice in a row to the same visiting hayseed." Stone's "trenchant and perceptive analysis" was outside the norm, said Hersh. "The overwhelming majority of the media fell in line . . . emphasizing Kissinger's exotic role in the secret diplomacy far more than the substantial issues."

As Stone tried so hard to tell Americans at the time, Vietnam should always stand as the tragic consequence of the arrogance of power in both the media and the government.

25

FROM
"WE SHALL OVERCOME"
TO "OFF THE PIGS"

O nce again, as history unfolded in tragedy, Stone had no desire to retain the remotest sense of neutrality. As the publisher of an opinion journal, Stone continued to lace his observations with hard facts that demolished government lies.

Stone was among an initial handful of antiwar protesters whose origins of dissent centered on civil rights, banning the H-bomb, and a moderating policy toward Cuba. By the late sixties, that nucleus grew to millions of anti–Vietnam War protesters around the world. Stone would deplore the senseless violence of destructive fringe groups who eventually destroyed the New Left. Earlier, he was among a tiny vanguard of old leftists respected by the young because he was no doctrinaire ideologue. And Stone was inspired by the New Left, who had no ties to the old crowd who had been cowed during the dark days of McCarthyism. "I was New Left before there was a New Left," he often quipped.

"The nice thing about the New Left was that they realized the complexities of the world and that no particular theory was going to fit exactly," said Stone in later life. This was by no means true of all elements in the movement. In 1963, Stone suddenly withdrew as moderator of a New York Town Hall discussion after hearing several of the participants speak in Washington. Their views, he said, "seem to me a mixture of naïveté, Negro nationalists' distortions (understandable enough in light of the Negroe's anguish, but still distortions) and out-of-this-world leftism." Many in this Maoist student sect were ejected from House hearings on travel to Cuba after shouting anti-American epithets. Stone also protested the ban but detested their militant posturing and stale leftist cant. He was now sufficiently well-known that the *New York Times* and the *Washington Post* reported the Town Hall flap. It was a "joke at the expense of our country when a congressional committee regards it as un-American to fight for freedom to travel," and "the students performed a public service in breaking the travel ban," he wrote. "But I do not wish to be identified with what I regard as hysterical exaggerations, hurtful to an honorable settlement between the United States and Castro's Cuba."

Despite his criticism of government actions, Stone was always the patriot, always referring to the United States as *we*. The writer who once called himself a radical wrote as a liberal in 1965, "We hope that the student movement will not be led astray by stunt-mongers and suicide tactics." Stone divided the peace movement into roughly three groups. One sought to persuade a wider public to end the war. The second were more concerned with *"testifying"* (Stone's emphasis) than in persuading; they fostered acts of moral disapproval such as refusing to pay taxes or serve in the military, obstructing the draft, halting troop trains. The third were "revolutionary forces" who sought solidarity with the Vietcong and "believe that peace can only be won by getting rid of the capitalist order." The intracommunist battles, from Tito to Mao, should persuade activists that all would not be peace and harmony if capitalism was destroyed and communism won, Stone archly observed. Nearing sixty, Stone now embraced conventional dissent: "Only the first [group] can change public opinion for the better."

Noting that elements of all three groups were present at any one demonstration, Stone cringed when he heard the "archaic echo of the thirties" from some youths. He hated the concept of fighting violence with violence and cautioned that in times of "rising tensions" a peace movement can become a "disguised vehicle for aggression and hatred. We're not going to calm our fellow citizens by jumping up and down, screaming. We're not going to aid the cause of peaceful coexistence by demonstrating that we cannot even coexist peacefully with our fellow citizens." Writing obscenities on the Pentagon or blowing up buildings solved nothing, he continually exhorted.

Stone thought it vital that the "respectables" march as an antidote to portrayals by hawks that the movement was composed only of long-haired, pot-smoking renegades. When he saw his friend and the widow of Drew Pearson, Luvvie, at one rally, Stone praised her sedate outfit. Taking her arm, he said, "Yes, we must always dress for peace."

* * *

In 1961, Stone experienced a new sensation. As he stood before Harvard students, he recalled, "I spoke at Harvard in the 1950s and there were virtually no students in the audience. Just older townspeople. Kids were afraid to come out for fear that if you were seen at a radical meeting, you'd be blacklisted." Observing one enthusiastic crowd in the sixties, Stone's sister, Judy, quipped that a generation had been skipped: "This is all of Izzy's old readers and their grandchildren." As the war spun on and Stone's stature grew, he crisscrossed the continent, from Harvard to Berkeley and in between on campuses across America's heartland. Organizers had to shift rooms to accommodate the overflow. Always nervous before a speech, Stone took lone walks. Then he would weave history, concepts, facts, and opinion in an unbroken stream without notes. Afterward, Stone was ready to party.

Todd Gitlin was in the 1961 Harvard audience when Stone spoke with "unillusioned sympathy" about Cuba. He "liked the fact that Stone was alert to Fidel's authoritarian tendencies" even as he recognized that the poor majority were aided by the revolution and urged students to mobilize against Kennedy's harsh policy. Gitlin began reading the Weekly, "which taught me, as it did many of my contemporaries, that the government lied. Over and over the antiwar movement could count on him to unravel the lies."

Gitlin drifted into friendship with Tom Hayden and others in the SDS band of "unabashed moralists" who were involved in civil rights and antinuclear movements. At the age of twenty, Gitlin became SDS president. The group were in their purest, short-haired infancy, wearing shirts and ties and skirts like all other youths in the early sixties. In October 1962, Gitlin was in a Washington audience when Stone spoke about the insanity of nuclear war on the eve of the Cuban missile crisis. Anxiety flooded his every word as Stone warned that "thousands of years of civilization were hanging by a thread."

"He was close to hysterical and that loomed very large in my sense of the world coming to an end," recalled Gitlin. As Gitlin and others drove to a small gathering afterward, they heard on the radio that Khrushchev and Kennedy had communicated and "they weren't going to blow up the world after all." Stone joined the young crowd, "which was very sweet of him." From that moment, a friendship with Stone grew. They ate in greasy spoons and Stone became a mentor.

By 1965, Weekly subscriptions had not yet reached twenty-one thousand. As the war continued, the movement swelled and so did Stone's readership. Knowledge of his newsletter grew by word of mouth as copies were passed from hand to hand, campus to campus, subscriber to potential new subscriber. That one simply could not know the truth without reading the *Weekly* was the word in peace circles in the United States, Britain, and Europe. Each year of the war added another ten thousand subscribers. By 1971 Stone was a rich publisher, read on Capitol Hill, in the State Department, and at the White House. As the FBI began its covert infiltration and attacks on the antiwar movement, it again stepped up its assault on Stone, checking with informants "familiar" with the CP and "related" activities. They rummaged through Stone's credit bureau records and D.C. police records (finding nothing). They collected articles about him from even the nation's smallest newspapers, which were now covering him. Editors were not particularly pleased with Stone's message: they should print more news instead of "selling soap." Thanks to a moribund media, he said, looking at reporters covering him in 1961, most people didn't know where Vietnam was.

He preached common sense: America would have to negotiate with China at some point, so the sooner the better; the country should demilitarize, send the Peace Corps to Cuba, withdraw troops from Vietnam. He chastised Russia and the United States for not trusting one another on nuclear disarmament and gave long speeches citing his verification scoop that both could detect atomic testing despite government lies that long-range detection was not possible.

After Hiroshima, Stone had joined an army of famed atomic scientists—including Ed Condon, Robert Oppenheimer, and Hans Bethe—urgently calling for civilian, not military, control of atomic experiments and pressing for international cooperation to halt the arms race. For seeking peace in the midst of Cold War hysteria, they were crucified by the media, the FBI, and McCarthyites, who dug up Communist connections from the thirties. Stone fervently defended them. Many lost their positions or were so besieged that they retreated from politics.

President Kennedy joined the huge propaganda campaign of fear, begun by Eisenhower, that had students ducking under desks in drills and their parents building backyard bomb shelters. Kennedy promulgated the insanity of surviving a major nuclear attack in one's fallout shelter with hoarded canned goods. "A fallout shelter for everybody," he recommended, "as rapidly as possible." Stone unceasingly ridiculed Dr. Edward Teller—"that kook"—and others who saw safety in stockpiling bigger bombs, securing congressional funding to build the Big One, the hydrogen bomb. On August 6, 1964, Stone spoke at a pacifist demonstration commemorating those who died in Hiroshima. Mass demonstrations seemed the only hope of changing policy, and on December 19, 1964, Stone was among members of nine groups who called for LBJ to begin an immediate cease-fire in Vietnam.

Stone filled a University of Maryland auditorium by 1965. "The policy of reprisal in Vietnam on which we have engaged is a confession that counterguerrilla warfare has failed," he said. No one ridiculed some of Stone's arcane references reflecting his advanced age: Washington warriors "probably put hair tonic on the hairs on their chest to show how virile and big they are when dealing with other people's lives." To which youths in his audience might have responded, "What's hair tonic?"

He called Ho Chi Minh a "very human man" and, naively, a leader who wanted a "Democratic state," not a Communist one. Stone was on safer ground when he discussed the U.S. role in killing millions of civilians, thousands of American soldiers, and ruining a country with no end in sight. In February 1965, four hundred students demonstrated and picketed the White House, then walked to a D.C. church for a rally addressed by Stone. This was a trickle of those to come.

Stone's name was now being usurped by strangers. While he seemed hopelessly bourgeois to some on the far left, one young Communist shouted to an audience at the Massachusetts Institute of Technology Socialist Club that the United States was a fascist regime. When challenged to a debate he bellowed, "I'll get I. F. Stone to debate for me!" The Los Angeles Fair Play for Cuba Committee distributed a 1963 newsletter that carried the text of an ABC-TV interview with Castro, which the *New York Times* "paper of record" had not covered, Stone noted. It was soon in his files to enlighten FBI agents.

Long a force in the National Committee to Abolish the Un-American Activities Committee (renamed in 1962 the National Committee to Abolish the House Un-American Activities Committee), Stone now had youthful comrades. Although he warned against "stunt mongers," he could not contain his joy at the antics of Jerry Rubin, Abbie Hoffman, and their Yippie cadre, who manipulated the media with acts too outrageous to ignore. For Stone, who had seen famous men cower before the HUAC and McCarthy committees, it was sheer joy to watch them strut into the HUAC chambers when they were subpoenaed for "treasonous" antiwar activities. Rubin, dressed in Revolutionary War costume, handed out copies of the Declaration of Independence to befuddled congressmen. He quipped that protesters who had not been subpoenaed suffered from "subpoenas envy."*

Stone had seen nothing like it in a lifetime of futile activism to end HUAC. "This new bunch of kids came along, who had never been members of the party, weren't haunted by their political past, weren't fearful about being asked to inform because they had nothing to inform about. They just threw the committee for a loss and made them look foolish, treating them with the derision, comedy, and buffoonery that they deserved, putting the HUAC in its place. I don't think the committee ever recovered.

"Before then you had the inquisitor and the heretic, that symbiotic relationship," when "counterclockwise Communist" informants held forth during the witch hunts. "The kids were different. They weren't ideologues in this sense." Stone uses a sports analogy, rather startling for him. "It's like a wrestling match where if your opponent doesn't do the thing you expect him to do, you don't quite know what to do. The committee suddenly seemed irrelevant and comical. They just pissed on them."

Stone was also fond of the Women Strike for Peace organization. "It was hard to pin down such nice ladies [Stone was still using the term in 1985]. They brought flowers to the committee." He recounted how their leader, Dagmar Wilson, answered committee questions: "'Would you have a Communist in the organization?' 'Yes.' 'Would you have a fascist?' 'Oh, I only wish we could reach them!'" Stone let out a burst of laughter.

Gitlin was interviewing Stone for his perceptive book *The Sixties: Years of Hope, Days of Rage,* but Stone was in no mood to examine the movement's deterioration. Characteristically, when Stone saw something to admire, he was not too interested in discussing the negatives. Rubin spent his last years apologizing for the sixties, trying to make it on the same Wall Street he had once ridiculed. In his eighties networking yuppie salons, business cards were passed around the way joints had once

---

*Rubin and Hoffman became national symbols for youths who longed for some levity in the movement, throwing dollar bills from the balcony onto the floor of the New York Stock Exchange in opposition to U.S. dollars spent on war, urging thousands of stoned peaceniks to levitate the Pentagon, marching in front of Judge Julius Hoffman calling out "Sieg Heil" at the conspiracy trial following the 1968 Democratic convention riots.

been. Such actions helped to paint the sixties counterculture as a sham, but Stone ignored the idea of any poseur qualities.

Both Rubin and Hoffman, the zanies of yesteryear, met tragic ends. Hoffman started as a dedicated civil rights activist, was arrested by the FBI for selling cocaine, went underground, reemerged, but tragically committed suicide in 1989. Five years later Rubin was struck by a car and killed as he jaywalked across Wilshire Boulevard.

Erwin Knoll, one of Stone's best friends and editor of the *Progressive,* said, "Izzy was always willing to give people the benefit of the doubt much more than I was." However, it would be wrong to regard Stone as credulous. At that first major anti–Vietnam War rally in April 1965, Stone spoke to the largest antiwar demonstration ever assembled to date. As Stone stood before twenty-five thousand in front of the Washington Monument, he felt red-hot anger as folk singer Phil Ochs derisively sang "Love Me, I'm a Liberal." Calling liberals cowards was no way to forge a wider coalition, Stone exclaimed. He shouted that he was a liberal and so was Senator Gruening, the Senate patriarch who had bravely voted against the Gulf of Tonkin resolution and was standing next to him. Stone would not placate the crowd who supported Ochs's song and yelled, "I've seen snot-nosed Marxist-Leninists come and go!"

On the other hand, Stone rebuked elders who were at that moment undermining SDS by tarring it as pro-Communist. On the eve of the 1965 march, some of the most trusted peace advocates and friends of Stone's, such as A. J. Muste and Norman Thomas, signed a press statement warning that peace groups should be independent from "any form of totalitarianism" and not receive "direction from the foreign policy of any government." Gitlin and other SDS organizers had no such intentions and urged widespread participation. Perhaps the "elders were desperate to build a maximum bloc against the war," thought Gitlin, but this could not explain why one of its organizers told Stone "the outlandish tale that the students intended to urinate on the White House."

Antiwar marchers grew from twenty-five thousand that 1965 spring day to half a million a few years later. Some protesters exponentially spun into lethal destruction along with the massive wreckage of Vietnam. Yet there was no truth to jingoistic claims that the antiwar movement "stabbed America in the back"; there was never, as Gitlin said, "an otherwise splendid and attainable victory on behalf of freedom and democracy in Vietnam." Escalating statistics tell the story: By the end of 1967 there were 486,000 American troops in Vietnam, and 1.7 million acres in South Vietnam had been defoliated. The once beautiful countryside was now so heavily cratered that it looked to some soldiers like the surface of the moon. A million and a half tons of bombs had been dropped on the North and South together. As Stone constantly wrote, Americans were supposed to be liberating the South, not bombing them to death. In 1968, Nixon's campaign mantra was peace, while he secretly readied nuclear bombs for North Vietnam. The United States dropped more bombs on Vietnam than it did in World War II and the Korean War combined. Of the fifty-eight thousand American war dead, some twenty thousand died after Nixon and Kissinger took office.

In 1964, Stone had warned young activists that marching for peace would be a long, slow struggle. Like others, he despaired as Nixon made a public show of ignoring protesters and the country remained passionately divided, but the antiwar movement ultimately did what the right said it did. It kept Johnson and Nixon from waging an intensely escalated nuclear war, which would have widened the conflict with disastrous global consequences.

Stone consistently showed up Nixon's lies in long essays in the *New York Review of Books*. He guessed correctly at Nixon's curdling paranoia and secrecy before it became common knowledge. One essay dealt with "a marriage of paranoias": Nixon, who always felt the media were against him, had been joined by the military-industrial complex. Stone recalled similar feelings among New Dealers "that the news media were one-sided. But there are crucial differences between the two periods. Poor people don't own newspapers. The news media now as then are in wealthy, mostly conservative and largely Republican hands." Unlike the rants against FDR, "it takes a lot of steam in the boiler before they turn against a Republican President." By 1969, mainstream media finally gathered up some steam, but many mass-circulation outlets remained pro-war and against the protesters.

"The Eichmann trial taught the world the banality of evil," wrote Stone, borrowing from Hannah Arendt. "Nixon is teaching the world the evil of banality." In 1970, Nixon disastrously waded into a group of protesting students and stiffly tried to engage them in sports banter. "The man so foolish as to talk to protesting students about football and surfing is the same man who (like Johnson) sees war . . . [as] a challenge to his virility."

Nixon, Agnew, and other hawks tapped into an older generation's anger, fear, and uncertainty about "these kids with long hair," despite that, or perhaps because, many of them were their very own children. There was something frighteningly unrecognizable about them. Some were arrogantly dismissive, most of them stoned, banding together in hippie garb, dashikis, long hair, love beads, sandals. University students rioted, occupied deans' offices, taunted "pigs" and national guardsmen, who were just another brand of draft dodgers in those days. Violence raged—police invaded a Black Panther lair and gunned down three unarmed members, sixty Weatherman were captured, black students with guns took over the student union at Cornell. Police with nightsticks swept through student mobs at Harvard Yard. They clubbed, teargassed, and jailed peaceful protesters, and well-organized hard hats, whose sons were in Vietnam, took out their wrath by beating "peaceniks."

Such images swirling on sensation-seeking TV did not of course capture the serious and peaceful contingents. (Nor the fact that most on campus remained conservative, according to polls.) In November 1969, a quarter of a million protesters marched past the White House in one of the largest demonstrations to date, and forty thousand participated in the March of Death that weekend. Behind seven drummers beating a funeral roll, they marched single file. Each wore a hand-lettered placard bearing the name of a soldier killed in Vietnam. On they came, wearing all those names of the dead, for thirty-eight hours. Being among them felt like a religious experience to Stone.

By then, a majority of Americans felt the war was a mistake, but this was no pro-peace referendum. Pop psychobabble never saw the complexities and divided the world into "freaks" and "straights." By 1969 blue-collar America rebelled, not because they necessarily felt the war was wrong but because too many of their sons had returned in pine coffins. Divisions shattered families and friendships: father and son, hawk and dove, peacenik mother and John Wayne father, those who went to war and those who went to Canada. That so many from various generations and backgrounds eventually chose dissent underscored the pathology of living through a war that few understood, conducted in subterfuge with no clearly defined military objectives, which was never even declared a war.

Stone admitted that he did not have the answers for the country's upheavals. But no one did. Media attention on flamboyant acts in the counterculture was made to order for Republicans, who continued to inflame voters for half a century with their derision of sixties "immorality." The FBI set up its illegal COINTELPRO (counterintelligence program), which included infiltration, wiretapping, black-bag jobs. Spies infiltrated the antiwar and civil rights movements, committing violent acts to destroy their peaceful image. They succeeded in doing great damage, but an unknowing public dismissed charges of infiltration as "crackpot" exaggerations. The Walker Report detailed the Chicago police gone berserk at the 1968 Democratic convention, citing "ferocious, malicious and mindless violence" and "gratuitous beating," but it was years before the public learned that "almost one in every six demonstrators was an undercover agent." Whether throwing feces and urine in hotel lobbies was done by FBI provocateurs or movement extremists was never known.

Americans now seem inured to betrayals—after the Pentagon Papers, COINTELPRO, Watergate, secret hoards of FBI files on countless citizens released through the FOIA, lies about Iran-contra, assassinations and covert wars in Latin America and Africa, bogus claims of Iraq's WMD, and once again, warrantless wiretapping in 2006. It seems hard to believe there was a more innocent era, but even such a perceptive observer as journalist/author William Greider recalled in 2004, "Again and again, [Vietnam] antiwar dissenters and civil-rights activists told me the FBI and CIA were spying on them, tapping their phones, infiltrating their ranks and disrupting their organizations. The stories I dismissed as paranoia all turned out to be true."

Stone was too busy writing about war and peace to pay much attention to the supercharged cultural revolution of sex, drugs, and rock 'n' roll that vast numbers of young either played at or took seriously. By 1970 war resistance had splintered and fringe groups pummeled each other. The Weathermen, numbering about three hundred, gained disproportionate attention from a media descending into sensationalism. Blowing up buildings and screaming "Off the pigs" brought instant fame to this ragtag bunch who managed to take over the SDS 1969 convention. The ultimate fascistic irony was their treatment of the First Amendment as they confiscated tapes and cameras, and threw out the media.

Among them was Stone's niece, Kathy Boudin, who participated in a 1969 Days of Rage confrontation with Chicago police. The goal of this women's group was to get arrested as a statement of solidarity with the poor and Black Panther militants. Kathy wore her helmet, waved a Vietcong flag, and waded into the police.

Weathermen slogans seemed designed to disgust rather than promote social change, and soon the majority of peace activists viewed the Weathermen as the lunatic left. "Smash monogamy" was their mantra for mandatory group sex, hetero- and homosexual. In a Washington speech, the incendiary leader (and Kathy's friend) Bernardine Dohrn glorified Charles Manson's desire to eat his "bourgeois" victims, including the murdered and pregnant actress Sharon Tate. Stone excoriated the "morbid development" of some, "a tendency to glorify violence for its own sake, as when they make Manson a hero, for killing 'bourgeois pigs,' i.e., people exactly like their fathers and mothers." He injected some psychology: *The ultimate menace they fear is their own secret selves in their own parents. This is what they are acting out on the stage of national politics.* Early SDS leaders bitterly saw in this offshoot mutation the ruination of their peaceful attempts to end the war, aid those in poverty, and provide racial equality. Stunned friends remembered Kathy as an earnest organizer of welfare mothers.

Then, on March 6, 1970, Boudin was in a third-floor sauna of a West Eleventh Street town house in New York's Greenwich Village when a bomb being assembled in the basement exploded, gruesomely ripping apart the two bombmakers and another friend on the ground floor. Boudin went screaming into the street naked and was taken in by a horrified neighbor. Bomb paraphernalia was found, including nails, which demonstrated a lethal intent to pierce the victims. In borrowed clothes, Boudin disappeared into the Weathermen underground for a decade, using countless aliases, allegedly still taking part in a few Weathermen bombings.

In 1980, Boudin surfaced infamously as the decoy in a U-Haul van that harbored six gun-toting blacks high on cocaine who had just killed a guard in a botched Brinks armored-truck robbery. At a New Jersey Turnpike roadblock, Boudin pleaded with the policemen to put away their guns. Six gunmen jumped from the back of the U-Haul, mowing down the defenseless officers. Families of the victims forever blamed Kathy, the white woman in the group declaring her innocence, which caused the police to disarm. Kathy could claim no youthful craziness for her participation. She was the mother of an infant and was nearing forty. With her father pleading her case, Kathy got twenty to life. For twenty-two years, Boudin taught in a literacy program, educated prisoners about AIDS, and pushed for prison reform. Released in 2004, she was sixty-two. Both her parents and Aunt Esther and Uncle Izzy were dead.

Her son, Chesa, who had been raised by Weathermen members Dohrn and Bill Ayers, had become a Rhodes Scholar.

Esther and Izzy could not reconcile the Kathy they knew with this outlaw. Stone was repelled by her participation in a wanton criminal act in which there was not even some twisted revolutionary rationale. He and Esther never once visited her in prison, although Stone occasionally sent her books. They seldom mentioned her.

When Kathy was arrested, Judy Stone felt that it was unnecessary for the *New York Times* to mention that Stone was her uncle, but her brother who had been so long in the business took it calmly. "Izzy said to me, 'But I am part of that story.' I guess you can't be a well-known uncle like Izzy and a father like Leonard and not be part of that story." Yet he never mentioned in print that Kathy was his niece.

Countless media ruminations have tried to explain what was in their childhood that would send Kathy into far-left violence and her brother, Michael, in the opposite direction of conservative politics and a federal judgeship. But it remained puzzling. Virginia Durr, the elegant civil rights activist, had housed Kathy for several days in earlier times and found her "very polite and pleasant" but "absolutely impenetrable." What puzzled Durr "is how such a smart girl could do such a dumb thing."

In 1970, Stone was anguished about the rash of bombings and bomb scares in New York City. When he appeared on the popular Dick Cavett TV show, he dismissed them as "children playing at revolution," recalled the producer, Bob Cunniff.

Shortly after the Greenwich Village explosion, Stone told college students that he was one of the few who had bothered to read the Weathermen Manifesto "down to the last cliché. Hogwash! You don't make revolutions out of half-baked ideas. Much of what the Black Panthers say is stupid, but I soberly think they are victims of a police conspiracy."

In a column awash in ambiguities, he sought to explain motivation but did not name his now famous fugitive niece, who had gone underground. "The Weatherman kids," a "far-out splinter group," should be viewed from "as many ways as possible. . . . They can be viewed as spoiled brats, in a tantrum with a world which will not change overnight . . . but they are also the most sensitive of a generation which feels in its bones . . . that the world is headed for nuclear annihilation and something must be done to stop it." Theirs was a "mishmash of ill-digested pseudo-Marxist rubbish . . . a St. Vitus' dance of hysterical politics." But "their criticism of 'conventional dissenters' like myself and our futility, as the war goes on, is hard to rebut. . . . These wild and wonderful—yes, wonderful! kids," he defiantly wrote, "also serve quite rational political ends." He returned to an old theme: radicals were necessary to shake up society's establishment. "But I do not believe in salvation by holocaust. Hate and hysteria certainly will not create a new man or build a better world. *Political suicide is not revolution.*"

Stone empathized with a perplexed older generation but added, "I must confess that I almost feel like throwing rocks through windows myself when I see Judge Julius Hoffman turn up as an honored guest at the White House and when I see Billy Graham like a smoother Rasputin dishing out saccharine religiosity there." Nixon and his entourage showed "no anguish, no awareness, no real comprehension . . . the dynamite that threatens us sizzles on a fuse that leads straight back to the White House."

Six months later, Stone was desolate. "During the depression I never felt the despair I am beginning to feel now about the future of our country." Stone's condemnation now was tougher. "Even the [past] revolutionaries had rational goals, not just a blind frustrated urge to destroy." Stone blamed Nixon for lacking FDR's leadership, which had helped quell Depression despair. A "loss of confidence extends into every sector of society. . . . The social landscape does not encourage long-range investment. Black and Chicano minorities are in revolt. . . . The police have become a target for snipers, as have firemen. . . . A tiny minority of firebrand youngsters is making good on its threat to 'bring the war home.' . . . Anarchy and barbarity, race war and gang rule, not utopia, lie at the end of the road on which our instant revolutionaries would put us. . . . One looks on, helpless to avoid the collision one sees coming."

Sounding like Dr. King, who had been slain two years before, Stone called for "mutual understanding and forgiveness. . . . You cannot beat men into angels, nor make them better by calling them 'pigs.' " Then Stone asked, "But how do you preach to youth the sanctity of human life when established society, its institutionalized violence and exploitation, treats it so lightly? . . . The craziest of our mixed-up kids are no crazier than the end-justifies-the-means morality of American imperialism."

Stone reprinted in a box, without comment, remarks by Senator McGovern: "What I personally resent most about some American radicals is their willingness to jeopardize the chances of constructive change by such antics as displaying Vietcong flags, disrupting courtrooms, shouting obscenities and other obnoxious patterns of conduct." Stone slugged the item "Radicalism—Or Posturing for the TV Cameras?"

Yet Stone could not forgive causes of counterviolence—unchallenged murders by authorities and the basic indifference "if not downright hostility of the white majority in this country" toward blacks. He cited the 1970 "killing of six blacks, all shot in the back, in Augusta, and the murderous fusillade against a black women's dormitory in Jackson, Miss., where two girls were killed." Stone asked why Nixon's top black officials had not walked out following the president's "skimpy message of protest" and Attorney General John Mitchell's trip to a "lily-white upperclass Delta Council meeting where he discussed the stock market!" Aaron Henry's bitter denunciation of that meeting ran in an early edition of the *Washington Star* but was promptly yanked. Stone reprinted Henry's comments: Mitchell "has done more than any one man to create the climate that makes white policemen feel they can shoot our people down." Stone also quoted Chicago grand jury evidence of police perjury and "wilful murder in the Black Panther raid which killed Fred Hampton and Mark Clark—but could find no evidence on which to indict!"

The whitewash of the National Guard murder of four Kent State students and the serious injury of nine others sent Stone into deeper depths. "What's a Little Murder (Of Blacks and Students)?" he caustically headlined his column on the President's Commission on Campus Unrest. While the report "honestly and thoroughly" showed that the "killings were unjustified and unnecessary," Stone added in italics, *"there is not the slightest chance that anything will be done about it."*

Stone scooped reporters by obtaining a copy of the unpublished grand jury report. He lauded the Knight *Beacon Journal* for exposing a "sensational" but nationally unreported speech by Ohio's Senator Young—the only senator who defended the students. He capitalized and boldfaced the sentence quoted by Young from the Justice Department summary of FBI findings: **WE HAVE REASON TO BELIEVE THAT THE CLAIM BY THE NATIONAL GUARD THAT THEIR LIVES WERE ENDANGERED BY THE STUDENTS WAS FABRICATED SUBSEQUENT TO THE EVENT.**

After the May shootings, Stone had visited Kent State, "a campus where you meet activists who never heard of *The Nation* and never read the *New Republic* and students who think themselves avant garde because they read *Time* and *Newsweek.*" Despite such Eastern intellectual sneering, Stone developed "respect and affection for the youngsters." He had found Vietnam War veterans "radicalized by their experience and frustrated by their parents' unwillingness to listen to them." That a grand jury could gloss over the National Guard killings on such a "politically backward" campus was a great tragedy. The handful of protesters were "average Americans, neither geniuses nor freaks." Stone demanded that a federal grand jury be convened because the weak-kneed Ohio grand jury report absolved the National Guard and Ohio authorities and instead astonishingly indicted twenty-five persons linked with the demonstration.

Stone had obtained the secret report containing FBI documents and disclosed the facts on Cavett's national television show. This occasioned an outraged letter to Hoover from someone involved in the Kent State affair, name blacked out. The writer requested a "full transcript of the investigation. I feel that if I. F. Stone, left wing pamphleteer, . . . can secure a full FBI and Justice Department report on the Kent State riot, and then read from it and display it on the Dick Cavett show, surely, I am entitled to a report that personally concerns me." Once again, Stone had stung Hoover, who wrote back, "You may be sure that we did not provide a copy to Mr. I. F. Stone." He told the letter writer to communicate with the Civil Rights Division of the Department of Justice, which had been given the report. Hoover's response still included its standard error: "I. F. Stone is the subject of a Security Matter–Communist investigation" and wrote for the *Daily Worker.* Of all the erroneous FBI contributions this was particularly blatant. Stone had never written for the Communist paper, and besides, it had folded in 1958.

Stone divulged chilling facts reported by one hundred FBI agents: none of the four killed or nine wounded students had "participated in any disorder at Kent or in the burning of the ROTC building on the commons of the University at any time." (Years later, parents who could never forget the news photos of their children, sprawled dead on the ground, were still waiting for an official apology.) Stone nailed Hoover for trying to cover up the report and praised the *Washington Post* and *Los Angeles Times* investigative reporter Jack Nelson for exposing charges against FBI infiltrators, acting as agent provocateurs, who committed arson and other unlawful acts that led to violent police action on other campuses.

* * *

As the war ground on and brought new media peace converts, Stone took satisfaction in quoting enraged editorials from an unusual source, the *Wall Street Journal*. He quoted from a fiery May 28, 1970, *Journal* editorial, headlining it "The Kind of Bums Nixon Likes" (the president had previously called the peaceful demonstrators and students "bums"). The *Journal* bashed Nixon for silence as hard hats went on a rampage in the financial district: "It is possible to imagine that the administration considers kicking bystanders in the head, swinging and throwing tools, spitting upon and assaulting individuals for making 'V' signs with their fingers, all less reprehensible than, say, throwing stones at armed helmeted National Guardsmen." Stone cheered, "Even Wall Street Lawyers Being Radicalized," when some formed a peace lobby.

Stone lashed out at a U.S. attorney's attack on the Chicago conspiracy-trial defendants, whom he called "fags," "sneaks," and "scum." Stone applauded senators who denounced Judge Julius Hoffman's "appalling ruling that the government had an automatic right to wiretap or bug the defendants without any prior authorization by a court." Equally repugnant was Agnew's characterization that they were "kooks" and "social misfits" who should be kept off the front page. "If the administration wanted to keep them off, it should have had more sense than to bring them to trial." Nixon was headed for deep trouble, prophesied Stone, who mocked his murky promises of troop withdrawal and peace talks. The "firm" withdrawal date was "always *Mañana*."

Both Lippmann and Stone were gripped by the same nightmare obsession, Vietnam, as were all observant Americans. In small bulletins Stone tried to address other salient issues, particularly Communist oppression. He sided with Soviet dissidents and said that it had been harder for writers under the Soviets "even than under the Czars." By 1971, Stone was blasting Castro: "Stalinist-Style Confessions Wrung from Revolutionary Poet." Famed Cuban poet Heberto Padilla was championed by Stone and international writers. His release from jail came only after "signing a confession as phony as the worst in the Stalin era. . . . Padilla's passionate concern for truth was too much" for Castro, whose "own vanity and megalomania have become enemies of a besieged revolution."

Stone took a skeptical view of Earth Day in 1970. Pollution was real but a "little exaggerated." Given the news that the United States had moved into Cambodia and officials seemed bent on sabotaging the SALT talks, Earth Day could be viewed as a "gigantic snow job" to distract attention as the country slipped into a wider war "and turn the youth off from more urgent concerns." Stone took his thoughts directly to the movement, voicing them as a speaker at the massive Earth Day rally. Today's global-warming activists would argue that this was one time Stone lacked prescience.

Late to address in depth the war's class nature, Stone now devoted much space to "the dirty deal the Army Gives the Draftee. . . . Army draftees were killed in Vietnam last year at nearly double the rate of non-draftee enlisted" men. Stone juxtaposed these facts with a CBS-TV account of "air-conditioned soldiers," the top brass, career officers, and NCOs living in relative luxury and safety in Long Binh. Reports of open rebellion among the draftees filtered into mainstream publications. Units were divided between heads (pot smokers) and juicers (beer drinkers), officers were fragged, racial discord was strong. Describing his unit, one soldier commented, "One-third are KKK, one-third are Black Panthers—and the rest of us duck a lot." Nihilistic messages and peace symbols were everywhere; cynicism about senseless killing was exemplified in a grim ditty, "Napalm Sticks to Kids." When VIP visitors touched down at one camp, they did not know that Army barbers had preceded them by helicopter to trim the GIs' hair and shave off their beards. But the Army couldn't control alienated GIs, who freely told the visitors how senseless and stupid the war was.

The more newspapers criticized Nixon, the more Agnew tore into them. "The Administration is trying to make independent reporting seem unpatriotic." Stone perceptively addressed an American problem that remains well into the twenty-first century: "There can be no generation of peace until we somehow curb the militarism and imperialism which gave us Vietnam and will create new Vietnams."

In the last days of spring 1971, Stone watched from the top of Capitol Hill the largest antiwar demonstration ever as half a million trudged in the sun. They looked like a "mass of brightly colored human confetti as far as the eye could see. . . . It took five hours for the last of the demonstrators to come within hearing range of the speakers." Stone was one of the speakers. The huge turnout was unexpected; Nixon had counted on apathy since replacing the draft with a lottery and promising to turn the war over to the South Vietnamese. "The peace movement has risen bigger than ever, from the ashes of Vietnamization," wrote Stone, but he worried that the protesters were "overwhelmingly white and middle class. There is a lot of missionary work to be done, in the ghettoes and out in the country."

Stone was overcome by "the stars of this year's demonstration." He devoted most of this edition to the Vietnam Veterans Against the War (VVAW) and their four-day encampment on the Mall, which "touched the heart of the country. . . . In an episode without parallel in the history of American constitutional law," Attorney General Mitchell had succeeded in getting an injunction forbidding them to sleep on the Mall, then "lost his nerve" and asked the judge to reverse the original order. Stone chuckled, "The failure of nerve is understandable." Stone recalled President Hoover's "biggest mistake," calling out the troops to drive the Bonus Marchers—tattered World War I veterans—out of a protest encampment in 1932. Nixon would have made his "biggest mistake . . . if police or troops had driven the VVAW out. . . . Pictures of legless veterans being carried out of the park could have precipitated riots in military encampments here and in Vietnam." Stone observed the remarkable shift among young GIs in this failing war. The 82nd Airborne Division sent word that they would join the vets rather than remove them. Active troops joined the thousand veterans, some of whom came in wheelchairs and on crutches, to participate in the VVAW candlelight procession and memorial service for the dead.

Stone was especially struck by a twenty-seven-year-old naval lieutenant and filled his newsletter with his testimony that week before the Senate Foreign Relations Committee. He called it the "most moving and eloquent we have heard in 30 years as a Washington correspondent." This was John Kerry, who defended antiwar members from Agnew's slam that they were "misfits." Said Kerry, "Those he called misfits were standing up for us in a way that nobody else in this country dared to."

Although Kerry's testimony was characterized as antiwar by Republicans who dredged up the "unpatriotic" slur again in 2004, much of Kerry's testimony was an impassioned plea for and defense of forgotten veterans. He spoke of atrocities that wars foster and "the hypocrisy in our taking umbrage over the Geneva Convention and using that as a justification for continuation of the war when we are more guilty than any other body of violations of those Geneva Conventions, in the use of free fire zones, harassment and interdiction fire, search and destroy missions, the bombings, the torture of prisoners." (Kerry referred to the conclusions of the Winter Soldier Investigation, in which other veterans had described personally committing or witnessing war crimes, and did not state that they were his own experiences.) But his anger was directed at the disgraceful treatment of wounded veterans "dying needlessly in VA hospitals" and in behalf of GIs who "come back and find the indifference of a country that really doesn't care. . . . Where are the leaders of our country? . . . Where are McNamara, Rostow, Bundy, Gilpatrick and so many others, where are they now that we, the men whom they sent off to war, have returned? . . . These men have left all the casualties and retreated behind a pious shield of public rectitude. They have left their reputations bleaching behind them in the sun. This Administration has done us the ultimate dishonor. They have attempted to disown us and the sacrifices we made for this country."

Kerry said, "Someone has to die so that President Nixon won't be, and these are his words, 'the first President to lose a war.' " Then Kerry asked the question that ignited his political career, "How do you ask a man to be the last man to die in Vietnam? How do you ask a man to be the last man to die for a mistake?"

At last Stone had found military heroes: "Just as the relative handful of the Resistance saved the honor of France so these thousand or more veterans of Vietnam will some day be seen as men who saved the honor of America." To the nation's discredit, it did not turn out that way; militarism remained ascendant.

The first time Daniel Ellsberg had seen or heard Stone was at the 1965 SDS antiwar rally held on a gorgeous spring day. He was concerned mostly about being seen on TV and having to explain to his bosses at the Pentagon why he was there; it was his first date with Patricia Marx, who was covering the rally for public radio. Four years later, tired of governmental lies, excuses, and cover-ups (including the secret bombing of Cambodia), the erstwhile Cold Warrior became a passionate activist who changed the course of history. In the fall of 1969, Ellsberg began smuggling out a seven-thouand-page top secret report that revealed the secrets and lies that had shaped three decades of America's policy on Vietnam.

In January of 1971, Ellsberg spotted Stone having lunch alone in the Senate cafeteria. Ellsberg introduced himself, told Stone he was a fan and the journalist motioned him to sit down. Ellsberg set his briefcase, bulging with his gold mine of secrets, next to his chair. As they talked about Vietnam, sudden tears came to Stone's eyes. He no longer knew what to say, he confided, because everything seemed so hopeless. Partly to "cheer him up," but also seeking his opinion, Ellsberg suddenly told Stone—"this hero of mine"—about the Pentagon Papers.

Reflecting on their meeting years later, Ellsberg had no explanation as to why Stone, the old bird dog, didn't pursue this incredible scoop and surmised that he probably felt these secrets needed a more establishment airing. Ellsberg's documents verified what Stone had long written. As Ellsberg urgently poured out his mission, Stone asked him if he was "ready to pay the consequences," which meant going to prison. Ellsberg, now married to Patricia Marx, had thought seriously about what might be a long sentence. As he stood up, Stone grabbed Ellsberg by the arm, tears again springing forth, and said, "Bless you for what you're doing." Recalled Ellsberg, "It meant a lot to me to hear that from him."

Stone agreed with Ellsberg's intent to seek out George McGovern and also suggested that he contact Gaylord Nelson, but Ellsberg failed that day to find any senator who would release the purloined documents. The saga of how Ellsberg's Pentagon Papers were published by the *New York Times,* the *Washington Post,* and other newspapers is now legendary. The publication resulted in a landmark Supreme Court decision and the trial of Ellsberg. Importantly, government-sanctioned spying on Ellsberg, attempts to plant derogatory information, and the Watergate plumbers' burglary of Ellsberg's former psychiatrist's office helped set in motion the crime that brought down Nixon.

As his lawyer, Ellsberg picked Leonard Boudin, after being dismissed by a Harvard law professor, Jim Vorenberg, who told Ellsberg he would not be a party to what sounded like "plans to commit a crime." Ellsberg recalled his fury. "I've been talking to you about 7,000 pages of documentation of crimes: war crimes, crimes against the peace, mass murder. Twenty years of crime under four presidents. And every one of those presidents had a Harvard professor at his side, telling him how to do it and how to get away with it!"

Contrary to some published accounts, it was another friend, not Stone, who suggested Boudin. After listening to Ellsberg, he said, "You know, I'm not a hero or a martyr. I'm a lawyer. But I've represented people like that. I'll be happy to represent you." After the stunning disclosures of Nixon's role in Watergate, Ellsberg's drawn-out case was dismissed.

Just before the Pentagon Papers made him famous, Ellsberg participated in the huge May 1, 1971, rally. Countless thousands, mostly young, came prepared: damp handkerchiefs to wipe teargassed eyes, sturdy shoes for running, lawyers' phone numbers written on their hands in case of arrest. By then, there was tacit support from a war-weary Washington. Taxi drivers, especially blacks, gave free rides to demonstration sites. Young Marines held rifles with one hand and gave the peace sign with the other. As demonstrators blocked the streets, some commuting workers smiled in their stalled cars and honked greetings. By noon, the demonstration to shut down the government was over. Yet police suddenly started mass arrests, not attempting to find out if the youths had been a part of the demonstrations. "Most of them hadn't," remembered Ellsberg. "If you were young and had long hair, all you had to do to get arrested in Washington that afternoon was to walk down the street in Georgetown. Tourists, students between classes, shoppers, the children of some members of Congress, all got swept up." A staggering number, thirteen thousand, were held in the football stadium into the night. Years later they got a small settlement for false arrest after a class-action suit.

At noon that day, Ellsberg and a band of activists, including Howard Zinn and Noam Chomsky, called Stone for lunch. "We all revered Stone." Ellsberg felt that there was "something odd," about Stone that day. "As I recall, he was not as enthusiastic about our actions as we would have hoped." It could have been that Stone was silently musing about what he could possibly add to the millions of words he had written against the war for so many exhausting years. Wrote Stone after lunch, "In all this anti-war theater perhaps the pantomime which most undercuts the war is Nixon's sudden honeymoon with Chou En-lai. The containment of China is what it's been all about for two decades since we began to pour out first treasure and then blood in south-east Asia. Hanoi was Peking's tool, and we had to stop those hordes in Vietnam or fight them— remember?—on the beaches of California. What was billed as the Asiatic Armageddon now dissolves into a ping-pong tournament. So why go on with the killing?"

Stone even seemed to match the ennui when he wrote, "What's left of the war but inertia?" His spirits revived when the Pentagon Papers were published. Perhaps, finally, the war might come to an end. It would take until 1973 to withdraw all troops. The war officially ended in 1975.

In December of 1971, Stone announced that he was giving up his nineteen-year-old newsletter. His heart was aching physically as well as emotionally. "I have decided to heed the familiar warning signals," said Stone. In what turned out to be a major delusion, Stone said he would be shifting "to a less exacting pace."

PART FIVE

Icon

26

FROM ICONOCLAST TO ICON

When he put the *Weekly* (now a biweekly) to bed for the last time, in the winter of 1971, Stone was ten days shy of sixty-four—"although I hate to admit it." Nimble in mind and spirit, Stone faced the terrors of failing health—severe angina pain and bad sight further clouded by a cataract. Not given to modesty at this stage, he reprinted tributes from the *Boston Globe,* the *Los Angeles Times,* the *New York Post,* and from U Thant, the secretary-general of the United Nations. As always, Stone wrote to his readers as if they were close friends. "You made possible an almost unique experiment in independent journalism. . . . Thanks to you I was able to carry on an uncompromising fight against the witch hunt and the war, against injustice and official duplicity." Those years of "isolation and loneliness" were "made easier to bear by the affection I felt from, and for, my readers."

In the last issue Stone reprinted golden oldies, including his Einstein eulogy and a wry comparison of the 1968 Poor People's March and welfare for the rich. To see the march in perspective, "remember that the rich have been marching on Washington ever since the beginning of the Republic. They came in carriages and they come in jets. They don't have to be put up in shanties. Their object is the same but few respectable people are untactful enough to call them handouts." Stone savored his sixteen-year-old eulogy to Einstein. "The man who sought a new harmony in the heavens and the atom also sought for order and justice in the relations of men. . . . He fought Fascism everywhere and feared the signs of it in our own country." Nothing would have pleased him more than the neighborhood children "who recall the cookies he gave them. . . . Newton and Copernicus and . . . Pythagoras, too, could sweep the heavens with their grasp—but none of them were remembered by so many humble friends, for so many simple human kindnesses. In this realm, far beyond politics and physics, Einstein reigns alone in warm human memory."

Stone had "dreamed of taking the flotsam of the week's news and making it sing," publishing an "urbane, erudite and witty" paper with "substance, but as light as a soufflé." He added, modestly, "Needless to say, I rarely felt that I had succeeded." As Stone achieved respectability, he seemed to ricochet from charming self-deprecation—referring to himself as "America's most widely un-read journalist"—to self-glorification—"What I've been writing is going to live among the five best writings in American journalism in this period," he said when his collected works were published in 1968. Stone seemed to be saying, so there, you establishment prigs.

By then, critics, journalists, and historians were demanding to know why Stone had never received a Pulitzer, especially for his work on Vietnam. Historian Henry Steele Commager honored Stone's 1968 collection and said, "It is of course absurd that he should not be on the editorial staff of one of the great national newspapers." Ben Bradlee seemed surprised at the suggestion: "Izzy would never have wanted to be here. He liked being on the outside." Still, as William Greider recounts, Stone possessed a strong establishment streak: "Izzy loved the *Post*. He was more forgiving than he should have been, although that was a different time, when it was being tough." Before Greider left the *Post* for *Rolling Stone* magazine, he called Stone for advice. "He urged me not to leave the *Post*. 'It's a great newspaper and you're inside and you should stay inside and write for it.'" Greider relayed Stone's thoughts to *Rolling Stone* editor Jan Wenner, a Stone admirer. "He was so upset he sent Izzy a subscription to convince him I had made the right move." Greider wrote piercing political pieces for *Rolling Stone,* acclaimed political books, and now writes for the *Nation,* where the rule, extracted years ago by Calvin Trillin from publisher Victor Navasky, was a "no diddling clause," which meant that editors could not change so much as a comma without the writer's permission. Greider retained what mattered to him and his friend Stone, the ability to be his own person and write what he thought.

Stone's success "restores our faith in the ability of the individual to make an impression on American life," said Commager, employing a customary comparison: Stone was a modern Tom Paine, an enlightened champion for the rights of man. Stone never fooled himself about nonexistent power—that a Nixon or LBJ would read the *Weekly* and rush to say, "Izzy's right, I am going to change my policy!" Still, by 1968, Stone was more influential than Lippmann. Stone did more than unveil the follies, deceptions, blunders, and immoralities of the Vietnam War; he explained them historically and with remarkable vision. He was long vindicated for his early dissent. By 1970, he was important enough to earn a blast by Agnew, who called the *Weekly* "another strident voice of illiberalism." Stone welcomed this "mere flea bite" from Agnew—"it does wonders for your circulation."

The college dropout was now safe enough to give a commencement speech and receive an honorary degree from Amherst. He spent a sleepless night walking around the city pondering what he would say. Just one student boycotted—David Eisenhower, the grandson of President Eisenhower and the son-in-law of President Nixon. Stone drew laughter when he said: "I really owe my academic eminence here today to David Eisenhower"—pause—"and the other radical activists of this class."

Although typically upbeat about closing the *Weekly*, in a moment of candor he said, "I was bored with Washington, with Nixon's banality, the whole thing." Stone said this in the final days of 1972 when it seemed as if nothing would stop Nixon or the war. It was six months after a strange burglary had occurred in Washington. The *Washington Post* put two unknown reporters on the story and kept them there, which was all the more reason for the media biggies to dismiss what they were uncovering. Watergate became the twentieth-century's premier journalism coup, which brought down the president. One reporter was Bob Woodward. The other was known to Stone since he was a toddler in the home of his friends Al and Sylvia Bernstein, Carl Bernstein. No one was prouder of them than Stone.*

About the time Nixon was exiting center stage in disgrace, Stone entered, trailed by fans in Europe, England, and the United States. He occupied a foremost place among influential journalists, writing for two publications consistently listed at the top in surveys of the most influential publications on Vietnam, the *New York Review of Books* and his own tiny *Weekly*. He was named one of the ten "leading influences of

---

*When FBI agent W. Mark Felt revealed that he was Deep Throat thirty-three years later, it reactivated media firestorms about using anonymous sources. However, Felt was only one source; Woodward and Bernstein laboriously slogged through documents and followed trails, much like Stone, who was Bernstein's model. But today's right-wing cable shows outdid even themselves. They featured Charles Colson and G. Gordon Liddy spouting disapproval of Felt's "disloyal" whistle-blowing, without mentioning that they were two of the ex-felons that Felt, Bernstein, and Woodward had helped send to jail for their roles in the Watergate scandal.

American intellectuals" on the war, with his friend Bernard Fall leading the list.

Ironically, however, the lover and practitioner of the written word achieved fame through two usurpers of leisure reading time, television and film. And he loved every minute of the limelight. The movie lover from silent-screen days felt as if he were in a dream sequence in 1974. "New Cannes Festival Star: I. F. Stone," exclaimed a *New York Times* headline. Wrote Vincent Canby, "When a 67-year-old American journalist gets as big a play from the press and the public as Federico Fellini, Jacques Tati, Jack Nicholson, Tony Curtis and Luis Buñuel there is no doubt that the festival has changed." Esther and Izzy were at the film festival for the showing of Jerry Bruck Jr's. documentary *I. F. Stone's Weekly.* Narrated by *New York Times* columnist Tom Wicker, the documentary captured Stone's personality and skewered everyone from LBJ to Walter Cronkite by juxtaposing film footage and comments about Vietnam with Stone's words. The journalist tossed off a crack before setting off from the festival for a speech at Oxford University: "I'd like to see a movie in which a boy and a girl kiss and then the camera cuts away. It'd be so revolutionary."

When people first heard Stone, they were often surprised by his soft, reasonable tone, given the passionate thoughts he expounded. In a serious vein he told one audience, "The American movies have done more to agitate the poor around the world than anything that Marx ever wrote or Lenin ever said. It's given them a picture of society with decent conditions, clean homes, toilets, to put it in the simplest terms. . . . The real agitation is the knowledge that only a few miles away . . . across the Rio Grande is heaven." Nothing there that a right-winger could disagree with. Then Stone added, in the same sweet tone, "The great ideals that have made our republic a shining light of history have been defamed and dirtied in Latin America by being associated with the imposition of dictatorships that made us look like a bunch of hypocrites."

After Bruck's documentary, there was no stopping Stone, hailed in art theaters across the country, in Europe, and on PBS-TV. The film propelled some students to enter journalism, including Max Holland, an American who saw it in far-flung Austria. "It turned Izzy from a figure of admiration into a cult figure," remarked Peter Osnos, who shared a portion of that fame through his appearance as Stone's former assistant. When Robert Redford was in the *Washington Post* newsroom during the filming of *All the President's Men,* he wowed starstruck Osnos by saying he had seen him in the film. It played for weeks in art theaters. At one showing, satirist Art Buchwald, Stone's friend, bent down in mock humbleness, kissing the hem of Stone's coat. Stone blushed from dimple to dimple, but, as friends said, he became "quite full of himself."

Young antiwar fans loved the juxtaposition of film footage in the Bruck documentary, most devastatingly that of Stone and Walter Cronkite. Known as the "most trusted" voice in television, Cronkite was soft on Vietnam War coverage until after the 1968 Tet debacle. Film clips show Cronkite doing a fawning man-in-the-news bio on South Vietnam's Air Force general Ky: "He doesn't even go out to lunch, but, like an American businessman, eats off the corner of his desk. He is a hero to the Vietnamese people." Following a shot of Cronkite's benign interview, the Bruck documentary inserts Stone's observations: one of Ky's heroes was Hitler, and "one of Ky's first acts was to suspend the press." Cronkite is filmed in a gung ho plane trip to an area that had been pummeled by B-52 strikes. Stone's voice is heard, collected from a speech demolishing the corrupt unsavoriness of American's South Vietnamese allies—"a pretty stinking crowd." He added, "The Vietnam War has been a terrible defeat for all the brand names we believe in—for General Electric and General Motors and AT and T—for all the great corporations" and the belief that technology would conquer all. "Here down in the jungle, way below, is this strange creature that we can't crush. . . . Isn't that wonderful that human beings can resist all this murderous technology."

In 1971, Stone and Cronkite were Polk Award winners. At the cocktail hour, Stone praised Cronkite for his recent Vietnam coverage; in that manner of celebrities who aren't sure to whom they are talking, Cronkite darted looks over and around Izzy. But Stone put all the other speakers to shame. He was "very happy to receive my first establishment award," then, unlike the platitudinous speakers before him, launched into a reality check about Polk: "One of those few American journalists who was not afraid to see beyond the murk of the Cold War. . . . He was *murdered* by the Greek police, who tried to blame it on the left." That was the real and true story that Stone hoped might come out "one of these days."

Stone seemed appealingly cool on TV. In one appearance alone he garnered nearly the number of subscribers as he had begun with back in 1953. He received four thousand new subscriptions overnight after denouncing the whitewashing of the Kent State murders on Dick Cavett's show. "He was very strong, furious about what can happen when government operates in secret and camouflage," said producer Bob Cunniff.

Cunniff, who left the *Today* show to become Cavett's producer, recalled how cowardly networks were about controversial guests in the sixties. "Most people had given up the fight. There really was no marketplace of ideas." He spoke about the 1968 Chicago convention coverage. "For two weeks, the cops were whopping any kid on the scene, on the grass, around the convention, anywhere. It wasn't that they 'suddenly lost control.' It was policy and I had been watching it." Cunniff suggested using some of this footage. "'Are you nuts?'" said his boss. "'They'd kill us for it.' Then, on that famous Wednesday when they were throwing kids into the wagons as though they were pieces of meat," the program used Cunniff's piece on police brutality. "As they ran the crawl at the end of the show, with the cops beating on the kids, we had a track of Frank Sinatra singing 'Chicago is my kind of town.' That shows how angry everybody involved with the program was." The public, who had heard the drumbeat from Nixon-Agnew calling protesters "bums," didn't agree. "The mail was twelve to one *against* us."

A *Weekly* fan, Cunniff "managed to smuggle" Stone onto the 1967 Thanksgiving *Today* show. He asked Stone how they could present him without offending "our middle-class audience." By then Stone was a packaging pro: " 'That's easy,' he replied. 'Just say I'm a modern-day version of Ben Franklin, I'm like a nice country editor who has interesting views.' And that's exactly how I wrote the introduction! So they suddenly saw this little guy with the thick glasses with interesting opinions, instead of some radical." Stone didn't hold back: "'How long are the American people going to keep putting up the money to bail out those whorehouse keepers in Saigon?' Now that's a rather precise way of making a point, isn't it?" said Cunniff, laughing. "Surprisingly, the mail was very favorable. Something about Izzy got to people, they liked him."

Cunniff liked Cavett because, unlike the sanitized king of nightly TV, Johnny Carson, he "put on a lot of interesting people." But it was grim to work with young nonreaders ("as you know, television is deeply uninformed") and "people at the top who said, 'You can't offend the powerful lobbies.'" Even so, Cavett enjoyed an irreverent popularity. When he featured Stone along with comedian David Frye, "David would do his hilarious imitations [of Nixon], and Izzy would come on, and it was just demolition all over the place. They had to hire a person just to answer Stone's mail, almost all of it totally pro-Izzy."

Like most everyone in Washington, Stone had an "ego wall" on which he framed accolades and awards. "His living room was a shrine to Izzy," Bud Nossiter recalled. Said Cunniff, "It pleased Stone that he was accepted." Nervous and focused before he went on the air, Stone rehearsed his ad-libs, which sounded off-the-cuff. Audiences were charmed by his frank comments, so unlike those of stuffy Washington scribes, such as his riff on what happens to gullible journalists in Washington. "If you're a 'solid' fellow and an 'up-and-coming' fellow, you find yourself at dinner parties agreeing with people," who go on about a "lot of half-baked nonsense and you shake your head very wisely and people see you shaking your head very wisely and they figure you're a very wise guy. . . . Pretty soon, you know, you're just caught up in the goddamnest mess of crap." After the show, a relaxed Stone loved to live it up in New York. One night he and Cunniff went to the Copenhagen Restaurant, where Stone pointed out to the producer all the varieties in the smorgasbord "like a herring salesman."

In 1978, Stone had the chutzpah to interview himself in an "Izzy on Izzy" *New York Times* feature. It is revelatory to see what questions Stone chose to ask himself. Whether he was thinking of the critics who assailed his early 1950s anti-anticommunist stance or not, this article strongly emphasized the evils of Communism. "Communism may solidify permanently into the greatest prison of the mind the world has ever seen, far more oppressive than the so-called Dark Ages of medieval Europe." Stone still added his caveat that Communism might be saved if a "synthesis, so to speak, of Marx and Jefferson can be achieved." A decade later the eighty-year-old Stone spoke in sad past tense: he "had always hoped" that such a melding could occur.

No one reveled in newfound glory more than Stone. College after college placed honorary doctoral degrees around his neck. When the University of Pennsylvania gave their former dropout his degree in 1970, Stone wore the black robes of the Philomathean Society, the group that had rejected him in 1927. Stone crowed, "It's a great day for the retarded. I am probably the only man who took forty-eight years to get his bachelor's degree." In his 1978 "Izzy on Izzy" article, Stone surprisingly addressed his inferiority about the lack of a college degree: "For many years I felt like Hardy's Jude the Obscure whenever I got near a college campus." His accumulating diplomas "eased my old feeling of downright Tobacco Road ignorance."

Most of the time, however, Stone was not reminiscing but busily raving to anyone who would listen about his new intellectual pursuits, learning Greek and Aramaic to better understand the earliest form of democracy.

By the time the *Weekly* ended, Stone the Obscure might have pondered how he had failed: widespread appreciation included a 1968 front-page feature in the conservative *Wall Street Journal,* mainstream editorial pages ran his comments, college youths listened at his feet. In 1969, he and Esther could afford to move into a larger elegant home in northwest Washington, with a walkway curving up a lush, hilly front lawn and a patio out back. The house was more like an adjunct to the Library of Congress with its collection of seven thousand books, the rare ones wrapped in plastic and lovingly transported by Stone. The office overflowed into upstairs bedrooms, a downstairs study, and a recreation room. When Stone slammed into the printing plant for the last time in December of 1971, in urgent perfectionist haste to eradicate every last typo in his final copy, he left a reminder—a dent in the wall from years of banging open the door. Stone was a "kindly man" the owner told Stone's writer and friend Nat Hentoff, "but he sure is serious about getting things right."

Stone dedicated the final issue to Esther, who had worked for so long, her desk topped with a cheery sign: "Good News Is on the Way." "Her collaboration, her unfailing understanding, and her sheer genius as a wife and mother, have made the years together joyous and fruitful."

Although he liked to promulgate the *Weekly* as a mom-and-pop venture, Stone hired assistants all through the sixties. He ran a rigorous boot camp, and the joke around town was that no one could last more than three days. One young poseur didn't even last that long. He said he was "sort of a 'communitarian anarchist,' " and their conversation went downhill from there. Growled Stone, "What the hell is that?"

"Izzy was notorious; extremely demanding, and did not have a great track record with assistants. One accomplishment of my callow youth was that I won the longevity prize, or at least tied with a predecessor," said Peter Osnos, who went on to a long career at the *Washington Post,* became the publisher of Random House's Times Books Division, and was the founder, publisher, and chief executive of PublicAffairs Books. Over one of his Chinese lunches near the printer's office, Stone interviewed Osnos. "I'm a terrible SOB to work for," he said. For $100 a week it was "made very clear that the job was everything from soup to nuts—I took out the garbage and ran errands and did all the truly menial stuff." Only later did Osnos know the "joy of having Izzy as a friend."

The most unnerving facet of the job, remembered by all assistants, was Stone's boot-camp reveille. Phone calls would start at 7:30 a.m. with the morning quiz: "Well, what did you see today?" "Well, why did you miss this on page thirty-nine of the *New York Times*?" Assistants who had envisioned an exciting life in the nation's capital instead went to bed with the *Congressional Record*, boning up for the morning's interrogation. "I felt I was back in school," said Chuck Nathanson, who worked for Izzy in 1963. "He had no sense of age or experience or status. It was pure competition all the time: 'he got it, he saw it, and I didn't.' He must have had in mind that he was educating this smart-aleck kid from Harvard, but it came across more as a fun kind of competition." Nathanson felt that Stone, like all writers, could use editing. "My pleasure in life was telling him things that I didn't think he could get away with, that cast suspicion or innuendos, and I'd ask him if there was any evidence." Stone was usually economical in his surgical strikes, but his occasional strolls into flamboyance were criticized by Nathanson. "Izzy put up with this and actually changed some things."

Stone carted a bulging accordion folder everywhere. Sitting in hearings, he would be talking to a friend, simultaneously glancing at newspaper articles, ripping them out and stuffing them into his folder. "He always looked like the Mad Hatter, rushing around late for a 'very important date,'" recalled Nathanson. It was hard to imagine Stone in repose. "He'd go on these afternoon walks and I'd ask, 'Do you compose while you're walking?' He'd joke, 'No, I try to keep from decomposing.' He waited until the last minute because he didn't want to get beat or miss anything. He'd be in his bathrobe, unshaven, furiously tackling a piece. It was usually beautifully written—he'd been chewing on it all week."

The main task was to cull every possible newspaper, document, and record, searching for items worthy of excerpting for Stone's boxes, the acidic shorts that often showed discrepancies in what officials were saying. It was an exhaustive struggle to write something Izzy found acceptable for his boxes. "He did not take lightly to someone writing in his *Weekly*. I felt I was writing on his skin," remarked Nathanson.

Stashed in the basement of Stone's home, assistants were summoned upstairs by a buzzer. Two or three times a day Osnos ran to the Hill and the State Department, read the AP wire, picked up releases and reports.

Since Stone wrote a newsletter, he was barred from the daily press gallery where the loftier journalists hibernated. Osnos was consigned to an obscure pressroom on the Hill. "When I worked for Izzy, there was nothing glamorous about it," he recalled. "It gave me no particular cachet, like if you worked for Scotty Reston. Later it became a badge of honor, but then most of mainstream journalists still thought of Izzy as a bit of a nudnik and he was 'tolerated.'"

Another assistant, Andy Moursand, recalled that as late as 1970 he was rebuffed by a *Washington Post* personnel department flunky, who said working with Stone didn't mean much—even as Izzy was being read and extolled by the best in the *Post* newsroom.

To every young staffer or journalist friend, Stone "spun this little conceit" that someday, my son, all of the headaches of producing a jam-packed four-page newsletter might be yours. No one thought for one minute that Stone would hand it over to anyone.

Stone left the business a wealthy man and in addition sold his mailing list and himself to the *New York Review of Books* for an undisclosed sum (but reputedly $75,000). "He did very well. We bought his mailing list—and Izzy. That was the deal," said journalist Walter Pincus, one of the investors in the magazine. Stone was proud to become a contributing editor of the *New York Review of Books*—"the finest review of its kind in the English language." Stone was not alone in this opinion, but the old promoter was also pitching a deal: "You will receive one issue of The Review for every two issues of the Bi-Weekly as long as your subscription lasts. (If you are already a subscriber to the New York Review, your present subscription will automatically be extended for the proper period. . . . I hope you will be reading and enjoying my articles in The New York Review.)" Stone loved to tell everyone he was a "rich capitalist" who had bought his wife a mink coat, but he now had a dilemma. He had to think about saving his money. "Pop was terrible at math and I don't think he understood or was really interested in economic systems except in the vaguest way," said his son Christopher. "I tried to explain to him about capital gains, but he was like so many people of his age who had been through the Depression. His dad losing everything had made a lasting impression." With guidance, Stone learned how to invest, warily, but wisely.

The financially free Stone and Esther romped on their *QE II* vacations like honeymooners, eating early, then napping so that they would be fresh for dancing all night. They went so often that their travel agent even knew which rooms they preferred. Esther and Izzy were on the *QE II* when the entire ship gathered in various lounges to witness the royal wedding of Princess Diana and Prince Charles in 1981. But Stone was having nothing to do with royalty worship. Instead he took the air on deck in grand style. Another loner sidled up and asked Stone why he wasn't watching the wedding. Stone looked puckishly at his shipmate. "I never thought I'd be able to say this, but for the first time in my life, I can truly say *I* am a republican."

A mellowed Stone recounted a cocktail hour spent with royal rightist William Buckley on board the *France* in the summer of 1971, a display of cordiality that convinced some Stone friends that he had gone dangerously soft. Noting that Buckley was aboard, "I wrote him a note, if only to avoid an awkward encounter." His letter humorously suggested that "since we were trapped on the same ship," Buckley "had the option of fighting a duel or letting me buy him a drink—and that I expected to hear from his seconds." The two met with their wives in the bar and had a "quite pleasant" exchange. "After a lifetime as a devoted Red-baiter, Nixon had just gone to Peking that summer. And so I said to Buckley, 'You and I are brothers in betrayal. You have been betrayed by Nixon and I have been betrayed by Mao Tse-tung.' " When Stone told that story in 1988 at the time when Reagan was meeting with Gorbachev, he quickly updated his comment: "I hope we're headed for some other great betrayals." Pleasantries aside, Buckley did not spare Stone in a *National Review* obituary that sneered at Stone's effort to join the scholars when he wrote his book about Socrates: Stone got to heaven and Socrates snubbed him.

Jack Beatty, author and former senior editor of the *Atlantic Monthly,* recalls a feistier Stone besting George Will, on a radio show. "For every quote from someone famous, Izzy could counter with another. For one dollop of Adam Smith, Izzy could quote Montaigne. Will was outdone on the pretension front. There was Izzy, with the Greeks tripping off his tongue, Herodotus, Thucydides, Heracleitus. . . ."

Stone seemed to waste little effort on ancient enemies. The British writer Christopher Hitchens was a young staffer at the *New Statesman,* a favorite haunt on Stone's trips to England. "Agnew had resigned, various people were under indictment. Almost every day there was a new rat in the bag, and it was clearly closing in around Milhous himself. It was press day and we were going to give Izzy lunch in the boardroom. Everyone was at the printer's but me, and they said, 'When Mr. Stone arrives, take him up to the boardroom, give him a drink, look after him until we get back,' and I thought, 'Wow, Izzy Stone!' I'd got Balliol College to subscribe to two copies of the *Weekly*. I completely miscalculated everything and made rather an ass out of myself—'Gee, Mr. Stone, I've been such an admirer for so long, you must be feeling great, what with the news and everything,' and he said, 'Well, what do you mean?' Continuing to josh him along, I said, 'Well, you know, Agnew's facing it and the others are getting bagged and indicted. It's *their* turn—you must feel wonderful!' And he said, 'Oh, that. No, I guess not. I just can't get used to being on the winning side. Never did like the feeling of being top dog.' I felt completely deflated. I felt very vulgar asking him to rejoice in these people's discomfiture. And I found out later that if I had known him at all, I would have known to expect that, he was not one to do any jeering."

Victor Navasky, the *Nation* publisher, Columbia journalism professor, and prize-winning author, tells charming stories about life with Izzy as a longtime friend and sometime editor, many of them now in his memoir, *A Matter of Opinion*. Navasky's first remembrance of Stone was as a teenager playing ball on Fire Island, watching a tennis ball soaring dangerously close to "I. F. Stone's porch," where the *PM* writer clacked out his prose. The word was out, no chasing after balls while Stone was writing. Navasky revered Stone. "Izzy saw what others missed, even though it was often in plain sight. Partly it was a matter of perspective. Izzy was always looking for evidence of the great forces and trends that shaped our history—'the fundamental struggles, the interests, the classes, the items that become facts.'"

In 1953, Navasky perceived an epicurean side to his hero. Navasky was one of the Swarthmore students who had invited Stone to speak. Stone agreed, "but requested a club-car ticket. . . . This seemed like an extravagance and out of keeping with my image of Izzy." Navasky realized later that it was "part of Izzy's charm that he never accepted the idea that in order to be a heretic, a maverick, a solo practitioner, it was necessary to be a martyr or a monk." Navasky realized that Stone's "insistence on his perks" sprang from a sense of "dignity, of self-confidence, of earned entitlement."

That sense of entitlement only grew with time. In 1987, Navasky asked Stone to keynote an international conference of investigative journalists in Amsterdam, sponsored by the *Nation* and a Dutch weekly. After Navasky's call, the *Nation*'s publisher, Hamilton Fish, phoned to cement the deal. Stone told him, "'We'd love to do it.' Hamilton, correctly concerned about matters budgetary, stuck his head into my office and asked, 'Who is this 'we'?" Expenses for both Izzy and Esther would be more than redeemed by Stone's drawing power, replied Navasky, although the budget was so tight that participants were ticketed on non-scheduled airlines, put up in a modest hotel, and transported to the conference center on the cheapest available buses. But all was not over.

Stone called. He and Esther "'have found that it's too much of a strain to fly going east, so we take the boat,' and it seemed the boat they always took was the *Queen Elizabeth II.*" And on it went: Stone beamed when he learned that the *QE II* was going to dock in England a few days before the conference. "'At our age,' he explained, 'we need a couple of days to get our land legs, and we have this little hotel in London which makes a nice base.'" Then came the romantic request to stay at the small pension where he and Esther had spent their honeymoon, "and if you could just locate that . . . ?" They did. The next call: by a wonderful coincidence some of Stone's family were going to be there at the same time, and what about finding a place for them? Next, if the *Nation* could just arrange for Stone to speak at a public forum in the famous cathedral in Amsterdam, "he would be pleased to donate his fee to help defray the costs of the conference."

Ultimately it was all worth it, said Navasky. Stone drew nearly a thousand Dutch for his speech, and seventy activist-journalists attended the conference. Stone gave a "truly inspirational" keynote and enthusiastically participated in discussions. The conference was such a success that follow-up conferences in London and Moscow drew hundreds of investigative reporters, activists, and scholars.

At the end of the conference, as caviar and vodka were consumed, Stone gleefully raised a toast: "Comes the revolution, we will all live like this."

Stone's *Weekly* had an afterlife of amazing resilience, remembered poignantly and passionately. "Izzy was one of my inspirations from way back," said Bill Kovach. "When I worked at the [*Nashville*] *Tennessean* I moonlighted as editor of the State Labor Council's newspaper and their file of Seldes's old *In Fact* and subscription to Izzy's newsletter were my most treasured reading material. One of the first things I did when I became chief of the Washington Bureau [of the *New York Times*] was to invite Izzy to a brown-bag lunch to talk with the staff." The year was 1979—and it was Izzy's "first invitation to the Times."

While they continued to admire Stone's work, some colleagues were personally stung by his criticisms. Some talented and hardworking journalists and authors felt Stone, in his David-versus-Goliath mode, took cheap shots at their expense in his quest to prove his independence and their lack of it. One State Department reporter said, "Izzy tends to think that if any of us comes up with a story, it was handed to us by the administration. That's annoying when you have dug . . . to get a story" the administration was concealing. "He also tends to see some of the omissions and inadequacies of the press as conspiratorial cover-ups when they are nothing more than ordinary human frailty." "I think Izzy took pot shots at his colleagues, often significantly uninformed shots," said Jack Raymond, a longtime *New York Times* reporter who considered Stone a close friend, until a "stinging revelation" exposed another side. "I was amazed one day to pick up his paper and find an attack on a piece of mine. For all intents and purposes he asserted that I was a handmaiden of the Pentagon. I was stunned that anyone could think that of me." Worse still was that "he wrote this without calling me to ask for an explanation of whatever I had written, which seemed perfectly clear. I brooded about it." They met soon after at a dinner party. As the evening was ending, the steaming Raymond, a tall man, bent down over Izzy and said, "I can't resist any longer. I'm mad about something." Stone replied, "What're you mad about?" "You suggest I am writing pap for a bunch of militarists . . . and I resent that." Izzy stopped him: " 'Ohhhhhhh, Jack! Why should you care about what I write in my little paper that few people see?' On hearing that, my heart sank." Not only had Stone ignored the larger moral question of impugning Raymond's writing, judgment, and integrity, he attempted to get off the hook by pretending that his little rag didn't matter. Raymond knew as well as Stone that in their circle the *Weekly* was a prized read.

On one hand, *Atlantic Monthly* editor Jack Beatty summed up the view of many: "That man died a moral hero." On the other, the gifted Robert Sherrill, longtime *Nation* writer and scourge, said, "To me he was no hero." Stone "lacked something" even though he was an "outstanding fellow, virtually always on the side of decency and fair play." A kindness, which Sherrill would expressly deny, was often hidden behind his curmudgeon exterior, but no one could write tougher letters to friends like editor Navasky if he felt like it. And who could resist his devastatingly witty assault on the *New York Times* for "renting its cranium" and fouling the op-ed page by running Mobil Oil's weekly ads?

Sherrill remembered a curdled experience as a writer for Stone (who never ran the article and "wouldn't pay me the lousy one hundred and twenty-five bucks he owed me and I was flat broke"). More unfair, in Sherrill's estimation, was a stinging attack on his book on Hubert Humphrey, *The Drugstore Liberal,* which Sherrill had dedicated to Stone. "Izzy has a hang-up. He doesn't think he can prove his honesty and objectivity unless he guts a friend." A dual dedication went to Stone and Sherrill's dead cat. "I regret that my cat was not mentioned first, ahead of Izzy, for he was much more loyal." There was this "little-shit side of Stone, which emerged." Given the dedication, Sherrill hardly expected Stone to "take complimentary notice" of the book, but neither had he "expected him to *attack* it. I had dug up some damned solid stuff about Humphrey's part in helping to crush the radical wing of the Democratic movement in Minnesota when he was starting out. Stone ignored that portion entirely and [in a *New York Review* book review that encompassed several books] jumped all over the title, *The Drugstore Liberal.* I assumed every goddamned fool, literate or not, would know it was a takeoff on the expression *drugstore cowboy*—a person who isn't what he claims to be. And then I explained it in the book jacket. But Izzy interpreted the title to mean that I was snickering at Humphrey's humble background. The whole thrust of my writing had always been against elitism and big shots. How could Izzy possibly have supposed that I was sneering at Humphrey's middle-class background as the son of a druggist who had himself worked in a drugstore?" Sherrill concluded that Stone "knifed my piddling book" to prove how "independent" and "objective" he was, that he "couldn't be bought off with the flattery of a dedication or some such from a struggling unknown." (Sherrill is being modest; his book on LBJ, *The Accidental President,* had made quite a splash by then.)

"I came to feel that there were two great drives in Izzy's life. One was to do good. The other was to promote himself. He was a great showman," said Sherrill. "He worked very hard to develop renown as the 'irritating little Jew who wears thick glasses.' There's nothing wrong with developing an act if it gets people's attention and helps you sell soap. He did a great deal of valuable service in the areas he picked to fight. Yet by the time I knew him and worked for him in the midsixties, he was not a populist," said Sherrill. He had become a "professional underdog—no, change that—he had become a *commercial* underdog. The issue that made Izzy famous—opposition to the Vietnam War—was not a populist issue if for no other reason than that the sons of the potential populists in this country were fighting it. Opposition, however broad it finally became, was founded on the Eastern liberal establishment—and Izzy was very much a part of that. No underdog there. No outsider there."

Others felt the shiv in the ribs from Stone. "He was always very good about encouraging the young," recalled Christopher Hitchens, "but when he was sure he was right, he was incredibly arrogant. At a dinner in London he was incredibly harsh to a woman editor. Told her she was talking rubbish. As it happens, I thought she was too, and you got the feeling that he would do that no matter whom he was talking to—just as he was unsnobbish about whom he was talking to, treating everyone alike, whether it was cabinet ministers or interns. He had this acid style and that was fine if it didn't become a thing in itself. But often he was just being crabby. You were being more or less told, 'Don't disagree with me, and if you do, you're a book burner,' which is kind of a parody of what he was famous for.

"He gave this editor a real pasting for her attitude toward censoring fascist speakers and writers. Stone took the straight First Amendment position, while the British equivalent of the ACLU had taken the view that it wouldn't defend people who were accused of crimes under the British Public Order Act, which does censor incitement. That is not so surprising in Britain since there is no First Amendment. Why would you defend the right for a fascist that you don't have yourself? When I heard the ACLU had defended the Nazis in Skokie, for example, I couldn't believe it because I didn't understand, not then living in the States, what the First Amendment meant in practice."

Stone was a fan of many mainstream truth-seeking talents of the era— Tom Wicker, Russell Baker, Anthony Lewis, Art Buchwald, CBS-TV's Morley Safer, Mary McGrory—as well as radical writer Andrew Kopkind. However, Stone was capable of memorable put-downs of colleagues, as in his review of Theodore White's fawning biographies of the powerful: "A man who can be so universally admiring need never lunch alone."

"I was alternately Izzy's hero and Izzy's villain, depending on whether what I wrote agreed or disagreed with him," recalled George Wilson, the *Washington Post*'s longtime Pentagon correspondent. In the early sixties, Wilson broke numerous tough stories. "Izzy would give me credit—and then he would put his own spin on it. He would say, 'Wilson said this . . . and this is what I think it means.' Which was all right—but just don't call him a reporter. There was only one side of the story for Izzy. He called once and said, 'There's so much I don't understand about the strategic missile race and you understand it and I would appreciate having lunch.' At lunch it became apparent that he really didn't want to learn anything. He just wanted to deliver a diatribe on the badness of the arms race."

Stone's friend Walter Pincus, an expert on atomic energy and the arms race for the *Washington Post,* felt the same way when trying to explain the intricacies to Stone. "Izzy would never study the history of the weapons. He did this once in a while on issues—just made a moral decision that it was wrong. But he didn't understand it." Pincus handled their disagreements quietly. "When he'd do a long piece in his *New York Review* phase and you really disagreed, you just wouldn't say anything. He loved talking about his pieces, and by not responding, that would be the signal you disagreed."

Other journalist friends felt that Stone was less concerned with an exchange of ideas than in clarifying his own thoughts. "He wasn't that interested in what you had to say. He used conversations as a means of sorting out his own ideas," said Jack Raymond.

Continued Wilson, "I didn't begrudge Izzy his opinion, but he was *not* a reporter in the sense of a guy who tried to put it down the middle. He had an agenda." Wilson was asked how, if Stone pointed out transgressions in transcripts or government lies, that was not "reporting" as well as serving an agenda. "You're trying to say he was a Morton Mintz [one of the revered *Washington Post* reporters and a friend of Stone's, who broke one business scandal after another in the last century]. I'm not ready to put Izzy in Mintz's class. Mintz would not take something as complex as the Vietnam War and write it as one way, black-and-white. He would investigate the cover-up and crassness of a drug company, and if he found evil, sure as hell he would put it in. But Izzy did a lot more interpretation than that.

"I had to take Izzy in small doses. He'd call: 'George, I got this story that all the other fellas missed. Helluva story.' I would have already heard that he had tried to sell it to someone else. He wanted us to pick it up and give him credit." Wilson was not without sympathy: "It's tough when you're all alone out there."

Part of Stone's charm was disingenuous oblivion to whatever pain or anger he might have caused, calling up to chat or praise a piece of work as if nothing had transpired. "It was hard to stay mad at Izzy," said Sherrill. And Raymond fondly recalled a "very nice, hardworking, thoughtful, scholarly man with a readiness to be amused."

Author, historian, and Greek classicist Garry Wills remembers Izzy as "totally delightful. My overall view is one of admiration. We were actually quite friendly—it's just that he stopped talking to me," said Wills with a laugh. Stone often called him in the middle of the night when struggling with his Greek studies. Then in 1978, at an Institute for Policy Studies dinner, Wills was startled at Stone's reaction to him. "Izzy was very uncomfortable. Finally he blurted out, 'I'm sorry. I just can't talk to you.'" The astonished look on Wills's face required an explanation: "'That Weinstein review was just such a betrayal of the cause.'"

Wills had written what Stone viewed as a soft essay on Allen Weinstein's book *Perjury,* about Alger Hiss, and Weinstein had critically reviewed another Hiss book in the *New York Review.* Stone angrily questioned Weinstein's charges that Hiss was guilty. He could never decide about Hiss's guilt or innocence, but argued that *Perjury* provided flawed evidence.

As a youth in a Jesuit seminary, Wills "didn't read newspapers. We certainly didn't read Izzy. We were very much for the Cold War and prayed for the conversion of Russia." William Buckley hired Wills for the *National Review* in 1957 and they soon clashed. "On civil rights we always differed, and on the Vietnam War we quickly differed." They parted company when Wills wrote an article defending the Berrigan brothers. "I long ago took the revisionist view that Truman was more responsible for the Cold War." While Wills was researching his book *Nixon Agonistes,* "Izzy became one of my heroes. He was one of the few people to make sense during the post–World War II anticommunist scare."

Eventually Stone's desire to talk with another devotee of ancient Greece overcame his anger. One night he called up Wills as if nothing had happened, asking his interpretation of a Greek passage, and the friendship continued. However, Stone was upset enough over Weinstein/Hiss to resign as contributing editor of the *New York Review of Books,* reasoning that his name could not remain on the masthead when he so severely disagreed. Yet nothing could change his close friendship with the *Review*'s publisher, Bob Silvers. Stone continued to contribute articles and later felt he had been precipitous when he'd resigned in anger.

At the time, Peter Osnos's wife was working part-time for Weinstein. "Like a dumbo, I thought I could fix it up and that Allen and Izzy would become friends," recalled Peter, who invited them both to dinner. "I made the surpassing mistake of not telling Stone until he got to the door that Weinstein would be there. "Izzy shook his hand but did not say a word to him during the entire evening."

Many younger writers were awed and somewhat intimidated by Stone when he became a huge success. Stone professed that he hated being viewed as an "oracle," but he loved that elevation. His coterie included the best of the next generation of journalists, who were inspired by Stone and defended him from arguments that he was not "objective." They make an excellent point that the critical eye is needed to counter what is being billed as the truth from official sources.

"Many miss the point that Stone wasn't just looking up facts and comparing them; he knew how to connect each piece of string, what to do with them when he found them," said Scott Armstrong, who began his career as an investigator for the Senate Committee on Watergate and was accustomed to examining records and documents. "I assumed all journalists did that. How naive I was." Stone acknowledged the many bright people in the business, but agreed with Armstrong, who said, "The urgency of deadlines, the need to get in the paper more often, tell the story fast, to stand well in their profession, kept them away from the truth. Izzy's advice was perseverance and patience. Keep honing it like a wood carving. Don't feel desperate when you get just a little piece of the puzzle.

"The *Washington Post* and contemporary newsroom mentality is to find the extraordinary 'Holy shit!' story. That was offensive to Izzy. He wouldn't give up ten pieces of the puzzle for the instant scoop. He preferred quieter scoops that meant something long lasting, constantly reading dozens of records in order to find enough material to establish some links and to ferret out what the government was accountable for. He looked at journalism as a political act. The reason you do it is to try to keep the political dialogue honest." Armstrong carried on Stone's crusade and founded the National Security Archive, a research institute that collects and publishes declassified documents acquired through the Freedom of Information Act (FOIA).

Some of the best in the business literally owe some of their success to Stone; two are Walter Pincus—*Washington Post* major investigative reporter for decades—and Don Oberdorfer—formerly with the *Post* and prize-winning author of several important works. In the long-ago late fifties, when they met Stone, they were just two eager and poorly paid novices, working in bureaus for small out-of-town papers. Pincus had worked in Army counterintelligence and was in the habit of checking records. He found phony claims for congressional expense accounts that had been filed and open to the press all along, "but nobody ever looked at them." He and Oberdorfer put together an account of how congress-men spent taxpayers' money on foreign jaunts and other personal perks.

Larry Stern, a fascinating and brilliant *Washington Post* editor given to inscrutable mumbling (reporters said they would have followed his instructions but they didn't know Zen), had become the ringleader of Stone's fan club and encouraged Pincus and Oberdorfer to show their congressional opus to Stone. He thought it was great and said, "Aim high!" He also told them to "lighten it up" and "get some humor in this."

After a rewrite, the novices peddled the piece to *Life* magazine. They were awed by the fancy New York offices and numbed by a wine-filled lunch and then they were told that *Life* was going to run it. Pincus said, "They offered, I think it was, five thousand dollars apiece! More than I had made in a full year. They were just as enthusiastic as hell. The high point came when they wanted to get a cab to take us back to the airport. We had to say we had other plans. We didn't want them to know we had snuck into town on Trailways. It was the classic two country hicks strik-ing it rich in the big city." The piece ran in *Life* magazine, June 1960, making some enemies on the Hill but a lifelong friend in Stone. "That was certainly a seminal event for Don and me. Izzy was the rock on which all that was built."

Pincus saw Stone as a role model for the kind of reporting he was perfecting himself. "Izzy really set the pattern for reading hearings. I still do it. It's the only way to report around Washington. He was constantly harping on that." Pincus enumerated the reasons why few reporters dig into documents: "One, they don't want to believe that someone would deliberately mislead them. Two, it takes a lot of work and time. Three, they don't want to be the object of opprobrium for writing critical pieces. People assume that you will be cut off. That's wrong. As long as you write critical pieces that are accurate, you gain respect. As long as they know that by not cooperating they're not going to stop you from writing anyway, many get the idea that it's better to cooperate. And by contacting them, they can't accuse you of not being fair."

Unlike Stone, Pincus developed friendships with powerful insiders but repeats an Izzy axiom: "Don't kid yourself when dealing with gov-ernment people that—because they invite you someplace—they like you. Manipulating is their role, ours is to get the real story. If you don't have the basic facts, then you are totally dependent on leaks and can easily be used."

Pincus's comment was made years prior to, but sounds greatly prophetic about, the 2002–3 pre-Iraqi-war coverage about weapons of mass destruction. More than a year after the war began and after the WMD excuse was exposed as bogus, both the *New York Times* and the *Washington Post* issued mea culpas about their credulous acceptance of Bushspeak. Pincus came out the hero. The words "in hindsight" and "in retrospect" were used extensively by editors apologizing for their refusal to challenge administration claims. In essence they were propaganda pawns for yet another president's rush to war with trumped-up charges. The *Times* editorial page and the *New Republic* magazine "expressed regret for some prewar arguments" after Michael Massing detailed major reporting lapses in the *New York Review of Books,* collected in his book of essays on abysmal media coverage, *Now They Tell Us.* The *Post*'s apology recognized that Pincus's "very prescient" piece questioning WMD arguments should have run on page one. Only through the insistence of assistant managing editor Bob Woodward was the piece run at all—buried on page seventeen. The incident brought back one of Stone's famous lines about the *Washington Post:* it was exciting to read, he once told David Halberstam, "because you never know on what page you would find a page-one story."

When the *Washington Post*'s Pentagon correspondent, Thomas Ricks, wrote in October 2002 that senior Pentagon officials had doubts and felt that risks were being underestimated about going to war, an editor, Matthew Vita, killed the story, primarily because the sourcing was "lots of retired guys." In a surpassing catch-22, Pincus's expertise went against him. Dismissive young editors complained that his dense, "cryptic" work needed heavy editing. Sounding like his mentor Stone, Pincus, seventy-one, said, "The main thing people forget to do is *read the documents.*" His decades of excellent reporting had also earned the confidence of many sources, including Hans Blix, the chief UN weapons inspector in Iraq, who resisted the rush to war.

Journalists contend that they are at the mercy of the president's bully pulpit, but when evidence surfaced, such as Britain's damaging Downing Street memo in 2005, which showed that the president was trying to "fix" intelligence information to justify going to war, many mainstream journalists again responded with a yawn.

Daniel Ellsberg said, as the war continued in Iraq, "Nobody has learned anything from the Pentagon Papers, Vietnam, Izzy, or anything." At the very time TV was doing the president's dirty work by denigrating candidate Kerry's words about Vietnam War atrocities, they were showing pictures of Abu Ghraib. "I am puzzled by the degree of servility and compliance from the press. Journalists recognize that officials mislead, are selective, ambiguous, try to misdirect you—but will say, 'They don't really lie.' *That is false.* They lie a lot. Journalists should always be asking, 'What is the real truth here? Why is he saying this to us?' It is inexcusable to take what they say at face value. You are talking not to pathological liars, you are talking to professional liars who should be looked at as skeptically as used-car salesmen or Pfizer or Merck spokesmen."

Ellsberg recalled a conversation with Anthony Lewis in 1972. "I asked him, 'Why do people repeat this BS in a servile, credulous manner?' Lewis said, 'In this town, the greatest thing a bureau chief can deliver to his visiting managing editor or publisher is a lunch with Henry Kissinger. If you can, you're in, and if you *can't,* you aren't. And if you write something Kissinger doesn't like, you won't get that lunch."

27

STONE VS. SOCRATES

Anyone passing the distracted older man—the "old duffer" he
called himself—on his daily five-mile round-trip hike to American University could be excused for thinking that he had no
more on his mind than searching for the next bus stop. They had no idea
of the "syntactical horrors" Stone was "silently undergoing in his head"
as he struggled with irregular verbs, the subjunctive, and declensions in
Greek. "I well remember that terrible morning in the basement stacks at
American University." Stone "discovered that Bishop Thirlwall, the great
Whig historian of Greece, had already learned Greek at the age of four.
Luckily, I was not armed, or I would have shot myself."

Stone recounted his desolation. "How could I dare, in my late 60's, to
begin the long and rocky ascent" of learning this intricate language? But
how could he write about the Greeks without knowing their language?
Then he discovered a few days later that Thomas Hardy didn't begin to
learn Greek until he was eighty. That "cheered me immensely. . . . I had a
full start of more than a decade on Hardy."

His painstaking task was aided by a virus. "If I hadn't been in bed I
would never have persevered." After recovering, Stone plowed through
nine months of bedtime reading to complete the first book of Homer's
Odyssey. In the morning, as always, Esther brought him breakfast on a tray
as he studied with magnifying glass at hand. He wrote out each line in
Greek and then parsed each word, ending up with over 250 pages of notes.
He had no true conception of Homer "until I dug into the original."

Stone once told Garry Wills, "'The one thing I envy you for is that
you can read Greek.' He called me up the day he started to take Greek
and said, 'I'm doing it?! I'm doing it!'" Stone was like an exultant child
learning to ride a bike. "For a long time he would call to discuss Greek,
certain passages he was reading, what is the best to read on Sappho and
so on." (The historian Bernard Knox was also often called for help.)

At the time, Wills was teaching at Johns Hopkins in Baltimore and writing for the *New York Review.* "Since he knew I stayed up late in those days, I would get the one a.m. phone calls that always started out, 'I hope I am not bothering you.' " For eight years, off and on, their nocturnal meanderings into ancient Greece continued. Stone would say, "Have you got a copy of the *Apology* nearby?' So I'd get it out and go over passages."

As if preparing for the dismissive reviews he would receive from a few scholars, Stone commented that, concerning most Greek studies, it was rare that "one does not find oneself caught in the crossfire of violent and sometimes ill-tempered controversy between equally respected scholars."

Since Socrates never wrote anything down, his thoughts and ideas were filtered through Plato, whose later writings on his master became increasingly interpretive. As Stone immersed himself, his dislike of the aristocratic Plato grew. Stone developed a "love-hate relationship with Plato," and the journalistic bird dog exclaimed to friends, "I am going to destroy Plato!"

Unlike many classicists, Stone saw Socrates not as an annoying but harmless dissenter of Athenian democracy but as a cold and dangerous demagogue who was done in by his arrogant rejection of commoners having a voice in their government.

"I don't think Izzy really understood Plato's philosophy," said Wills. "I don't think he was interested in metaphysics, and he was looking at a severely limited aspect of Plato—the politics—and even then only as it figured with Socrates." Wills nonetheless had great admiration for Stone's spirit and enjoyed a "shared enthusiasm and the sharing of ideas. Izzy just loved it and worked hard at it."

Stone may not have had a deep interest in metaphysics, but he was always entranced with someone who studied philosophy. The first night Scott Armstrong met Stone, Armstrong was sitting next to Esther at a dinner party and mentioned that he had been a philosophy major. Esther excitedly called across the table, "Izzy! *Izzy!* There's a philosopher over here!" Ignoring any polite protocol, Stone swiftly vacated his seat and moved next to Armstrong. "Izzy was full of the Greeks and Romans. I couldn't keep up. I'd long since forgotten Greek philosophy except passages of major Greek works."

Was Stone supercilious? Armstrong laughed. "Izzy could be obnoxious but he was never supercilious. If he was bored, he was more than willing to dominate a conversation, and he was not one to put up with chitchat. When the conversation didn't interest him, Izzy would impolitely cut through it to get back to the person who had said the last thing that interested him. He did that often." Other friends were the writers Judith and Milton Viorst. Being an informed listener was essential. "If you saw Izzy, you had better have read the paper that day. This was what it was all about," said Judith. "He was passionate about the news and issues, and his capacity for moral indignation was amazing." Armstrong saw a paradox: "I had the sense that he was probably more bored with academicians than any group you could name—Izzy really loved the company of journalists—yet he wanted the rigor of structured intellectual conversation." Around that time, Judy Martin, aka Miss Manners, joined Stone, Larry Stern, and Alan Barth for lunch. Barth, unflinching editorial writer and friend of younger journalists, was dying of cancer, a subject that was studiously avoided. Stone held forth: "Izzy was translating the *Trojan Women*, quoting first in Greek—in this perfectly awful accent—and then giving this most beautiful translation," recalled Martin.

After a lingering lunch, when the foursome went to get their coats, no one was in the checkroom. Stone jumped behind the door and began finding and distributing coats. One of the others joked, "Do we tip you for our coats?"

"Yes!" Izzy replied instantly. "I'm working my way through Homer!"

Stone was not above getting a provocative buzz going and once said, "The secret of lively publishing is to get readers mad at you." When Stone interviewed himself for the *Times,* he asked, "Was Sappho a lesbian?" He puckishly replied, "I refuse to answer such low porno questions about her." (Stone went on to extol her poems.)

Stone's breezy elegance led to a serendipitous meeting with budding book agent Andrew Wylie, who loved serious works but rapidly learned they were hard sells. Applying for a job as a book editor in 1979, he was asked, "What have you read recently?" "Thucydides," he replied. "How about James Michener? Or James Clavell?!" the editor boomed. "Clearly," thought Wylie, "I was not qualified for the job." Searching for a way to read what he wanted and still "make a living," Wylie started on his own rocky agent's road after "two years tutelage" with an agent who knew how to dicker.

"The first author I wanted to represent was I. F. Stone. I'd read an interesting essay he'd written on the trial of Socrates, so I rang him up and arranged to visit him straightaway." The next day Wylie was pitching himself to Stone in line at the writer's favorite cafeteria. "The most im-

portant thing," said Wylie, "is to get *paid.* If you get $100,000, the pub-
lisher will print a lot of copies and will make sure the bookstores put
your book in the front of the stores. If you're paid less, they'll print fewer
copies, and you'll end up spine-out in the back of the store." Wylie was
on a roll. "Why should the worst writers have the best deals? If enough
people are given a chance to find you, you'll be a bestseller!" Stone was
not so much impressed with this staccato pitch as he was in getting him
to leave him alone, thought Wylie, but he closed the deal. "So I had my
first client. I went to see his publisher." Random House had republished
a series of Stone's columns in 1967 and in 1973 when he was a hot ticket.
However, the publishers were not sold on *The Trial of Socrates.* According to Wylie, an editor told him, " 'This is the Reagan era. No one knows
who Socrates was, and no one cares about Izzy.' I said, 'I'm sure you're
right. So will you revert the rights to his backlist?' " (Some of Stone's previous books were out of print, others were selling modestly.) Wylie sold
the bundle to Little, Brown for $105,000, "at the time, a fairly strong ad-
vance." The collected works sold well and *Socrates* became a surprise best
seller. Wylie had "learned two things: It's okay to ignore the prevailing
climate and follow your interests; and, or rather, but: every time you
must be paid."

Stone's jokes about becoming a "recycled freshman" and the "world's
oldest freshman" when he began his Greek studies at American University hid deep anxiety. By now, Dr. Bernard Lown was caring for Stone.
More than anyone except Esther, Stone conveyed to this Boston cardiol-
ogist his deepest fears and thoughts. "Izzy felt his life was over because he
had serious coronary artery disease. He didn't think he would survive a
major operation. He was very troubled by angina. I didn't think he had
been treated properly. Even then the premier medicine was nitroglycerin.
If you teach a person properly how to use it, then in the majority of cases
the patient is empowered, self-reliant, and knows that the angina pain
can be relieved and [need] not be limited by it."

Stone respected Lown on many levels. The cofounder of International
Physicians for the Prevention of Nuclear War (IPPNW), Lown shared the
1985 Nobel Peace Prize with a controversial Russian doctor. He founded
the Lown Cardiovascular Research Center in Brookline, Massachusetts,
and was a longtime professor of cardiology at the Harvard School of
Public Health. Lown invented the defibrillator, the mechanism that
jump-starts a heart undergoing cardiac arrest, but he was no scientific

automaton. In his book *The Lost Art of Healing,* he argued that scientific breakthroughs had obscured that vital art and called for a compassionate and synergistic relationship between doctor and patient. His patients were famous leftists—John Kenneth Galbraith, Noam Chomsky, Stone's brother-in-law Leonard Boudin. At least one was infamous; a Mafia don sent Lown cases of unparalleled rare wines after Lown saved his life.

His politics appealed to Stone, but Lown says, "Izzy was more interested in my philosophy about medicine than in my philosophy about politics." (Stone once joked to Lown that Lenin had advised comrades not to go to a Bolshevik doctor because "he's too involved with the movement to be a good doctor.") "He was interested in how you manage the patient with coronary artery disease without the need to resort to invasive procedures. He dreaded surgery."

In his book, Lown emphasized the necessity of building confidence by drawing out a patient when taking his case history. Stone was a disaster. "I could not get a history on him. He'd always want to share this or that and he'd jump up and down and tell me about everything else. One day the whole hour was lost. He'd just discovered what Sappho meant for a little couplet, and he was like a little boy who'd discovered sex or God knows what. 'Do you realize that for two and a half thousand years nobody knew what Sappho meant, and now I know?' And the way he traced it down from some Roman writer who utilized a similar word and an incorrect Germanic translation of it! He knew and it made sense and he regaled me for an hour with it."

A frustrated Lown kept asking, " 'What about your angina? What are you doing about medication?' Nothing was forthcoming." Lown realized that behind the facade, Stone, facing retirement, was "extraordinarily depressed" that first time he saw him. Stone always said retirement was a "vestibule to death" unless one had something compelling to do. "He had to be engaged in a big way. When he wrote an article about Socrates, I said, 'This is a marvelous book you've got to write,' and he said, 'I intend to.' "

Despite Stone's public enthusiasm, Lown sensed that Stone was reluctant on two levels to complete that "long and lonely" project, as Stone described it. "He was beginning to lay out the second book—on freedom of speech and thought—before finishing the first." Psychologically, Lown thought, Stone was building into his life some continuity (such as another book) because he was "scared of dying. He wanted to live because his searching brain had still a lot of uncompleted business like a book about freedom of speech through the ages. But he was too scared to finish *The Trial of Socrates* because he was convinced if he finished it, he'd die."

On a second level, Stone had more anxiety than he publicly admitted about the reaction of scholars. "He once called me in the wintertime," said Lown. "He was invited to lecture at Princeton to a conclave of scholars about Socrates, and he didn't want to go in the worst way. 'I'm having a lot of angina, do you think I should go?' He felt, of course, that I would say, 'Don't go.' But then it became clear to me that if he didn't go, he would think later that it was a terrible moral defeat of cowardice. I said, 'You've got to go.' He always was sort of self-abnegating as a Greek scholar. 'Who am I? A little Jewish boy who's pretending to be a scholar,' he told me, then added that he always wanted to be a scholar." Stone called Lown at midnight after the speech, bubbling that the event was great. " 'He'd had a standing ovation, the scholars didn't pick him apart.' "

Over the years, Stone's letters to his doctor were remarkable in their attention to life outside of Stone's health—comments about the SALT treaty, snippets of Greek carefully handwritten with correct accent marks, tirades on a speech by Caspar Weinberger (then secretary of defense). "His parallel is stupid in the extreme. In Hector's farewell to Andromache . . . Homer towered above the silly illusions of the Pentagon."

When in Boston, Stone often stayed with Lown and his wife and became a central figure in their social life, joining friends such as historian Howard Zinn, MIT professor Noam Chomsky, and Moshe Barash, prize-winning author and professor of art at Hebrew University of Jerusalem. Both Stone and Barash hoped to be there at the same time. "When they'd get together, it was something I wished I had taped. One would quote a source, and the other would quote a better source. And Greek this and Latin that, and we would sit there, out of it—resenting it a little bit for being so Philistine but enjoying the joy of these two who were real scholars."

Above all, remembers Lown, "Stone was very, very anti-Soviet. You cannot imagine how full of vehemence he was by the time I met him. It was the fact that this noble socialist idea got covered with dung by the Soviet Union that he hated. 'The Soviets appropriated a good idea, a noble vision of humankind, and corrupted it to such an extent that it will not be resuscitated for the longest time.' For Izzy, 'it was a crime of the worst sort' because he felt it 'set back humankind maybe a century.'

"He was foremost above all else a Jeffersonian Democrat, writ large." In 1982, Stone wrote to Lown, still using decade-old *Weekly* stationery,

"Bravo for your temerity in challenging this shibboleth of Soviet civil defense." (Explained Lown later, "It was a fake and I pointed it out on a big television show in Moscow.") Stone continued, "The whole picture is soured for me by (1) the stupidity of Soviet bureaucrats in choosing this very week-end of our U.S. demonstration against nuclear war in New York to arrest the handful of Soviet peace activists and (2) their continued persecution of Sakharov, whose theory of convergence and his own intrinsic moral eminence could be the world's greatest force for coexistence. Moscow's double standard in all this turns my stomach."

Lown made international waves for his antinuclear alliance with Russians well after the era of Cold War hysteria and just four years before the collapse of the Berlin Wall. A moment of high drama engulfed the 1985 Oslo presentation of the shared Nobel Peace Prize, given to Lown and his Russian colleague, Yevgeny Chazov, in honor of the 135,000 antinuclear doctors and health professionals in the international organization that Chazov and Lown had founded five years previously. Hostile journalists grilled them at a crowded press conference for representing a group that declined to take a stand on Soviet human rights violations. Suddenly, a Russian journalist fell to the floor stricken by cardiac arrest. The two cardiologists jumped from the podium, ripped off their coats, and took turns pounding on the supine journalist's chest, "all the while shouting in Russian and English for drugs and equipment." The duo saved his life. Few journalists missed the symbolism in this widely reported incident. Columnist Ellen Goodman expounded on this "medicine as metaphor" moment of U.S.-Soviet cooperation and quoted Lown's comparison: "It is the same with the threat of nuclear war. You treat it first and ask questions later."

Lown defended his participation with Chazov, the personal physician to Kremlin leaders who had signed a letter twelve years before condemning the dissident physicist Sakharov for his campaign against Soviet human rights violations. "We disagree on many aspects," Lown told reporters at Oslo, "but we have risen above the partisanship of the Cold War to inform the world that this merry-go-round to oblivion must stop. Broadening the agenda would break up our movement. We have found a small oasis of common interest that we pursue with obsessive intensity." Lown was appalled when European leaders urged the Nobel committee to rescind their award because of Chazov's association. "There are enormous forces around us that enjoy and profit from the Cold War," said Lown, halting the press conference as he choked back tears. "We all have to die someday. What we in IPPNW are trying to redress is the danger that we all may die in the same instant."

Recalled Lown, "I got enormous attacks," and he developed empathy for what Stone had experienced in the past. "When the whole cultural enterprise turns against you, how difficult it is to keep your sanity, let alone your conviction." A bright spot was Stone's enthusiastic support. "Izzy was really delighted when we got the Nobel. Sometimes when you get honored, important people will congratulate you, but there's a little edge of resentment. That was never there with Izzy."

Despite the snubs that Stone had earlier received from a rather parochial band of Washington correspondents, he always enjoyed a broad collection of friends among international scholars, intellectuals, and journalists and was important far beyond that small world. Said Lown, "I do a lot of world-hopping, and I'll come across all sorts of people who either knew Izzy or knew of his work. And when I would say I was his doctor, oh, boy, did I become distinguished. In an instant! Forget the Nobel Prize!"

The current state of affairs was not abandoned by Stone in his pursuit of Socrates. From 1972 on, Stone's mind and speeches and many articles—written for the *New York Review of Books*, the *Nation*, the *New York Times*, the *Washington Post*, the *Washington Star*, and other welcoming establishment papers—focused on Reaganomics, the Iran-contra arms-for-hostages scandal, Star Wars, the Pentagon, the machinations of über-lobbyist Henry Kissinger, the lack of free expression in Cuba, Maoist China, and the Eastern bloc. He signed *New York Review of Books* letters from the early seventies until the year he died, along with other famous leftists, supporting imprisoned dissidents in Czechoslovakia and Poland.

The CIA—whose charter prohibits domestic spying—nonetheless tracked Stone's writing and speeches and underlined comments such as the following: "The 'dirty-tricks' division of the CIA is our international device for violating international law." Stone said frequently, "Stalin made it a practice to bump off the head of the secret service every two years or so. That was really therapeutic." Stone wrote, "I think we ought to get rid of the CIA altogether, lock, stock and burglar's kit." He roused student audiences by saying, "The CIA and its bag of dirty tricks must go."

Stone despised post-Vietnam covert operations long before they were exposed in congressional hearings and said, "There are so many secret organizations and secrecy in American government that a perfect clone of Ollie North was slipped into the same job as he had, the National Security Council—Negroponte, who ran the illegal activities for the contras in Honduras." (Illustrating that it is hard to keep a bad man down, the current President Bush appointed John Negroponte the director of national intelligence in 2005, despite his part in the covert funding of the contras and his alleged cover-up of human rights abuses carried out by CIA-trained operatives in Honduras in the 1980s.)

Stone said toward the end of his life, "There is very little sense of history in this generation. This country got along very well without the FBI for over a century. The year after I was born," Teddy Roosevelt established the Bureau "by executive order behind the back of Congress." Members had turned it down because they "didn't want to establish a secret police. Inevitably such organizations become a means of inhibiting the exercise of freedom of liberties and intimidate people." Stone then was off on an Aristotle comparison about secret women spies in the agora known as "long ears."

While he polished up his words for print, young audiences loved it when Stone let fly with slangy expressions such as "We've got the Middle East so covered that a camel can't belch without our having a record of it" and "With the satellites, a farmer in the Soviet Union can't squeeze a cow's teat without our knowing about it. . . . The CIA has made the U.S. look like the world's biggest Mafia while helping to trap it into one serious mistake after another. . . . The CIA will go down in the books as a vain attempt to change history by institutionalizing assassination." Such Stone critiques were kept in CIA files.

On network television Stone decried Reaganomics: "The elderly are suffering, the minorities are suffering, the poor are suffering. The cities are going to pot. Public services are suffering. There's not anybody in that whole damn Reagan team that ever has to stand in the rain and wait for a bus to get anywhere. . . . When you come to town with all these rich friends who have ranches . . . and homes in Cape Cod and they're always flying all over the world . . . and they import hairdressers and couturiers and cooks for their big parties, and you tell the poor, 'Hey, times are bad, folks, you've got to pull in your belt!' And the poor sucker that can't afford a forty-nine-cent cup of coffee . . . has to pull in his belt. Inflation's a real problem, but why should only the poor suffer? . . . Reagan's cut the poor and handed out an absolutely unreasonable, unwise tax cut to the rich."

Stone also felt that "there's a great danger that this administration is going to stumble into war." Stone's fear of an accidental nuclear holocaust was matched by his wariness of the Soviets. The revelations on Stalin had soured Stone forever. He did not succumb to "Gorbymania," arguing vehemently with friends that Gorbachev spoke "a lot of drivel" and provided no new ideas. Stone had passionate shouting matches with his friend Arthur Cox, then secretary of the American Committee on U.S.-Soviet Relations, who had served in the State Department and the CIA. Cox said Stone was too lenient earlier and too wary later. "He was wrong about the Russians years before and he is wrong now!" declared Cox. Gorbachev was trying to reform the unreformable, a decayed society. Neocons give Reagan full credit for Russia's collapse, but a major factor was the USSR's own quagmire, their costly Afghanistan war against Islamic fundamentalists and Taliban terrorists, including Al Qaeda, which the United States was helping.

Far ahead of officials who followed the CIA's inaccurate reports, Stone predicted five years before it happened that the Soviet Union would collapse from within. He applauded Reagan's dealings with Russia. "There is some good in everybody. Nixon, the great Red-baiter, who would have expected he was going to open the door to China? And Reagan, the great opponent of the evil empire, who would have dreamt that he would head for a summit with Gorbachev and draw back from the nuclear abyss? . . ." Stone chuckled. "The kooks that are the core of his support were ready to read the riot act to him."

Even while immersed in Socrates, Stone kept his one good eye on the coverage of politics. "Izzy was outraged throughout about the Iran-contra coverage," recalls Scott Armstrong. "He would call and complain that the press was missing it. Izzy was watching Iran-contra like a hawk—'How can people be so blind?' It was the perfect example of a scandal that would rankle his ass. His grievances were like those of someone covering it—not the grievances of a person who had left it all behind."

Stone's eyes were so bad by then that he stashed magnifying glasses all over the house and relied on Esther to read to him. Still, he could remember the exact date of an article. His reference points remained clear and crisp. "He'd remember a good line or a bad line like we would remember a dinner party when someone threw a glass or did something outrageous," marveled Armstrong. Stone wistfully eyed the new time-saving research offered by the National Security Archive (even though he often remarked that relying on FOIA was a "kind of sissy journalism"). He sighed, "I could have saved thirty years of my life if I had a resource like this."

* * *

Stone had become a doting grandfather and played the jolly uncle to the children of friends. He retained a special tolerance for bright youths eager to learn. "Izzy was so hungry for minds that he could influence," recalled Armstong. Cox remembered a long car ride when he was essentially the silent chauffeur; Stone turned all his attention to Cox's young son, who was taking a great-books course. Stone had a manner of talking to the young as if they were equals; the two discussed the *Iliad* as if they were longtime chums. "When Izzy was learning the Apple computer, one of the few who had one was my son, Nick," recalled Judith Viorst. "Every morning at seven a.m. Izzy would call Nicki and I would tell him, 'You are not allowed to grumble. This is a great man, so get up and answer.' Only a young intellectual kid would say, as Nicki did, 'You know, he's really a smart guy! He picks up this stuff very well.' It was very thrilling to see this whole new generation discuss Izzy."

Armstrong invited him to the National Security Archive to speak on a hot summer's day. Stone, then nearing eighty, insisted on walking the stretch from his house to Dupont Circle in plus-ninety-degree heat. "He got a little off course and went two extra unnecessary blocks." Before the final eye operation in his last months, Stone was close to blind in one eye and seeing poorly out of the other. He once fell down the steps, cutting himself. Esther pasted huge letters on his typewriter keys. When computers came into existence, Stone filled the screen with letters the size of license plates. Esther wore red hats so he could see her in an audience. She warned him of cracks in the sidewalk.

On this day, Stone was thrilled that the students knew about Iran-contra and "understood his every allusion," said Armstrong. Stone talked for two hours and fifteen minutes, but still did not want to leave. He explored the computers, asking countless questions. Remembering a point he wanted to make forty-five minutes before, he tracked down the woman who had asked a question and expounded for fifteen minutes more. Armstrong finally persuaded Stone to take a ride home. "He was so revved up by the experience that he could not stop talking about 'the kids.' It was like the mind of a twenty-five-year-old on speed. Stone wanted to come back, but I didn't want to impose. He called back in the fall and demanded, 'How come you haven't invited me back to speak to your people?'"

The ever-present Israeli/Arab impasse remained a heavy concern. Stone always tried to joke when he was ostracized by American Jews and called a Jew hater, acknowledging in the seventies that "finding an American publishing house willing to publish a book that departs from the standard Israeli line is about as easy as selling a thoughtful exposition of atheism to the *L'Osservatore Romano* in Vatican City."

In 1988, Stone was still saying, "I just can't understand why one is allowed to be sympathetic toward one's own fellow refugees but not to open your heart to another people's refugees. The Palestinian Arabs are a wonderful part of the Arab world. They supply intellectuals, professionals, engineers, scientists. . . . It would be so wonderful if we could feel about them as brothers. I don't see how it is possible to uphold the right of a Jewish state in Palestine and deny the same right to the Palestinians to determine what they want to do with the occupied territories. It runs against *everything* that's best in the Bible and in the Jewish tradition. . . . There is a saying in Yiddish: 'If you don't have *rachmones*—that is, compassion—how can you call yourself a Jew?' I think the test of that in the Middle East is the Jewish attitude toward the Arabs. If we harden our hearts and shut our minds to injustice, we will become a very different people; whatever the reaction of the Arabs is, the Jewish people themselves would be changed. Everything that [comes from] the Diaspora—toleration, separation of church and state, brotherhood of peoples of all different beliefs and backgrounds—these things are being trampled on in Israel, I am sorry to say. If something isn't done pretty soon, the lines may harden, each side will destroy its own moderates, and then will move on to destroy each other."

At eighty, Stone was still making waves. He acknowledged that Arafat and other Arab leaders did not recognize the state of Israel, then argued, "Israel wants them to recognize Israel but refused to give a quid pro quo. You can't negotiate peace by telling them who they should accept as their leader. . . . They are up against the same plight that surrounded European Jews after World War II: no state, no passport, no recognition. They need a state of their own, the right to self-determination, and the respect that comes with being recognized.

"Look," Stone said to a San Francisco City Arts and Lectures audience, "there's risk in peace, there's risk in war, there is no way to live without risk. I believe the risks of peace and conciliation are superior to the risks of war and hatred."

Stone continued to give discomfort to all camps as every man's Jeremiah. Booed and shunned by some Jews, Stone nonetheless derided a group of pro-PLO leftists for an "oversimplified" and wrongheaded view. He exclaimed, "Israel was a great experiment." Stone's position was not without personal consequences. His son Christopher remembers walking into a party and being assailed for whatever Stone was currently writing on Israel. When Stone became a star of Cavett's TV show, producer Cunniff felt that the only time he saw Stone conflicted was on questions about Israel. "He sort of admitted after we got off the air that he had pulled his punches. I think he was feeling the pressure."

Obviously sensitive years later, Stone reprinted in his final newsletter an article he had written just after the 1967 Six-Day War, mentioning in the headline that it had been "So Unfairly Distorted." Wrote Stone on June 12, 1967, "Israel's swift and brilliant military victory only makes its reconciliation with the Arabs more urgent. . . . It was a moral tragedy—to which no Jew worthy of our best Prophetic tradition could be insensitive—that a kindred people was made homeless in the task of finding new homes for the remnants of the Hitler holocaust. Now is the time to right that wrong, to show magnanimity in victory. . . . Abba Eban [Labor member of the Israeli Knesset and foreign minister from 1966 to 1974] exultantly called the sweep of Israel's armies 'the finest day in Israel's modern history.' The finest day will be the day it achieves reconciliation with the Arabs."

Toward the end of his life Stone recalled, "I was a hero when I spoke up for Jewish refugees, and then when I began to speak up on Arab refugees, I was not kosher any longer." His public pattern was to make light of criticism: "I think it's a basic law of human history that anybody that tries to be a good human being is going to get in trouble sooner or later with his own tribe." However, Stone once said in private that being attacked by Jews was "just about the only thing that hurt my feelings all those years."

In 1979, Abba Eban continued to argue with Stone in print when Stone's *Underground to Palestine* was republished. "Stone seems to believe that the Arabs could have been brought to accept Zionism by Jewish benevolence and self-abnegation, rather than by coming to terms with Jewish strength and stability. . . . Alas, the evidence points in the opposite direction." Eban mentioned his various meetings with Arab leaders who told him they would bow only to Israel's force. Eban derided Stone for one-sidedness in not condemning PLO terrorism: "That Israeli reluctance to accept the PLO state as a neighbor has anything to do with the PLO's policy of killing Israelis . . . is a thought that goes unrepresented in Stone's book."

Stone abhorred the name-calling that occurred over this heated subject and deplored Jews claiming anti-Semitism when anyone disagreed. Another friend and Jew who felt the ire of the Jewish community was Joe Rauh. "One night Izzy and I were bragging about who got the biggest shaft from the conservative Jewish community. He starts talking about what the mainline, rich Jewish community had done to him for being for a Palestinian state—which was a mighty independent position for a Jew then. He had a lot of guts to say that. Then I told him about the head of the Union of American Hebrew Congregations who calls me one day saying he wants to give me an award for my fight for civil rights." The group had planned to release Rauh's speech but refused to after seeing his draft, which Rauh characterized as "a polite but tough criticism of the Jewish community for being against affirmative action." On top of that, they changed the order of the program so that Rauh, the honoree, did not speak last. The final speaker then attacked Rauh *from the platform! It was most embarrassing." Did Stone concede you were the winner? "Izzy?! Oh, Christ, no. Not Izzy. But we had a good laugh."

Still, Stone was capable of crying and losing composure when giving speeches about the troubles between the Palestinians and the Israelis. In 1988, Stone praised the *Washington Post* and the *New York Times* for their "very good coverage" and "courageous" editorials and applauded elements in the American Jewish community who saw that change was necessary. "I read a terrible story of a bulldozer brought up by the Israeli Army in an obscure village I'd never heard of . . . where a suspect sought by the Army . . . was suspected of taking refuge in an Arab farmer's olive orchard, and the Army brought out a bulldozer and proceeded to level the gardens and the orchard, and the climax of the story was the difficulty it had in dealing with one olive tree . . ." Stone fell silent before his New York audience, then began haltingly, his voice strangled with tears. "and it didn't want to give . . . it took a lot of work to put chains on the olive tree and link it up to the bulldozer and finally tear it up. And, ah"— Stone again fought back tears—"the olive tree seemed like a symbol, because in the background of this dispute are certain elements in the Israeli community who would like to uproot the Arabs and drive them out, as well as the olive trees. . . . My God," Stone exclaimed, "have we so quickly forgotten about the Hitler occupation of Europe? Have we so quickly forgotten that the Geneva Pact which now governs the treatment of occupied populations and territories is an effort to prevent what happened in occupied Europe?"

Stone's difficulty with "pious lying" surfaced when he attended a memorial for Lippmann. Fulsome praise for Lippmann filled the room. Then Stone got up and bellowed, "He was on the wrong side of Sacco and Vanzetti!" Stone peered at the blur of an audience and added that it was a tremendous fault that Lippmann never wrote about the holocaust. Stone sat down to utter silence. After taking a shot at their hero, Stone blithely walked out. Said Esther, "Izzy left me to face everybody."

But Stone was an equal-opportunity deflator. When young leftists were making a documentary on the 1930s American Communist Party, they eagerly asked Stone to say a few words about the Communists he had known back then. They waited for the oracle. Stone blasted the "pissant sectarians" of yesteryear. "They had no appreciation of Thomas Jefferson. This is the greatest country in the world, freedom of press, freedom of religion." Stone went on and on, disconcerting the young filmmakers in high fashion.

No matter the depth of his outrage or despair at the world order, Stone's personal humor often ruled, sometimes with sparkling original cracks, and sometimes with corny jokes. Jack Beatty was among his younger friends. "I remember telling him that my wife was going to have a baby; she was thirty-nine and it was late in the game for both of us." Beatty imitated Stone's voice: " 'Jack! You need a michloch.' I asked, 'Michloch?' thinking it was some Yiddish word. And Izzy said, 'Yeah, *mick lock*—an Irish chastity belt.' " All the old lover of burlesque needed, as he chortled away, was a rim shot on the drum.

In an exchange of ideas, "you couldn't keep up," said Beatty. "If he was losing on facts, he'd repair to the theory behind it—'Well, that may be true, but as *Kropotkin* said in his letter to' . . . and you'd be thinking, 'Huh?' He was a very wily guy. You had to have a kind of brass-bound ego to be around him, because he would, invariably, put you down, because the dialectic was his game. And he was into winning." To some, Stone was never much of a philosopher. Philosophy fascinated him principally when he could use it to address issues. "He wanted to elucidate issues in intellectual terms; he wanted to examine ideas and theories to pry open *reality* rather than just as ends in themselves."

During the 1980s Jack and his wife often became chauffeurs for the Stones, who loved movies as much as they did, although Stone hated *Tootsie*, the Dustin Hoffman film that was universally acclaimed and uproariously funny. As they walked out of the movie, Stone ranted about how this idea "was old at the time of the Greeks" in plays about men pretending they were women. "It's an insult! An extended cliché!" In a way, Stone was showing off; what was good enough for the Greeks and Shakespeare was certainly good enough for Hollywood. Paradoxically, after a long day of using his brain, Stone felt entitled to lose himself in bad old westerns that offered nothing new from the days of the silent screen.

In the early eighties, while standing in line for movies, squads of boomers who recognized Stone from antiwar rallies would come up to tell him how much they admired him. If any remained around to talk, Stone would start in on Socrates.

Stone demonstrated his love of research into antiquity in a run-on sentence at the age of eighty. "I started by spending a year studying the two great English revolutions of the seventeenth century, then had to understand the Reformation to understand what happened then, and my hero, John Milton, was a leading character in that century—and when I got to the Reformation, I felt I had to understand the premonitory movements that foreshadowed it in the Middle Ages, people like Abelard, and when I saw what the rediscovery of Aristotle in the twelfth century had done to free men's minds, I moved back to ancient Athens. [Short intake of breath.] I thought I would do a cursory study of freedom of thought in antiquity based on standard sources, and I discovered everything was involved in controversy and that you couldn't make valid political or philosophical inferences from the translations. So I set out to learn the ancient Greek. . . ." Stone "got through the Gospel of St. John and then to the *Iliad* and then I got into business and set out to read the poets . . . and then I fell in love with the Athenians. I couldn't understand, how could they possibly have condemned a philosopher to death for his ideas? . . . I set out to explain how it might have happened."

Stone felt he had produced "a lot of new insights of some value," and Christopher Lehmann-Haupt wrote in the *New York Times*, "The case Mr. Stone makes is impressive. . . . His reasoning is persuasive," although "one feels slightly bothered that Mr. Stone's indictment never comes completely into focus." The reviewer joined several others who praised the book's liveliness. The *New York Times* called it "an intellectual thriller," and the Hellenic scholar who had advised Stone, Bernard Knox, said in the *Atlantic Monthly* it was a "challenging investigative probe of the evidence." "His common-sense reading of ancient texts is irradiated with love for democracy," wrote Thomas D'Evelyn in the *Christian Science Monitor*, who nonetheless criticized Stone as being "blind to what inspired Socrates."

To the anguish of many an author, publications can perversely utilize unfairly biased reviewers. That was Stone's fate when the *Wall Street Journal* chose Sidney Hook, whose animus had begun in 1939 when Stone and other leftists assailed Hook for equating Stalin's totalitarianism with Hitler's. Hook cuttingly disparaged both the author and the book, saying that Stone's achievement "is somewhat marred by the display of the spirit of a little Jack Horner, so proud of some of his magical feats of philological analysis that he can't help strewing the pages of a popular book with recondite Greek words." Hook sniffed, "But this touch of pedantry is a common and forgivable offense in autodidacts." Stone joked, "What's wrong with being self-taught—except that I never paid the professor." Hook mocked the speech that Stone wrote for Socrates and added, "Mr. Stone's jeering remarks about Plato's philosophical doctrines are those of a cultural philistine."

In public Stone said of Hook, "I don't have animosity toward him." (In private to author Cottrell, he referred to him as "that bastard.") "Socrates got into trouble because a lot of snotty rich kids—who didn't believe in democracy—followed him along and imitated his negative dialectic. Twice they overthrew the democracy and imposed a terrible reign of terror on the city . . . those young, disaffected aristocrats in league with the Spartans who overthrew the democracy," said Stone, were one reason some of the Athenians condemned Socrates. Stone said he was not condoning the death sentence but trying to explain how it came about because, in his estimation, an arrogant Socrates could not fathom that commoners had a right to free speech. "Socrates appealed to his 'right' as a 'superior' man to speak. I think if he had appealed to the fundamental traditions of ancient Athens and its belief in freedom of speech, he could have been acquitted."

Stone was defensive over some of the reviews. "Anyone who finds something new in Thucydides or some other classic that the establishment scholars have overlooked is sure to be mugged for his temerity and impudence in making such discoveries. . . . Having trounced him severely for his labors, his unwelcome labors, they will continue to overlook the discoveries as if they had never been made."

Navasky categorized three essential opinions of Stone's reviewers: "First, there are those who seem to have understood what he was about" and cited as an example the *Nation* critic John Leonard's description: "'This altogether engaging do-it-yourself philological meander and owner's manual on free speech and class animus in ancient Athens.' Second there are those I think of as pedants who ask, 'Where does a mere journalist, even one who in his seventies has taken the trouble to learn ancient Greek, get off writing about such a subject?' And finally, there are those, also scholars/pedants, who concede that Izzy was or is a great journalist and then go on to ask, 'Where does a merely great journalist get off, etc., etc., etc.' I think there's been a fundamental misunderstanding here. . . . Izzy was less a conventional journalist, even a 'merely great one,' than he was a scholar."

Stone himself argued that one had to factor in bias when examining any historical interpretation. For example, said Stone, Whig and Tory scholars in seventeenth-century England presented "two different points, both are valid and part of the truth."

Mostly Stone had a rousing good time of it all, basked in his best-seller status, and spoke to fans all around the world, reiterating his old phrase: it was all "a lot of fun."

Each year Stone eagerly participated in his numerous birthday celebrations, treating them as if they should be international holidays. During a Q-and-A session after his speech in San Francisco at the City Arts and Lectures series in January 1988, Stone was cut off in midsentence by laughter. Being trundled onstage was a cake in the sagging stage of candle meltdown. Stone had turned eighty a few weeks before.

"I'll make a confession," said Stone. "This is the first speech I've made since I was eighty years old. I was thinking, 'What the hell are eighty years in the lifetime of humanity? Have I really learned anything?' " He paused. "I don't know. I'm not sure."

The premier autodidact told an applauding audience, "You know, Michelangelo died in his eighties and he said something very wonderful. He sighed and said, 'And I had just begun to learn the alphabet of my profession.' "

28

THE LAST OF THE
GREAT FOG CUTTERS

When you are younger, you get blamed for crimes you never committed, and when you're older, you begin to get credit for virtues you never possessed. It evens itself out.

—I. F. Stone

Stone's capacious memory, erudition, and historical acumen that helped him define modern issues continued to function until the end of his life. The frenetic deadlines of journalism had suited Stone, yet his experience with Socrates expanded his desire. "I think he was trying to provide himself at the end of his life with an opportunity to do more scholarship and deal with ideas," said his son Christopher. The year after *The Trial of Socrates* was published, Stone hoped to write his opus on freedom of speech and thought. It was sure to have a Stone twist. He puckishly told his son he had a great idea "but he wasn't going to share it." Said Christopher, emotionally, "It was wonderful that he thought like that . . ." Unable to finish the sentence, Christopher choked up, then said, "That was consolation, that he was getting ready and that he would have worked on it."

Although few outside of his immediate family knew—nor did obituaries or tributes mention it—Stone had developed colon cancer. As always, talk of illness was verboten. Even friends like journalism critic and professor Ben Bagdikian thought that Stone's rapid exit for a bathroom one day was caused by an emotional response to just another heated discussion on what was wrong with the world. "For a guy who would go public with the rumblings of the earth, he just kept to himself all sorts of problems too long," recalled Christopher. "He was having diarrhea and stomach cramps, and after he ate he had pain—all of which most people would act upon."

At the age of eighty-one, Stone's most obvious physical problem, his eyesight, was finally helped by a successful cataract operation. To the family, it became clear that his eyesight was now a lesser problem. Stone was shortening his walks, even taking cabs because of stomach cramps, but he did not tell his doctors. He let his colon problem advance until an exploratory operation was necessary. On May 22, 1989, he went in for colon surgery. "His heart wasn't in bad shape, but there is always a risk," said Christopher, so Stone had "the colon crew and the heart crew." He came through the operation in "great spirits." Told that he had cancer, Stone was amazingly accepting. He knew that people sometimes lived with cancer for several years and he was ready to tackle his new book.

An astounded nurse heard Stone's first words when he came to after general anesthesia: "What's happening in China?" Stone had been transfixed by the massive Tiananmen Square protests that spring. Seven weeks of student-led pro-democracy demonstrations in China had captured worldwide interest; in one demonstration on May 4, one hundred thousand students and workers peacefully marched in Beijing demanding democratic reforms and protesting government corruption. As early as two years before, Stone had held a flickering candle in front of the White House in a show of solidarity for the budding democratic movement. "Pop resisted the romanticization of the American students in the Vietnam War, but there was no resistance to the Chinese students—although I can tell you that their notion of the Bill of Rights was *très* fuzzy at best. A lot of them wanted material goods," said Christopher. "At any rate, Pop wasn't going to look that carefully at it. The idea of freedom breaking out in Beijing was 'wonderful, just wonderful.'"

As Christopher swung through the Boston airport on his way to his father's side at Boston's Brigham and Women's Hospital, he saw on television that indelible image of a slim, young Chinese man dwarfed by the line of tanks he was halting by standing still in the middle of their path. Christopher wanted to tell his father, knowing that he would be cheered and would grasp some of the symbolism: "That's your life, Pop, that's you!"

But Stone had experienced terrible heart fibrillations a few days after the operation and was now in intensive care. He did not greet Christopher's news with customary enthusiasm. This was an ominous barometer. Patients in hospitals were often gauged by how well they were eating, said his son. "If their appetite picks up, they're on the mend. If it wanes—trouble. Dad's appetite that waned was his appetite for news." This was a man who "gorged on news. Plate after plate of news and snacks of documents and dispatches in between. But he lost the hunger." As doctors checked for customary vital signs, Stone's family watched for their real ones, waiting for Izzy to "tear a lusty two-column swath out of the *New York Times*, perhaps to the tune of 'Hey, goddamn it!' But he didn't."

His life-support system, the smell of newsprint, lingered as papers piled up all over the room. Then on his last full Sunday, Stone told his daughter, "Cut off the [Boston] *Globe*." On June 3 and 4, troops and tanks rolled into Tiananmen Square, violently crushing the revolt. The estimate of civilians slaughtered in the area surrounding the square ranged from four hundred into the thousands. "Dad just couldn't talk about what was happening to the students. I had never shielded Dad from news, but I had to listen to the radio and not tell him what was happening. It was all just too painful."

On June 18, 1989, Izzy Stone died at the age of eighty-one of heart failure.

The wire-service tickers as always issued news bulletins from around the world that day—from Beijing, Lima, Rome, London, Paris, and, from Boston, one item, the death of Stone. In San Francisco the city board of supervisors adjourned the next day out of respect for the memory of the late journalist, who would surely have chuckled at such governmental sanction. There were memorial services in New York and Washington, editorials and columns blossomed with tributes to Stone, some of them with a requisite line about his misappraising Russia. Some fans recognized a rather frenzied hypocrisy as the establishment that had so long ignored him burst with eulogies. "Some of the honorifics made my stomach turn," said the *Nation*'s Alexander Cockburn. "Mainstream institutions that wouldn't have touched him for his most heterodox and important work during the wars in Korea and Vietnam came loping forward to appropriate him as someone wrongheaded at times but still the conscience of the trade, as though the trade had a conscience and as though they themselves were better because of Stone." Then they continued to produce "the sort of shifty fact-mangling that Stone excelled in exposing." He accused mainstream writers of taming Stone in order to "haul [him] into the realm of the respectables." Tom Wicker, a true friend of Stone's and a tough observer himself, did not escape Cockburn's wrath. Wicker had written that Stone so presciently saw that "bombing North Vietnam was an ineffective substitute for winning the ground war in South Vietnam." "*Wrong*," said Cockburn. That's what some journalists were saying. "Stone was saying the war was a criminal enterprise and the United States should get out." Or, as Stone would say, "Get the hell out." Stone always said America's "peace-by-quickie-bombardment" was as morally wrong as it was militarily stupid.

An apt phrase was coined when writer Elizabeth Drew called Izzy journalism's great "fog cutter." Cutting through the fog of manipulative, distorted, and lying governmental prose was his true specialty, and he always loved the irony that the State Department was located in a section of Washington called Foggy Bottom.

For Esther, life without Izzy was unbearable. Unlike widows who become the keeper of the flame, Esther drifted into the privacy of her life with close friends and family. Especially devoted were son Jeremy and his wife, B.J., who visited daily. Eleven years after Izzy died, Esther died in a Potomac, Maryland, nursing home in November 2000 at the age of ninety-one. She had been as determined as her husband to keep their little weekly afloat for its lifetime of nearly twenty years. Said their son Jeremy, Esther was Stone's "main substantive administrative assistant, subscription manager, advertising manager, and chief cook and bottle washer."

Another family member who fell into sadness after Stone's death was brother-in-law Leonard Boudin. At a New York memorial service for Stone, packed with six hundred fans, he gave an uncharacteristically unfocused speech, even though he delivered one line that made his listeners chuckle, describing Izzy as "the only genius I knew of with a functioning sense of humor." He traced some golden moments in Izzy's career: his book on Kent State; his 1941 attacks on American conglomerates selling to Germany; his slicing prose: "Mr. Roosevelt is a master of the art of changing the subject." Said Boudin, "He was a man of extraordinary moral and, yes, even physical bravery" who had covered wars in Israel. He knew a "tremendous amount of constitutional law . . . one of the great losses the Supreme Court has had is that it never had Izzy on it. He not only had legal learning but a sense of history which very few justices have, and a writing style which the most liberal justice can't touch." He remembered Izzy talking with the great scholar his uncle Louis Boudin, when Izzy was in his early twenties. "There was no subject on which these two men—the young and the old—were not able to converse virtually as equals."

Leonard and Stone were the most unusual of brothers-in-law, sharing decades of standing side by side for causes as well as trying hard to top one another at family gatherings; two men with outsize egos and talents to match. "By any rational measures, [Boudin] was among the greatest civil liberties lawyers of his time," remarked the *Nation*. "Whole areas of constitutional law bear his mark." He and Stone were founders of the Emergency Civil Liberties Committee. Stone fought as hard as Boudin did for one of Boudin's greatest achievements during the fifties, winning a 1958 case that established that passports could no longer be withheld on political grounds. When other lawyers refused to represent victims of McCarthyism, Boudin, who was himself no radical, took them on. He continued to champion the liberties of civil rights leaders and anti-Vietnam warriors— Benjamin Spock and Daniel Ellsberg, Julian Bond and Paul Robeson— and of leftist governments such as Chile under Allende and Cuba.

As the *Nation* said, "Boudin was to the practice of law" what Stone was to the practice of journalism during the fifties—"a lone individual who kept his bearings and acted as a guardian of important public values at a time of general institutional default."

"At the end they became very close," recalled Leonard's widow, Jean. "Always talking together, always joking. They made fun about other people's anecdotes that they were always so competitive." That autumn, after Stone died, Boudin became ill. "As a joke, the last thing I said to Leonard in the hospital when he could still understand me," recalled Jean, "was 'Leonard, I just want to tell you, you're just competing with Izzy,' and he laughed."

Five months after Stone died, so did Leonard, at age seventy-seven, of a heart attack.

Respect for I. F. Stone among serious journalists lived on long after those memorial testimonials seventeen years ago. Carried away at the time, Robert Kaiser, an executive editor at the *Washington Post*, said of his good friend that Stone "had changed the way journalism is performed." As we have so appallingly witnessed, such sentiments are in no way true. But Stone did change, inspire, and rally around him a number of the absolute best remaining journalists. He gave readers a fresh and dissenting voice, speaking for some and converting others along the way. He introduced healthy skepticism to the trade back when even the best were willing to believe that what their country was doing in Vietnam was just or timidly approached the correctness of the civil rights movement or did not explore Israel's approach to Palestinians or took the official word of hypocrisy surrounding the Kent State and Jackson State murders. In many instances he had a special wisdom that could see on deadline what the results of a political act would be in the future. It wasn't just that time proved him right—he was often right at the time.

Stone's no-holds-barred attitude was especially attractive to younger writers. Said Scott Armstrong, "Izzy gave you a gift, encouraging you to 'persevere and convince other people. That is what journalism is all about.'" Said Eric Alterman, "His inability to countenance conventional wisdom inspired a similar skepticism in those who spent time with him." Colman McCarthy said that for anyone who knew and talked with Stone he was the "hydraulist—a lifter of your mind, a raiser of ideals that you'd forgotten you had or believed were better off without." Commented Jack Beatty, "He was so revered by all of us because, in a world where talk is cheap and there are many cheap talkers, Izzy actually believed in what he wrote and said. There was a kind of integrity that is missing today. He was in no way apologetic, although he could admit to making mistakes." Stone's bad eyesight became a metaphor for his earlier enthusiasm for the USSR, long since abandoned. Said Beatty, "There was that one-eyed quality—but what a marvelous view most of the time."

Stone's last written words, in fact, published a few months before he died, were about the evils that existed in Russia, going against the grain once more, when everyone else was hailing glasnost and the reforms of Gorbachev. "One of his great themes, a kind of obsession, was the misuse of psychiatry to persecute people in the Soviet Union," recalled his editor and cofounder of the *New York Review of Books,* Bob Silvers. Stone indignantly badgered and sometimes shamed members of the international psychiatric community for "their crime of silence" as political prisoners were locked up in mental wards in the Kremlin.

This was the last of seventy pieces—loping walks through history and the present—that Izzy wrote for the *New York Review.* Silvers's introduction to Stone was at a newstand kiosk in Paris in 1955, where Silvers spied a copy of the *Weekly.* He never forgot the passion Stone poured into an article on the murder of Emmett Till and how America needed a black Gandhi to lead it against a terrible racial sickness. A few years later Silvers, then at *Harper's* magazine, proposed that Stone write an article on King, "who seemed almost miraculously to be the man inspired by Gandhi that Izzy had hoped for." No, said his editor; Izzy was "too doctrinaire." Silvers recalled "the editor was absolutely wrong" and such conventional perceptions were grossly unfair. A man who could conceive of a "black-American Gandhi was anything but doctrinaire."

With the enthusiasm of a cub reporter, Stone continued to tac
view assignments until a few months before he died, always begging
few more words or paragraphs because he had just found the m
amazing point to add after reading a newspaper from Germany or a.
"article by young labor leaders in Tunisia." His semi-apology and argument always were that it "wasn't going to be a Fulbright," his brilliant
and long three-part *Review* study of Senator William Fulbright that ran
to eighteen thousand words. Stone wrote the first article on Vietnam.
Today, the *New York Review of Books* is continuing the tradition by publishing the best exposés of America's media failures of yet another war.

The *Nation* magazine rushed to create an I. F. Stone award for student
journalism in the hope that the young would be inspired by Stone's
legacy—a commitment to human rights, exposing injustices and explosive facts ignored by the mainstream media. Through the years, other institutions honored Stone, and twelve years after his death, UC Berkeley's
graduate school of journalism inaugurated an I. F. Stone endowment
with a schoolwide forum following the 9/11 terrorist attacks. The endowment, funded by computer executive Steve Silberstein, supports
teaching fellows, scholarships, and internships, with a focus on human
rights reporting, free expression, and investigative journalism. The politically active businessman read the *Weekly* as a youth and remained impressed: Stone was a "hard-hitting, get-at-the-facts, don't-fall-for-BS-
propaganda" journalist, Silberstein said.

In that vein, teaching fellows have included Lowell Bergman, Barbara
Ehrenreich, David Rieff, and Jonathan Mirsky, whose own "muckraking
carefully researched writing resulted, after many years, in me being
thrown out of China." The regular contributor to the *New York Review of
Books* said, "I used to spend a few summer weeks with the Stones on Fire
Island when I was in college." Mirsky remembers that he and Stone were
both scheduled to speak at Washington, D.C.'s first big teach-in in 1965.
Each had fifteen minutes to speak, and Stone rushed in and asked if he
could take Mirsky's fifteen minutes because he needed thirty minutes to
say what was so vastly important to him. "Only Izzy could have gotten
away with that kind of thing," said Mirsky years later. "I sat admiringly
while he used my time." In a new century, he enjoyed having a UC
Berkeley fellowship honoring Stone.

On permanent display in Berkeley's North Gate Hall, locked in a glass
case, like some relic from an ancient Egyptian tomb, is Stone's battered

upright typewriter, along with letters from Eleanor Roosevelt and ...rt Einstein. Orville Schell, the Chinese scholar and dean of the grad-...te school, hopes that some students who pass by will be intrigued ...nough to learn about I. F. Stone and what he did.

As long as there are deans like Orville Schell, and modern-day visiting journalists, such as Mark Danner of the *New York Review of Books,* at least some young students will know what real reporting is all about. A brilliant collection of essays by Michael Massing, *Now They Tell Us: The American Press and Iraq,* describes what Massing calls the "unseen war" because of government censorship and the hordes of journalists who practiced self-censorship and boosterism as if the Gulf of Tonkin lies had never happened. In the preface, Orville Schell excoriates the press, who "with a few notable exceptions" failed to scrutinize either the administration's pre-invasion excuse for war or "its failures afterward." It looks today as if we have distressingly come full circle to the days when Stone wrote on the fringe. "The few dissenting voices," said Schell, "were confined to the margins of the media."

All too few in the media, said Schell, remembered I. F. Stone's admonition: "If you want to know about governments, all you have to know is two words, 'governments lie.'"

What Stone detractors got so terribly wrong is reflected in a sneering end to an unsigned *New Republic* obituary: "In old age he may finally have come to understand that all of his best work—all the digging, ferreting, the polemicizing, the triumphant use of official documents to refute official pretenses—had been made possible by the distinctive openness of the society in which he lived."

Stone knew that long before whoever wrote this silly comment was born. He never stopped praising the American freedoms that allowed him to speak and to think as he did. That is why he fought so hard against those who were bent on destroying them.

And that is precisely why he should be remembered.

ACKNOWLEDGMENTS

My incomparable, beloved husband, Jack Gordon, was the inspiration for and the driving force behind this book. He endured an off-again, on-again literary ménage à trois, with Izzy seemingly forever present in our marriage. They were kindred souls in their fight for justice and in their wise and witty approach to problems. Brilliant and courageous, Jack risked his political career as he battled McCarthyism, pushed for civil rights and civil liberties, equality for women, better education, programs for the poor, an end to the Vietnam War. An early subscriber to *I. F. Stone's Weekly,* Jack kept pushing me to the finish line when I would despair, insisting that this book was important. I could not have finished it without his endless reassurances, kindness, vast input, and love. Just as it was completed, Jack tragically and shockingly left all of us who loved him, run over by a car while walking near our home in early winter darkness. The mistakes and misjudgments of this book are mine; all that is good in it belongs to this man I so loved.

I am also extremely indebted to the Stone family, particularly Izzy's brother Lou, sister, Judy, daughter, Celia, and son Christopher, who gave me so much of their time and provided me with indispensable family material, specifically some letters, photographs, and a delightful family chronicle written by Lou and chapters of an unfinished memoir by his deceased brother, Marc. The Stone genes have produced a warm, smart, and gregarious collection in addition to Izzy. Some of the anecdotes that I had heard through personal interviews were enhanced by accounts given to the Stone family for an "I. F. Stone" memorabilia collection following Izzy's death in 1989. His two memorial services in New York and Washington, D.C., produced wonderful reflections by Leonard Boudin, Victor Navasky, Christopher Stone, Celia Gilbert, and Robert Silvers, among others. Douglas B. Rauschenberger, director of the Historical Society of Haddonfield, provided me with a priceless copy of Stone's fourteen-year-old endeavor *Progress.*

I was also very lucky to have known Izzy and Esther as neighbors in Washington, D.C., to have interviewed him and Esther for the *Washington Post,* and to have heard him speak on numerous occasions.

Todd Gitlin, historian, media critic, and author, not only supplied personal stories and observations of his long association with Stone, but graciously gave me his tape of an unpublished interview with Izzy that adds fresh thoughts and insights to previously published material. So did Bill Thomas, who gave me the "outtakes" of an interview with Stone for the *Baltimore Sun.*

The most idyllic place in the world to write is Bellagio, Italy, where I was fortunate enough to be a Ford Foundation Bellagio Center scholar in 1992, which made it possible to research and shape the section on the thirties. I thank its New York director, Susan Garfield, and our hospitable Italian host, Gianna Celli.

Countless books informed my thinking and are listed in the bibliography. Nothing was more vital than the collected works of Izzy's decades of writing. The real difficulty was the hopeless task of picking the best out of those millions of wonderfully written and researched ideas, themes, and opinions. Three other books deserve special mention. Andrew Patner's *I. F. Stone: A Portrait* is a small gem of taped interviews that captures the essence of Izzy in conversation, coupled with Patner's cogent editing and comments. My book would be most incomplete without Patner's work. Robert Cottrell's 1992 *Izzy: A Biography of I. F. Stone,* expanded from a meticulously researched doctoral thesis, is also an insightful look at Stone. Historian Ronald Steel's brilliant biography of Walter Lippmann was invaluable for the comparison material I have used to highlight the insider-versus-outsider approach to journalism. Three additional books were also especially helpful on the history of twentieth-century media: David Halberstam's *The Powers That Be,* Richard Kluger's *The Paper,* and Phillip Knightley's all-embracing study of war correspondents and war coverage, *The First Casualty.*

Andy Moursund, one of Stone's former assistants, provided his insights and also a treasure trove of leftist and historical memorabilia from his Georgetown Book Store in Bethesda, Maryland. Thanks to Andy, I was able to amplify the collected works of Stone with a near complete set of *I. F. Stone's Weekly,* numerous original copies of *PM,* ancient copies of *Fortune* and *Collier's,* and a rare original copy of Stone's *Business as Usual,* written in 1941.

Research on the Cold War era became unending when previously secret archives from Russia, China, and North Korea were made available in the last days of the twentieth century. The Woodrow Wilson Institute's Cold War History Project was an outstanding source for new perspectives of scholars who added fascinating dimensions to earlier accounts of the Korean War. The Venona Files, decrypted Russian KGB memos from the early to midforties, released by the CIA in 1995 and 1996, cast new light on Russian spying operations within the U.S. government. And I am even grateful for the malevolent J. Edgar Hoover. Without his frenzied vendetta against Stone, I would not have been able to cull from five thousand pages of Izzy's file. Through the Freedom of Information Act I obtained documents on Stone from the Central Intelligence Agency, the Department of State, the U.S. passport division, the Departments of the Army and Air Force, and the U.S. Postal Service, many of which were included in the Federal Bureau of Investigation file.

I was also fortunate to interview some of the finest practitioners of twentieth-century journalism, authors, historical luminaries, and family friends, some of whom have since died. I include them with fond memories, along with the living who gave of their time and insights on Izzy.

Bill Kovach, James Dickenson, Nicholas Von Hoffmann, Scott Armstrong, Helen Thomas, and Studs Terkel read portions of the early manuscript and provided wise and invaluable advice.

My personal interview list includes Martin Agronsky, Sara Alpern, Gar Alperovitz, Madeleine Amgott, Patrick Anderson, Scott Armstrong, Ben Bagdikian, Bill Bailey, Harriet Baskin, Jack Beatty, Al and Sylvia Bernstein, Carl Bernstein, Barbara Bick, Kai Bird, Jean Boudin, Ben Bradlee, David Brinkley, Felicity Bryan, Noel Buchner Jr., Jill Lit Capron, Arthur Cox, Bruce Craig, Bob Cunniff, Helen and Richard Dudman, Daniel Ellsberg, Dorothy Fall, Margaret Hartel Farrington, John Henry Faulk, Jules Feiffer, John Kenneth Galbraith, Todd Gitlin, Sam Grafton, William Greider, Bernd Greiner, Dorothy Healy, Joseph Heller, Christopher Hitchens, Max Holland, Roy Hoopes, Irving Howe, Toby Ingersoll, Molly Ivins, Robert Kaiser, Oleg Kalugin, Stanley Karnow, Shirley Katzander, Murray Kempton, Penn Kimball, Erwin Knoll, Max Lerner, Dr. Bernard Lown, Christopher Lydon, Colman McCarthy, Morton Mintz, Richard Moose, Andy Moursand, Chuck Nathanson, Victor Navasky, Connor Cruise O'Brien, Peter Osnos, Luvvie Pearson, Charlie Peters, Robert Pierpoint, Walter Pincus, Rutherford Rudd Poats, Shirley

Povich, David Prensky, Peter Pringle, Victor Rabinowitz, Marcus Raskin, Joseph Rauh, Douglas B. Rauschenberger, Jack Raymond, James "Scotty" Reston, Ruth Rosen, Harrison Salisbury, George Seldes, Robert Sherrill, Ruth Smallberg, Al Spivak, Larry Spivak, Christopher, Ann, and Jessica Stone, Judy Stone, Louis and Deena Stone, Paul Sweezy, Helen Thomas, Mildred Traube, John Vanderchek, Judith Viorst, Nicholas Von Hoffman, George Vournas, Michael Watts, Rae Weimer, Roger Wilkins, Garry Wills, George Wilson, Thomas Winship.

Izzy's voice and personality have been preserved on tape and television, memorably so in Jerry Bruck Jr.'s 1973 documentary *I. F. Stone's Weekly.* Stone appears in a PBS documentary of Huey Long, early *Meet the Press* radio shows housed in the Library of Congress, and in interviews on *The Dick Cavett Show* on ABC-TV. His voice is heard on the Kronos Quartet recording *Howl U.S.A.*, Nonesuch label (6/4/96), "Cold War Suite from How It Happens." I have utilized portions of these plus Stone's speeches toward the end of his career, in 1988, at the National Press Club, the Nation Institute in New York, and the City Arts and Lectures series in San Francisco.

When I first began this book in 1990, some young friends spent hours at the Library of Congress looking up musty newspaper clippings; among the best, who have gone on to their own careers, are Chantal Botana and Ed Pressman. Other researchers were Laure Demongeot and Jessie Moskal. I also salute the many writers of today's media Web sites and magazines and newspapers that hold accountable today's politicians and the media for their present-day follies, in the tradition of I. F. Stone. Among today's concerned Stone followers who assisted me in tracking a vital source was Andre Carothers.

Olwen Price and her band of efficient dictationists at the *Washington Post* typed many rambling interviews. Shirley Coombs helped type the bibliography.

This book is my third that has been edited by Lisa Drew; I don't think there is another editor in the business who provides such enthusiastic and wise counsel and editing. Her retirement leaves a major hole in publishing. My many thanks go to Lisa and her assistant, Samantha Martin.

While I am critical of today's mass media, I was exceptionally privileged to have worked in a more golden age of print journalism. Shirley Povich, that legendary *Washington Post* sportswriter, made the phone call that changed my life and brought me from Detroit to the now defunct *Washington Star,* where I worked for city editor Sidney Epstein, a drill sergeant of a boss who terrified us all into getting the facts. After a stint with Charlotte Curtis at the *New York Times,* I was hired by Ben Bradlee. The *Washington Post* was my home for twenty-three years, from 1968 to 1991. Ben remains in my view the all-time best editor, bar none; tough as hell but fair. Shelby Coffey honed my early writing, and Eugene Patterson always gave encouragement. All along the way I experienced the joy and awe of working with principled, dedicated, and fun-loving colleagues, too numerous to mention adequately in this space.

Finally, friends and family kept reminding me that there was a life outside of researching and writing, yet still managed to encourage me to persevere, among them my agent Ronald Goldfarb, Nicholas Von Hoffmann, Sharon and Gar Alperovitz, Melanie Sommers and Jonathan Gordon, Michael Siegel, Leah Siegel and Eric Loehr, Carole Hampton, Ruth Gibson, Mollie and Jim Dickenson, Cathy Wyler and Richard Rymland, Janet Donovan, Dorothy Fall, Norman and Grace Mark, Marthena Cowart, and Gayle and Chuck Hodges. And no one made me laugh harder through it all than the two new members of my grandchildren brigade, Teagan Samantha Loehr and Gaby Gordon.

NOTES

Abbreviations for frequently used references in notes:

IFS—I. F. Stone
CG—Celia Gilbert
CS—Christopher Stone
JJS—Jeremy Jay Stone
LS—Lou Stone
JS—Judy Stone
MM—Myra MacPherson
Steel, *Lippmann*—Ronald Steel, *Walter Lippmann and the American Century*
Patner, *Portrait*—Andrew Patner, *I. F. Stone: A Portrait*
Cottrell, *Izzy*—Robert Cottrell, *Izzy: A Biography of I. F. Stone*
Stern, *Maverick*—J. David Stern, *Memoirs of a Maverick Publisher*
Record—*Philadelphia Record*
Post—*New York Post*
Compass—*New York Daily Compass*
Review—*New York Review of Books*
Torment—*In a Time of Torment.* Collection of I. F. Stone's works compiled mostly from the *New York Review of Books*
Haunted Fifties—Stone's collection of *Compass* and *Weekly* columns
Polemics—*Polemics and Prophecies.* Collection of Stone's work for *New York Review of Books* and other publications after the *Weekly* folded
The Weekly Reader—*I. F. Stone's Weekly Reader.* Collection
The Weekly—MM's extensive collection of original *I. F. Stone's Weekly*

Original dates of Stone's *Weekly* columns are cited either in notes or in the book.

FBI files: In four decades of surveillance, memos were classified under a myriad of numbering systems. They were released to this author over more than a decade, 1990–2002, out of sequence and in no particular order. There are approximately five thousand pages, many of which were repeats or redacted or indicated as missing. Therefore citing such numbers would be of no value in identifying specific memos to readers. I have either categorized them by the date of the memo or the date of incidents referred to in the memo; they are so identified in the body of the text or in chapter notes. In addition, some information appeared in "The Secret War Against I. F. Stone" by MM in the *Washington Post* Outlook section, August 21, 1994, C-1, and the *Washington Spectator*, July 1995.

FYI: The permanent number assigned to MM's Freedom of Information Act request is FOIPA No. 335,111. Years of appeals requesting severely redacted and missing pages were only partially successful.

Foreword: The Importance of Being Izzy and the Death of Dissent in Journalism

xi In 2004, Philip Roth: Roth, *Plot Against America*.

xi "Uncanny echoes": I. F. Stone voice sampling from radio commentary and lecture at the Ford Hall Forum, broadcast on NPR, 4/12/83. Incorporated by Scott Johnson in his composition for the Kronos Quartet. Featured on the Kronos Quartet recording *Howl U.S.A.*, Nonesuch label, 6/4/96, "Cold War Suite from How It Happens (The Voice of I. F. Stone)."

xii "This kind of list": Quotes and paragraph information: Felicity Barringer, "Journalism's Greatest Hits: Two Lists of a Century's Top Stories," *New York Times*, 3/1/99.

xii He is a lone "courageous" voice: Michael Cross-Barnet, "The *New York Times* Shafted My Father," *Los Angeles Times*, 6/26/05.

xii "reliance at home and abroad": Stone, *Truman Era*, xxiv, 12/8/52.

xiii "It is not a private quarrel": IFS, Herbst Theater, San Francisco, 2/5/88. Audiotape provided by City Arts and Lecture, Inc.

xiii "Almost every generation": Stone, *Truman Era*, 110, "Free Speech Is Worth the Risk," *Compass*, 5/18/49.

xiv forwarding address was in care of Charles de Gaulle: Murray Kempton to MM, 8/25/91.

xiv "Walter was more engaged": James Reston to MM, 11/12/90.

xv Unless otherwise noted, quotes and comments from author Nicholas Von Hoffman are from numerous personal interviews and conversations spread over several years. "He defied the social fears": E-mail to MM, 6/19/05.

xv "We are a discouragingly timid lot": Koppel on *Nightline*, 9/27/89; in Lee and Solomon, *Unreliable Sources*, 337.

xvi "give you a lot of crap": Patner, *Portrait*, 101.

xviii "Reporters are not here": Bill Plante, PublicEye, CBSNews.com, 8/14/07.

xviii "A newspaperman ought to use": Stone, *Truman Era*, xviii.

xviii "reporters were not stenographers": Armstrong to MM, 1/20/90.

xviii "News is something": Ivins, *Who Let the Dogs In?*, xvii.

xix "going to sit on your ass": IFS, unpublished portion of interview with Bill Thomas for the *Baltimore Sun*, 1/2/83. Tape given by Thomas to MM.

xix Scotty Reston recalled his tribute: Reston to MM, 11/12/90.

xxii "'Screw you, you sons of bitches'": IFS to MM, *Washington Post*, 7/9/79.

xxii "to the notion of genius": Lydon to MM, e-mail, 8/3/04.

xxii "Socrates had delivered *it* to the jury": IFS, SF speech, 2/5/88.

xxiii "great risks in a free society": IFS, San Francisco City Arts and Lecture Series, 2/4/88.

xxiv "get extremely discouraged": Knoll to MM, 5/25/90.

xxiv "I don't think the primary": IFS, S.F. speech, 2/5/88.

xxv "monstrous assault": Bill Moyers, National Conference on Media Reform, 1/12/07.

xxv "Aren't they synonymous?": *American Morning*, 3/31/04. Transcript number 033102CN.V74 CNN (as reported in *Fair*).

xxv "shoe leather reporting": "'Talking Points Memo' drove the U.S. attorneys story, proof that Web writers with input from devoted readers can reshape journalism," Terry McDermott, *Los Angeles Times*, 3/17/07. [It is impossible to name the thousands of blogs that provide opinion, transcripts, reports and news, but a few are AlterNet, Daily Kos, The Huffington Post, Salon.com, Amerika.com, TruthOut, Truthdig, EFF, Deep Links, MoveOn.org. Apologies to those I missed.]

xxvi "just knowing Izzy is out there": Ivins, numerous conversations with MM; this comment in 2004.

xxvi "change the odds a little": Nat Hentoff, *Washington Post*, 6/24/89; "You mustn't feel": Hentoff, *Editor & Publisher*, 5/26/89.

xxvi "I don't have a pessimistic": Stone's comments to end of chapter, S.F. speech, 2/5/88.

Chapter 1: Coming to America

3 saw tears in Stone's eyes: CS to MM, 12/90 and 8/31/91.

4 "huddled against the canal wall": Serge, *Memoirs of a Revolutionary*, 1.

4 Driven into poverty: Sachar, *Course of Modern Jewish History*, 281–85.

5 "One-third [of you] will die out": Ibid., 285.

5 "sensation-mongering anti-Semitic journal": Ibid., 286–88.

5 Kishinev pogrom details: Ibid., 287.

6 Feinstein never spoke: Information on the Stone/Feinstein history comes from several sources: "The Family," history written by Stone's brothers, Lou and Marc; unpublished memoirs of Marc; numerous MM interviews with Stone's son Christopher, brother Lou and his wife Dina Stone, sister Judy

Stone, Harriett Baskin (granddaughter of Izzy's uncle Shumer); Haddonfield Historical Society director.

6 Historical background for Russian Jews: Several sources, notably Chamberlin, *Soviet Russia;* Sachar, *Course of Modern Jewish History;* Aleichem, *In the Storm;* Singer, *Love and Exile;* and Howe, *World of Our Fathers.*

7 "Death to the Jews!": Aleichem, *In the Storm,* 206–7; "America," 214–15.

8 In the decade from 1900 to 1910: Howe, *World of Our Fathers.*

9 Just as German Jews had earlier: Ibid.

9 Yiddish was "piggish jargon": Birmingham, *"Our Crowd,"* 292.

9 A 1903 report: Beard and Beard, *New Basic History,* 379.

10 Collecting millions in revenues: Cook, *The Muckrakers.*

10 "happy condition of Philadelphia": Costello and Feldstein, *Ordeal of Assimilation.*

10 "Sell anything that can": Birmingham, *"Our Crowd,"* 35.

Chapter 2: Beginnings

12 "a dumpling of a man": Derek Shearer, *In These Times,* 6/13/78.

12 "Good God," he said: Jack Beatty to MM, 1/91.

12 "When you grow up": IFS to MM, *Washington Post,* 7/9/79.

13 "the indisputable favorite of his mother": Ernest Jones, *The Life and Work of Sigmund Freud,* vol. 1 (1953; repr. New York: Basic Books, 1981), 5.

13 But that pampered childhood: Unless otherwise noted, family and Haddonfield history throughout chapter: LS, "The Family,"1987 unpublished history; MM interviews with LS, 1989–91; MM interviews with JS, 7/9/90, and several subsequent conversations; and MM interview with Douglas B. Rauschenberger, director, Historial Society of Haddonfield, 2/1/91. Unless otherwise specified, all comments and quotes from Lou and Judy Stone in this chapter are from interviews with MM.

13 greeted surprised strangers in Yiddish: Patner, *Portrait,* 117.

15 "Hi, I saw you": LS to MM, 1989. Also in "The Family."

17 "Izzy was a child": Raskin to MM, 12/4/89.

17 He was very much afraid of ghosts: JS to MM, 7/9/90.

18 "I was kind of a freak": Dick Polman, *Philadelphia Inquirer, Daily Magazine,* 1/28/88.

18 Izzy would sit in a trolley car: IFS to MM, *Washington Post,* 7/9/79; one of the "biggest thrills": "Portrait of a Man Reading," *Washington Post Book World,* 2/14/71.

18 "I've been on a Horace binge": IFS to MM, *Washington Post,* 7/9/79.

18 "I remember coming home": *Washington Post Book World,* 2/14/71.

19 "There were very few places": Patner, *Portrait,* 9.

19 "He's not *sports*": Ibid.

19 Katy would whisper in Yiddish: LS to MM, 1990.

19 "He was full of tricks": Ibid.

20 "You could always tell the politics": Patner, *Portrait,* 118.

20 "he prized wit": CG to MM, 10/24/05 e-mail.

20 "he was going his own way": LS to MM.

20 "Do not permit your children": Uncle Shumer information, ibid.

20 "It's full of barbarism": *Washington Post Book World,* 2/14/71.

21 "complain to God in his own tongue": Nils Gunnar Nilsson, foreign journalist, written comments for Stone family memorial collection.

21 "I shall always remember": LS, *Family Flyer* bulletin; copy of IFS eulogy given by LS to MM.

21 "the children . . . had no role models": Hertzberg, *Jews in America,* 196.

21 "The only political act": Patner, *Portrait,* 118.

22 "on their library table I found": Ibid., 36.

22 "In their children there awoke": Hertzberg, *Jews in America,* 197; "confront their tormentors": Ibid., 203.

22 "Contrary to popular mythology": Ibid., 198.

22 Marc . . . "strived in many ways": "The Family."

22 Katy slipped money: LS to MM; "The Family."

23 "He was not stern": LS to MM.

23 Marc had no desire: Marc Stone, unpublished memoir; LS to MM.

24 "quite friendly to me": Patner, *Portrait,* 161.

24 "He was not popular": Farrington to MM, 2/11/90. All following quotes and comments by Farrington are from this interview.

24 "I had four years": *Washington Post Book World,* 2/14/71.

25 third from the end, that is: In various articles Stone repeats that he finished forty-ninth out of fifty-two. However, the *Shield* yearbook records a total of fifty-six, which would make Stone's third-from-the-end finish even more impressive.

25 "School interfered with my reading": IFS to MM, *Washington Post,* 7/9/79.

26 tracking down an out-of-town reporter: IFS phone call to MM, 3/8/88.

26 "Izzy never looks back": *New York Times,* 12/7/71, 43.

26 "He was a very private person": CS to MM, 8/31/91. Unless otherwise noted, all Christopher Stone comments in this chapter are from author's interview.

26 "I was a cocky": IFS to MM, 7/79.

27 "What made Izzy tick?": Raskin to MM, 5/90.

27 "It's a help": "I. F. Stone Talks to Joe Pichirallo," *Washington Post,* 1/13/85.

28 "monument to opinionation": MM, *Washington Post,* 7/9/79.

28 could not abide the color: Jill Lit Stern's daughter, Jill Capron, to MM, 1/29/91.

28 Izzy startled her speechless: Ibid. This story has reached legendary proportions in the Stern and Feinstein-Stone families. Some versions do not include Spinoza, but all concur that the incident happened when Izzy was about thirteen.

Chapter 3: Boy Publisher

29 "fashioned herself an intellectual": Jill Capron to MM, 1/29/91. Unless otherwise noted, references to and quotes from Jill Capron in this chapter are from this same interview. The "assimilationist" story: LS to MM.

29 The Stern mansion, built in 1816: Stern, *Maverick.*

29 "a great influence in my life": *Washington Post Book World,* 2/14/71.

30 "had it been the reverend": Kaplan, *Whitman,* 102.

30 "resist much and wage 'heavy' war": Ibid., 103.

30 Izzy quoted from *Antigone*: IFS conversation with MM, 7/79.

30 "To stay in power": Copy of *The Progress,* Historical Society of Haddonfield.

30 "I was a strong Wilsonian": Unpublished 1985 interview with Todd Gitlin, historian, author, and a founder of SDS (Students for a Democratic Society).

31 encouraged the passage of the Espionage Act: Moynihan, *Secrecy.*

32 "between meditative squirts": Stone, *Truman Era,* xviii.

32 "worked my way down": Stan Isaacs, *Newsday,* 1/20/68.

32 "The smell of a newspaper": Stan Isaacs, *Newsday,* 1/29/68.

32 "I was a natural bird dog": Bill Thomas, *Baltimore Sun,* 1/2/83.

32 "mostly Yiddish, but it's good": *Washington Post Book World,* 2/14/71.

33 "Were just going" to "ablative, by the way": IFS letter given to MM by LS.

34 "a cross between Randolph Hearst": "Stone Talks Pichirallo," 1/13/85, MM 7/79.

35 rational persuasion to "army of reformers": Pells, *Radical Visions,* 4.

35 "My introduction to radicalism": IFS to Todd Gitlin, unpublished taped interview, 12/85. Given to MM by Gitlin.

35 "There was a big market": Ibid.

36 Visiting Russia, Russell witnessed: Aaron, *Writers on the Left,* 59. Unless otherwise noted, information on Kropotkin is from this source.

36 In that long ago, revolutionaries: Ibid.

36 "Vladimir Ilyich, your concrete": Pyetr Kropotkin, as quoted in Ashley Montagu foreword to *Mutual Aid.* Kropotkin "abnormal violence"; Monatgu.

37 mainstream papers . . . lied to the American public: Knightley, *First Casualty,* provides a vivid recounting of America's newspapers during the end of World War I and the early days of the Russian Revolution.

37 Karl Marx has been: Kamenka, *Portable Karl Marx.*

37 "I am not a Marxist": David McLellan, *Karl Marx: An Intimate Biography* (New York: Harper & Row, 1973). Quoted in Heilbroner, *Worldly Philosophers,* 151.

37 "wherever . . .": Wording varies slightly in two accounts of the *Manifesto*: Kamenka, *Portable Karl Marx,* and Wilson, *To the Finland Station.*

37 Marx saw "Communism" as: Karl Marx, *Communist Manifesto* (1848).

37 At that time, the concept: Grun, *Timetables of History.*

37 In one Manchester factory in 1862: Heilbroner, *Worldly Philosophers,* 159. Heilbroner's observation several years ago that sweatshops were a thing of the past did not reckon with the new gilded age in the latter years of the twentieth century and the early twenty-first century. Corporate globalism rivals the greed and avarice of nineteenth-century robber barons in its exploitation of third-world workers and the obscene salaries of CEOs in the United States. The double exploitation by Nike is but one example: children make tennis shoes in overseas sweatshops for pennies, and the shoes are then advertised to

appeal to America's youth and sold for more than $100 a pair to ghetto teens dealing in drugs or stealing to acquire them.

38 "from each according to his capacity": Kamenka, *Portable Karl Marx.*

38 "so many of these predictions": Heilbroner, *Worldly Philosophers,* 164.

38 which exceeds even that of the robber-baron: In 1998, the thirteen thousand richest families in America had almost as much income as the 20 *million* poorest households combined; those thirteen thousand families had incomes three hundred times that of average families. Paul Krugman, "The Class Wars, Part 1—for Richer," *New York Times Magazine,* 10/20/02. The disparity has only gotten worse.

38 "lost that faith when I saw": "Gadfly on the Left," *Wall Street Journal,* 7/14/70.

38 But Stone was no economist: CS to MM.

38 In truth, "socialist" Stone: Max Holland, interview with MM.

38 "was sort of a socialist": Unpublished Gitlin interview,1985.

38 "eating cold kasha": "Why I Was for Wallace," *Truman Era,* 66–68.

39 Vilified by opposition: Rivers, *Opinion Makers.*

39 "Jefferson brought the Enlightenment": Bill Thomas, *Baltimore Sun,* 1/2/83.

39 "In ancient Greek society": Ibid.

39 "In no other society": I. F. Stone, "Izzy on Izzy," *New York Times,* 1/22/78.

39 "the most eloquent defense": Ibid.

40 Stone's favorite passage is: Milton, *Areopagitica.*

Chapter 4: Raking the Muck and Red, White, and Blue Patriotism

41 "a man who made a million bucks": Unpublished portion of Bill Thomas interview with Stone for *Baltimore Sun,* 1/2/83; given to MM by Thomas.

41 Stone admired the exceptions: Aronson, *Packaging the News.*

42 "looted on a scale unrivaled": Cook, *Muckrakers,* 13.

42 "gave voice": Ibid., 11.

42 "All muckraking, crusading": Seldes, *Even the Gods Can't.*

42 "my heart has been with the working class": John Graham, *"Yours for the Revolution,"* 289.

42 "Gold is God": Ibid.

42 "I met him once": IFS to Gitlin, 1985.

42 in 1913, paid circulation reached 760,000: Information in *Appeal to Reason* and also Aronson, *Deadline for the Media,* among several sources.

43 The *New York Times* reported Debs's conviction: Articles reprinted in Rovere, *Loyalty and Security.* The complete 1/11/19 statement in *"Yours for the Revolution,"* 289–92.

44 "fugitive mention": Johnpoll and Johnpoll, *Impossible Dream,* 4.

44 three "diametrically opposed tendencies": Ibid., 5.

45 "Individualism" sanctified America's financiers: Beard and Beard, *New Basic History.*

46 "I don't propose to": Cook, *Muckrakers,* 45.

46 She found sources who talked: The legendary story of Ida Tarbell is well recounted in Cook, *Muckrakers*, 65–96.

47 While Tarbell was all cool steel: Ibid.

48 "Hour after hour": Sinclair, *Jungle*, 72.

48 "There was no heat": Ibid., 79.

48 everlastingly bitter: Sinclair, *Brass Check*, 32–38.

49 "The lobbyists of the packers": Ibid., 47.

49 Sinclair persisted in vain: Ibid.

49 "To see this whole affair": Stone, *Truman Era*, 89.

49 "I'll tell ya what": Terkel to MM, 1/15/04.

50 "an attack upon the bourgeoisie": London, introduction to *Martin Eden*.

50 Sinclair's cutting observation: Baskett, introduction to *Martin Eden*.

51 "Muckraking in America came": Cook, *Muckrakers*, 152.

51 Four years later, the party: Although the vote for Eugene Debs was larger in 1920 than in 1912, 923,000 to 901,062, the number represented a smaller percentage of the total presidential vote.

51 One of the worst class battles: Weinstein, *Decline of Socialism*.

52 In many strike centers: Ibid.

52 In San Diego: *Impossible Dream*, 302.

52 Debs deplored the union: Ibid., 304.

53 "People who believed that": Mabel Dodge Luhan, *Movers and Shakers*, 89.

53 "heavy-set young man": Steel, *Lippmann*, 53.

53 "The struggle under the competitive": Graham, "*Yours for the Revolution*," 14.

54 Reporters who sought truth: Crozier, *American Reporters on the Western Front*.

54 It was upheld by the Supreme Court: *Impossible Dream*, "*Yours for the Revolution*," *Loyalty and Security in a Democratic State*.

54 "They give you 90 days": *New York Times*, 7/14/17.

54 The *New York Herald Tribune* aligned: *Impossible Dream*, 308.

55 The ugliness of war hysteria: Quotes of Debs and trial and other information in this paragraph in Graham, "*Yours for the Revolution*," 285, 288–92.

55 "the master class": Ibid., 285.

55 Germany was not alone: Fischer, *Russia's Road from Peace to War*.

56 "from the very beginning": Graham, "*Yours for the Revolution*," 285.

56 "The war did no good": T. S. Mathews, review of *All Quiet on the Western Front*, *New Republic*, 6/19/29.

56 Debs was released on Christmas: Graham, "*Yours for the Revolution*," 288.

56 "inspired by Bolsheviks": Ibid., 286.

57 Boudin had gone from: Johnpoll and Johnpoll, *Impossible Dream*, 312.

57 "gave the kibosh to the left": IFS to Gitlin, 1985.

57 "crawling into the sacred corners": Graham, "*Yours for the Revolution*," 286.

57 "these foreign leeches": David H. Bennett, *The Party of Fear*, 189.

57 In 1919, when two anarchists: Gentry, *J. Edgar Hoover;* and Cox and Theoharis, *The Boss*.

57 *Times* specialized in lopsided coverage: One opposing comment came from the future New York mayor Fiorello La Guardia: "A very useful word is *Bolshevism*. Easy to say, hard to define, but most potent as an epithet." *New York Times*, 5/28/20.

58 Indignation crackled in a report: *To the American People: Report upon the Illegal Practices of the U.S. Department of Justice*, issued in 1920 and recounted in Johnpoll and Johnpoll, *Impossible Dream;* Graham, *"Yours for the Revolution";* Coser and Howe, *American Communist Party;* and Bennett, *Party of Fear*, 192–93. (In this century, abuses of the Patriot Act touched off a historical revisit to the Palmer Raids by various publications, which observed marked similarities.)

58 "so determined" and "so dangerous an attack": Steel, *Lippmann*, 167.

Chapter 5: Newspaperman in Knee Pants

60 "a little Jewish boy": Patner, *Portrait*, 33.

60 "he had an unusually developed": J. David Stern's Oral History, 1972, Columbia University.

61 "Izzy was always getting": Ibid.

61 "I was a dangerous radical": Stern, *Maverick*, 141.

61 Arthur Brisbane, Hearst's widely: Ibid., 156.

61 "diddled it up a bit": Patner, *Portrait*, 33.

62 in 1923, New York City had: Kluger, *Paper*.

63 "I was a nonsports kid": Patner, *Portrait*, 34.

63 some newsmen were owned: Jake Lingle met an untimely death when he got caught in the cross fire between rival mobs. Lingle, an Al Capone gang member, was, wrote George Seldes, the "liaison officer" between Colonel McCormick's *Tribune* and Capone. This explained how a newspaper reporter could wear a belt studded with no less than $50,000 worth of diamonds. Seldes, *Witness*, 203.

63 "Something has been lost": Howard Kurtz, *Washington Post*, 11/9/91.

63 "in the early 1930s": Patner, *Portrait*, 104.

63 trinkets as the Pulitzer Prize: Walter Winchell once griped that columnist Arthur Krock won the Pulitzer essentially by walking across the street and picking up a "handout"—the phrase for a public relations release—in the guise of Franklin D. Roosevelt's self-serving interview with Krock, who took no notes because of his phenomenal memory.

63 Pulitzer Prize winner Bayard Swope: Steel, *Lippmann*, 200.

64 "*bore* to be a virgin?": Diggins, *American Left*.

64 "there was not a socialist": Seldes, *Witness*, 123–24.

64 "a mass murderer of newspapers": Liebling, *Press*, 10.

65 Radio revolutionized politics: Allen, *Only Yesterday*.

65 Frankfurter was deeply critical . . . Lippmann: Steel, *Lippmann*, 225.

65 Davis got 8 million: James Weinstein, *Decline of Socialism*.

65 "As a radical": IFS to Todd Gitlin, 1985.

66 "fine line of credit": *This Fabulous Century, 1920–1930* (New York: Time-Life Books, 1969).

66 not making whoopee: Pells, *Radical Visions.*

66 mocked by "highbrows": Ibid.; and Aaron, *Writers on the Left.*

67 "Widely dispersed . . .": Aaron, *Writers on the Left.*

67 a generation of lost working men: Seldes, *Witness*, 250.

67 "yawned at Socialism in 1925": Allen, *Only Yesterday.*

67 "He was a good antifascist": Patner, *Portrait*, 34.

68 Jews at Harvard . . . in 1900: Hertzberg, *Jews in America*, 246.

68 "It still breaks my heart": IFS to MM, 7/79.

68 Stone was the "most alive": Cottrell, *Izzy*, 26.

69 "The ministers were a nice": Patner, *Portrait*, 103–4.

69 *What about the murder":* Of the many versions Izzy told, this one to Todd Gitlin, in an unpublished taped interview, 1985, was among the best.

69 received a monthly bribe: Seldes, *Witness.*

70 Matteotti was killed just: Ibid., 217.

70 In the 1920s, the *New York:* Kluger, *Paper*, 294–95.

70 "My job was to shake": Patner, *Portrait*, 34.

70 Information for Sacco-Vanzetti history: Joughin and Morgan, *Legacy of Sacco and Vanzetti.*

71 "I kept thinking, what would": IFS to MM, *Washington Post*, 7/9/79.

72 "Sacco, Vanzetti Dead": *New Masses* III symposium, October 1927, 9.

72 "dismissed as partisan": Steel, *Lippmann*, 233.

72 Outraged by Lippmann's detachment: O'Connor, *Heywood Broun.*

72 All material on Broun from O'Connor, *Heywood Broun.*

72 "waltzed up to this Napoleonic pip-squeak": IFS to MM, *Washington Post*, 7/9/79.

73 "It was just a damn": Ibid.

73 "I was fifteen when he": All quotes and references to Jean Boudin in this chapter are from Jean Boudin interview with MM, NYC, 6/29/90.

75 Esther's trauma: CS; JJS to MM.

75 "you wear the mantle of greatness": Esther's letter 4/12/47 to IFS: CG to MM, 10/25/05.

75 "I would go on and on": IFS to MM, *Washington Post*, 7/9/79.

75 "a lot of gibberish": Cottrell, *Izzy.*

76 "except run a Linotype": Stone, introduction to *Haunted Fifties*, 4.

76 "first thing I made her do": IFS to Joe Pichirallo, *Washington Post*, 1/13/85.

76 "Portrait of My Mother": Alice James Books, *Bonfire*, 1983, Celia Gilbert, by permission, CG to MM, 10/29/05.

Chapter 6: Crashing into the Thirties

81 "just two young kids": IFS to MM, 7/9/79; "darling little apartment": Jean Boudin to MM, 6/20/90.

81 incessantly pushing: Cottrell, *Izzy;* and LS to MM.

81 Stern had bought the *Philadelphia Record:* Stern, *Maverick.*

82 The turmoil didn't end: Cottrell, *Izzy;* and Sam Grafton to MM, 6/24/90.

82 Stone's salary jumped: Cottrell, *Izzy.*

82 On "Black Tuesday": Thomas and Morgan-Witts, *The Day the Bubble Burst.*

83 "no precedent": Ibid., 395. All information on the crash is from this work.

84 "The home they never moved into": LS, "The Family"; LS to MM, 1990.

84 this "calamitous time": Unless otherwise noted, all information on the Depression, Katy, and her illness in this chapter are from LS, JS, and CS to MM.

85 In 2005, studies: Benedict Carey, "Hypomanic? Absolutely. But Oh So Productive!" *New York Times,* 3/22/05, Science section, 1.

87 "turning the conversation": Stern, *Maverick,* 188.

87 Rin Tin Tin's death: *Record,* 8/10/32.

88 "the philosophy of Jesus": Ibid., 2/32.

88 Roosevelt's political finagling: Burns, *Lion and Fox;* Miller, *FDR;* and Steel, *Lippmann.*

88 "only . . . candidate with any chance": *Record,* 4/20/32.

89 "DISTORT FACTS AND DISGUISE NEWS": Ibid., 5/29/32.

89 "remarkably varied lot": Burns, *Lion and Fox,* 132.

89 tumultuous 1932 Chicago convention: Ibid., 136–37.

90 "Meet Our Next President": *Record,* 7/3/32.

90 "Victory for All of Us": *Record,* 11/9/32.

90 "magnificently blundering chapter": Ibid., 11/8/32.

91 "there was an excitement" to "FDR was an *aristocrat*": IFS to Gitlin, 1985.

91 "Some—by no means all": Krugman, *New York Times Magazine,* 10/20/02.

91 the historic whirlwind: Burns, *Lion and Fox;* Miller, *FDR;* and Steel, *Lippmann.*

92 The controversial Agricultural Adjustment Act: *Post,* 3/16/33.

92 "FDIC turned out": Stern, *Maverick,* 196.

92 By January 1934, 20 million: Miller, *FDR;* and Burns, *Lion and Fox.*

93 "What the nation did not" to "seven years' itch": *American Mercury* 16, no. 113 (May 1933).

Chapter 7: New Deal, New Life, *New York Post*

95 "Izzy was always excited about": Traube to MM, 6/23/90.

96 "Whatever happened in the world": Gibson, *Clifford Odets,* 124; Leof history: Ibid.

96 "We stayed up all night": Boudin to MM, 6/24/90.

97 "goddamnest bunch of Wall Streeters.": Cottrell, *Izzy,* 42.

97 "When Stern bought the *Post*": Unless otherwise noted, all information from or about Sam Grafton in this chapter is from an interview with MM, NYC, 6/24/90.

97 "joy to work for": Patner, *Portrait,* 36.

98 "Roosevelt Heads Notables": Stern, *Maverick,* 221.

98 "We were a forceful": Ibid., 223.

98 "He would beg us all": Traube to MM, 6/23/90.

99 "It is so rarely that": IFS column in *Press Time* (New York: Books, Inc., 1936), a book of *Post* classics.

99 "except her private parts": *Post*, 6/22/35.

99 In 1937, burlesque was closed: Minsky and Macklin, *Minsky's Burlesque;* and Corio, *This Was Burlesque.*

100 "The real perspective is this": IFS to Gitlin, 1985.

101 Stern "hated Communists": Stern's daughter, Jill Capron, interview with MM, 1/29/91.

101 "I felt a newspaperman": IFS to Gitlin, 1985.

102 It showed how corruption: Thomas and Blanchard, *What's the Matter with New York.*

102 "It was *wonderful*": IFS to Gitlin, 1985.

102 dinner with "three great scholars": Patner, *Portrait,* 31–32.

103 *Rancors Aweigh:* Information on Pegler and Dorothy Thompson: White, *FDR and the Press.*

103 "I can appreciate what": Ibid., 2.

103 Hearst termed them all Communists: Ibid., 95.

103 The most vicious personal attack: Ibid., 45.

104 "planned collectivism" to "nothing could be worse": Steel, *Lippmann,* 315–17.

104 After the landslide: *Post,* 2/8/37.

104 FDR was "drunk with power": Steel, *Lippmann,* 319.

104 "FOR CONTINUATION OF THE": *Post,* 2/9/37.

105 In 1934, life expectancy: U.S government statistics.

106 "Why They Riot": *Post,* 4/9/34.

106 "This sabotage of the recovery": *Post,* 12/3/36.

107 "when you walk along": LS to MM, 1990.

108 "clanking of Phi Beta Kappa": O'Connor, *Heywood Broun,* 141.

108 Bankhead . . . stood on her head: A brilliant book on newspapers is *The Paper* by Richard Kluger, which provided such rich background and anecdotes in this chapter. (Bankhead: 295; match game: 296; Beebe, 247.)

109 Then came Heywood Broun: O'Connor, *Heywood Broun,* 185.

109 "rich New York *columnist*": Ibid., 187.

109 In New York in 1933: Leab, *Union of Individuals.*

110 "I joined up": Patner, *Portrait,* 38.

110 Publishers defined "professionals": Leab, *Union of Individuals,* 40.

110 On April 8, 1934, Stern: Ibid., 117.

110 "resisted . . . sniffed . . . jeered": O'Connor, *Heywood Broun,* 185.

111 "the one which has made": *Press Time,* 181.

111 "five dollars to make": Stern, *Maverick,* 242.

111 "the Guild was asking things": Patner, *Portrait,* 38.

111 "rammed the pay cut": O'Connor, *Heywood Broun.* The American Newspaper Guild struggled for years—troubled by few funds, balking publishers, and Communist infiltration when it was forced to join the CIO to survive. But it

gave reporters a foothold on the ladder of decent wages, hours, and job security that lasted long enough for publishers to develop a conscience, or at least
a competitiveness, that brought many of them in line with other professional
salaries. Today the ANG is but a weak vestige, as most newspapers have
crushed the union shop.

112 "Macy's—owned by Jews": Patner, *Portrait*, 37, 38.

112 "At a signal from the magistrate" to "good reactionary fashion": Isador Feinstein, "How to Make a Riot," *New Republic*, June 27, 1934.

113 "Powerful and militant unions": *Nation*, 9/12/35, 288; and 9/18/35, 316.

114 titled "Not Fit to Print": *Nation*, 12/25/35, 741.

114 "Millions of Americans are": *Nation*, 2/12/36, 187.

115 "told me that the fight": LS to MM.

115 "Geoffrey Duprion": Cottrell, *Izzy*, 69.

115 "It was just about the": IFS to MM, *Washington Post*, 7/9/79.

115 "He could summon up": CS to MM, 6/31/91.

116 "seriously misread the New Deal": Steel, *Lippmann*, 324.

117 "the national government had acted": Burns, *Lion and Fox*, 267.

Chapter 8: American Dictators and (Not Always) Popular Fronts

118 "The Fascist experience": Unless otherwise noted, comments of Stone's in
this section are from 1985 unpublished interview with Todd Gitlin.

119 "Only Nazi hoodlums": *Post*, 5/3/34.

119 "The right of free speech": Steel, *Lippmann*, 314.

120 the Messiah of the Rednecks . . . to "Even though you hated every word": 1985
PBS documentary on Huey Long, RKB/Florentine Films, by Ken Burns, produced by Ken Burns and Richard Kilberg, written by Jeffrey C. Ward, narrated
by David McCullough. Includes Betty Carter's quotes in this chapter.

121 "He certainly was an extremely": Stone in PBS documentary.

121 His own brother: Sherrill, *Gothic Politics*.

121 His "dee-duct box": Ibid., and Brinkley, *Voices of Protest*.

122 Two weeks after Long: *Post*, 8/29/35.

123 During the height of his power: Brinkley, *Voices of Protest*, 129.

123 "Jew Deal": Alan Brinkley in *Voices of Protest* contends that Coughlin's slur
did not surface until after his popularity waned and attributes the "Jew Deal"
line to 1938. Other historians refer to the use of this slur in 1935 at the height
of his popularity.

123 even Stone's father supported: LS to MM.

123 "pigs swilling in the trough": Brinkley, *Voices of Protest*, 117.

123 radicalism was abhorrent: Ibid., 240.

124 "in the light of another great orator": *Post*, 9/3/35, 10.

124 Even famed lawyer . . . to "is overhung by peril": *Post*, 9/10/35, editorial.

124 "It's a terrible thing to say": IFS in Long PBS documentary, 1985.

125 "There was genuine fear": Wechsler, *Age of Suspicion*, 140–41.

125 "This was particularly true of" to "have lasted very long inside": Ibid.

126 "You can't blame all": IFS to Gitlin, 1985.

126 "For the majority of writers": Aaron, *Writers on the Left*.

126 "Once you kicked somebody out": Bailey to MM, 4/4/90. All Bailey information and quotes in this chapter are from this interview.

127 "For a Jew to scab": Howe, *Margin of Hope*, 8.

127 "We were so filled with hope": Interview with MM, 2/8/96.

128 "shocking testimony": *Post*, 11/11/36.

129 "too large for a coffin": Alan Brinkley review of Bruce Nelson's *Workers on the Waterfront: Seamen, Longshoremen, and Unionism in the 1930's* (University of Illinois Press, 1990), in *Review*, 6/28/90.

130 "not so much for the sake": Pells, *Radical Visions*.

131 turned the case over: Henry Moon, *American Communist Party*, 213.

131 Socialists were no longer: Pells, *Radical Visions*.

131 "During the Popular Front": Klehr, *Heyday of American Communism*, 252.

132 Dewey had attacked: Phillips, *Truman Presidency*, 217, 240–41.

132 "unscrupulous as McCarthy": *Haunted Fifties*, 64; and *The Weekly*, 3/8/54.

132 During the popular front, less radical: Aaron, *Writers on the Left*, 178.

133 The League of American Writers read: Ibid., 353.

133 "sucked into it by a friend": Grafton to MM.

133 *Waiting for Lefty* information and quotes: Gibson, *Clifford Odets*, 316–17.

134 "The whole place bristles with guns": *Post*, 7/5/35.

134 While Odets sat in prison: Gibson, *Clifford Odets*.

Chapter 9: Hitler, Lippmann, Izzy, and the Jews

135 "At a very early time": Greiner to MM, 6/23/91.

135 "most statesmanly Jewish pundit": Lipstadt, *Beyond Belief*, 109.

135 "Our ignorance was inexcusable": Shirer, *Nightmare Years*, 137.

136 From the first days: Morse, *While Six Million Died*, 152–53.

136 "Peace Hangs Upon a Thread": *Post*, 7/26/34, editorial.

137 When correspondents during the early: Information from Lipstadt, *Beyond Belief*.

137 Roosevelt himself remained scandalously silent: Beschloss, *Conquerers;* Morse, *While Six Million Died;* and Lipstadt, *Beyond Belief*.

137 "showed a surprising insensitivity": Steel, *Lippmann*, 331–33.

137 Shirer shared none of Lippmann's: Shirer, *Nightmare Years*.

138 "the Jews by their parvenus?": Steel, *Lippmann*, 331.

138 "one of America's foremost *publicists*": *Record*, 4/5/33.

138 "Germany's Future Dark as Dictator": Ibid.

138 The State Department had . . . caved: Ibid., 4/3/33.

139 As late as 1939: Steel, *Lippmann*, 373, 331–33.

139 "The dispassion, if not indifference": Lipstadt, *Beyond Belief*, 276.

139 "one German-Jewish reader": Patner, *Portrait*, 37.

140 "He criticized the Jews": Steel, *Lippmann*, 188.

140 "could not say that Walter": Halberstam, *Powers That Be*, 370.

141 "don't you think it's too Jewish?" Ibid., 32.

141 "paper not seem too Jewish" . . . and references to Arthur Krock, Sulzberger, and Frankfurter: Halberstam, *Powers That Be*, 216–17; "we have too many Jews in Europe": Salisbury, *Without Fear or Favor*, 401; The advancement of Jews was "not encouraged": Kluger, *Paper*, 385.

141 *Herald Tribune*'s edict on European coverage: Kluger, *Paper*.

142 "insane amounts as reparations": *Record*, 3/24/33. Fifty years after World War II ended, this consensus was challenged by some revisionist historians who argued that the Versailles treaty should not be blamed for Hitler's rise and the war. And, indeed, Stone had placed part of the blame for Hitler's success on Germany's squabbling leftist movements, who had not united against him. Margaret MacMillan, *Paris 1919: Six Months That Changed the World* (New York: Random House, 2002).

142 "Germany was . . . deprived" to "bloody civil war": *Record* 3/24/33.

142 "There was never any revolt": IFS to Gitlin, 1985.

142 "the twilight of Capitalism and Democracy": *Record*, 1/31/33, 8.

143 "kind of lightning rod which": Steel, *Lippmann*, 330.

143 Lippmann "would not go against": Steel, *Lippmann*, 326; "no less confused": Ibid., 328.

144 "BERLIN IS ANGERED": *New York Times*, 7/28/35, 1.

144 "pirate" flag . . . Judge Brodsky's comments: Lipstadt, *Beyond Belief*, 58.

144 "Nazi secret police took": *Post*, 9/10/35, 10.

144 "More feigned than real": Ibid., 7/27/35.

145 he assailed Hitler's "mad charges": *Post* collection *Press Time*, 172–74.

146 "is an obscenity": *New York Times*, 2/03.

146 "Many government officials": Lipstadt noted that the *Washington Post*'s publisher, Eugene Meyer, was "adamantly opposed" to special demands for rescuing Jews. *Beyond Belief*, 228, fn. 35; Halberstam, *Powers That Be*, 517; and "Bystander to Genocide," *Village Voice*, 12/18/84, 30.

146 "Democracy in Germany has received": Morse, *While Six Million Died*, 284. MM's comment "might have saved countless victims" is from a reading of Kai Bird's *The Chairman*. This biography of John McCloy (assistant secretary of war) emphasizes several controversies in his career including the internment of the Japanese in World War II and the decision not to bomb railroads into Auschwitz.

147 "even to extermination": Morse, *While Six Million Died*, 156.

147 Hitler was "seeking to rid": *New York Herald Tribune*, 7/28/35.

147 "it is inconceivable": Morse, *While Six Million Died*, 177.

148 refused all pleas: Information on Nazi Olympics from *New York Times, Post, Washington Post*, and other periodicals of the period.

148 "sons of bitches": Povich to MM, 7/15/93.

148 "only one more sign": *Post*, 9/25/35.

148 "to send a signal": *Post*, 10/22/35.

148 "Jew baiting is officially" . . . to "expressed his admiration": Shirer, *Nightmare Years*, 237.

149 Lindbergh . . . winter's stay in Berlin: *Post,* 11/15/38.

149 "sets Frenchman against Frenchman": IFS, "1937 Is Not 1914," *Nation,* 11/6/37.

149 "swaggered" into a café: Accounts from Shirer, *Nightmare Years,* 299–301.

150 "Numerous papers": Lipstadt, *Beyond Belief,* 101.

150 "Germany's Moral Leprosy": *Post,* 11/15/38.

150 "the rise of National Socialism": William Norman Grigg, *American* 17, no. 14 (7/2/01). Reference to *Wall Street and the Rise of Hitler* by Dr. Antony Sutton.

150 On May 13, 1939, the *St. Louis:* MM, *Nation,* 3/92.

Chapter 10: "My Heart Is with the Spanish Loyalists"

152 "A *war* was coming": IFS to Gitlin, 1985.

153 "total failure to report the Communist": Knightley, *First Casualty,* 213. One of the best books to detail the attitudes and actions of correspondents at war.

153 "We didn't want to listen": IFS to Gitlin, 1985.

153 "The . . . *Daily Mail*": Orwell, *Homage to Catalonia,* 56, 57.

153 "failure of correspondents": Knightley, *First Casualty,* 215. For background on poor coverage by the *Herald Tribune,* see Kluger, *The Paper,* 224, 276, 288, 294–95.

153 "We didn't have much patience": IFS to Gitlin, 1985.

154 "wounded men . . . nurses, wives": Orwell, *Homage to Catalonia,* 174.

154 "intentionally misleading" and "liquidate": Ibid., 158. Orwell's leftist British paper, the *New Statesman,* refused to publish his accounts. Left-wing publishers turned down *Homage to Catalonia.* When finally published in Britain, it sold only six hundred copies and was not published in the United States until years later.

154 "whatever faults": Ibid., 181.

154 Spain would be a "grim prelude": *Post,* summer 1936.

155 "Even as Eden spoke": Ibid., 1/21/37.

155 "The logic of everything": Steel, *Lippmann,* 340.

155 "work out their own salvation": Ibid., 337.

155 would be "too severe" . . . through "status quo": *Post,* 1/19/37.

156 "simple and disinterested" truce: Steel, *Lippmann,* 337.

156 "it wasn't one of the things": Ibid., 338.

157 "strafing city after city": Payne, *Civil War in Spain,* 140.

157 machine-gunned to death: Ibid., 141–42.

157 "neutrality was so strictly enforced": Ibid., 143, 146.

157 The *Manchester Guardian* . . . "increasing respect": Orwell, *Homage to Catalonia,* 65.

158 "more blood than you would think": Knightley, *First Casualty,* 202.

158 "carnival of treachery": Hemingway's biographer, Carlos Baker, cited in Knightley, *First Casualty,* 214.

158 "was, on balance" to "nothing but Insurgent": Ibid., chap. 9, "Commitment in Spain," 192–216.

158 "I would always opt for honest": Ibid.

159 Survivors of the International Brigade: Payne, *Civil War in Spain.*

160 Stalin deserted the Loyalists: Ibid., 182.

160 "They *made* us leave": Bailey to MM.

160 "Mothers! Women!": Payne, *Civil War in Spain,*183.

160 "Spain made possible a vicarious": Moon, *American Communist Party,* 366–67.

160 "I hate fascism" to "nothing else can": *Nation,* 9/18/37 (Stone under the byline Geoffrey Stone).

Chapter 11: When Tyrants Ruled

163 "The great anomaly of the time": Von Hoffman to MM, 2001.

163 "a *great* disillusionment": IFS to Gitlin, 1985.

164 "resort to the methods of Fascist thugs": *Post,* 12/7/34.

164 "prominence of the Soviet Union": *Post,* 1/26/37; IFS comments: Cottrell, *Izzy,* 67. Stone was not alone in his ambiguity. Only years later did technology provide evidence to substantiate what was long surmised: bloodstain traces were found on confession documents, corroborating that they were extracted by torture.

164 "far better sense than his": Steel, *Lippmann,* 325. Lippmann's December 1937 column, "from the dominion that Russian communism has exercised over their minds," quoted on p. 325.

164 "pessimism of the intellect": Knoll to MM, 5/25/90.

164 "decayed, semi-feudal": IFS, *Nation,* 11/6/37, 496.

165 "peasants and proletariats": *Fortune,* March 1932.

166 " 'Liquidation' under the Russian constitution": *Post,* 7/22/37.

166 "He had somehow united": Klein, *Heyday of American Communism,* 358.

166 "fellow traveling": Attitude of Stone from Cottrell, *Izzy;* Patner, *Portrait;* family interviews with MM.

166 "came out four square against": Stern, *Maverick,* 245.

167 "Extremists and muddleheads": Ibid.

167 "sworn to destroy our system": *Post,* 2/15/38.

167 "they certainly appreciate you": Stern, *Maverick,* 246–47; and Jill Capron to MM.

167 "spokesman for the Kremlin": IFS, "Chamberlain's Russo-German Pact," *Nation,* 9/23/39, 313.

168 "fashionable liar": Taylor, *Stalin's Apologist,* 210.

168 Duranty's glowing reports of Russia's: Ibid.; and Bassow, *Moscow Correspondents.*

168 no press conferences: Taylor, *Stalin's Apologist;* and Bassow, *Moscow Correspondents.*

168 bothered Salisbury for decades: Salisbury to MM, 10/18/91.

169 "the famine is mostly bunk": Taylor, *Stalin's Apologist,* 210.

169 "Millions Feared": *New York Herald Tribune,* 8/21/33, 8; "Any talk of famine": *New York Times,* 9/14/33. As quoted in Taylor, *Stalin's Apologist.*

169 "The Famine the *Times* Couldn't Find": *Commentary,* 1983, 32–40.

169 "Had Duranty, a Pulitzer Prize": Taylor, *Stalin's Apologist*, 240.

169 "sufficiently remarkable": Taylor, *Stalin's Apologist*, 267.

169 "the threads of a conspiracy": Joseph Davies, *Mission to Moscow*, 181, as quoted in Taylor, *Stalin's Apologist*, 266.

169 "Duranty did what we considered": Prensky to MM, August 1992.

170 "horrifying travesty": Larina, *This I Cannot Forget*, 74.

170 stories about a fight for principle: LS, Sam Grafton, Jill Stern Capron to MM.

171 creates further confusion: J. David Stern's Oral History, 1951, Columbia University.

172 "wanted me to write an editorial": Patner, *Portrait*, 32.

172 "I guess he didn't want": Ibid., 35.

172 "He was very bitter": Jill Stern Capron to MM.

173 "drop a bomb" to "factional disarmament": Freda Kirchwey, *Nation*, 5/27/39.

173 Stone took a harsher stance: *Nation*, 8/10/39.

174 "no one" was "more outraged": Cottrell, *Izzy*, 73. (Legendary quote used by many sources.)

174 "dishonest action of his entire career" and IFS admission: Ibid., 77.

174 through with "fellow traveling": Ibid., 78; letters to Blankfort, 10/15/39 and 10/21/39.

174 angry two-thousand-word *Nation* article: IFS, "Chamberlain's Russo-German Pact."

174 had dismissed: IFS wrote the following: One *New York Sun* dispatch was discounted by the left "on the ground that the *Sun* is anti-Soviet. Similar reasons made it easy to brush aside" H. R. Knickerbocker's piece in "the Hearst-owned International News Service." Stone praised the Hearst columnist: "The agreement since signed exactly fits [Knickerbocker's] description," although Knickerbocker "seemed skeptical of his own story." Comments on Duranty followed. *Nation*, 9/23/39.

175 "If Chamberlain had": IFS, *Nation*, 9/23/39.

175 In later years: Shirer, *Nightmare Years*, 405–8.

175 "history with its face lifted": IFS, "The Chicken or the Egg," *Nation*, 11/4/39.

176 "Did I feel duped?": All quotes in this chapter from Max Lerner from interview with MM, 4/14/91.

Chapter 12: *Nation* on the Brink

181 his letters to Blankfort: Information in this paragraph, Cottrell, *Izzy*, 72.

181 "a press agent *and* an independent": Patner, *Portrait*, 36.

182 a $500 advance from Modern Age: Cottrell, *Izzy*, 86.

182 was hired as publicist: Patner, *Portrait*, 35, 36.

182 It was a modest house: Dorothy Fall to MM, 2002.

182 A monstrous military building: Brinkley, *Washington Goes to War*, 75.

183 "But I just left him drowning": Ibid., 231.

183 "moralistic approach to politics and politicians": IFS, "Free Inquiry and Free

Endeavor," *Nation*, Christmas edition, *One Hundred Years*, 41. Also Alpern, *Freda Kirchwey*, 33.

183 The daughter of progressive parents: Warren Olivier, "Oh Stop That Freda!" *Saturday Evening Post*, 2/9/46, 22.

184 "she is really Mrs. Evans Clark": *Saturday Evening Post*, 2/9/46, 100.

184 "was very hard": Alpern, *Freda Kirchwey*, 37, fn. 20.

184 "Freda was under the damn": Madeline Amgott to MM, 6/27/94.

185 thousands of pacifists: *Saturday Evening Post*, 2/9/46, 102; Max Lerner to MM, 4/14/91.

185 Half a century later, historians: The best book on Bush-family German connections is by historian Kevin Phillips, *American Dynasty* (New York: Viking, 2004).

185 Stone choked on his "ostentatious": IFS, *Truman Era*, 124–25, 8/7/48.

186 Stone bitingly attacked Secretary of State: IFS, *Nation*, 9/30/40.

187 "basis for blackmail?": Ibid., 10/12/40, 319.

187 "The Nazis were ready": Ibid., 3/9/40.

187 "Only 12 percent": Brinkley, *Washington Goes to War*, 46; 1939 Roper poll.

188 hanged Pepper in effigy: Claude Pepper to MM, 1989; and Seldes, *Witness to a Century*, 97, 105.

188 "but there was also" to "odd . . . for so fervent a democrat": IFS, "Wheeler's Cliveden Set," *Nation*, 3/8/41.

189 Many on the left rested easier: John Kenneth Galbraith to MM, 5/29/96.

189 "the experience of being disastrously wrong": Galbraith, *Life in our Times*, 162.

189 "The automobile industry was" to "assume that this is a deal?": Galbraith to MM, 5/29/96.

190 "most intractably independent of reporters": Galbraith, *Life in our Times*, 158.

190 "Izzy was not vilified": Galbraith to MM, 5/29/96.

190 "Stone pressed his receiver": Brinkley, *Washington Goes to War*, 173. Although there may have been some embroidery, Brinkley told MM (7/6/94) the incident was relayed to him by a reporter who was present.

191 "We are going into this war lightly": *Nation*, 12/13/41, 603–4.

191 remained Hitler's one ace: Freda Kirchwey, "Hitler's Double-Talk," *Nation*, 11/5/41; and Freda Kirchwey, "End of the Comintern," *Nation*, 5/29/43.

192 "There was a time": Alpern, *Freda Kirchwey*, 154. (Memo from FK to IFS, 6/8/43, Freda Kirchwey papers, Schlesinger Library, Radcliffe College.)

192 "Talks with a Cabinet member": Alpern, *Freda Kirchwey*, 154.

192 "Washington Gestapo" to "Molotov, in the White House?" *Nation*, 7/17/43, part 1 of Stone series, 64–66.

193 "In the middle of a war": Alpern, *Freda Kirchwey*, 154. (FK to IFS memo, 7/20/43.)

194 "The quality of the work": *Nation*, part 2 of Stone series, 7/24/43, 92–95.

Chapter 13: Great Expectations

196 Stone always praised his World War II: Patner, *Portrait;* and IFS to MM, 1988.

196 Stone's exposé of profiteering . . . to "two years in jail or both": Hoopes, *Ralph Ingersoll*, 255; and IFS, *War Years*, 109.

197 "I just loved the guy": Patner, *Portrait*, 74.

197 "Ralph absolutely *adored* Izzy": All Toby Ingersoll quotes and information in this chapter are from her interview with MM, 9/25/91.

197 As Wolcott Gibbs wrote: *New Yorker*, 5/2/42, 22.

197 VRM (Very Rich Men): David Margolick, *Vanity Fair*, January 1999, 122; other information, *New Yorker* profile, 5/2/42.

197 blood from black donors could not: Margolick, *Vanity Fair*. All Rae Weimer quotes and comments are from Weimer interview with MM, 3/2/90.

197 exposed the Standard Oil Company: *New Yorker*, 5/2/42. Sources on Stone's reporting: *PM* copies; Roy Hoopes to MM, 6/90, and his *PM* documents given to MM; Rae Weimer to MM; Shirley Katzander to MM; and Penn Kimball to MM.

198 "Dear Ralph" . . . Eleanor Roosevelt praised: Hoopes, *Ralph Ingersoll*, 256.

198 "war with Japan was imminent": *New Yorker*, 5/2/42.

198 He flunked the physical: As noted in Stone's FBI file, copy obtained by MM.

198 "The paper was often sloppy": Margolick, *Vanity Fair*, January 1999.

198 "All you could do is": Shirley Katzander to MM, 2/17/90.

198 Kimball discovered: Kimball, *File*, 112; and Kimball to MM, 11/26/90.

199 The rush to *PM*: Kimball, *File*, 82; Hoopes, *Ralph Ingersoll*; Rae Weimer, interview with MM; Richard H. Minear, Art Spiegelman (introduction), *Horton Saves the World; Dr. Seuss Goes to War: The World War II Editorial Cartoons of Theodor Seuss Geisel* (New Press, 1999); Margolick, *Vanity Fair*, January 1999, 128.

199 *PM* pioneered color . . . to . . . 450,000 copies: Margolick, *Vanity Fair*, January 1999; and Hoopes, *Ralph Ingersoll*, 226.

200 "immaterial" to the takeover publishers: collection of Liebling, *Press*, his *New Yorker* "Wayward Press" pieces, 24–25; "birth of a new whooping Crane": 42.

200 "One of the good things" to "bother to read them": Ibid., 45–46.

200 "I really liked Marshall Field": Patner, *Portrait*, 74.

200 "He got us to write": Ibid., 73.

201 "concentrating pretty heavily on": Margolick, *Vanity Fair*, January 1999; and Weimer to MM.

201 "we were trying to be": Patner, *Portrait*, 76.

201 "I never was aware": Heller, interview with MM, 4/4/92.

202 "Their [the Jews] greatest danger": Lindbergh's speech in *PM*, 10/5/41, 8–10; "a bid for anti-Semitism": Anne Morrow Lindbergh, *New York Times* obituary, 2/8/01, by Eric Pace.

203 "ability to say little": IFS, *War Years*, 25, 10/5/40.

203 "Hull and the undemocratic": Ibid., 103, 1/3/42.

203 what Stone had already written: *Time*, 2/9/43.

203 "Izzy would never get angry": Amgott to MM, 6/26/94; "no youth in his eyes": IFS, *War Years*, 176, 8/7/43.

203 "Hull's whole demeanor": Amgott to MM, 6/26/94; *"I think his name is Feinstein": Congressional Record*, 478, 2/1/43; "communistic publication known as *PM*": Cottrell, *Izzy*, 106.

204 "those who have dared": *Time*, 2/8/43, 16; "dabbling in dirty waters": *Nation*, 2/6/43.

204 "You can count on my": Cottrell, *Izzy*, 89–90; Stone to Lerner, 3/27/41 letter in Max Lerner Papers, Sterling Library, Yale University. Also Lerner to MM.

205 "second abusive display of yours": Cottrell, *Izzy*, 90, fn. 24; "We cannot afford to throw overboard": Ibid., 107, fn. 16; "it was hardly advisable": Ibid., 90, fn. 23; "violence of your language": Ibid.

206 *"PM's* editors were not humorous men": Liebling, *Press*, 46.

207 substantive results: Stone's exposés cited in *PM* file indexes and documents; given to MM by Ingersoll's biographer, Roy Hoopes.

208 "a murder of a people so appalling": Navasky, *Matter of Opinion*, 195.

208 "smearing Ralph as a party-liner": Patner, *Portrait*, 75; biggest public fight: Hoopes, *Ralph Ingersoll*, 219; "failure has gone to his head": several sources.

208 "This whole affair": Hoopes, *Ralph Ingersoll*, 321; "I hated having to fire people": Patner, *Portrait*, 75.

208 "He would just pay": Reid to MM, 1991.

209 "They are the ones who": Stone comment with MM in 1988; also often-voiced similar quotes to many interviewers.

209 Bick discovered: Bick's story was related to MM, 2/18/91; a version was sent to the Stone family after Stone's death in 1989, given to MM by Stone family.

Chapter 14: Living with Izzy

211 "Dad's life pulsed": NYC memorial service for IFS, July 12, 1989.

211 "My father worked": CG in May/June 1978 issue of *Saturday Evening Post*, 56, excerpt from *Working It Out*, edited by Sara Ruddick and Pamela Daniels (New York: Pantheon Books, 1977).

211 "some kind of a Purple Heart": MM, *Washington Post*, 7/9/79, B1.

212 "Sometimes Izzy could be impossible": JS to MM, 7/28/90. Unless otherwise noted, JS quotes and comments in this chapter are from this interview.

212 "I thought Izzy was an enormously": Nathanson to MM 9/3/91. Nathanson's comments and quotes in this chapter are all from interview with MM.

212 "She is the most perfect": Moursand to MM, 5/26/90.

212 "Izzy's negatives": Osnos to MM, 9/26/91.

213 Jean imitated Esther's delicate voice: Jean Boudin to MM, 6/20/90.

213 "This is the best thing": Viorst to MM, 9/20/91.

213 "She's an angel and I": Cottrell, *Izzy*, 209, Stone letter to Blankfort.

214 "You know, my daughter": Esther Stone to MM, 7/9/79.

214 "That's what Esther": IFS to Joe Pichirallo, *Washington Post*, 1/13/85.

215 "Sex is *madly* important": Esther Stone to MM. 7/9/79; "so wise and so accepting": Comment of Jessica's mother, Ann, wife of Christopher Stone, to MM, 8/31/91.

215 "Esther is so much more": IFS to MM, 7/9/79.

215 "was the mirror image": CG in May/June 1978 issue of *Saturday Evening Post*, 56.

215 "There was an enormous bond": CG to MM, 12/2/05, e-mail interview.

216 "blossomed into lectures": CS at IFS memorial service, NYC, 7/12/89; Stone's walking conversations are vividly quoted in Patner, *Portrait*.

216 "I hate to pass a beggar": Patner, *Portrait*, 49.

217 "turned for love and unmatched": CS; Esther "saw into the heart": CG; "from whom he drew his zest": CS, both speaking at IFS memorial service, 7/12/89.

217 "rather difficult": CS, IFS memorial, 7/12/89; "shot by Jews": Family anecdote recounted to MM.

217 Helen Dudman, a lifelong friend: Interview with MM, 6/90.

218 "Isn't this *fun*, kids?": CS essay, *Saturday Evening Post*; and CS to MM.

218 "I *need to practice*" to "*and* the state of Israel": Amgott to MM, 6/27/94.

218 "Thank God Izzy had": JS to MM, 9/7/90.

218 "He never talked about them": Pincus to MM, 5/2/90.

218 "He was always" to "rich and famous lifestyle": JS to MM, 9/7/90.

219 "I'm very proud now": CS to MM, 8/31/91; also, anecdotes about meeting Einstein and Jean-Paul Sartre visiting the home in Paris.

220 "He just sat there, quietly": Smallberg to MM, 9/3/92.

220 Neither parent disciplined the children to "following his own will": This section from CS to MM, 8/31/91. Unless otherwise specified, the remainder of quotes and comments by Christopher Stone are from this interview.

221 "As long as I was" to "projected onto me": CG, *Saturday Evening Post* excerpt, with the exception of "Poetry was woven," which is from Gilbert's tribute to her father at the NYC memorial service, 7/12/89.

223 "I need to deliver . . .": CG to MM, 12/2/05, e-mail interview.

223 "She didn't want to listen": Toby Ingersoll to MM, 9/25/91. Also, further quotes.

224 "If he didn't like this": *New Yorker* profile of Katharine Hepburn, July 14 and 21, 2003, 58.

225 "The secret of the power": CG, NYC Memorial, 7/12/89.

225 "only other newspapermen": Foreword to IFS, *Truman Era*, xix.

225 One week he missed: Patner, *Portrait*, 73–74.

225 "I rarely had doubts" to "unregenerate and cheerful": Foreword to IFS, *Truman Era*, xix.

226 "He used to revise a thousand times": Moursand to MM, 5/26/90.

226 "too perfect to be pleasant": IFS, *War Years*, 227, 5/20/44 column on Thomas E. Dewey; "required a strong stomach": Ibid., 238, 7/8/44 column; "a man could be half Jewish": *The Weekly*, 8/19/68; and *Polemics*, 43.

227 "He would surprise you completely": Pringle interview with MM, 1992.

Chapter 15: Blood and Billions and Going Underground

229 "goodbye to a great and good": IFS, *War Years*, 272–75, 5/21/45, "Farewell to F.D.R."

229 "I hate to confess it": Ibid., 274, 4/21/45.

229 "So long as Mr. Roosevelt": Ibid., 278–79, "Notes Before 'Frisco," 4/21/45.

230 "I was a mainline journalist": IFS to Gitlin, 1985.

230 "goggle-eyed as any" to "we owe World War II": IFS, *War Years*, 282, 5/5/45.

230 "Dear Dolly: I love you": IFS letter to Esther, given by CC to MM, 12/2/05 e-mail.

231 "With the exception of Czechoslovakia": IFS, *Truman Era*, 32–35, 11/23/47.

232 "invited personal friendship": McCullough, *Truman*, 425.

232 "combines a tremendous": Mortimer, *World That FDR Built*, 32.

232 "was capable of being kind": MM profile of Averell Harriman, *Washington Post Potomac Magazine*, 9/7/75.

233 "little bit of a squirt": McCullough, *Truman*, 451.

233 "I liked the little": Ibid.; Stalin's "worthless" comment: Ibid., 452 (Stalin as told to Nikita Khrushchev as quoted in his memoirs).

233 "the idea embodied in the": IFS, *War Years*, 26.

234 "additional bombs would be delivered": McCullough, *Truman*, 457.

234 dropping the bomb was unnecessary: See Gar Alperovitz, *The Decision to Use the Atomic Bomb and the Architecture of an American Myth*. On the contrary, the Discovery Channel still tells the story essentially as it was told during the Truman years, as do other sources.

234 "terrible racistic implications": ISF, *Truman Era*, 52, 7/22/49 column.

234 "the mammalian world's death warrant" to "sowed the whirlwind": McCullough, *Truman*, 456.

234 "More terrifying than" to "faces pinched by hunger": IFS, *War Years*, 17, 8/13/45.

235 Eleanor Roosevelt . . . through "a potential war breeder": Roosevelt, *My Day*, 112, 1/3/47.

236 Frankfurter who did nothing . . . to . . . on light industry and agriculture: Simons, *Jewish Times*, 50–51.

236 "'turn the Reich into a goat pasture'": IFS, *Truman Era*, 50, 8/18/48.

236 "Merely to refuse a loan": Ibid., 31–32, 12/13/46. Report ignored by the media: The House Special Committee on Postwar Economic Policy and Planning, 12/46.

236 "To make German revival": Ibid., 28–29, 7/17/46.

236 he marveled at Stone's writing: Greiner to MM, 6/23/91; *PM*, 10/17/43.

237 "The rebirth of I. G. Farben": IFS, *Truman Era*, 29, 7/17/46.

237 "ignominiously in S.S. uniforms": Ibid., 324; "treated far worse than": Ibid., 325, "The Plight of the Jews," 10/6/45.

237 "drunk on the beauties": Ibid., 331–32, "Palestine Pilgrimage," 12/8/45.

237 He "hated" Egypt . . . to "state in Palestine": Ibid., 332–36, "Palestine Pilgrimage," 12/8/45.

238 "no more gangsters": *Nation*, 1/12/46, 34–35.

238 The group allowed him: IFS, *Underground to Palestine*, "Summons to Adventure," 9.

239 "inescapably—the world being": IFS, introduction to *Underground to Pales-*

tine, xi. Because numerous paragraphs in the following text refer to *Underground to Palestine,* only the pages will be identified.

239　"I felt a defeatist spirit": 48.

240　"'We knew when the people were dead'": 20; "I committed a primitive": 107.

240　"Hans Christian Andersen": 31; they had been in the Nazi: 35.

240　"miracle of whole Jewish families": 53; "we were only more Jews to kill": 71.

241　The story of teenagers Abram and sister, Sarah: 61–64.

241　"This man is an Aryan": 100–101.

241　"I just loved it!": Katzander, who housed Stone in Paris, in interview with MM; "I wish there were photographs": Nat Hentoff, *Washington Post,* 6/24/89, 27.

242　Stone finally reached Italy: 108–30.

243　The trip across the Mediterranean to Palestine: 131–214.

243　you *have* to write her story: IFS conversation with MM, 8/80.

244　"Soon they were all smiles": Har-Shefi to MM, *Washington Post,* 8/26/80.

244　"our youngest, ten": *Underground,*146.

244　"the luxury of our excesses": Har-Shefi to MM, *Washington Post,* 8/26/80.

245　"three dimensional reporting": From the back cover of the Pantheon edition of *Underground to Palestine.*

245　"It was in effect boycotted": "Confessions of a Jewish Dissident," addition, p. 234, of the Pantheon edition of *Underground to Palestine.*

Chapter 16: Guilty Until Proven Innocent

246　"you cannot kill an idea": "ABC's of an Effective Foreign Policy," 8/27/47.

246　"three simple ideas are being hammered": IFS, *Truman Era,* 36, "Remolding the Public Mind," 8/1/47.

246　"To listen in on": Ibid., 36–37, "Blessed Land: Blind People," 9/14/47.

246　"America being mobilized emotionally": Ibid., xxvii.

247　"terrible" mistake: Bernstein, *Loyalties,* 196; Rauh verification to MM.

247　"Each department and agency": "Code of Federal Regulations, Title 3—The President 1943–1948 Compilation," also listed as "3 CFR, 1943–1948 Compilation: Prescribing Procedures for the Administration of an Employees Loyalty Program in the Executive Branch of the Government."

248　"As much as anyone he": Garry Wills, "Keeper of the Seal," *Review* 38 no. 13 (7/18/91), review of *Counsel to the President: A Memoir* by Clark Clifford with Richard Holbrooke.

248　"a lot of baloney": Bernstein, *Loyalties,* 197–98.

248　"an impossible situation": Mortimer, *World That FDR Built,* 69.

249　"free peoples who are resisting": Steel, *Lippmann,* 438; "coalition of crooks, incompetents": Cottrell, *Izzy,* 159, IFS column.

249　"The military assistance program": IFS, *Truman Era,* 177–78, "Can Diplomacy Ever be 'Total'?" 3/15/50.

249　Lippmann's reaction to the Truman Doctrine: Steel, *Lippmann,* 438. Press favorable reaction: McCullough, *Truman,* 348.

249 "a military shopping service for dictators": *PM*, 7/20/47.

249 "for the sake of the future": *PM*, 9/29/47, as cited in Cottrell, *Izzy*, 133.

249 "The world is not going Communist": IFS, *Truman Era*, 41; *PM*, 10/5/47.

249 "at least as old as Jesus": Ibid., 39–40; *PM*, 10/5/47.

250 "all claimed to have been": Liebling, *Press*, 143.

250 "'I . . . left the party out of'": *Compass*, 2/12/52.

250 "sprinkling of priests": "Budenz: Portrait of a Christian Hero," *Compass*, 4/23/50.

250 "Around the hearing table": IFS to Gitlin, 1985.

251 "It was a dreadful": Rabinowitz to MM, 6/20/90.

252 "The purpose of independence": *Compass*, 2/28/50.

252 "Petty little dictators": Patner, *Portrait*, 46.

252 "outlawry, suppression and terror": *PM*, 1/22/48.

252 "I'd feel like a stultified ass": Navasky, *Naming Names*, 287–88.

253 "From the first to last": IFS, *Truman Era*, 94–96, "The Shadow Cast at Foley Square," 10/14/49; "appalling anthology of fatuity": *Compass*, 10/17/49.

253 "Washington was becoming more": IFS, *Truman Era*, xxviii, 12/8/52.

254 "not a member of the Communist Party" to "instances as that of I. F. Stone": IFS FBI files, 12/28–31/50.

254 "No group likes nonconformists": Patner, *Portrait*, 48, 49.

254 "Jew-baiting suspended priest": IFS, *Truman Era*, 108–11, 5/18/49 column.

254 "He considered me to be": Rabinowitz to MM, 6/20/90.

255 "Russians are really very paranoid": Patner, *Portrait*, 47.

255 "Foreigners who met him": Jonathan Mirskey, "Unmasking the Monster: *The Private Life of Chairman Mao*," *Review* 41, no. 19 (11/17/94). In the midnineties, Mao was unmasked in the memoirs of his personal physician as a vicious psychopath and venereal-diseased despot who delighted in defiling young girls without regard to his affliction. In the midfifties half a million people were falsely accused of being "rightists"; many faced a "torturously slow and painful death" of hard labor.

255 "irrespective of ideology": IFS, *Truman Era*, 78–79, 1/4/50 column.

255 "for all the welcome good sense": Ibid.

256 The China Lobby was bankrolled: Steel, *Lippmann*, 469.

256 "half his normal size": IFS, *Truman Era*, 175; *Compass*, 3/15/50.

256 "when Stalin turned the spigot": Ibid., 86–88, 10/22/48 *PM* column.

257 "Negro and white citizens": IFS FBI file, 12/13/51.

257 "I respect the rights": Informant's report to FBI, 7/25/51.

257 "Red Underground" column: IFS, *Truman Era*, 194–95, 11/11/51.

258 "playing Moscow's game": McCullough, *Truman*, 667; Wallace drew roaring ovations: Culver and Hyde, *American Dreamer*.

258 "remarkably *dumb* in some ways": IFS to Gitlin, 1985.

258 "When the Communists go": IFS, *Truman Era*, 160–61, 2/28/50.

259 "Why I Was for Wallace": Ibid., 66–68, 8/25/48.

259 "Wallace was on the right trail" to "a lot of squishy slogans": IFS to Gitlin, 1985.

260 "pity for America" to "feeling awkward about it": IFS, *Truman Era*, 98–101, "The Tactics of the Crawl," 3/23/50.

260   "Toward an American Police State": "The Master Plan for American Thought Control," *Compass,* 3/13/52.

261   "organized campaign" to "scared and sterile radio": IFS, *Truman Era,* 88–89, "Red Channels," 6/25/50.

261   "some poor Red or 'Near-Red' ": Cottrell, *Izzy,* 157, "Me and Marxism: Invitation—to a Dog Fight," 11/14/49.

261   "Quit following the Red line": Ibid., *Meet the Press* interview with Patrick Hurley, 8/15/45, 157.

262   "rubbish of the Cominform": Ibid., "Me and Marxism," 11/14/49.

262   Izzy was a "legitimate reporter": Lawrence E. Spivak to MM, 2/18/92.

262   "I resigned one sentence": Hoopes, *Ralph Ingersoll,* 328.

262   "was a gallant defeat": Ibid., 330.

262   "newspapers as a matter of course": Roy Hoopes to MM, 12/5/89.

262   Liebling's "grim duty": Liebling, *Press,* 47.

262   "On all the papers I worked for": IFS to John Greenya, *Washington Star,* 11/8/70.

263   "our all-out Tory press": Liebling, *Press,* 51; "The small circulation of the": IFS, *Truman Era,* 217, 4/4/52.

263   "The red label cannot": IFS, *Truman Era,* 163, 2/28/50.

Chapter 17: A Hot War and a Cold Murder

264   "There is hypocrisy on both sides": Two accounts of his speech in Stone's FBI files, apparently by two different informants. They repeat his essential theme, although quotes varied and there were glaring errors. For example, Stone's vitriolic references to Chiang Kai-shek's "Kuomintang" government were recorded as comments about the "Comintern." (Reports on the forum on "Facts About Korea" sponsored by the National Council of the Arts, Sciences and Professions, 8/3/50, the Carnival Room, Capitol Hotel, in NYC.)

264   termed the invasion a "Soviet War Plan": David Rees, in what was for many years the standard history of the war, described the North Korean invasion as a "Soviet war plan." David Rees, *Korea: The Limited War* (Baltimore: Penguin, 1964), 19. Similarly, David Dallin concluded that Stalin "planned, prepared and initiated" the attack. David Dallin, *Soviet Foreign Policy After Stalin* (Philadelphia: J. B. Lippincott, 1961), as quoted by Kathryn Weathersby in the Cold War International History Project.

264   Syngman Rhee, "deliberately provoked": *Compass,* 6/15/51; "possible" American suspects: *Compass,* 6/9/52—also contained in Stone's FBI files.

265   "It's hard to believe": Patner/*Portrait,* 65.

265   "At no point in his": On March 28, 1949, Kim Il Sung visited Stalin—seeking help in attacking the south, whose armies had been making forays into northern territory. Stalin said no; the Chinese civil war continued to drain the Red Army and it could not be counted on to help. He greatly feared U.S. involvement. Once again paranoia reigned; Stalin incorrectly thought the

United States' imminent withdrawal of troops in South Korea was to pave the way for the South to attack the North. In reality both Rhee and the United States thought such a move would so weaken South Korea's defense that the withdrawal was delayed. Militants in the South Korean government hoped to provoke an incident with the North to force the United States to leave its troops in place and become involved in the fight. Like Russia, Washington was determined to avoid this. However, Stalin's ambassador in North Korea sent repeated warnings that the United States had assisted Rhee in expanding his forces, further alarming Stalin. By January 1950, Stalin was cautiously entertaining Kim's pleas to attack the South. Circumstances were more favorable; after the Chinese Communists were victorious, Stalin decided that the United States would not intervene in Korea for several reasons—among them that the United States had not used force to prevent the Communist victory in China and that Russia now had nuclear weapons. (For precise accounts and specific documents, including translated Russian communiqués, see Woodrow Wilson International Center for Scholars, Cold War International History Project, Kathryn Weathersby, Working Paper No. 39, July 2002, as well as many other papers published by the History Project regarding the Korean conflict. Web site: http://wwics.si.edu.)

265 Fifty-year-old Russian documents: Woodrow Wilson Institute Cold War International History Project, Virtual Archive Working Paper #8: "Soviet Aims in Korea and the Origins of the Korean War, 1945–50: New Evidence from Russian Archives," by Kathryn Weathersby.

265 "in the simplistic propaganda": IFS, *Hidden History,* Stone's preface to 1952 edition, xxi.

266 "seeking to restrain": Wrote Bruce Cumings, "Indeed, two key Russian Embassy officials seeking to restrain Kim used language almost identical to that which John Foster Dulles used with Rhee in his June 1950 discussions in Seoul (both, upon hearing Kim or Rhee declaim their desire to attack the other side, 'tried to switch the discussion to a general theme,' to quote from document #6)." For a full account of their differences as well as these excerpts, see "Cumings and Weathersby Exchange on Korean War Origins," July 1995, Woodrow Wilson Cold War International History Project.

266 Truman "abruptly reversed": Cold War International History Project, Virtual Archive Working Paper #8.

267 "developments" along the thirty-eighth parallel: IFS, *Hidden History,* 9.

267 In 1954, Colonel W. A. Perry: Files on IFS released under FOIA by the U.S. Army, memo written March 12, 1954.

267 "uttered a word of warning": IFS, *Hidden History,* 21. "This is only a surmise": Ibid.

268 "almost prostrate with its inferiority": Steel, *Lippmann,* 475 (Lippmann, 4/30/51 and 5/21/51).

268 "heavily documented rubbish": *Post,* 5/11/52.

268 "prove their apostasy": Patner, *Portrait,* 48, 49.

268 "no blind-ideologue Communist crap": Poats comments to MM, 9/27/91.

269 "timely parallels": Bernhardt J. Hurwood, coauthor of *Korea, the Land of the 38th Parallel, Saturday Review of Books,* 11/1/69.

269 "except for a few books": Cited in Chen Jian, *China's Road to the Korean War: The Making of the Sino-American Confrontation* (New York: Columbia University Press, 1994).

269 "The comfortable notion" to "and American superiority": IFS, *Hidden History,* 341; "easy Buck-Rogers-style victory": Ibid., 342.

269 reneging on his promise of aid: Forty years later, the Chinese scholar Chen Jian noted newly released Communist archives that verified that an alarmed Mao decided to commit troops immediately after the South Korean army crossed the thirty-eighth parallel and the next day, September 30, 1950, General Douglas MacArthur issued his unconditional-surrender demand to Kim Il Sung. At that point, Stalin, still concerned about an escalated war, withdrew his promise "to offer the Chinese an air umbrella in Korea," wrote Chen Jian. This created "tremendous difficulties for Mao" before the Soviet leader acquiesced. Mao was devastated when Stalin initially withdrew his promise of assistance—although Jian concluded that Mao's entry into the war was inevitable. In the long run, wrote Jian, "The Soviet 'betrayal' at a crucial juncture strengthened Mao's belief in self-reliance and sowed a seed for the future split between China and the Soviet Union." Jian, *China's Road.*

269 "But in those days": Poats to MM, 9/27/91.

270 Mao would have entered the war: Especially interesting on this point is Chen Jian's *China's Road to the Korean War.*

270 "sheer statistical slapstick": IFS, *Hidden History.* 327; "the public had grown so sour": Ibid., 335.

270 "One could almost feel" to "peace upon the economy": Ibid., 346–47.

270 "sheer poppycock": Richard Rovere, *Post,* 5/11/52.

270 "The great watershed that": Murray Kempton to MM, 9/24/91.

271 "somewhat contorted": Stanley Karnow to MM, 1991.

271 "if not days, after Stalin died": Ongoing interviews, Pierpoint to MM, October 1991, and e-mail interview, 12/07/03.

271 "a drawn-out war": Stalin memo to Mao, 6/5/51, Cold War International History Project, document #95. Historian Weathersby wrote in 1995, "The evidence thus suggests that Stalin's desire to continue the war in Korea was a major factor in the prolongation . . . ; immediately after his death the three communist allies took decisive steps to reach an armistice agreement."

271 "If there is peace in Korea": *Wall Street Journal,* 11/27/51. Quoted in IFS, *Hidden History,* 346.

271 "purposely trying to avoid": Reston, *New York Times,* 11/16/51. Quoted in IFS, *Hidden History,* 325.

271 "I do not believe them": *Compass,* 7/3/52.

272 "who happen to be old friends": Steel, *Lippmann,* 487.

272 "explicit and detailed": Cold War International History Project, Virtual

Archive, "New Russian Evidence on the Korean War Biological Warfare Allegations: Background and Analysis," by Milton Leitenberg.

272 "I am inclined" to "that ring quite phoney": *Compass*, 7/3/52.

272 "had a gift for making the war": Stone quoted in *Saturday Review of Books*, 11/1/69, by Bernhardt J. Hurwood.

272 Film sent to New York: Robert Pierpoint, CBS-TV reporter in Korea, to MM (ongoing interviews, October 1991, e-mail interviews in January 2004); Poats tried carrier pigeons: Knightley, *First Casualty*, 338; "I don't recall anybody": Poats to MM, 9/27/91.

273 "neutralism was a bad word": Patner, *Portrait*, 62.

273 Acheson appalled Reston: Steel, *Lippmann*, 473.

273 could not resist a quick stiletto . . . to "took nerve": IFS, *Compass*, 10/19/49.

274 "this goddamn town" to . . . disruption of school and friendships: CS and Richard Dudman to MM.

274 "Were this any place but Paris": IFS, *Truman Years*, 209 (*Compass*, 10/1/50).

274 worn-out his father looked: CS to MM. Comments and quotes from Christopher Stone in this chapter are from interviews with MM.

275 "just a kid": Karnow to MM; sister referrred to as "crazies": JS to MM, 5/2/04. Comments and quotes from Karnow in this section are from interviews with MM, 1991–92.

275 "very dramatic scene": JS to MM, 7/9/90.

276 a lucky break: CS to MM, 10/25/05.

277 feeding Hoover personal letters: Curt Gentry, *J. Edgar Hoover*, 234.

277 He lampooned a ludicrous *Collier's* edition: *Compass* columns, 10/23/51, 10/28/51.

277 "The Crime of Hush-Up": *Compass* Polk columns, 8/5/52, 8/7/52.

278 His body was found: Keeley, *Salonika Bay Murder*.

278 Walter Lippmann headed the committee: In addition, the Overseas Writers Association special committee included James Reston of the *New York Times*, William Paley and Joseph C. Harsch of CBS, the columnist Marquis Childs, Ernest Lindley of *Newsweek*, and Eugene Meyer, then owner of the *Washington Post*.

278 "feeble bit of whitewash": *Compass*, 8/8/52.

278 "had as big a stake" to "journalistic stuffed shirts": Ibid.

278 "accepted a verdict": Ronald Steel, "Casualty of the Cold War," *Review* 38, no. 15 (9/26/91).

279 "To a surprising degree": Steel, *Lippmann*, 487.

279 "For men with few illusions": *Compass*, 8/7/52.

279 "A cardinal point": Ibid.

279 "a decent and fine young man": *Compass*, 7/7/52; "military monster" and "poor investment": Steel, "Casualty."

279 exposed this sham endorsement: *Compass*, 7/7/52; Donovan declared himself: bound report of the Overseas Writers of the Special Committee to Inquire into Polk's Murder, 75; "vocal dissenter was I. F. Stone": Steel, "Casualty."

280 "has been all but forgotten": *Compass*, 7/6/52.

281 "there is no improving on": Lydon, *New York Times* book review, 4/7/96, of Elias Vlanton with Zak Mettger, *Who Killed George Polk?* (Philadelphia: Temple University Press, 1996).

281 "their role in its unfolding": *Compass*, 7/10/52.

281 "I do not have" to "don't remember that either": Reston to MM, 11/12/90.

281 "particularly Lippmann, should have": Steel, "Casualty."

Chapter 18: Chasing Izzy

285 endless spying on Stone: See the introductory note on page 490 regarding Stone's FBI files.

287 "like exposing Gypsy Rose Lee": IFS to MM, *Washington Post*, 7/9/79.

288 "really had a pathological hatred": FBI agent to MM, 1991. Requested anonymity.

289 Files were kept on many of America's great twentieth-century writers: An excellent book on this subject is Natalie Robins, *Alien Ink*.

289 "stark, raving mad": Robins, *Alien Ink*, 160.

290 tortured motions to subscribe: FBI bulletin, 12/28/53.

290 "failed to establish any espionage" to "nasty" treatment: FBI memo, 11/22/54.

290 "NO!" Hoover angrily scrawled: FBI memo, 3/28/53.

291 "Hoover's closet is well stocked": *The Weekly*, 9/5/53; *Haunted Fifties*, 25.

291 arrested on a "morals charge": Robins, *Alien Ink*, 175.

291 "a very active homosexual": Gentry, *J. Edgar Hoover*, 347.

291 "spousal relationship": Richard G. Powers, *G-Men*, quoted in Robins, *Alien Ink*, 67.

292 "the same mishmash": *Haunted Fifties*, 25, 9/5/53.

292 "dirty business": *Compass*, 6/13/49.

292 "Secret police agents are very dangerous": San Francisco speech, 2/5/88.

292 Bentley was a bitter defector: The best recent book on Bentley is Kathryn S. Olmsted's *Red Spy Queen*.

294 *"the extent of his relation"*: FBI memo, 10/17/46; "identified Stone as a close contact": FBI memo, 10/18/46.

294 "Stone doesn't get that sense": FBI memo, 7/11/45; letter from Boston Field Office classified as information "received from FBI informant."

295 "Isn't it about time": *Daily Worker*, 4/18/44; "Stone thought the United States": Informant at Stone speech of the Midwest Committee for the Protection of the Foreign Born, quoted in MM, "Secret War," *Washington Post*, 8/21/94.

295 More important than character flaws: Numerous sources on Bentley, specifically Goodman, *Committee*, and Olmsted, *Red Spy Queen*.

296 Clark knew the grand jury: Olmsted, *Red Spy Queen*, 117–18.

297 "I have kept silent": *Compass*, 5/15/52.

298 seeking the death penalty was a ploy: Lamphere, *FBI-KGB War*. The Bureau had evidence it did not reveal at the trial. Lamphere, its chief spy chaser, helped decipher decrypted KGB codes that led to the twentieth century's

most infamous spy couple. Even at the time Lamphere wrote his 1986 memoir, the U.S. government was keeping most of the decoded messages secret. (See chapter 19, "Lies and Spies.")

298   In 1997, the Russian who: Alessandra Stanley, "K.G.B. Agent Plays Down Atomic Role of Rosenbergs," *New York Times,* 3/16/97, 9.

300   "I don't think any Commie": IFS FBI file, 5/25/47.

300   "Greetings, FBI agents and fellow subversives": Stone's speech at the National Council of the Arts, Sciences and the Professions rally against the H-bomb, Carnegie Hall, 2/13/50; trailed by a midget: MM, "Secret War"; FBI FOIA files.

301   "To accept ideological interrogation": *The Weekly,* 6/29/53.

301   "People are afraid to look": Ibid., 12/21/53.

302   "The only honorable way": Rick Perlstein, "Architects of America's Red Scare," *New York Times,* 8/20/01.

302   Reagan could thank his lucky: Reagan "passionately espoused the New Deal, and by 1938 he had swung so far toward the idealistic left that he tried to join the Hollywood Communist Party. He was quickly rejected, on the shrewd ground that he was not Party material (too garrulous, too patriotic)." Edmund Morris, "The Unknowable: Ronald Reagan's Amazing Mysterious Life," *New Yorker,* 6/28/04.

302   "I could answer": *"I'd Hate Myself in the Morning"—A Memoir: Ring Lardner Jr.* (New York: Thunder's Mouth Press/Nation Books, 2000), 9.

302   "Where's the hammer": Goulden, *Best Years,* 306.

303   "YOU DON'T HAVE TO": Ibid., 307.

303   "Izzy felt the First" to "work unmolested in America": Faulk to MM, 2/90.

303   "known Soviet Agent": Ivins, *Who Let the Dogs In?,* 350; "so much anticommunist": Ibid., 351.

304   "Pop hated sellouts": CS to MM.

304   discussing a column of Stone's: On 2/14/46 Anne White engaged in political gossip with a friend in Washington about Stone's column regarding Harold Ickes's dramatic resignation from the cabinet and whether Ickes had been nasty at the press conference when Stone grilled him; she couldn't tell from the newspaper account. The friend said that he had been "nasty," but that the fracas with Stone was "minor" in this "exciting" press conference—FBI memo titled "concerning activities of Harry Dexter White," 3/11/46; Stone's invitation to Harry Dexter White's House: 11/4/46 Gregory Espionage-R file.

305   "having denied him the true": Quoted in Craig, *Treasonable Doubt,* 214.

305   "I certainly knew" to "which bred him": IFS, *Truman Era,* 48–50 (*Compass,* 8/18/48).

Chapter 19: Lies and Spies

307   Two long 1944 memos: Russian memos concerning Lippmann, aka Imperialist: Venona File #36, New York 696-7 to Moscow, 5/16/44, 283–84 of officially released documents.

307 Another memo involving *I* . . . to "Poland as essential": Venona #41, New York 847b-848 to Moscow, 6/15/44, 295–97, released by United States 1995–96.

308 On December 23, the journalist: This report includes the puzzling code name of another unidentified "journalist" as "Bumblebee"; to this author's knowledge, that code was used only for David Greenglass, who fingered his brother-in-law Julius Rosenberg as an atomic spy and was not a journalist. Hence, this list of coded journalists talking with Sergei may be in error.

309 Lippmann's meetings with Pravdin: In fact, Haynes and Klehr dismiss Lippmann as having "had no sympathy for communism" without even mentioning the cables of his discussions with Sergei. They only mention that the CPUSA-KGB had placed agent Mary Price as his secretary "to find out what sources and additional information lay behind" his columns. Haynes and Klehr, *Venona*, 241, 99.

311 does not begin to describe him: Novak's outing of former ambassador Joseph Wilson's CIA wife during the Iraq war earned him the sobriquet "douche bag of journalism" by Comedy Central's *Daily Show* host Jon Stewart. Other journalists refused to use information peddled by the White House to discredit Wilson's accurate claim that WMD information was fraudulent, purposely leaked to damage Wilson and his wife's career.

311 Novak fumed on CNN: Brent Kendall, *Guardian*, 4/12/03.

311 "hardly enough to pay for the postage": Jeremy J. Stone's replies to accusations expounded in the early nineties by *Accuracy in Media, Human Events*, and other publications that would be libelous if Stone were alive; Jeremy J. Stone, e-mail to MM, 10/27/05.

313 "the Venona papers standing alone": *Washington Star* book review of Schecter and Schecter, *Sacred Secrets*.

313 "The hardest part": Persico, *New York Times*, 1/03/99.

314 "throughout the forties and fifties": Coulter, *Treason*, 99.

314 virtually frozen overnight: Weinstein and Vassiliev, *Haunted Wood*, 106.

315 "There is no evidence": Haynes and Klehr, *Venona*, 249.

315 "It has now been overwhelmingly": Coulter, *Treason*, 97.

315 she consistently refers to Stone: Ibid., 97–98.

315 "Stone was likely predisposed": Philip Nobile, " 'I Lied': Testing the Intellectual Honesty of Eric Alterman," *New York Press*, 1/19/99.

316 "too few of those dealing": Jacob Weisberg, "Cold War Without End," *New York Times Magazine*, 11/28/99.

316 FDR avoided official channels: Weinstein and Vassiliev, *Haunted Wood*, 160; White "doesn't pass information": Ibid., 169.

316 "only the American and Soviet": West, *Democracy Matters*, 55.

317 "The Future of the Reich": *PM*, 3/19/45.

317 The FBI tried frantically: FBI memo, 3/27/45.

317 "inconceivable" that the Red Army: Steel, *Lippman*, 405, quoting Lippmann in *U.S. Foreign Policy*, 1943.

317 White actually opposed: "White warned that shutting down the Ruhr would exile millions of Germans and harm the rest of Europe." Morgenthau replied,

"Sure it's a terrific problem. Let the *Germans* solve it. Why the hell should *I* worry about what happens to their people?" Beschloss, *Conquerors*, 104. On White's role, see Craig, *Treasonable Doubt*, 268. "'Let the Germans stew'" to "his Semitic grievances": Ibid., 161.

318 "They all are" to "that of a 'Scotchman'?": Olmsted, *Red Spy Queen*, 131.

318 In 1962, JFK: Reeves, *President Kennedy*, 346–47.

320 disaster of 9/11: Excellent on this subject is former senator Bob Graham's *Intelligence Matters*.

320 "Now then," Moynihan asked: Moynihan, *Secrecy*, as quoted in Sam Tanenhaus, *New York Times* book review, 5/4/98.

320 "This is absurd": R. W. Apple Jr., "Government Is Overzealous On Secrecy, Panel Advises," *New York Times*, 3/5/97.

321 "It is not known at": Information on FBI tracking Stone from FOIA files, Number HQ 65-60654—Section 1–4: Several copies were sent: two to the Bureau, two to the New York bureau, one to Los Angeles, one to San Francisco and three to the Washington Field Office. Date when report was made, 2/28/51, details first two months surveillance of that year. Deleted pages indicated as "copies destroyed," 12/1/60.

322 "as an espionage investigation": FBI files, 3/16/51.

323 "typewritten specimens" to ... "comparison purposes": FBI file, 6/8/51.

324 "Communists convicted after violating": IFS, *Compass*, 7/21/51.

325 "appeared to be dependent": FBI files, 7/11/51.

326 "We had no clandestine relationship": Kalugin to MM, 5/24/03.

326 "tweak his [Hoover's] nose": Gentry, *J. Edgar Hoover*, 719.

326 During the fierce battle: Peters, *Five Days in Philadelphia*, 91–92.

326 "not feed him disinformation": Kalugin to MM, 5/24/03.

327 "No. What I told you": Ibid.

327 "I always maintained" to "on the fringe": Kalugin to MM, 6/6/03.

328 "you didn't want Izzy": Galbraith to MM, 5/28/96.

Chapter 20: A Guerrilla Warrior during the Fifties Fetish

329 "little market for 'exposing'": *Haunted Fifties*, 175–76, 11/14/55.

329 "the place haunted" to "free speech of both": IFS foreword to *Truman Era*.

330 "'left wing press'": *The Weekly*, 3/15/54 (*The Weekly Reader*, 42).

330 "even his own Senate colleagues": *Haunted Fifties*, introduction, xx.

330 "Outgoing Democrats and incoming Republicans": "Who Will Watch This Watchman?" *The Weekly*, 1/17/53, 4.

330 "I hope General Eisenhower": *The Weekly*, 1/17/53. Conversations with MM and other interviewers about fearing *The Weekly* wouldn't last.

331 "a subversive fellow": *Haunted Fifties*, xx.

331 "It was a hard time": Knoll to MM, 5/23/90.

331 Izzy and Esther letters to Celia: Given to MM by CG, 10/05 e-mail.

332 "his secretary:" MM, "Gathering No Moss," *Washington Post*, 6/9/79, B1.

332 "There was this perception": Brinkley to MM, 12/9/93.

332 "He had a wonderful style": Feiffer to MM, 5/91.

333 "more than *one* subscriber": Abourezk to MM, 4/06.

333 "It just wasn't worth it": Patner, *Portrait*, 81–82.

333 "phone call to a friend": *The Weekly*, 4/7/53; "mushes forward": Ibid., 4/28/53.

334 "Keep Your Diamonds": Ibid., 12/2/68.

334 " 'buried in this goddamn city' " to "feel the cold stares": CS to MM, 8/31/91.

335 "Dick, I don't think": Information, quotes from Dudman, interview with MM, 5/91. (Dinner-party anecdote was also relayed to Stone family.)

335 "write something new" to "he liked acceptance awfully well": Dudman to MM, 5/91.

336 "He was bloody lonely": Nossiter to MM, 10/26/91; "pissing match with a skunk": CS to MM, 12/8/91, and in letter to MM.

336 "I was sort of laughing": CS to MM, 12/8/91.

337 "Ours was Wilson's last": Martin to MM, 12/9/91.

337 "McCarthyism was nowhere": Miller to Stone family memorial; "we had to cancel Izzy's": Martin to MM, 12/9/91.

337 Finlay Lewis anecdote: Lewis to MM, 9/28/05 e-mail.

338 "My *sister* was Joe McCarthy's" to "seems strange today": Brinkley to MM, 12/9/93.

338 "It's a cliché": Spivak to MM, 5/18/90.

339 "While we were all running": Kempton to MM, 9/24/91.

339 red-hot conflict of interest: "The J. Edgar Hoover–McCarthy Axis," *The Weekly*, 10/5/53.

340 "one final well-flung custard pie": Ibid., 5/25/53.

340 "he saw Eisenhower": *The Weekly Reader*, 42, 3/15/54.

340 "Those like Walter Lippmann": Ibid., 2/54, 4.

341 "You could get canned if": Kempton to MM, 9/24/91.

341 "When the dissemination of ideas": IFS at Embassy Auditorium, Los Angeles, 4/22/54, furnished by an informant, Stone's FBI file (Bufile 100-27078). He spoke under the auspices of the Citizens Committee to Preserve American Freedom. Also the next day, 4/23/54, in San Francisco, sponsored by Californians for the Bill of Rights.

342 Stone opposed American intervention: *The Weekly*, 5/3/54.

342 "This hounded mutual aid organization": Ibid., 5/10/54.

342 Stone pummeled the *Times*: Column by Michael Cross-Barnet, an editor at the *Baltimore Sun*, in *Los Angeles Times*, 6/26/05.

343 "fungoid growth": *Haunted Fifties*, 179, 1/28/57.

343 "This town was so scared": Joseph Rauh information and quotes, interview with MM, 3/6/90. (Barth was a gentle idol to reporters at the *Washington Post* well into the seventies; his outstanding editorials, collected in *The Loyalty of Free Men*, remain vivid examples of the best and bravest in American journalism opinion pieces.)

344 "I'm going to subpoena": Rovere, *Senator Joe McCarthy*, 58; "It was also, of course": Ibid., 166; "how McCarthy butchered the truth" Ibid., 169.

344 "just because they are usually" to "it is up to the diner to refuse it": Ibid., 167.

344 "did not relieve us of complicity": Howard Kurtz, *Washington Post*, 11/9/91.

344 "If no one's reading you": Spivak to MM, 5/18/90.

345 "One of my in-laws is a Commie" to "gift of historical imagination": Kempton to MM, 9/24/91.

345 "only for being a bully": *The Weekly*, 3/15/54; "For the first time": Ibid., 3/8/54.

346 "we were just brought up": Seldes to MM, 11/6/91. Seldes might have agreed that this 1906 payoff was chump change even after factoring in inflation compared with today's Liars for Hire—so-called journalists who were on the payroll of the Bush administration as propagandists to plug its side of the story. When this practice was revealed, Bush expressed no ethical concern.

346 "granddaddy of us investigative reporters": Stone's remark reprinted by *Fair*, September/October 1995; "five-buck liberal who subscribes": Ibid.

346 "to divorce himself" to "cancel or not renew": Seldes to MM, 11/6/91.

347 "I'm very proud": Colman McCarthy, *Washington Post*, 5/10/82.

347 "his sodden end": *The Weekly*, 5/13/57.

Chapter 21: Confessions

348 "great leader": *The Weekly*, 3/14/53.

348 "too hideous to be credible" to "warmongers depend": Ibid., 4/11/53.

349 "*This is not a good*" to "it and the Soviet press": Ibid., 5/28/56.

350 "not figments of hostile propaganda" to "they get new orders": Ibid.

351 Stone was a "nasty" critic: IFS FBI file Bufile 100-37078; "expeditious attention": FBI memo dated 6/18/56.

351 It was suggested that: New York FBI office to Hoover, 6/29/56.

351 couldn't even make contact: WFO FBI memo, 7/31/56.

351 "Under no circumstances": FBI orders in memo, 9/27/56.

352 "deeply rooted in Russia's" to "on the same planet": *The Weekly*, 3/14/56.

352 "undeviating fellow traveler": Column is in Stone's FBI file.

352 Spain had set them up as: Applebaum, *Gulag*, xxxiv.

353 "has built a distorted picture": *The Weekly*, 3/14/53.

353 "Soviet camps became the notorious": Applebaum, *Gulag*, 93.

353 "No one wants to admit": Ibid., xxii.

354 " 'I can't speak' " to "his being a radical": CS to MM, 8/31/91.

354 "reasons for Izzy's significance" to "against all on the left": Rauh to MM, 3/6/90.

356 "liberal court of Earl Warren" to "beyond hope of exorcism": *The Weekly*, 6/24/57.

356 "Civilized people of the world": MM, "The Hybridization of Hungary," *Washington Post*, 11/4/86, D1.

356 "For those of us" to "party apparatus exudes": *The Weekly*, 10/29/56.

357 "It was a joy to see": Ibid., 12/17/56.

357 "Faced at last with the": Ibid.

357 "hands-off policy" to "sentimental nonsense to the Pentagon": Ibid., 12/3/56.

358 "condone preventive war" to "*our* tyrant friends in Nicaragua": Ibid., 11/12/56.

358 "I . . . am a hypocrite": Ibid.

Chapter 22: A Bloody Revolution at Home

359 "successful experiment in Apartheid": *Torment,* 153.

359 *Brown et al. v. Board of Education* . . . to "not be ended overnight": *The Weekly,* 5/24/54.

360 "Now I know how" to "of that [outside] pressure": Several sources, including books on civil rights and the PBS documentary *Early Civil Rights Struggles: The Murder of Emmett Till*; and compilation by Lisa Cozzens, 1997–98, on Web site http://www.watson.org/~lisa/blackhistory/early-civilrights/emmett.html.

361 "maniacal murder" to "Negro to lead us": *The Weekly,* 10/3/55.

361 no longer joined blacks: Ibid.

361 "suddenly [felt] no longer alone": Ibid., 9/16/63.

362 "not even a glass of" to "us darkies to lunch?": IFS, *Truman Era,* 132, 12/20/48.

363 Story of the Stones' maid: CS to MM.

363 "showed him all the rooms": Holeman's 1988 memo obtained by MM from the National Press Club archives.

363 "We were anxious" to "contemptuous of the rest of us": Rogers to MM, 10/10/91.

364 "regurgitate the same drivel" to "collaborationist": Thomas W. Lippman, *Washington Post,* 6/19/81.

364 "Pete was an *in*former": Rogers to MM, 10/10/91.

364 stirred up trouble: The best books on Martin Luther King and the civil rights movement remain Taylor Branch's Pulitzer Prize–winning *Parting the Waters, Pillar of Fire,* and *At Canaan's Edge.*

364 "solve the race problem amicably": Steel, *Lippmann,* 552–53.

365 "Rowan's obtuse and ugly comment": *Torment,* 118 (*Review,* 11/11/65).

365 "Amid the hand-wringing": *The Weekly,* 10/7/57.

366 "A Piece of Foreign Correspondence" to "strong supporters of Governor Faubus": Ibid., 9/29/59.

367 "begins to burn the brand": Ibid.

368 "I hated the whole" to "inflicted on my friends": Bernstein, *Loyalties,* 95–96.

369 "cynically suggested that the shotgun": *The Weekly,* 10/3/55.

369 "not one single student" to "stirred up by Jews": Ibid., 10/8/62.

369 "the inevitable result of agitation": Wilkie, *Dixie,* 120; "I killed that nigger": Ibid., 156.

369 "Looking back": Ibid., 128.

370 "loquacious Senators" to "Negroes weren't so pushy": *The Weekly,* 9/30/63.

370 that ten years later: Ibid., 11/9/64.

371 "Why is J. Edgar Hoover?": Ibid., 6/1/59.

371 "Mr. Hoover's boundless enthusiasm": Stone's speeches as reported by informant to FBI, memo dated 1/21/60, document #266, Stone file.

372 not subject to judicial interference . . . and "it's bunk": Cottrell, *Izzy*, 175; lawsuit against Eastland: *The Weekly*, 12/12/55.

372 "police state" tactics: Ibid., 11/27/61.

372 "rubbing, scrubbing, shining" to . . . newspapermen apologized: Conference sponsored by the University of South Florida, St. Petersburg, attended by MM, June 3–6, 2004.

372 "They and a few white sympathizers": *The Weekly*, 6/4/62.

373 "but a nigger": Wilkie, *Dixie*, 143.

373 "sexual sickness" to "leaking 'red' smears": *Torment*, 384, 4/5/65.

374 "Mississippi Negroes are excluded": *The Weekly*, 1/11/65.

374 "I could hear people screaming" to . . . found not guilty: Ibid., 6/22/64.

375 reason to rejoice . . . to "lobbyist for civil rights": Ibid.

376 "It is no small" to "some Oriental despot": Ibid., 5/8/67.

376 "He stood in the line" to "a lost race speaking": Ibid., 4/15/68.

376 "troubles may be beginning" to "integration cannot be stopped": Ibid., 10/7/57.

Chapter 23: Affairs of the Heart, Plus Kennedy, Khrushchev, and Castro

378 "Can you not talk": Stone's operation, CS to MM, 8/21/91.

379 "at the center of the storm": *The Weekly*, 11/20/67.

380 "the Stone goes rolling on!": Quoted by Andrew Patner in *Salon* letters to editor, 1/8/98; Patner, *Portrait*, 121.

380 "Izzy has tremendous influence": Stan Isaacs, *Newsday*, 1/20/68.

380 "Nixon Was Wrong About Vietnam": *The Weekly*, 2/1/60.

381 "We do not remember": Ibid., 7/18/60.

381 "giddy arrogance": Ibid., "Our Feud With Fidel," 1/16/61.

381 "on the brink of war": Ibid., 1/8/62.

382 "you, sir, are a": Johnson, *Bay of Pigs*, 139.

382 did not die in the invasion: MM, "The Sad Death of Pepe San Roman," *Washington Post*, 10/17/89.

382 "pulling down an iron curtain": *The Weekly*, 1/14/63.

383 "the better they like you": Reeves, *President Kennedy*, 106.

383 "It's *still* my view": IFS to Gitlin, 1985.

384 "just the arrogant bully": Ibid.

384 When he came back: Stan Isaacs, *Newsday*, 1/20/68.

384 "I might as well make": *The Weekly*, 1/16/61.

385 "To face the November" to "interests are simply ignored": *Torment*, 19–23 (*Review*, 5/14/66).

386 "Castro alone" to "misleading than the doped": *The Weekly*, 1/21/63.

386 "I moved up" to "last Yankee imperialist": Ibid., 1/7/63.

387 "I think my crime": IFS to Gitlin, 1985.

388 "are Communists" to "No comment": *Binghamton* (NY) *Evening Press*, 12/8 and 12/9/61. Collected in Stone's FBI file.

388 "delighted by his wit" to "where we really are": *The Weekly*, 12/9/63.

389 "wrote no eulogy": Steel, *Lippmann*, 542–43.

390 "I don't care about": Personal recollection, Raymond Marcus, 7/95, http://karws.gso.uri.edu/JFK/The_critics/Marcus/Marcus_on_Stone.html.

390 "The hope is that men": *The Weekly*,12/9/63.

390 "No Democrat more deserved": Ibid., 9/24/64.

Chapter 24: The Haunting War

391 "Let the Government Deceive": *The Weekly*, 5/8/61.

391 "he was terribly distressed": Vanderchek to MM, 4/15/90.

392 "my faithful burned" to "their accounts with God": *The Weekly*, 11/1/65.

392 In the *Post*'s excised account: Leroy F. Aarons and William J. Raspberry, *Washington Post*, 11/4/65.

393 appointment of Dean Rusk: Stan Isaacs, *Newsday*, 1/29/68.

393 "Anti-Guerrilla War" to "Diem in South Vietnam?": *Torment*, 173, 5/22/61.

394 "pro-American" to . . . financed by the United States: Ibid., 178–88, 10/28/63.

394 "lost opportunities" to . . . National Liberation Front: Ibid., 218, 3/8/65.

395 "laid it on" *The Weekly*, 4/22/65.

395 a coup with "plausible deniability": Reeves, *President Kennedy*, 638.

395 "free elections": *The Weekly*, 11/11/63.

395 "a test of American will": Steel, *Lippmann*, 557.

396 "few Americans are aware" to *"attack might have been provoked"*: *Torment*, 202, 8/24/64.

396 "like a barroom brawl": Ibid., 203–6, 9/28/64.

397 nuclear warfare while lying: Ellsberg, *Secrets*, 201.

397 "minutes to write six alternative": Ibid., 41–43.

397 "very devastating" to the administration: Ellsberg to MM, 3/10/05.

397 "Unfortunately few will" to . . . captured from the United States: *Torment*, 212–18, 3/8/65.

397 "Stone added it all up": Ellsberg to MM, 3/10/05. The meager list included six Chinese and two North Vietnamese machine guns, one Czech and four Soviet pistols, four Chinese mortars, less than a hundred rifles and guns, two bazookas, two Chinese rocket launchers, sixty-four submachine guns, twenty-four French submachine guns "modified" in North Vietnam, two machine guns made in North Vietnam, sixteen helmets, a uniform, and an undisclosed number of mess kits, belts, sweaters, and socks.

398 "counterfeit phrases of this kind": *The Weekly*, 7/11/66.

398 "disarmed by assurances": Gitlin, *Days of Rage*, 267.

398 "leveled every urban": *Torment*, 98, 1/20/66.

399 *"without nuclear weapons"*: Ellsberg, *Secrets*, 62.

399 "Bobby Kennedy thought": Dorothy Fall comments and observations, several talks with MM, 1990 through 2004; "contrary to officialdom": Fall to MM, 2/17/04.

400 "gave him an ineradicable interest": *The Weekly*, 3/13/67.

400 "Bernard was outspoken": Dorothy Fall, e-mail to MM, 2/18/04.

400 "There is hardly a writer": *The Weekly*, 3/13/67.

401 "President Kennedy's administration": Knightley, *First Casualty*, 375–76. See chapter on correspondents in Vietnam, pp. 373–401.

402 No *Time* readers saw: Ibid., 379.

402 "immoral until the very end": Halberstam and Mohr comments, ibid., 380–81; original source for Halberstam, Aronson, *Press and the Cold War*, 182; for Mohr, Nora Ephron, "The War Followers," *New York* magazine, 11/12/73.

402 "'none of this means anything'": Knightley, *First Casualty*, 423.

402 "to be skeptical of any official statement": *Torment*, 313 (*Review*, 4/22/65).

402 "Conventional journalism": Knightley, *First Casualty*, 423; original source, *Esquire*, April 1970.

402 "sat down to write the": Osnos to MM, 9/26/91.

403 "our enemy in this conflict?": Knightley, *First Casualty*, 402; original quote from Don Oberdorfer, *Tet* (1971).

403 "saving of civilian lives" to "ponji-stick journalism": *Torment*, 393–96, 1/9/67.

404 "Oh, I loved that": All of Salisbury comments to MM, 10/18/91.

404 "Salisbury would have been": Wilson to MM, 10/01/91.

405 "'There's a little snag'": Dudman to MM, 5/91. Also in letter Dudman sent to Stone family for a collection of reminiscences on Stone.

405 "I did run into opposition": Kalb to MM, e-mail, 2/23/05.

406 "I've been pulling my punches": Steel, *Lippmann*, 569.

406 "had misled me" Ibid., 571; "messianic megalomania": Ibid., 577.

406 "From these dissident journalists": Ibid., 576.

406 too many administration dolts present: Dorothy Fall to MM, 6/94.

406 "His sense of isolation increased": Steel, *Lippmann*, 580.

407 "one declining and one ascending": Patner, *Portrait*, 139.

407 "The company . . . with the biggest": MM, *Long Time Passing*, 52.

408 "I sent them a good boy": Knightley, *First Casualty*, 393, quoting Hersh. Also used by Hersh in present speeches.

408 "The real crime is higher up": *Polemics*, 386–89 (*Review*, 12/15/69).

409 "Unthinking enthusiasm, blind devotion": *Torment*, 364, 11/1/65.

409 "so twist the truth" to "honorable record": *Polemics*, 307–11, 3/4/68.

410 "This has been Nixon's war": *The Weekly*, 11/17/69.

410 "if they had the guts": Ibid., 1/12/70.

411 "a con man offering the Brooklyn": *Review*, 3/9/72.

411 Stone's . . . "perceptive analysis": Hersh, *Price of Power*, 485.

Chapter 25: From "We Shall Overcome" to "Off the Pigs"

412   "The nice thing about the New Left": IFS to Gitlin, 1985.

412   "seem to me a mixture": *Washington Post* and *New York Times*, 9/14/63.

413   "The students performed" to "hysterical exaggerations": *Washington Post*, 9/14/63.

413   "stunt-mongers and suicide tactics" to "with our fellow citizens": 6/23/65.

413   "we must always dress for peace": Luvvie Pearson to MM, 6/14/91.

414   "I spoke at Harvard": IFS to Gitlin, 1985.

414   "which taught me . . . that the": Gitlin, *Sixties*, 90.

414   "which was very sweet of him": Gitlin to MM, 9/9/91.

415   "A fallout shelter for everybody": Kennedy quote, information, *Detroit News* compilation of articles on its Web site, 2005.

416   "The policy of reprisal": Speech, 2/17/65, in Stone's FBI file.

416   "I'll get I. F. Stone to debate": Informant report of speech, Stone FBI file.

417   "This new bunch of kids" to "They just pissed on them": IFS to Gitlin, 1985.

417   "hard to pin down such": IFS to Gitlin, 1985.

418   "Izzy was always willing": Knoll to MM, 5/25/90.

418   "I've seen snot-nosed Marxist-Leninists": Gitlin, *Sixties*, 183.

418   "students intended to urinate": Ibid., 182.

418   "otherwise splendid and attainable victory": Ibid., 263.

419   "a marriage of paranoias": The pro-Nixon *New York Daily News* circulation was far bigger than the *New York Times* and *New York Post* combined. Two out of three D.C. papers were pro-Nixon conservative (the *Washington Star* and the *Daily News*). So was the *Washington Post*, wrote IFS, "on alternate days." *Polemics*, 484–87, 12/1/69.

419   "the evil of banality": *The Weekly*, 5/18/70.

421   "demonstrators was an undercover agent": MM, *Long Time Passing*, 108.

421   "The stories I dismissed as paranoia": William Greider, *Nation*, 5/3/04.

421   they confiscated tapes, cameras: MM, *Long Time Passing*, 109. Original source, Patrick Sale, *SDS* (New York: Random House, 1973).

421   planned a 1969 Days of Rage: Susan Stern, *With the Weathermen: The Personal Journey of a Revolutionary Woman* (New York: Doubleday, 1975).

422   "Smash monogamy" and support for Manson: MM interview with Weathermen sources, 2006. Susan Braudy's secondary sourcing on Kathy Boudin places her at center stage in several instances. However, it should be noted that there are inaccuracies in Braudy's details of I. F. Stone, including the wrong year of his death, identifying his brother by a son's name, crediting him with introducing Daniel Ellsberg to brother-in-law lawyer Leonard Boudin, and stating that Esther wrote *Weekly* unsigned editorials. Therefore no information from this book, *Family Circle*, about Stone is included.

422   intent to pierce the victims: FBI report cited in Braudy, *Family Circle*, 210.

423   "do such a dumb thing": Ibid., 312.

423   "down to the last cliché": Sandy Grady, *Philadelphia Bulletin*, 4/12/70.

423   "The Weatherman kids" to "back to the White House": *The Weekly*, 3/23/70.

424 "frustrated urge to destroy" to "Posturing for the TV Cameras?": Ibid., 9/70.

425 Stone could not forgive causes: Ibid., 6/1/70.

426 "left wing pamphleteer": Letter and Hoover's response in IFS FBI file, 11/5/70.

426 none of the four killed : *The Weekly,* 11/2/70.

426 charges against FBI infiltrators: Jack Nelson, *Los Angeles Times,* 9/11/70.

427 quoted from a fiery May 28: *The Weekly,* 6/1/70.

427 "fags," "sneaks," and "scum" to "bring them to trial": Ibid., 3/9/70.

427 Castro, whose "own vanity": Ibid., 5/17/71.

427 "gigantic snow job": Ibid., 5/4/70.

428 "trying to make independent reporting": Ibid., 6/1/70.

428 "create new Vietnams": Ibid., 5/3/71.

430 "last man to die for a mistake": Ibid., Kerry's testimony, 4/22/70, abbreviated by Stone.

430 "men who saved the honor": Ibid.

430 militarism remained ascendant: Iran-contra scandals faded and Oliver North, Elliott Abrams, and John Negroponte found their way into another Republican militaristic administration, that of George W. Bush. Imperialistic preemptive war became popular in the new century. A new generation of media who were infants then and still know little about the Vietnam War joined in the frenzy of vilifying presidential candidate Kerry in 2004. Misleading and inaccurate Swiftboat ads, paid for by Bushites, trampled his war record, trashed his testimony. Sadly, Kerry did not mount a vigorous defense of his noble bygone words or actions, as an inane dispute swirled around whether he deserved his third Purple Heart, while Bush's ducking the war went mostly unnoticed.

431 "this hero of mine": Ellsberg, *Secrets,* 358–59.

431 "Bless you for what you're doing": Ibid., 359; and to MM 3/10/05.

431 "telling him how to do it": Ellsberg, *Secrets,* 383.

432 "If you were young": Ibid., 380–81.

432 "something odd," about Stone: Ellsberg to MM, 3/10/05.

432 "In all this anti-war theater": *The Weekly,* 5/3/71.

Chapter 26: From Iconoclast to Icon

435 "the affection I felt from": "Notes on Closing, But Not on Farewell," *The Weekly,* final edition, 12/14/71.

435 "untactful enough to call": Ibid. (Original ran 5/12/68.)

435 "alone in warm human memory": Ibid.

436 "rarely felt that I had succeeded": Ibid.

436 "five best writings": IFS to Stan Isaacs, "Thunder on the Left," *Newsday,* 1/29/68.

436 "He liked being on the outside": Ben Bradlee to MM, 10/1/91.

436 "He was so upset he sent Izzy": Greider to MM, 10/4/90.

437 "it does wonders for your circulation": John Greenya, *Washington Star,* 9/8/70.

437   "I was bored with": Karl Meyer, *New Statesman,* 12/22/72.

437   at the top in surveys: Cottrell, *Izzy,* 284–85.

438   "When a 67-year-old" to "It'd be so revolutionary": Vincent Canby, *New York Times,* 5/23/74.

438   "a bunch of hypocrites": The voice sampling of IFS is from his lecture at the Ford Hall Forum and broadcast on NPR, 4/12/83. Incorporated by Scott Johnson in his composition for the Kronos Quartet at the suggestion of its first violinist, David Harrington. A portion was first performed at Lincoln Center in April 1991. It has since been expanded, continues to be performed, and is featured on the Kronos Quartet recording *Howl U.S.A.,* Nonesuch label, 6/4/96, "Cold War Suite from How It Happens (The Voice of I. F. Stone)".

438   "from a figure of admiration": Quotes and comments by Peter Osnos in this chapter are from interview with MM, 9/26/91.

439   "He doesn't even go" to "all this murderous technology": Transcript of *I. F. Stone's Weekly* documentary by Jerry Bruck Jr., 1973.

439   "He was *murdered* by": IFS, Jerry Bruck documentary.

439   "secret and camouflages": All Cunniff quotes and comments in this chapter from his interview with MM, 6/21/91.

440   "His living room was a": Nossiter to MM, 9/26/91.

441   "the goddamnest mess of crap": Stone on *Cavett,* in Bruck documentary.

441   "greatest prison of the mind": IFS, "Izzy on Izzy," *New York Times,* 1/22/78.

441   "downright Tobacco Road ignorance": IFS, "Izzy on Izzy."

442   "serious about getting things right": Nat Hentoff, *Village Voice,* 12/23/71.

443   "back in school": All quotes and comments by Chuck Nathanson to MM, 9/3/71.

444   "That was the deal": Pincus, 5/2/90.

444   "articles in The New York Review": Final *Weekly,* 12/14/71.

444   "Pop was terrible at math": CS to MM, 8/31/91.

445   "*I* am a republican": Jack Beatty to MM, 2/4/91.

445   "I wrote him" to "some other great betrayals": San Francisco Arts and Lectures series, 2/5/88. Buckley-Stone portion of the anecdote told in slightly different form in Karl Meyer, *New Statesman,*12/22/72.

445   "For every quote from": Beatty to MM, 2/4/91.

445   "every day there was a": Hitchens to MM, 5/18/90.

446   "I. F. Stone's porch": Navasky to MM, 1/16/90.

446   "Izzy saw what others missed": Navasky, *Matter of Opinion,* 196. This entertaining book (see bibliography) should be read in its entirety, but good excerpts are posted on the *Nation* Web site.

446   "Partly it was a matter": Comments of Navasky in various columns and speeches including conversations with MM, 1/16/90.

446   "requested a club-car ticket" to "earned entitlement": *Nation,* 7/2/03.

446   Stone to keynote . . . to "Comes the revolution": Navasky, *Matter of Opinion,* 289–91.

447   "Izzy was": Bill Kovach to MM, 10/21/05 e-mail interview.

448   "if any of us comes up": Stan Isaacs, *Newsday,* 1/20/68.

448   "I think Izzy took pot shots": Raymond to MM, 10/4/91, plus following comments.

448   "renting its cranium": Bob Sherrill, quoted by Navasky, *Matter of Opinion,* 231.

449   a curdled experience . . . to "No outsider there": Combination of interview with MM for *Washington Post,* 7/9/79, follow-up interview, and Sherrill letter to MM, 1994.

450   "At a dinner in London he": Hitchens to MM, 5/18/90.

450   "need never lunch alone": Stone softened this by adding that "the skillful courtier in White never swallows the superlative reporter." *Review,* 8/15/65.

450   "I was alternately Izzy's hero": Wilson to MM, 10/1/91.

451   "Izzy would never study": Pincus to MM, 5/2/90. Interview includes subsequent comments in this chapter.

452   "totally delightful" to "one of my heroes": Wills to MM, 11/19/90.

453   "Many miss the point": All of Scott Armstrong's comments, interview with MM, 1/20/90.

454   "Izzy was the rock": Pincus *Life* magazine anecdote and comments on journalism to MM, 5/2/90.

455   should have run on page one: For the entire account see Howard Kurtz, "The Post on WMDs: An Inside Story; Prewar Articles Questioning Threat Often Didn't Make Front Page," *Washington Post,* 8/12/04, A.01.

455   *"read the documents":* Ibid.

456   "Nobody has learned anything": Ellsberg to MM, 3/10/05.

456   Ellsberg recalled a conversation: Ibid.

Chapter 27: Stone vs. Socrates

457   "shot myself" to "dug into the original": IFS, "Izzy on Izzy," *New York Times,* 1/22/78.

457   "'the one thing I envy'" to "go over passages": Wills to MM, 11/19/90. Subsequent Wills comments in this chapter are from this interview.

458   "the crossfire of violent": IFS, "Izzy on Izzy."

458   "Izzy was full of the Greeks": Armstrong to MM, 1/20/90. Subsequent Armstrong comments in this chapter are from this interview.

459   "If you saw Izzy, you": Judith Viorst to MM, 9/20/91. Subsequent Viorst comments are from this interview.

459   "the *Trojan Women*" to "my way through Homer": Martin to MM, 12/8/91.

459   "Was Sappho a lesbian?" IFS, "Izzy on Izzy."

459   "What have you read" to "you must be paid": Andrew Wylie, *Washington Post Book World,* 5/9/04.

460   "Izzy felt his life was over": Unless otherwise noted, all references and quotes of Dr. Bernard Lown regarding Stone are from Dr. Lown's interview with MM, 5/29/96.

461   "vestibule to death": IFS to MM, 7/79.

463   "Moscow's double standard in all": IFS letter to Lown, 11/1/82.

463   a Russian journalist fell to: William Drozdiak, "2 Nobelists Aid Heart Victim in Oslo Drama," *Washington Post,* 12/10/85, 1.

463   "medicine as metaphor": Ellen Goodman, *Boston Globe,* 12/17/85.

463   "We disagree on many aspects": Drozdiak, *Washington Post,* 12/10/85.

464   "the 'dirty-tricks' division": IFS, *Washington Star,* 2/24/80. In IFS CIA file.

464   "That was really therapeutic": San Francisco Arts and Lectures series, 2/5/88.

464   "a perfect clone of Ollie North" to known as "long ears": Ibid.

465   "camel can't belch" to "institutionalizing assassination": *Oregonian,* 4/8/76.

465   "The elderly are suffering": Ed Bradley, *60 Minutes.*

466   "He was wrong about Russia": Cox to MM, 9/89. Also subsequent comments.

466   "The kooks that are the": SF speech, 2/5/88.

466   "Izzy was outraged" to "so hungry for minds": Armstrong to MM, 1/20/90.

467   "Every morning at seven a.m.": Viorst to MM, 9/20/91.

469   Christopher remembers walking: CS to MM, 8/3/91.

469   "I was not kosher": SF speech, 2/5/88.

469   "hurt my feelings": IFS to MM, 9/79.

469   "Stone seems to believe": Abba Eban, *Washington Post,* 2/25/79.

470   "Izzy?! Oh, Christ, no": Rauh to MM, 3/6/90.

470   "I read a terrible story": The Nation Institute and The New School present "A Conversation with I. F. Stone at 80," 2/88.

471   Said Esther, "Izzy left me": Dorothy Fall to MM, 1996; Jack Beatty to MM, 2005.

471   " 'Jack! You need a michloch' ": Beatty to MM, 5/28/96.

472   "I set out to explain how": S.F. speech, 2/5/88.

472   "blind to what inspired Socrates": *Christian Science Monitor,* 1/20/88.

473   Hook cuttingly disparaged: *Wall Street Journal,* 1/20/88.

473   In private, he referred to him: Cottrell, *Izzy,* 313.

473   "Socrates got into trouble" and "two different points, both are": S.F. speech, 2/5/88.

473   "Anyone who finds something new": National Press Club, 3/24/88.

474   "Izzy was less a conventional journalist": Navasky, introduction to Stone, Nation Institute speech, 1988.

Chapter 28: The Last of the Great Fog Cutters

475   "I think he was trying": CS to MM, 1991.

476   "Pop resisted the romanticization": Ibid.

476   "That's your life, Pop" to "Cut off the *Globe*": CS, NYC memorial service.

477   "I had never shielded Dad": CS to MM, 1991.

477   "Some of the honorifics" to "United States should get out": Alexander Cockburn, *Nation,* 9/10/89.

478   as morally wrong as it: Colman McCarthy, *Washington Post,* 6/24/89.

478   "main substantive administrative assistant": "Esther M. Stone, 91, Widow of Journalist," obituary, *New York Times,* 9/12/00.

479   "greatest civil liberties lawyers" to "institutional default": *Nation,* 12/18/89.

480 "Izzy gave you a gift": Armstrong to MM, 1/20/90; "His inability to countenance": Alterman; he was the "hydraulist": McCarthy, *Washington Post*,
6/24/89; "He was so revered": Beatty to MM, 5/28/96.

480 "One of his great" to "anything but doctrinaire": Bob Silvers, IFS memorial
service, NYC.

481 "don't-fall-for-BS-propaganda": Silberstein comments in "I. F. Stone Honored at North Gate," *North Gate News,* Fall 2001.

481 "Only Izzy could have gotten": Mirsky e-mail to MM, 2005.

482 "The few dissenting voices" to " 'governments lie' ": Orville Schell, preface to
Massing, *Now They Tell Us,* in *Review,* 2004.

482 "In old age he may": Unsigned obituary, *New Republic,* 7/10/89, 10.

BIBLIOGRAPHY

Books by I. F. Stone

The Haunted Fifties. Great Britain: Merlin Press, 1963.

The Hidden History of the Korean War: 1950–1951. Merlin Press, 1951. Boston and Toronto: Little, Brown and Company, 1998 (reprint).

The I. F. Stone's Weekly Reader. Ed. Neil Middleton. New York: Random House, 1973.

In a Time of Torment. New York: Random House, 1967.

Polemics and Prophecies: 1967–1970. Boston, Toronto, and London: Little, Brown and Company, 1970.

The Trial of Socrates. Boston and Toronto: Little, Brown and Company, 1988.

The Truman Era: 1945–1952. Boston, Toronto, and London: Little, Brown and Company, 1988.

Underground to Palestine and Reflections Thirty Years Later. New York: Pantheon Books, 1978.

The War Years: 1939–1945. Boston, Toronto, and London: Little, Brown and Company, 1988.

About I. F. Stone

Cottrell, Robert C. *Izzy: A Biography of I. F. Stone.* New Brunswick, NJ: Rutgers University Press, 1992.

Patner, Andrew. *I. F. Stone: A Portrait.* New York: Anchor Books, 1990.

Selected Bibliography

Aaron, Daniel. *Writers on the Left: Episodes in American Literary Communism.* New York: Harcourt, Brace & World, 1961.

Abramson, Rudy. *Spanning the Century: The Life of W. Averell Harriman, 1891–1986.* New York: William Morrow and Company, 1992.

Alderman, Ellen, and Caroline Kennedy. *In Our Defense: The Bill of Rights in Action.* New York: William Morrow and Company, 1991.

Aleichem, Sholem. *In the Storm.* New York: G. P. Putnam's Sons, 1984.

Allen, Frederick Lewis. *Only Yesterday: An Informal History of the 1920's.* New York, Hagerstown, San Francisco, and London: Harper & Row Publishers, 1931.

Alpern, Sara. *Freda Kirchwey: A Woman of The Nation.* Cambridge, MA, and London, England: Harvard University Press, 1987.

Alperovitz, Gar. *Atomic Diplomacy: Hiroshima and Potsdam.* New York: Penguin Books, 1985.

———. *The Decision to Use the Atomic Bomb and the Architecture of an American Myth.* New York: Alfred A. Knopf, 1995.

Alterman, Eric. *What Liberal Media? The Truth About Bias and the News.* New York: Basic Books, 2003.

Applebaum, Anne. *Gulag: A History.* New York: Anchor Books: 2003.

Aronson, James. *Packaging the News: A Critical Survey of Press, Radio, TV.* New York: International Publishers, 1971.

————. *Deadline for the Media: Today's Challenge to Press, TV, and Radio.* Indianapolis and New York: Bobbs-Merrill Company, 1972.

Baker, Russell. *The Good Times.* New York: William Morrow and Company, 1989.

Ballard, William, et al. *Views from the Socially Sensitive Seventies.* American Telephone and Telegraph Company, 1973.

Barnard, Harry. *Eagle Forgotten.* New York: Duell, Sloan and Pearce, 1938.

Barnet, Richard J. *The Giants: Russia and America.* New York: Simon and Schuster, 1977.

Barth, Alan. *The Loyalty of Free Men.* New York: Viking Press, 1951.

Bassow, Whitman. *The Moscow Correspondents: Reporting on Russia from the Revolution to Glasnost.* New York: Paragon House, 1988.

Bayley, Edwin R. *Joe McCarthy and the Press.* New York: Pantheon Books, 1981.

Beard, Charles A., and Mary R. Beard. *The Beards' New Basic History of the United States.* New York: Doubleday and Company, 1944.

Bennett, David H. *The Party of Fear: From Nationalist Movements to the New Right in American History.* New York: Vintage Books, 1995.

Bernstein, Carl. *Loyalties: A Son's Memoir.* New York: Simon and Schuster, 1989.

Beschloss, Michael. *The Conquerors: Roosevelt, Truman and the Destruction of Hitler's Germany: 1941–1945.* New York: Simon and Schuster, 2002.

Bessie, Alvah. *Inquisition in Eden.* New York: Macmillan, 1965.

Bird, Kai, and Martin J. Sherwin. *American Prometheus: The Triumph and Tragedy of J. Robert Oppenheimer.* New York: Alfred A. Knopf, 2005.

Birmingham, Stephen. *"Our Crowd": The Great Jewish Families of New York.* New York, Evanston, and London: Harper & Row, 1967.

Boorstin, Daniel J. *The Decline of Radicalism: Reflections on America Today.* New York: Random House, 1969.

Bradlee, Ben. *A Good Life: Newspapering and Other Adventures.* New York: Simon and Schuster, 1995.

Branch, Taylor. *Parting the Waters: America in the King Years, 1954–63.* New York: Simon and Schuster, 1988.

————. *Pillar of Fire: America in the King Years, 1963–65.* New York: Simon and Schuster, 1999.

————. *At Canaan's Edge: America in the King Years, 1965–68.* New York: Simon and Schuster, 2006.

Braudy, Susan. *Family Circle: The Boudins and the Aristocracy of the Left.* New York: Alfred A. Knopf, 2003.

Bray, William G. *Russian Frontiers: From Muscovy to Khrushchev.* Indianapolis and New York: Bobbs-Merrill Company, 1963.

Brenman-Gibson, Margaret. *Clifford Odets: American Playwright: The Years from 1906–1940.* New York: Atheneum, 1981.

Brinkley, Alan. *Voices of Protest: Huey Long, Father Coughlin and the Great Depression.* New York: Alfred A. Knopf, 1982.

Brinkley, David. *Washington Goes to War*. New York: Alfred A. Knopf, 1988.

Brody, David. *Steelworkers in America: The Nonunion Era*. New York: Harper Torchbooks, 1960.

Broun, Heywood Hale. *Whose Little Boy Are You?: A Memoir of the Broun Family*. New York: St. Martin's/Marek, 1983.

Browder, Earl. *Build the United People's Front*. New York: Workers Library Publishers, 1936.

Buffone, Samuel J., et al. *The Offenses of Richard M. Nixon: A Guide for the People of the United States*. New York: New York Times Book Co., 1974.

Burns, James MacGregor. *Roosevelt: The Lion and the Fox*. New York: Harcourt, Brace & World, 1956.

Calmer, Alan, ed. *Proletarian Literature in the United States: An Anthology*. New York: International Publishers, 1937.

Cannon, Lou. *Reporting: An Inside View*. California: California Journal Press, 1977.

Chamberlin, William Henry. *Soviet Russia: A Living Record and a History*. Boston: Little, Brown and Company, 1930.

Cooke, Alistair. *The Vintage Mencken*. New York: Vintage Books, 1955.

Corio, Ann. *This Was Burlesque*. New York: Madison Square Press, Grosset & Dunlap, 1968.

Coser, Lewis, and Irving Howe. *The American Communist Party: A Critical History, 1919–1957*. Beacon Hill and Boston: Beacon Press, 1957.

Costello, Lawrence, and Stanley Feldstein. *The Ordeal of Assimilation: A Documentary History of the White Working Class*. Garden City, NY: Anchor Books, 1974.

Coulter, Ann. *Treason: Liberal Treachery from the Cold War to the War on Terrorism*. New York: Crown Forum, 2003.

Cox, John Stuart, and Athan G. Theoharis. *The Boss: J. Edgar Hoover and the Great American Inquisition*. Philadelphia: Temple University Press, 1988.

Craig, R. Bruce. *Treasonable Doubt: The Harry Dexter White Spy Case*. Lawrence: University Press of Kansas, 2004.

Crankshaw, Edward. *Khrushchev Remembers*. Boston and Toronto: Little, Brown and Company, 1970.

Criley, Richard. *The FBI v. the First Amendment*. Los Angeles: First Amendment Foundation, 1997.

Crosland, Mrs. Newton, and Frederick L Slous. *Dramatic Works of Victor Hugo*. P. F. Collier, Publisher, no copyright listed.

Crozier, Emmet. *American Reporters on the Western Front, 1914–1918*. New York: Oxford University Press, 1959.

Culver, John C., and John Hyde. *American Dreamer: A Life of Henry A. Wallace*. New York and London: W. W. Norton & Company, 2000.

Descartes, René, et al. *The Rationalists*. Garden City, NY: Dolphin Books, 1960.

Deutscher, Isaac. *Russia in Transition and Other Essays*. New York: Coward-McCann, 1957.

Diamond, Edwin. *The Tin Kazoo: Television, Politics, and the News*. Cambridge, Mass.: The MIT Press, 1977.

Dies, Martin. *The Trojan Horse in America*. New York: Dodd, Mead & Company, 1940.

Diggins, John Patrick. *The American Left in the Twentieth Century*. New York: Harcourt Brace Jovanovich, 1973.

———. *The Rise and Fall of the American Left.* New York and London: W. W. Norton & Company, 1992.

Dilling, Elizabeth. *The Red Network.* Chicago: Published by author, 1934.

Donner, Frank J. *The Age of Surveillance: The Aims and Methods of America's Political Intelligence System.* New York: Alfred A. Knopf, 1980.

Dos Passos, John. *1919.* New York: Washington Square Press, 1961.

Draper, Theodore. *American Communism and Soviet Russia.* New York: Vintage Books, 1986.

Edel, Leon. *Edmund Wilson: The Thirties.* New York: Farrar, Straus and Giroux, 1980.

Ehrlich, Anne, and Paul Ehrlich. *One With Nineveh: Politics, Consumption, and the Human Future.* Washington, D.C.: Island Press, 2004.

Einstein, Albert. *Ideas and Opinions.* New York: Crown Publishers, 1954.

Ellsberg, Daniel. *Secrets: A Memoir of Vietnam and the Pentagon Papers.* New York: Viking Penguin, 2002.

Faulk, John Henry. *Fear on Trial.* Austin: University of Texas Press, 1983.

———. *The Uncensored John Henry Faulk.* Austin: Texas Monthly Press, 1985.

Fischer, Louis. *Russia's Road from Peace to War: Soviet Foreign Relations, 1917–1941.* New York, Evanston, and London: Harper & Row Publishers, 1969.

Fleming, Thomas. *The New Dealers' War: F.D.R. and the War within World War II.* New York: Basic Books, 2001.

Franken, Al. *Lies: And the Lying Liars Who Tell Them.* New York: Dutton, 2003.

Freedman, Max. *Roosevelt & Frankfurter: Their Correspondence, 1928–1945.* Boston and Toronto: Little, Brown and Company, 1967.

Friendly, Fred W. *Due to Circumstances Beyond Our Control.* New York: Random House, 1967.

Fulbright, Senator J. William. *The Arrogance of Power.* New York: Random House, 1966.

Galbraith, John Kenneth. *A Life in Our Times.* Boston: Houghton Mifflin Company, 1981.

———. *Money: Whence It Came, Where It Went.* Boston: Houghton Mifflin Company, 1975.

Gans, Herbert J. *Deciding What's News: A Study of CBS Evening News, NBC News, Newsweek and Time.* New York: Pantheon Books, 1979.

Gelb, Arthur. *City Room.* New York: G. P. Putnam's Sons, 2003.

Gelbspan, Ross. *Break-ins, Death Threats and the FBI: The Covert War Against the Central America Movement.* Boston: South End Press, 1991.

Gentry, Curt. *J. Edgar Hoover: The Man and the Secrets.* New York and London: W. W. Norton & Company, 1991.

Ghiglione, Loren. *The American Journalist: Paradox of the Press.* Washington, DC: Library of Congress, 1990.

Gitlin, Todd. *Inside Prime Time.* New York: Pantheon Books, 1985.

———. *The Sixties: Years of Hope, Days of Rage.* Toronto, New York, London, Sydney, and Auckland: Bantam Books, 1987.

Goldman, Eric F. *The Crucial Decade—and After, 1945–1960.* New York: Alfred A. Knopf, 1960.

Goodman, Amy, and David Goodman. *The Exception to the Rulers: Exposing Oily Politicians, War Profiteers, and the Media That Love Them.* New York: Hyperion, 2004.

Goodman, Walter. *The Committee.* New York: Farrar, Straus and Giroux, 1968.

Gornick, Vivian. *The Romance of Communism.* New York: Basic Books, 1977.

Goulden, Joseph G. *The Best Years: 1945–1950.* New York: Atheneum, 1976.

Graham, John. *Introduction to "Yours for the Revolution": The Appeal to Reason, 1895–1922.* Lincoln: University of Nebraska Press, 1990

Graham, Robert, and Jeff Mussbaum. *Intelligence Matters: The CIA, the FBI, Saudi Arabia, and the Failure of America's War on Terror.* New York: Random House, 2004.

Greider, William. *The Soul of Capitalism.* New York: Simon and Schuster, 2003.

Grun, Bernard. *The Timetables of History: A Horizontal Linkage of People and Events.* New York: Simon and Schuster, 1979.

Gwertzman, Bernard, and Michael T. Kaufman. *The Collapse of Communism.* New York: Random House, 1990.

Halberstam, David. *The Best and Brightest.* New York: Ballantine Books, 1993.

———. *The Fifties.* New York: Villard Books, 1993.

———. *The Powers That Be.* New York: Alfred A. Knopf, 1979.

Halper, Albert. *Union Square.* New York: Viking Press, 1933.

Haynes, John Earl, and Harvey Klehr. *Venona: Decoding Soviet Espionage in America.* New Haven and London: Yale University Press, 2000.

Hecht, Ben. *A Child of the Century.* New York: Signet Books, 1954.

Heilbroner, Robert L. *The Worldly Philosophers: The Lives, Times and Ideas of the Great Economic Thinkers.* New York: Simon and Schuster, 1986.

Hellman, Lillian. *Scoundrel Time.* New York: Bantam Books, 1977.

Hentoff, Nat. *The War on the Bill of Rights: And the Gathering Resistance.* New York: Seven Stories Press: 2003.

Hersh, Seymour M. *The Price of Power: Kissinger in the Nixon White House.* New York: Summit Books, 1983.

Hertsgaard, Mark. *On Bended Knee: The Press and the Reagan Presidency.* New York: Farrar, Straus and Giroux, 1988.

Hertzberg, Arthur. *The Jews in America: Four Centuries of an Uneasy Encounter.* New York: Simon and Schuster, 1989.

Hesse, Hermann. *Magister Ludi: The Glass Bead Game.* New York: Bantam Books, 1969.

Hodgson, Godfrey. *America in Our Time: From World War II to Nixon—What Happened and Why.* New York: Vintage Books, 1976.

Hofstadter, Richard. *The American Political Tradition.* New York: Vintage Books, 1954.

Homer. *The Odyssey.* New York: Mentor Books, 1937.

Hoopes, Roy. *Ralph Ingersoll: A Biography.* New York: Atheneum, 1985.

Hougan, Jim. *Spooks: The Haunting of America—The Private Use of Secret Agents.* New York: William Morrow and Company, 1978.

Howe, Irving. *A Margin of Hope: An Intellectual Autobiography.* San Diego, New York, and London: Harcourt Brace Jovanovich, 1982.

———. *World of Our Fathers: The Journey of the East European Jews to America and the Life They Found and Made.* New York and London: Harcourt Brace Jovanovich, 1976.

Huberman, Leo, and Paul M. Sweezy. *Cuba: Anatomy of a Revolution.* New York: Monthly Review Press, 1960.

Hyma, Albert, and J. A. Rickard. *Ancient, Medieval & Modern History.* New York: Barnes & Noble, 1957.

Ivins, Molly. *Who Let the Dogs In?: Incredible Political Animals I Have Known.* New York: Random House, 2004.

Johnpoll, Bernard K., and Lillian Johnpoll. *The Impossible Dream: The Rise and Decline of the American Left.* Westport, CT, and London: Greenwood Press, 1981.

Johnson, Haynes. *The Bay of Pigs: The Leaders' Story of Brigade 2506.* New York: W. W. Norton & Company, 1974.

Josephson, Matthew. *The Robber Barons: The Great American Capitalists, 1861–1901.* New York: Harcourt, Brace and Company, 1934.

Joughin, G. Louis, and Edmund M. Morgan. *The Legacy of Sacco and Vanzetti.* New York: Harcourt, Brace and Company, 1948.

Kahn, Gordon. *Hollywood on Trial.* New York: Boni & Gaer, 1948.

Kalb, Marvin. *One Scandalous Story: Clinton, Lewinsky, & 13 Days That Tarnished American Journalism.* New York: Free Press, 2001.

Kamenka, Eugene. *The Portable Karl Marx.* New York: Penguin Books, 1988.

Kane, Joseph Nathan. *Facts About the Presidents.* New York: Permabooks, 1960.

Kaplan, Justin. *Lincoln Steffens: A Biography.* New York: Simon and Schuster, 1974.

———. *Walt Whitman: A Life.* New York: Harper Perennial Classics, 2003.

Keeley, Edmund. *The Salonika Bay Murder: Cold War Politics and the Polk Affair.* New Jersey: Princeton University Press, 1989.

Kimball, Penn. *The File.* New York, San Diego, and London: Harcourt Brace Jovanovich, 1983.

Klehr, Harvey. *The Heyday of American Communism: The Depression Decade.* New York: Basic Books, 1984.

Klingaman, William K. *1919: The Year Our World Began.* New York: Harper & Row, 1987.

Kluger, Richard. *The Paper: The Life and Death of the New York Herald Tribune.* New York: Vintage Books, 1986.

Knightley, Phillip. *The First Casualty.* New York and London: Harcourt Brace Jovanovich, 1975.

Koestler, Arthur. *Darkness at Noon.* New York: Macmillan, 1941.

Kovach, Bill, and Tom Rosenstiel. *The Elements of Journalism: What Newspeople Should Know and the Public Should Expect.* New York: Crown Publishers, 2001.

Kropotkin, Petr. *Mutual Aid: A Factor of Evolution.* Boston: Porter Sargent Publishers, 1902.

Krugman, Paul. *The Great Unraveling: Losing Our Way in the New Century.* New York: W. W. Norton & Company, 2003.

Kurth, Peter. *American Cassandra: The Life of Dorothy Thompson.* Boston, Toronto, and London: Little, Brown and Company, 1990.

Lader, Lawrence. *Power on the Left: American Radical Movements Since 1946.* New York and London: W. W. Norton & Company, 1979.

Lamphere, Robert. *The FBI-KGB War: A Special Agent's Story.* New York: Random House, 1986.

Landis, Arthur H. *The Abraham Lincoln Brigade.* New York: Citadel Press, 1968.

Larina, Anna. *This I Cannot Forget: The Memoirs of Nikolai Bukharin's Widow.* New York and London: W. W. Norton & Company, 1993.

Lash, Joseph P. *Eleanor and Franklin: The Story of Their Relationship, Based on Eleanor Roosevelt's Private Papers.* New York: Signet Books, 1973.

Lasswell, Harold D. *Psychopathology and Politics.* New York: Viking Press, 1960.

Leab, David J. *A Union of Individuals: The Formation of the American Newspaper Guild, 1933–1936.* New York: Columbia University Press, 1970.

Lee, Martin A., and Norman Solomon. *Unreliable Sources: A Guide to Detecting Bias in News Media.* Carol Publishing Group, 1990.

Lekachman, Robert. *The Age of Keynes.* New York: McGraw-Hill Book Company, 1975.

Levi, Primo. *If Not Now, When?* New York: Penguin Books, 1986.

Lewis, John. *Marxism and Modern Idealism.* New York: International Publishers, 1945.

Liebling, A. J. *The Press.* New York: Ballantine Books, 1961.

Linton, Calvin D. *The Bicentennial Almanac: 200 Years of America.* Tennessee and New York: Thomas Nelson Inc., Publishers, 1975.

Lipstadt, Deborah E. *Beyond Belief: The American Press and the Coming of the Holocaust, 1933–1945.* New York and London: Free Press, 1986.

Liveright, Horace. *Washington Merry-Go-Round.* New York: Liveright Inc., 1931.

London, Jack. *Martin Eden.* New York, Chicago, and San Francisco: Holt, Rinehart and Winston, 1936.

Luhan, Mabel Dodge. *Movers and Shakers.* New York: Harcourt, 1936.

Lukas, J. Anthony. *Nightmare: The Underside of the Nixon Years.* London, Toronto, and New York: Bantam Books, 1976.

Lundberg, Ferdinand. *Imperial Hearst: A Social Biography.* New York: Modern Library, 1937.

Lyons, Eugene. *The Red Decade: The Stalinist Penetration of America.* Indianapolis and New York: Bobbs-Merrill Company, 1941.

MacPherson, Myra. *Long Time Passing: Vietnam and the Haunted Generation.* Garden City, NY: Doubleday, 1984.

Martin, Bernard. *A History of Judaism: Volume II, Europe and the New World.* New York: Basic Books, 1974.

Masses. Vols. 9–10, November 1916–December 1917. Reprint. Millwood, NY: Kraus, 1980.

Massing, Michael. *Now They Tell Us: The American Press and Iraq.* Preface by Orville Schell. New York: New York Review of Books Publications, 2004.

Mayfield, Sara. *The Constant Circle: H. L. Mencken and His Friends.* New York: Dell Publishing, 1968.

McCarthy, Colman. *Inner Companions.* Washington, DC: Acropolis Books, 1975.

———. *Involvements: One Journalist's Place in the World.* Washington, DC: Acropolis Books, 1984.

McClure, Robert D., and Thomas E. Patterson. *The Unseeing Eye: The Myth of Television Power in National Politics.* New York: G. P. Putnam's Sons, 1976.

McCullough, David. *Truman.* New York: Simon and Schuster, 1992.

McKeon, Richard. *Introduction to Aristotle.* New York: Modern Library, 1947.

McWilliams, Cary. *Brothers Under The Skin.* Boston and Toronto: Little, Brown and Company, 1964.

Miller, James. *"Democracy Is in the Streets": From Port Huron to the Seige of Chicago.* New York: Simon and Schuster, 1987.

Miller, Nathan. *F.D.R.: An Intimate History.* New York: Doubleday, 1983.

———. *The Roosevelt Chronicles: The Story of a Great American Family.* New York: Doubleday, 1979.

Milton, John. *Areopagitica.* In *The Complete Poetry and Selected Prose of John Milton.* New York: Modern Library, 1950.

Minor, Dale. *The Information War.* New York: Hawthorn Books, 1970.

Minsky, Morton, and Milt Macklin. *Minsky's Burlesque.* New York: Arbor House, 1986.

Morris, Roger. *Richard Milhous Nixon: The Rise of an American Politician.* New York: Henry Holt and Company, 1990.

Morse, Arthur D. *While Six Million Died.* New York: Random House, 1968.

Mortimer, Edward. *The World That FDR Built: Vision and Reality.* New York: Macmillan Publishing Co., 1988.

Moynihan, Daniel Patrick. *Secrecy: The American Experience.* New Haven: Yale University Press, 1998.

Navasky, Victor S. *Kennedy Justice.* Kingsport, TN: Kingsport Press, 1971.

———. *A Matter of Opinion.* New York: Farrar, Straus and Giroux, 2005.

———. *Naming Names.* New York: Penguin Books, 1991.

Neider, Charles, ed. *The Complete Humorous Sketches and Tales of Mark Twain.* New York: Doubleday, 1961.

Newman, Robert P. *Owen Lattimore and the "Loss" of China.* Berkeley and Los Angeles: University of California Press, 1992.

The New York Review of Books: January 1967–January 1968. New York: Arno Press, 1969.

The New York Times. The Pentagon Papers. Toronto, New York, and London: Bantam Books, 1971.

Oberdorfer, Don. *The Two Koreas: A Contemporary History.* Reading, MA: Addison-Wesley, 1997.

O'Brien, Michael. *McCarthy and McCarthyism in Wisconsin.* Columbia and London: University of Missouri Press, 1980.

O'Connor, Richard. *Heywood Broun: A Biography.* New York: G. P. Putnam's Sons, 1975.

The Official U.S. Senate Report on Senators McCarthy and Benton. Boston: Beacon Press, 1953.

Olmsted, Kathryn S. *Red Spy Queen: A Biography of Elizabeth Bentley.* Chapel Hill: University of North Carolina Press, 2002.

Orwell, George. *Homage to Catalonia.* San Diego, New York, and London: Harcourt Brace Jovanovich, 1952.

Payne, Robert. *The Civil War in Spain.* New York: Putnam's, 1962.

Pells, Richard H. *Radical Visions and American Dreams: Culture and Social Thought in the Depression Years.* Middletown, CT: Wesleyan University Press, 1973.

Peters, Charles. *Five Days in Philadelphia: The Amazing "We Want Willkie!" Convention of 1940 and How It Freed FDR to Save the Western World.* New York: Public Affairs, 2005.

Phillips, Cabell. *The Truman Presidency: The History of a Triumphant Succession.* New York: Macmillan, 1966.

Plato. *The Republic.* London: Penguin Books, 1987.

Pomerantz, Charlotte. *A Quarter-Century of Un-Americana.* Chicago: Chicago Center, 1997.

Postman, Neil. *Amusing Ourselves to Death.* New York: Penguin Books, 1985.

Powell, Jody. *The Other Side of the Story.* New York: William Morrow and Company, 1984.

Rayback, Joseph G. *A History of American Labor.* New York: Macmillan, 1959.

Reed, John. *Ten Days That Shook the World.* New York: Penguin Books, 1977.

Reeves, Richard. *President Kennedy: Profile of Power.* New York: Simon and Schuster, 1993.

Remnick, David. *Lenin's Tomb: The Last Days of the Soviet Empire.* New York: Random House, 1993.

Rivers, William L. *The Opinion Makers.* Boston: Beacon Press, 1965.

Robins, Natalie. *Alien Ink: The FBI's War on Freedom of Expression.* New York: William Morrow and Company, 1992.

Roosevelt, Eleanor. *My Day: The Best of Eleanor Roosevelt's Acclaimed Newspaper Columns, 1936–1962.* New York: Da Capo Press, 2001.

Roth, Philip. *The Plot Against America: A Novel.* New York: Houghton Mifflin Company, 2004.

Rovere, Richard H. *Loyalty and Security in a Democratic State.* New York: The New York Times, Arno Press, 1977.

———. *Senator Joe McCarthy.* New York: Harper and Row, 1959.

Sachar, Howard M. *The Course of Modern Jewish History: The Classic History of the Jewish People, from the Eighteenth Century to the Present Day.* New York: Vintage Books, 1990.

Salisbury, Harrison E. *A Time of Change: A Reporter's Tale of Our Time.* New York: Harper & Row, 1988.

———. *Without Fear or Favor.* New York: Times Books, 1980.

Sanders, Ronald. *The Downtown Jews: Portraits of an Immigrant Generation.* New York: Dover Publications, 1969, 1987.

Satin, Joseph. *The 1950's: America's "Placid" Decade.* Boston: Houghton Mifflin Company, 1960.

Schecter, Jerrold, and Leona Schecter. *Sacred Secrets: How Soviet Intelligence Secrets Changed American History.* Washington, DC: Brassey's, 2002.

Schlesinger, Arthur M., Jr. *The Imperial Presidency.* Boston: Houghton Mifflin Company, 1973.

Schmidt, Benno C., Jr. *Freedom of the Press vs. Public Access.* New York, Washington, and London: Praeger Publishers, 1976.

Schmidt, Karl M. *Henry A. Wallace: Quixotic Crusade, 1948.* New York: Syracuse University Press, 1960.

Seldes, George. *Even the Gods Can't Change History: The Facts Speak for Themselves.* Secaucus, NJ: Lyle Stuart, 1976.

————. *Witness to a Century: Encounters with the Noted, the Notorious, and the Three SOBs.* New York: Ballantine Books, 1987.

Serge, Victor. *Memoirs of a Revolutionary: 1901–1941.* London and New York: Oxford University Press, 1963.

Shawcross, William. *Sideshow: Kissinger, Nixon and the Destruction of Cambodia.* New York: Simon and Schuster, 1979.

Sheehan, Neil. *A Bright Shining Lie: John Paul Vann and America in Vietnam.* New York: Random House, 1988.

Sherrill, Robert. *The Accidental President: The Election Year Blockbuster on LBJ.* New York: Pyramid Books, 1968.

————. *Gothic Politics in the Deep South.* New York: Ballantine Books, 1968.

Shipler, David K. *Russia.* New York: Penguin Books, 1983.

Shirer, William L. *20th Century Journey: The Nightmare Years, 1930–1940.* Boston and Toronto: Little, Brown and Company, 1984.

Simons, Howard. *Jewish Times: Voices of the American Jewish Experience.* New York, London, Toronto, Sydney, and Auckland: Anchor Books, Doubleday, 1988.

Sinclair, Upton. *The Brass Check: A Study of American Journalism.* Published by the author, 1916.

————. *The Jungle.* New York: Viking Penguin Books, 1985.

Singer, Isaac Bashevis. *Love and Exile: An Autobiographical Trilogy.* New York: Farrar, Straus and Giroux, 1984.

Sperber, A. M. *Murrow: His Life and Times.* Toronto, New York, London, Sydney, and Auckland: Bantam Books, 1986.

Spragens, William C. *The Presidency and the Mass Media in the Age of Television.* Washington, DC: University Press of America, 1978.

Steel, Ronald. *Walter Lippmann and the American Century.* New York: Vintage Books, 1980.

Stendhal. Trans. C. K. Scott Moncrieff. *The Red and the Black.* New York: Modern Library, 1953.

Stern, J. David. *Memoirs of a Maverick Publisher.* New York: Simon and Schuster, 1962.

Stone, Judy. *The Mystery of B. Traven.* Los Altos, CA: William Kaufmann, 1977.

Taylor, S. J. *Stalin's Apologist, Walter Duranty: The New York Times's Man in Moscow.* New York and Oxford: Oxford University Press, 1990.

Terkel, Studs. *Hard Times.* New York: Avon Books, 1970.

Terrill, Ross. *China in Our Time: The Epic Saga of the People's Republic, from the Communist Victory to Tiananmen Square and Beyond.* New York: Simon and Schuster, 1992.

This Fabulous Century: Volume IV, 1930–1940. New York: Time-Life Books, 1969.

Thomas, Gordon, and Max Morgan-Witts. *The Day the Bubble Burst: A Social History of the Wall Street Crash of 1929.* New York: Doubleday, 1979.

Thomas, Norman. *After That New Deal What?* New York: Macmillan, 1936.

————, and Paul Blanchard. *What's the Matter with New York: A National Problem.* New York: Macmillan, 1932.

TIME Capsule/1923. New York: Time Incorporated, 1967.

TIME Capsule/1929. New York: Time Incorporated, 1967.

Toland, John. *The Last 100 Days.* New York: Random House, 1966.

Tussey, Jean Y. *Eugene V. Debs Speaks.* New York: Pathfinder Press, 1972.

Viorst, Milton. *Fire in the Streets: America in the 1960s.* New York: Simon and Schuster, 1979.

Von Hoffman, Nicholas. *Citizen Cohn: The Life and Times of Roy Cohn.* New York: Doubleday, 1988.

Wallace, Irving, and David Wallechinsky. *The People's Almanac.* New York: Doubleday, 1975.

Warren, Robert Penn. *Homage to Theodore Dreiser: On the Century of His Birth.* New York: Random House, 1971.

The Washington Post. The Presidential Transcripts. New York: Dell Books, 1974.

Wasserman, Harvey. *America: Born & Reborn.* New York: Collier Books, 1983.

Wechsler, James A. *The Age of Suspicion.* New York: Random House, 1953.

Weinstein, Allen. *Perjury: The Hiss-Chambers Case.* New York: Alfred A. Knopf, 1978.

———, and Alexander Vassiliev. *The Haunted Wood: Soviet Espionage in America—the Stalin Era.* New York, Modern Library, 1999.

Weinstein, James. *The Decline of Socialism in America, 1912–1925.* New York and London: Monthly Review Press, 1967.

West, Cornel. *Democracy Matters: Winning the Fight Against Imperialism.* New York: Penguin Press, 2004.

West, Nigel. *Venona: The Greatest Secret of the Cold War.* London: HarperCollins Publishers, 1999.

Wheen, Francis. *Karl Marx: A Life.* New York and London: W. W. Norton & Company, 2001.

White, Graham. *FDR and the Press.* Chicago: University of Chicago Press, 1979.

Wilkie, Curtis. *Dixie: A Personal Odyssey through Events That Shaped the Modern South.* New York: A Lisa Drew Book/Scribner, 2001.

Wills, Garry. *Inventing America: Jefferson's Declaration of Independence.* New York: Doubleday, 1978.

———. *Nixon Agonistes: The Crisis of the Self-Made Man.* Boston: Houghton Mifflin, 1970.

Wilson, Edmund. *The Thirties.* New York: Farrar, Straus and Giroux, 1980.

———. *To the Finland Station: A Study in the Writing and Acting of History.* New York: Doubleday, 1940.

Wolfe, Tom. *The Kandy-Kolored Tangerine-Flake Streamline Baby.* New York: Farrar, Straus and Giroux, 1965.

Wreszin, Michael. *A Rebel in Defense of Tradition: The Life and Politics of Dwight Macdonald.* New York: Basic Books: 1994.

INDEX